The Mail Order Gardener

The Mail Order Gardener

A Complete Guide to Sources of Flowers, Vegetables, Trees, Shrubs, Tools, Furniture, Greenhouses, Gazebos, and Everything Else a Gardener Could Wish For

HAL MORGAN

A Steam Press Book

PERENNIAL LIBRARY

HARPER & ROW, PUBLISHERS, New York
Cambridge, Philadelphia, San Francisco, Washington
London, Mexico City, São Paulo, Singapore, Sydney

Produced by Steam Press, Watertown, Massachusetts

Written and designed by Hal Morgan with the assistance of Bruce Morgan, staff writer, and Michelle Menken, research assistant

Copy editors: Polly Cone and Katherine Ness

Composition: DEKR Corp., Woburn, Massachusetts

Illustrations on pages 11, 24, 67, 74, 94 top, 172, 180, 183, 192, 238, 247, and 267 courtesy of the Massachusetts Horticultural Society Library.

FIRST EDITION

Library of Congress Cataloging-in-Publication Data

Morgan, Hal.
  The mail order gardener.

  1. Gardening equipment industry—United States—
Directories. 2. Horticultural products industry—
United States—Directories. 3. Mail-order business—
United States—Directories. I. Title.
HD9486.5.U62M67 1988 635'.029'473 87-45649
ISBN 0-06-055113-5   88 89 90 91 92 MPC 10 9 8 7 6 5 4 3 2 1
ISBN 0-06-096241-0 (pbk.) 88 89 90 91 92 MPC 10 9 8 7 6 5 4 3 2 1

Contents

Part III
SOCIETIES AND MAGAZINES

Introduction

OUR FIRST GARDENS were garden-center productions—the plants and seeds all came from local nurseries and gardening-supply stores. On our third-floor window ledges and eventually in real dirt, these collections of herbs and flowers were a source of quiet pride and satisfaction to us. But, as we tried new plants and watched them grow, we noticed that some other people's gardens held more exotic specimens—pink irises, blue poppies, French tomatoes, and Japanese radishes. Where did these come from?, we wondered. Experienced gardeners seemed to have secret sources of rare and unusual plants.

As our gardening efforts have expanded, we've discovered that the secret of those arresting gardens lies in the mail. Garden centers stock the most popular varieties of the most popular flowers and vegetables, and some have excellent selections. But the range of their offerings doesn't come close to what can be ordered by mail. A good garden center might offer seeds for a dozen tomato varieties, but one mail-order firm sells more than 300 (the Tomato Seed Company, Inc., page 31). A local nursery may offer five or six different daylilies; many mail-order suppliers sell several hundred in colors ranging from pale pink to creamy yellow and wine red. And the gardener planning an apple orchard may choose from scores of mail-order suppliers offering both rare antique varieties and the latest introductions. We admit that our own garden is still well stocked with easily found favorites like snapdragons and alyssum, but it also holds a growing array of unusual beauties bought by mail.

As we've delved into the world of mail-order gardening, we've discovered an unanticipated benefit: our New England winters have grown more bearable and have begun to seem much shorter. Seed catalogs start to filter into the house in December and January, and a little later the nursery lists arrive. Instead of looking out glumly at the stalks of withered perennials and wondering how we'll ever get the car out of the driveway with that spreading slick of ice, we retreat into the pleasures of planning for spring. We make garden diagrams and tentative lists of plants, then redraw them and fix on different arrangements until we have it just right. When a new catalog arrives with something yet more enticing, we push the imaginary roots around to fit everything in.

Next the seeds arrive—often in the midst of a howling blizzard—and we draw up a schedule and begin to plant. While the snow piles up outside, we have spring in mind with tiny sprouts of pansies, delphiniums, and larkspurs on the windowsills. The catalogs that enticed us with their color pictures and glowing descriptions now serve as guides for propagating, thinning, and pinching back. March, instead of being the most miserable month of the year, has become a period of planting frenzy indoors and a time to send off orders for perennial plants and strawberries.

At some point our search for interesting mail-order sources for our own garden turned into a mission to find *every* mail-order source, with the goal of assembling the information in a directory accessible to all gardeners. For the past two years we've combed the advertising sections of gardening magazines and specialty journals and worked our way through the catalog files at horticultural societies. For immeasurable help in this effort we are most particularly indebted to the Massachusetts Horticultural Society library and to its librarian, Walter Punch. The library has kept up files of nursery and seed lists for more than a hundred years, and its archive is a treasure trove for both the historical researcher and the home gardener trying to find a source for a specific rose or tomato.

We've written to more than 3,000 merchants of plants, seeds, and supplies from all over the world asking for price lists and information. The immediate result has been an extended feast of the best kind of mail. We've also found that this universe of suppliers is a slippery one to get a grip on; companies seem to come and go almost weekly. From the letters, lists, and catalogs we received we've compiled this directory, which we hope will be both useful and enjoyable to read. We know it can be no match for the catalogs themselves.

We should note that although we were in touch with all of the listed suppliers in 1987, we've only ordered from a small sampling. By including them here we are in no way vouching for the quality of their products or the character of their business practices. When in doubt, test an unfamiliar company with a small order. If you're satisfied with what you receive, buy more confidently the second time around.

Good luck, and happy gardening.

Buying Plants from Overseas

Because of the danger of importing crop-damaging diseases with plants and seeds sent from abroad, both the United States and Canadian governments enforce restrictions on the importation of all plant material and of some seeds. Most flower seeds may be imported without any special paperwork or inspection, but vegetable seeds and live plants are subject to some stringent regulations.

To import plants into the United States, gardeners will need to obtain an import permit from the Department of Agriculture. The permit is free unless the plants are being ordered for resale. To get an application, write to Permit Unit, USDA-APHIS-PPQ, 665 Federal Building, Hyattsville, MD 20782. Explain which plants you intend to import, giving the botanical name if possible, and specify the country from which you intend to import them. The Permit Unit will then send you an application and an information package, or, in some cases, will let you know that importation of the plant is prohibited or will require a special post-entry quarantine.

In general, most garden plants, like roses and ornamental shrubs, and most houseplants may be imported from most countries. Citrus plants are prohibited, and other fruit trees may only be imported from certain countries. Most garden seeds may be imported without special paperwork, but seeds for woody plants (trees and shrubs) require an import permit and may be subject to quarantine. Gladiolus bulbs grown on the continent of Africa or in Italy, Malta, or Portugal are prohibited. Seeds for some crop plants imported from some countries are either prohibited or are subject to quarantine. All plants must be shipped bare root (without soil), and all plants and seeds will be checked by Department of Agriculture inspectors upon entry into the United States.

Further regulations, enforced by the Department of the Interior, restrict the importation of endangered and threatened plants. When you send for an import permit application you'll receive a list of these species and the special rules that govern their sale.

Canadian gardeners are subject to many of the same restrictions when ordering plants from abroad. To get an application for an import permit, write to Agriculture Canada, Plant Products and Plant Health Division, Permit Office, Ottowa, ON, Canada K1A 0C6. Local offices of Agriculture Canada, Plant Health Division, will also supply the necessary forms and information. When writing, specify which plants you want to order and from which countries. You'll get information on any restrictions along with the import permit application. The permit is free.

Somewhat looser regulations govern trade in plant material between the United States and Canada, though plants and certain vegetable seeds are still subject to restrictions.

PART I:

Plants and Seeds

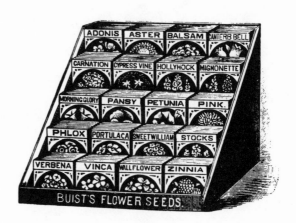

General Flowers and Vegetables

Abundant Life Seed Foundation
P.O. Box 772, Port Townsend, WA 98368
Telephone: 206-385-5660

Catalog price: $1

A non-profit organization devoted to saving the seed of older vegetable varieties, garden flowers, and native plants, all raised for seed without chemicals. In 1986 the foundation put out a rescue call for the vanishing Oxheart carrot and, as a result of the response, expects to have enough seed to sell by 1988. Its annual seed list, published in January, also includes a selection of books.

Ahern Hybrid Seeds, Inc.
P.O. Box 3158, La Jolla, CA 92038
Telephone: 619-474-8080

Catalog price: free

A select offering of hybrid vegetable seed, including Maui Special and Vidalia Sweet onion and Celebrity tomato. Ahern sells only one or two varieties of each vegetable, but seems to have chosen the biggest and the tastiest specimens. The firm also sells "space-saver hybrids" for those with small gardens.

Alberta Nurseries & Seeds Ltd.
Box 20, Bowden, AB, Canada T0M 0K0
Telephone: 403-224-3544 or 3545

Catalog price: free

A big color catalog of flower and vegetable seed, general nursery stock, and gardening supplies. Flowers get the lead-off position in the booklet—a dozen pages of garden annuals, from ageratum to zinnia. The selection is generally limited to the popular flower types, but a few unusual plants make the list, and a fair number are sold in individual-color packets as well as in mixes. The vegetable department is about as extensive. It covers the important bases and gives special attention to short-season varieties for northern growers. The nursery offerings range from fruit trees and berry plants to hardy shrub roses, lilacs, evergreens, and garden perennials. U.S. customers will have to content themselves with the seed section of the list. No nursery stock is exported.

Allen, Sterling & Lothrop
191 U.S. Route 1, Falmouth, ME 04105
Telephone: 207-781-4142

Flower and vegetable seed with an emphasis on short-season types for northern growers. The catalog is illustrated with quaint line drawings, and growing tips are offered for all vegetables. The firm sells its wares from a good-size gardening-supply store as well as by mail, so some items in the catalog are simply listed without description or price. Seed potatoes, dahlia roots, and blackberry bushes are among the plants offered this way. The back portion of the catalog lists a big inventory of gardening supplies—fertilizers, seed-starting trays, Maine-made barrels and tubs, baskets, and canning supplies—but with no prices given.

Allium Farms
Box 296, Powers OR 97466

Catalog price: free

Elephant garlic for planting or for eating. The cloves are sold by the pound, and shoppers can choose from premium size or smaller seed cloves. Every order is sent with a garlic recipe book.

Alston Seed Growers
Littleton, NC 27850

Catalog price: free

A few old-time vegetable varieties presented in an attractive letterpress-printed brochure. Corn is the specialty here, in five different varieties, but Alston also sells seed for Moon-and-Stars watermelon ("so rare it's almost forgotten"), Everlasting tomato, and Birdhouse gourd.

Angel Seed Company
P.O. Box 26540, Fraser, MI 48026
Telephone: 313-294-0001

Catalog price: $1, deductible from first order

Herb, flower, and vegetable seed, presented in a small descriptive catalog. Herbs are perhaps the strongest suit here; seed for almost 50 types are offered, including lemon mint, valerian, and several scented basils. (Tarragon seed is also sold, but with no notice that it is the inferior Russian strain). The vegetable offerings concentrate on such exotics as tomatillo, Atlantic Giant pumpkin, and Giant Walking-Stick cabbage. The flowers include about 20 perennials and biennials, and no annuals.

Archia's Seed Store
P.O. Box 109, 106-108 E. Main Street, Sedalia, MO 65301
Telephone: 816-826-1330

Catalog price: free

Vegetable and flower seed, gardening supplies, and some nursery stock, sold by mail or at the seed store. Archia's encourages shoppers to buy in person, but they'll gladly fill any and all orders that come by mail, and the descriptive catalog lists hundreds of seed offerings. Vegetables are the chosen favorites here. Half the catalog and most of the pictures are devoted to edible crops; the flower offerings are crammed into two unillustrated pages. The gardening supplies offered include hose-repair kits, fertilizers, insecticides, pots, and beekeeping equipment.

Aurora Garden & Pets
3604 Jefferson, Texarkana, AR 75502
Telephone: 501-774-3771

Catalog price: 50¢

A vegetable seed list that lets gardeners order exactly the quantities they need, from 30¢ packets to 50-pound sacks. A table on the first page gives the amount of seed needed to plant a 100-foot row, and shoppers can multiply and divide to determine their precise needs. Beans are Aurora's specialty, and a list of more than 60 varieties takes up the front section of the catalog. Plenty of choices are also available among the other offerings—especially tomatoes, peas, corn, peppers (both hot and sweet), melons, and okra.

Becker's Seed Potatoes
Rt. 1, Trout Creek, ON, Canada P0H 2L0

Catalog price: free

Thirty-five potato cultivars, sold as seed eyes or as whole seed. Spring shipment only. Canadian orders must be received by May 15, U.S. orders by April 10. To reduce the risk of freezing, shipments are not sent out until late April.

Bishop Farm Seeds
Box 338, Belleville, ON, Canada K8N 5A5
Telephone: 613-968-5533

Catalog price: free in Canada, not sent to U.S.

Canadian orders only. Vegetable, flower, and grain seed for backyard gardeners and commercial farmers. Local customers will also find a big selection of gardening supplies at the retail store.

Blue Corn Nursery
Rte. 10, Box 87R, Santa Fe, NM 87501

Catalog price: long self-addressed stamped envelope

Seed for several ancient corn varieties, including blue corn from the Taos and Santa Clara pueblos, white corn from the Taos pueblo, and both miniature and full-size ornamental corn.

Robert Bolton & Son
Birdbrook, Halstead, Essex, England CO9 4BQ
Telephone: 44-440-85-246

Catalog price: free

More than 50 named varieties of sweet peas, all grown at Bolton's Birdbrook nursery and sold in packets of either ten or 20 seeds. The catalog is not illustrated, but each plant is carefully described, including flower color and size, stem length, and scent. U.S. and Canadian customers must send payment in sterling or charge orders to a Visa or Access card.

Bountiful Gardens
5798 Ridgewood Road, Willits, CA 95490

Catalog price: free

U.S. distributors of vegetable and herb seed from Chase Organics of England. Chase grows all its seed organically and offers only open-pollinated varieties—no hybrids. Bountiful Gardens also sells a smattering of flower seed and loads of supplies and books of interest to organic gardeners.

Brown's Omaha Plant Farms, Inc.
P.O. Box 787, Omaha, TX 75571

Catalog price: free

Onion, cabbage, cauliflower, brussels sprout, and broccoli plants shipped from October to May. The business also operates under the names W. G. Farrier Plant Co., Omaha Plant Farms, and Jim Brown Plants.

Bunton Seed Co.
939 E. Jefferson Street, Louisville, KY 40206
Telephone: 502-584-0136

Catalog price: $1

A big glossy catalog of flower and vegetable seed, mostly illustrated with black-and-white photographs, but with some color plates. Most of the flowers are sold in color mixes, but some, such as delphinium, larkspur, and zinnia, are also sold in single-color packets. The bulk of the catalog is devoted to vegetables, a nice blend of modern hybrids and older varieties. A full-service supplier, Bunton also sells tools, seed-starting supplies, fertilizers, pots, grass seed, and bird feeders.

Burgess Seed & Plant Co.

905 Four Seasons Road, Bloomington, IL 61701

Catalog price: free

An all-purpose color catalog of vegetable seeds and plants, ornamental trees and shrubs, roses, fruit trees, berry plants, and houseplants. The widest choice of offerings is found among vegetable seeds; Burgess sells more than two dozen varieties of tomato, and 15 types of corn. The nursery stock is a bit more limited, especially when compared to nursery specialists, but there is plenty to choose from, and the prices are more than reasonable.

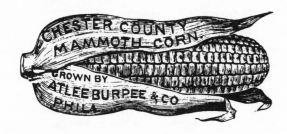

W. Atlee Burpee Company

300 Park Avenue, Warminster, PA 18974
Telephone: 215-674-4915

Catalog price: free

Burpee, the largest of all the mail-order gardening suppliers, has practically everything. The firm's primary business is flower and vegetable seed (many varieties are Burpee's own creations), but the spring catalog is also full of such extras as lilies, roses, fruit and nut trees, garden tools, and seed-starting supplies. Shoppers should watch for mentions of Burpee's leaflets, described in short paragraphs scattered throughout the catalog. Once free, these now cost 20¢ to 40¢, but they're packed with useful information.

A separate fall catalog, mailed in the summer, lists bulbs and perennial plants.

D. V. Burrell Seed Growers Co.

P.O. Box 150, Rocky Ford, CO 81067
Telephone: 303-254-3318

Catalog price: free

A good list of flower and vegetable seed aimed at the commercial grower, but with reasonably priced packets for the home gardener. Burrell's specialty is melons, and, if you're planning a section of your garden for watermelon, muskmelon, or cantaloupe, give this catalog a look. Thorough planting and growing instructions are given for most plants listed.

The Butchart Gardens

Box 4010, Sta. A, Victoria, BC, Canada V8X 3X4
Telephone: 604-652-4422

Catalog price: 40¢, deductible from first order

Seeds for the flowers grown at the famous Butchart Sunken Garden (a garden planted in an old limestone quarry). The list encompasses a wide array of annuals and perennials for borders, rock gardens, and hanging baskets, including the Himalayan blue poppy (*Meconopsis betonicifolia*), the pure

blue gentian salvia (*S. patens*), the dwarf Thumbellina zinnia, and a strain of nigella (love-in-the-mist).

Thomas Butcher

60 Wickham Road, Shirley, Croydon, Surrey, England CR9 8AG
Telephone: 44-1-654-3720 or 4254

Catalog price: free

A huge list of flower seed forms the bulk of this extensive catalog. Common garden flowers are listed along with rare varieties, houseplants, and exotic greenhouse plants. Shoppers will find seed for several varieties each of begonia, chrysanthemum, cyclamen, hibiscus, primula, and streptocarpus, to name just a few of the more than four hundred species sold. A more limited selection of herb, vegetable, tree, and shrub seed is tucked in the back of the catalog. Order by credit card to simplify foreign currency exchange.

Butterbrooke Farm

78 Barry Road, Oxford, CT 06483-1598
Telephone: 203-888-2000

Catalog price: long self-addressed stamped envelope

A seed cooperative that offers non-hybrid vegetable seed at low prices. All seeds are untreated and therefore free of the poisons used by many commercial seed growers. The list is not long, but Butterbrooke has all the basics necessary for a full vegetable garden.

Chiltern Seeds

Bortree Stile, Ulverston, Cumbria, England LA12 7PB

Catalog price: $2 in cash

An encyclopedic catalog of all manner of seed, listed alphabetically by botanical name. No pictures help guide the seed shopper, but the descriptions are a pleasure to read, and the vast scale of the offerings more than makes up for the lack of illustrations. With seed for garden perennials, flowering annuals, vegetables, trees, shrubs, and succulents, the 200-page catalog seems to have just about everything. A bias toward flowering plants makes the Chiltern selection particularly delightful for anyone planning an exceptional flower border.

The reader who takes the time to search will find a wide range of old-fashioned sweet peas (introduced by a brief history of the plant's discovery and cultivation), more than two dozen viola, violet, and pansy cultivars, almost 300 British wildflowers, and seed for Japanese cedar, Indian bean tree, and many rhododendron species.

The gigantic selection makes Chiltern a valuable source of supply, but the text of the catalog is almost as great a treasure. Besides giving thorough descriptions of each plant's requirements and growth habits, the writers offer hundreds of delightful asides. We learn, for instance, that nasturtiums have long been thought to have phosphorescent properties and that Linnaeus observed a plant emitting bright flashes of light. We are also treated to translations of many of the Latin names. Did you know that *Lampranthus spectabilis* means "shining flower worth seeing"? Or that the botanical name for the sensitive plant, *Mimosa pudica*, means "bashful mimosa"?

U.S. and Canadian orders must be accompanied by a bank check in sterling or charged to a Visa or Access card.

Comstock, Ferre & Co.
236 Main Street, P.O. Box 125, Wethersfield, CT 06109
Telephone: 203-529-6255

Catalog price: free

One of America's oldest gardening suppliers, Comstock, Ferre (pronounced "ferry") has been selling seeds since 1820. The firm doesn't broadcast its history throughout its catalog, but the list does have a comfortable tried-and-true appeal, what with the black-and-white drawings and old engravings that appear on most pages. The offerings are about evenly balanced between vegetables and flowers, with a selection of classic herbs added to round out the list.

The Cook's Garden
Moffits Bridge, P.O. Box 65, Londonderry, VT 05148
Telephone: 802-824-3400

Catalog price: free

Vegetable and herb seed for the serious kitchen garden. Forty lettuce varieties are listed, with 14 different chickories, six unusual sprouting and romanesco broccolis, and peppers that range in color from yellow to brown to purple to red. Many of the selections are from France and Italy, but a few American vegetables are sold; these include such favorites as Lincoln peas, Sweet 100 tomatoes, and Buttercrunch lettuce.

The Country Garden
Rt. 2, Box 455A, Crivitz, WI 54114
Telephone: 715-757-2045

Catalog price: $2 for descriptive catalog, free price list

If you're a flower gardener who pays close attention to color, Country Garden may have some answers for you. The offerings are precise color varieties rather than random mixes, and the hues are carefully described to help you avoid color clashes. The catalog contains a wide assortment of annual and perennial flower seed, more than 1,500 varieties in all, including dozens of different sweet pea strains and a big selection of calendula and poppy varieties.

A fall bulb list supplements the spring seed catalog.

C. A. Cruickshank Inc.
1015 Mt. Pleasant Road, Toronto, ON, Canada M4P 2M1
Telephone: 416-488-8292

Catalog price: free

Canadian representatives for Thompson & Morgan seeds (see page 00). Cruickshank sells only a selection from Thompson & Morgan's flower seed list, but a wealth of other offerings makes this a catalog that demands time and attention. Here gardeners can find dozens of tuberous begonias, dahlias, gladioli, lilies, daylilies, and wildflowers sold as bulbs, tubers, and plants, as well as scores of other plants, from orchids to miniature roses to gloxinias. All are well described, with growing instructions, and many entries are illustrated with drawings or color photographs. Cruickshank can export almost all its offerings to U.S. customers.

A separate iris list is sent out in April, and a fall bulb catalog is mailed in August.

William Dam Seeds
P.O. Box 8400, Dundas, ON, Canada L9H 6M1
Telephone: 416-628-6641

Catalog price: $1 in U.S., free in Canada

Supplier of flower and vegetable seed, with an especially good selection of short-season varieties. Many European vegetable strains are included along with the familiar best-sellers. The catalog, illustrated with both color and black-and-white photographs, provides some instructions for plant care. All seeds can be shipped to the U.S.

Dan's Garden Shop
5821 Woodwinds Circle, Frederick, MD 21701

Catalog price: free

Flower and vegetable seed in a catalog well illustrated with black-and-white photographs and drawings. Cultural instructions and good descriptions are given for each listing, as are the number of seeds per packet and per ounce, and, for vegetables, the length of row each packet or ounce of seeds will sow. Seed-starting supplies and plastic pots are also offered.

De Giorgi Company, Inc.
P.O. Box 413, Council Bluffs, IA 51502
Telephone: 712-323-2372

Catalog price: $1

Ninety-two pages of flower and vegetable seed make up this chunky catalog. De Giorgi saves money on printing by using cheap paper and old black-and-white illustrations and passes the savings on to you. Even premium hybrid varieties sell for less than $1 a packet, and many seeds can be had for 50¢. What the catalog lacks in beauty it makes up for in information. Every plant listing includes a good description, and almost all offer detailed growing directions.

Howard Dill
400 College Road, Windsor, NS, Canada B0N 2T0

Catalog price: free

Giant pumpkin seed. See "Growing the Big Ones," page 32.

Dominion Seed House
Georgetown, ON, Canada L7G 4A2

Catalog price: free to Canadian customers

Canadian orders only. A huge color catalog of flower and vegetable seed, bulbs, garden perennials and berry plants, tools, pots, fertilizers, pest controls, books, and seed-starting supplies. The firm has lots to offer in just about every category. Most offerings are illustrated, all are fully described.

Fred & Eleanor (Ellis) Doty
P.O. Box 940, Canby, OR 97013
Telephone: 503-266-9684

Catalog price: free price list

Pansy and columbine seed sold in 100-seed packets. The pansies are a large-flowered, ruffled type (Oregon Giants) in a mix of colors. The columbines are a mix of cultivars, described in the brochure as a blend of the Mrs. Scott Elliott hybrids and "other choice strains."

A Garden for Kids

Can you remember the thrill of having your first garden? Why not share that excitement with the children in your life? Several seed companies offer special seed collections for kids, and some catalogs sell special kid-size tools.

Henry Field Seed & Nursery Co. (page 18), Gurney Seed & Nursery Co. (page 19), and T & T Seeds Ltd. (page 30) all sell packets of vegetable and flower seeds selected especially for kids and priced to fit their budgets. The Field "Conglomeration" packet and the T & T "Kiddies Big Assortment Packet" cost just a dime each; Gurney's "Giant Jumble Seed Packet" goes for only a penny. Not just any dime or penny will do, however. To get the packets kids have to tape their own money to their parents' orders. Field also requires children to pen the word "Conglomeration" on the order form themselves. All three companies throw a little of everything into the mix, steering clear of plants that take special care to propagate. (The Field collection is limited to vegetables; the other two include flowers.) The packets can yield everything from pumpkins and watermelons to radishes and carrots and flowers from alyssums to zinnias. The packets seem like a great idea and a kind of guessing game that makes kids wonder just what it is they've planted.

Suttons Seeds Ltd. (page 30) presents a British approach to children's gardening. The firm offers separate flower- and vegetable-seed collections for kids, each in a normal-priced packet that parents will have to buy. No pumpkins or watermelons find their way into these packets; consideration has clearly been given to the amount of space the children will be allowed in the garden. The selections include carrot, lettuce, radish, nasturtium, and calendula seeds.

The W. Atlee Burpee Company (page 15) sells a children's garden kit called the "Kinder-Garden." It contains a black plastic mat (40 by 48 inches) with holes punched and marked for planting beans, beets, carrots, cucumbers, lettuce, onions, snap peas, radishes, spinach, tomatoes, turnips, marigolds, and zinnias; a packet of each of those seeds; anchor stakes; and a leaflet with instructions and ideas for kids' gardening.

Inspiration and ideas for gardening with children can also be found in profusion in a videocassette and booklet

set from the Brooklyn Botanic Garden (page 193) titled *Get Ready, Get Set, Grow! A Kid's Guide to Good Gardening.* The package sells for $32.45 postpaid (plus sales tax for New York residents) and includes a 15-minute video and two booklets, one for kids and one for supervising adults. Check prices after 1988.

If you feel like going all the way in setting up a child gardener, you might think about some child-size tools. Plow & Hearth (page 241) offers a set of four tools with 30-inch handles (leaf rake, garden rake, shovel, and hoe), and Smith & Hawken (page 241) offers a set of three tools (spade, fork, and garden rake) that are beautifully made, with T-grip ash handles and forged solid-socket heads. Smith & Hawken also sells a child-size Adirondack chair, brightly colored washable clogs made from rubber-like plastic, and the Suttons children's seed collections (see above).

Early's Farm & Garden Centre

P.O. Box 3024, Saskatoon, SK, Canada S7K 3S9
Telephone: 306-931-1982 (or 800-667-1159 within Saskatchewan)

Catalog price: free in Saskatchewan, $2 elsewhere, deductible from an order of $25 or more

Flower and vegetable seed and a wide selection of gardening supplies in a glossy color catalog. The firm has a big gardening-supply store at 2615 Lorne Avenue in Saskatoon.

ECHO

17430 Durrance Road, N. Fort Myers, FL 33917

Catalog price: long self-addressed stamped envelope

A non-profit organization that has worked for several years to develop new food crops for small farmers in Third World countries. In 1987, in an effort to raise money for its ongoing research efforts, ECHO began to offer North American farmers seed for some of its more successful plants. About 30 seeds were listed in the 1987 brochure, from egusi, an African melon, to spineless prickly pear cactus, the pads of which can be eaten raw. Descriptions and instructions for raising the plants help shoppers decide what might be appropriate for their gardens.

Elysian Hills

Rt. 1, Box 452, Brattleboro, VT 05301
Telephone: 802-257-0233

No catalog

Seed for the Gilfeather turnip, described as "an unusually mild, delicately flavored, oblong, white" variety. For a packet, send $1 and a long self-addressed stamped envelope. One packet (approximately 50 seeds) will plant a 50-foot row.

Farmer Seed & Nursery Co.

818 N.W. 4th Street, Faribault, MN 55021
Telephone: 507-334-1651

Catalog price: free

Color catalog of vegetable seed, flowering bulbs, and general nursery stock—fruit and shade trees, ornamental shrubs, roses, hedges, and berry plants. Farmer's inventory includes many favorites, but doesn't extend to unusual varieties. The firm also sells tools, canning equipment, and gardening supplies.

Fern Hill Farm

P.O. Box 185, Clarksboro, NJ 08020

Catalog price: long self-addressed stamped envelope

Seed for Dr. Martin pole lima beans, an heirloom variety. Seed can be ordered untreated or treated with the fungicide thiram. For an extra charge, the farm will even ship germinated seed, timed to arrive just as spring planting begins.

Henry Field Seed & Nursery Co.

Shenandoah, IA 51602
Telephone: 605-665-4491

Catalog price: free

A color-saturated catalog of vegetable and flower seed, fruit, nut, and shade trees, berry plants, ornamental shrubs, hedges, roses, and flowering garden plants. Popular varieties abound in this list, along with such bizarre attractions as yard-long cucumbers, midget corn (grows four-inch ears), and a flowering crab apple grafted to bloom in five different colors. Several pages are devoted to gardening supplies. A center spread of customer testimonials with pictures of homegrown harvests is a regular feature of Field's catalog.

Fisher's Garden Store

P.O. Box 236, Belgrade, MT 59714
Telephone: 406-388-6052

Catalog price: free

Vegetable and flower seed selected for high altitudes and short growing seasons. Some of the vegetable varieties, such as Mountaineer winter squash, Glacier sweet corn, and Early Set tomatoes, are Fisher originals.

The Fragrant Path

P.O. Box 328, Ft. Calhoun, NE 68023

Catalog price: $1

A real charmer of a seed catalog, filled with fragrant and old-fashioned plants and with other "rarities" that have found favor with the proprietors. The catalog has a personal flavor to it; its descriptions are spiced with opinion and with quotes from the likes of Izaak Walton and Thomas Jefferson. On modern petunias, for example, the writer notes that "some of the large ruffled ones are quite abominable, as after they have faded, they hang on the plant like soiled tissue." The firm offers an old-fashioned mixture as an alternative. We had good success with seeds for some unusual flowers and herbs that we ordered in 1987.

Garden City Seeds

P.O. Box 297, Victor, MT 59875
Telephone: 406-961-4837

Catalog price: $1

Open-pollinated vegetable seed for northern growers; a blend of old favorites, heirloom varieties, and modern introductions. The catalog is exceptionally informative, providing organic pest- and disease-control measures for all vegetables and full directions for saving seed. Some of the heirloom varieties—such as Mandam Bride corn from the Mandam Indian tribe of Minnesota—will be difficult to find elsewhere. The seeds are not treated, and some are organically grown in Montana.

Gardeners' Choice
County Road 687, Hartford, MI 49057
Telephone: 616-621-2481

Catalog price: $1

A hard-sell catalog of "amazing" vegetables, flowers, trees, and houseplants, crowded with bold headlines ("Yes! Bushels of Meaty Walnuts from This *Soaring* Shade Tree") and dramatic color illustrations. If you are in the market for seven-pound onions, asparagus "thicker than a man's thumb," "roof-high" climbing tomatoes, or "dinner plate" dahlias, then Gardeners' Choice may be for you.

Gardenimport
P.O. Box 760, Thornhill, ON, Canada L3T 4A4
Telephone: 416-731-1950

Catalog price: $2

Gardenimport is the North American distributor of Suttons Seeds (see page 00), and the firm backs up its offerings from the British seed house with an attractive inventory of bulbs and perennial plants. The $2 catalog fee buys four gorgeous color booklets—the spring and fall lists for two years. An elegant design combines sharp color photographs with antique engravings. The text describes each listing and occasionally proffers growing advice. Among the special attractions here are Suttons's famous sweet peas, a nice selection of primulas, some tasty European vegetables, and a wide-ranging inventory of bulbs and tubers—from gladioli, dahlias, and tuberous begonias to lilies, narcissi, and tulips. The firm sells a good selection of irises, daylilies, and heirloom peonies. Although Gardenimport presents only a selection of what it considers the most outstanding features of Suttons's list—some 300 flowers and vegetables—it will fill special orders for other Suttons seeds.

Giant Watermelons
P.O. Box 141, Hope, AR 71801

Catalog price: free

Seed for giant watermelons. See "Growing the Big Ones," page 32.

Gleckler's Seedsmen ✔
Metamora, OH 43540

Catalog price: free

The offbeat is the rule for vegetables from Gleckler's. Here you'll find seeds for foot-long sweet peppers, three-foot carrots, purple broccoli, pink celery, white-skinned cucumbers, and striped eggplant. Many varieties are imported from Europe and the Far East. If you're looking for something different for the garden, you may want to try Gleckler's.

Good Seed
P.O. Box 702, Tonasket, WA 98855

Catalog price: $1

Heirloom seeds are offered alongside modern introductions in this 64-page catalog. A seed-saving philosophy pervades the list: no hybrids are sold, only open-pollinated varieties. New varieties are not offered for mere novelty; they must have proved their merits. And tremendous effort has clearly been made to seek out rare old-timers. Eight different native American corns are offered, along with such classic 19th-century vegetables as Stowell's Evergreen sweet corn (the original sweet corn introduced in 1840), Ice Cream watermelon (recently rescued and sold again beginning in 1987), and Thomas Laxton peas. Extensive instructions are given for starting and raising all seeds. Seed-saving tips are offered, and the 1987 catalog contained a long essay on soil care. Several pages are given over to flower and herb seed.

Grace's Gardens
10 Bay Street, Westport, CT 06880

Catalog price: 50¢, deductible from first order

Jane Grace calls hers the "world's most unusual seed catalog," and she's not far from the mark. More a flier than a catalog (it all fits on a single folded page), the list features a "big" theme: big tomatoes, giant pumpkins, yard-long beans, and 18-inch cucumbers. By 1987 Ms. Grace had dropped many of the old-fashioned offerings of her earlier lists in favor of newer (and bigger) selections, but she still sells the Abraham Lincoln tomato.

Grianán Gardens
P.O. Box 14492, San Francisco, CA 94114

Catalog price: $1, deductible from first order

A collection of flower and herb seed with an appealing Victorian flavor. Old-fashioned favorites mingle with recent innovations in an attractive catalog illustrated with 19th-century engravings. The Himalayan blue poppy is here, along with moonflower, gas plant, and Japanese anemone. The firm is working to offer more of its seeds in individual color choices rather than in mixes. In 1987 it sold snapdragons, strawflower, verbena, and sweet peas separated by hue.

Gurney Seed & Nursery Co.
Yankton, SD 57079

Catalog price: free

Everything is pictured in color in Gurney's oversize seed and nursery catalog—every strawberry, corn, and tomato variety, every rose and dahlia, even peat pots and canning jars. And the firm seems to sell practically everything for the garden, from seeds to trees to tools. Gurney says its catalog contains more than 4,000 items but we came out with a tally closer to 2,000. Either way, these pages offer a tremendous volume of choice and hours of winter reverie. (We ordered a heavy-duty nutcracker for shelling black walnuts, and we can attest that it works.)

The best deal in the Gurney catalog—the "Giant Jumble Seed Packet"—is available only to kids. It costs only a penny, but it has to be a child's own penny, taped to a parent's order. Inside is a "fun mix of flower and vegetable seeds," which we're told might hold surprises like sunflowers, watermelons, peas or squash, or practically anything else that grows easily.

Halifax Seed Company Ltd.
Box 8026, Halifax, NS, Canada B3K 5L8
Telephone: 902-454-7456

Catalog price: $1, free within Atlantic Canada

A seed supplier serving Atlantic Canada, Halifax Seed Company deals primarily in vegetable seed, but also sells flower and herb seed, some roses, perennials (as plants), berry plants, bulbs, and tubers. Several pages in the black-and-white catalog are devoted to tools and other gardening supplies. No plants, bulbs, or tubers are shipped outside Atlantic Canada.

Harris Seeds
Moreton Farm, 3670 Buffalo Road, Rochester, NY 14624

Catalog price: free

Joseph Harris launched his seed business back in 1879, but the current thick color catalog has a distinctly modern look. The emphasis here is on the new rather than the old: most of the vegetables sold are modern hybrids, and the shopper has to search to find any old garden standards. The catalog is split evenly between flower and vegetable offerings, all presented in an easy-to-read format with good-size color illustrations. In addition to its voluminous seed list, Harris sells clematis plants, gladiolus corms, and an array of tools and gardening supplies.

Hastings
P.O. Box 4274, Atlanta, GA 30302-4274
Telephone: 404-524-8861

Catalog price: free

"Seedsmen to the South" is Hastings's motto, and seeds for many warm-climate and heat-resistant vegetables and flowers are offered along with trees and shrubs suitable for southern planting. Three pages of beans open this color catalog, which also includes many varieties of okra, corn, collards, southern peas, tomatoes, and sweet potatoes. Such sun-loving flowers as portulaca, ornamental peppers, cosmos, and zinnia are sold as seed.

The nursery stock includes roses, berries, ornamental trees and shrubs, and fruit and nut trees. Fifteen apple varieties are offered, plus 12 pecans, 11 peaches, and cherries, pears, nectarines, persimmons, and plums.

Heirloom Garden Seeds
P.O. Box 138, Guerneville, CA 95446
Telephone: 707-869-0967

Catalog price: $2

From the name, mail-order shoppers might expect to find old-time favorites and plants appropriate to the gardens of historic Williamsburg in this catalog. Indeed, the heirloom gardener will find many tempting delights here, such as Oxheart carrots, Bantam corn, angelica, soapwort, and scarlet pimpernel. But readers will also come across some surprises. The firm stretches the meaning of "heirloom" to reach the corners of horticultural history, and it has pulled out such oddities as pleurisy root (once eaten boiled with buffalo

meat), wormwood (the controversial ingredient in absinthe), and kudzu vine (recommended for container growth only). The catalog makes for fascinating reading.

Herb Gathering Inc.
5742 Kenwood, Kansas City, MO 64110
Telephone: 816-523-2653

Catalog price: $2, deductible from first order

French vegetable seed, herb seed, and fresh herbs "for the tastefully creative." The gardening cook will have much to choose from on these pages and while browsing can learn the French names for many vegetables and herbs. For the floral craftsperson, Herb Gathering has assembled a collection of flowers and other ornamental plants suited to drying for wreaths and bouquets.

High Altitude Gardens
P.O. Box 4238, Ketchum, ID 83340
Telephone: 208-726-3221

Catalog price: $2, deductible from first order

Short-season vegetable seeds for mountain and northern gardeners, along with a big selection of wildflower and grass seeds. The owners point out that their fast-growing vegetables may also be attractive to low-altitude customers who garden at vacation homes and who need a crop to ripen in just a few weeks. The wildflower listings take up 20 pages of the catalog and include more than 120 species. The firm offers a number of regional wildflower mixes and will custom blend mixes based on answers to a questionnaire.

Horticultural Enterprises
P.O. Box 810082, Dallas, TX 75381-0082

Catalog price: free

A hot-yellow poster-style brochure helps put gardeners in the mood for a mouth-scorching assortment of chile peppers. Seeds for more than 30 varieties are offered (with a few sweet peppers thrown in to prevent overheating). To complement the pepper harvest, the firm sells seed for such south-of-the-border favorites as chia, jicama, tatume, and epazote.

J. L. Hudson, Seedsman
P.O. Box 1058, Redwood City, CA 94064

Catalog price: $1

Poring over the J. L. Hudson catalog, the reader gets the impression that this is more of a mission than a business. Clearly a tremendous effort has gone into collecting seed for the many hundreds of species and varieties listed, and into describing them in such a thorough and eccentric way. Where else can a gardener find seed for skunk cabbage (the stinky American swamp plant), lemon grass (used as a flavoring in Thai cooking), and semilla de chintallauha (an antidote for black widow spider bites)? Hudson has seed for the Himalayan blue poppy and for several related meconopsis species. The catalog also lists seed for more than 60 acacias and a dozen amaranths, for Bloody Butcher field corn, Japanese radishes, and Black Valentine bush beans. For the perennial border Hudson sells Russell lupines by color, digitalis species and cultivars, and a score of campanulas. For your greenhouse you can order seed for palms, passionflowers, and

dozens of plants we've never heard of. All are listed by botanical name (a brief index to common names offers some help to the non-expert) and described in a wonderfully peculiar, quasi-academic style. This catalog is an anomaly and a delight—a terrific alternative to mainstream seed sources.

Ed Hume Seeds
P.O. Box 1450, Kent, WA 98032

Catalog price: free

Short-season vegetable and flower seed (which, of course, can also be grown where the summers are longer). This is a catalog for the general home gardener rather than the specialist. All plants are listed by common names, and seeds are sold only by the packet, not in bulk quantities. The seeds are priced very reasonably, and all are untreated. Someone at the firm has a special interest in dahlias; the catalog lists almost 50 varieties.

Illinois Foundation Seeds
P.O. Box 722, Champaign, IL 61820
Telephone: 217-485-6260

Catalog price: free

A color brochure presenting seed for several varieties of hybrid sweet corn. All have a high-sugar gene, which makes for extra sweetness when the corn is eaten freshly picked and for corn that keeps its sweetness longer when stored or shipped. Seed is sold in three-ounce packets or by the pound.

International Growers Exchange
P.O. Box 52248, Livonia, MI 48152

Catalog price: $5, deductible from first order

We wonder if there are any plants that International Growers Exchange does *not* sell. Thick spring and fall lists seem to cover everything from orchids and succulents to wildflowers and perennials. The selection of unusual bulbs in the fall catalog is as big as any we've seen, and the wildflower offerings are truly impressive. Dozens of orchid species from around the world are offered, along with pages of perennial listings, herb plants and seeds, begonias, gloxinias, bromeliads, and more than 100 native Japanese alpines. About the only things missing are trees and vegetables. Most of the plants are listed with only brief descriptions. Some of the more common types can be ordered only by the dozen.

Island Seed Co.
P.O. Box 4278, Sta. A, Victoria, BC, Canada V8X 3X8

Catalog price: $2, deductible on orders of $15

General flower and vegetable seed presented in a thick descriptive catalog with few illustrations. Growing instructions are given for all plants; for tomatoes this advice runs to three pages. The flower seed tends to be sold in color mixes, though some plants, such as marigolds, sweet peas, and wallflowers, can be ordered by specific color.

Johnny's Selected Seeds
305 Foss Hill Road, Albion, ME 04910
Telephone: 207-437-9294 or 4301

Catalog price: free

Vegetable seed with an emphasis on short-season varieties for northern growers. Each variety is thoroughly described, and cultural information is given for each vegetable type. Johnny's list of vegetables looks to be a match for any competitor, with 35 varieties of tomato, 25 of corn, and 23 of lettuce. The approach of the business is to provide honest information rather than a hard sell, and we have friends who swear by the quality of the seeds. Estimates of the number of seeds per packet and the length of row the packet will sow are given for each seed type—a tremendous help in matching a seed order to a garden plan. All seed is sold untreated.

Johnny's also sells gardening supplies, books, and some flower seed.

Johnson Seed Co.
P.O. Box 172, Dousman, WI 53186

Catalog price: two first-class stamps

Jim Johnson puts out this homegrown vegetable seed list himself, offering a blend of heirloom varieties and more recent introductions. Jacobs Cattle bean is here, as is Moon-and-Stars watermelon, Mammoth Sandwich Island salsify, and Stowell's Evergreen sweet corn. Almost 200 listings in all.

J. W. Jung Seed Co.
335 S. High Street, Randolph, WI 53957-0001
Telephone: 414-326-3121

Catalog price: free

J. W. Jung started his seed business back in 1907, and at this writing he still lives next door to the firm's headquarters and still keeps tabs on the company's progress. He turned 100 in May 1987.

The oversize color catalog displays a full line of vegetable and flower seed, along with a substantial selection of nursery stock, including berry plants, fruit trees, ornamental trees and shrubs, roses, wildflowers, perennials, and houseplants. The firm sells bulbs for lilies, gladioli, irises, and dahlias, and an ample assortment of gardening supplies. The mix of illustrations in the catalog is delightful—new color photographs appear on the same page as hand-tinted engravings a century old. And that mix of pictures mirrors the blend of old and new in the seed selection. Jung doesn't make a big deal of its heirloom seeds; it tends to feature the hybrids. But the old-timers are shuffled in there on every page.

Kalmia Farm

P.O. Box 3881, Charlottesville, VA 22903

Catalog price: free

Hardy perennial onions offered in a summer catalog for fall planting. The farm has rescued the potato onion from relative obscurity (it was popular in the 19th century) and now claims to be the biggest supplier of that plant. Kalmia Farm offers two other types that are winter hardy into Canada: multiplier and Egyptian top onions. So as not to seem narrow-minded, the farm sells several different shallots and garlics and a number of flowering alliums.

Kilgore Seed Company

1400 W. First Street, Sanford, FL 32771

Catalog price: $1

Florida gardeners will appreciate the growing tips given in the Kilgore catalog. A month-by-month vegetable planting guide shows when to set seeds out in the Florida garden, and another chart shows how much seed and how much garden space you'll need to grow a crop of vegetables to feed two or four people.

Vegetables—specifically those that grow well in the South—are Kilgore's main strength. Along with standard varieties popular throughout the country, gardeners will find such southern specialties as blackeye, crowder, and purple-hull peas, Floradel and Tropic tomatoes, and Florida Giant watermelon. Several pages of the catalog are devoted to flower seed.

Kitazawa Seed Co.

1748 Laine Avenue, Santa Clara, CA 95051-3012

Catalog price: free

This firm sells seed for 50 oriental vegetable varieties. Gardeners with a taste for oriental cooking will find seed for several different daikons (Japanese radishes), mustards, and Chinese cabbages, along with Japanese melons for pickling and Japanese squash. The small flier has no pictures, but gives good descriptions.

The Kusa Research Foundation

P.O. Box 761, Ojai, CA 93023

Telephone: 805-646-5536

Catalog price: $1, deductible from first order

Seed for rare cereal grain crops, many of which have been in use for centuries but aren't found on the lists of major seed

suppliers. Among the foundation's offerings are Candlestick millet, widely grown in India and Africa, Dragon's Claw millet, a "staple food of strong hard-working peasants," Chilean lentils, White Pearl grain sorghum, and hulless barley.

Lagomarsino Seeds

5675-A Power Inn Road, Sacramento, CA 95824

Telephone: 916-381-1024

Catalog price: free

This firm concentrates on vegetable seed. The brochure lists about 300 choices, from chicory to Chinese cabbage to popular tomato and bean varieties. No pictures or descriptions are included to help with the selection. A separate list of flower seeds (more than 100 types) and of tree seeds can be had by calling or writing.

Lakeland Nursery Sales

Unique Merchandise Mart, Building 4, Hanover, PA 17333

Catalog price: free

Serious gardeners may have trouble dealing with the Lakeland catalog; it is a bit like a plant-oriented *National Enquirer*. But we appreciate the tabloids, and we get a kick out of the Lakeland catalog. Roses, fruit trees, decorative trees and shrubs, vegetables, and flowers are offered in a presentation that makes even ordinary plants seem exotic. Climbing tomatoes are made to seem like an incredible innovation. The Thundercloud plum tree is headlined "Purple Passion Makes Any Yard More Exciting." And a scented geranium is sold as a "deodorizer plant." Of course many of the offerings really are strange—mammoth strawberries with fruit the size of peaches, dogwoods and roses grafted to bloom in three colors, giant redwood tree seedlings, and potato-tomato combinations that yield two crops from a single plant. You can't get much stranger than that!

McGregor Nursery Sales, at the same address, sells many of the same items in a more sober, less attention-grabbing catalog. McGregor offers more trees and shrubs and fewer vegetables.

D. Landreth Seed Company

P.O. Box 6426, Batimore, MD 21230

Telephone: 301-727-3922 or 3923

Catalog price: $2, deductible from first order

David Landreth launched his seed business in 1784 with an ad in a Philadelphia paper announcing his newly imported stock. That first list included "most of the approved broccolis, . . . peas and beans of every curious . . . kind, . . . short top'd, best salmon and real turnip-rooted radishes, . . . a variety of sweet herb and a curious collection of best flower seeds, in small lots or assortments."

The firm still sells all that and quite a bit more. The emphasis in the catalog is on vegetable seed. A fair selection of flower seed is offered, but is crammed into a list at the back of the booklet without pictures or descriptions. The vegetables get more respectful attention, with black-and-white pictures, growing instructions, and clear descriptions. In addition to the "approved broccolis," shoppers will find most of the popular varieties of tomatoes, beans, carrots, beets, and lettuce.

Lands-End Seeds
P.O. Box 216, Crawford, CO 81415

Price list: free

One of North America's smallest seed houses, Lands-End sells only seed for a white soup bean and root cuttings for horseradish, comfrey, and Jerusalem artichoke. All are grown in Crawford, Colorado, at a 6,800-foot elevation. Planting instructions are sent with orders.

Le Jardin du Gourmet
Box 77, W. Danville, VT 05873

Catalog price: free

Herb, vegetable, and flower seed. See "The 22¢ Seed Packet," page 24.

Le Marché Seeds International
P.O. Box 190, Dixon, CA 95620
Telephone: 916-678-9244

Catalog price: $2

The name is French for "the market," and a garden grown from these seeds will produce feasts of vegetables and herbs of the types found in the produce markets of France, Italy, and the Orient. Some American favorites, like Illini Gold sweet corn and Oxheart tomato, have been thrown in for good measure, along with some specialties of other parts of the world, such as jicama and tomatillo from Mexico. The cosmopolitan gardener/chef will appreciate the opportunity to choose from a range of chicories, cornichons, Asian eggplants, and European lettuces. The catalog is an oversize affair, illustrated with attractive drawings and sprinkled with recipes and growing suggestions.

Orol Ledden & Sons
P.O. Box 7, Sewell, NJ 08080-0007
Telephone: 609-468-1000

Catalog price: free

A general catalog of flower and vegetable seed with more than 600 listings. Gardeners can choose from 16 cantaloupe varieties, 14 types of corn, and more than 30 tomatoes. Most of the flower seeds are sold as color mixes, though the more popular kinds, like marigolds, zinnias, and petunias, can be had in specific colors. The firm carries a full line of gardening supplies—tools, fertilizers, insecticides, and pots. Those who live in the area can visit the Ledden store at the corner of Atlantic and Center avenues in Sewell.

Letherman's Inc.
1221 Tuscarawas Street E., Canton, OH 44707
Telephone: 216-452-5704

Letherman's is a commercial seed supplier, but most of the seeds it carries can also be purchased in relatively small quantities, roughly two to four times the size of a standard packet. Home gardeners with spacious plots may want to consider the firm as a seed source, since it offers a substantial choice of varieties, particularly among the vegetables. More than 50 tomato varieties and 60 plus types of corn are listed.

Libby Creek Farm
P.O. Box 177, Carlton, WA 98814
Telephone: 509-997-0071

Catalog price: long self-addressed stamped envelope

Spanish Roja garlic offered for eating or for planting. Seed garlic is in short supply, so place your order early, by the end of June, to be sure you're not left out.

Liberty Seed Co.
P.O. Box 806, New Philadelphia, OH 44663
Telephone: 216-364-1611

Catalog price: free

General flower and vegetable seed from an old family-owned company. Vegetables are offered in larger-than-average packets at reasonable prices. Hybrid tomatoes, for example, are sold in 50-seed packets rather than in the standard packet of 30. The vegetable selection is substantial: 34 corn varieties, 27 tomatoes, and 15 muskmelons. The flower offerings are somewhat more limited, but all the popular types are available. All vegetable and flower varieties are described, and a few are pictured in color. Some planting and growing information is provided.

Lindenberg Seeds Ltd.
803 Princess Avenue, Brandon, MB, Canada R7A OP5

Catalog price: free

Vegetable and flower seed and some nursery stock, including a good selection of short-season vegetables. The nursery offerings include roses, grapes, berries, and a few perennials and roots and tubers for peonies, dahlias, lilies, begonias, and gladioli. U.S. customers can order seeds only and have to pay an export handling charge ($3 per order in 1987).

Lockhart Seeds
3 North Wilson Way, P.O. Box 1361, Stockton, CA 95201
Telephone: 209-466-4401

Catalog price: $1

This firm sells primarily to commercial vegetable growers and offers no flower seed at all. However, many of the listings are available in packets or in quantities small enough for the home gardener, so some may want to consider Lockhart as a seed source. The only restriction is a $10 minimum order. The emphasis here is on modern hybrids. The only non-hybrid corn in the catalog is an ornamental type for drying.

Long Island Seed & Plant
P.O. Box 1285, Riverhead, NY 11901

Price list: free

A simple postcard serves as a price list and catalog for this firm, which sells vegetable seed with a novel twist. Rather than offer dozens of heirloom and hybrid varieties, Long Island combines many different types in a single mix. A packet of carrot seed will produce diverse bunches of carrots, and gardeners may have fun trying to figure out what they've grown. The tomato mixes are separated into cherry types, medium determinate types, and large indeterminate types so that growers can choose more precisely what they want.

McFayden Seeds

P.O. Box 1800, Brandon, MB, Canada R7A 6N4
Telephone: 204-726-0759

Catalog price: free to Canadian customers, not sent to U.S.

The name says seeds, but McFayden sells much more. A good selection of vegetable seed covers the first quarter of the catalog; flower seed and bulbs take up the next few pages; then the list turns to nursery stock—20 colorful pages of perennials, roses, fruit trees, berry plants, and ornamental trees and shrubs. A fall catalog offers even more bulbs for

fall planting. McFayden carries a big inventory of gardening and kitchen supplies, including grinders and stuffers for sausage making and a ravioli press. Canadian orders only.

Earl May Seed & Nursery Co.

Shenandoah, IA 51603
Telephone: 712-246-1020 or 800-831-4193

Catalog price: free

Vegetable and flower seed and nursery stock laid out in a bright color catalog with illustrations of just about everything. Most of the popular vegetables are here, with the balance tipping toward the hybrids. Only a few annual flower seeds are sold (half the choices are marigolds and zinnias), but a number of perennials are offered as plants. The nursery line is more extensive than at most of the big seed companies. Fruit and nut trees, roses, berry plants, grapevines,

The 22¢ Seed Packet

Raymond Saufroy stumbled onto the idea of tiny seed packets almost by accident, but the inexpensive packages have proved a boon for his business and a popular money saver for the small-scale gardener. Saufroy founded Le Jardin du Gourmet in 1954 as a mail-order supplier of shallots, herbs, and other continental gourmet delights. Over the years he's also carved out a niche as a source of seeds for hard-to-find European herbs and vegetables such as chervil, bergamot, radicchio, and endive.

In 1978 *Family Circle* offered to print a small feature on Le Jardin du Gourmet, but only if Saufroy put together an inexpensive sample package that readers could order by mail. He decided on a $1 collection that included eight small herb-seed packets and copies of his favorite French recipes. Fifty thousand readers sent Saufroy their dollars that first month, and many wanted to know if he sold other little seed packages.

Since then Le Jardin du Gourmet has expanded its offering of 22¢ seed packages. Gardeners with limited space may now choose from 65 varieties of herbs, 200 different vegetables, and 25 garden flowers. The smaller packets are just the thing for apartment dwellers, window-box gardeners, and anyone who wants to sow just a few plants rather than a whole row or wants try out some unfamiliar items.

Le Jardin du Gourmet also offers standard-size seed packages at prices that range from 60¢ to $1.25. And, if

the anticipation of delicious herbs and salads proves too much to bear as you leaf through the catalog, you may add a tin of mussels, snails, or pâté to your order.

The catalog is free. Or send for the "Get Acquainted Offer": for $3.50 you'll get eight herb-seed packets (basil, caraway, chervil, chives, dill, roquette, savory, and sorrel), a half pound of shallots, some garlic, and recipes and planting instructions for everything.

Le Jardin du Gourmet

Box 77, West Danville, VT 05873

shade and ornamental trees, flowering shrubs, and hedges make up a hefty chunk of the catalog. The firm carries the usual assortment of seed-starting supplies, fertilizers, tools, and kitchen aids, as well as some unusual items: wind-sock flamingo "decoys," martin houses, and Gardena-brand sprinklers.

Mellinger's Inc.

Vegetable seed. See under *Trees and Shrubs*, page 159.

The Meyer Seed Company

600 S. Caroline Street, Baltimore, MD 21231
Telephone: 301-342-4224

Catalog price: free

The Meyer catalog seems at first glance to be geared to the commercial grower. Only a few of the vegetable varieties listed are described and pictured; most are simply named in the price chart, where the number of days from planting to maturity is also given. But all the seeds are sold in packets as well as in larger quantities, and the firm welcomes orders from home gardeners. Meyer offers most of the standard vegetable varieties—some old-timers and a lot of hybrids— and a somewhat more limited menu of flower seed. Several pages of gardening supplies fill the back of the catalog.

Midwest Seed Growers

505 Walnut Street, Kansas City, MO 64106
Telephone: 816-842-1493

Catalog price: free

A vegetable and flower seed catalog for commercial and large-scale home gardeners. All seed is sold by weight; the smallest quantities are the equivalent of several packets. Corn, for example, can be bought only in quantities of a pound or more, and most tomatoes are sold in quantities of at least an ounce. (The more expensive hybrids are available in smaller lots.) If you have long rows to fill, you may want to take a look at this list.

Mountain Seed and Nursery

P.O. Box 9107, Moscow, ID 83843
Telephone: 208-882-8040

Catalog price: $1, deductible from first order

Vegetable seed for short-season growers in a simple descriptive catalog. Not all varieties are described, but basic cultural information is given for each vegetable type. The selection ranges from old favorites to new hybrids, covering two dozen early-ripening tomatoes (many of them developed at the University of Idaho), 16 varieties of corn, and 15 peas. The firm also publishes a native seed list under the name Northplan Seed Producers (see entry under *Wildflowers*, page 178).

Mountain Valley Seeds & Nursery

1798 N. 1200 E., Logan, UT 84321
Telephone: 801-752-0247

Catalog price: free

General garden seed in a descriptive, lightly illustrated black-and-white catalog. Hybrids predominate on the vegetable end of the list, the offerings selected to bear well in short-season areas. The list is not as extensive as some. Only eight to-matoes are sold, for example, but among them are the popular Sweet 100 and Celebrity varieties. The flower list fits on just four pages and is largely confined to favorites sold in color mixes.

Nationwide Seed & Supply

4801 Fegenbush Lane, Louisville, KY 40228

Catalog price: free

A small selection of vegetable seed sold in reasonably priced packets. Most of the standard varieties are priced at less than 50¢ per packet, and all the hybrids cost less than $1. The catalog describes each variety and illustrates a few.

Native Seeds/SEARCH

3950 W. New York Drive, Tucson, AZ 85745

Catalog price: $1

In a way this is the ultimate heirloom seed catalog. Native Seeds/SEARCH is a non-profit organization devoted to saving and furthering the use of traditional crops of the Southwest. The group has collected seed for more than 300 vegetable varieties grown by American Indians in the region and offers them for sale in a fascinating descriptive booklet. Desert gardeners can choose from strains that have been grown in their region for hundreds, even thousands, of years. Scores of different corn types are offered, including several blue corns, as well as a number of ancient chiles, amaranths, gourds, tomatillos, and tobaccos. The huge bean selection puts Burpee to shame.

Those interested in furthering the cause can become members for a $10 annual fee. Members receive a quarterly newsletter and are eligible to join the growers' network.

Neal's Open-Pollinated

Rt. 2, Mt. Vernon, IA 52314
Telephone: 319-895-8171 or 6059

Catalog price: long self-addressed stamped envelope

Seed for Reid's yellow dent corn, an open-pollinated variety used primarily as livestock feed, sold by the bushel (56 pounds).

Nichols Garden Nursery

1190 N. Pacific Highway, Albany, OR 97321
Telephone: 503-928-9280

Catalog price: free

Herbs take center stage at the Nichols nursery. They stand alone in the first few pages of a catalog that also carries a big selection of vegetable seed, a smaller choice of flower seed, and some gardening supplies. The herb seed offerings include many intriguing edibles, such as Thai basil, Florence fennel (harvest the root), and cardoon, as well as such medicinal curiosities as mole plants ("drives moles from the neighborhood"), and mugwort ("good moth repellent"). And, since many herbs don't grow well from seed, the nursery sells a big selection of plants—French tarragon, English lavender, winter savory, and handfuls of mints and thymes. The vegetable listings touch on the usual favorites, and delve a little deeper than normal into spicy offerings like peppers and radishes and foreign leafy greens like chicory, celtuce, and mizuna.

Ontario Seed Company, Ltd.
P.O. Box 144, 16 King Street S., Waterloo, ON, Canada N2J 3Z9
Telephone: 519-886-0557

Catalog price: free in Canada, $2 for U.S. customers

Flower and vegetable seed in an illustrated black-and-white catalog. Vegetables take up the bulk of the listings, encompassing a familiar mix of old and new varieties (two dozen corn choices and as many tomatoes). The featured vegetable for 1987 was the Red Robin tomato, a compact plant suitable for raising in pots. The flower selection rarely strays from standard favorites, most offered in color mixes. In the 1987 catalog the flower illustrations frequently appeared without proper captions and so far from the listings that they were almost useless as aids to selection. Tools, gardening supplies, seed-starting necessities, books, and fertilizers fill the back of the catalog.

P & P Seed Company
14050 Gowanda State Road, Collins, NY 14034

Catalog price: free

Seed for giant pumpkins. See "Growing the Big Ones," page 32.

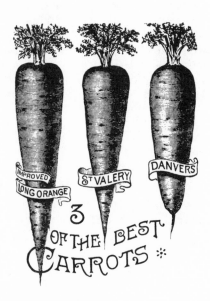

3 OF THE BEST CARROTS

Park Seed Co.
Cokesbury Road, Greenwood, SC 29647-0001
Telephone: 803-223-7333 or 4946

Catalog price: free

As a one-stop source of flower and vegetable seed and basic gardening supplies, Park is hard to beat. The 1987 catalog ran to a gigantic 132 pages, all plastered with color plates of the hundreds of varieties listed. Flower seeds have gained the upper hand here. They take up the first two-thirds of the catalog and stretch from the very popular to the downright unusual. Gardeners wanting a packet of yellow French marigolds will find them easily. A little searching will turn up some more offbeat treasures, like a lilac-colored lisianthus, dwarf delphiniums, and the Himalayan blue poppy. The vegetable offerings are a match for those in any of the big cat-

alogs—nearly 40 different tomatoes in 1987 and 20 corn varieties. (Heirloom seed savers will be disappointed in the emphasis given to hybrids. Of the 1987 corn listings, for example, only one was an open-pollinated strain.)

Perhaps the best feature of the Park catalog is the center spread: a combination index and germination/culture guide. Every plant in the catalog is listed in the guide, and a coded system gives detailed instructions for starting seed and growing plants to maturity.

In addition to seeds, Park sells nursery stock for garden perennials, roses, clematis vines (16 varieties), and perennial herbs and carries a limited selection of gardening supplies. Spring bulbs are scattered alphabetically through the spring seed catalog. A separate catalog of bulbs for fall planting is mailed in early summer.

Patrick's Nursery & SunGarden Seeds
P.O. Box 130, Ty Ty, GA 31795
Telephone: 912-382-1122 or 1770

Catalog price: free

Fruit and nut trees, berry plants, grapevines, and vegetable seed, the selections made with the southern grower in mind. Fruit varieties for the Deep South account for about half the nursery stock, and these varieties are broken out so that gardeners can find them easily. The vegetable seed prices were among the lowest we found in 1987.

Peace Seeds
2385 S.E. Thompson Street, Corvallis, OR 97333

Catalog price: $1 for seed list, $6 for annual *Catalog and Research Journal*

Peace Seeds has come up with an entirely different way of organizing a seed list, a reflection of the firm's novel approach to the seed business. All plants—flowers, vegetables, trees, and shrubs—are filed in a single list by botanical name, including species, genus, family, order, and superorder. A gardener looking for Buttercrunch lettuce seeds, for example, would need to know that lettuce, *Lactuca sativa*, belongs to the superorder *Asteriflorae* (unless he's willing to scan for common names the way we did). The effect is to give a sense of where plants fit into the natural order (we learned that marigolds and zinnias are close relatives of lettuce and burdock), but it certainly makes things difficult to find. The list includes seed for almost 600 different plants, from hybrid and heirloom vegetables to wildflowers and trees.

The *Catalog and Research Journal* offers descriptions of all plants on the seed list, as well as "an informative way of looking at the plant kingdom based on evolution."

The Pepper Gal
10536 119th Avenue N., Largo, FL 33543

Catalog price: long self-addressed stamped envelope

A regular inferno of pepper seed! Dorothy L. Van Vleck is the Pepper Gal, and she has managed to collect seed for more than 250 pepper varieties. These are about evenly divided among sweet, hot, and ornamental types. Gardeners who can't make up their minds when faced with such a daunting list might want to try one of the mixtures. Ms. Van Vleck refers to those special pepper fans who supply her with seed as her "pepper friends." Maybe you'll get the bug and join their ranks.

Peter Pepper Seeds
P.O. Box 415, Knoxville, TN 37901
Telephone: 615-524-5965

Catalog price: long self-addressed stamped envelope

"Hot and unusual peppers" and a few related curiosities. The flier shows pictures of the dozen or so pepper selections, and some of them are indeed unusual looking. As a side dish, Peter Pepper sells seed for pepper tomatoes—hollow tomatoes for stuffing—loofah sponges, and castor bean plants.

Piedmont Plant Co.
P.O. Box 424, Albany, GA 31703
Telephone: 912-435-0766 or 883-7029

Catalog price: free

If you've missed all the deadlines for ordering and starting seed for your garden, this firm will ship you vegetable plants. Choose from tomatoes, peppers, onions, cauliflowers, broccolis, eggplants, leeks, brussels sprouts, beets, lettuces, collards, and cabbages. Tomatoes are offered in the biggest range of choice—15 varieties, both hybrid and standard. Some of the plants are sold by the dozen, others in a minimum quantity of 50.

Pinetree Garden Seeds
New Gloucester, ME 04260
Telephone: 207-926-3400

Catalog price: free

Pinetree Garden Seeds has built its business entirely around the home gardener. The owners realize that most backyard gardeners like to try a little of this and a little of that, and that few people have room for hundred-foot rows of even their favorite varieties. The answer: reasonably sized seed packets at low prices. Vegetable, herb, and flower seed are generally priced below 50¢ per packet here—some as low as 25¢. The prices are low because the packets have fewer seeds, generally about half what you'd get from other companies. If you want the equivalent of a full-size packet, just order two. At these prices you'll still come out ahead.

The owners test new varieties before listing them in the catalog, and the result is a selection of proved successes and some refreshingly honest opinions. About Sweet 100 tomatoes the catalog writer comments, "I admire the yield but don't like the flavor as much as the plain old red cherry types."

In 1987 the firm added garden perennials to the catalog, all field grown and wintered at the Maine nursery. Spring and fall bulbs are offered, along with a selection of tools and gardening supplies and dozens of useful books.

Plants of the Southwest
1812 Second Street, Santa Fe, NM 87501
Telephone: 505-983-1548

Catalog price: $1

A fascinating catalog of seed for dry-region and mountain plants that defies our categorizing system. The focus is on plants that grow well in the Southwest; the list spans native grasses and wildflowers, trees and shrubs, heirloom and new short-season vegetables, and ancient food crops. Wildflowers take up the most room in the catalog, with more than 100 offerings (including 19 penstemon species). Propagation and cultural instruction is given for each listing. Some plants are pictured in line drawings, and all are well described.

Pony Creek Nursery
Tilleda, WI 54978
Telephone: 715-787-3889

Catalog price: free

Flower and vegetable seed, berry plants, fruit trees, ornamentals, and shade trees all rolled into a single newspaper-format catalog. The key to Pony Creek is savings. The firm sells full-size seed packets at competitive prices—most of the non-hybrids at about 50¢ per packet in 1987. Here strawberry plants cost a third less than those offered by most strawberry specialists, and four- to five-foot grafted apple trees are listed for less than $10.

Porter & Son
1510 E. Washington Street, P.O. Box 104
Stephenville, TX 76401-0104

Catalog price: free

The Porter catalog doesn't beat about the bush. Tomatoes are the most popular vegetable the firm sells, and tomatoes come first in the catalog (more than 40 varieties, including the firm's own Porter breed). Watermelons and cantaloupes, two other specialties, come right behind. Porter sells seed for southern growers, and southern favorites get strong play here. Almost 40 different peppers are listed, and nine okra varieties. The flower seed selection isn't nearly as extensive as the vegetable end of the list. Porter sells irrigation equipment, fertilizers, pest-control chemicals, and a few books.

Premium Seed & Horticultural Supply Co.
915 E. Jefferson Street, Louisville, KY 40206

Catalog price: $1.50

Vegetable seed and some flower seed in a catalog that concentrates on gardening supplies (see entry under *Greenhouse Supplies*, page 216). The seed selection covers most of the popular hybrids and standard varieties. Seeds can be bought by the packet or in larger quantities. The packet prices are comparatively low.

Raber's Greenhouse & Nursery

P.O. Box 212, Route 62, Berlin, OH 44610

Catalog price: free

Strawberry plants, vegetable seed, and a limited selection of flower seed. The catalog gives terse descriptions in tiny type and no cultural direction. The strawberry selection is perhaps the strongest on the list, with 25 varieties offered. The vegetable seed department carries most of the popular varieties. Those living in the area can visit the garden center for a much larger choice of nursery stock.

Rawlinson Garden Seed

269 College Road, Truro, NS, Canada B2N 2P6

Telephone: 902-893-3051

Catalog price: free in Canada, $1 for U.S. customers (deductible from first order)

General vegetable and flower seed in a black-and-white catalog with good descriptions. The firm carries most of the favorites and some short-season varieties popular in the Maritimes, like Earlivee sweet corn and Scotia tomato. Rawlinson sells the record-setting Atlantic Giant pumpkin, developed in Nova Scotia by Howard Dill. The flower seed department is growing, but still lags behind the vegetables. Only one snapdragon variety is offered (the miniature Magic Carpet), and Dragonfly is the only columbine sold.

The Redwood City Seed Company

P.O. Box 361, Redwood City, CA 94064

Telephone: 415-325-7333

Catalog price: 50¢

Seed for old-fashioned open-pollinated vegetables, herbs, berries, and other "useful plants." The entire list is something of a curiosity; the overall effect is very similar to the catalog of J. L. Hudson, a Redwood City neighbor. Unusual offerings are presented with informative tiny-type descriptions and 19th-century woodcuts. Among the vegetables are the Oxheart carrot, Hopi blue corn, Queen Victoria rhubarb, and four types of amaranth. Peppers are apparently something of an obsession. They take up several columns, and, for the spicy varieties, owner Craig Dremmann has worked out a "hotness scale." Among the other "useful plants" are dye plants, medicinal herbs, such old-timers as broom corn and marsh mallow, and curiosities like ololiuqui ("seeds were of major importance to the Aztecs"). The firm also sells books.

W. Robinson & Sons Ltd.

Sunny Bank, Forton, Nr. Preston, Lancs., England PR3 OBN

Telephone: 44-524-791210

Catalog price: free

Home of the "Mammoth" vegetables, a trade name for especially large varieties ("For kitchen or show, Mammoth seeds are the ones to sow"). Mammoth blanch leeks have been grown to weights of over five pounds, and the firm claims that its Mammoth red onion is "the largest red onion in cultivation." Only seed is sold. The prices are higher than those of most North American suppliers. Payment by Visa or Access card will simplify exchange rates.

P. L. Rohrer & Bro., Inc.

P.O. Box 25, Smoketown, PA 17576

Telephone: 717-299-2571

Catalog price: free

Vegetable, flower, and crop seed for the home gardener and the commercial grower. The vegetable and flower seed is sold by the packet or the pound; the grass and grain seed is sold by the sack. The selection at Rohrer's tends to favor the market grower, and the descriptions point out those plants that bear especially big or salable yields. Fifteen varieties of corn are sold, all of them hybrids, and six different tomatoes. The flower selection fits easily on two pages.

Roswell Seed Company, Inc.

115-117 S. Main, P.O. Box 725, Roswell, NM 88201

Telephone: 505-622-7701

Catalog price: free

The headline on this list reads "Seeds in Bulk," but Roswell also sells very affordable seed packets for the small-scale gardener. In fact, most of the vegetable seed packets in 1987 cost just 35¢. The firm concentrates on crops that will do well in the Pecos Valley, and the list is particularly strong on watermelons, okra, and hot peppers. (Alfalfa seed, another specialty, is sold only in bulk.) Only a dozen flower types are listed in the catalog, but the firm sells a wide selection of packets from various wholesale suppliers, and customers can request "any rare variety or type" not in the regular stock. The firm sells a full line of fertilizers, pesticides, and fungicides.

S & H Organic Acres

P.O. Box 757, Newberg, OR 97132

Telephone: 503-538-6530

Catalog price: free

Marlene & Jim Courselle have found an unusual niche for themselves in the mail-order gardening business. They sell only garlic, shallots, and specialty onions. We're not sure we'd dare to dine with them, but their catalog is a treat. The king of their list is called elephant garlic, and its bulbs often weigh a pound or more. The Courselles send out their biggest bulbs to people who plan to eat them. Gardening customers get smaller bulbs, which are more economical for planting.

Sanctuary Seeds
2388 W. 4th Avenue, Vancouver, BC, Canada V6K 1P1
Telephone: 604-733-4724

Catalog price: $1

Untreated non-hybrid vegetable and herb seed in an elegant countercultural catalog. By steering clear of hybrids, the firm has found its way to an unusually strong selection of heirloom vegetables and old garden favorites. The herb offerings outnumber the vegetables, though a close inspection turns up some plants that might be more accurately filed under "flowers." Sweet peas, snapdragons, and baby's breath are classified here as medicinal herbs. Perhaps their healing power lies in their beauty. All the plants are described, and some growing advice is offered for the vegetables. The bulk of the catalog is devoted to packaged herbs, natural vitamins, health foods, and books.

Seeds Blüm
Idaho City Stage, Boise, ID 83706
Telephone: 208-343-2202

Catalog price: $2

Seeds Blüm (pronounced "seeds bloom") has put together one of the most entertaining, informative, and engaging seed catalogs we found. The pages are filled with lively line drawings, personal observations, and loads of unusual offerings that have struck the fancy of owner Jan Blüm. Vegetables are grouped by botanical family—cabbages, turnips, and brussels sprouts appear together in the mustard family, for example. That little shakeup from the standard alphabetical listing sets readers to browsing, and a slow browse is the proper way to approach this catalog. With the tomatoes and potatoes (nightshade family) are potato gift boxes—gourmet blue- and yellow-fleshed potatoes elegantly packed for shipping anywhere in the U.S. Among the corn and sorghum listings (grass family) is an aside explaining that corn kernels planted in the same direction will yield a field of cornstalks with their leaves oriented in the same direction. The firm sells many heirloom varieties and encourages gardeners to try them and to try saving seed on their own. There is even a seed-finding service to help track down favorite plants no longer listed in catalogs.

The pleasures of browsing continue in the flower section of the list, where plants are categorized by their uses. Nasturtiums and hollyhocks are found under "edible flowers," sweet peas and poppies in the "cutting garden." Most fun are the collections, which, even if you don't order them, offer plenty of planting ideas. "The evening patio," for instance, is a collection of night-blooming plants that inspired us to plant moonflowers in pots on our balcony last summer.

Seeds Blüm sells a nice assortment of books on gardening and cooking and a number of intriguing gifts. In addition to the potato box mentioned above, the firm sells a cornbread gift box (it includes Hopi blue and Bloody Butcher cornmeal), a specialty bean box, and a sorghum gift pack.

Seedway
Hall, NY 14463-0250
Telephone: 716-526-6391

Catalog price: free

A glossy color catalog of vegetables and flowers, with hybrid vegetables in the spotlight. The firm sells 28 varieties of hybrid corn and as many hybrid cabbages (though most of the cabbages are sold in bulk only to commercial growers). Each variety is described in a couple of sentences, and an effort is made to point out those plants best suited to the home garden. The flower department carries the popular varieties, mostly in color mixes.

Shepherd's Garden Seeds
7389 W. Zayante Road, Felton, CA 95018
Telephone: 408-335-5400

Catalog price: $1

Seed for European and oriental vegetables and herbs, chosen with the discriminating kitchen gardener in mind. Renee Shepherd started this business as an alternative to the trend among larger seed companies toward varieties best suited to commercial growers—vegetables that ripen simultaneously for machine harvesting and that are tough enough for shipping. Ms. Shepherd has chosen her vegetables for their flavor, their tenderness, and their eating qualities. She offers Precovil peas from France, Fino Verde Compatto basil from Italy, Grenadier cabbage from Holland, and Japanese Red Beard onions. She has also kept a sharp eye out for suitable American varieties and has included a number of tasty homegrown selections: Camp Joy cherry tomatoes, developed by a small farming cooperative, Sugar Baby watermelons, and Silver Queen corn. All of the offerings are well described, with an abundance of growing advice, and the catalog is sprinkled with recipes.

The flower seed department is far smaller than the vegetable operation, but selections have been made with care. Varieties have been divided into three sections: cottage garden flowers, edible flowers, and flowers for drying. All can be bought in individual packets or in collections.

R. H. Shumway's
P.O. Box 1, Graniteville, SC 29829
Telephone: 803-663-6276

Catalog price: $1

Roland H. Shumway launched his seed business back in 1870 with a few seeds from a Jerusalem cherry tree given to him by his mother. Today the R. H. Shumway catalog is still illustrated by engravings from the firm's 19th-century catalogs, and the vegetable list is still stocked with old-fashioned favorites. (The firm's slogan, "The Pioneer American Seedsman," is a little misleading. It is the name the business operated under in its first years. Several American seed firms have longer histories.) One of Shumway's special prides is the Abraham Lincoln tomato, developed at the firm's seed farms in 1926 and "rebred" in 1986 to "restore its purity." The list also takes in a number of modern vegetable varieties and hybrids. A "General Store" section at the back of the catalog offers a selection of tools, fertilizers, and gardening supplies. If you're on the mailing list for the full "deluxe" catalog, you'll be able to order flower seed. The catalog we were sent lists only vegetables. No catalogs are mailed after January 20.

Siberia Seeds

Box 2026, Sweetgrass, MT 59484
or Box 3000, Olds, AB, Canada T0M 1P0

Catalog price: long self-addressed stamped envelope

Tomato seeds for northern growers, a mix of heirlooms and newer varieties. The firm takes its name from the Siberian tomato, a strain that comes from Siberia and that sets fruit at temperatures as cold as 38°F. U.S. customers should write to the Sweetgrass, Montana, address, Canadian customers to the address in Olds.

Southern Exposure Seed Exchange

P.O. Box 158, North Garden, VA 22959

Catalog price: $2

Vegetable seed, with an emphasis on heirloom varieties. The firm sells some hybrid varieties, such as Silver Queen corn and A-Plus carrots, but these take a back seat to the older strains that can be carried on by seed savers. Among the tomato offerings (which include no hybrids at all) are several family heirlooms. Brandywine comes from an Amish family and has been passed down through the generations since at least 1885. Mortgage Lifter was created in the early 1930s by M. C. Byles of Logan, West Virginia. The plants became a local legend for their large, tasty fruit, and Mr. Byles sold enough seedlings to pay off the mortgage on his house. This catalog is full of such stories, which accompany sound descriptions of all varieties and detailed planting advice.

A small list of flowers includes a few precious heirlooms of its own, and we are told that this part of the list is growing. A handful of antique apples are sold, along with some gardening supplies and a selection of books.

Steele's Pansy Gardens, Inc.

8653 S. Lone Elder Road, Canby, OR 97013
Telephone: 503-266-9540

Catalog price: long self-addressed stamped envelope

Seed for large-flowered Mastadon pansies in a choice of a dozen colors or in color mixes. Steele's sells by the packet, the ounce, or the pound.

Stokes Seeds Inc.

P.O. Box 548, Buffalo, NY 14240-0548
Telephone: 416-688-4300

Catalog price: free

At 160 pages, the 1987 Stokes catalog weighed in near the top of the scale among the general flower and vegetable seed lists. The firm strives to keep up with the latest introductions, and the list is crowded with new strains and hybrids— more than 150 of the 1987 offerings were new to the catalog. Each vegetable type is introduced by a lengthy growing guide, and the flowers receive similar, though not quite as detailed, instructions. Among Stokes's specialties are its 50 hybrid corn varieties and 40 coleus selections. Most of the flowers can be bought separately by color as well as in mixes.

Sunrise Enterprises

P.O. Box 10058, Elmwood, CT 06110-0058

Catalog price: $1

Oriental vegetable seed in a bilingual (English and Chinese) catalog. Black-and-white photographs show many of the offerings, and the text explains how they are used in the kitchen. Planting tips are sent with the seeds. More detailed instructions, including recipes, can be ordered for a nominal fee. Customers can request these in either English or Chinese editions.

Suttons Seeds Ltd.

Hele Road, Torquay, Devon, England TQ2 7QJ
Telephone: 44-803-62011

Suttons is one of Britain's premier seed houses, and it carries an exceptionally nice selection of flower seed and some attractive vegetable offerings. Canadian customers should order through Gardenimport, of Thornhill, Ontario (see page 19), and U.S. customers may want to route their orders through Canada as well because of import restrictions on orders from England. Sweet peas, for example, which Suttons stocks in profusion, cannot be sent from England to the U.S., but they can be sent from Canada. The vegetable section of the Suttons list provides a refreshing outlook on some of our North American standards. The Sweet 100 tomato is referred to with a hint of disdain as "particularly popular with children."

T & T Seeds Ltd.

P.O. Box 1710, Winnipeg, MB, Canada R3C 3P6
Telephone: 204-943-8483

Catalog price: $1

A small color catalog of vegetable and flower seed. The choice of varieties is not gigantic—only 11 tomatoes and eight corn cultivars—but it covers the territory from asparagus to zinnia. For only 10¢, children can order the "Kiddies Big Assortment Packet," a mix of all types of flower and vegetable seed, but the dime has to be sent in with a larger order from Mom and Dad. Canadian customers may choose from a nice assortment of gardening supplies, bulbs, and nursery stock—shade and fruit trees, roses, berry plants, and garden perennials. Only seeds are shipped to the U.S.

Territorial Seed Co.

P.O. Box 27, Lorane, OR 97451
Telephone: 503-942-9547

Catalog price: free

Seed for growers west of the Cascades, where cool summers and mild, wet winters call for a particular assortment of vegetable and flower varieties. Territorial's tomatoes, for example, ripen early and bear fruit even without much hot summer sun. And a number of cabbages and lettuces are offered for year-round harvesting. Flowers have been chosen for ease of growth. All can be sown directly in the garden, and all mature quickly. Along with popular garden varieties like cosmos and alyssum, the list includes such Northwest natives as thimble flower (*Gilia capitata*) and Oregon camas. Local shoppers can visit the company store and model vegetable garden at 80030 Territorial Road (second mailbox on the right, south of Lorane).

Texas Onion Plant Co.
P.O. Box 871, Farmersville, TX 75031

Catalog price: free

Onion plants sold in 50-plant bunches. Choose from a sweet Vidalia type, a Bermuda type, a Spanish type, and a sweet Texas red. Shipping season lasts from January to June.

Thompson and Morgan
P.O. Box 1308, Jackson, NJ 08527
Telephone: 201-363-2225

Catalog price: free

Thompson and Morgan haughtily titles its spring booklet *The Seed Catalog*, and the boast is not groundless. As a source of flower seed the catalog has few rivals. Its more than 200 pages are crowded with 4,000 plus offerings, many of them illustrated by crisp color photographs. A British firm, Thompson and Morgan stocks a wide array of flowers popular in England, some of which are difficult to find in North America. Sweet peas are offered in a pastel rainbow of colors along with more than 70 primulas, 50 pansy cultivars, and 35 campanulas. Plants that might be featured as rarities or exotics on some lists are simply filed alphabetically here with a minimum of fanfare. (This is not to say that Thompson and Morgan is above exaggeration. We planted the firm's touted "black" pansies last spring and they turned out to be a lovely shade of purple.)

The vegetable section is confined to a mere 40 pages at the end of the catalog. All the popular types are here, but in a smaller range of choice than we'd become used to among the flowers. Only eight varieties of sweet corn are listed, for example, and just two watermelons. The catalog closes with several pages of tree and shrub seed, one feature of which is a selection of trees suited for bonsai cultivation.

Canadian customers should order through C. A. Cruickshank, Thompson and Morgan's Canadian representative (see page 16).

Tillinghast Seed Co.
P.O. Box 738, La Conner, WA 98257
Telephone: 206-466-3329 or 3552

Catalog price: free

Tillinghast dabbles in a little of everything, it seems. The flower and vegetable catalog has some of the flavor of the rambling general store that has served as the firm's headquarters since 1885. The store holds a florist shop, a kitchen shop, a gourmet coffee and candy shop, a garden shop, a wildlife gallery, and a library. The catalog wanders from vegetable and flower seed to bulbs, roses, fruit trees, perennial plants, tools, and canning supplies. And all the catalog departments are quite well stocked. Buyers have a choice of more than 60 roses, including hybrid teas, floribundas, climbing and shrub varieties, and miniatures. Among the bulbs are more than 30 dahlias and 25 tulips. The vegetable selection has been carefully chosen with the Northwest climate in mind. All plants are well described. Some are illustrated in color, and growing directions are offered throughout.

Tomato Growers Supply Co.
P.O. Box 2237, Fort Myers, FL 33902

Catalog price: free

You won't find pepper seed in this catalog. Or corn or beans. Tomato Growers Supply sells tomato seed only, plus supplies for growing the perfect crop. You can choose from old varieties, new varieties, giant beefsteaks, and tiny cherries—125 different tomatoes in all. A six-page introduction gives a history of the tomato in cultivation, and step-by-step directions for raising the plants.

The Tomato Seed Company, Inc.
P.O. Box 323, Metuchen, NJ 08840

Catalog price: free

If you thought 125 tomato varieties seemed like a lot, how about 300? That's how many tomatoes Martin Sloan sells in his encyclopedic Tomato Seed Company catalog. And, if readers aren't satisfied with his selection, he'll try to hunt down long-lost favorites. We wonder if there really are any tomatoes he hasn't already found. Tomato fanatics can choose from European varieties, modern American hybrids, and heirlooms. Mr. Sloan sells Mortgage Lifter, a popular old southern variety, and Goldie, which dates back to about 1800. He sells Cabot, a popular early type from Nova Scotia, and Marbi, a processing variety for tropical or subtropical areas. He sells Marglobe, Marmande, Oxheart, Brandywine, and Beefmaster tomatoes, along with scores we'd never heard of before.

Tregunno Seeds Limited
126 Catharine Street N., Hamilton, ON, Canada L8R 1J4
Telephone: 416-528-5983 or 5984

Catalog price: free to Canadian customers

Tregunno sells garden seeds by mail to Canadian customers only and really seems to direct its catalog to residents of Ontario. The order form notes that shipping is free to all points in Ontario, but neglects to mention the mailing costs to other provinces. Both vegetable and flower lists are quite

Growing the Big Ones

If you've ever strolled through the produce displays at a country fair, you've surely been thunderstruck by the size of the prize-winning pumpkins, squashes, and watermelons. And, if you have even a spark of ambition as a gardener, you've probably entertained a passing thought of trying to grow one of these monsters yourself. Every summer gardeners around the world join in a spirited competition to raise the largest vegetable of all, with the spotlight focused most intensely on the race for the world's largest pumpkin.

The World Pumpkin Confederation encourages this rivalry by putting up large cash prizes every year and coordinating the efforts of workers at a number of festivals and fairs that sponsor annual weigh-offs. In addition to the satisfaction and the fame, the grower of the largest pumpkin can earn up to $4,000 in prize money, depending on where the entry is registered. The biggest squash and watermelons can each reap more than $1,000.

Anyone thinking of raising giant vegetables will first need some pedigreed seeds. For the past few years the winning pumpkins have all been Atlantic Giants, a strain developed by Howard Dill of Windsor, Nova Scotia. Dill himself has won the biggest prize money twice; others using his seeds have won in other years.

Many seed companies now offer Atlantic Giant pumpkin seed. Those serious about growing winners may want to order directly from Howard Dill or from P & P Seed Company, a firm that offers seeds harvested from parent pumpkins that weighed in at a minimum of 400 pounds. (P & P Seed Company operates from the same address as the World Pumpkin Confederation. It's run by Peter and Paul Waterman, brothers of Ray Waterman, who heads the confederation.)

According to the World Pumpkin Confederation, the seedlings should be pampered with an indoor start in sterile potting soil, then raised under grow lights until the third leaf appears, when they should be set out in the garden. Space the seedlings 15 to 20 feet apart in deeply tilled, well-fertilized, sandy loam and in a spot that gets full sun all day. If the soil is not rich enough, condition it with generous quantities of peat moss, com-

post, and aged cow manure. One or two fruits should be singled out on each vine, and the rest picked off as they appear. Deal with pets, insects, and diseases as you would for any vegetable in the garden.

If you manage to raise a contender (one that tips the scales at more than 450 pounds), contact the confederation to find out how to enter it in an accredited show. Official weigh-offs are held in October at pumpkin festivals and country fairs in Topsfield, Massachusetts; Buffalo, New York; Barnesville, Ohio; Hope, Arkansas; Elk Grove Village, Illinois; Windsor, Nova Scotia; Blenheim, Ontario; and Vancouver, British Columbia.

Watermelons don't earn as much prize money as pumpkins, but a winner can still take home a fat check, and all competitors can enjoy giving it their best effort. Seed from 200-pound parents may be purchased from Giant Watermelons, a firm run by members of the Bright family, who have a number of weigh-off trophies on their mantle. Eleven-year-old Jason Bright grew a 260-pounder to set the world record in 1985.

If you want to learn more about raising these Goliaths of the garden, subscribe to the World Pumpkin Confederation's quarterly newsletter. Each issue has articles, growing tips, and ads from suppliers, and complete details are given on entering pumpkins, squash, and watermelons in shows. An annual subscription costs $10.

All the firms below send free information.

Giant Watermelons
P.O. Box 141, Hope, AR 71801

Howard Dill
400 College Road, Windsor, NS, Canada B0N 2T0

P & P Seed Company
14050 Gowanda State Road, Collins, NY 14034

World Pumpkin Confederation
14050 Gowanda State Road, Collins, NY 14034
Telephone: 716-532-5995

extensive. Almost 40 tomato varieties are offered, and nearly 50 petunias. The firm sells a big selection of fertilizers, insecticides, and fungicides and an assortment of tools and other gardening supplies.

Tsang & Ma
P.O. Box 294, Belmont, CA 94002
Telephone: 415-595-2270

Catalog price: free

Tsang & Ma suggests that we "try something ancient," meaning some of the firm's seeds for oriental vegetables. Offerings range from daikon and bok choy to mao gwa (Chinese fuzzy gourd) and perilla (an aromatic herb). To help you make a meal of your harvest, the firm sells oriental sauces and seasonings and a selection of pots, pans, and cooking utensils.

Otis Twilley Seed Co., Inc.
P.O. Box F65, Trevose, PA 19047
Telephone: 215-639-8800

Catalog price: free

The catalog is headlined "Wholesale Prices," but all Twilley's flower and vegetable seeds are sold in packets as well as in bulk. Since Twilley does sell to commercial growers, however, its selection is biased toward cultivars suited to large-scale planting, with a heavy emphasis on hybrids. The featured tomatoes, for example, are types that fruit at one time for convenient one-sweep harvests. Petunias and marigolds each rate three pages in a flower section that concentrates on the most popular varieties. Color illustrations abound in this catalog. The descriptions include no cultural instructions.

Vermont Bean Seed Co.
Garden Lane, Fair Haven, VT 05743-0250
Telephone: 802-265-4212

Catalog price: free

The folks at Vermont Bean Seed Company sell vegetable seeds, and they do it well. The catalog is clearly written and illustrated, full of horticultural advice, and crammed with vegetable offerings, from hybrid tomatoes to heirloom beans. The bean selection is a source of particular pride here. Some 60 varieties are described in the catalog, many of them old-fashioned types like the Vermont cranberry bean, the Swedish brown bean, and the soldier bean. Unusual greens are another specialty, and the firm has put together a fascinating collection of oriental and European greens to be cooked or used in salads. While the firm has a deep interest in saving and popularizing heirloom varieties, it does not shy away from modern hybrids. Most of the corn offerings are hybrids, as are about half the tomatoes. Flower seed and gardening supplies take up the last few pages of the booklet.

Vesey's Seeds Ltd.
P.O. Box 9000, Charlottetown, PE, Canada C1A 8K6
or P.O. Box 9000, Houlton, ME 04730-0814
Telephone: 902-892-1048

Catalog price: free

Short-season vegetable seed in a catalog with both color and black-and-white illustrations. The selection is limited to those varieties that have proved themselves to northern gardeners. Only ten tomatoes are offered, but among them are the Canadian favorites Scotia, Cabot, and Tiny Tim. The only watermelon sold is New Hampshire Midget. A small selection of flower seed is presented in a color section, and some tools and gardening supplies are offered. U.S. customers should write to the Houlton, Maine, address, Canadian customers to Charlottetown.

Willhite Seed Co.
P.O. Box 23, Poolville, TX 76076
Telephone: 817-599-8656

Catalog price: free

If melons are in your garden plans, take a look at the Willhite catalog. The firm sells all manner of vegetable seed, from beans to corn to tomatoes, but the company's heart is in its melons. Pages of watermelons, cantaloupes, and muskmelons follow the regular vegetable listings. Some of the hybrids were created by Willhite's owner, Lee Coffey. All plants are described (often with the commercial grower in mind), and many are illustrated in color. Cultural instruction is confined to a planting chart that tells how deep to plant seeds and how many will be needed to plant a 100-foot row or an acre. Commercial growers may order seed in bulk; smaller packets are sold for home gardeners.

Wilton's Organic Seed Potatoes
P.O. Box 28, Aspen, CO 81612

Catalog price: free

Seed potatoes. The minimum order is for five pounds of red or russet potatoes. Those who write will receive an order form and a return envelope.

Wyatt-Quarles Seed Co.
P.O. Box 739, Garner, NC 27529
Telephone: 919-832-0551

Catalog price: free

Vegetable and flower seed in a descriptive catalog brightened by occasional black-and-white and color illustrations. The collection is aimed at the southern gardener and is strongest in the melon, corn, and tomato departments. Planting instructions are given for each vegetable type. (Growers outside the Carolinas will have to be careful not to follow these directions too literally. The catalog tells us to plant garden peas "during January in the East," meaning eastern North Carolina.) The flower seed selection is of medium range and includes packets separated by color for such popular plants as petunias, zinnias, and impatiens. Separate bulb catalogs are mailed in the summer and early spring. These full-color booklets offer a fairly wide array of tulips, daffodils, gladioli, dahlias, begonias, and lilies.

African Violets and Other Gesneriads

Alice's Violet Room
Rt. 6, Box 233, Waynesville, MO 65583
Telephone: 314-336-4763

Catalog price: 25¢

A concentrated listing of more than 200 violets, grouped beneath the rubrics of a couple dozen hybridizers. The plants are spread among single, double, semidouble, miniature, and semiminiature varieties. Blossom color may be white, blue, pink, red, reddish plum, peach, or just about any combination of these tints you can imagine. The nursery stresses that its plants are grown in a special potting soil that tends to produce a compact root system. Shipping season is May and June for spring, September and October for fall.

Annalee Violetry
29-50 214th Place, Bayside, NY 11360
Telephone: 718-224-3376

Catalog price: $1

More than 100 varieties of violets neatly sorted into six camps in a four-page brochure. Standard and show varieties claim the bulk of the listings, but chimera (sometimes known as pinwheels or radials), variegated foliage, trailer, miniature and semiminiature, and the nursery's own hybrids also nab a portion of the space. Each entry receives a tight line of description. Minimum order is three plants.

Jeanne P. Bohn
P.O. Box 174, Hygiene, CO 80533

Catalog price: 25¢ coin

For those willing to do a little propagating at home, this nursery offers African violet leaves freshly cut from mature plants. Several score varieties are listed without description on three typewritten pages. Multicolor and fantasy blossoms—in single, double, and semidouble form—make up the lone category here. The variegated stock plants have been fed a high-nitrogen fertilizer to speed propagation.

Elizabeth Buck
9255 Lake Pleasant Road, Clifford, MI 48727
Telephone: 517-761-7382

No catalog

Although she provides neither price list nor catalog, Ms. Buck does sell African violet leaves taken from 600 or so of the newest varieties from leading hybridizers in the U.S. and Canada. Serious hobbyists may want to write or call for more explicit information.

Buell's Greenhouses, Inc.
P.O. Box 218, Weeks Road, Eastford, CT 06242
Telephone: 203-974-0623

Catalog price: 25¢ plus long self-addressed envelope with two first-class stamps

A vast selection of African violets and gloxinias aimed at the gesneriad specialist. The narrow, rather fussy booklet lays out almost a thousand violet listings with a code that details bloom color, shade, border, edge, type (double, semidouble, etc.), and plant size. By assembling this data in your mind, you begin to picture what a particular variety might look like. A smaller group of gloxinias follows the violets; individual entries here get the full prose treatment.

Cape Cod Violetry
28 Minot Street, Falmouth, MA 02540
Telephone: 617-548-2798

Catalog price: $1, deductible from first order

Several hundred African violet leaves and plants from a dozen different hybridizers. A grouping of 30 or so unusual striped-blossom varieties (intended for the collector) heads the list. Green blossoms, miniatures and semiminiatures, and trailers offer additional generic clumps that keep the six pages of this computer-generated catalog tidy. For true violet nuts, the catalog ends on a festive note: an assortment of violet-printed luncheon napkins, plastic-coated plates, guest towels, greeting cards, and bumper stickers.

Country Girl Greenhouse
P.O. Box 83, Rt. 14, Sterling, CT 06377
Telephone: 203-564-8227

Catalog price: $1

A slapdash catalog whose contents are printed so thickly and darkly that they are all but unreadable. The violets here may be purchased either at blooming size or by the leaf, in chimera, classic, semiminiature, miniature, and trailing varieties. Of these, the classics claim the largest share, with roughly 200 listings. The catalog also lists a good selection of African violet species and other gesneriads—including episcia, columnea, and streptocarpus. A medley of plant tonics, vases, jewelry, and cross-stitch kits consumes eight pages toward the end.

Davidson-Wilson Greenhouses
See under *Houseplants*, page 106.

Fischer Greenhouses

Oak Avenue, Linwood, NJ 08221
Telephone: 609-927-3399

Catalog price: 35¢

After 40 years of shipping African violets by mail, a firm tends to have the kinks worked out. This colorful 12-page catalog is a visual treat, with scads of flowers crisply pictured in bright rows. Single, trailing, ruffled, plain, and many other types appear among the hundred choices here. Companion gesneriads (such as streptocarpus, episcia, and columnea) supplement the mix. A three-page stretch of light stands, fertilizers, insecticides, books, and other violet supplies addresses your practical needs.

Lorraine Friedrich

9130 Glenbury, Houston, TX 77037
Telephone: 713-448-8976

Catalog price: 50¢

A haphazard list of violets and other gesneriads that cuts from columneas to semiminiature violet trailers. Five typewritten pages spell out the details: dozens of genera, all told, with African violets getting the upper hand. Most listings are available as full-size plants, but "leaves with little babies" present a second option in some cases.

Glasshouse Works

See under *Tropical Plants*, page 169.

Goodman Greenhouses

4780 Falstaff Road, Greenwood, CA 95635
Telephone: 916-333-1454

Catalog price: two first-class stamps

Four extra-long, closely printed pages offering a good assortment of African violets and gesneriads. Entries are coded to convey color, leaf and flower type, and plant size. Violet standards, miniatures, semiminiatures, and trailers take up slightly more than half the list; other gesneriads (aeschynanthus, columnea, nematanthus, and a few more), the remainder. Plants are generally 2½-inch stock, shipped in plastic pots. Minimum order is one case of 25 plants.

Green Mountain African Violets

Neal Road, Rt. 1, Box 43-A, White River Junction, VT 05001

Catalog price: 50¢

A simple, easy-to-decipher catalog listing nearly 100 violets, from a nursery that prides itself on cultivating its plants in a "home-like atmosphere." Several dozen standard and show varieties lead off. Listings specify type, color, and special qualities; personal commentary enriches the description. Variegated standards (20 or so), little romance (ten), trailing varieties (ten again), plus miniatures and semiminiatures (a total of four), complete the slate, all offered as unrooted leaves. A handful of columneas and episcias, as well as a modest stock of growers' supplies, also appear.

Hortense's African Violets

12406 Alexandria, San Antonio, TX 78233
Telephone: 512-656-0128

Catalog price: 25¢

Seventy violet hybrids split evenly between standard and smaller forms. Entries consist of two or three lines of sharp description. Violets are available either as starter plants or fresh-cut leaves, with a $10 minimum order.

Innis Violets

8 Maddison Lane, Lynnfield, MA 01940
Telephone: 617-334-6679

Catalog price: 50¢, deductible from first order

This brochure sets out a smorgasbord of recent violet hybrids from eight hybridizers in the U.S. and Canada. Standards, miniatures, semiminiatures, and trailing types are offered, all as leaf cuttings only. Growers' supplies—pots, trays, rings, fertilizer, and terrariums—have a whole page to themselves.

International Growers Exchange

See under *General Flowers and Vegetables*, page 21.

Jeannette's Jesneriads

2173 Leslie Street, Terrytown/Gretna, LA 70056
Telephone: 504-393-6977

Catalog price: long self-addressed stamped envelope

Fifteen violet varieties listed on a single sheet of paper, from a hybridizer who's been plying her trade for just a few years now. Starter plants only—shipped in 2¼- to 3-inch pots—are offered here. Entries are simply but amply described; semidouble forms predominate, and pink and purple hues have the edge. All foliage is glossy green, non-variegated show type.

JoS Violets

402 Dundee, Victoria, TX 77904
Telephone: 512-575-1344

Catalog price: long self-addressed stamped envelope

More 100 violets in both starter plant and leaf form have sunk roots in this five-page catalog. A list of standards—with doubles and semidoubles most plentiful—claims a majority of the total roster. Miniatures, semiminiatures, chimeras, and trailers win their share of attention, too. A one-page offering of violets from Hortense's African Violets (check listing above) is included with this catalog.

Karleen's Achimenes

1407 W. Magnolia Street, Valdosta, GA 31601
Telephone: 912-242-1368

Catalog price: $1.50

A collectors' list of more than 250 achimenes cultivars. Brief descriptions identify the size and color of each variety, but buyers will have to have some experience to distinguish among them all. Related gesneriads—gloxinias, eucodonias, sinningias, and smithianthas—are also sold.

Kartuz Greenhouses

See under *Houseplants*, page 106.

Kent's Flowers

320 W. Eagle, Arlington, NE 68002
Telephone: 402-478-4011

Catalog price: 50¢

A descriptive list of about 50 violet varieties, with top billing given to hybrids by Gordon Boone. Standards, miniatures, and semiminiatures all appear, most of them offered as leaves, but a few available as starter plants. To offset Boone's stardom, Bryant, Baker, Johnson, Granger Gardens, Smith, Sorano, Susan's, Pittman, Jeannette's Jesneriads, and Nadeau get cameo hybridizer roles. The nursery will begin selling its own hybrids in 1988.

Lauray of Salisbury

See under *Houseplants*, page 106.

Lloyd's African Violets

2568 E. Main Street, Cato, NY 13033
Telephone: 315-626-2314

Catalog price: 50¢ in coin

A smattering of violets from eight different hybridizers. Fredette Originals (18 offerings), "Happy Harold" Rienhardt (18) Wrangler's by Winston Smith (16); plus hybrids from Sandra Williams (14), Rob's Mini-O-Lets (14), Dick Wasmund (13), Meek's (10), and Lloyd's (five), make up the list. With the exception of Rienhardt—which offers only leaves—all varieties are available either as starter plants or by the leaf. In addition to the named hybrids, a limited supply of unusual chimera violets is available here.

Lyndon Lyon Greenhouses, Inc.

14 Mutchler Street, Dolgeville, NY 13329-0249
Telephone: 315-429-8291

Catalog price: $1

This colorful booklet just might make a believer out of someone who's never cared much for African violets. A medium-size list built around a snug portrait gallery in which nearly 100 violets shine like buttons against a background of pure black, the catalog has that kind of persuasive punch. The listings are divided among four groups: new violets, older favorites, companion plants, and chimeras. Violets are sensibly sorted out by color of bloom and described with plenty

of exclamation points. Fantastic! Outstanding! Lovely! But the photographs prove the adjectives correct. Plants only (shipped in 2½-inch pots) are available, with a minimum order of three.

McKinney's Glassehouse

89 Mission Road, Eastborough, Wichita, KS 67207
Telephone: 316-686-9438 or 684-5333

Catalog price: $1.50

A wide range of gesneriads from many different genera. African violets from Lyndon Lyon Greenhouses lead off the list, offered as rooted cuttings or leaves. Good selections of aeschynanthus, codonanthe, columnea, episcea (80 choices), gesneria, kohleria, nautilocalyx, nematanthus, and sinningia species and cultivars fill out the rest of the descriptive catalog—several hundred offerings in all. A simple drawing accompanies a cultural introduction to each genus.

Marvelous Minis

30840 Wentworth Street, Livonia, MI 48154
Telephone: 313-261-6767

Catalog price: $1, deductible from first order

A simple ten-page catalog showcasing miniature, semiminiature, and trailing African violets, available as starter plants or rooted cuttings from a host of hybridizers. Featured here: Carol's Violets, Ralph Robinson, Lyon Greenhouses, Bugtussle Violets, Ethel Champion, and others. The violet buffet is well stocked with every imaginable size, color of bloom, and foliage type. Terrarium and dish-garden plants—begonias, gesneriads, ficus, and ferns—are also listed.

Mary's Violet Joy

3200 W. 82nd Terrace, Leawood, KS 66206
Telephone: 913-642-4357

Catalog price: $1

These violets have been screened for their symmetry and show potential. Ruby Cox, Jeannette's Jesneriads, and Ralph Robinson are three hybridizers showcased at the front of this stapled roster. Standard varieties gathered from many sources, together with miniatures, semiminiatures, and trailers, complete the rich selection—more than 200 entries in all. Seed and growers' supplies take up a page of their own.

Mighty Minis
7318 Sahara Court, Sacramento, CA 95828
Telephone: 916-421-7284

Catalog price: $1, deductible from first order

A big list of small things. More than 600 African violet miniatures scroll past on a dozen italic-typed pages. About 150 trailing varieties appear in a clump as the finale. The listings here are careful to note the hybridizer, type and color of bloom, and foliage characteristics. Freshly cut leaves only are shipped—no plants.

Miree's Gesneriads
70 Enfield Avenue, Toronto, ON, Canada M8W 1T9
Telephone: 416-251-6369

Catalog price: $1, deductible from first order

A gesneriad grower who delves into the unusual and stays away from the common (not a single African violet makes it onto the list). Aeschynanthus, columnea, episcia, kohleria, and miniature sinningia types, some of them Miree's own hybrids, are all well represented. All are ably described, and a few words of cultural instruction introduce each genus. The 1987 list included a few miniature begonias, and the nursery plans to expand that part of the business for 1988, with more listings and a number of "tiny miniatures." Plants and cuttings can be sent to U.S. as well as Canadian customers.

Patty's Plant Place
2550 S. 391 Street W., Rt. 2, Cheney, KS 67025
Telephone: 316-542-0371

Catalog price: 50¢

Five pages packed from stem to stern with several hundred African violet varieties. A score of hybridizers—including Granger Gardens, Hortense, Champion, and Winston Smith—plump up the listings here. Each one-line entry notes the violet's source, bloom size and color, and foliage type. Standards, miniatures, semiminiatures, and trailers are offered, both as starter plants and leaves. Columneas and episcias are also available.

Petrovffsky Greenhouses
14867 Indian Springs Road, Penn Valley, CA 95946
Telephone: 916-272-1454

Catalog price: 50¢, deductible from first order

This 22-page booklet, in clotted dot-matrix print, sets out several hundred African violets: standards, miniatures and semiminiatures, standard and miniature trailers, and pinwheels. Featured hybridizers here are the two Irenes—Fredette and Lineberg. A small coterie of "companion plants" (meaning episcias, aeschynanthus, columneas, and nematanthus) wait to meet their chosen violets at the back of the catalog.

Plant Factory
2414 St. Charles Place, Cinnaminson, NJ 08077
Telephone: 609-829-5311

Catalog price: long self-addressed stamped envelope

About 50 nicely described violets fill this small catalog. Single, double, and semidouble blossoms—variegated, streaked, and solid in hue—appear side by side in the listings. Both plants and freshly cut leaves are available. Accessories and growers' supplies—including a light and moisture meter, insecticide, and plastic pots—complete the range.

The Plant Kingdom
See under *Houseplants*, page 107.

Plants 'N' Things
Pollock Road, Rt. 2, Keswick, ON, Canada L4P 3E9
Telephone: 416-476-7011

Catalog price: $1

A huge selection of gesneriads from a nursery that offers leaves and cuttings only. Roughly 500 listings darkly line 20 extra-long pages. Nearly half are African violets; the remainder are episcias, aeschynanthus, codonanthes, sinningias, and other gesneriads. Growers' supplies of all sorts complete the selection.

Pleasant Hill African Violets
Rt. 1, Box 73, Brenham, TX 77833
Telephone: 409-836-9736

Catalog price: 75¢

Freshly cut African violet leaves are available in profusion from this Texas grower. More than 500 varieties from 18 hybridizers (Gordon Boone, Irene Fredette, Winston Smith, etc.) are distinctly arrayed across a dozen typed pages. Extensive comment, often with a comforting note of authority, attends each violet listed here. Standards, miniatures, semiminiatures, and trailers are all available—in addition to a smattering of other gesneriads.

Rainwater Violets
937B S.E. Third, Lee's Summit, MO 64063
Telephone: 816-524-0131

Catalog price: 50¢

This lucid booklet states its case and gets out of the way in an exemplary fashion. Fantasies, multicolors, and "tutones" dominate the list, which is set in unusually large type and

gently spaced on the page. The contents here include the nursery's own hybrids, along with others from Irene Fredette and Ruby Cox. Standards, miniatures, semiminiatures, trailers, and chimeras are all available in small groupings of a dozen or so.

Ray's African Violets
Rt. 1, Box 244, College Station, TX 77840
Telephone: 409-690-1407

Catalog price: free

A generous sampling of miniature and semiminiature violets from a nursery that specializes in diminutive beauties. Roughly a quarter of the space here is given over to trailing varieties—described as "naturally branching violets with three or more crowns at maturity." Descriptive text is chock full of tender enthusiasm. Both plants and leaves are available; the minimum order is $12.

Roberts' Gesneriads
5656 Calyn Road, Baltimore, MD 21228
Telephone: 301-788-7723

Catalog price: $2

Hundreds of gesneriads populate this densely written 32-page catalog. After a lengthy introductory statement that tells you probably more than you really want to know about the nursery business ("I have found these past couple of years that the paperwork mountain has become a heavy burden"), the listings unreel from achimenes right through to trichantha. Sinningias—vegetatively propagated—are the house specialty.

Suni's Violets
4 South Meadow Woodlake, Dept. SP, Woodbury, CT 06798

Catalog price: $1

This unkempt catalog is like an African violet general store where you have to stand in dim light craning your neck for a while before the wares emerge. A wild medley of typefaces, numerous boxed tips, arrows pointing hither and yon, and a general abundance of marginal chatter make for a pleasant ramble. What does it boil down to? Well over 100 standard and miniature violets, in leaf, plant, and plantlet form (the nursery sends its plantlets barerooted and claims that they thrive as well as potted specimens). Growers' supplies are also displayed.

Sunshine Orchids International
Fruitland Road, Barre, MA 01005
Telephone: 617-355-2089

Catalog price: $1, deductible from first order

A gesneriad nursery with a somewhat misleading name. A few orchids are offered (seven in 1987), but they are completely overwhelmed by the almost 200 African violets and the scores of other gesneriads. The nursery is particularly proud of its three dozen columnea cultivars, ("some not found anywhere else") and of its many nematanthus offerings.

Susan's Bloomers
P.O. Box 3094, Champaign, IL 61821

Catalog price: 50¢

A selection of miniature African violets simply set forth on a single page. Listings are organized by color of bloom: blues, fuchsias, lavenders and purples, multicolors, pinks (the largest bunch), reds and roses, and whites. Descriptive text is lean. The hundred-or-so violets are sold either as freshly cut leaves or potted plants.

Tiki Nursery
P.O. Box 187, Fairview, NC 28730
Telephone: 704-628-2212

Catalog price: $1, deductible from first order

A catalog packed with nearly 1,000 brief listings, of which approximately a third are African violets in standard, miniature, and trailing forms. In addition to violets—available by the plant or leaf—this 30-page booklet offers a wealth of gesneriads (such as columneas and sinningias) and "exotics" (begonias and fuchsias, for example). Most plants are shipped in 2¼- or 3-inch pots; minimum order is $15.

Tinari Greenhouses
P.O. Box 190, Huntingdon Valley, PA 19006
Telephone: 215-947-0144

Catalog price: 35¢

Color photographs go a long way toward explaining the charm of African violets—as is proved by this small, nicely balanced catalog from a firm that's been mailing them out for more than forty years. Standard, miniature, semiminiature, and trailing varieties are listed here, and most appear in muted but lovely group shots as well. All plants are grown and shipped in 2¼-inch plastic pots.

Tomara African Violets
Rt. 3, Box 116, Fayette, MO 65248
Telephone: 816-248-3232

Catalog price: 30¢

A smorgasbord of several hundred violet varieties gathered from all over the map. More than 30 widely scattered hybridizers have contributed the fruits of their labor to this array, which breaks down into standard, variegated, miniature, and semiminiature sectors. Fredette hybrids claim a page of their own, but otherwise the catalog is salted with a jumble of famous initials (e.g., GB, LL, WS). Plants and plants alone are offered here.

Travis' Violets
P.O. Box 42, Ochlocknee, GA 31773
Telephone: 912-574-5167 or 5236

Catalog price: $1, deductible from first order

Here's a small booklet refreshingly printed in violet-colored ink—why didn't anyone else think of this?—that scans very nicely. Hortense's Honeys and Fredette Originals are the brightest stars, but the galaxy includes Lyndon Lyon hybrids plus those of the nursery itself and many others. A couple hundred listings altogether, in standard, miniature, and semi-miniature forms. Most violets are available either as plants or as leaves.

The Violet House
African violet seed. See under *Indoor Gardening Supplies*, page 225.

The Violet Showcase
3147 S. Broadway, Englewood, CO 80110
Telephone: 303-761-1770

Catalog price: $1

A wide range of African violet standards starting with Alamo Red ("bright red double blossoms") and ending with Zapped ("hot coral pink semidouble flowers usually with lots of purple speckles"). Trailers, pinwheels, miniature, and semi-miniature types also get a nod in these listings. A dozen or so Fredette Originals head the roster. Both starter plants—shipped in 2¼-inch plastic pots with wicks—and leaf cuttings are available.

Violets c/o Cookie
2400 Knightway Drive, Gretna, LA 70053
Telephone: 504-392-8094

Catalog price: long self-addressed stamped envelope

A score of standard African violets marked by variegated foliage. Each plant on the list is simply and clearly described, and the number of stems is noted in some cases. Blooms are single, double, and semidouble; their colors range from pale pink through blue to fuchsia and lavender. Two-tone blossoms are common.

Violets Collectible
1571 Wise Road, Lincoln, CA 95648
Telephone: 916-645-3487

Catalog price: $1

Roughly 1,000 violets, offered either as plants or leaves, are packed into this 18-pager, which draws its listings from a wide sweep of hybridizers (including Baker, Champion, Munk, Lyon, Granger, and Boone). The bulk of the catalog is given over to standard varieties, alphabetically arranged. Each of these is tartly evoked in a tiny line of text. Miniatures and semiminiatures are bunched together with trailers at the rear of the booklet.

Volkman Bros. Greenhouses
2714 Minert Street, Dallas, TX 75219
Telephone: 214-526-3484

Catalog price: long self-addressed stamped envelope

A hundred plus standard, miniature, and semiminiature African violets, many of them the nursery's own introductions. Lovely color photographs unlock the charm of perhaps a third of the offerings here. Most of the catalog showcases a mix of accessories for the violet gardener, including potting soil, plastic trays, wick saucers, and pest controls. The company also offers elaborate aluminum plant stands.

Wilson's Violet Haven
3900 Carter Creek Parkway, Bryan, TX 77802
Telephone: 409-846-8970

Catalog price: $1

More than a dozen African violet breeders are represented in this ten-page catalog. Some names you may recognize: Boone, Bryant, Champion, Sisk, Fredette, Hortense, Ness, Nortex, Scott, Lyons, Whitaker, Williams, and Smith. A medley of other contributors follows. Most plants are standards, but a smattering of miniatures and trailers also make the list.

Zaca Vista Nursery
1190 Alamo Pintado Road, Solvang, CA 93463
Telephone: 805-688-2585

Catalog price: $1

A crisp array of hundreds of violet varieties set forth in a 16-page booklet. Almost all are standards. While the listings are for cuttings only, starter plants may be specially ordered from "currently available listings" updated and mailed every six to eight weeks (to receive the latest "CAL," send a stamped self-addressed business-size envelope). Minimum order is $20.

Alpines and Rock-Garden Perennials

Alpenflora Gardens
17985 40th Avenue, Surrey, BC, Canada V3S 4N8
Telephone: 604-576-2464

Catalog price: $2

Alpenflora Gardens' 1987 list of alpines, rockery plants, and other choice perennials presented about 500 plants by botanical and common names, with a one-word description of flower color and an indication of height at maturity. Experienced gardeners probably made some discoveries on the list—a couple of dozen sedum species were offered and a nice selection of dianthus cultivars—but beginners might have been put off. By 1988 the nursery hopes to issue a color catalog with descriptions that will make the plants accessible to a wider audience.

Alpine Plants
See under *Garden Perennials*, page 86.

Appalachian Wildflower Nursery
See under *Wildflowers*, page 173.

Baldwin Seed Co.
Alaskan natives. See under *Wildflowers*, page 173.

P. & J. Christian
Minera, Wrexham, Clwyd, N. Wales
Telephone: 44-978-366399

Catalog price: $1 note or three International Reply Coupons

Choice bulbs, corms, and tubers for discriminating gardeners. Before even writing for the catalog, customers in the U.S. and Canada should be aware that the Christians ask export customers to order at least £25 of bulbs and charge £10 for a health certificate and about £8 for shipping on top of that. It all adds up to a major investment in bulbs. Why would anyone bother? The nursery offers scores of fall-flowering crocus types, more than 30 tulip species, a selection of cyclamen species, and several dozen fritillaria, as well as many exotics we don't pretend to recognize. Plants are listed by botanical name with a few words of description.

Holden Clough Nursery
Holden, Bolton-by-Bowland, Clitheroe,
Lancs., England BB7 4PF
Telephone: 44-2007-615

Catalog price: $2

More than 1,200 alpines and herbaceous perennials take up the first half of this compact booklet. Plants are listed by botanical name, with brief but adequate descriptions. Heaths and heathers, shrubs, vines, and conifers crowd the rest of the pages. The firm asks export customers for a minimum order of £80. Import permits must be supplied, and packing and shipping are charged at cost. (See *Buying Plants from Overseas*, page 9.)

Coènosium Gardens
See under *Trees and Shrubs*, page 150.

Colorado Alpines, Inc.
P.O. Box 2708, Avon, CO 81620
Telephone: 303-949-6464

Catalog price: $2, deductible from first order

Container-grown perennials selected for cold hardiness. Most are natives of the western U.S. and Canada, but some European and Asian alpines are mixed in as well as some cultivated varieties. Plants are wintered outside at a 7,500-foot elevation, so tender varieties don't appear on this nursery's list. Eleven columbine species are offered, and 18 primulas, along with several hybrids and named varieties. The nursery ships from March to November.

The Cummins Garden
See under *Azaleas and Rhododendrons*, page 44.

Daystar
See under *Trees and Shrubs*, page 151.

Eastern Plant Specialties
Dwarf conifers, dwarf azaleas, and rock-garden perennials. See under *Azaleas and Rhododendrons*, page 44.

Eco-Gardens
See under *Garden Perennials*, page 87.

Far North Gardens
See under *Primroses*, page 136.

Foxborough Nursery
Dwarf conifers. See under *Trees and Shrubs*, page 153.

Glendoick Gardens Ltd.
Dwarf rhododendrons and conifers. See under *Azaleas and Rhododendrons*, page 45.

Holly Hills, Inc.
Dwarf conifers. See under *Azaleas and Rhododendrons*, page 46.

W. E. Th. Ingwersen Ltd.
E. Grinstead, W. Sussex, England RH19 4LE
Telephone: 44-342-810236

Catalog price: two International Reply Coupons for seed list

The Ingwersen nursery catalog is a dense, small-type affair, with an array of plants sure to set the avid rock gardener drooling. Unfortunately, in 1987 the firm suspended plant exports and will now ship only seeds to overseas customers. If the seed list is as extensive as the nursery list, this may still be an important source for rock gardeners.

International Growers Exchange
See under *General Flowers and Vegetables*, page 21.

Klaus R. Jelitto
P.O. Box 560 127, D 2000 Hamburg 56, Germany
Telephone: 49-41-03/8-97-52

Catalog price: two International Reply Coupons

Adventurous gardeners with some knowledge of German may find some unusual offerings in this catalog, which includes seed for hundreds of rock-garden and alpine plants and other garden perennials. Plants are listed by botanical name, and even we, who are basically monolingual, could easily flip to the selections of campanula, dianthus, and primula (more than 50 species and cultivars are offered of each). We couldn't read the descriptions, however, and though we could decipher the price for packets, grams, and larger quantities, it was harder to figure out shipping costs and special import requirements. A coded propagation guide is keyed to lengthy texts in different languages (including English) at the back of the catalog.

L. Kreeger
91 Newton Wood Road, Ashtread, Surrey, England
KT21 1NN

Catalog price: $2 in cash

Mr. Kreeger sells seed for alpine plants, but will deal with serious rock gardeners only and prefers to limit his catalog mailings to members of rock-garden societies. Please don't trouble him unless you are a bona fide alpine enthusiast able to recognize rare plants by botanical name and prepared to grow difficult specimens from seed.

Lamb Nurseries
See under *Garden Perennials*, page 89.

Maver Nursery
See under *Garden Perennials*, page 89.

Montrose Nursery
P.O. Box 957, Hillsborough, NC 27278
Telephone: 919-732-7787

Catalog price: $1

One of the few spring catalogs we received in 1987 that opened with pleasant words about the weather—and winter weather at that. (Custom almost demands some critical words about crippling droughts, floods, or bitter cold.) The nursery's typed and amply descriptive list spans dozens of cyclamens (some of them rare and endangered species) and about 150 other perennials and shrubs—about half of them alpines and smaller plants suitable for rock gardens.

Mountain West Seeds
See under *Wildflowers*, page 177.

Owl Ridge Alpines
5421 Whipple Lake Road, Clarkston, MI 48016
Telephone: 313-394-0158

Catalog price: 50¢

Rock-garden perennials and wildflowers in a descriptive list that helpfully separates plants that require sun from those that thrive in the shade. Experts will be at home with the botanical listings, but novices may find it disconcerting that no common names are used. Among the offerings are *Arabis koehleri*, a low-growing Oregon native with purple flowers, a number of phlox, campanula, and primula species and cultivars, and an interesting list of unusual iris species.

Rakestraw's Perennial Gardens & Nursery
3094 S. Term Street, Burton, MI 48529
Telephone: 313-742-2685

Catalog price: $1, deductible from first order

A small booklet that manages to describe scores of sedums, dwarf conifers, and rock-garden perennials without resorting to eye-straining micro-type. Plants are listed by botanical name—followed by the common name if one exists—and the list darts from genus to genus without lingering long in any one spot. Aside from the strong sedum selection, the nursery's collection ranges widely. Among the offerings: *Erinus alpinus*, *Draba repens*, and *Lychnis alpina*—all diminutive rock-garden plants—and small selections of hostas, campanulas, and primulas.

Rice Creek Gardens
1315 66th Avenue N.E., Minneapolis, MN 55432
Telephone: 612-574-1197

Catalog price: $1

A densely typed descriptive list that takes some concentration to read, but one that covers a lot of ground and can fill a lot of garden needs. Rock-garden perennials take up the most space, and the listings are sensibly broken down into larger and smaller plants and into plants that prefer sun and varieties that grow in shade. Some 400 offerings are spread among those categories, many of them suitable for the perennial border as well as the rockery. A selection of larger border perennials is offered—such as *Aster × frikartii* and *Coreopsis verticillata* 'Moonbeam'—that are apparently too big for even the most spacious rock garden. The nursery also sells very nice selections of groundcovers, dwarf and weeping conifers, dwarf ferns, and small ornamental shrubs.

Rocknoll Nursery
9210 U.S. 50, Hillsboro, OH 45133-8546
Telephone: 513-393-1278

Catalog price: two first-class stamps

An extensive and rambling list of rock-garden plants, wildflowers, garden perennials, dwarf evergreens, flowering shrubs, and groundcovers. Thirty sempervivums are inexplicably listed in a separate category from the 300 or so "rock plants," and big inventories of iris, hosta, and daylilies are found pages away from the rest of the garden perennials. The iris collection is focused on dwarf, Japanese, and "interesting" Siberian types, and includes a number of species iris. The daylily selection is as well chosen, offering Stella d'Oro and some other choice hybrids by Peck, Henry, Soules, and others.

Rocky Mountain Seed Service
See under *Wildflowers*, page 180.

R. V. Roger Ltd.
The Nurseries, Whitby Road, Pickering,
N. Yorkshire, England YO18 7HG
Telephone: 44-751-72226

Catalog price: $1 cash

An excellent collection of trees, shrubs, roses, alpines, and heathers. Unfortunately, we cannot tell from the catalog whether or not the nursery will export plants or what it might charge for this service. Serious rock gardeners and heather enthusiasts may want to inquire, as the nursery has a great deal to offer in both areas.

Seedalp
P.O. Box 282, CH-1217 Meyrin 1, Geneva, Switzerland
Telephone: 41-22-82-4878

Catalog price: free

Another European seed source for garden perennials and alpines. More than 1,000 plants are listed by botanical name, with a code that explains which ones are suited for the rockery, which for the perennial border, which need shade or moisture, and when the plants will bloom. Happily, the key to the code is given in English as well as French and German. Payment must be made in Swiss francs.

Siskiyou Rare Plant Nursery
2825 Cummings Road, Medford, OR 97501
Telephone: 503-772-6846

Catalog price: $2

A fat descriptive catalog of "alpines and other dwarf, hardy plants for the woodland and rock garden." Hundreds of alpines, perennials, wildflowers, and dwarf shrubs are listed together alphabetically by botanical name. Good collections of dwarf conifers and hardy ferns rate their own categories. Among the listings are a number of heaths and heathers and nice selections of phlox, lewisia, penstemon, and saxifraga. Several violas native to western drylands are another uncommon offering.

Solar Green, Ltd.
Rt. 1, Box 115A, Moore, ID 83255
Telephone: 208-554-2821

Catalog price: $1.50

Patty Slayton is a relative newcomer to the mail-order nursery business, but she's already built up an impressive list of 150 alpines, many of them rare and hard-to-find species. She collects seed in the mountains of Idaho and trades with British alpinists for seed from botanical expeditions in Europe and Asia. (All her stock is originally grown from seed, none from plants collected in the wild.) Her list is a fascinating mix of unusual western natives, plants from mountainous regions around the world, and some popular perennial cultivars. Spring and fall price lists are sent with a descriptive catalog, though the information in the catalog is often too general to be really useful. Ms. Slayton recommends that shoppers consult an illustrated book on alpines before ordering. She also discourages orders from warmer regions, where she feels her plants may not survive.

Southwestern Native Seeds
See under *Wildflowers*, page 180.

Joel W. Spingarn
Dwarf conifers. See under *Trees and Shrubs*, page 164.

Stonehurst Rare Plants
Dwarf conifers. See under *Trees and Shrubs*, page 165.

Surry Gardens
See under *Garden Perennials*, page 92.

Washington Evergreen Nursery
Dwarf conifers. See under *Trees and Shrubs*, page 166.

We-Du Nurseries
See under *Garden Perennials*, page 93.

Wildwood Gardens
Dwarf trees and shrubs. See under *Bonsai*, page 57.

Azaleas and Rhododendrons

Baldsiefen Nursery
P.O. Box 88, Bellvale, NY 10912
Telephone: 914-986-4222

Catalog price: $3, deductible from first order

A limited but choice selection of rhododendrons and azaleas from a broad range of hybridizers. The thick descriptive catalog offers an education in rhododendron culture, starting with the choice of a planting site and continuing through planting, fertilizing, pruning, and fending off pests and diseases. The booklet explains who the major hybridizers were (and are), gives lengthy descriptions of each offering, and pictures a few of the blooms in color. Baldsiefen sells proved winners rather than the latest novelties and includes such classics as Gibraltar and Scintillation. The stock is generally on the large side, which means that prices are a little higher than average, but also that plants are closer to blooming age. All plants are shipped balled and burlapped.

Benjamin's Rhododendrons
18402-A N. Tapps Highway, Sumner, WA 98390

Catalog price: $3

A big list of more than 600 rhododendron hybrids, each briefly described, including notes on cold hardiness, bloom season, color, and growth habit. A scoring system rates each plant for the quality of flower, foliage, and overall habit and performance. (1 means not worth growing, 5 perfect in all respects. Some 5's are on the list; we didn't notice any 1's.) A more limited, but still extensive list of rhododendron species is found at the back of the catalog. The owners are expanding this section of the inventory, so look for even more species offerings in the future. Most plants sold are smaller specimens, in the four- to eight-inch range, and most are types that will grow best in milder climates (zones 6 to 9).

The Bovees Nursery
1737 S.W. Coronado, Portland, OR 97219
Telephone: 503-244-9341 or 9381

Catalog price: $2, deductible from first order

An excellent selection of rhododendrons and azaleas from a respected grower. The plants are chosen from a broad range of hybridizers and parent types. Among the offerings are a number of *yakushimanum* hybrids and a nice inventory of rhododendron species. A separate list of vireya rhododendrons is sent out on request. A glossary explains the sometimes cryptic terms of the rhododendron subculture, and a short essay gives some background on the key collectors and hybridizers. Each plant is decribed in a few sentences; color, size, growth habit, fragrance, and cold hardiness are noted. Plants can be had as one-, two-, three-, or four-year-old specimens; the price rises with the age.

Boyer Nurseries
See under *Trees and Shrubs*, page 148.

Briarwood Gardens
14 Gully Lane, Rt. 1, E. Sandwich, MA 02537
Telephone: 617-888-2146

Catalog price: $1

Briarwood Gardens is a small, sharply focused nursery, one of the prime suppliers of Dexter rhododendrons. The firm is authorized by Heritage Plantations to take cuttings from the original Dexter plants, and the catalog lists 80 different Dexter varieties. A few non-Dexter hybrids are offered, including Melanie Shaw, a touted Briarwood introduction with a deep purple blossom. The catalog describes each plant briefly and features a few with more lengthy texts. (The featured plants are changed from year to year so that regular customers can learn more about a range of the hybrids.) Plants are on the small side; most can be had as juniors and yearlings only.

Bull Valley Rhododendron Nursery
214 Bull Valley Road, Aspers, PA 17304
Telephone: 717-677-6313

Catalog price: $1.60

A good array of Leach and Dexter hybrid rhododendrons, along with a smattering of others, such as Gable and Cowles hybrids. Plants are described by flower color only, and the firm headlines its list "Plants for the Serious Collector!" The exclamation point is intended to discourage idle inquiries from beginners. The nursery interrupts its shipping season to assure that no plants arrive at empty houses during the American Rhododendron Society convention.

Cardinal Nursery
Rt. 1, Box 316, State Road, NC 28676
Telephone: 919-874-2027

Catalog price: free

A wide-ranging rhododendron list that covers most of the major hybridizers and some that are less familiar—more than 500 offerings in all. Many are hardy into zone 5, and quite a few will survive freezes of -25° F. The list is weighted toward the eastern types created by Dexter, Gable, Leach, and Shammarello, but the firm also sells quite a large selection from British, Dutch, and Northwest hybridizers. Plants are on the small side, and prices are reasonable.

Carlson's Gardens
P.O. Box 305, South Salem, NY 10590
Telephone: 914-763-5958

Catalog price: $2, deductible from first order

Carlson's little booklet offers a strong selection of azaleas, including Knapphill-Exbury hybrids, and a broad array of evergreen types from a number of hybridizers. A more limited rhododendron inventory is largely confined to Leach, Gable, and Dexter hybrids. The nursery carries a particularly good array of azalea petites and dwarf rhododendrons. The catalog describes each offering briefly, without illustrations. Gardeners interested in particular plants can write for color photographs, which are sold at a nominal fee.

Carroll Gardens
See under *Garden Perennials*, page 87.

L. C. Case
14 Lockeland Road, Winchester, MA 01890

Catalog price: long self-addressed stamped envelope

Rhododendron seed for serious growers who are ready to take on the extra work of raising plants from seed. Case concentrates on hybrids bred for severe climates, and he seems to favor yellow blooms. The list is sent out in November.

V. O. Chambers Nursery
26874 Ferguson Road, Junction City, OR 97448
Telephone: 503-998-2467

Catalog price: free

A thick descriptive catalog of rhododendrons and azaleas, including a good selection of rhododendron species. Both old favorites and newer hybrids make the list of rhododendron hybrids, which runs to more than 350 names. Scintillation and Nova Zembla share space with *arboreum* and *williamsianum* crosses. The azalea list includes almost 100 cultivars, including a number of Kurume, Satsuki, and Greenwood hybrids. All plants are well described in a couple of sentences.

Chiltern Seeds
See under *General Flowers and Vegetables*, page 15.

The Cummins Garden
22 Robertsville Road, Marlboro, NJ 07746
Telephone: 201-536-2591

Catalog price: $1, deductible from first order

Hybrid and species rhododendrons and azaleas in a catalog with brief descriptions. The selection is largely confined to the most popular cultivars from a wide range of hybridizers. In 1988 the nursery will add a number of dwarf rhododendrons to the list. A companion plant section includes dwarf conifers, hollies, heaths, mountain laurel, and some perennials suited to the rock garden.

Daystar
See under *Trees and Shrubs*, page 151.

Bill Dodd's Rare Plants
P.O. Drawer 377, Semmes, AL 36575

Catalog price: long self-addressed stamped envelope

A small nursery specializing in native azalea species and first-generation hybrids with native parents. Mr. Dodd complements these offerings with a list of companion trees and shrubs that includes mountain laurel, sourwood, loblolly bay, and bigleaf magnolia. The list is a two-page typed affair without descriptions. Most of the offerings are best suited to southeastern gardens.

Peter B. Dow & Company
Seeds. See under *Native Plants of Australia and South Africa*, page 119.

Eastern Plant Specialties
P.O. Box 40, Colonia, NJ 07067
Telephone: 201-388-3101

Catalog price: $2, deductible from first order

Unusual rhododendrons and azaleas, dwarf conifers, rock-garden perennials, and native plants. The nursery has sought out uncommon rhododendron and azalea hybrids, including a good selection of dwarf azaleas, and offers them with a solid inventory of rhododendron species and mountain laurel cultivars. Each listing is described in a short paragraph that gives the necessary details of cold tolerance, size, flower color, bloom season, and growth habit. The dwarf conifer listings have been crammed into a smaller space with tiny type and abbreviated descriptions. The nursery grows hundreds of dwarf conifers and only allows room in the catalog for a select few, so don't be afraid to ask if you don't see what you want.

Flora Lan Nursery
Rt. 1, Box 357, Forest Grove, OR 97116
Telephone: 503-357-3500

Catalog price: free

The folks at Flora Lan haven't wasted any time or money on a fancy catalog, but their computer-type listing includes a very nice selection of rhododendrons in a range of sizes at reasonable prices. About 200 hybrids are listed in a chart that shows the cold hardiness, mature height, and flower color of each. A more limited array of azaleas, Japanese maples, camellias, magnolias, heaths, and other "companion plants" are listed without any descriptions at all.

Girard Nurseries
See under *Trees and Shrubs*, page 154.

Glendoick Gardens Ltd.
Perth, Scotland PH2 7NS

Catalog price: $1

Rhododendron connoisseurs may want to explore the offerings of this Scottish nursery. Roughly 500 rhododendron hybrids and species are listed, among them almost 200 dwarf types and nearly 150 larger species. *R. arboreum*, the 40-foot tree-like species is on the list, as is the six-inch *R. keiskei* 'Yaku Fairy'. A smaller selection of azaleas, camellias, dwarf conifers, and perennials is offered to complete the garden. The minimum order for export is £75, and an import permit must be obtained by the buyer. (See *Buying Plants from Overseas*, page 9.)

The Greenery
14450 N.E. 16th Place, Bellevue, WA 98007
Telephone: 206-641-1458

Catalog price: $1

An exceptionally good collection of species rhododendrons, most of them suited to the conditions of the Pacific Northwest. A somewhat smaller selection of hybrid rhododendrons and azaleas is also offered. The descriptions don't note cold hardiness or mature size, so buyers may need to shop with a reference book at hand.

Greer Gardens
1280 Goodpasture Island Road, Eugene, OR 97401-1794
Telephone: 503-686-8266

Catalog price: $2

One of the larger rhododendron growers, Greer Gardens puts out a colorful descriptive catalog that will interest both ex-perts and beginners. Hybrid rhododendrons are the stars of Greer's show; more than 500 named cultivars are listed, from new *yakushimanum* hybrids to old favorites like Nova Zembla. The rhododendron species list is almost as extensive, covering some 200 plants. All offerings are thoroughly described, including plant size, hardiness, parentage, and detailed notes on foliage, bloom, and growth habit. A rating system scores each plant for its flower and overall growth. Greer also offers a good inventory of hybrid azaleas, two dozen vireya rhododendron species and hybrids, and a wide selection of ornamental maples, conifers, and other landscaping trees and shrubs. In a two-page section at the back of the catalog the firm has picked out a number of trees and shrubs suitable for bonsai culture, among them conifers, maples, and azaleas.

Hager Nurseries, Inc.
Rt. 5, Box 2000, Spotsylvania, VA 22553
Telephone: 703-582-5031

Catalog price: two first-class stamps and a long self-addressed envelope for price list, $4 for descriptive catalog

More than 1,400 azalea hybrids from a broad range of hybridizers; a few of the offerings are Hager's own creations. The price list is simply a list of names, introduced by a few words about each of the hybridizers. The full catalog gives a brief description of each variety, with flower color, growth habit, size, bloom season, and cold hardiness noted. Plants are available in container sizes from one quart to two gallons. Larger plants are sold, but these must be picked up at the nursery.

Hall Rhododendrons
1280 Quince Drive, Junction City, OR 97448
Telephone: 503-998-2060

Catalog price: $1

A well-known grower with a massive list of rhododendron species and hybrids. More than 1,200 are listed in the catalog, and even more are being propagated at the nursery. Among the offerings are several dozen *yakushimanum* forms and crosses. A broad range of hybridizers is represented, and the plants are sold in a wide choice of sizes, from two- to five-year-old specimens. Short descriptions cover the pertinent points of mature size, cold hardiness, foliage, and flower. A rating system judges the quality of each listing. The firm is the creator of the Hall box, a device widely used for forcing rhododendrons. The box is pictured on the catalog cover, but does not seem to be available for sale. Hall does sell aluminum plant labels and playing cards printed with color pictures of rhododendrons.

James Harris Hybrid Evergreen Azaleas
538 Swanson Drive, Lawrenceville, GA 30245

Catalog price: long self-addressed stamped envelope

A limited selection of Mr. Harris's own evergreen azalea hybrids. No hardiness information is given on the descriptive list, but other growers note these hybrids as being hardy to zone 7. The nursery also sells a handful of native azalea species. The hybrids are sold as transplants (very small plants), and the species as year-old specimens.

Harstine Island Nursery

E. 3021 Harstine Island N. Road, Shelton, WA 98584
Telephone: 206-426-2014

Catalog price: send want list with long self-addressed stamped envelope

This nursery publishes no list or catalog, but responds instead to customers' want lists. More than 800 rhododendron varieties are grown, mostly hybrids, as well as an extensive inventory of azaleas, ornamental maples, and dwarf conifers.

Hass Nursery

24105 Ervin Road, Philomath, OR 97370
Telephone: 503-929-3739

Catalog price: $2

An extensive inventory of evergreen azalea hybrids, more than 500 cultivars in all. About half the offerings are Satsuki hybrids, originally from Kairyo Nursery in Japan and propagated by Hass from specimens growing at Brookside Garden in Wheaton, Maryland. A far smaller selection of rhododendrons complements the azalea list. Many of Hass's plants are unusual types, and many are hardy only in zones 7 to 9. The novelty of the offerings will make the list of particular interest to experienced growers, though the adequate descriptions and cultural information also make it accessible to beginners.

Hillhouse Nursery

Kresson-Gibbsboro Road, R.D. 1, Marlton, NJ 08053
Telephone: 609-784-6203

Catalog price: free

Linwood azalea hybrids, created by the late G. Albert Reid at the Fischer Greenhouses in Linwood, New Jersey, and grown at Hillhouse Nursery by Reid's close friend Theodore Stecki. Most of the plants are hardy to 0° F, a few to -5° and even -10°. Hillhouse also sells a limited selection of Girard, Exbury, and Glenn Dale hybrids. All plants are sold in 3-inch pots.

Hillier Nurseries (Winchester) Ltd.

See under *Trees and Shrubs*, page 155.

Holly Hills, Inc.

1216 Hillsdale Road, Evansville, IN 47711
Telephone: 812-867-3367

Catalog price: two first-class stamps

A small but interesting collection of evergreen azalea hybrids created in the 1970s by H. R. Schroeder. All are hardy to at least -15° F, and all have survived the hottest summers Evansville has seen this century. The parentage is given for each, along with a description of growth habit and flower. The nursery also sells a small but select group of rhododendron hybrids (including the popular Yaku Princess) and a selection of American hollies and dwarf conifers.

Horsely Rhododendron Nursery

7441 Tracyton Boulevard N.W., Bremerton, WA 98310
Telephone: 206-692-9588

Catalog price: free

A small list of rhododendron species and hybrids; some of the crosses are the nursery's own. Two plants are singled out for full descriptions: Arthur Horsley, a low white-flowering cross of White Swan and Nestucca, and One Thousand Butterflies, a compact pink-flowered plant. The balance of the list is typed out with only a code to indicate flower color. A few Exbury azaleas are tacked on to the end of the list.

Hortica Gardens

Satsuki and Kurume azaleas. See under *Bonsai*, page 56.

Hydon Nurseries Ltd.

Clock Barn Lane, Hydon Heath, Godalming,
Surrey, England GU8 4AZ
Telephone: 44-48632-252

Catalog price: $3

A big catalog of rhododendrons, including an impressive offering of species, for the serious collector willing to handle the import paperwork. Hydon sells such tree forms as *R. arboreum* and *R. fortunei*, along with dwarf species like *R. impeditum* and *R. calostrotum*. The firm lists about 100 rhododendron species in all and nearly 300 hybrids, among them more than a dozen *yakushimanum* crosses. Descriptions note flower, foliage, size, growth habit, and bloom season (in Britain). The guide to hardiness is by a British system, and North American buyers will want to do some further research before ordering. Hydon mentions no minimum order for export, but the cost of the shipping and the extra work involved in obtaining an import permit make small orders uneconomical. For information on customs regulations see *Buying Plants from Overseas*, page 9.

Justice Gardens

107 Hight Drive, Watkinsville, GA 30677
Telephone: 404-769-8379

Catalog price: free

A broad selection of important rhododendron and azalea hybrids, organized by hybridizer on a photocopied list without descriptions of any kind. Plants are sold in small sizes—rooted cuttings or liners—and at good prices.

Millais Nurseries

Crosswater Farm, Churt, Farnham, Surrey, England
GU10 2JN

Catalog price: $1

Specialists may want to take a look at the Millais catalog, but beginners should steer clear. The nursery offers a reasonably good selection of hybrid and species rhododendrons and a more limited choice of azaleas. Many of the rhododendrons are the tender types from Nepal that cannot survive the temperature extremes found in most regions of North America. (They grow well in the Pacific Northwest.) The abbreviated descriptions include a British hardiness classification that does not translate easily to North American climatic conditions.

Mowbray Gardens

3318 Mowbray Lane, Cincinnati, OH 45226
Telephone: 513-321-0694

Catalog price: free

Two typewritten sheets present a small collection of rhododendrons, most of them Leach hybrids. Plants are offered as one-, two-, or three-year-old stock.

E. B. Nauman, Nurseryman

688 St. Davids Lane, Schenectady, NY 12309

Catalog price: free

A limited list of hybrid rhododendrons and azaleas (described by the nursery as a "specialized catalog"). A total of 30 named varieties are offered. Most of the rhododendrons are hardy in zone 5; a few will survive in zone 4. Three mountain laurel hybrids and a dwarf Canadian hemlock were offered in 1987. Nauman sells small plants, so customers must be willing to wait a couple of seasons for flowers.

North Coast Rhododendron Nursery

P.O. Box 308, Bodega, CA 94922

Catalog price: $1

Rhododendrons for mild climates, offered in a detailed descriptive catalog. Almost 50 species are listed, most of them natives of the eastern Himalayas, southern China, Burma, and Southeast Asia, areas with a climate similar to that of coastal California. The roughly 100 hybrids sold are crosses of warm-climate types, and all have performed well in hot dry California summers. Plants are sold as two-, three-, or four-year-old specimens.

Nuccio's Nurseries

P.O. Box 6160, Altadena, CA 91001
Telephone: 818-794-3383

Catalog price: free

A strong selection of azaleas and camellias for mild climates. The azalea department includes 200 Satsuki hybrids and an array of Kurumes and Belgian hybrids. A few dozen of Nuccio's own hybrid azaleas are also listed. Almost 400 camellias are offered, from *japonica* types to *sasanquas*, *reticulatas*, and *rusticanas*. The nursery sells a good selection of camellia species. Descriptions are generally quite short, and most do not include information on cold hardiness.

Orlando S. Pride Nurseries

See under *Trees and Shrubs*, page 162.

Alfred A. Raustein

230 Union Avenue, Holbrook, NY 11741
Telephone: 516-588-0989

Catalog price: free

A small nursery that grows a wide array of rhododendrons from most of the major hybridizers, all hardy in Holbrook, New York (zone 6b). Among them are a number of German introductions that we haven't seen elsewhere. Mr. Raustein grows each plant in small quantities and asks shoppers to inquire about price and availability before sending in their orders.

Roslyn Nursery

211 Burrs Lane, Dix Hills, NY 11746
Telephone: 516-643-9347

Catalog price: $2

A thick catalog of rhododendrons, azaleas, and such companion plants as mountain laurel, holly, andromeda, ferns, and conifers. The emphasis here is on hybrid and species rhododendrons for colder climates, where winter temperatures drop to -5° F and below. More than 400 rhododendron hybrids are offered as well as almost 100 species. The azalea list is also quite extensive, including more than 300 evergreen types and 100 deciduous hybrids. The rhododendron descriptions include a code to hardiness, which notes those plants that will survive in zones 4 and 5, but the azalea list simply notes that the plants have endured winters at the nursery (zone 6). The nursery sells plants in a range of sizes, from four to 30 inches, the price rising with the height.

F. W. Schumacher Co.

Rhododendron and azalea seed. See under *Trees and Shrubs*, page 163.

Gordon W. Severe Nursery

Rt. 4, Box 173-1, Millsboro, DE 19966
Telephone: 302-945-2912

Catalog price: free

A huge list of azalea hybrids from a range of hybridizers, presented on a computer printout by name only without descriptions. Among the strengths of the list are the 450 Glenn Dale hybrids and the 350 Satsuki hybrids, which are offered by special arrangement with Brookside Garden. Plants are sold as seedlings and transplants. The minimum order is 25 plants.

Sonoma Horticultural Nursery

3970 Azalea Avenue, Sebastopol, CA 95472
Telephone: 707-823-6832

Catalog price: $1.50

Sonoma Horticultural Nursery sells more than 300 rhododendron hybrids and 100 species in a descriptive catalog. The offerings include both hardy and tender types (all the plants have survived summer heat of over 100° F and most will endure much colder winters than they experience in Sebastapol). Cold hardiness is noted for each listing, along with information about flower color, growth habit, bloom season, and mature size. Among the species listings are tree forms and such dwarf types as *R. nakaharai* and *R. pemakoense*. The nursery sells a number of vireya hybrids and more than 200 hybrid azaleas. Rhododendrons are sold as two- or three-year-old specimens; azaleas come in gallon or two-gallon containers.

Sorum's Nursery

Rt. 4, Box 308J, Sherwood, OR 97140
Telephone: 503-628-2354

Catalog price: free

Sorum's is a smaller nursery with a limited but wide-ranging inventory of rhododendrons. Plants are separated on the list into dwarf and full-size types and grouped by flower color, but no further description is offered. Stock can be ordered in sizes from ten to 30 inches. The firm also sells ficus and pieris. A small list of evergreen azaleas is available on request.

Stillpoint Gardens

See under *Shade Plants*, page 146.

Stubbs Shrubs

23225 S.W. Bosky Dell Lane, West Linn, OR 97068-9198
Telephone: 503-638-5048

Catalog price: $2, deductible from first order

Stubbs Shrubs specializes in evergreen azaleas, listing almost 300 hybrids in a descriptive catalog. The text notes the hybridizer or grouping, flower color, mature size, and growth habit of each offering, but neglects to note cold hardiness. A helpful introduction gives some background on the major hybridizers and groupings, explaining where Kurume, Satsuki, and North Tisbury types originated. Plants are sold primarily as rooted cuttings. Larger plants are available on special request.

The Sweetbriar

P.O. Box 25, Woodinville, WA 98072
Telephone: 206-821-2222

Catalog price: $2, deductible from first order

For the past few years The Sweetbriar has been trimming back its retail mail-order business. The 1984 catalog had nice descriptions of about 150 rhododendron and azalea offerings, but by 1987 the nursery was down to an irregular list with no descriptions at all, sent to new customers with a copy of the older catalog.

Thomasville Nurseries, Inc.

See under *Roses*, page 144.

Transplant Nursery

Parkertown Road, Lavonia, GA 30553
Telephone: 404-356-8947

Catalog price: free

Transplant Nursery offers a wide range of rhododendrons and azaleas in its slim descriptive catalog. The inventory delves especially deeply into native deciduous azaleas and Dexter rhododendrons. The nursery offers two dozen native azalea species, along with a number of crosses between them. Nearly 150 Dexter hybrids are listed. Other offerings include Robin Hill, Kurume, Pennington, Kehr, Carla, North Tisbury, Harris, Glenn Dale, and Satsuki azaleas, and a handful of *yakushimanum* crosses. Descriptions deal with flower color only and don't mention cold hardiness or mature size. Plants come in either gallon or two-gallon containers.

Vireya Specialties Nursery

2701 Malcolm Avenue, Los Angeles, CA 90064
Telephone: free

Catalog price: free

The growing popularity of vireya rhododendrons got the best of this nursery in 1987. The entire inventory of 36 varieties sold out in the fall of 1986 and none were available for spring shipment. The catalog is mailed in early August, and interested shoppers should pounce when it arrives.

Washington Evergreen Nursery

See under *Trees and Shrubs*, page 166.

Wayside Gardens

See under *Garden Perennials*, page 92.

Westgate Gardens Nursery

751 Westgate Drive, Eureka, CA 95501
Telephone: 707-442-1239

Catalog price: $1, deductible from first order

Without a word of introduction this catalog launches into a descriptive list of nearly 800 rhododendron hybrids and species, all mixed together according to the law of the alphabet. Parentage is given for the hybrids, and notes on mature height, cold tolerance, and flower color are provided for all. The occasional hybrid is tolerant to -15° F, but most of the offerings will succumb in winter temperatures below -5°.

Whispering Pines Nursery
74 County Street, Lakeville, MA 02347
Telephone: 617-947-0705

Catalog price: free

A small but interesting collection of hybrid rhododendrons from a range of hybridizers. The simple list notes only color and cold hardiness. Most of the offerings are hardy to -10° F, and a number will survive at -25°. The exception is a vireya hybrid that can't even tolerate a cool breeze. Plants are available in one-, two-, or three-year-old sizes.

Whitney Gardens & Nursery
P.O. Box F, Brinnon, WA 98320-0080
Telephone: 206-796-4411

Catalog price: $1

A fat descriptive catalog that could serve as a beginner's text on rhododendrons and azaleas for milder climates. Four hundred rhododendron hybrids, nearly 100 species, and almost 200 azalea hybrids are sold. The descriptions cover cold hardiness, bloom season, mature height, and fragrance and go into some detail about flowers, foliage, and growth habit. A few of the choicer offerings are pictured in color or black-and-white photographs. Among the rhododendron offerings are almost 100 *yakushimanum* hybrids, some of them Whitney's own creations. The rhododendron species list includes a number of tree-like plants, such as *R. rex* from southern China and *R. sidereum* from Burma. The nursery is open to visitors year-round, but the owners recommend late April and early May as the peak bloom season.

Woodland Nurseries
See under *Trees and Shrubs*, page 167.

Bamboos

American Bamboo Company
345 W. Second Street, Dayton, OH 45402

Catalog price: free

A number of varieties of phyllostachys bamboo for outdoor planting in northern areas. The featured species in the spring of 1987 was *P. bissettii*, according to the nursery, "one of the most hardy bamboos." All plants are field grown at the nursery, though a heavy layer of mulch is recommended where temperatures drop to -10° F.

Endangered Species
See under *Tropical Plants*, page 168.

Fruitland Nurseries
L. C. Helm, Rt. 2, Box 490, Thomson, GA 30824

Catalog price: free

Ten bamboo species, ranging from the tiny *Sasa pygmaea*, which grows to a height of only two feet, to *Phyllostachys bambusoides*, which can reach maturity at 60 feet in just five years. Mr. Helm writes a paragraph or so about each of his plants, including notes on cold hardiness, light and soil requirements, and the size and density of the foliage. Rhizomes are shipped from February through mid-March.

Garden World's Exotic Plants
See under *Tropical Plants*, page 169.

Louisiana Nursery
See under *Trees and Shrubs*, page 158.

Northern Groves
3328 S.E. Kelly, Portland, OR 97202
Telephone: 503-232-1860 or 231-7322

Catalog price: long self-addressed stamped envelope

Nearly 50 species and varieties of hardy bamboo. Only a handful are hardy below -10° F, but if you live in an area where the thermometer stays above 0° all winter you can take your pick of the entire list. The offerings are sensibly arranged by mature height; plants that grow to a mature size of two to six feet are all grouped together, as are species that soar to heights of 30 to 70 feet. Plants are shipped in gallon, three-gallon, or larger containers.

Steve Ray's Bamboo Gardens
909 79th Place S., Birmingham, AL 35206
Telephone: 205-833-3052

Catalog price: free

An educational catalog of 30 bamboos, most of them hardy to about 0°F. Each plant is fully described in a paragraph of text and pictured in a black-and-white photograph. Several pages at the back of the booklet present a course in bamboo culture. Mr. Ray concentrates primarily on the medium-size and larger bamboos, but offers a few dwarf types to make the list complete.

Sunset Nursery

4007 Elrod Avenue, Tampa, FL 33616
Telephone: 813-839-7228 or 837-3003

Catalog price: long self-addressed stamped envelope

Forty bamboo species and varieties on a simple typed list with notes on mature size and cold hardiness. Both tiny and tall plants are offered, the toughest hardy to -10° F, the most tender to just 27°. A two-page cultural guide accompanies the list.

Tradewinds Nursery

P.O. Box 70, Calpella, CA 95418
Telephone: 707-485-0835

Catalog price: free

Fifteen bamboo species from a grower who's specialized in these plants for almost two decades. This new nursery was formed after the demise of an earlier venture called Panda Products Bamboo Plantation. In 1987 Tradewinds had a big inventory of Moso bamboo (*Phyllostachys pubescens*), the species most widely cultivated in China today. It grows to a height of 75 feet and will survive chills down to 0° F. A few other tall types are offered, as are a range of medium-size and small species.

Tripple Brook Farm

Cold-hardy bamboo. See under *Garden Perennials*, page 92.

Upper Bank Nurseries

P.O. Box 486, Media, PA 19063
Telephone: 215-566-0679

Catalog price: one first-class stamp

Ten species of hardy bamboo, presented on a single typed sheet by botanical name only. Interested customers will have to inquire further or do some reading to find out how tall each grows and how deep a chill it will survive.

Begonias

Antonelli Brothers

2545 Capitola Road, Santa Cruz, CA 95062

Catalog price: $1

Tuberous begonias from one of the leading hybridizers and growers in the field. In 1987 the nursery promoted its new strain of miniature begonia, developed from old multiflora types. The firm is also proud of its ruffled picotee hybrids, which it introduced in 1954. In addition to those forms, Antonelli Brothers offers rose, giant double ruffled, rose picotee, and hanging-basket picotee types. All are available as seeds or tubers and can be had in color assortments or by separate hue. Canadian customers are charged an extra paperwork fee and are asked to send an official Canadian agriculture mailing label.

Atkinson's Greenhouses

Rt. 2, Box 69, Morrilton, AR 72110

Catalog price: 50¢

More than 100 named begonia cultivars, sold as rooted plants (most taken from 2-inch pots for shipping). The list gives a brief description of the foliage and flower of each offering. Shoppers looking for particular cultivars will have to hunt through several pages, as the names are not in strict alphabetical order. A few other flowering and foliage houseplants and a selection of cacti and succulents bring up the rear of the list.

Blackmore & Langdon

Pensford, Bristol, England BS18 4JL
Telephone: 44-272-33-2300

Catalog price: $2 in cash

A choice inventory of tuberous begonias and delphiniums from a noted grower of both plants. Many of the begonias are pictured in the compact color catalog, and the exquisite blooms might even lure beginners to part with the steep asking prices. Begonias are shipped as dormant tubers, and, though the catalog includes no specific export instructions, the firm should be able to ship these to the U.S. and Canada economically. The named delphinium cultivars can be sent as plants only (they don't come true from seed) and, unfortunately, are costly to export except in quantity. Mixed seeds from choice varieties are also offered, and gardeners on the wrong side of the Atlantic may have to settle for these.

C. A. Cruickshank Inc.

See under *General Flowers and Vegetables*, page 16.

Fairyland Begonia Garden
1100 Griffith Road, McKinleyville, CA 95521
Telephone: 707-839-3034

Catalog price: 50¢

Rex, tuberous, and other hybrid and species begonias. Fragrant tuberous begonias are a mini-specialty offered in a choice of four cultivars created by the nursery's owners. These commanded a premium price in 1987, and three were sold out by the time we got our catalog in February. The roughly 100 begonia offerings are each described in a paragraph of text that sometimes rises to enthusiastic heights. A couple dozen lilies are also listed; they range in price from mixtures at $5 for a 10-bulb sack to a rare new oriental hybrid set at $100 per plant. Those who want an element of mystery in their gardening can order lily seed and see what colors come up.

G & G Gardens
See under *Fuchsias*, page 85.

Glasshouse Works
See under *Tropical Plants*, page 169.

Robert B. Hamm
P.O. Box 160903, Sacramento, CA 95816

Catalog price: $3 for a year of newsletters and price lists

Mr. Hamm specializes in "unusual plants," some for garden planting and some for indoor culture. He concentrates particularly on unusual begonias; in his spring 1987 list he offered 50 cultivars. But he grows and sells much more—from succulents and tropical plants to herbs and scented geraniums.

International Growers Exchange
See under *General Flowers and Vegetables*, page 21.

Kartuz Greenhouses
See under *Houseplants*, page 106.

Lauray of Salisbury
See under *Houseplants*, page 106.

Logee's Greenhouses
55 North Street, Danielson, CT 06239
Telephone: 203-774-8038

Catalog price: $3, deductible from order of more than $25

We first came across the Logee's catalog soon after we noticed a spectacular Martha Washington geranium in a green-house. The memory of the hours we spent poring over the exotic listings and the rich color photographs is still fresh in our minds, as is the disappointment we felt when we found out elsewhere that the geraniums we wanted would not bloom in our New England summer heat. The catalog will make any plant lover drool, but unfortunately, it is a bit lighter on growing instruction than it is on description. The nursery grows more than 500 begonia varieties, about evenly split among rex, fibrous, and rhizomatous types, with a very few wax and tuberous types tacked on almost as an afterthought. Gesneriads, camellias, bougainvilleas, peperomias, and tender ferns are also well represented on a list that extends to all manner of ornamental plants for windowsill and greenhouse culture.

Miree's Gesneriads
Miniature begonias. See under *African Violets and Other Gesneriads*, page 37.

The Plant Kingdom
See under *Houseplants*, page 107.

John Scheepers, Inc.
See under *Bulbs*, page 63.

Wyatt-Quarles Seed Co.
See under *General Flowers and Vegetables*, page 33.

Berry Plants

Ahrens Strawberry Nursery
Rt. 1, Huntingburg, IN 47542-9589
Telephone: 812-683-3055

Catalog price: free

Twenty-eight varieties of strawberries for the home grower or those with larger aspirations. The old standards are here— Earliglow, Sparkle, and Catskill—along with new varieties and some strains geared to the special needs of commercial growers. A chart helps shoppers compare offerings for flavor, firmness, size, and disease resistance. The minimum order is 25 plants of a single variety. Ahrens also carries other fruit-bearing nursery stock—blackberries, raspberries, boysenberries, gooseberries, currants, blueberries, and a selection of fruit trees.

Alexander's Nurseries
376 Wareham Street, Middleboro, MA 02346
Telephone: 617-947-6390

Catalog price: long self-addressed stamped envelope

A dozen varieties of highbush blueberries, available as root cuttings or two- to four-year-old plants. Alexander's also sells lilacs, herbs, and perennials in a supplemental list.

W. F. Allen Co.
P.O. Box 1577, Salisbury, MD 21801
Telephone: 301-742-7122

Catalog price: free

Allen's has been in the strawberry business since 1885, and, judging by the testimonials in the catalog, the firm still satisfies its customers each spring. Fifteen varieties are listed—old favorites and new introductions—and a few are pictured in delicious color photographs. All are exhaustively described, with disease resistance, freezing quality, and flavors compared. The minimum order is 50 plants—25 each of any two varieties. Blueberries, raspberries, blackberries, and asparagus round out the list.

Ames' Orchard and Nursery
See under *Trees and Shrubs*, page 147.

Beaverlodge Nursery Ltd.
Berry plants for Canadian customers. See under *Trees and Shrubs*, page 148.

Blue Star Laboratories
Rt. 13, Box 173, Williamstown, NY 13493
Telephone: 315-964-2294

Catalog price: free

Earliblue, Bluetta, Spartan, Patriot, Blueray, Bluejay, Bluecrop, and Northland blueberry bushes. Minimum order for a single variety is five plants. The nursery also sells asparagus transplants.

Blueberry Hill
Rt. 1, Maynooth, ON, Canada K0L 2S0

Catalog price: free

Native lowbush blueberries (*Vaccinium angustifolium*) for home garden planting. "This plant is hardy throughout most of the U.S. and Canada," the leaflet notes, "but requires a period of winter chill for best fruit production." Plants can be shipped to U.S. as well as Canadian customers.

Boston Mountain Nurseries
Rt. 2, Box 405-A, Mountainburg, AR 72946

Catalog price: free

A berry nursery with a specialty in brambles—blackberries, raspberries, tayberries, boysenberries, dewberries, gooseberries, and youngberries. The firm sells almost 20 different blackberry and raspberry cultivars. Strawberry plants, grapevines, and blueberry bushes are also offered in a more limited range of choices.

Boyer Nurseries
Strawberry plants. See under *Trees and Shrubs*, page 149.

Brittingham Plant Farms
P.O. Box 2538, Salisbury, MD 21801-2538
Telephone: 301-749-5153

Catalog price: free

Twenty-four varieties of strawberries sold as plants in the spring. The catalog gives an excellent description of each type, illustrated with a huge photograph of the berry. A chart compares ripening seasons, flavor, freezing qualities, firmness, and disease resistance. To complete your berry patch,

Brittingham sells raspberries, blackberries, blueberries, and grapes.

Buntings' Nurseries, Inc.
P.O. Box 306, Selbyville, DE 19975
Telephone: 302-436-8231

Catalog price: free

Thirty-five varieties of strawberries in an informative catalog with six full pages of tips on planting and care and the biggest comparative chart of all the strawberry brochures. Earlier catalogs have had big color pictures, but Buntings' now seems to have chosen a less glossy and more educational format. There's much to learn here, and plenty of berries to choose from. Asparagus, rhubarb, and horseradish are offered too.

California Nursery Company
Grapevines. See under *Trees and Shrubs*, page 149.

Cooley's Strawberry Nursery
Route 3, Box 530, Bald Knob, AR 72010
Telephone: 501-347-2026 or 724-5630

Catalog price: free

Twenty different strawberries sold in lots of 100 or more. The firm seems to aim its sales pitch at the larger grower, but its orientation toward large-scale farmers might also save small-scale gardeners some money. Cooley's price for 100 plants is lower than many competitors' prices for 50.

Dyke Bros. Nursery
Rt. 1, Box 251-S, Vincent, OH 45784
Telephone: 614-678-2192

Catalog price: free

Blueray, Berkeley, and Coville blueberries, and Cheyenne blackberries, sold singly or by the thousand. Orders must be placed by March 15 for spring delivery.

Edible Landscaping
See under *Trees and Shrubs*, page 151.

Emlong Nurseries Inc.
See under *Trees and Shrubs*, page 152.

The Fig Tree Nursery
Berry plants for southern growers. See under *Trees and Shrubs*, page 152.

Finch Blueberry Nursery
P.O. Box 699, Bailey, NC 27807
Telephone: 919-235-4664

Catalog price: free

Seventeen varieties of highbush rabbiteye blueberry, including Tifblue, Woodard, Southland, Climax, Garden Blue, Delite, Alice Blue, and Premier. The price list comes with a page of cultural information. Shipments are made from October 15 through May.

Dean Foster Nurseries
P.O. Box 127, Hartford, MI 49057
Telephone: 616-621-2419

Catalog price: free

A strawberry specialist with some unusual offerings on the side. The big color catalog lists almost 100 strawberry varieties, including a few recommended for hanging baskets and trellises. (The runners produce fruit without rooting.) The nursery also sells a big selection of raspberries and blackberries—among them a white blackberry and three gold raspberries—fruit and nut trees, shade trees, evergreens, grapevines, Jerusalem artichoke, horseradish, and a hybrid tamarillo.

Fowler Nurseries, Inc.
See under *Trees and Shrubs*, page 152.

Golden Bough Tree Farm
See under *Trees and Shrubs*, page 154.

Greenmantle Nursery
See under *Trees and Shrubs*, page 154.

Hartmann's Plantation Inc.
P.O. Box E, Grand Junction, MI 49056
or P.O. Box 524, Earleton, FL 32631
Telephone: 616-253-4281 (Michigan) or 904-468-2087 (Florida)

Catalog price: free

Hartmann's runs a bi-climatic blueberry operation, selling highbush types for northern growers from its Michigan center and rabbiteye bushes for southern gardeners from its Florida nursery. Northerners (zones 7 to 3) have a somewhat larger field of choice: more than 30 varieties are sold from Michigan, compared to 17 listed in the Florida catalog. The two nurseries print separate catalogs. Both give full descriptions of the plants offered. Minimum order is $20.

Highlander Nursery
Blueberry Lane, Pettigrew, AR 72752
Telephone: 501-677-2300

Catalog price: free

Ten different highbush blueberry cultivars presented in a simple flier. No information is given about the varieties beyond an estimate of their fruiting season (early, middle, or late). One smaller plant is offered, the miniature Top Hat blueberry, which grows to a height of only two feet. No minimum order.

Inter-State Nurseries
See under *Trees and Shrubs*, page 156.

Ison's Nursery & Vineyards
See under *Trees and Shrubs*, page 156.

Johnson Nursery
See under *Trees and Shrubs*, page 157.

Kelly Nurseries
See under *Trees and Shrubs*, page 157.

Wm. Krohne Plant Farms
Rt. 6, Box 586, Dowagiac, MI 49047
Telephone: 616-424-3450 or 5423

Catalog price: free

The Krohne brochure doesn't show a single picture of a berry. A comparative chart helps buyers choose from the 19 varieties offered. In 1987 the nursery added Lester, Jewell, Tristar, and Tribute plants to its inventory. Prices are quite competitive.

Lakeshore Tree Farms Ltd.
Berry plants for Canadian customers. See under *Trees and Shrubs*, page 157.

Lewis Strawberry Nursery
P.O. Box 24, Rocky Point, NC 28457
Telephone: 919-675-2394 or 9409

Catalog price: free

This nursery carries more than 40 strawberry types, including many recommended for southern growers. The only information about the different varieties is given in the form of a comparative chart that rates flavor, firmness, freezing quality, and disease resistance. For more detailed descriptions gardeners will have to look elsewhere. Prices are quite low, but the minimum order is 100 plants.

McConnell Nurseries, Inc.
See under *Trees and Shrubs*, page 158.

McFayden Seeds
Berry plants for Canadian customers. See under *General Flowers and Vegetables*, page 24.

Makielski Berry Nursery
7130 Platt Road, Ypsilanti, MI 48197
Telephone: 313-434-3673

Catalog price: free

Raspberries and blackberries are the featured attractions at this family-owned nursery, which carries 22 varieties. The 1987 wares were appropriately presented in a raspberry-red descriptive booklet illustrated with occasional drawings. To complement its raspberry line, the nursery sells currants, gooseberries, blueberries, strawberries, grapevines, and fruit trees.

Earl May Seed & Nursery Co.
See under *General Flowers and Vegetables*, page 24.

Mellinger's Inc.
See under *Trees and Shrubs*, page 159.

Michigan Bulb Co.
See under *Garden Perennials*, page 90.

Miller Nurseries
See under *Trees and Shrubs*, page 159.

Morden Nurseries Ltd.
See under *Trees and Shrubs*, page 159.

Walter K. Morss & Son
Rt. 2, Boxford, MA 01921
Telephone: 617-352-2633

Catalog price: free

A simple, unillustrated brochure listing more than 20 strawberry varieties, 15 raspberries, as many blueberries, and a dozen grapes. The plants are described in a few sentences, though most of the discussions center on productivity and fruit size and appearance, concerns that are more important to commercial growers than to home gardeners. The minimum order is 25 strawberry plants of a single variety, five raspberries, or two blueberries.

New York State Fruit Testing Cooperative Association, Inc.
See under *Trees and Shrubs*, page 160.

Nourse Farms, Inc.
Box 485, R.F.D., S. Deerfield, MA 01373
Telephone: 413-665-2658

Catalog price: free

Nourse sells 32 varieties of strawberry, 18 raspberries and blackberries, horseradish roots, rhubarb, and asparagus. The best-selling home garden strawberries are here—like Catskill, Sparkle, and Earliglow—along with such new strains as Blomidon and Cornwallis. The catalog is one of the few without a comparative chart, but each variety is fully described, and the center spread of the booklet is given over to growing tips.

Pacific Berry Works
P.O. Box 54, Bow, WA 98232
Telephone: 206-757-4385

Catalog price: free

A select list of strawberries, raspberries, blackberries, and tayberries for northwestern growers. The nursery offers an especially strong collection of day-neutral everbearing strawberries, plants that will bear fruit year-round if temperatures are right. Most strawberry nurseries offer one or two of these.

Pacific Berry Works sells six varieties. The minimum order is 25 strawberry plants or five raspberry or blackberry plants.

Patrick's Nursery & SunGarden Seeds
Berries and grapes for southern growers. See under *General Flowers and Vegetables*, page 26.

Peaceful Valley Farm Supply
See under *Trees and Shrubs*, page 161.

Pony Creek Nursery
See under *General Flowers and Vegetables*, page 27.

Rabbiteye Farms Nursery
Homerville, GA 31634
Telephone: 912-487-5504 or 2278

Catalog price: free

Seven rabbiteye blueberry varieties offered on a straight price list without descriptions. Five plants is the minimum order.

Raber's Greenhouse & Nursery
Strawberry plants. See under *General Flowers and Vegetables*, page 28.

Raintree Nursery
See under *Trees and Shrubs*, page 162.

Rayner Bros.
P.O. Box 1617, Salisbury, MD 21801
Telephone: 301-742-1594

Catalog price: free

Twenty-five strawberry varieties, ten blueberries, and ten raspberries and blackberries in a color catalog replete with growing advice for the home gardener. With all the hyperbole that's printed in most garden catalogs, it is refreshing to read the occasional words of caution in this one. The features as well as the faults of each of the strawberries are pointed out in the text. We learn that Scott and Surecrop may produce too many runners, that fresh Pocahontas berries are too tart for many palates, and that Raritan's color is a bit light when frozen. The minimum strawberry order is 25 plants of a single variety. Other offerings include asparagus plants, grapevines, and a small selection of dwarf fruit trees.

Rider Nursery
Strawberry plants. See under *Trees and Shrubs*, page 163.

St. Lawrence Nurseries
See under *Trees and Shrubs*, page 163.

Square Root Nursery Co., Inc.
4764 Deuel Road, Canandaigua, NY 14424
Telephone: 716-394-3140

Catalog price: free

Grapes and winemaking supplies from a grower in the heart of New York's vineyard country. Almost 50 grape varieties are offered, from dessert types to European wine cultivars. Most of the plants listed will survive north to zone 5, and a few extra-hardy types are sold for zone 4 gardeners. Plants are sold individually and in collections. No minimum order.

Stark Bro's Nurseries & Orchards Co.
See under *Trees and Shrubs*, page 164.

Stegmaier Orchards, Inc.
Rt. 8, Box 108, Cumberland, MD 21502
Telephone: 301-722-5266

Catalog price: long self-addressed stamped envelope

Red and black raspberries and thornless blackberries, fifteen varieties in all. The price list is a small card without descriptions. The minimum order is 25 plants of a single variety.

Sunny Rows Plant Farm
Rt. 1, Box 189C, Currie, NC 28435
Telephone: 919-283-5605

Catalog price: free

More than 40 strawberry varieties, with a special emphasis on plants suited to the southern climate. The nursery carries a number of varieties, such as Atlas, Earlibelle, and Sentinel, developed by the North Carolina Agricultural Research Service. The catalog includes other cultivars from Florida and California that bear well in the Gulf states. Northern gardeners are given a nod with such strains as Sparkle and Catskill. The minimum order is 25 plants of a single variety.

T & T Seeds Ltd.
Berry plants for Canadian customers. See under *Trees and Shrubs*, page 165.

Waynesboro Nurseries
See under *Trees and Shrubs*, page 166.

Windy Ridge Nursery
Hardy northern berries. See under *Trees and Shrubs*, page 166.

Womack's Nursery Co.
Grapes for Texas growers. See under *Trees and Shrubs*, page 167.

M. Worley Nursery
See under *Trees and Shrubs*, page 167.

Bonsai

The Bonsai Associates, Inc.
Unpruned starter plants. See under *Bonsai Supplies*, page 191.

Bonsai Creations
Pre-bonsai and trained bonsai specimens. See under *Bonsai Supplies*, page 191.

The Bonsai Farm
13827 Hwy. 87 South, Adkins, TX 78101
Telephone: 512-649-2109

Catalog price: $1

A nice selection of pre-bonsai starter plants, such as Bahama black olive, bald cypress, and Chinese elm, offered in an illustrated catalog equally rich with tools, supplies, and bonsai containers. Dozens of shears, graving chisels, grafting knives, and specialized root and knob cutters are pictured.

Brussel's Bonsai Nursery
8365 Center Hill Road, Olive Branch, MS 38654
Telephone: 601-895-7457

Catalog price: $1

Pre-bonsai and trained bonsai plants and trees, from inexpensive seedling trees to decades-old specimens that cost hundreds of dollars. Those who want a head start on the seedlings but can't afford the fully cultured trees can choose

from an assortment of "semispecimens"—six- to 20-year-old plants that have been partially trained. The nursery sells a good selection of ceramic pots, along with a basic assortment of tools and supplies.

Coènosium Gardens
See under *Trees and Shrubs*, page 150.

Forestfarm
See under *Trees and Shrubs*, page 152.

Girard Nurseries
See under *Trees and Shrubs*, page 154.

Greer Gardens
See under *Azaleas and Rhododendrons*, page 45.

Hortica Gardens
P.O. Box 308, Placerville, CA 95667
Telephone: 916-622-7089

Catalog price: 50¢

Trees and shrubs suitable for bonsai training or for normal container and garden planting. The list spans almost 200 azalea hybrids—the bulk of them Satsuki and Kurume cultivars—along with more than 40 Japanese cultivars of *Acer palmatum* and scores of other trees and shrubs, with some hollies, heathers, and other plants thrown in for a change of pace. Most offerings are sold as young plants, but some can be had as older, partially trained bonsai specimens.

Hughes Nursery
See under *Trees and Shrubs*, page 156.

Matsu-Momiji Nursery
P.O. Box 11414, Philadelphia, PA 19111
Telephone: 215-722-6286

Catalog price: $1.25

Japanese black pines, spruces, maples, and other plants for bonsai culture. The black pines are the nursery's real specialty, offered in 35 named cultivars, though unfortunately they cannot be shipped to many western states. In addition to its many starter plants, the firm also stocks a few mature trained plants. The spring 1987 list included a Colorado blue spruce collected from the Grand Canyon and grown in a bonsai container for more than a decade and a foot-tall Japanese black pine with a three-inch trunk, priced at more than $1,000. A large collection of containers is available at the nursery (but not by mail).

Miniature Plant World
See under *Houseplants*, page 106.

D. Orriell, Seed Exporters
Seed for Australian native plants. See under *Native Plants of Australia and South Africa*, page 119.

Pacific Northwest Bonsai Farm
2322 Mousebird Avenue N.W., Salem, OR 97304

Catalog price: $1

A nice range of deciduous and and evergreen trees and shrubs sold as young seedlings or rooted cuttings. Bonsai practitioners can thwart the plants' growth, and home landscapers can raise them to full size. The firm made an arrangement in 1986 to take over the retail business of Brooks Tree Farm (see entry under *Trees and Shrubs*, page 149), and offers many of the same tree species. In 1988 Pacific Northwest plans to begin offering its large stock of potted plants to mail-order customers. We assume these will include older specimens and perhaps some that have been partially trained for bonsai.

The Plant Kingdom
See under *Houseplants*, page 107.

Shanti Bithi Nursery
3047 High Ridge Road, Stamford, CT 06903
Telephone: 203-329-0768

Catalog price: free

For the bonsai enthusiast who wants to enjoy mature specimens before the eyesight fails, Shanti Bithi offers imported plants that range from relative youngsters to crooked and thickened geriatrics. Prices range from about $70 for attractive but still wispy examples of *Juniperus chinensis* and *Acer palmatum* to almost $2,000 for twisted stumps of *Acer buergeranum* and *Pinus pentaphylla*. Many of the mature specimens are pictured in color so that shoppers won't have to invest blindly. A few species are available as starter plants at non-bonsai prices. Shanti Bithi also sells a nice selection of books, tools, supplies, and ceramic containers.

Wildwood Gardens
14488 Rock Creek Road, Chardon, OH 44024
Telephone: 216-286-3714

Catalog price: 50¢

More than 100 different trees and shrubs offered as young stock for bonsai training or for planting in rock gardens. Among them are several Kurume azaleas, some unusual hemlock cultivars, and a number of flowering quinces. The nursery also grows and imports trained bonsai, and the list includes many partially and fully trained specimens. Starter plants are priced between $4 and $25, mature bonsai up to $500.

Bromeliads

Alberts & Merkel Bros., Inc.
See under *Tropical Plants*, page 168.

Bird Rock Tropicals
6523 El Camino Real, Carlsbad, CA 92009
Telephone: 619-438-9393

Catalog price: long self-addressed stamped envelope

More than 100 tillandsia species and cultivars laid out in a typed list without descriptions. Bromeliad enthusiasts will recognize these names, but beginners will need to do some research.

Arthur Boe Distributor
P.O. Box 6655, New Orleans, LA 70114
Telephone: 504-362-6809

Catalog price: long self-addressed stamped envelope

A one-page specialty list of approximately 50 tillandsias. All plants listed have been freshly collected from tropical rain forests. Listings are by botanical name and specify blooming time (where appropriate) and growing conditions (from low, arid land to high, humid climes) for each type. Minimum order $20.

Frank Cornelison
225 San Bernardino Street, N. Fort Myers, FL 33903
Telephone: 813-995-4206

Catalog price: one first-class stamp

Almost 200 bromeliad species and hybrids from a range of genera—cryptanthus, aechmea, neoregelia, billbergia, tillandsia, vriesea, and others. Plants are listed by botanical name only, without descriptions. Many other specimens are available, so collectors looking for specific plants should send their want lists.

Dane Company
4626 Lamont, Corpus Christi, TX 78411
Telephone: 512-852-3806

Catalog price: long self-addressed stamped envelope

A collector's list of bromeliads spanning a number of genera. Aechmea, billbergia, cryptanthus, neomea, and tillandsia are all well represented, and more than 100 neoregelia species and varieties are listed. Offerings are named and priced without descriptions.

Golden Lake Greenhouses
10782 Citrus Drive, Moorpark, CA 93021
Telephone: 805-529-6895

Catalog price: $1

A big catalog of bromeliads of just about every type. Strengths include more than 100 aechmeas and as many neoregelias in an array of species, naturally occurring varieties, and hybrids. The list also touches somewhat more lightly on dyckia, cryptanthus, billbergia, tillandsia, quesnelia, and other genera. Most plants are listed by name only, though some include one- or two-word notations. Several dozen hoyas are offered, as well as such jungle cactus as rhipsalis and epiphyllums.

Jerry Horne
See under *Tropical Plants*, page 169.

International Growers Exchange
See under *General Flowers and Vegetables*, page 21.

G. Kohres
Tillandsia seed. See under *Cacti and Succulents*, page 68.

Werner Krauspe
P.O. Box 49621, Los Angeles, CA 90049
Telephone: 213-472-6501

Catalog price: long self-addressed stamped envelope

A long list of almost 300 tillandsias presented by name only. Beginners will need to consult a reference book to find out even basic information about flower color. A dozen or so vrieseas, aechmeas, billbergias, and other bromeliads add a touch of variety. The firm also goes by the name of W. K. Quality Bromeliads.

Paul P. Lowe
5741 Dewberry Way, W. Palm Beach, FL 33415

Catalog price: $1

A typed listing of bromeliads that brings in representative samples of the aechmea, cryptanthus, guzmania, neoregelia, vriesea, and tillandsia genera. Each offering is given a few words of description that include notes on foliage and flower. Plants are sold as unrooted cuttings (or "pups") unless extra rooted specimens are on hand. A few orchid species and hybrids are offered for the adventurous grower.

New World Bromeliads, Inc.
P.O. Box 14442, Gainesville, FL 32604
Telephone: 904-372-4576

Catalog price: free

Bromeliads from a range of genera, presented on a plain flier with type reduced in order to fit all 130 offerings on a single page. Aechmea, neoregelia, tillandsia, and vriesea species and crosses are offered in the greatest numbers; a few other genera make the list. Discounts apply to orders of a dozen or more plants (in any assortment). The nursery plans to have a more comprehensive list of some 500 bromeliads available by early 1988.

Rainforest Flora, Inc.
1927 W. Rosecrans Avenue, Gardena, CA 90249
Telephone: 213-515-5200

Catalog price: long self-addressed stamped envelope

A single-page specialty list of more than 100 unmounted tillandsias listed alphabetically by botanical name. Not one word of description breaks the rank and file order of the listings, which range widely in price; this is an index for the connoisseur. Minimum order $30.

Seaborn Del Dios Nursery
Rt. 3, Box 455, Escondido, CA 92025
Telephone: 619-745-6945

Catalog price: $1, deductible from first order

Six hundred bromeliads in a botanical-name list for the serious collector. Twenty-seven genera are represented, though many of them by only one or two species. Most of the attention settles on aechmeas (180 choices), billbergias, cryptanthus, neoregelias (160 selections), nidulariums, and tillandsias. Plants can be shipped to almost any country.

Alvim Seidel
See under *Orchids*, page 131.

Shelldance Nursery
2000 Cabrillo Highway, Pacifica, CA 94044
Telephone: 415-355-4845

Catalog price: $1

This lengthy list of 800 bromeliads is more of a starting point for negotiation than a catalog. Many of the plants listed aren't always available, and many unlisted plants are. Since the sizes of the available plants vary constantly, no prices are quoted. Collectors are advised to give the nursery a want list, and more up-to-date information will be sent. Beginners can let Shelldance pick out an assortment.

Tropical Imports
43714 Road 415, Coarsegold, CA 93614
Telephone: 209-683-7097

Catalog price: long self-addressed stamped envelope

Located below the snow line and above the valley fog in the Sierra Nevada foothills, this nursery claims to offer the largest selection of tillandsias in the world. Their one-page roster contains more than 200 species and varieties listed by name alone. Plants are shipped at nearly mature size, and come complete with instructions on proper care.

Guy Wrinkle/Exotic Plants
See under *Tropical Plants*, page 171.

Bulbs

Amaryllis, Inc.
1452 Glenmore Avenue, P.O. Box 318, Baton Rouge, LA 70821
Telephone: 504-924-5560 or 4521

Catalog price: $1

An enticing array of amaryllis bulbs presented as garden plants (northern gardeners will have to be content forcing them indoors in the winter). If you love the drama of massive amaryllis blossoms but are tired of seeing the same standard colors, this catalog offers more than 50 new choices. The catalog has no pictures, just brief descriptions.

Bakker of Holland
Louisiana, MO 63353-0050
Telephone: 314-754-4525

Catalog price: free

Bursting with color, this catalog skips across tulips to daffodils, irises, amaryllis, hyacinths, and crocuses. Bright blooms fill every page. In addition to the major varieties, smaller listings of border and miscellaneous bulbs—including anemones, foxtail lilies, snowdrops, and mountain bells—enable you to touch up a garden in style. A helpful seasonal map of the U.S. shows likely blossoming dates for bulbs, depending on your location.

Ballydorn Bulb Farm
Killinchy, Newtownards, Northern Ireland
Telephone: 44-238-541250

Catalog price: $1 (free to American Daffodil Society members)

Daffodil bulbs for the discerning gardener in a special export catalog with prices in U.S. dollars. Ballydorn offers dozens of exotic cultivars, most of them the bulb farm's own introductions. Along with the familiar yellows and whites, you'll find oranges, reds, and pinks in many combinations. Prices range from $1.20 to more than $30, and a minimum of $7 is charged for overseas shipping.

Bonnie Brae Gardens
Jeanie (McKillop) Driver, 1105 S.E. Christensen Road, Corbett, OR 97019
Telephone: 503-695-5190

Catalog price: free

A small listing of about 30 daffodils, broken into three types: standards (the largest category), intermediates, and miniatures. Each entry notes the flower's color and hybrid source. Orders should be sent before September 15 to guarantee fulfillment.

Borbeleta Gardens
See under *Lilies*, page 117.

Breck's
6523 N. Galena Road, Peoria, IL 61632

Catalog price: free

Breck's has been in the gardening business since 1818, making it one of this country's oldest garden houses. The firm started out in Boston as Joseph Breck & Co., selling garden seeds and fruit trees. In 1849 a few "bulbous roots" were listed in the catalog. They must have sold well. Two years later bulbs took up the first four pages of the catalog, and by 1868 Breck's carried more than 150 varieties of gladioli. Today Breck's operates from Peoria, Illinois, and remains one of the country's leading suppliers of flowering garden bulbs.

A lavish color catalog displays exotic varieties of daffodils (including one named Pistachio, with a "luminous chartreuse-yellow" flower), a rainbow of hyacinths and tulips, and a wide assortment of other bulbs. Far from resting on its laurels, Breck's is among the most vigorous direct-mail marketers in the gardening world. If you're a regular mail-order shopper, Breck's has probably already sent you a catalog.

Breck's is affiliated with Spring Hill Nurseries, which offers trees, shrubs, and garden perennials in a spring catalog (see entry under *Trees and Shrubs*, page 164.)

Bundles of Bulbs
112 Greenspring Valley Road, Owings Mills, MD 21117
Telephone: 301-363-1371

Catalog price: $2

Scores of tulips, narcissi, lilies, and other bulbs for fall planting. Clear drawings identify each tulip and narcissus type (species, kaufmanniana, fosterana, triumph, etc., for the tulips; each of the divisions up to 11 for the narcissi). The text describes colors and notes which bulbs are suitable for forcing.

W. Atlee Burpee Company
See under *General Flowers and Vegetables*, page 15.

Carncairn Daffodils Ltd.
Carncairn Lodge, Broughshane, Ballymena, Co. Antrim, Northern Ireland BT43 7HF
Telephone: 44-266-861216

Catalog price: free

An impressive selection of daffodils from a true specialist—almost 300 varieties in all. Shipping alone will cost at least $7, so don't write to Carncairn unless you take your daffodils seriously. But, if you plan to plant in quantity, or if you are looking for something unusual, this catalog might have what you need. Each listing is carefully described. Prices range from $1 to $30 per bulb.

P. & J. Christian
See under *Alpines and Rock-Garden Perennials*, page 40.

Cooper's Garden
See under *Irises*, page 109.

The Country Garden
See under *General Flowers and Vegetables*, page 16.

C. A. Cruickshank Inc.
See under *General Flowers and Vegetables*, page 16.

Daffodil Mart
Rt. 3, Box 794, Gloucester, VA 23061
Telephone: 804-693-3966

Catalog price: $1, deductible from first order

Only daffodils appear in this densely packed 28-page price list, and there are almost 400 varieties in all. Bulbs are listed twice: first alphabetically with a coded descriptive system that condenses flower type, color, bloom season, and height into seven or eight characters, then in a descriptive list or-

ganized by flower type. The cross-checking is a little confusing at first, but all the information is there. Prices range from $2 to $55 per bulb, with discounts given for quantity orders.

Peter de Jager Bulb Co.
188 Asbury Street, Box 2010, S. Hamilton, MA 01982
Telephone: 617-468-4707

Catalog price: free

Shaded in pastel blocks, the pages in this comprehensive catalog make for easy reading. Daffodils (trumpet, long-cupped, short-cupped, species, double-flowering, triandrus, collar, and poeticus, among other types) and tulips (Darwin, triumph, early and late double, parrot, and botanical, just to name a few) are the two largest sections here. Crocus, hyacinth, and lily plants also turn up briefly. Light, clear photographs crowd the margins; commentary is thorough and exact.

Doornbosch Bulb Co.
132 South Street, Hackensack, NJ 07601
Telephone: 201-489-6808 or 6809

Catalog price: free

Flowering bulbs sold by the hundred and by the thousand. If you are planning a large tulip bed or a big planting of narcissus, Doornbosch's prices are very good. The list includes 200 tulips of many types, 75 daffodils and narcissi, along with crocuses, anemones, bearded irises, gladioli, dahlias, tuberous begonias, gloxinias, and amaryllis. (Though we doubt many home gardeners will want to order amaryllis bulbs or gloxinia tubers by the hundred.)

Dutch Gardens, Inc.
P.O. Box 200, Adelphia, NJ 07710
Telephone: 201-391-4366

Catalog price: free

Royal Gardens, of Farmingdale, New Jersey, merged with Dutch Gardens, of Lisse, Holland, in 1987, and this is the resulting company. The spring and fall catalogs that Dutch Gardens sent out in 1987 were among the most beautiful we received. Gorgeous color photographs show each flower to its best advantage, and most of the pictures are given an entire page to themselves. The fall list includes more than 80 tulips, 28 daffodils and narcissi, and amaryllis in ten colors, along with crocuses, anemones, alliums, irises, and fritillarias. On the spring list are dozens of dahlias, gladioli, tuberous begonias, and lilies, plus a selection of gloxinias, hostas, astilbes, peonies, freesias, and bleeding hearts. Prices are low, compared to other catalogs that sell in small quantities. The minimum order is $20. We should note that some bugs have yet to be worked out: we ordered a lily with a pretty lavender bloom, which turned out to have bright yellow flowers.

Murray W. Evans
3500 S.E. Manthey Road, Corbett, OR 97019
Telephone: 503-695-5141

Catalog price: long self-addressed stamped envelope

A daffodil grower and hybridizer, Evans offers about 100 of his own creations in a four-page descriptive list. The profiles of the offerings are more complete and more helpful than those of most specialty lists, encompassing form and poise, in addition to color, height, and bloom season. Evans points out which of his cultivars are suited for show and which for the garden and gives the parentage of each. Prices range from $2 to $20 per bulb. Evans sells about 80 of Bill Pannill's hybrids, squeezed onto the end of the list without descriptions.

French's, Bulb Importer
Route 100, Pittsfield, VT 05762-0565
Telephone: 802-746-8148

Catalog price: free

A typed descriptive list that offers a good selection of imported tulips, hyacinths, crocuses, irises, lilies, narcissi, and daffodils. Some more unusual bulbs are also listed, including 20 varieties of freesia, eight of amaryllis, and a selection of camassias, chionodoxas, calla lilies, gloxinias, and fritillarias. French's also carries an interesting collection of seeds for flowering houseplants, among them winter-flowering pansies and sweet peas, kalanchoe, schizanthus, and several varieties of primula. The catalog ends with a small selection of tools.

Gardenimport
See under *General Flowers and Vegetables*, page 19.

Gary's Perennials
1122 Welsh Road, Ambler, PA 19002
Telephone: 215-628-4070

Catalog price: free

Nearly 100 Holland bulbs pack this catalog, which comes in two parts, a printed brochure and an accompanying color photo gallery. The nursery prides itself on the size and quality of its offerings. Whether it's daffodils ("the largest size attainable") or tulips you're after ("our tulip bulbs measure 12 cm. and up"), the emphasis is on jumbo dimensions. Ten types of tulips, including early, bunch-flowering, fancy fringed, and Darwin hybrid, appear among hyacinths and daffodils. A scattering of other perennials—notably narcissus, Dutch iris, and galanthus—are each represented by one or two varieties.

Gladside Gardens
See under *Gladioli*, page 95.

Russell Graham, Purveyor of Plants
See under *Garden Perennials*, page 88.

J. N. Hancock & Co.
Jackson's Hill Road, Menzies Creek, Victoria,
Australia 3159
Telephone: 61-3-754-3328

Daffodil fans should know about the extensive offerings available here, drawn from a collection that's been tended for the past 70 years. Hundreds of daffodils spill across the 40 pages of the catalog. Most divisions and nearly all imaginable color mixes—traditional yellow, lemon green, bright cup, pink, and white—are represented on the carefully detailed roster. Occasional color portraits reveal the delicacy of bloom and subtle tint these flowers are noted for.

Hatfield Gardens
Daffodils. See under *Daylilies*, page 78.

International Growers Exchange
See under *General Flowers and Vegetables*, page 21.

John D. Lyon, Inc.
143 Alewife Brook Parkway, Cambridge, MA 02140
Telephone: 617-876-3705

Catalog price: free

A four-page list of unusual bulbs, each entry accompanied by a quick, precise description of bloom color. Crocuses are a specialty here; the list includes both spring- and fall-blooming types, many of them hard-to-find species and varieties. A dozen fritillaria species, a handful of *Iris reticulata* cultivars, and more than 30 narcissi are other areas of strength. Shoppers will also find alliums, anemones, colchicums, corydalises, freesias, galanthi, scillas, and tulips.

McClure & Zimmerman
1422 W. Thorndale, Chicago, IL 60660
Telephone: 312-989-0557

Catalog price: free

This catalog is a gold mine for the bulb enthusiast. A thorough sampling of bulb types—from crocuses and daffodils through tulips, amaryllis, and lilies—packs 27 tightly organized pages. Tasteful line drawings and occasional black-and-white photographs supplement the text. A broad array of miscellaneous and small bulbs (including alliums, cyclamens, gladioli, irises, and hyacinths) enrich your options.

McFayden Seeds
Supplier to Canadian customers. See under *General Flowers and Vegetables*, page 24.

Maver Nursery
See under *Garden Perennials*, page 89.

Mellinger's Inc.
See under *Trees and Shrubs*, page 159.

Messelaar Bulb Co., Inc.
P.O. Box 269, Ipswich, MA 01938
Telephone: 617-356-3737

Catalog price: free

Imported Dutch bulbs in a big color catalog. Many varieties of tulips are pictured (including single and double early, Darwin, large-flowering cottage, double peony, and parrot), together with a nice selection of daffodils, narcissi, crocuses, irises, and miscellaneous bulbs. A small batch of lilies and a few hybrid amaryllis (for indoor forcing) are featured at the back of the catalog.

Michigan Bulb Co.
See under *Garden Perennials*, page 90.

Miller's Manor Gardens
Daffodils. See under *Irises*, page 112.

Grant Mitsch Novelty Daffodils
P.O. Box 218, Hubbard, OR 97032
Telephone: 503-651-2742

Catalog price: $3, deductible from first order

A catalog for daffodil lovers to drool over. Several hundred crosses are showcased here—meticulously described and clearly photographed. All daffodil divisions from 1 to 12, with the exception of division 10 (species, wild forms, and their hybrids), have at least a few representatives on the scene; division 2 (large cups) is the largest single grouping. The shapes and multihued blooms of these flowers will amaze those who've seen daffodils only in the general bulb catalogs.

Charles H. Mueller
Star Route, Box 21, New Hope, PA 18938
Telephone: 215-862-2033

Catalog price: free

Two small, cleanly printed brochures stocked with nearly 400 spring-, summer-, and autumn-flowering bulbs. The spring list (mailed in June) stresses autumn crocuses, colchicums, sternbergia, and cyclamens, but also includes dahlias, gladioli (both exhibition and miniature), cannas, acidantheras, hostas, lilies, daylilies, and tuberous begonias. The fall list (mailed in September) runs through tulips, crocuses, daffodils (including many show types), hyacinths, and a few wildflowers. Introductory notes for each plant type are brief but helpful. The nursery maintains an even bigger "catalog" in the form of its show garden. Open in April and May, it displays 1,300 spring-flowering bulbs in bloom, and all of them are for sale.

Oakwood Daffodils
2330 W. Bertrand Road, Niles, MI 49120
Telephone: 616-695-6873

Catalog price: free

American-grown, Midwest-acclimated daffodils for garden and show are summarily packaged here on ten stapled pages devoid of photographs. Each variety offered is fully described, and the parentage and blooming time noted. Prices range widely, from less than $1 to more than $50.

Park Seed Co.
See under *General Flowers and Vegetables*, page 26.

Pinetree Garden Seeds
See under *General Flowers and Vegetables*, page 27.

Clive Postles Daffodils
The Old Cottage, Purshull Green, Droitwich,
Worcestershire, England WR9 0NL

Catalog price: $1

Exhibition and garden daffodils, presented in a meticulous fashion. More than 100 detailed entries fill this rather dainty catalog, half of which is given over to the hybrids of John Lea. In the descriptive text the words "elegant," "superb," and "lovely" recur. Elite parentage is stressed throughout. The bulbs range in price from £1 to £35; U.S. and Canadian customers must pay a minimum freight charge of £5.

Potterton & Martin
The Cottage Nursery, Moortown Road, Nettleton, Caistor,
Lincolnshire, England LN7 6HX
Telephone: 44-472-851792

Catalog price: $1

Approximately 500 dwarf bulb offerings, neatly laid out and nicely described, make this catalog a nifty resource for those who favor small-scale effects in their garden plots. The listings proceed through patches of anemone, crocus (both autumn and spring flowering), iris, narcissus, trillium, and tulip. About half the offerings are species, the balance hybrids and named cultivars. All receive a few words of description.

small-bulbed zephyranthes, fragrant tiger lilies, irises, gladioli, caladiums, and hymenocallis—in addition to a score of perennials—expand the range here. Most varieties appear in luscious color shots, beaded with dew, on pages of creamy white.

Wayside Gardens
See under *Garden Perennials*, page 92.

M. and C. Willets
P.O. Box 446, Moss Landing, CA 95039
Telephone: 408-728-2852

Catalog price: $1, deductible from first order

Two catalogs of Iridaceae bulbs—sparaxis, moraea, ixia, and galaxia—will be issued in 1988, one in the spring and the second in the fall. No lists were mailed in 1987, so we can't offer further information.

Nancy R. Wilson, Species & Miniature Narcissus
571 Woodmont Avenue, Berkeley, CA 94708

Catalog price: free

A brisk listing of several dozen narcissus offerings. Species narcissi begin the single-page list; each entry includes a line or two of description, noting the plant's color, shape, and country of origin. On the flip side, miniature hybrids appear. Detailed remarks concerning proper care of both species and miniatures fill the bottom third of the page.

Wyatt-Quarles Seed Co.
See under *General Flowers and Vegetables*, page 33.

Cacti and Succulents

Abbey Garden
4620 Carpinteria Avenue, Carpinteria, CA 93013
Telephone: 805-684-5112 or 1595

Catalog price: $2

More than 1,000 cactus and succulent species raise their prickly heads and exhibit their bright blooms in this vast, often astonishing catalog. The abundant color photographs and the boxed notes of explanation about individual genera make a sortie through these 48 pages an education in exotic plant life. Dozens of categories, from aloe to turbinicarpus (small globular plants from Mexico), fill the roster here. Collections—selected by the nursery—are offered at bargain prices.

Altman Specialty Plants
553 Buena Creek Road, San Marcos, CA 92069
Telephone: 619-744-8191

Catalog price: $1

These succulents have to be seen to be believed—and even then you're not quite sure. "We are about to expose you to the neatest, most bizarre plants in the world," the owners proclaim on the first page. Next thing you know, you're up against specimens resembling golf balls, zippers, snowflakes, Christmas trees, tiger jaws, leaky umbrellas, panting tongues, rosebuds, stepping stones, tendrils of hair, turtle shells, and the northern lights. There are several hundred types altogether. Each genus gets interesting, detailed commentary, dealt out with a touch of humor. Black-and-white snapshots pack every page; a few illustrations in the middle of the catalog are in color.

Anything Grows Greenhouse
Euphorbia milii hybrids. See under *Tropical Plants*, page 168.

Apacha Cactus
3441 Road B, Redwood Valley, CA 95470
Telephone: 707-485-7088

Catalog price: free

A no-frills listing of cacti and succulents. Entries consist solely of botanical names and prices, and there are no illustrations, so this catalog does not represent a good bet for cactus novices (a casual browser would feel like someone wandering in the desert without a map). Plants are seed-grown or propagated specimens suitable for 3- or 4-inch pots.

Arid Lands Plants
5755 East River Road, Suite 115, Tucson, AZ 85715
Telephone: 602-628-2597

Catalog price: long self-addressed stamped envelope

Six precisely pictured cacti make this slim brochure a treat to open and peruse. Your choices here are few, but all of them are seductive: the fatly bristling golden barrel cactus; the erect, spiny Mexican fence post; the fast-growing silver torch; the Turk's cap, known for its crown-like cephalium; the bishop's cap, with its showy yellow flowers; and the majestic saguaro. A starter kit (4-inch stoneware container, seed for four cacti, soil packet, and instructions) is temptingly priced.

Atkinson's Greenhouses
See under *Begonias*, page 50.

Aztekakti

P.O. Box 26126, El Paso, TX 79926
Telephone: 915-858-1130

Catalog price: three first-class stamps

Two long pages listing several hundred North American, South American, and Mexican cactus and succulent seeds by botanical name. The minimum order is 100 seeds; larger allotments of 1,000, 10,000, 50,000, and 100,000 are also available in most cases. Cactus genera that stand out here include echinocereus, ferocactus, mammillaria, and thelocactus. A small group of succulents (including agave and yucca strains) and desert and subtropical trees supplements the cacti. Seeds are guaranteed to come from the most recent harvest, either from wild plants or nursery-grown stock.

Bentleys Botanical Gardens

P.O. Box 12442, La Crescenta, CA 91214
Telephone: 818-249-2182

Catalog price: $2, deductible from first order

A classy, sparely filled catalog containing dozens of succulents and cacti from a family-run firm that's been in business since the turn of the century. Each listing here merits a clear color photograph the size of a postage stamp, together with the plant's botanical name, common name, and a terse description. Aloe, crassula, echeveria, kalanchoe, and sedum plants are pictured among the succulents. The cactus offerings span lobivia, mammillaria, notocactus, opuntia, and rebutia species. A couple of "cactus characters," resembling bristly Mr. Potato Heads, defy description and must be seen in their top hats to be fully appreciated.

CTP

Cactus seed. See under *Trees and Shrubs*, page 149.

Cactus by Dodie

934 E. Mettler Road, Lodi, CA 95242
Telephone: 209-368-3692

Catalog price: free

More than 1,000 cactus species jam this catalog, which comes down to 20 stapled, typewritten pages of botanical names. There are two introductory pages of blurred black-and-white specimen shots, but other than that, you're on your own among these closely packed genus declensions reminiscent of Latin class (*Acanthocalycium: glaucum, peitscheranum, variflorum, violaceum*). Some richly represented categories here include gymnocalycium, mammillaria, and parodia. About 200 succulents bring up the rear, just ahead of a nice selection of books devoted to the care of cacti and their cousins.

Cactus by Mueller

10411 Rosedale Highway, Bakersfield, CA 93308
Telephone: 805-589-2674

Catalog price: $1, deductible from first order

A very basic listing of 1,000 plus cactus and succulent species, arranged alphabetically. The catalog doesn't waste time on niceties—here's the name, here's the price, take it or leave it. Mammillarias are the single largest cacti group, while haworthias edge out crassulas and stapelias among the succulents. Rooted plants only (not unrooted cuttings) are available here, and all plants are shipped bare root.

Cactus Data Plants

9607 Avenue S-12, Littlerock, CA 93543
Telephone: 805-944-2784

Catalog price: $1, deductible from first order

This plain little booklet, from a nursery that specializes in globular cactus types from North America and Mexico, offers an outstanding selection of mammillarias. Nearly 300 species, mostly propagated from plants collected by field explorers, claim five of the catalog's 20 pages. Dozens of other genera—including echinocereus, ferocactus, and opuntias—also appear. Black-and-white photographs scattered throughout fail to do justice to the great delicacy of these plants. A handful of succulents, as well as a listing of helpful-sounding books, bring up the rear.

The Cactus Patch

P.O. Box 71, Radium, KS 67571
Telephone: 316-982-4670

Catalog price: 25¢

An amiable and discursive five-page listing of hardy cacti suited to cold climates. "Here we are, just 13 years from that year 2000, which 50 years ago did seem to be at least a million years away," the catalog begins. This chatty tone persists throughout the text, which provides a brief, well-written paragraph for each of the cacti. Opuntias win top billing here. The selection includes both rooted and unrooted pads and cuttings.

California Epi Center

See under *Epiphyllums and Hoyas*, page 82.

Chiltern Seeds

See under *General Flowers and Vegetables*, page 15.

Mrs. D. T. Cole

Swakaroo Nursery, P.O. Box 85046, Emmarentia, Tvl., 2029 South Africa

Catalog price: $1 in cash

An excellent collection of lithops seed, offered in a simple list.

Desert Nursery
1301 S. Copper, Deming, NM 88030
Telephone: 505-546-6264

Catalog price: one first-class stamp

This catalog is a mass of dark ink aimed at those who know their way around the prickly cactus patch; beginners will be lost. Several hundred cacti are listed in tightly packed typewritten lines on four stapled pages. Mammillaria and opuntia species stand out. Rooted and unrooted cuttings, as well as larger plants, are available.

Desert Plant Co.
P.O. Box 880, Marfa, TX 79843
Telephone: 915-729-4943

Catalog price: $2

Cacti from the Southwest presented with all the subtlety of a billboard. More than 40 species are gathered one to a page in this chunky booklet, each introduced with a black-and-white photograph and a bold headline. Echinocactus, mammillaria, epithelantha, opuntia, and yucca are among the genera represented.

Desert Theatre
17 Behler Road, Watsonville, CA 95076
Telephone: 408-728-5513

Catalog price: two first-class stamps

A "dramatic" selection of cacti and succulents—intended primarily for collectors—explains the thespian name. The contents are divided evenly between the two main camps, with approximately 200 listings in each. A terse description (e.g., "fleshy, dark green leaf from Somalia") is all you get to steer by. Plants are ranked as small, medium, or large, depending on pot size; all varieties shipped bare root.

Peter B. Dow & Company
Seeds. See under *Native Plants of Australia and South Africa*, page 119.

Endangered Species
See under *Tropical Plants*, page 168.

Philip Favell
P.O. Box 3567, San Diego, CA 92103

Catalog price: free

Aloe fanciers have a true pal in this gentleman, who presents more than 40 species of the graceful, burn-salving plant in alphabetical order on a single typewritten page. Sizes offered range from seedling (suitable for a 2-inch pot) to large (for planting in a gallon container).

Phyllis Flechsig Cacti & Succulents
619 Orpheus Avenue, Encinitas, CA 92024
Telephone: 619-753-5942

Catalog price: $1, deductible from first order

A vast supply of nursery-propagated plants, including some very rare specimens, laid out in a darkly printed 18-page catalog. Echinocereus (a family of low-growing, multiheaded cacti), epiphyllum hybrids developed by the nursery, rhipsalis

(tree dwellers native to tropical forests), and the ever-popular mammillarias are a few of the stars spotlighted here. More than 200 assorted succulents balance the cacti. Each variety is tartly evoked; there are no photographs.

Glasshouse Works
See under *Tropical Plants*, page 169.

Glenna's Greenhouses
851 E. 170th Street, South Holland, IL 60474
Telephone: 312-333-2248

Catalog price: free

A simple typed roster of lithops and cactus seeds. Nearly a dozen lithops are listed by name and marked to indicate either a white or yellow flower. Almost 30 cacti appear by name alone. Seeds are priced per packet of 25; limited amounts of fresh seed, gathered from the nursery's own plants, are also available at slightly higher cost.

Greenlife Gardens Greenhouses
See under *Epiphyllums and Hoyas*, page 83.

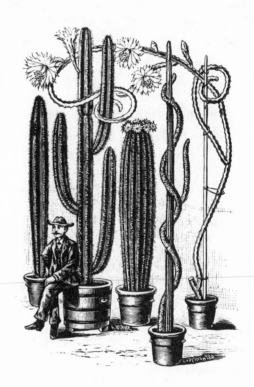

Grigsby Cactus Gardens
2354 Bella Vista Drive, Vista, CA 92084
Telephone: 619-727-1323

Catalog price: $2, deductible from first order

This catalog, strong on data but weak on allure, presents an encyclopedic array of succulents and cacti. Approximately 1,000 choices, including many rare specimens, are neatly listed (and pictured) in its 40 pages. The splendor of these plants will need to remain in your imagination, for their appearance here is rather drab and lusterless. Fertilizer, pots, cactus tweezers, pumice, and soil are also advertised.

Robert B. Hamm
See under *Begonias*, page 51.

Highland Succulents
Eureka Star Route, Gallipolis, OH 45631
Telephone: 614-256-1428

Catalog price: $2

Succulents of every stripe fill this ample catalog, a gold mine for the specialist or collector. Agave, crassula, echeveria, euphorbia, haworthia, and pachypodium species comprise the major categories to sift through; scores of options lie in wait beneath each heading. Many specimens are pictured in small, sharp, black-and-white photographs. Plants are shipped year-round.

Intermountain Cactus
2344 S. Redwood Road, Salt Lake City, UT 84119
Telephone: 801-972-5149

Catalog price: long self-addressed stamped envelope

A short listing of cold-hardy cacti, many of them accustomed to rugged Rocky Mountain conditions. Opuntia and echinocereus species, offered either in pad or clump form, take top honors. Ball and barrel cacti are also available, some of them as mature plants.

International Growers Exchange
See under *General Flowers and Vegetables*, page 21.

K & L Cactus Nursery
12712 Stockton Boulevard, Galt, CA 95632
Telephone: 209-745-4756

Catalog price: $2, deductible from first order

Flowering desert and jungle plants are the main order of business in this catalog, evenly split between cacti and succulents. Aloes, crassulas, echeverias, euphorbias, haworthias, lithops, and mesembryanthemums make up the succulent group; each category offers scores of choices. In the second half of the booklet hundreds of cacti strut their stuff, among them 100 epiphyllum hybrids. There are many photographs, including some in color. An excellent assortment of handbooks and guides has been gathered on the final pages.

Kimura International, Inc.
18435 Rea Avenue, P.O. Box 327, Aromas, CA 95004
Telephone: 408-726-3223

Catalog price: free

Nearly 1,000 cactus and succulent plants from around the world wedged into 14 pages as dry as the Sonoran Desert—an environment better suited to the specialist than the browser. Each listing is specified by botanical name, size, and price. Specimens are shipped in 2- to 8-inch pots. More than 70 black-and-white snapshots slightly enhance the package.

G. Kohres
Bahnstrasse 101, D-6106 Erzhausen/Darmstadt, West Germany
Telephone: 49-6150-7241

Catalog price: one International Reply Coupon

Seed for thousands of cactus and succulent species and for more than 100 tillandsias. Plants are listed by botanical name only and can be ordered in 20-seed packets or in larger quantities. A few words of introduction in English explain terms and ordering procedures.

Lauray of Salisbury
See under *Houseplants*, page 106.

Living Stones Nursery
2936 N. Stone Avenue, Tucson, AZ 85705

Catalog price: $1.50

Owners Jane Evans and Gene Joseph took over Ed Storm's lithops and mesembryanthemum collection after Storm's death in 1987, and they plan to carry on his business with little change. They'll be selling more than 100 lithops species, many of them rare types grown from seed collected by Desmond Cole of Johannesburg, a noted authority on the genus. They'll also carry lithops hybrids, along with hundreds of mesembs, asclepiads, and other hybrids. Ed Storm's catalog was filled with sharp black-and-white photographs; we assume the new nursery will follow his lead.

Marvin's Cactus
4410 W. Easton Place, Tulsa, OK 74127
Telephone: 918-587-8338

Catalog price: free

More than 100 cactus genera—many represented by only one or two species—are listed on these six typewritten pages. Mammillarias are the top dog, with echinocereus strains taking second place. A smaller batch of succulents races by. Seeds for select varieties (both cacti and succulents) are offered at the back of the catalog.

Mesa Flora Nursery
HC1, Box 4159, Yucca Valley, CA 92284
Telephone: 619-364-2232

Catalog price: $2, deductible from first order

This catalog lays out more than 500 cacti and succulents in rather cursory style. The majority of the listings are given over to cactus plants, from acanthocalycium to weingartia, with stops at cereus, echinocereus, lobivia, notocactus, and rebutia. Text is abbreviated; most entries consist of botanical name and a glancing description. The photographs (several per page) are basic stuff and won't entice anyone who hasn't already decided to buy. Cactus and succulent seed mixtures bring up the rear.

Mesa Garden
P.O. Box 72, Belen, NM 87002
Telephone: 505-864-3131

Catalog price: two first-class stamps

Simply a huge compendium of seeds and plants for the cactus and succulent grower. Several thousand coded entries line the pages of the main seed catalog (mailed in January) in tidy rows—and reveal, in abbreviated form, tips on when to plant, at what temperature, and how patient to be about the results. Many listings also specify where the seeds were collected. A spring plant list, sent out in April, lists seedlings of North and South American cacti, along with many mesembryanthemums and other succulents. A fall supplement holds more mesembryanthemums and a number of additional seeds and plants. Specify which of the lists you want.

Mohave Joshua Co.
P.O. Box 3222, Kingman, AZ 86402
Telephone: 602-757-2818

No catalog

This outfit sells seed for the Joshua tree (*Yucca brevifolia*), a native of the Mojave Desert. A single packet of a dozen seeds cost $2 (postpaid) in 1987; three packets sold for $5.

New Mexico Cactus Research
P.O. Box 787, Dept. 121, Belen, NM 87002
Telephone: 505-864-4027

Catalog price: long self-addressed stamped envelope

A mini-list of seed mixtures drawn from 70 popular cactus and succulent genera. Some of these mixtures, such as the mammillaria cactus blend, offer several hundred species— and correspondingly various spines, colors, and shapes—in a single packet. Perhaps a more typical example, the ferocactus mix, contains about 30 different types. Succulents take up a third of the list. Seeds are sold in small packets or in larger quantities.

The Pantree
1150 Beverly Drive, Vista, CA 92083

Catalog price: 50¢

Approximately three dozen succulent species adorn this simple list. Euphorbias (with 120 entries), crassulas (21), and aloes (17) are three of the categories most fully loaded with choices. All plants here have been propagated by the nursery and most are available in 3-inch pot size, shipped bare root.

Quality Cactus
P.O. Box 319, Alamo, TX 78516
Telephone: 512-464-2357 or 800-237-5326

Catalog price: two first-class stamps

This catalog presents a list of cactus and succulent seeds so darkly jumbled it resembles a garden plot where bristling weeds have won the war. Hundreds of seeds are available on three oversize pages, but good luck finding them—and figuring out how to order. Only a fraction of the seeds listed are in stock at any given time.

Rainbow Gardens Nursery & Bookshop
See under *Epiphyllums and Hoyas*, page 83.

Redlo Cacti SP
2315 N.W. Circle Boulevard, Corvallis, OR 97330
Telephone: 503-752-2910

Catalog price: $1, deductible from first order

This catalog chides and guides you through a prickly maze of more than 200 rare cacti and succulents. Notes on proper care are generously provided. How much light does a cactus need? "For most houseplants, I feel that if you can't take a snapshot of it without special film or added flash, it isn't getting enough light," says Lorne E. Hanna. "Even more light is required by most succulents." This is typical of the catalog's idiosyncratic voice. The listings reveal emphatic judgments: on a single page, the closing remarks for three different mammillarias are "one of my favorites," "doesn't appeal to me," and "go easy with the water!" All plants here are seed grown or nursery propagated; none are field collected.

Rocky Waters Farm
4383 Pool Road, Winston, GA 30187
Telephone: 404-942-3114

Catalog price: $1, deductible from first order

A rich assortment of more than 1,000 cacti and succulents sold as rooted cuttings, mature plants, or seedlings. The catalog is laid out in alphabetical order by botanical name only, without a hint of description. Mature plants predominate here, but many varieties are available in at least two sizes (or forms). Plants are shipped from April to October.

Sand Ridge Greenhouse
Rt. 2, Box 604, Collinsville, OK 74021

Catalog price: free

"Cacti make ideal houseplants," says this catalog right at the start. "They require only the most simple care that even the busiest gardener can easily find time for." Thus primed, we are free to scan the 50 plus cactus offerings arrayed below.

Mammillarias gobble more than half the list, but notocactus, parodia, echinocactus, and astrophytum species (among others) also get a nod. Plants are shipped in 3-inch plastic pots, along with a detailed culture sheet.

Schulz Cactus Gardens
1095 Easy Street, Morgan Hill, CA 95037
Telephone: 408-683-4489

Catalog price: free

This catalog makes light reading; there's not an adjective in sight, and the heart of the booklet is dots (. . .) linking specimens and their cost. Echinocereus, gymnocalycium, mammillaria, matucana, and thelocactus are well represented, with mammillaria spreading over five of the eight-page total. All plants are greenhouse grown from seed (no field-collected specimens).

Shein's Cactus
3360 Drew Street, Marina, CA 93933
Telephone: 408-384-7765

Catalog price: $1

Collectors on the trail of exotic cactus strains will want to know about this roster listing nearly 1,000 species of more than 50 genera. Distractions are few. Botanical name and price for page after page make up the skeletal list. A handful of succulents—aloes, haworthias, and lithops, among other types—ring the curtain down. The nursery does not ship during winter months.

Singers' Growing Things
17806 Plummer Street, Northridge, CA 91325
Telephone: 818-993-1903

Catalog price: $1.50, deductible from first order

A neat, voluminous offering of seed-grown succulents. Euphorbias (including jatrophas and monadeniums) and sansevierias are richly represented in this 24-page illustrated booklet. Plant sizes range from rooted cuttings to 8-inch and larger pots. Tips on succulent care are plentifully supplied.

Southwest Seeds
200 Spring Road, Kempston, Bedford, England MK42 8ND
Telephone: 44-234-58970

Catalog price: two International Reply Coupons

A British nursery specializing in wild-collected desert plant seeds drawn from the American Southwest, Mexico, and

Africa is an oddity worth checking out. Perhaps 2,000 seeds (many in short supply) are set forth in this 12-page booklet. The selection is global, with South American cactus seeds knocking up against Texas succulents. According to the catalog, all seeds are packed and ready for "quick despatch" to any destination.

Southwestern Native Seeds
See under *Wildflowers*, page 180.

Succulenta
P.O. Box 480325, Los Angeles, CA 90048

Catalog price: $2

A series of four- and five-page stapled lists detailing current selections issue from this nursery at irregular intervals. The spring 1987 list contained scores of variously priced succulents, with special depth in haworthia strains. Each plant is fully described. A small patch of cacti—14 species, all told—bristled at the end of the list. All plants here are nursery propagated; none have been collected in the wild.

Sunnyvale Cactus
679 Pearl Street, Reading, MA 01867
Telephone: 617-944-5959

Catalog price: long self-addressed stamped envelope

Winter-hardy cacti capable of thriving and blooming at 0° F (and colder—down to -25°) are the unlikely heroes here. The catalog notes, which equal the listings in length, point out that many cactus species are native to cold climates and may be observed flourishing in frosty locales from Canada to the Andes. Twenty or so unrooted opuntia cuttings fill a two-page slate. Planting instructions and cultural tips—tough as they are, these cacti do require some special attention—are mailed with each order.

Taggarts Enterprises, Inc.
Rt. 3, Box 29, Hennessey, OK 73742
Telephone: 405-853-2253

Catalog price: $2.50, deductible from first order

A short list of cacti and succulents from a nursery just breaking into the mail-order business. Cacti take up perhaps two-thirds of the listings, with more than 40 species offered. The succulent portion of the list scans more quickly; a dozen offerings appear, and euphorbias lead the pack. Most plants are available in either 2- or 3-inch pots.

Tripple Brook Farm
Cold-hardy cacti. See under *Garden Perennials*, page 92.

Tucson Succulents
P.O. Box 5681, Tucson, AZ 85705

Catalog price: one first-class stamp

Seed-grown succulents, many of whose seeds have been collected from plants growing in the Sonoran Desert, make up this crisp botanical listing. Approximately 200 species—the bulk of them from the Cactaceae family—march right along in alphabetical order, with here a word of explanation and there a descriptive line. Plant sizes range from small (2- to 3-inch pot) to extra large (8-inch and larger pots).

Guy Wrinkle/Exotic Plants
See under *Tropical Plants*, page 171.

Y. O. Ranch Cactus Co., Inc.
P.O. Box 1443, Ingram, TX 78025
Telephone: 512-367-5110 or 5679

Catalog price: free

Hundreds of cactus and succulent plants spread across a dozen darkly inked pages, with unusually vivid descriptions of each specimen. "Texas native, slow grower, grey and very wrinkled, flower hot pink, endangered species," reads a typical entry—in this case for *Ariocarpus fissuratus*. Sizes offered range from 2- to 8-inch pots.

Roy Young
23, Westland Chase, West Winch, King's Lynn,
Norfolk, England PE33 0QH
Telephone: 44-553-840867

Catalog price: two International Reply Coupons (four for air mail)

Nearly 1,000 cactus and succulent seeds, available by the packet, are listed in this bright, chipper catalog. Astute collectors may be able to sniff out a rare item or two from among the close-set lines of small type: conophytum, echinocereus, lithops, mammillaria, parodia, and rebutia species are the honored guests.

Carnivorous Plants

Black Copper Kits
266 Kipp Street, Hackensack, NJ 07601

Catalog price: 25¢

A small brochure presenting a limited array of carnivorous plants and terraria: pitcher plant rhizomes; Venus flytrap plants and bulbs; and terrarium pebbles, soil, and sphagnum moss. Information and culture sheets on the care of carnivorous plants and terraria are also available.

Carolina Exotic Gardens
Rt. 5, Box 283-A, Greenville, NC 27834
Telephone: 919-758-2600

Catalog price: $1

Carnivorous plants and seeds mingle freely in this modest list. Popular varieties turn up—Venus flytrap, pitcher plant, and cobra lily—together with butterworts and sundews (including rare South African and Australian types). Seeds are sold in 25- to 35-seed packets. Pre-mixed terrarium sets of plants, complete with soil sufficiently acidic for planting, make easy choices for beginners.

Cedar Ridge Nurseries
P.O. Box 464, Allison Park, PA 15101
Telephone: 412-443-9073

Catalog price: free

"Deep in the Asian jungle, far below the canopy, where sunlight intrudes only for a short time after the death of some great tree, a strong and sinewy vine winds its way into the middle layer of the forest." So begins this somewhat overheated but lushly detailed 18-page catalog, devoted ex-

clusively to the charms of nepenthes, or Asian pitcher plants. The nursery claims to be the leading propagator/distributor of the genus in North America. Several dozen species (and some hybrids) appear, each with its country of origin noted and its character evoked. Most are from Borneo, Malaysia, or the Philippines. Remarks on cultivation are thorough and exact.

Hungry Plants
1216 Cooper Drive, Raleigh, NC 27607

Catalog price: 50¢

Carnivorous plant tissue cultures sold by the test tube. Drosera, pinguicula, sarracenia, and nepenthes species are mentioned by botanical name only on a single page. The average number of plants per tube ranges from five to more than 20. Not much here for the casual browser, but those seeking rare specimens may strike pay dirt.

Marston Exotics
Turners Field, Compton Dundon, Somerton,
Somerset, England TA11 6PT
Telephone: 44-458-42192

Catalog price: $1 in cash

This fat little booklet lifts the lid on the carnivorous plant showcase and presents a host of bewildering specimens—from Venus flytrap (described by Darwin as "one of the most wonderful plants in the world") to pitcher plants and bladderworts. Eleven different species, including some quite rare ones, are featured, each with a discursive paragraph or two of introduction. Line drawings effectively convey the sheer oddity of these plants.

Orgel's Orchids
Rt. 2, Box CB K-6, Miami, FL 33187
Telephone: 305-233-7168

Catalog price: free

A big list of more than 100 carnivorous species clumped on two pages; nepenthes (both seedlings and mature plants), sarracenias, droseras, and pinguiculas are included. Plants are presented by botanical name only, but the breadth of the offerings will make this list worth cross-checking with a good reference book.

Peter Pauls Nurseries
Chapin Road, Canandaigua, NY 14424
Telephone: 716-394-7397

Catalog price: free

Woodland and carnivorous plants sold in complete terrarium kits or individually as plants, rhizomes, or seeds. Among the carnivorous offerings are Venus flytrap (sold as plants or bulbs), cobra lilies, butterworts, sundew, and several nepenthes and sarracenia species. Color photographs enhance the package.

World Insectivorous Plants
P.O. Box 70513, Marietta, GA 30007-0513
Telephone: 404-973-1554

Catalog price: 50¢

A rich selection of carnivorous plants neatly presented in a 12-page catalog and classed according to relative ease of care. Each of the several dozen species listed—sundews, pitcher plants, butterworts, bladderworts, and nepenthes—appears in a tidy line drawing about the size of a quarter. Notes are copious and reassuring. If you care to subscribe to the *Carnivorous Plant Newsletter*, a slot is open on the order form. This catalog is an excellent place to begin, for those braced to enter "a strange, forgotten, sometimes bizarre botanical world. . . ."

Chrysanthemums

Bluestone Perennials
See under *Garden Perennials*, page 86.

Dooley Mum Gardens
Rt. 1, Hutchinson, MN 55350
Telephone: 612-587-3050

Catalog price: free

Garden chrysanthemums from a grower that manages to pull the plants through some tough northern winters. About 80 varieties are offered in a descriptive list that occasionally lets its verbiage run to three sentences. Flower color, type, and size, plant height, and bloom season are always mentioned, and sometimes we get a few additional words. Autumn Sunset was "everyone's favorite last fall," Centerpiece has "long stems which make excellent cut flowers," and Ruby Red is rated "the best ruby red cushion to date." For gardeners who haven't tried enough mums to form their own opinions, such comments can be helpful.

Huff's Gardens
P.O. Box 187, Burlington, KS 66839
Telephone: 316-364-2933

Catalog price: free

An impressive list of hardy garden chrysanthemums that spans hundreds of named cultivars. Descriptions cover the important details of flower size, bloom season, and plant height. Flower color and form are evoked in a few carefully chosen words. The list is helpfully broken down by flower type into such categories as "regular incurve," "anemone," "pompon," and "cascade," and broken down further by color within those groupings. The organization should help those who know what they're after scan quickly to the selections most likely to be of interest. Plants are sold as rooted cuttings, and big discounts are offered on orders of ten or more of a single variety.

Indigo Knoll Perennials
See under *Garden Perennials*, page 89.

King's Mums
P.O. Box 368, Clements, CA 95227
Telephone: 209-759-3571

Catalog price: $1

A glossy catalog of almost 200 chrysanthemums, each well described and a few pictured in color. The offerings are separated by flower type, and gardeners can use this organization to track down the garden or show specimens they are interested in. Reflex types, for example, will do fine in an outdoor bed, while the exotic spider blooms will require extra care. A few particularly hardy garden varieties have been singled out in a special grouping. King's is the U.S. agent for H. Woolman Ltd. (see page 00), and should be able to supply any mum from that catalog.

Lamb Nurseries
See under *Garden Perennials*, page 89.

Mums by Pashka
12286 E. Main Road, North East, PA 16428
Telephone: 814-725-9860

Catalog price: free

This wholesale grower selects a few of the many chrysanthemums it cultivates for the nursery trade and offers them by mail to retail customers. The price list separates the named varieties by color and gives short descriptions.

Sunnyslope Gardens
8638 Huntington Drive, San Gabriel, CA 91775
Telephone: 818-287-4071

Catalog price: free

The curly petaled blooms on the cover of this catalog look like creatures from another planet, and they demonstrate the nursery's interest in exhibition chrysanthemums. The main list of 120 "recent and prize-winning" plants is divided only by color, so shoppers will have to scan for special flower types. Big lists of cascade, spider, and thread-like varieties follow, along with more limited selections of spoon, pompon, and garden types. Many of the offerings are pictured in color; all are adequately described.

Ter-El Nursery
See under *Garden Perennials*, page 92.

Thon's Garden Mums
4811 Oak Street, Crystal Lake, IL 60014
Telephone: 815-459-1030

Catalog price: free

Color photographs the size of postage stamps line the edges of every page, helping shoppers choose from about 120 garden mums. Few of the fragile-looking exhibition types are pictured—the emphasis here is on sturdy and hardy performers for the flower bed. Ample descriptions point out the features of all plants, and a code in the margin allows readers to scan for selections by height and bloom date.

H. Woolman Ltd.
Grange Road, Dorridge, Solihull, W. Midlands,
England B93 8QB
Telephone: 44-5645-6283

H. Woolman has been one of the world's leading chrysanthemum growers and hybridizers for more than a century, and the color catalog pictures scores of exotic and many-hued varieties. The firm will export large orders, but would prefer that customers deal with its North American agent, King's Mums (see page 00).

Dahlias

Alpen Gardens
173 Lawrence Lane, Kalispell, MT 59901
Telephone: 406-257-2540

Catalog price: free

A massive list for the dahlia enthusiast. More than 250 varieties are sold, but each is listed with only a cursory description and no picture, as shoppers are expected to know their dahlias. The list is broken down by flower size (from giant to miniature) and by type of flower, ranging from water lily, ball, and pom to single, orchid, and peony. Tubers are shipped in early April only, so don't miss the season.

Bateman's Dahlias
6911 S.E. Drew Street, Portland, OR 97222
Telephone: 503-774-4817

Catalog price: free

Almost 200 dahlia varieties in an unillustrated price list. Brief descriptions detail color, flower type and size, and plant height and occasionally highlight special characteristics, such as strains that flower freely or are particularly good for cutting.

Bedford Dahlias
65 Leyton Road, Bedford, OH 44146
Telephone: 216-232-2852

Catalog price: one first-class stamp

A charming little booklet loaded with dahlias and winsome personality. More than 100 varieties are listed and briefly evoked by means of coded entries suggesting plant size and bloom color. Jokes, anecdotes, and sage axioms also pepper the pages; the proprietor recently retired after teaching high school chemistry for 40 years, and he seems to have picked up a habit of telling sharp-witted tales in the classroom.

Blue Dahlia Gardens
G. Kenneth Furrer, San Jose, IL 62682
Telephone: 309-247-3210

Catalog price: free

Despite the name, Mr. Furrer has not yet come up with the elusive blue dahlia. But he offers several hundred varieties with red, yellow, bronze, purple, and white blooms, conveniently grouped in his catalog by the size of the plants—from extra large to subminiature. A dozen new introductions are extensively described, and nine are pictured in cameo photographs.

Campobello Dahlia Farm
Rt. 1, Box 243, 1085 Prison Camp Road,
Campobello, SC 29322-9335
Telephone: 803-472-4672

Catalog price: free

A concentrated listing of dahlias in a brief, handsome format, from a farm set in the foothills of the Cherokee Mountains. Many sizes and types of dahlias are represented in a neatly typeset roster of approximately 100 varieties. Certain entries

are available by the plant, some by the root, and one or two by pot root. (Campobello recently absorbed the former Ruschmor Dahlia Gardens in Rockville Center, New York.)

Connell's Dahlias
10216 40th Avenue E., Tacoma, WA 98446
Telephone: 206-531-0292

Catalog price: $1, deductible from first order

A catalog that's as colorful as a fireworks display. Thirty-six big, brassy photographs set the pulse to racing. Unfortunately, the text stumbles the reader up; the listings are packed into bristling thickets of hard-to-read type. It's all here, once you sort it out: several hundred dahlias of every known dimension and hue. A sampling of gladioli finishes the list off on a high note.

C. A. Cruickshank
See under *General Flowers and Vegetables*, page 16.

Dahlias by Phil Traff
1316 132nd Avenue E., Sumner, WA 98390

Catalog price: free

A listing of about 100 dahlias, each nicely described. The size and color of the blooms are indicated by means of abbreviations ("ASC" is a large semi-cactus, for example; "MFD" means "miniature formal decorative") and a sentence or two of text. Phil Traff and some of his helpers appear in a group shot on the back page that lends a genial note to the business at hand.

Dutch Gardens, Inc.
See under *Bulbs*, page 60.

Ferncliff Gardens
S.S. 1, Mission, BC, Canada V2V 5V6
Telephone: 604-826-2447

Catalog price: free in Canada

For Canadian customers only. A thoroughly detailed listing of dahlias, gladioli, irises, and peonies from a nursery that has been in business for most of a century. Dahlias are classed according to size and appearance; exhibition types and cutting varieties have been starred. Decorative, cactus and semi-cactus, ball, miniature, pompon, and low-growing bedding flowers are available. The gladiolus, iris, and peony listings exhibit a parallel richness. None of the offerings are shipped to the U.S.

Garden Valley Dahlias
406 Lower Garden Valley Road, Roseburg, OR 97470
Telephone: 503-673-8521

Catalog price: one first-class stamp

A casual list of approximately 100 dahlias, evenly distributed in size from AA (ten inches or more in diameter) to pom (two inches or less). Entries specify flower size, type, and color. A page of cultural hints completes the brochure.

Gardenimport
See under *General Flowers and Vegetables*, page 19.

Gladside Gardens
See under *Gladioli*, page 95.

Golden Rule Dahlia Farm
3460 State Route 48N, Lebanon, OH 45036
Telephone: 513-932-3805

Catalog price: free

More than 100 farm-grown dahlia roots and plants selected for their reliability. Listings range from a large orange semi-cactus to a small yellow formal decorative variety. Roots appear more often than plants, but some listings offer both. The nursery boasts that it has perfected a method of packing green plants that gives "100% satisfaction."

Homestead Dahlia Farms
P.O. Box 1051, Poulsbo, WA 98370
Telephone: 206-697-6578

Catalog price: two first-class stamps

A three-page typewritten list of assorted dahlias, arranged alphabetically. All blossom types are represented, and all sizes; pompons and miniatures receive separately headed sections at the end of the general roster. Text is minimal—typically one or two words devoted to color. Several paragraphs on the best method of dividing dahlia clumps contain helpful advice.

Hookland's Dahlias
1096 Horn Lane, Eugene, OR 97404
Telephone: 503-688-7792

Catalog price: free

Nearly 200 crisply presented dahlia varieties. This brochure unfolds as a coded, alphabetical list that indicates size and type of flower plus a jot of further description. Gift tubers are included in orders of $10 or more.

Ed Hume Seeds
See under *General Flowers and Vegetables*, page 21.

Kordonowy's Dahlias
P.O. Box 568, Kalama, WA 98625
Telephone: 206-673-2426

Catalog price: free

Approximately 700 dahlias fill this blunt booklet. The effect is a little numbing: 16 consecutive pages of tightly packed listings, all in capital letters. It's like reading an endless botanical telegram. Large dahlias seem to dominate the list, but it eventually works down to miniature and pompon sizes. Special collections at reduced rates are also available.

Lamson's Dahlias
Rt. 4, Box 4275, Selah, WA 98942
Telephone: 509-697-8552

Catalog price: two first-class stamps

Someone's been doing a lot of typing. Twenty pages of it add up to a sensibly organized, if not especially alluring, catalog. Most of 1,000 hardy dahlias unfold according to size—starting huge and working down toward bottlecap diameter. A wealth of colors, types, and sizes reward the patient wanderer.

Legg Dahlia Gardens
1069 Hastings Road, Geneva, NY 14456
Telephone: 315-789-1209

Catalog price: free

From the heart of the Finger Lakes region, here's a compilation of 200 dahlias cleanly set forth. Listings are sensibly grouped by size of bloom. At the center of the catalog there's a convenient bargain hunter's guide to seven collections. The nursery stresses that all stock offered has been grown on its farm, and any varieties failing to make the grade have been pruned from the list.

Mohawk Dahlia Gardens
90714 Marcola Road, Springfield, OR 97478
Telephone: 503-747-0141

Catalog price: one first-class stamp

A small, balanced list from a nursery that's new to the mail-order business. Two typewritten pages show what's available: at least a handful of dahlias in each of nine groupings segregated by size (B's and BB's offer the greatest selection). Varieties in short supply have been marked with asterisks; prices are moderate.

Nicholls Gardens
See under *Irises*, page 113.

Pennypack
Stanley Johnson, Cheltenham, PA 19012

Catalog price: free

The dahlias in this lean catalog are bred to meet exhibition standards. The largest category consists of giant show varieties, evoked according to a nine-point size and a 15-point (as opposed to the usual five- or six-point) type scale. "Description brief but quality high," notes the catalog in a sort of floral haiku. Dwarf, miniature, and pompon varieties balance the big guys. Most listings are for rooted cuttings, but plants also turn up.

Red Barn Dahlias
2035 E. Newton Street, Seattle, WA 98112
Telephone: 206-322-0386

Catalog price: two first-class stamps

Nearly 200 dahlias of every size and hue, unveiled in a relaxed manner on five stapled pages. "This is our third year of unending sunshine and blue skies on Vashon Island," exclaims the proprietor right at the start, setting everyone at ease. The unfussy tone carries over into the listings. "Came from England several years ago," reads the entire text for one miniature. Elsewhere, a water lily's color is evoked as "wine (sort of) red." A couple of mixed-size collections supplement the roster.

John Scheepers, Inc.
See under *Bulbs*, page 63.

Sea-Tac Gardens
20020 Des Moines Way S., Seattle, WA 98148
Telephone: 206-824-3846

Catalog price: 25¢ or long self-addressed stamped envelope

A lean listing of 150 plus dahlias arranged by bloom size on a couple of pages. Flower type and bloom color are quickly noted in code ("FD Dk R" indicates a formal decorative, dark red dahlia, for example). Minimum order is $10.

Shackleton's Dahlias
30535 Division Drive, Troutdale, OR 97060
Telephone: 503-663-5718

Catalog price: one first-class stamp

An abbreviated listing of approximately 100 dahlias. All types and sizes are shuffled into the catalog's alphabetical mix. Except for the nine introductions, which merit a bit of boastful text, commentary here is limited to plant height, bloom size, flower type, and a word or two on blossom color.

Sunburst Show Gardens
P.O. Box 457, 357 Winthrop Street, Rehoboth, MA 02769
Telephone: 617-252-3259

Catalog price: free

Dahlias sold by collections only, featuring best of show and recent introductions (priced from $10 to $20 per root). Available grades are fancy and extra fancy; those gardeners seeking particular sizes and colors will be accommodated if possible.

Swan Island Dahlias
P.O. Box 800, Canby, OR 97013
Telephone: 503-266-7711

Catalog price: $2, deductible from first order

This nursery has been vending dahlias for over 50 years. The glossy 40-page catalog informs us that dahlias were discovered growing in the Mexican mountains by members of the Cortez expedition during the early 16th century—and then proceeds to give us several hundred reasons why we should be grateful. The photographs are large, bright, and wonderful. Listings here run to finely detailed mini-paragraphs. All flower sizes and types appear; collections are temptingly priced.

Van Bourgondien Bros.
See under *Bulbs*, page 64.

Wyatt-Quarles Seed Co.
See under *General Flowers and Vegetables*, page 33.

Daylilies

Adamgrove
See under *Irises*, page 107.

Alpine Valley Gardens
2627 Calistoga Road, Santa Rosa, CA 95404
Telephone: 707-539-1749

Catalog price: one first-class stamp

A big list of daylilies at low prices. If you've wanted a daylily border along the driveway but didn't think you could afford it, this catalog might make you reconsider. More than 200 varieties are listed, many priced at $2 or $3 a plant. Some of that savings is reflected in the catalog, which has no pictures. Flowers are described in a few words, and an abbreviated code provides height, flower size, and bloom season.

American Daylily & Perennials
P.O. Box 7008, The Woodlands, TX 77387
Telephone: 713-351-1466

Catalog price: $3, deductible from first order

Gorgeous color photographs abound in this glossy catalog, a good source for mail-order shoppers who want to see what they are buying. More the 400 cultivars are listed, each of them at least briefly described and about 100 of them pictured. Some of the newer introductions cost up to $50, but a number of plants are priced in the $5 range. The firm offers collections at reduced rates and gives quantity discounts on a few yellow and gold varieties it feels are suitable for mass plantings. Cannas and Louisiana irises are offered in a more limited range of cultivars. The nursery is only open to the public during its annual "bloom festival" one weekend each year.

Barnee's Garden
Rt. 10, Box 2010, Nacogdoches, TX 75961
Telephone: 409-564-2920

Catalog price: free

A typed list of about 300 daylilies for the aficionado. Many of the plants are priced within the range of the average gardener ($6 to $10 each), but many more are recent introductions for the serious collector. Barnee's Garden bought the Bob Dove Daylily Garden and now sells a selection of Dove's creations. Some of these, such as the Super Ballerina and the Nacogdoches Lady, sold for $100 a plant in 1987. A brief color description is given for each flower, with an abbreviated guide to height, bloom size, and season. Plants are shipped in early spring and early fall. A separate iris list, which contains more than 250 varieties, is mailed in the summer.

Myron D. Bigger
See under *Peonies*, page 135.

Borbeleta Gardens
See under *Lilies*, page 117.

Brand Peony Farm
See under *Peonies*, page 135.

Lee Bristol Nursery
P.O. Box 5, Gaylordsville, CT 06755
Telephone: 203-354-6951

Catalog price: long self-addressed stamped envelope

A nice list of more than 100 daylily varieties, a few of them the nursery's own introductions. Catalog illustrations are limited to several black-and-white drawings, but all the plants are well described. Prices are reasonable, mostly in the $5 range. Shipments are made from April to November.

Ed Brown's Corner Oaks Garden
6139 Blanding Boulevard, Jacksonville, FL 32244
Telephone: 904-771-0417

Catalog price: free

The featured selections at Corner Oaks Garden are Mr. Brown's own hybrids, most of which are small plants with soft-colored, ruffled blooms. These new introductions are illustrated with miniature black-and-white photographs. The rest of the list, some 300 named cultivars, is presented with abbreviated descriptions. Among the hybridizers, Guidry, Spalding, Munson, and Gates are well represented. The nursery caters to the more serious collector. Very few plants are priced at less than $10, and quite a few carry tags of more than $50. Darrel, a 1986 introduction with seven-inch butter-yellow blossoms, sold for $150 in 1987.

Busse Gardens
See under *Garden Perennials*, page 86.

Caprice Farm
See under *Peonies*, page 135.

Cooper's Garden
See under *Irises*, page 109.

Cordon Bleu Farms
P.O. Box 2033, San Marcos, CA 92069

Catalog price: $1

A collector's list of about 500 daylilies, briefly described and priced between $5 and $100. The nursery carries a strong selection of miniature and small-flowered types.

The Country Greenery
Box 200, Glen Mills, PA 19342
Telephone: 215-687-0679

Catalog price: free

Two hundred daylilies on a typewritten list that will be of most interest to experts. Plants are only briefly described, and the emphasis is on relatively expensive recent introductions. The savvy beginner can, however, find some deals here. Stella d'Oro, for example, the popular long-blooming miniature, was priced at just $5 in 1987.

Daylily World
P.O. Box 1612, Sanford, FL 32771
Telephone: 305-322-4034

Catalog price: free

E. David Kirchoff and Morton L. Morse have a passion for doubles, and although we admit to no fondness for these curiosities, we're sure many gardeners will appreciate them. Among the stars here are a yellow and red double called Handyman, and Amadeus, a scarlet tetraploid that won an A.H.S. honorable mention in 1986. The main list of 600 plus cultivars incudes offerings from many different hybridizers, with very short descriptions.

Eco-Gardens
See under *Garden Perennials*, page 87.

Englerth Gardens
Rt. 2, Hopkins, MI 49328-9641
Telephone: 616-793-7196

Catalog price: free

A long and affordable list of daylilies, hostas, and Siberian irises. Five hundred daylilies are offered, the majority priced between $3 and $5. Beginners may have some trouble working through the coded descriptions, and the catalog includes no pictures, but the prices should make it worth the extra effort. You'll find 150 hostas and 30 Siberian irises, also at fair prices.

Floyd Cove Nursery
11 Shipyard Lane, Setauket, NY 11733
Telephone: 516-751-1806

Catalog price: $1

The American Hemerocallis Society maintains a national display garden at Floyd Cove Nursery, and visitors are welcome from June to September. Call first to be sure someone will be there. Owners Pat and Grace Stamile lead off their list with a handful of their own introductions: tetraploids on the red end of the spectrum and heavily ruffled diploids in pinks and soft yellows. The main list of almost 700 cultivars includes names from a range of hybridizers at prices from $5 to $200.

Garden Perennials
See under *Garden Perennials*, page 88.

Gardenimport
See under *General Flowers and Vegetables*, page 19.

Greenwood Nursery
P.O. Box 1610, Goleta, CA 93116

Catalog price: $3

A glossy color catalog that gives buyers a glimpse of at least some of the daylilies offered. Happily, the pictures aren't limited to the newest and most expensive cultivars. El Tigre, a big reddish-orange flower, rated a photograph in 1987 though priced at only $4 (the bottom of the scale here). Whether pictured or not, the plants are well described. About High Lama, for example, the catalog notes, "Pale mauve lavender flowers that are round, broad petaled and sensuously smooth. Cream green throat. Fine substance, branching." Plant height, flower size, and bloom season are noted in abbreviations. Among the roughly 500 offerings are a score of doubles and a good selection of miniatures.

Hahn's Rainbow Iris Garden
See under *Irises*, page 110.

Hatfield Gardens
22799 Ringgold Southern Road, Stoutsville, OH 43154
Telephone: 614-474-5719

Catalog price: $1.50

A specialist's catalog of daylilies, daffodils, hostas, and bearded irises. Descriptions are kept to a minimum; with the varietal name included, they rarely run beyond a single line. More than 300 daylilies are offered, almost all of them

priced between $7.50 and $50 in 1987. The 300 daffodils are described in an uninviting code. Fragrant Rose, for example, is listed with the notation, "4(Duncan)2W-GPP," which we interpret as "double daffodil, corona replaced by additional perianth segment; introduced by Duncan; early bloom; white perianth, green and pink corona." The bulb cost $40 in 1987. The hosta list includes some 200 varieties, the iris list almost 100.

Hem Haven Nursery
P.O. Box 192, Fairhope, AL 36533
Telephone: 205-928-3340

Catalog price: free

A dense typewritten list with lots of capital letters and a minimum of space between lines. Some 250 daylilies are offered, most of them at reasonable prices—$3 to $5 in 1987. Shoppers will have to cope with a coded system of description that manages to give all pertinent details on a single line.

Hickory Hill Gardens
Rt. 1, Box 11, Loretto, PA 15940
Telephone: 814-886-2823

Catalog price: $1

A good source of daylilies for the specialist and a list worth examining even if you're just looking for some unusual plants for a perennial border. More than 500 cultivars are listed, most in the $4 to $6 range (with some specimens going for much more). The nursery also sells a small selection of irises and hostas and a few garden perennials.

Holiday Seeds
See under *Hostas*, page 104.

Homestead Division of Sunnybrook Farms
See under *Hostas*, page 104.

Hughes Garden
2450 N. Main Street, Mansfield, TX 76063
Telephone: 817-478-8144

Catalog price: long self-addressed stamped envelope

Two hundred daylilies on a list with brief, often abbreviated descriptions. Tom Hughes is a hybridizer as well as a grower, and a number of his offerings are his own creations. It is difficult to tell which ones he hybridized, however, as he has neglected to credit the sources of his plants. Information about height and bloom season is only irregularly included.

Iron Gate Gardens

Rt. 3, Box 250, Kings Mountain, NC 28086
Telephone: 704-435-6178

Catalog price: $2, deductible from first order

New and recent hosta and daylily introductions for those who want the latest innovations. More than 500 daylilies are listed, including dozens of Pauline Henry's dramatic multi-color Siloam hybrids. A few blooms are pictured in color; all offerings are described in a few words. Prices rarely dip below $15, and most are in the $20 to $50 range. The hostas are somewhat less expensive—some can be had for $4 and $5—but the list does include some very costly novelties.

Jernigan Gardens

Rt. 6, Box 593, Dunn, NC 28334
Telephone: 919-567-2135

Catalog price: long self-addressed stamped envelope

A neat, typewritten list of daylilies, hostas, and bearded irises. The 300 daylily listings are reasonably priced. McPick, a pretty apricot-flowered miniature, sold for just $1.50 in 1987, and Stella d'Oro was priced at $4. The majority of the daylily offerings fell into the $2 to $5 price range. The nursery does sell some more expensive novelties for those who want to keep ahead of their neighbors. The hosta list spans more than 100 offerings; the iris list contains 50 plus. Descriptions are abbreviated and coded to include information about size, bloom season, foliage, and fragrance.

Joiner Gardens

33 Romney Place, Wymberly, Savannah, GA 31406
Telephone: 912-355-3996

Catalog price: long self-addressed stamped envelope

More than 250 daylilies in a list that assumes some expertise. Descriptions include bloom season, height, bloom size, and color, and, occasionally, a few additional words of praise. Quite a few plants are Joiner's own introductions, but many other hybridizers are represented. 1987 prices ranged from $3 up to $50. Many attractive plants are offered on the low end of the price scale, and even beginners may want to give this list a try. Stella d'Oro, for example, was offered at $5 in 1987, and Littleness, a good light yellow miniature, sold for just $3. Shipments are made year-round.

Klehm Nursery

See under *Peonies*, page 135.

Lenington-Long Gardens

7007 Manchester Avenue, Kansas City, MO 64133
Telephone: 816-454-9163

Catalog price: two first-class stamps

George Lenington is an accomplished hybridizer, and his nursery's list naturally enough starts off with almost 200 of his own introductions. Lenington award-winners from past years include Mavis Smith, a pale cream flower flushed with pink, and Little Kewpie, a tiny light gold bloom. Marsh's Chicago tetraploids are well represented on the general list, which includes 300 varieties from a number of different hybridizers. Lenington-Long carries a good selection of recent introductions, but the classics have not been neglected. Many tried and true varieties can be had for less than $5.

Louisiana Nursery

Rt. 7, Box 43, Opelousas, LA 70570
Telephone: 318-948-3696 or 942-6404

Catalog price: $2 (specify daylily and iris list)

More than 400 daylilies crowd the pages of this collector's list. Among them are some old favorites and some of the latest and most expensive new introductions. One 1987 listing, a large pink-flowered tetraploid called Booger, sold for $200. Louisiana irises lead the pack in the iris section of the catalog. Four native species are offered in a variety of colors, along with more than 100 cultivars. The nursery sells a good selection of hybrids of *Iris virginica*, *I. spuria*, and *I. pseudacorus*. All offerings are briefly described. A separate catalog of perennials, trees, and shrubs can be had for $3.50 (see entry under *Trees and Shrubs*, page 158).

Maple Tree Gardens

See under *Irises*, page 112.

Meadowlake Gardens

Rt. 4, Box 709, Walterboro, SC 29488
Telephone: 803-844-2359 (after 8 P.M.)

Catalog price: $2, deductible from first order

Meadowlake Gardens rails against the soaring prices of new daylily introductions. The nursery makes an effort to sell its newest plants at reasonable rates, but even here shoppers will have to dig deep for the funds to buy the latest novelties. In 1987 Meadowlake offered new introductions from a number of hybridizers at prices ranging from $25 to $100. The main list is one of the biggest in the business, spanning almost 1,200 varieties. The catalog presents each with a short description, occasionally expanded into two or three sentences, and pictures some specimens in black-and-white photographs. Some older varieties were priced as low as $5 in 1987, but most of the listings were set between $10 and $40. A separate list of Japanese irises is available on request.

Melrose Gardens

See under *Irises*, page 112.

Miller's Manor Gardens

See under *Irises*, page 112.

Moldovan's Gardens

38830 Detroit Road, Avon, OH 44011
Telephone: 216-934-4993

Catalog price: two first-class stamps

This nursery sells only daylily and hosta introductions by Steve Moldovan and Roy Woodhall. Because of their prices, these will be of more interest to serious collectors than to casual gardeners. Two 1987 daylily introductions were priced at $200, and even the older varieties rarely dropped below $20. The hostas, all recent cultivars introduced between 1981 and 1983, were priced in the $50 range.

Nicholls Gardens

See under *Irises*, page 113.

Oakes Daylilies

Corryton, TN 37721
Telephone: 615-689-3036 or 687-1268

Catalog price: free

A monumental list of daylilies from virtually every hybridizer. A total of 1,300 cultivars are arranged alphabetically in the list, with pertinent statistics noted in abbreviated form. The nursery sells almost 50 of Marsh's Chicago hybrids and as many of Henry's Siloam varieties. Prices range from $3 for older types like McPick and Jest to $200 for Moldovan's 1984 introduction, Mirishka. Oakes maintains an official American Hemerocallis Society display garden, where visitors can see a nearly complete collection of past award-winners in all categories. Most of these are also for sale by mail.

Pilley's Gardens

2829 Favill Lane, Grants Pass, OR 97526
Telephone: 503-479-8623

Catalog price: free

A densely typed list that tries both the eyes and the concentration, but one that holds some treasures and some bargains. Among the 600 offerings are more than 40 of Pauline Henry's Siloam hybrids, a good collection of Munson introductions, and some Moldovan creations at reasonable prices. Those shopping for the latest will find new introductions priced up to $200, but those looking for savings can choose from a wide array of tested favorites for under $5. In 1987, Stella d'Oro was offered for $2.50, and dozens of varieties could be had for $2 and $3. The nursery is open to visitors by appointment only.

Powell's Gardens

Eight hundred daylily cultivars. See under *Garden Perennials*, page 90.

Renaissance Gardens

9329G Westbury Woods Drive, Matthews, NC 28105
Telephone: 704-541-8534

Catalog price: free

Judith and Robert Weston concentrate on smaller plants in their hybridizing efforts. In 1987 they were particulary proud of Cowrie Shell, a cream-colored miniature with a pink blush and spinach-green throat. Their general list includes 250 plants from a range of hybridizers. In 1987, Ruffles Elegant, a tall, lilac-pink Munson creation, commanded the top price of $100; a handful of older varieties were offered at $4. Shoppers will have to master the system of coded descriptions in order to get through the typed list.

Rocknoll Nursery

See under *Alpines and Rock-Garden Perennials*, page 42.

Saxton Gardens

1 First Street, Saratoga Springs, NY 12866

Catalog price: two first-class stamps

The specialty here is cold-hardy daylilies. Winter temperatures at the nursery sometimes drop to -50° F, and Saxton has come up with its own Adirondack hybrids that are able to survive the bitter cold. Each plant on this comparatively small list is nicely described, and a few are pictured in color. Most of the 1987 offerings cost only $4 and $5, placing them well within the reach of the average gardener.

Seawright Gardens

134 Indian Hill, Carlisle, MA 01741
Telephone: 617-369-2172

Catalog price: $1, deductible from first order

Our own daylily border came from Seawright Gardens, though we have to admit that we bought the plants at the nursery rather than by mail. The mail-order list is a 20-page typed affair with extensive descriptions of each of about 300 offerings. Special attention is given to the eyed and blotched tetraploids of the late Don Stevens, plants like Bandit Man, a light orange flower with a red eyezone and gold throat, and Black Eyed Susan, a canary-yellow bloom with a deep red throat blotch. 1987 prices ranged from $4 to $50. The nursery, at 201 Bedford Road, is open to the public seven days a week from May through August.

Shields Horticultural Gardens

P.O. Box 92, Westfield, IN 46074
Telephone: 317-896-3925

Catalog price: free (request daylily list)

This typewritten list gives the vital statistics of each of its 200 offerings, but not enough detail is provided on the finer distinctions to give shoppers a sound basis for their decisions. Color descriptions are limited to a word or two—"yellow" or "red," or occasionally "light yellow" or "Chinese red"—and no information is given about flower shape, texture, or pattern. That criticism aside, the list includes a nice range of hybrids at reasonable prices. About half the 1987 offerings were listed at $5, and the costliest hybrid went for $35. A separate list of tender summer-flowering bulbs is available on request (see entry under *Bulbs*, page 63.)

Solomon Daylilies
105 Country Club Road, Newport News, VA 23606
Telephone: 804-595-3850

Catalog price: free

A big list of almost 900 daylilies, presented in a chart that includes key data but no detail. The inch-wide space allotted for flower color limits descriptions to two or three words. The nursery is aware that this is a problem and will lend slides to interested customers. The inventory spans most of the major hybridizers, and prices are moderate—mostly in the $5 to $10 range.

Soules Garden
5809 Rahke Road, Indianapolis, IN 46217
Telephone: 317-786-7839

Catalog price: 50¢, deductible from first order

Seven hundred daylily cultivars presented in a coded descriptive list. The text is often confined to a couple of words, but where necessary the writer has allowed it to spill over onto a second line. Real Wind, for example, is described as "pinkish orange; wide, deep rose halo; gold, green heart." Some of Soules's own creations get even more extensive treatment. 1987 prices ranged from $3 for some older varieties up to $200 for one desirable Munson introduction. The nursery modestly offered its own 1987 introductions well below $100. Stella d'Oro, our measuring stick, sold for $5.

Soules also carries a sizable inventory of hostas, which are described a little more fully than the daylilies. The list includes a good selection of species, and a collection of hybrids that should interest collectors as well as casual gardeners.

Springhead Gardens
Rt. 3, Box 1700, Madison, FL 32340
Telephone: 904-929-4107

Catalog price: 25¢

Edna Welsh's typewitten list of daylilies and houseplants is on the spare side, without much information beyond the names of the plants and their color. But she has also kept her prices to a minimum, and for this we can forgive all faults. The daylily selection includes just 60 varieties, all of them priced between $1 and $5 in 1987. If you're willing to leave the choice up to her, you can get an even better price on an assortment of 15 plants. The houseplant list includes night-blooming cereus, peperomia, lantana, and several begonia cultivars, all priced at $1 in 1987.

Stillpoint Gardens
See under *Shade Plants*, page 146.

Margaret Sullivan
408 Riverside Drive, Fredericksburg, VA 22401
Telephone: 703-373-7118

Catalog price: long self-addressed stamped envelope

A typed list of more than 300 daylilies, each with two or three words that note the color of the blooms (in a very basic fashion) and point out miniatures and ruffled types. The selection is moderately priced—from a 1987 high of $25 to a low of $2.50.

Thomasville Nurseries, Inc.
See under *Roses*, page 144.

Thundering Springs Daylily Garden
P.O. Box 2013, Dublin, GA 31040
Telephone: 912-272-5122 or 1526

Catalog price: free

Elmer and Evelyn Brown have managed to fit a lot of information in a little space. They've crowded 600 daylily varieties into a small 12-page booklet that includes reasonably good indications of flower color. The list is hard to read, but it's free, and the selection is a good one. The emphasis here is on reliable performers rather than expensive novelties. About half the plants sold for $5 or less in 1987, and none went for more than $45. The Browns maintain an American Hemerocallis Society display garden. Visitors are welcome from mid-May to the end of June, but should call ahead if coming from any distance.

Tranquil Lake Nursery
45 River Street, Rehoboth, MA 02769-1395
Telephone: 617-252-4310 or 336-6491

Catalog price: 25¢

A limited but selective list of daylilies and irises at reasonable prices. The nursery offers 250 daylilies on a list filled with award-winners and quality cultivars. Each is nicely described in a way that gives mail-order shoppers a good idea of what the plants will look like. Of Ruffled Apricot, for example, the catalog notes, "Enormous wide petalled apricot with lavender pink midribs and brilliant apricot throat. Heavily ruffled. A classic flower and a super breeder." Many good plants can be had for $5 or less (Stella d'Oro was $4 in 1987), and enthusiasts will find plenty of new and recent introductions priced between $25 and $50. The nursery also sells a smaller selection of Siberian and Japanese irises and a handful of *I. pseudacorus* cultivars.

Turnipseed Nursery Farms
See under *Ivies, Groundcovers, and Climbing Vines*, page 116.

Valente Gardens
Rt. 2, Box 234, E. Lebanon, ME 04027
Telephone: 207-457-2076

Catalog price: one first-class stamp for price list, $1 for catalog

A small list of daylilies, hostas, and Siberian irises. Both price list and catalog offer descriptions in abbreviated form, the catalog also providing cultural instructions. Approximately 50 daylily cultivars are offered, almost as many irises, and about a dozen hosta varieties. Valente also sells a good selection of garden perennials at the nursery, and some of these may be available by mail in 1988.

Andre Viette Farm & Nursery
See under *Garden Perennials*, page 92.

The Vine and the Branch
See under *Irises*, page 114.

Wayside Gardens
See under *Garden Perennials*, page 92.

Gilbert H. Wild and Son, Inc.
Sarcoxie, MO 64862-0338

Catalog price: $2

A big color catalog of daylilies and peonies. Nearly 1,000 daylilies are offered, more than half of them Wild's own introductions. Although many of Wild's creations are attractive, the selections from other hybridizers are surprisingly limited, given the scope of the catalog. Only two of Marsh's Chicago hybrids are sold, and just three of Henry's Siloam varieties. Except for that drawback, the catalog is a valuable resource, particularly for beginners and general home gardeners. All plants are described in detail, and many are pictured in big color photographs. 1987 prices ranged from $3 to $50, and a number of the plants were available at a discount in larger quantities. Stella d'Oro sold for $12.50.

The peony section of the catalog is just as colorful, if a little less extensive. More than 100 varieties are offered, from old classics to relatively recent introductions. Wild has been active in hybridizing peonies, but the firm sells a good selection from a number of other sources as well.

Wimberlyway Gardens
7024 N.W. 18th Avenue, Gainesville, FL 32605-3237
Telephone: 904-372-4922

Catalog price: $2

Wimberlyway is the nursery of Ida Munson, Bill Munson, Betty Hudson, and Elizabeth Hudson Salter, and its catalog is dominated by their introductions, dozens of which have won American Hemerocallis Society awards. Most of the plants listed are new or recent creations, and, as a result, most are relatively expensive. The newer plants are described in detail, and some are pictured in black-and-white photographs. Older plants and those from other hybridizers are simply listed with coded descriptions. The nursery plans to add color to the catalog, perhaps by 1988.

Epiphyllums and Hoyas

Beahm Epiphyllum Gardens
2686 Paloma Street, Pasadena, CA 91107
Telephone: 818-792-6533

Catalog price: 50¢, deductible from first order

Epiphyllums, hoyas, and rhipsalis jam this prolix catalog. Hundreds of epiphyllums, roped off into sections according to color of bloom, claim the first 14 of 17 stapled pages here; cuttings are generally from six to ten inches long and well rooted. A small group of unrooted rhipsalis cuttings comes next. Finally, the hoyas trail their glossy, delicately scented vines across most of a page. Notes throughout the catalog are unusually detailed and carry such warnings as "DON'T repot epiphyllums when they are in bud or bloom" at every turn.

California Epi Center
P.O. Box 1431, Vista, CA 92083
Telephone: 619-758-4290

Catalog price: $2, deductible from first order

A rich selection of flowering jungle cacti, offered either as plants or rooted cuttings. Epiphyllums, predominantly night-blooming species, lead off. The text in this 48-page booklet is copious and detailed. Entries are organized by plant size and color of bloom, so that white and cream blossoms on medium to extra-large orchid cacti, for example, make up a category with 22 options. In addition to the epiphyllums, Christmas cacti, night-blooming cereus, haworthias, and rat-tail cacti are also listed. Many of the specimens appear in bright color photographs.

Phyllis Flechsig Cacti & Succulents
See under *Cacti and Succulents*, page 67.

Green: Plant Research
Hoyas. See under *Tropical Plants*, page 169.

Greenlife Gardens Greenhouses
101 County Line Road, Griffin, GA 30223
Telephone: 404-228-3669

Catalog price: $1

This catalog is a loosely organized hodgepodge that darts among cacti, succulents, myrtles, and ferns, but seems most distinguished by its offering of more than 40 hybrid epiphyllums. Although not pictured, these are carefully—and fervently—described. Dwarf crape myrtles, a species native to the Orient, constitute another specialty of the house; seven varieties are listed with detailed notes on care. Black-and-white photographs capture the looks of selected cacti, sedums, ivies, and ferns.

Grimshaw's (Epi Time) Nursery
2362 Coco Palm Drive, Tustin, CA 92680
Telephone: 714-838-0836

Catalog price: long self-addressed stamped envelope

More than 250 epiphyllum cultivars sold as unrooted cuttings or as small rooted plants. Listings in an abbreviated format carry notes about flower size, shape, and color. Two pages of introductory text offer full instructions for planting and care of the cuttings and for maintenance of established plants.

Hill-n-Dale
6427 N. Fruit Avenue, Fresno, CA 93711
Telephone: 209-439-8249

Catalog price: 50¢ in stamps

A broad selection of hoya cuttings loosely arranged on a number of single pages. More than 100 species are listed, together with a dozen dischidias. The whole presentation is casual: several pages include hoya groupings under informal headlines like "The Good Bloomers" and "The Small Ones."

Hurst Nursery
12059 Lambert Avenue, El Monte, CA 91732
Telephone: 818-444-5296

Catalog price: 50¢

A massive list of epiphyllum hybrids, some the nursery's own introductions, but many the creations of other noted growers. More than 350 cultivars are offered, each evoked in a couple of lines of text. Ber-Tee, for example, is described as a "winning combination of rippled growth with a long-lasting flower. Light to dark shades of red, highlighted with purple. Clean growth. Blooms heavy."

K & L Cactus Nursery
Epiphyllum hybrids. See under *Cacti and Succulents*, page 68.

Rainbow Gardens Nursery & Bookshop
P.O. Box 721, La Habra, CA 90633-0721
Telephone: 213-697-1488

Catalog price: $2, deductible from first order

For devotees of orchid cacti, this lovely booklet is a real windfall. The epiphyllums are sensibly organized by hue: white and cream; yellow; pink, rose, and lavender; red; orange, amber, and copper; and purple. Other flowering tropical cacti, including Christmas, rattail, and wicker-work species, are also granted a spot in the catalog's sun. Scores of dazzling color photographs brighten the text and give browsers something to ponder. (A listing of more than 200 volumes on cacti and succulents, published as a separate booklet, is well worth asking for.)

Rainforest Plantes et Fleurs, Inc.
1550 Rycroft Street, Honolulu, HI 96814
Telephone: 808-942-1550

Catalog price: free

A straightforward list of several dozen rare hoya cuttings precisely described in a line or two. "Fuzzy, dull yellowish flowers deeply recurved with 45 flowers per umbel. Fragrance resembles peaches," suggests the text for *H. coriacea*.

San Luis Gardens
4816 Bridgecreek Road, San Luis Obispo, CA 93401
Telephone: 805-544-3122

Catalog price: free

Nearly 100 hoya species and cultivars, offered as cuttings, are described in detail. Prices range from cheap (around $3) to think-it-over (around $35), with most entries falling in between. All cuttings exhibit two or more nodes.

Ferns

Charles Alford Plants
Staghorn ferns. See under *Tropical Plants*, page 168.

Conley's Garden Center
See under *Wildflowers*, page 174.

The Crownsville Nursery
See under *Garden Perennials*, page 87.

Eco-Gardens
See under *Garden Perennials*, page 87.

Fancy Fronds
Judith J. Jones, 1911 4th Avenue W., Seattle, WA 98119
Telephone: 206-284-5332

Catalog price: $1

More than 50 hardy ferns laid out in an informative descriptive catalog printed on an appropriate fern-green paper. About half the offerings are marked with a symbol indicating sufficient cold hardiness for planting in northeastern and midwestern gardens, and the specific requirements of each plant are spelled out in the text. A few drawings sprinkled through the catalog call attention to particularly attractive species.

Foliage Gardens
2003 128th Avenue S.E., Bellevue, WA 98005
Telephone: 206-747-2998

Catalog price: $1

Ferns for indoor and outdoor culture roll out on a typed list with a text that explains what they look like and what growing conditions they prefer. The inventory ranges from difficult and exotic specimens like *Pityrogramma triangularis* and *Asplenium trichomanes* 'Dwarf Form' to more common types such as ostrich fern and autumn fern.

Glasshouse Works
See under *Tropical Plants*, page 169.

Russell Graham, Purveyor of Plants
See under *Garden Perennials*, page 88.

Griffey's Nursery
See under *Wildflowers*, page 175.

Holbrook Farm & Nursery
See under *Garden Perennials*, page 89.

Jerry Horne
See under *Tropical Plants*, page 169.

North Eastern Ferns and Wild Flowers
See under *Wildflowers*, page 178.

Novelty Nurseries
P.O. Box 382, Novelty, OH 44072
Telephone: 216-338-4425

Catalog price: free

Rare or hard-to-find hardy ferns, all of which the nursery has pulled through its zone 5 winters. Among the offerings are dragon's-tail fern (*Asplenium ebenoides*), recurved broad buckler fern (*Dryopteris dilatata* 'Recurvata'), and tassel fern (*Polystichum polyblepharum*). We assume the rest of the listings are about as unusual as these, as we recognize none of the names (except the Japanese painted fern) from reading other catalogs.

Oakridge Nurseries
See under *Wildflowers*, page 178.

Rice Creek Gardens
Dwarf ferns. See under *Alpines and Rock-Garden Perennials*, page 41.

John Scheepers, Inc.
See under *Bulbs*, page 63.

Strand Nursery Co.
See under *Wildflowers*, page 180.

Varga's Nursery
2631 Pickertown Road, Warrington, PA 18976
Telephone: 215-343-0646

Catalog price: $1

A wholesale fern grower that for the past few years has also offered its extensive inventory to retail customers by mail. Shoppers will have to peruse this list with a reference book close at hand. Two hundred tropical ferns and 30 hardy types are listed by botanical name only, with a code that supplies basic information about mature size and notes which are evergreen and which deciduous types.

Wayside Gardens
See under *Garden Perennials*, page 92.

We-Du Nurseries
See under *Garden Perennials*, page 93.

Wildginger Woodlands
See under *Wildflowers*, page 181.

Woodlanders, Inc.
See under *Trees and Shrubs*, page 167.

Yerba Buena Nursery
See under *Wildflowers*, page 181.

Fuchsias

Barbara's World of Flowers
3774 Vineyard Avenue, Oxnard, CA 93030
Telephone: 805-659-4193

Catalog price: $4

We suspect that Barbara has put such a steep fee on her catalog to weed out idle requests from fuchsia novices. The 36-page list (bound between fuchsia covers) is really intended for those deeply involved in the hobby. Hundreds of cultivars are offered, with key characteristics briefly noted in a few words and a string of coded symbols.

G & G Gardens
6711 Tustin Road, Salinas, CA 93907

Catalog price: $1, deductible from first order

If a fuchsia catalog is printed on colored paper, you might expect the obvious choice of fuchsia pink. G & G Gardens has chosen lavender and peach instead, perhaps to make a point about the color of its fuchsia offerings, which range even further afield—from flaming orange to deep violet. More than 100 named cultivars are listed, with a couple of concise

and helpful sentences of particulars on each. A few fuchsia species are also sold, along with a small but nicely varied collection of tuberous begonias.

Hidden Springs Nursery
Rt. 14, Box 159, Cookeville, TN 38501
Telephone: 615-268-9354

Catalog price: 40¢ (specify herb and fuchsia list)

The text of the fuchsia catalog describes about 70 cultivars, notes which varieties flower in summer heat, and offers a few paragraphs of cultural instruction. The herb list is not so wordy. Without any description at all, it lists more than 100 herbs, scented geraniums, and sedums. Among the offerings are a dozen different mints and as many thymes. A separate list of fruit trees and berry plants can be had for 45¢ (see entry under *Trees and Shrubs*, page 155).

Merry Gardens
See under *Herbs*, page 101.

Wanda's Hide-away
See under *Geraniums*, page 95.

Wileywood Nursery & Florist
17414 Bothell Way S.E., Bothell, WA 98012
Telephone: 206-481-9768 or 775-9768

Catalog price: free

A descriptive list of almost 150 fuchsia varieties serves as Wileywood's catalog, though the firm plans to put together something more finished "maybe next year." Until then the list will work just fine, as the writers have taken the time to describe each plant in some detail.

Garden Perennials

Alexander's Nurseries
See under *Berry Plants*, page 52.

Alpine Plants
P.O. Box 245, Tahoe Vista, CA 95732
Telephone: 916-546-5518

Catalog price: $1

A sensibly designed, well-written catalog of some 60 perennials for rock garden and border, many of them Sierra natives, along with about 30 shrubs and a handful of evergreen trees. Selected perennials are identified with crisp line drawings, while each of the trees is shown as a stately silhouette, with detailed close-ups of the cone and needles. To aid indecisive customers, a few of the plants are featured as nursery favorites, among them blue flax, alpine wallflower, yellow monkeyflower, and creeping buttercup.

Appalachian Wildflower Nursery
See under *Wildflowers*, page 173.

Blackmore & Langdon
Delphiniums. See under *Begonias*, page 50.

Kurt Bluemel, Inc.
See under *Grasses*, page 97.

Bluestone Perennials
7211 Middle Ridge Road, Madison, OH 44057
Telephone: 216-428-7535

Catalog price: free

A nicely illustrated color catalog of perennial plants at reasonable prices. Cultural information is given for each listing, along with a good description. From delphiniums to lupines to chrysanthemums to groundcovers, the 48-page catalog has much to offer. Shipments are made from late March to June. Plants are container grown and generally small. Some will not flower until their second summer.

Breck's
See under *Bulbs*, page 59.

W. Atlee Burpee Company
See under *General Flowers and Vegetables*, page 15.

Busse Gardens
Rt. 2, Box 238, Cokato, MN 55321
Telephone: 612-286-2654

Catalog price: $1, deductible from first order

A massive catalog of garden perennials, illustrated with black-and-white drawings. Plants are only briefly described, but the key facts of plant height, flower color, light requirements, and bloom season are given for each listing. Among the perennial offerings are more than 300 daylily cultivars (including many miniatures), almost 200 hostas, as many irises, and 100 peonies.

Camelot North Nursery & Greenhouses
Rt. 2, Box 398, Pequot Lakes, MN 56472
Telephone: 218-568-8922

Catalog price: $1, deductible from first order

A long list of garden perennials sold as field-grown clumps from May through September. The unillustrated list gives plant height, flower color, light preference, and bloom season, but little further description, so shoppers will have to know what they are looking for. The wide selection and the good prices make this an attractive supplier for the informed gardener.

Canyon Creek Nursery
3527 Dry Creek Road, Oroville, CA 95965
Telephone: 916-533-2166

Catalog price: $1

A wide-ranging list of flowering perennials, including several named viola cultivars from Richard Cawthorne in England and a selection of old-fashioned violets. Because the nursery has relatively mild winters, the list includes some plants not offered by competitors from harsher climates. Out of consideration for their customers to the north, Canyon Creek takes care to point out those plants that can't take the cold.

Carroll Gardens

P.O. Box 310, Westminster, MD 21157
Telephone: 301-848-5422 or 800-638-6334

Catalog price: $2

A thick catalog crammed full of perennials, lilies, herbs, wildflowers, roses, trees, and shrubs. No color illustrations, but some clear line drawings do the job. With its detailed cultivation instructions and garden diagrams, this catalog could serve as a handbook for planning and growing a perennial garden.

Some sections of the catalog compare well with other complete specialty catalogs. More than 150 rose cultivars are offered in an eight-page section that gives full instructions for year-round care. Similar advice is given with the long lists of lilies and rhododendrons.

Chiltern Seeds

See under *General Flowers and Vegetables*, page 15.

Clifford's Perennial & Vine

Rt. 2, Box 320, East Troy, WI 53120
Telephone: 414-642-7156

Catalog price: $1, deductible from first order

Field-grown, year-old perennials that should bloom in their first season after planting. All the basics are here: foxgloves, delphiniums, columbines, oriental poppies, lilies, irises, daylilies, and peonies—some of them available in unusual varieties. Mixed in among the old favorites are some harder-to-find plants, such as plume poppy (*Macleaya cordata*) and blackberry lily (*Belamcanda chinensis*). Orders must be received in time for the brief shipping seasons, April 10 to May 20 and September 15 to October 30.

Cooper's Garden

See under *Irises*, page 109.

The Country Garden

See under *General Flowers and Vegetables*, page 16.

Country Gardens

74 South Road, Pepperell, MA 01463
Telephone: 617-433-6236

Catalog price: $1

Field-grown perennials, most at least a year old, listed in a 20-page descriptive catalog. In 1987 the nursery started offering English hand-pollinated delphinium hybrids, a welcome alternative to the Round Table varieties so widely sold. Country Gardens also sells a good selection of campanula and salvia species and old-fashioned viola cultivars. Shipments are made in the spring and fall.

The Crownsville Nursery

P.O. Box 797, Crownsville, MD 21032
Telephone: 301-923-2212

Catalog price: $2, deductible from first order

A thick descriptive catalog of garden perennials, ferns, wildflowers, and herbs—more than 600 offerings in all. Among the attractions are almost 50 hostas, three dozen Japanese and Siberian iris cultivars, hybrid delphiniums grown from hand-pollinated English seed, and several hibiscus varieties. The nursery changes its stock of offerings every year—in 1987 a quarter of the listings were new to the catalog—so the list is full of surprises each spring.

Earthman Nursery

P.O. Box 281, Brimfield, IL 61517
Telephone: 309-682-1770

Catalog price: free

Earthman does most of its business directly from its garden center, but will arrange to ship plants to customers who live too far away to visit. The catalog lists about 100 garden perennials, including delphiniums, chrysanthemums, hostas, and more than a dozen daylilies. The nursery also sells a selection of groundcovers, grasses, and ornamental shrubs. Each plant is briefly described. None are illustrated.

Eco-Gardens

P.O. Box 1227, Decatur, GA 30031
Telephone: 404-294-6468

Catalog price: $1 (stamps accepted)

A typed list of perennials, wildflowers, ferns, daylilies, hostas, bulbs, water plants, trees, and shrubs. Descriptions are kept to a minimum, so shoppers may have to check a reference book or inquire further to know just what the offerings are and what conditions they will need in order to grow. Most descriptions do mention zone hardiness. Roughly 400 plants, many of them unusual species and cultivars, made up the 1987 list, and the nursery plans to add about 100 new offerings for 1988. Many of the perennials are suitable for either woodland plantings or for the rock garden, and the daylilies and hostas are all small varieties.

Far North Gardens

Seed for more than 1,000 wildflowers and garden perennials. See under *Primroses*, page 136.

Flowerland
Wynot, NE 68792

Catalog price: long self-addressed stamped envelope

Field-grown perennials in a simple list with very brief descriptions. Zone hardiness is not specified, but the nursery is located in southern zone 4, so plants should be hardy at least that far north. Prices are quite low. As an introductory offer, the nursery will sell fifteen plants of its choice to new customers for $5.95, postpaid. (Check price if ordering after 1988.)

Forestfarm
See under *Trees and Shrubs*, page 152.

The Fragrant Path
See under *General Flowers and Vegetables*, page 18.

Garden Perennials
Rt. 1, Wayne, NE 68787
Telephone: 402-375-3615

Catalog price: $1, deductible from first order

Gail Korn put out her first catalog of garden perennials in 1986, and she's already worked out most of the bugs. Her 24-page list gives good descriptions and plenty of cultural advice, and she's added occasional line drawings to help shoppers pick out what they want. Plants are listed by botanical name, but a common-name index inside the front cover makes it easy to find plants by either system. The inventory covers the territory from sedums and sempervivums to chrysanthemums and pinks, most of the offerings available in a choice of cultivars. Daylilies get special attention, with well over 100 offerings. All plants are field grown and shipped bare root. All have toughed out at least one zone 4 winter. The nursery's prices are reasonable: most plants

cost less than $3, and many are less than $2. The daylilies are a little more expensive, but still in a fair range of $3 to $5.

Garden Place
P.O. Box 388, Mentor, OH 44061-0388
Telephone: 216-255-3705

Catalog price: $1

Forty pages of perennials in a catalog with very brief descriptions and no illustrations—almost 800 listings to choose from. A guide at the back of the catalog indexes all plants by color, height, and sun requirements. Only field-grown plants are sold, and all are shipped bare root. The nursery welcomes visitors year-round (on weekdays only), but suggests the month of August as the optimum time to view plants in flower.

Gardenimport
See under *General Flowers and Vegetables*, page 19.

Russell Graham, Purveyor of Plants
4030 Eagle Crest Road N.W., Salem, OR 97304
Telephone: 503-362-1135

Catalog price: $2, deductible from first order

The Graham list, with its many garden perennials, wildflowers, ferns, specialty bulbs, lilies, and ornamental grasses, does not fit easily into our categories. But we had to put it somewhere, so here it is. The 30-page catalog is weak on description but strong on the diversity of its offerings. More than 50 ferns are listed, all winter hardy and suitable for outdoor planting. The wildflowers include a choice of violet species, trilliums, wild geraniums, and trout lilies. Among the garden perennials are foxtail lilies, primulas, and columbines. All the plants are field grown, and all are dug and shipped while dormant in the spring or fall.

Bulbs are a true specialty, and the serious daffodil enthusiast can write for a separate list of more than 100 novelty and show varieties, most of them hybridized by Murray Evans or Bill Pannill. Included in the regular catalog are a number of miniature narcissi, several Japanese and American irises, and two dozen lily species.

Grianán Gardens
See under *General Flowers and Vegetables*, page 19.

Hauser's Superior View Farm
Rt. 1, Box 199, Bayfield, WI 54814
Telephone: 715-779-5404

Catalog price: free

Mr. Hauser was not boasting about his view when he named his nursery: his farm sits on a hill overlooking Lake Superior. That puts him about as far north as you can get in Wisconsin and means that his field-grown plants have survived zone 4 chills. No money has been wasted printing pictures or descriptions on this list; only the name and price are given and sometimes the color. Beginners may be thwarted by the lack of information, but for those who know their perennials, Mr. Hauser's selection is fairly wide ranging, and his prices are reasonable—in 1987 most plants were $8 to $12 per dozen.

Holbrook Farm & Nursery

Rt. 2, Box 223B, Fletcher, NC 28732
Telephone: 704-981-7790

Catalog price: $2, deductible from first order

A family-run nursery with a sizable array of offerings, presented in a clear, well-written catalog. The personal touch of owner Allen Bush pervades the booklet. A photograph of his daughter graces the cover, and the plant descriptions are peppered with his advice, observations, and opinions. The perennial list seems to include a little of everything, from spiderworts to heathers to daylilies. Some wildflowers, ferns, and shrubs are also offered.

Hortico, Inc.

723 Robson Road, Rt. 1, Waterdown, ON, Canada L0R 2H0
Telephone: 416-689-6984

Catalog price: free (request perennial list)

Hortico's primary business is wholesale, and the prices in the list are per 100 plants, but the nursery will sell smaller quantities, even single plants, for an additional charge. The list covers almost 1,000 different species and varieties, including nearly 200 irises and a limited selection of ferns, wildflowers, and ornamental grasses. Descriptions are held to a minimum (height and color), so shoppers may have to consult the list with a reference book at hand. Most plants can be exported to the U.S.

Hortico sends out separate lists of roses (see entry under *Roses*, page 140) and shrubs (see entry under *Trees and Shrubs*, page 156).

J. L. Hudson, Seedsman

See under *General Flowers and Vegetables*, page 20.

Imperial Flower Garden

202 N. 4th Street, Box 255, Cornell, IL 61319
Telephone: 815-358-2519

Catalog price: free

If the Wicked Witch of the West had done her poppy shopping at Imperial Flower Garden, she could have put Dorothy and her friends to sleep in a dazzling rainbow-hued field. We never knew poppies came in so many colors! Dozens of named varieties are offered (all oriental), in tints from carmine to apricot to watermelon pink to white. Plants are shipped when dormant in August and September. The nursery also grows a large assortment of beardless irises—Siberian, Japanese, and species—and a smaller selection of daylilies. The unillustrated catalog gives cultural instructions and color descriptions.

Indigo Knoll Perennials

16236 Compromise Court, Mt. Airy, MD 21771
Telephone: 301-489-5131

Catalog price: $1, deductible from first order

A new nursery specializing in exceptional perennials. The inventory is not vast, but the several dozen selections are all choice varieties, and it would be hard to make an ill-advised order. Among the offerings are a few low-growing *Aster novi-belgii* cultivars, several excellent dianthus types, and an array of carefully chosen chrysanthemums. The text gives

plenty of information about each plant, and a good measure of advice and opinion.

International Growers Exchange

See under *General Flowers and Vegetables*, page 21.

Inter-State Nurseries

See under *Trees and Shrubs*, page 156.

Kelly Nurseries

See under *Trees and Shrubs*, page 157.

Lamb Nurseries

E. 101 Sharp Avenue, Spokane, WA 99202
Telephone: 509-328-7956

Catalog price: free

An extensive collection of garden perennials and rock-garden plants presented in a descriptive catalog devoid of illustrations. More than 500 species and varieties fill the list, ranging from anemones to zauschnerias. Those plants suitable for the rock garden (or for the front of the perennial border) are clearly marked, so that alpine enthusiasts can scan the pages and easily find items of interest. Particularly big selections of campanulas, chrysanthemums, penstemons, violets, sedums, and sempervivums are offered. Plants are listed by botanical name, but common names are always mentioned, and the descriptions are clear enough to make the catalog useful even to the rank beginner.

Louisiana Nursery

See under *Trees and Shrubs*, page 158.

McConnell Nurseries, Inc.

See under *Trees and Shrubs*, page 158.

Maver Nursery

Rt. 2, Box 265B, Asheville, NC 28805
Telephone: 704-298-4751

Catalog price: $3 for general list

Maver puts out several computer-type lists, which, in combination, offer seed for almost 6,000 different plants. The $3 general list includes 4,300 alpines, perennials, wildflowers, ornamental grasses, and bulbous plants. (Each of those five categories is also broken down into a separate catalog for specialists, available at $1 each, $2 for the perennial list.) Another 1,000 trees and shrubs are to be found on the $1 tree and shrub list. The selection is vast, but these really are just lists of botanical names and prices, so shoppers will need to have reference books at hand to decipher the offerings. The owners have published a reference book themselves, which looks like the perfect tool for cracking their lists. Descriptions of 5,000 plants include propagation and cultural instructions, natural habitat, and uses in the garden. The book sold for $27 postpaid in 1987.

Mellinger's Inc.
See under *Trees and Shrubs*, page 159.

Michigan Bulb Co.
1950 Waldorf, N.W., Grand Rapids, MI 49550-0500
Telephone: 616-453-5401

Catalog price: free

In the spring of 1987 the Michigan Bulb Company expanded its previously small brochure to a full 36-page catalog, which was filled with sharp color photographs of ornamental trees and shrubs, fruit trees, roses, berry plants, irises, lilies, begonias, geraniums, houseplants, a few vegetable seeds, and a big selection of garden perennials. The fall list was back down to four pages, with tulips, daffodils, and a smattering of the most popular nursery offerings. As we write, the firm is still deciding how extensive its catalog and offerings will be in 1988.

Milaeger's Gardens
4838 Douglas Avenue, Racine, WI 53402-2498
Telephone: 414-639-2371

Catalog price: $1, deductible from first order

A colorful descriptive catalog, titled *The Perennial Wishbook*, that could serve as a starter perennial reference book. Roughly 500 species and cultivars are offered. Each plant type is prefaced in the catalog by cultural remarks, each listing is described, and many are illustrated by clear color photographs. In addition to garden perennials, the nursery

sells perennial herbs, wildflowers, and more than 150 rose cultivars. Most plants are two- or three-year-old field-grown specimens, shipped bare root, but some, such as delphiniums, are shipped in 3-inch pots after a year of growth. Prices are quite reasonable, and they include shipping.

Mo's Greenhouse
185 Swan River Road, Big Fork, MT 59911
Telephone: 406-837-5128

Catalog price: $1.50, deductible from first order

A perennial catalog with groundcovers and alpines mixed in. A few line drawings appear, more as decorations than as aids to identification. All plants are well described, with cultural instruction and zonal hardiness noted. Readers are told whether the plants are field-grown specimens (shipped bare root) or grown and shipped in 3½-inch pots. In some cases, shoppers can choose between the two. Among the offerings are about two dozen daylilies, a rainbow of bearded irises, and Russell lupines sold by color.

Mohn's, Inc.
P.O. Box 2301, Atascadero, CA 93423

Catalog price: two first-class stamps

A color catalog of hybrid poppies, the results of crosses between oriental and California poppies. The nursery claims that its plants will each produce between 25 and 100 flowers over a blooming season of three to four months. Heights range from one to six feet, and the plants have the perennial qualities of their parents.

Montrose Nursery
See under *Alpines and Rock-Garden Perennials*, page 41.

Nature's Garden
Rt. 1, Box 488, Beaverton, OR 97007

Catalog price: $1, deductible from first order

This is one of the few nurseries that sells the Himalayan blue poppy (*Meconopsis betonicifolia*) in plant form. Those of you who have struggled with the difficult seedlings of this species and have seen the flowers only as pictured in books will appreciate what a treasure this discovery is. The nursery sells roughly 100 perennials, many of them suited to woodland plantings or rock gardens. Two lists are sent out each year, one in the spring and one in the fall. If you request both, the $1 catalog fee is not deductible from an order, but goes instead to pay for the second mailing.

Park Seed Co.
See under *General Flowers and Vegetables*, page 26.

Pinetree Garden Seeds
See under *General Flowers and Vegetables*, page 27.

Powell's Gardens
Rt. 3. Box 21, Princeton, NC 27569
Telephone: 919-936-4421

Catalog price: $1.50

A daunting list of irises, daylilies, hostas, and garden perennials. Last-minute additions have been written in between the single-spaced typed lines, and the effect does not invite browsing. But then, this is not a catalog for the casual gardener. More than 1,000 iris cultivars are listed, almost 800 daylilies, and about 350 different hostas. To fully appreciate the list, gardeners must have some expertise, as the descriptions tend to be telegraphic. A hosta fan will undoubtedly be excited by this description of the cultivar Regal Rhubarb: "L-Upright gr.; petiole burg.!" The plant sold for $100 in 1987. Almost all the irises are tall bearded cultivars, many of them Powell introductions. A handful of Japanese, Siberian, and spuria irises are tacked on at the end of the list. The Powell breeding efforts are also apparent in the daylily list.

The descriptions of the garden perennials are terse, but a little less cryptic. With a good book at hand, the list will be far less frustrating. And with roughly 1,000 species and varieties to choose from, it is worth making the extra effort.

The Primrose Path
Rt. 2, Box 110, Scottdale, PA 15683
Telephone: 412-887-6756

Catalog price: $1.50

The search for unusual and hard-to-find garden perennials has led owners Charles and Martha Oliver to sink their trowels into a wealth of native plant material. The fast-expanding list is now an equal mix of cultivated varieties and wild species. All plants are grown at the nursery (none of the native plants have been collected in the wild), and all are dug to order and shipped in a sphagnum wrapping. True to its name, the nursery offers a choice of primula species and varieties and plans to add more to the list each year. The catalog carries a total of about 300 offerings, all described with cultural instructions, some illustrated with line drawings. A special section helps you plan a border for summer-long color. Indexes point out plants suited to the special conditions of the rock garden and the woodland and note flowers that attract hummingbirds and butterflies.

Putney Nursery, Inc.
See under *Wildflowers*, page 179.

Reno Nurseries
2718 Washington Street, Dubuque, IA 52001
Telephone: 319-556-4503

Catalog price: free

A brief descriptive list of garden perennials, with a choice of about 25 different plants. Many of the listings are sold only in mixes rather than by color or strain, and this allows the nursery to offer them at comparatively low prices. Deals can be had on daylilies, Asiatic lilies, and chrysanthemums, if you aren't fussy about color.

Rice Creek Gardens
See under *Alpines and Rock-Garden Perennials*, page 41.

Rocknoll Nursery
See under *Alpines and Rock-Garden Perennials*, page 42.

C. Scholz
Postfach 130 173, D-4800 Bielefeld 13, West Germany

A huge list of perennial seeds—more than 1,200 species and varieties in all. Plants are listed by botanical name, and very brief descriptions are given in German. With a reference book at hand, the list turns out to be a valuable resource. Thirty-seven campanulas are offered, for example, and 12 meconopsis species. Payment must be made in German currency.

Seedalp
See under *Alpines and Rock-Garden Perennials*, page 42.

Select Seeds
81 Stickney Hill Road, Union, CT 06076

Catalog price: $1

"Seeds of old and rare perennials." An attractive premise for a seed company, and one that Select Seeds delivers on wonderfully. Marilyn Barlow got into the seed business while restoring the landscape and gardens around her 1835 house. Her quest for historically correct plants led her to the research library at Old Sturbridge Village in Sturbridge, Massachusetts, where she studied early 19th-century gardening texts and catalogs. She then sought out seed sources for the flowers grown in colonial and Victorian gardens and has put together an appealing list of more than 100 "documented" varieties for period garden restoration. Her catalog lists plants by botanical name and gives antique common names, some of which are really delightful (*Viola tricolor* has been called heart's-ease, love-in-idleness, and jump-up-and-kiss-me; *Lobelia siphilitica* was once known as Indian tobacco). Short descriptions note special cultural requirements, fragrant varieties, and flowering seasons. Ms. Barlow plans to offer seed collections as well as individual packets in 1988.

Shady Oaks Nursery
See under *Shade Plants*, page 146.

Soergel Greenhouses
2573 Brandt School Road, Wexford, PA 15090-7931
Telephone: 412-935-2090

Catalog price: free

Randy and Beth Soergel offer more than 200 different garden perennials, only 70 of which appear on their price list. Because the list doesn't include everything they sell, the Soergels encourage shoppers to send their want lists. A color flier sent with the price list shows what 40 of the plants look like in bloom. The nursery is located 20 miles north of Pittsburgh and is open to visitors who want to see the entire perennial line.

Stillpoint Gardens
See under *Shade Plants*, page 146.

Surry Gardens
P.O. Box 145, Surry, ME 04684
Telephone: 207-667-4493

Catalog price: free price list, $2 for descriptive catalog

The five-page price list is a daunting affair, with more than 700 offerings set out in columns of botanical names. The full descriptive catalog is almost overwhelming. The nursery sells nearly 50 different campanulas, more than 30 primulas, and dozens of dianthus and delphinium cultivars. The Himalayan blue poppy (*Meconopsis betonicifolia*) is on the list, along with a pure white variant. And more than a dozen anemone species are offered.

Mail-order customers looking at the full catalog must be careful not to get too excited about particular offerings until they check the mail-order price list. Many of the plants described in the catalog can only be purchased at the nursery. Off limits to long-distance shoppers are the more than 100 old-fashioned roses, the dozens of daylily cultivars, and the many rhododendron and azalea offerings.

T & T Seeds Ltd.
Perennial plants for Canadian customers. See under *General Flowers and Vegetables*, page 30.

Ter-El Nursery
P.O. Box 112, Orefield, PA 18069

Catalog price: $1

A small family-run nursery specializing in groundcovers, perennials, and hardy chrysanthemums. Groundcover offerings include bronze ajuga, English ivy, aegopodium, and a couple of sedums. Ten named varieties make up the chrysanthemum list, and the perennial inventory takes in hostas, daylilies, arabis, peonies, veronicas, and coneflowers. The list is smaller than some, but the nursery grows many other unlisted plants in small quantities. If you don't see what you want, ask for it.

Thompson and Morgan
See under *General Flowers and Vegetables*, page 31.

Tillinghast Seed Co.
See under *General Flowers and Vegetables*, page 31.

Tripple Brook Farm
37 Middle Road, Southampton, MA 01073
Telephone: 413-527-4626

Catalog price: free

We've had some trouble pigeonholing this nursery, with its list of perennial herbs, cold-hardy bamboos and cacti, trees, shrubs, wildflowers, and ferns. The owners have made it their mission to seek out little-known and hard-to-find plants that they feel deserve wider use in the garden. Among their recommendations are a handful of prickly pear cacti hardy to zone 4, the Asian yellow daylily (*Hemerocallis lilioasphodelus*), and several mulberry cultivars.

Van Bourgondien Bros.
See under *Bulbs*, page 64.

Andre Viette Farm & Nursery
Rt. 1, Box 16, Fishersville, VA 22939
Telephone: 703-943-2315

Catalog price: $2

More than 1,500 perennial offerings crowd the pages of this barely descriptive price list, which should be consulted with a reference book at hand. The plants are helpfully divided into those that prefer sun and those that tolerate shade. Each listing is followed by data on height, color, and bloom season. Separated from the main listings are massive offerings of daylilies (500 varieties), irises (300 bearded, Siberian, and Japanese cultivars), hostas (100), and peonies (100). No plants are shipped to Canada, and California gardeners can order only daylilies and tall bearded irises.

Wayside Gardens
Hodges, SC 29695-0001
Telephone: 800-845-1124

Catalog price: $2

The Wayside Gardens catalog is a virtual encyclopedia of perennials, ornamental trees and shrubs, and flowering bulbs. The color-drenched pages and full descriptions make this a terrific beginner's guide to perennials and landscape plants; the wide-ranging selection makes it an ever-important source for the veteran. Shoppers can chose from an array of azaleas, roses, flowering cherries, groundcovers, clematis vines, ornamental grasses, wildflowers, daylilies, peonies, lilies, hostas, ferns, and hibiscus, to name just some of the offerings, most of them pictured in sharp color photographs. A fall catalog presents tulips, daffodils, irises, and many other spring-blooming flowers. A tendency toward hyperbole in the descriptions is really not unusual among catalog writers, but thrifty shoppers might do well to compare Wayside's claims to those of its competitors. The Stella d'Oro daylily, for example, was billed in 1987 as "rare" and given a price a bit higher than average.

Weddle Native Gardens
3589 G Road, Palisade, CO 81526
Telephone: 303-464-5549

Catalog price: long self-addressed stamped envelope

More than 100 garden perennials in a straight botanical-name price list. Plants are sold in flats, 4½-inch pots, or gallon containers. The list touches on most of the popular species and dwells on columbines, which are sold in several colors (separately or in a mix) in both a standard-size variety and a miniature.

We-Du Nurseries
Rt. 5, Box 724, Marion, NC 28752
Telephone: 704-738-8300

Catalog price: 50¢

Richard E. Weaver, Jr., and Rene A. Duval, the "We" and "Du" of the company's name, have put together a fascinating collection of more than 500 garden perennials, wildflowers, and ferns. Weaver and Duval believe that native plants deserve wider use in the garden, and they have mixed a strong collection of southeastern natives in with their perennial listings. Along with cardinal flower, for example, they sell great blue lobelia and its white variant (*Lobelia siphilitica* 'Alba'), and two related southeastern species, *L. elongata* and *L. puberula*, described as "very graceful" and "more elegant" than the more common species. Other areas of strength include alliums, trilliums, epimediums, species irises, and hardy orchids. Rock gardeners and woodland planters will find many unusual offerings here, all well described with cultural directions.

White Flower Farm
Litchfield, CT 06759-0050
Telephone: 203-496-1661 (customer service), 9600 (orders), or 9624 (plant questions)

Catalog price: $5, deductible from first order

White Flower Farm is the upper-crust Yankee of garden catalogs. It holds its nose up in the mail-order nursery business the way *The New Yorker* does on the magazine rack. It costs a little more to join this club—the $5 catalog fee is higher than most—but once you're in, the upkeep isn't bad. The fee is deductible from the first order, the catalogs are sent free to regular customers, and the plant prices aren't unreasonable.

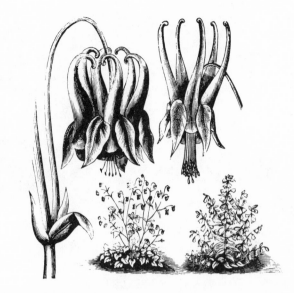

The Garden Book, the firm's 100-page catalog, offers an education in perennial flower gardening. Its clear color photographs show most of the important flower types, and the chatty descriptions explain what is good and bad about them all. Even more valuable are the lengthy and detailed cultural instructions, which are better than those found in most books on perennials. One small deceit colors our opinion of this catalog. Amos Pettingill, the purported author of the text, is actually an invention. His rambling, personable style is a calculated effect created over the years by a number of anonymous scribes.

White Flower Farm's selections range from Blackmore & Langdon delphiniums (sold by color or in a mix) to rhododendrons, daylilies, cinquefoils, ferns, and daphnes. Just a few species and varieties are offered of each, and these are billed as the finest available. Of the five rhododendrons listed, for example, Mr. Pettingill writes, "The varieties offered below meet all of the criteria for ornamental shrubs—handsome foliage, compact form, winter hardiness, and full-flowering habit. These are treasures for any garden, but devils to propagate, so stocks remain limited." The bold headlines and exclamation points of the coarser catalogs won't be found on these pages, but the subtler approach of sale by enticement may be even more dangerous to the pocketbook. Supplies, tools, books, and teak garden furniture can be found in an appendix at the back of the catalog.

Woodlanders, Inc.
See under *Trees and Shrubs*, page 167.

Geraniums

Cook's Geranium Nursery
712 N. Grand, Lyons, KS 67554
Telephone: 316-257-5033

Catalog price: $1, deductible from first order

Hundreds of geraniums get the descriptive treatment in this little booklet that includes double, single, and fancy-leaved zonal types, Lady Washingtons (or regals), miniatures and dwarfs, ivy-leaved and scented varieties, and such novelties as bird's-egg, cactus-flower, stellar, and deacon varieties. One interesting group is made up of species pelargoniums and garden hybrids of wild strains. Gardeners familiar with only the common red and pink zonal types will be amazed at the range of bloom color—from white, salmon, and apricot to pale violet and deep burgundy.

Davidson-Wilson Greenhouses
See under *Houseplants*, page 106.

Fox Hill Farm
444 W. Michigan Avenue, Box 9, Parma, MI 49269-0009
Telephone: 517-531-3179

Catalog price: $1 (specify scented geranium catalog)

This nursery issues two brochures that lay out some 350 herbs, fragrant plants, and scented geraniums, with particular strength in hardy perennials. The scented geranium list makes a charming introduction to these aromatic curiosities. The booklet cites a representative sampling of rose-, citrus-, spice-, mint-, and pungent-scented plants. Advice on how to pot, water, fertilize, and generally maintain scented geraniums is helpfully provided, but you may not require this counsel at all. "They thrive on benign neglect," the catalog

concedes. See entry under *Herbs*, page 100, for description of Fox Hill's herb offerings.

Lake Odessa Greenhouse
1123 Jordan Lake Street, Lake Odessa, MI 48849
Telephone: 616-374-8488

Catalog price: free

Stepping into the Lake Odessa Greenhouse must present both pleasure and confusion to the nose. The nursery sells almost 50 varieties of scented geraniums in fragrances from cinnamon and strawberry to balsam and citronella. Descriptions try to differentiate among varieties such as Prince Rupert, with its "lemon scent," Lady Mary, which has a "light lemon scent," and Mabel Grey, tagged with a "bitter lemon odor." (We have a Mabel Grey on our porch, and had never thought of its smell in such harsh terms.) A few rosebud, tulip, dwarf, and variegated geraniums offer an unscented respite.

Logee's Greenhouses
See under *Begonias*, page 51.

Lost Prairie Herb Farm
Scented geraniums. See under *Herbs*, page 101.

Merry Gardens
See under *Herbs*, page 101.

Parsley's Cape Seeds
Seed for native South African pelargoniums. See under *Native Plants of Australia and South Africa*, page 120.

Rust-En-Vrede Nursery
Seed of pelargonium species. See under *Native Plants of Australia and South Africa*, page 120.

Shady Hill Gardens
821 Walnut Street, Batavia, IL 60510-2999

Catalog price: $1, deductible from first order

Almost 900 geranium cultivars and species from a nursery that does its best to satisfy all the desires of geranium fanciers. Indecisive types had best keep this catalog at bay. Zonal, stellar, cascade, regal, fancy-leaf, deacon, scented, ivy-leaf, miniature, dwarf—all the familiar types are listed here—

Heaths and Heathers

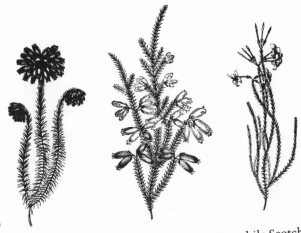

Holden Clough Nursery
See under *Alpines and Rock-Garden Perennials*, page 40.

The Cummins Garden
See under *Azaleas and Rhododendrons*, page 44.

Daystar
See under *Trees and Shrubs*, page 151.

Heathers Wild Flower Seeds
South African erica seed. See under *Native Plants of Australia and South Africa*, page 119.

Heaths and Heathers
P.O. Box 850, Elma, WA 98541
Telephone: 206-482-3258

Catalog price: long self-addressed stamped envelope

More than 100 heaths and heathers of all shapes and sizes. More than a dozen varieties of bell heather (*Erica cinerea*) form low-growing bushes, while three tree-heath species grow six to eight feet tall. Winter heath (*E. carnea*) opens its blooms

from November to May—even north to zone 4—while Scotch heather (in 40 varieties) and Cornish heath take charge through the summer and fall. Plants are shipped in 2¼-inch rose pots practically year-round, with breaks only in the dead of winter and the heat of summer.

Parsley's Cape Seeds
Erica species native to South Africa. See under *Native Plants of Australia and South Africa*, page 120.

Protea Seed & Nursery Suppliers
See under *Proteas*, page 137.

R. V. Roger Ltd.
See under *Alpines and Rock-Garden Perennials*, page 42.

Siskiyou Rare Plant Nursery
See under *Alpines and Rock-Garden Perennials*, page 42.

Von Lyncker Nurseries Ltd.
Seed for South African erica species. See under *Native Plants of Australia and South Africa*, page 120.

and listed in profusion. More than 40 species are offered for those interested in exploring pelargonium genealogy.

Sunnybrook Farms Nursery
Scented geraniums. See under *Herbs*, page 103.

Tansy Farm
Scented geraniums. See under *Herbs*, page 103.

Wanda's Hide-away
14812 84th Avenue N.E., Bothell, WA 98011
Telephone: 206-488-2405

Catalog price: $1

Wanda Blake sells about 30 miniature geranium varieties and as many fuchsias in her typed catalog. She describes each of the geraniums with a few words on flower and foliage, but presents the fuchsias by name only.

Well-Sweep Herb Farm
Scented geraniums. See under *Herbs*, page 103.

Young's Mesa Nursery
2755 Fowler Lane, Arroyo Grande, CA 93420
Telephone: 805-489-0548

Catalog price: $2, deductible from first order

Bill and Kay Young's fascination with geraniums began with miniatures, and their impressive catalog opens with a selection of more than 300 of these diminutive charmers. The list rambles on to hundreds of full-size zonal, scented, fancy-leaf, ivy-leaf, stellar, bird's-egg, regal, and other types, and seems to contain just about everything a geranium lover could ask for. All plants are shipped in either 2¾-inch or 4-inch pots. No seeds or cuttings are offered, and the firm does not sell wholesale.

Gladioli

BioQuest International
South African gladiolus species. See *Native Plants of Australia and South Africa*, page 119.

Connell's Dahlias
See under *Dahlias*, page 74.

Dutch Gardens, Inc.
See under *Bulbs*, page 60.

Ferncliff Gardens
See under *Dahlias*, page 74.

Gardenimport
See under *General Flowers and Vegetables*, page 19.

Gladside Gardens
61 Main Street, Northfield, MA 01360
Telephone: 413-498-2657

Catalog price: $1, deductible from first order

Although gladioli are the first order of business here, a profusion of dahlias, canna lilies, and exotic bulb- and tuber-grown flowers fill pages of the typewritten list. The nursery publishes a spring list only and does not sell

bulbs for fall planting (tulips and daffodils, for example). Among the more unusual listings are sacred lily of India (*Amorphophallus rivieri*), taro (*Colocasia esculenta*, the plant from which poi is made), and the blue and white lily-of-the-Nile (*Agapanthus africanus*). A total of 120 gladiolus varieties are sold, ranging from miniatures to giants and from species to new introductions.

Harris Seeds
See under *General Flowers and Vegetables*, page 20.

Mellinger's Inc.
See under *Trees and Shrubs*, page 159.

Noweta Gardens ✔
900 Whitewater Avenue, St. Charles, MN 55972
Telephone: 507-932-4859 or 3210

Catalog price: free

An oversize color catalog of gladioli in every hue imaginable and in sizes from miniatures ("pixiolas" or "tiny tots" at this nursery) to standards. Carl Fischer is the guiding hand behind the business; the 1987 booklet featured a close-up of his face in the centerfold and a three-page letter from him that touched on subjects as diverse as the weather and the

moral fiber of the nation. More than 100 varieties were offered in 1987—after summer floods that wiped out almost 50 others.

Parsley's Cape Seeds
Seed for South African gladiolus species. See under *Native Plants of Australia and South Africa*, page 120.

Pleasant Valley Glads
163 Senator Avenue, P.O. Box 494, Agawam, MA 01001
Telephone: 413-786-9146 or 789-0307

Catalog price: free

A big list of gladiolus hybrids—more than 400 named varieties—that describes each plant nicely but includes no pictures. Miniature types take up almost half the catalog, and these seem like an appealing option for gardeners who feel the normal gladioli blooms command too much attention in a flower bed. Those who want the real thing can choose from scores of standard and large varieties.

Rust-En-Vrede Nursery
Seed of gladiolus species. See under *Native Plants of Australia and South Africa*, page 120.

John Scheepers, Inc.
See under *Bulbs*, page 63.

Summerville's Gladiolus World-Wide
Rt. 1, Box 449, Glassboro, NJ 08028
Telephone: 609-881-0704

Catalog price: free

Summerville's chunky little booklet offers about 250 gladiolus cultivars, each well described in a paragraph of text. Miniatures make up about a quarter of the list. A few featured plants are pictured in color on both sides of the cover; most of them are new introductions.

Van Bourgondien Bros.
See under *Bulbs*, page 64.

The Waushara Gardens
Plainfield, WI 54966
Telephone: 715-335-4462

Catalog price: $1

Almost 150 gladiolus varieties for both home gardeners and commercial growers, presented in a catalog that manages good descriptions by resorting to tiny type. Be sure the light is bright and that your glasses are on before settling down with this booklet. Selected offerings are pictured in color, though the printing quality varies widely from year to year. The 1984 catalog unfolded into a huge, brilliantly colored poster depicting dozens of bloomstalks, but the 1987 brochure included just a few dark and somewhat muddy photographs.

Wright Iris Nursery
See under *Irises*, page 115.

Wyatt-Quarles Seed Co.
See under *General Flowers and Vegetables*, page 33.

Grasses

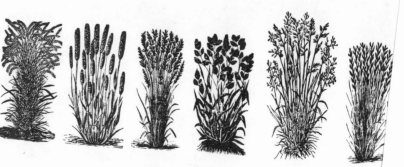

Kurt Bluemel, Inc.
2740 Greene Lane, Baldwin, MD 21013
Telephone: 301-557-7229

Catalog price: $1

An extensive list of ornamental grasses, sedges, and rushes—almost 200 species and varieties. The nursery has subspecialties in marsh and water plants—including such mud lovers as sweet flag, bog bean, bullrush, and rice—and garden perennials. Among the perennial offerings are several Japanese anemones, 30 astilbe cultivars, wild ginger, bleeding heart, goatsbeard, and loosestrife in a choice of five colors.

Church's Greenhouse & Nursery
522 Seashore Road, Cape May, NJ 08204
Telephone: 609-884-3927

Catalog price: free

Cape beach grass plants sold by the thousand. The grass is recommmended to beachfront property owners as a natural erosion controller. The minimum order of 1,000 plants comes to more than $150, so write only if you are considering a big planting.

Horizon Seeds, Inc.
P.O. Box 886, Hereford, TX 79045
Telephone: 806-258-7280

Catalog price: free

Horizon will send out its annual seed guide to anyone who asks. Tucked at the back, after pages of corn, sorghum, and other grains for commercial growers, is an excellent list of native prairie-grass seed. More than 80 different species and locally occurring strains are offered. The only catch is that the seeds have to be ordered through local Horizon dealers, which the firm will happily locate for you. Contact either the Hereford office or the branch office at P.O. Box 81823, Lincoln, NE 68501 (402-475-1232).

Lafayette Home Nursery, Inc.
Native prairie grasses. See under *Wildflowers*, page 175.

Maver Nursery
See under *Garden Perennials*, page 89.

Native Plants, Inc.
Seed for native grasses. See under *Wildflowers*, page 177.

Northplan Seed Producers
Native grass seed. See under *Wildflowers*, page

Plants of the Southwest
See under *General Flowers and Vegetables*, pa

Prairie State Commodities
P.O. Box 6, Trilla, IL 62469
Telephone: 217-235-4322

Catalog price: 50¢

Corn, clover, alfalfa, and grass seed sold in 5
The grass seed is likely to be of most interest
least in the quantities offered). Choices run fr
perennial ryegrass to redtop and Park Kentuc

R & R Beachgrass
Beaver Dam Acres, Rt. 1, Box 3, Lewes, DE 1

Catalog price: free

American beach grass culms sold by the hu
thousand. The nursery is prepared to fill
50,000 culms or more.

Sharp Bros. Seed Co.
Healy, KS 67850
Telephone: 316-398-2231

Catalog price: free

A big selection of grass seed, including d
species, listed by common name only in a
terested customers will have to inquire furt
and shipping rates. The company has branc
rillo, Texas (806-352-2781), and Greeley, C
4710).

Stock Seed Farms
See under *Wildflowers*, page 180.

Zoysia Farm Nurseries, Inc.
3617 Old Taneytown Road, Taneytown, M

Catalog price: free

Zoysia grass plugs, promoted (vigorously)
weed-free low-maintenance alternative
grasses.

Herbs

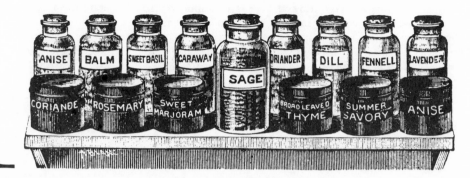

ABC Herb Nursery
Rt. 1, Box 313, Lecoma, MO 65540
Telephone: 314-435-6389

Catalog price: one first-class stamp (or a quarter)

An alphabetical index of more than 100 herbs, this little booklet evokes a stroll across a meadow. Each herb is listed simply with a line describing the plant's uses, and the entries skip from winter savory ("beans, vinegars, meats") to lemon balm ("tea, punch, jelly, salad, aroma") in a way that makes one feel like crushing and sniffing everything in sight. Collections of herbs are offered at bargain rates. In addition, information sheets that include herb care and storage tips may be purchased for a nominal fee.

Alexander's Nurseries
See under *Berry Plants*, page 52.

Belché Herb Co.
P.O. Box 1305, Schenectady, NY 12301

Catalog price: free

A dozen herbal seeds sold by the packet. Emphasis here is on culinary varieties, and the plants cited—chives, sweet basil, parsley, and thyme for example—appear with comments on their kitchen uses. "Superb fresh in or on anything!" exclaims the text for Greek oregano. "I like it on broiled chicken breast."

Caprilands Herb Farm
534 Silver Street, Coventry, CT 06238
Telephone: 203-742-7244

Catalog price: free

Caprilands promises "everything for the herb gardener" and delivers the goods from its 18th-century barn in central Connecticut. Herbal craft items (pillows, pads, hangers, and scented wreaths), cards, seasonings, dolls, ornaments—and, of course, plants—are offered here. Dozens of helpful books on herb gardening round out the selection in this eight-page catalog, quaintly printed in a squint-inducing typeface reminiscent of a colonial broadsheet.

Casa Yerba Gardens
Star Route 2, Box 21, Days Creek, OR 97429
Telephone: 503-825-3534

Catalog price: $1

A rich offering of rare and unusual herb seeds and plants from a farm that grows its plants organically, without chemical fertilizers or insecticides. Several hundred seed varieties are available, together with a smaller number of plants. Each entry in the 30-page catalog is carefully notated to show the plant's (eventual) uses, estimated height, and recommended sowing time. The text also includes some general instructions for growing herbs from seed, which beginners may find useful—and reassuring. "Generally, herbs will thrive in most garden soils with a minimum of care," the catalog remarks. Gift certificates are available.

Catnip Acres Farm
67 Christian Street, Oxford, CT 06483
Telephone: 203-888-5649

Catalog price: $2

This catalog raps its ruler on the desk, then advances to the blackboard to give a most complete lesson in herbs, from A (angel's trumpet) to Y (yarrow). By the time you work your way through these 18 orderly and detailed pages, you'll know plenty. A distinctive feature of the catalog is its historical depth. Each of the several hundred seeds is listed with a discursive paragraph that often includes a tantalizing nugget; Scotch broom, we learn, has branches which "are nearly leafless and were once used to make brooms and for thatching. The flowers and tops were used to flavor beers, the seeds roasted for a coffee substitute." Butterfly weed, so named because it attracts butterflies to the garden, "is also known as 'pleurisy root' due to its use during the 1800s as an expectorant in treating this disease." A browser's delight.

Companion Plants
7247 N. Coolville Ridge Road, Athens, OH 45701
Telephone: 614-592-4643

Catalog price: $2, deductible from first order

A comprehensive and balanced catalog featuring 300 plus herb plants and a third as many seeds. Most plants are de-

scribed in a line or two of text; the seeds are simply named. According to the catalog, most of the seed offered is harvested from the nursery's own stock, but some is gathered from wild plants. The nursery will occasionally harvest seed by special request; it's best to inquire about availability and price.

The Crownsville Nursery
See under *Garden Perennials*, page 87.

Dabney Herb Farm
Box 22061, Louisville, KY 40222
Telephone: 502-893-5198

Catalog price: $2

A somewhat clumsily assembled guide to many hundreds of herbal plants, seeds, and bulbs, this catalog daunts the casual reader. Listings are organized by family—rosemary, sage, thyme, and so forth. A description of each plant's characteristic features and mature height are given. Dried botanicals, described as "food quality," answer a need for those who don't care to grow their own herbs. Other items—cinnamon sticks, juniper berries, sandalwood chips, etc.—are available for crafting and potpourri uses.

Dionysos' Barn
Box 31, Bodines Road, Bodines, PA 17722
Telephone: 717-995-9327

Catalog price: 50¢

A single page printed on both sides, this sheet packs in roughly 100 different herbs offered as plants—some with commentary, but most pinned down by common name and Latin name—nothing more. Entries are marked to indicate whether they are annual, biennial, or perennial.

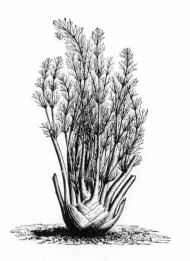

Fox Hill Farm
444 W. Michigan Avenue, Box 9, Parma, MI 49269
Telephone: 517-531-3179

Catalog price: $1 (specify herb list)

A simple price list of more than 300 herbs, fragrant perennials, and scented geraniums, all sold as plants. (The scented geraniums rate a separate descriptive catalog. See entry under *Geraniums*, page 94.) Among the herb listings are two dozen thymes, six santolinas, six varieties of English lavender, and three different wormwoods.

Fragrant Fields
Dongola, IL 62926
Telephone: 618-827-3677

Catalog price: $1, deductible from first order

A terse listing of scores of potted herbs offered without commentary. Basic varieties such as sweet basil, marjoram, and sage are available by the tray (3½-inch pots, 18 pots per tray). Mixed trays of three herbs each form a second option here. Scented geraniums are also proffered in mixed trays selected by the nursery.

Goodwin Creek Gardens
Box 83, Williams, OR 97544

Catalog price: 50¢

A stylish eight-page brochure with more than 250 organically grown perennial herbs and everlastings. Both plants and seeds are offered by this small family farm located at the foot of Grayback Mountain in southwestern Oregon. Grasses, lavenders, mallows, mints, sages, thymes, and yarrows are all here; each plant listing includes a terse summation of growth habit, height, and general uses. A handful of delicate line drawings enliven the catalog; those interested in further herbal research will find a recommended reading list on the back page.

Halcyon Gardens Herbs
P.O. Box 124-M, Gibsonia, PA 15044

Catalog price: $1

Seed for more than 50 herbs, both rare and common, fill this little booklet, which bills itself as "a guide to growing herbs." After stating the case for herbs generally ("perhaps the most delightful and beneficial group of plants on the planet"), the catalog explains step by step how to plant, propagate, and harvest them. Listings include all herbal types: culinary, fragrant, medicinal, ornamental, and tea. Stress is on quality and purity; many culinary herbs—such as French sorrel—are imported from Europe for this reason. Descriptions are thorough and extend the herbal welcome.

Robert B. Hamm
See under *Begonias*, page 51.

Happy Hollow Nursery
221 Happy Hollow Road, Villa Rica, GA 30180
Telephone: 404-459-4144

Catalog price: $1

Several dozen herb plants presented in an orderly chart format. Scanning from left to right: plant name ("bee balm"), height ("2-3'"), description ("opposite leaves, pointed shaped with serrated margins"), growing conditions required ("moist soil, partial shade"), and general remarks ("spreads quickly"). Most plants are grown in 2¼-inch pots. A group of herb-laden recipes occupies a page at the back of the catalog.

Hemlock Hill Herb Farm
Hemlock Hill Road, Litchfield, CT 06759-0415
Telephone: 203-567-5031

Catalog price: 50¢

This little booklet is as dainty as a pot of herbs on a windowsill. The nursery sells plants only—no seeds, products, or books—and the 40 or so varieties are lovingly described. Line drawings every few pages illustrate sweet bay, marjoram, sage, tarragon, and winter savory. It's hard not to like a catalog that says of borage: "Plant it in a clump. Then when you are bone weary and ready to relax with a martini, drop one of the flowers in your drink."

The Herb Cottage
Washington Cathedral, Mt. St. Alban, Washington, DC 20016
Telephone: 202-537-8982

Catalog price: free

This simple list includes a small selection of herb seed packets, along with kitchen items, cards, charts, gardening materials, toys—even gift wrap. In business since 1927, the Herb Cottage originally sold dried and potted herbs, books, fragrances, and jelly. Now they carry bookmarks, too. A single folded-and-stapled page briskly notes the possibilities.

Herb Gathering Inc.
See under *General Flowers and Vegetables*, page 20.

Hidden Springs Nursery
See under *Fuchsias*, page 85.

J. L. Hudson, Seedsman
Herb seed. See under *General Flowers and Vegetables*, page 20.

International Growers Exchange
Perennial herb plants. See under *General Flowers and Vegetables*, page 21.

Lost Prairie Herb Farm
805 Kienas Road, Kalispell, MT 59901

Catalog price: $1

A simple, easy-to-read listing of approximately 200 herb plants, scented geraniums, garden perennials, and natural pest controls. Among the first group are a dozen mints, ten different basils, angelica, germander, hyssop, and sweet woodruff. Each offering is nicely described, with culinary and medicinal uses pointed out along with suggestions for decorative use in the garden. About a dozen scented geraniums are offered, in fragrances from gooseberry to coconut. Minimum order is four plants.

McLaughlin's Seeds
P.O. Box 550, Mead, WA 99021-0550

Catalog price: $1 (specify herb list)

A descriptive catalog of aromatic, culinary, and decorative herbs, as well as cutting flowers and garden perennials. The booklet for some reason did not get to us by press date. A

separate wildflower catalog (which we did receive) is sent out for $1 (see entry under *Wildflowers*, page 176).

Meadowbrook Herb Garden
Route 138, Wyoming, RI 02898
Telephone: 401-539-7603

Catalog price: $1

More than 250 herbs and other "useful" plants are presented with a flourish in this classy 12-page catalog. Only the seeds are available by mail, however; these are marked with an asterisk in the listings and constitute perhaps half the total. Popular collections of herb seeds—culinary, medicinal, everlasting, tea herbs, and wildflowers—are also available.

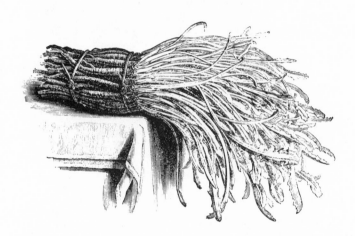

Meadowsweet Herb Farm
Shrewsbury, VT 05738
Telephone: 802-492-3566

Catalog price: free

This elegant brochure may be suitable for leaving casually displayed on a coffee table for the neighbors to see; it's that attractive. Finely typeset, printed in two colors, and filled with seductive line drawings of bonnets, baskets, and wreaths, the Meadowsweet catalog resembles a Victorian hope chest. The emphasis here is on the decorative and culinary uses of herbs. No plants are shipped; however, seeds for more than 50 herbs are offered. Gift certificates are available in any amount.

Merry Gardens
P.O. Box 595, Camden, ME 04843
Telephone: 207-236-9460

Catalog price: $1 (specify catalog #1, herbs and geraniums)

Some 200 herb plants, along with geraniums, ivies, and fuchsias, are cited in this neatly ordered eight-page booklet. Unfortunately, none of the herbs are described beyond a code to indicate which are perennials and which are annuals. Informational leaflets (such as "Herbs for Indoors" and "Fragrant Plants"), available for a nominal fee, may answer your questions on care and cultivation. The firm also publishes a list of indoor plants that it will send out for $2 (see entry under *Houseplants*, page 106.)

The Mix Niche
Rt. 1, Box 1620, McIntyre, GA 31054

Catalog price: $1

Dried herbs, quilting supplies, and seashells take up most of this catalog, but buried in the center are almost 100 herb plants, from French tarragon to hyssop. Most are for use in cooking, teas, or potpourris; few medicinal plants make the list.

Nash's Plant Farm
Rt. 2, Box 546, Batts Neck, Stevensville, MD 21666
Telephone: 301-643-5196

Catalog price: $1

A brief listing of annual and perennial herbs that can be devoured at a glance. Fewer than 100 varieties, all told, each with a word or two of description: "Roots yield dye, nice ground cover," reads the line on bedstraw. A card containing planting tips, inserted in the nursery's nuts-and-bolts brochure, has some good advice for the novice herb fancier: "Be sparing with both water and fertilizer on your herbs—lush, rapid growth may look good; but the plants won't have as much taste and fragrance if they're pushed too fast with extra feeding."

Nichols Garden Nursery
See under *General Flowers and Vegetables*, page 25.

Putney Nursery, Inc.
See under *Wildflowers*, page 179.

Rasland Farm
N.C. 82 at U.S. 13, Godwin, NC 28344
Telephone: 919-567-2705

Catalog price: $1.50

With its ruled headlines, its blend of typefaces, its boxed listings, and its handful of black-and-white photographs, this catalog has the feel of a small-town newspaper. The heart of the news here is a range of more than 100 culinary, fragrant, medicinal, and ornamental plants. In addition, the nursery offers wreaths, sachets, dried bouquets, potpourri supplies, and herbal oils. Those unable to find solace in their gardens may want to seek relief through a series of meditation tapes available from the nursery. No kidding! One even includes music composed, performed, and recorded by two members of the Tippett family, owners of Rasland Farm.

The Redwood City Seed Company
Herb seed. See under *General Flowers and Vegetables*, page 28.

Richters
Goodwood, ON, Canada L0C 1A0
Telephone: 416-640-6677

Catalog price: $2

This handsome 80-page catalog has it all, from seed collections to culinary herb posters for the wall. Bergamot, comfrey, dill, ginseng, lavender, marigold, and mint plants are typical of the fare in the lavishly detailed booklet. Delicate line drawings bring abstract botanical names into focus at regular intervals. Hundreds of varieties—available as plants, seeds, or sometimes both—are listed. Gourmet vegetables (such as artichoke, chicory, and leek plants) and wildflowers also get a spot in the sun. Finally, pest controls, garden tools, dried herbs, and a 14-page library of reference books trot past toward the back of the catalog. An herbal browser's delight.

The Rosemary House
120 S. Market Street, Mechanicsburg, PA 17055
Telephone: 717-697-5111 or 766-6581

Catalog price: $2

"We have had a few letters telling us our catalog 'needs help,'" the nursery confesses right up front. You'll be able to see why. A stunning hodgepodge of literally thousands of items jammed together according to no discernible scheme, this catalog takes the cake for plenitude. It's like an attic presided over by a dotty aunt. Perfumes, wire whisks, oils, herbal charts, reference books, mustard mix: don't ever say you've seen it all until you plow though these 24 pages. Herb seeds, botanicals, and herb plants are available in profusion—if you can find them.

Sanctuary Seeds
See under *General Flowers and Vegetables*, page 29.

Sandy Mush Herb Nursery
Rt. 2, Surrett Cove Road, Leicester, NC 28748
Telephone: 704-683-2014

Catalog price: $2, deductible from first order

Fine italic calligraphy sets the tone in this richly informative catalog. Several hundred plants are organized as neatly as recipes in a file box; marginal commentary abounds. "The novice herb grower might very well wish to start with a selection of herbs most appealing as a group," a section on "Choosing Herbs" remarks. "The following specialty lists might . . . help you in deciding which herbs best suit your interests and growing conditions." Three pages (of 50) are given over to an illustrated display of herb garden patterns. A smattering of seeds, books, and cards rounds out the catalog.

Shepherd's Garden Seeds
Seed for culinary herbs. See under *General Flowers and Vegetables*, page 29.

Sunnybrook Farms Nursery
9448 Mayfield Road , P.O. Box 6, Chesterland, OH 44026
Telephone: 216-729-7232

Catalog price: $1, deductible from first order

Herbs dominate this catalog from a nursery that has been in the same family since 1928, when a prominent Cleveland pediatrician named Dr. Harold Ruh first set up shop. Roughly 200 herbs, tersely described, are supplemented by a somewhat smaller listing of scented geraniums (50 types), ivies (90 varieties), and houseplants. Black-and-white photographs add clarity to evocations of such items as an old-fashioned European coiled straw beehive.

Tansy Farm
5888 Else Road, Rt. 1, Agassiz, BC, Canada V0M 1A0
Telephone: 604-796-9316

Catalog price: $2

A well-organized, well-written booklet describing the more than 300 plants grown at Tansy Farm. This nursery prides itself on offering the best and largest selection of herbs and scented geraniums available anywhere in Canada. Listings for each variety spell out the plant's relative hardiness, life span, height when in flower, light requirements, and common uses. Helpful tips on plant cultivation and care—most drawn from firsthand experience—bracket the listings and amplify this catalog's appeal. Orders are shipped to U.S. and Canadian addresses.

Taylor's Herb Garden
1535 Lone Oak Road, Vista, CA 92084
Telephone: 619-727-3485

Catalog price: $1

Glossy pages and lush color photographs—here a field of sweet lavender, there a clump of borage—make this small, beautifully produced catalog a treat to thumb through. Dozens of herbs are offered, each with a paragraph of descriptive text. Recipes using herbs as key ingredients are dotted throughout the booklet. In an introductory note, the Taylors contend that their nursery's plants, all grown out of doors in that famous California sun, tend to be healthier, hardier specimens than those cultivated in a greenhouse. The firm also offers seed for almost 200 herbs.

Triple Oaks Nursery and Florist
Franklinville, NJ 08322
Telephone: 609-694-4272

Catalog price: free

More 200 fresh herb plants are available from this nursery, but only a fraction of these are named on the single typewritten page that serves as a catalog. Herb baskets and wreaths, potpourri supplies, dried herbs, herb books, and fragrant herbal oils steal most of the attention here. If you already know exactly what you want to order, this rudimentary index may be worth having; otherwise, go visit the place in person and take a look around.

Tripple Brook Farm
See under *Garden Perennials*, page 92.

Village Arbors
1804 Saugahatchee Road, Auburn, AL 36830
Telephone: 205-826-3490

Catalog price: $1

An alphabetical listing of more than 100 herbs, scented plants, and perennials. Entries are brief but engaging: catnip is described as "inimical to insects, exciting to cats and soothing to humans when brewed into a tea." The herbs—sold by the pot—show special depth in the basil, lavender, and mint families. Growing conditions are noted for each plant listed. Ten herb collections, some handmade dried herb wreaths, and selected useful reference books complete the selection.

Well-Sweep Herb Farm
317 Mt. Bethel Road, Port Murray, NJ 07865
Telephone: 201-852-5390

Catalog price: 75¢

A rich selection of almost 1,000 herb plants, scented geraniums, and garden perennials in a 34-page booklet that doesn't delve into descriptions. Common name, botanical name, and price; that's all you get. Among the many strengths on the list are almost 50 thymes, 38 varieties of rosemary, and 34 different lavenders. The scented geraniums are offered in a range of more than 80 named varieties. Bunches of dried flowers and a handful of herb seeds are also available.

West Kootenay Herb Nursery
Rt. 2, Bedford Road, Nelson, BC, Canada V1L 5P5
Telephone: 604-352-9479

Catalog price: $1 (Canadian customers only)

More than 100 herb plants gathered in a plain, homespun booklet and listed alphabetically, from agrimony to yerba buena. Owing to "consistent bad luck" with the U.S. postal service, the firm no longer ships beyond Canadian borders. Gardeners to the north may find plenty to sniff through here, however.

Wyrttun Ward
Beach Street RFD, Middleboro, MA 02346
Telephone: 617-866-4087

Catalog price: $1

Wyrttun Ward is not the exotic name of this nursery's owner. It means "herb keeper," *wyrttun* being an archaic Anglo-Saxon word for "herbs." The lavender-colored descriptive catalog is evenly split between herb and wildflower offerings, listing about 100 of each. All plants are shipped in 3-inch pots. Among the herbs are such edible flavorings as French tarragon, sweet cicely, and thyme, dye plants like woad and bedstraw, and a number of medicinal herbs. The wildflower list includes Dutchman's breeches, showy ladyslipper, toadflax, and mayapple.

Hostas

Busse Gardens
See under *Garden Perennials*, page 86.

Caprice Farm
See under *Peonies*, page 135.

Donnelly's Nursery
Rt. 7, Box 420, Fairview, NC 28730
Telephone: 704-298-0851

Catalog price: free

Fifty hosta varieties, from Antioch to Zounds. Each offering is described in a few words that manage to conjure up a rough picture of the foliage and flower. A smaller list of ivies is presented with a more cursory text.

Eco-Gardens
See under *Garden Perennials*, page 87.

Englerth Gardens
See under *Daylilies*, page 78.

Fairway Enterprises (Garden Division)
114 The Fairway, Albert Lea, MN 56007

Catalog price: long self-addressed stamped envelope

Three dozen hosta cultivars typed out in a simple descriptive list. Most of the 1987 offerings were Minks, Aden, and Smith hybrids, and most were priced between $20 and $50 a plant.

Hatfield Gardens
See under *Daylilies*, page 78.

Hildenbrandt's Iris Gardens
See under *Irises*, page 110.

Holiday Seeds
4276 Durham Circle, Stone Mountain, GA 30083
Telephone: 404-294-6594

Catalog price: $1 in cash or stamps

A hosta specialist who also dabbles in ferns, irises, lilies, and daylilies. Forty hosta cultivars and species are typed out on the main list with the basic particulars as to foliage and bloom. Several new introductions that are relatively expensive ($25 to $50) merit a few extra words of description and praise. Most of the hostas can be bought as either plants or seeds, though the seed end of the operation may not last

much longer, to judge by the discouraged note we received from the proprietors. The 1987 list carried about 20 daylily cultivars offered as plants and an equal number, with named parents, as seeds. Other unnamed daylilies are offered as seedlings at bargain rates, as are unlabeled hostas, bearded and Siberian irises, and lilies. A small fern selection rounds out the list; these include lady, Christmas, Japanese painted, and Japanese climbing ferns.

Homestead Division of Sunnybrook Farms
9448 Mayfield Road, Chesterland, OH 44026
Telephone: 216-729-9838

Catalog price: $1

In 1986 the Homestead Division moved its operation into a new building. The reason: co-owner Jean Ruh's sheep had completely taken over the old shed. The Ruhs sell more than 150 hosta species and cultivars in a clear descriptive list that includes the requisite notes on foliage and flower and occasionally gives some background on parentage and history. Several other shade-tolerant plants are offered, among them nearly 100 English ivies, a handful of epimediums (which like even deeper shade than hostas), and Japanese painted ferns. More than 50 daylilies are also listed, to fill in brighter spots.

Iron Gate Gardens
See under *Daylilies*, page 79.

Jernigan Gardens
See under *Daylilies*, page 79.

Klehm Nursery
See under *Peonies*, page 135.

Maroushek Gardens
120 E. 11th Street, Hastings, MN 55033
Telephone: 612-437-9754

Catalog price: 50¢

Eighty hosta species and cultivars make up the mail-order branch of this perennial nursery. Foliage and flower are decribed in short notes, and an introduction explains how to care for the plants. A few new hybrids are offered for collectors at prices well above the reasonable level of the bulk of the list. A good selection of rock-garden perennials and clematis vines can be bought at the nursery (but not by mail).

Moldovan's Gardens
See under *Daylilies*, page 79.

Piedmont Gardens
533 Piedmont Street, Waterbury, CT 06706
Telephone: 203-754-8534 or 3535

Catalog price: 50¢

Sixty-five hosta varieties, divided in a descriptive list into large- and small-leaf categories. Some of the featured hybrids are the firm's own creations. Older varieties are offered at very good rates—quite a few for $2 or less a plant. The nursery also sells a few wildflowers and ferns for shade planting.

Powell's Gardens
350 hosta cultivars. See under *Garden Perennials*, page 90.

Rocknoll Nursery
See under *Alpines and Rock-Garden Perennials*, page 42.

Savory's Greenhouses
5300 Whiting Avenue, Edina, MN 55435
Telephone: 612-941-8755

Catalog price: $1

This neat catalog describes more than 250 hosta varieties and pictures a few of them in color. The nursery is as active in hybridizing as it is in production growing, and a good number of the offerings are its own introductions. Prices range from a low of $3 for common types like *H. undulata* 'Erromena' and *H. lancifolia* to $50 and $75 for a few of Savory's newer hybrids.

Shady Oaks Nursery
See under *Shade Plants*, page 146.

Soules Garden
See under *Daylilies*, page 81.

Stillpoint Gardens
See under *Shade Plants*, page 146.

Valente Gardens
See under *Daylilies*, page 82.

Andre Viette Farm & Nursery
See under *Garden Perennials*, page 92.

Houseplants

Arthur Eames Allgrove
P.O. Box 459, Wilmington, MA 01887
Telephone: 617-658-4869

Catalog price: 50¢

Terrarium lovers should know about this man, a genuine New England eccentric, and his wealth of offerings. Allgrove's charming, chatty brochure ("Talk about a busy year. Well, this has been the one to beat all," he reports in his foreword) features fully stocked terrariums as well as the ingredients for stocking them yourself, if you care to. Partridgeberry, rattlesnake plaintain, shining club moss, striped pipsissewa, shinleaf, and rainbow fern are all for sale. In addition, the nursery handles handcrafted sheet moss and grapevine baskets and wreaths, perfect for a touch of cheer over the holidays.

Color Farm
2710 Thornhill Road, Auburndale, FL 33823
Telephone: 813-967-9895

Catalog price: 50¢

Almost 100 coleus cultivars, either heirlooms or modern crosses from old-fashioned parents. Catalog entries are arranged by color.

C. A. Cruickshank
See under *General Flowers and Vegetables*, page 16.

Davidson-Wilson Greenhouses
Rt. 2, Crawfordsville, IN 47933
Telephone: 317-364-0556

Catalog price: free

This eye-opening catalog presents an exotic range of houseplants, with special strengths in geraniums and African violets. Hundreds of flowers are listed, many with accompanying color photographs. From nutmeg-scented geraniums and chocolate-brown Lady Washingtons to white and deep red violets, the range of choice is amazing. Begonias, impatiens, and fuchsias are also available.

Dunford Farms
P.O. Box 238, Sumner, WA 98390

Catalog price: free

A postcard introduces you to the complete inventory here: three varieties of agapanthus and alstroemeria.

French's, Bulb Importer
Houseplant seeds. See under *Bulbs*, page 61.

Greenlife Gardens Greenhouses
See under *Epiphyllums and Hoyas*, page 83.

International Growers Exchange
See under *General Flowers and Vegetables*, page 21.

Kartuz Greenhouses
1408 Sunset Drive, Vista, CA 92083
Telephone: 619-941-3613

Catalog price: $2

Gesneriads and begonias crowd the pages of this catalog, illustrated with occasional line drawings. Most of the gesneriad genera are represented—achimenes, episcia, lysionotus, sinningia, saintpaulia, and others—along with an enticing selection of begonias, miniature plants for terrariums, and unusual tropicals for indoor growth (or for outdoor container culture). The firm sells almost 500 begonia and gesneriad varieties and species.

Lauray of Salisbury
Undermountain Road, Salisbury, CT 06068
Telephone: 203-435-2263

Catalog price: $2

A rich resource for those who have advanced beyond the novice stage of gardening, this 50-page catalog brims with more than 1,000 orchids, begonias, gesneriads, succulents, and cacti. Each plant is evoked in a few words. Browsers would be well advised to look elsewhere—there is not a single photograph to linger over—but serious gardeners can tap a wealth of offerings here. Minimum order is $10.

Lifetime Nursery Products
1866 Sheridan Road, Highland Park, IL 60035
Telephone: 312-432-0830

Catalog price: free

A quarantine on Florida citrus trees has cut deeply into the offerings of this nursery since 1985. As of this writing, the firm sells amaryllis and daffodil bulbs and ficus (fig) trees.

Logee's Greenhouses
See under *Begonias*, page 51.

Marvelous Minis
Terrarium and dish-garden plants. See under *African Violets and Other Gesneriads*, page 36.

Merry Gardens
P.O. Box 595, Camden, ME 04843
Telephone: 207-236-9460

Catalog price: $2 (specify houseplant list)

A homespun catalog detailing several hundred houseplants. Flowering plants (including aubutilon, acacia, oleander, and impatiens), oxalis, vines, gesneriads, foliage plants, and ferns and mosses are the key headings here. Telegraphic descriptions abound, and simple line drawings give a general idea of what a handful of the offerings look like. The firm also publishes an herb plant list for $1 (see entry under *Herbs*, page 101).

Michigan Bulb Co.
See under *Garden Perennials*, page 90.

Miniature Plant World
45638 Elder Avenue, Box 7, Sardis, BC, Canada V2R 1A5
Telephone: 604-795-3492

Catalog price: $2

What can you say about a catalog that advises you to play country music for your miniature roses? This is a quirky, offbeat booklet from a nursery that's specialized in miniatures since 1971. Offerings include several hundred shamrocks, roses, succulents, bonsai plants, and ivy vines for use in terrariums and dish gardens. The tone of the booklet is scruffy and informal, as though you were being led through a greenhouse by its rumpled owner. ("Oh, here we are at the potting bench," the writer remarks at one point. "'Scuse me while I clear away these empty coffee cups and apple cores.") Line drawings and black-and-white photographs supplement the text.

The Plant Kingdom
Box 7273, Lincoln Acres, CA 92047
Telephone: 619-267-1991

Catalog price: $1

A densely printed 30-page catalog sans photographs, this reference booklet will be most useful to the expert gardener. Nearly 1,000 varieties are available, including begonias, gesneriads, miniature and dwarf plants, rare and exotic specimens (acalyphas, durantas, and iochromas, among others), bonsai, and vines. Patrick J. Worley, the mastermind behind all this propagation, describes the catalog as "an almost bewildering selection of plants," and he's certainly got that right. Knowledge of basic horticultural techniques is presumed; not a good bet for the beginner.

Rhapis Gardens
P.O. Box 287-PB, Gregory, TX 78359
Telephone: 512-643-2061

Catalog price: $1

A classy, distinctive catalog from a nursery that specializes in named cultivars of *Rhapis excelsa*, a miniature palm.

Originally imported to Japan from China in the 1600s and reserved for use among the Japanese nobility, these small ornamental palms have since become prized for their beauty, versatility, and long life. Dozens of varieties are featured (and pictured) in this carefully detailed catalog. In addition to rhapis palms, the 30-page booklet lists several tropical cousins—including polyscias, cissus, and cycas—as well as designer pots to plant them in.

Rhapis Palm Growers
31350 Alta Vista, P.O. Box 84, Redlands, CA 92373
Telephone: 714-794-3823

Catalog price: $2

A select offering of more than 50 rhapis palms. Each variety is clearly described, and about half are pictured in an accompanying booklet of color photographs—unfortunately, printed in Japanese. These exquisite, slow-growing dwarfs do not come cheap (many list for several hundred dollars or more), but they are said to bring pleasure for a lifetime.

Springhead Gardens
See under *Daylilies*, page 81.

Irises

Adamgrove
Rt. 1, Box 246, California, MO 65018

Catalog price: $1

A big descriptive catalog of irises and daylilies, with black-and-white photographs of featured plants. In 1987 the firm took charge of the iris inventory of the late David Sindt, including his small bearded hybrids and a strong collection of iris species. Seventy species and wild-collected variants are listed, among them more than a dozen strains of the tiny *Iris pumila*. The nursery also carries a big inventory of dwarf and miniature iris hybrids. More than 100 dwarf bearded iris cultivars are offered, and more than 30 *pumila* hybrids. Two hundred cultivars make up the daylily list, among them some unusual doubles. Adamgrove was particularly proud of one 1987 introduction with a bloom color it described as "the fiery black of a charred log." Bearded irises are shipped in July and August, beardless irises and daylilies in August and September.

Aitken's Salmon Creek Garden
608 NW 119th Street, Vancouver, WA 98685
Telephone: 206-573-4472

Catalog price: $1, deductible from first order

A nicely balanced selection of irises that includes a smattering of Siberian, Japanese, and Pacific Coast varieties along with a wealth of bearded strains. Black-and-white photographs supplement the minimal text.

American Daylily & Perennials
Louisiana irises. See under *Daylilies*, page 76.

Anderson Iris Gardens
22179 Keather Avenue N., Forest Lake, MN 55025
Telephone: 612-433-5268

Catalog price: free

Several hundred tall bearded irises sway through these 18 typewitten pages with notes on petal colors and blooming times. The 1987 prices ranged from $25 (for the hot red Cayenne Pepper) to $2 for a number of older introductions. The nursery also offers about 50 different peonies.

Avonbank Iris Gardens
Radford University, P.O. Box 5691, Radford, VA 24142
Telephone: 703-639-1333

Catalog price: free

A chatty, informal catalog offering several dozen tall bearded irises, with a stress on remontant (reblooming) and remontant-bred types. Each flower merits a fat paragraph of discussion, often featuring personal remarks. "This iris pleases me more each year," a sample entry confides. "It is very faithful and prolific both spring and fall. The light creamy-yellow flowers do not carry their color far, but are admirable at close range." A handful of "space-age" irises (horned, spooned, and flounced) are also listed here.

Baldwin's Iris Gardens
621 S. Third Avenue, Walla Walla, WA 99362

Catalog price: $1

Almost 400 tall bearded irises, supplemented by a somewhat smaller group of shorter cultivars. Each plant is described in an abbreviated entry.

Barnee's Garden
See under *Daylilies*, page 77.

Bay View Gardens
1201 Bay Street, Santa Cruz, CA 95060
Telephone: 408-423-3656

Catalog price: $1

Hundreds of irises neatly packaged in a 16-page catalog with a color shot on the cover. Bearded varieties predominate, but the beardless selection includes Pacific Coast, Louisiana ("the most vibrant colors in irisdom"), and spuria types. A clever grouping scheme descends the ladder from elite through chic, contemporary, and classic before landing in universal—the cheapest category of all.

Borbeleta Gardens
See under *Lilies*, page 117.

Brand Peony Farm
See under *Peonies*, page 135.

Randy and Shelley Brown's Iris Garden
186 W. 800 N., Sunset, UT 84015
Telephone: 801-773-8067

Catalog price: one first-class stamp

A big array of 200 plus tall, standard, and dwarf bearded irises laid out in a fine-print brochure. Each entry is simply described.

Brown's Sunnyhill Gardens
Rt. 3, Box 102, Milton-Freewater, OR 97862
Telephone: 503-938-3010

Catalog price: free

A mixed roster of bearded irises on a five-page typed list. Tall varieties grab the lion's share of the listings; border and intermediate types sneak in every so often. Apart from the slate of recent introductions, which garner a paragraph each, descriptions here are terse.

Busse Gardens
See under *Garden Perennials*, page 86.

Cal Dixie Iris Gardens
14115 Pear Street, Riverside, CA 92504
Telephone: 714-780-0335

Catalog price: $1

A dense compendium of tall bearded irises, beginning with select varieties and dropping through successively cheaper rungs to a group of 300 varieties bargain priced at $1.50. Those willing to pay more can choose from more than 1,000 other names higher up the price scale (which tops out with a few $25 selections). Border, intermediate, and standard dwarf bearded varieties make up smaller categories. The list ends with a selection of arilbred irises (hybrids of bearded and aril types). All listings, even for the cheapest offerings, include a few words on the bloom characteristics.

Cape Iris Gardens
822 Rodney Vista Boulevard, Cape Girardeau, MO 63701

Catalog price: free

This smartly detailed catalog covers the iris waterfront. Several dozen recent introductions are described at length, and then hundreds of other tall bearded introductions tick past in a more cursory fashion. Dwarf, intermediate, and border bearded; Siberian; and spuria varieties round out the list. A very few iris species are offered in a note almost hidden on the last page.

Caprice Farm
See under *Peonies*, page 135.

Chehalem Gardens
P.O. Box 693, Newberg, OR 97132-0693
Telephone: 503-538-8920

Catalog price: free

Fanciers of spuria and Siberian irises will want to delve into the offerings here, presented with copious notes on cultivation and care. Listings are divided about half and half between the two camps—55 and 47 varieties, respectively. Each plant merits a line or two of text.

Comanche Acres Iris Gardens
Rt. 1, Box 258, Gower, MO 64454
Telephone: 816-424-6436

Catalog price: $1

In 1987 Comanche Acres bought the iris stock of Gilbert H. Wild & Son and that year included the colorful pages of the Wild catalog along with its own more modest brochure. We're not sure how the catalog will be handled in 1988. The Comanche Acres inventory now includes several hundred tall and border bearded irises, several dozen smaller bearded types, and a nice selection of Louisiana irises. All offerings are well described using a code system and a few evocative words.

Cooley's Gardens, Inc.
P.O. Box 126, Silverton, OR 97381
Telephone: 503-873-5463

Catalog price: $2, deductible from first order

A silken gallery of blooms, this catalog is a pleasure to hold—and behold. Sixty-five slick pages proffer hundreds of life-size color shots, arranged as frames around paragraphs of descriptive text. Tall bearded irises only.

Cooper's Garden
212 W. County Road C, Roseville, MN 55113
Telephone: 612-484-7878

Catalog price: one first-class stamp

Siberian iris, Louisiana iris, and wild iris species in a specialist's list with only brief descriptions. The species list is extensive, and the collector will undoubtedly find some treasures here. A few wild lily species are also offered, along with more than 70 daylily cultivars (at good prices) and a rich selection of garden perennials. Bulb fanciers can send a self-addressed stamped envelope in the summer for a separate list of daffodils.

Cottage Gardens
11314 Randolph Road, Wilton, CA 95693
Telephone: 916-687-6134

Catalog price: 25¢

Honest Abe would feel utterly at home in this plain cabin, where everyone is bearded and tall. Several hundred varieties are presented simply and clearly across 12 pages. The nursery's latest introductions emerge in great detail; otherwise the adjectives are used sparingly.

Country View Gardens
13253 McKeighan Road, Chesaning, MI 48616
Telephone: 517-845-7556

Catalog price: long self-addressed stamped envelope

A lucid array of more than 350 bearded irises, with special depth in medians and dwarfs. The listings are arranged according to plant height—beginning at the miniature dwarf bearded level and working up to the tall types. No orders accepted after August 1.

Carrie Criscola
Rt. 2, Box 183, Walla Walla, WA 99362
Telephone: 509-525-4841

Catalog price: one first-class stamp

Gardeners who know their way around the iris plot may want to peruse these listings; novices won't be able to figure them out. More than 500 flowers are listed by name alone. The majority here are tall bearded types; a single page of dwarfs and intermediates suffices for fanciers of smaller plants.

C. A. Cruickshank Inc.
See under *General Flowers and Vegetables*, page 16.

Deming Iris Gardens
4122 Deming Road, Everson, WA 98247
Telephone: 206-592-5008

Catalog price: $1

A fat little booklet containing hundreds of bearded iris cultivars from tall to miniature dwarf types. Descriptive text is thorough. A handful of blurry black-and-white photographs provide some visual relief. Japanese, *chrysographes* (a species native to China), and Pacific Coast iris seedlings are also offered.

Englerth Gardens
Siberian irises. See under *Daylilies*, page 78.

Ensata Gardens
9823 E. Michigan Avenue, Galesburg, MI 49053
Telephone: 616-665-7500

Catalog price: one first-class stamp

Japanese irises predominate in this thin catalog. More than 100 cultivars are briefly listed and described, supplemented by about 15 Siberians. For those baffled by the selection, the nursery pitches a representative mix of ten—singles, doubles, pastel, dark, and white—at a bargain rate.

Ferncliff Gardens
See under *Dahlias*, page 74.

Foss Iris Gardens
6045 St. Croix Avenue, Minneapolis, MN 55422
Telephone: 612-545-5107

Catalog price: free

A straightforward booklet presenting a modest clump of bearded irises side by side with an even smaller bunch of daylilies. Plants come listed by varietal name and several words of description; "hardy Minnesota" iris strains are featured.

Garden of the Enchanted Rainbow
Rt. 4, Box 439B, Killen, AL 35645
Telephone: 205-757-1518

Catalog price: one first-class stamp

Several hundred bearded irises—"classics," medians, and rebloomers—are densely listed here. Entries have been coded to reveal blooming times, appropriate soil (alkaline or acidic), and hardiness. Flower colors are described in two or three words.

Gardenimport
See under *General Flowers and Vegetables*, page 19.

Grandview Iris Gardens
HC 86, Box 91, Bayard, NE 69334
Telephone: 308-586-1471

Catalog price: one first-class stamp

A full roster of about 400 tall bearded irises, described by color only and offered at attractive prices (from $1.50 to $8.00 in 1987). A rack of bargain specials are sold at even lower rates.

Hahn's Rainbow Iris Garden
200 N. School Street, Desloge, MO 63601
Telephone: 314-431-3342

Catalog price: $1, deductible from first order

This personable catalog features a bright hand-colored cover in four shades of ink. Inside, 1,000 or so iris varieties—overwhelmingly tall and border bearded types—spill forth in dot-matrix print. A tiny selection of smaller bearded cultivars, together with 70 or 80 daylilies, winds things down on a more manageable note.

Hamner's Iris Gardens
960 N. Perris Boulevard, Perris, CA 92370
Telephone: 714-657-3501

Catalog price: free

A colorful slate of 100 plus tall bearded cultivars on five pages of various pastel hues. A single alphabetical listing contains most of the specimens; following the general list, a "quality collection" department offers several others at reduced cost. Descriptions here range from very short ("ruffled medium blue self") to quite detailed, especially for the new introductions.

Hatfield Gardens
See under *Daylilies*, page 78.

Hildenbrandt's Iris Gardens
HC 84, Box 4, Lexington, NE 68850-9304
Telephone: 308-324-4334

Catalog price: two first-class stamps

More than 1,000 bearded irises listed in rudimentary fashion, with a heavy emphasis on tall types. Most varieties are mentioned by name alone; others receive a snippet of description. Oriental poppies, peonies, hostas, and lilies supplement the iris fare.

Holiday Seeds
Unlabeled seedlings. See under *Hostas*, page 104.

Hortico, Inc.
See under *Garden Perennials*, page 89.

Illini Iris
Rt. 3, Box 5, Monticello, IL 61856
Telephone: 217-762-3446

Catalog price: $1

Siberian and bearded iris varieties mixed with peonies and daylilies in a spirited listing. More than 100 cultivars, most of them irises, blossom on the four pages of the brochure. The stamp of the proprietor's personality sneaks into the text here and there—the language transcends the botanical. One iris is described as looking "pink from afar," and another new introduction has been "named for my favorite Dixieland song." One could do worse than to order flowers from a man who has the nerve to name an iris "Muskrat Ramble."

Imperial Flower Garden
Beardless irises. See under *Garden Perennials*, page 89.

Inter-State Nurseries
See under *Trees and Shrubs*, page 156.

Iris

109 Sourdough Ridge Road, Bozeman, MT 59715

Catalog price: 25¢ or long self-addressed stamped envelope

A smallish band of hardy mountain-grown irises, suited for gardens that endure cold winters. The nursery owner dubs them "survivors" in her opening line. Bearded varieties grouped by color of bloom occupy two simply typed pages here. Seven of the 70 or more listings are Dykes Medal winners.

Iris Acres

Rt. 4, Winamac, IN 46996
Telephone: 219-946-4197

Catalog price: 50¢

More than 1,000 irises on a long typed list that looks more like the work of a gardener than of a secretary. Tall beardeds cover the first dozen sheets, and reblooming types follow. Descriptive text is marred by overstrikes and faint vowels; only a masochist would browse through these lines. On the other hand, irises do not grow from a typewriter. The nursery prides itself on the hardiness of its rhizomes and guarantees replacement if they fail.

Iris Country

118 S. Lincoln Street, Wayne, NE 68787
Telephone: 402-375-3795 or 4436

Catalog price: 50¢, deductible from first order

Approximately 500 tall bearded irises put forth with all the clarity and flair of a phone book. Listings are arranged alphabetically and printed small. Dotted lines connect the variety's name and . . . price. Especially vigorous and dependable varieties are marked with an asterisk.

The Iris Pond

7311 Churchill Road, McLean, VA 22101

Catalog price: $1

A generous selection of both bearded and beardless irises, spread over five closely printed pages. Bearded types predominate, but nearly 100 beardless Siberian, Japanese, and species irises give you your money's worth in that camp, too. Each listing receives a line of descriptive text. Introductory notes to the catalog explain that yes, the nursery plantings do in fact surround a large pond.

Iris Test Gardens

1010 Highland Park Drive, College Place, WA 99324

Catalog price: 50¢

More than 500 tall bearded irises laid out in a 16-page alphabetical list with minimal commentary. Many of the offerings are the nursery's own hybrids; double rimmers are a house specialty.

The J-Lot Gardens

1156 N. Main, Joshua, TX 76058
Telephone: 817-295-4074

Catalog price: two first-class stamps

An easygoing collection of cheaply priced spring-blooming and reblooming irises presented on separate stapled lists.

Roughly 150 alphabetical entries appear on each of the two lists, with the individual varieties described in a cursory fashion. The tone of the material is offhand and refreshingly casual. "Everybody makes mistakes and I am no exception," remarks the proprietor. "If you receive a plant which does not bloom true to name, write me, describe the bloom and I can usually give you its correct name as well as send the correct plant or refund your money."

Jernigan Gardens

See under *Daylilies*, page 79.

Joe Pye Weed's Garden

Jan Sacks & Marty Schafer, 45 Elm Street, Bedford, MA 01730
Telephone: 617-275-7723

Catalog price: free

This nursery has recently taken over handling Bee Warburton's iris introductions, which are displayed on a couple of typed pages. Siberians and median beardeds are the two largest categories here—carefully described and offered with enthusiasm.

Keith Keppel

P.O. Box 8173, Stockton, CA 95208
Telephone: 209-463-0227

Catalog price: 50¢

Several hundred irises offered in a tidy booklet. Tall beardeds dominate the list, but intermediate and border bearded types also show up under their own, much smaller headings. Listings are careful to note parentage; those irises that have been imported—usually from France and Australia—are noted with an asterisk.

Kirkland Iris Garden

725 20th Avenue W., Kirkland, WA 98033
Telephone: 206-828-4907

Catalog price: free

A generous spread of median bearded irises from a nursery that specializes in them. Little prior knowledge is presumed, and friendly explanations of unfamiliar terms and procedures abound.

Klehm Nursery

See under *Peonies*, page 135.

Laurie's Garden

41886 McKenzie Highway, Springfield, OR 97478
Telephone: 503-896-3756

Catalog price: one first-class stamp

Hundreds of beardless irises crowded onto four typed pages. Crested, Japanese (the largest single group), Siberian, and water irises (suitable for damp, acidic soils) are the chief seams in this botanical mine. Descriptive lines here have a quirky charm and reflect the kinks of the writer's personality. The typist renders one name as "Blashed Snow Ball" and then asks rhetorically, "Could that be splashed? Horrible name . . . lovely flower!" Mixed packets of seeds are available for each of the iris types. The nursery does not ship plants in the spring.

Long's Gardens

P.O. Box 19, Boulder, CO 80306
Telephone: 303-442-2353

Catalog price: free

More than 300 tall bearded irises presented in a catalog that is brisk and sensible, but minus allure. Varieties are listed alphabetically with scanty descriptions. A handful of "shorter-than-tall" interlopers appear at the back of the booklet. For gardeners who live within driving distance of Boulder, the nursery sponsors a bargain basement "you select and you dig" operation during the bloom season (late May and early June).

Louisiana Nursery

See under *Daylilies*, page 79.

Maple Tree Gardens

Ponca, NE 68770
Telephone: 402-755-2615

Catalog price: free

Siberian, arilbred, and bearded irises presented in a neatly typed brochure. Parentage, color of bloom, and plant size are noted in the terse descriptions for each variety. In addition to irises, the nursery sells more than 100 daylilies.

Maryott's Gardens

1073 Bird Avenue, San Jose, CA 95125
Telephone: 408-971-0444

Catalog price: $1

A profuse jumble of bearded irises fills this stout little catalog. Hundreds of tall, border, intermediate, and standard dwarf varieties appear, each one nicely described. A handful of photographs, including more than a dozen in color, lend appeal to the booklet.

Maxim's Greenwood Gardens

2157 Sonoma Street, Redding, CA 96001
Telephone: 916-241-0764

Catalog price: free

Page after page of irises in a broad range of types. Nearly 1,000 offerings baffle and bemuse the browser here: tall beardeds first and foremost, and medians. Maxim's also features more than 70 Japanese irises, 50 Louisiana varieties, as many Pacificas, a nice selection of Siberians, and a few spuria cultivars. Two dozen daylilies are also listed. Collections and cut-rate deals abound.

Meadowlake Gardens

Japanese irises. See under *Daylilies*, page 79.

Melrose Gardens

309 Best Road S., Stockton, CA 95205
Telephone: 209-465-8578

Catalog price: $1

A picture gallery that offers more than a dozen crisply photographed irises (in color) and vivid descriptions at every turn. Nearly 100 varieties are listed in a glossy brochure that unfolds to become a pleated guide to the iris world. Arilbred (an unusually rich selection), Louisiana, spuria, and bearded irises—they're all here for the picking. Most of the offerings are recent introductions, and prices tend to be on the high side.

Mid-America Iris Gardens

P.O. Box 12982, Oklahoma City, OK 73157
Telephone: 405-946-5743

Catalog price: $1

"With each year of growing iris comes more rewards than I could ever have imagined," writes owner Paul Black at the start of his genial and voluminous catalog. "New customers become tomorrow's friends and the friends I have are certainly one of the greatest rewards given to me." Next he dedicates the 34-page booklet to his sister and brother-in-law. All this generosity sets a sunny tone that lingers as you leaf through nearly 1,000 iris varieties (about ten percent of which are lusciously pictured in color). Tall beardeds predominate here, but smaller bearded types also get their due.

Miller's Manor Gardens

3167 E. U.S. 224, Ossian, IN 46777
Telephone: 219-597-7403

Catalog price: free

This catalog details 1,000 ways to happiness for bearded-iris fans. From miniature dwarf to tall, the bearded varieties parade past; aril-medians, Siberians, and a few species iris also appear on these 24 tightly packed pages, which average several words of description per specimen. More than 100 daylilies and almost as many daffodils claim turf at the back of the booklet.

Mission Bell Gardens

2778 W. 5600 South, Roy, UT 84067

Catalog price: free

A hearty selection of tall bearded irises that skips from Acapulco Gold ("ruffled deep yellow self") to Winterscape ("gorgeous blossoms of blue-white with orchid infusion, matching beards"). The several hundred varieties are clearly and precisely laid out. In addition to the tall guys, a handful of intermediate and border beardeds are listed. Minimum order $25.

Moonshine Gardens

P.O. Box 1019, Clearlake Oaks, CA 95423
Telephone: 707-998-3055 or 743-1570

Catalog price: free

Move over, Marcel Proust. This bearded-iris catalog brims with 500 exhaustively detailed descriptions that rival the jottings of the wan Frenchman in his cork-lined room. Each listing receives a fat paragraph of evocation that may include simple effusiveness, oblique anecdotes, botanical pondering, or rambling commentary. Rich reading for those who like to stay up late with a catalog. Rebloomers are a priority here, with roughly a third of the catalog entries falling into that camp.

Nicholls Gardens

4724 Angus Drive, Gainesville, VA 22065
Telephone: 703-754-9623

Catalog price: free

A small booklet containing both bearded and beardless irises, with almost 500 selections to choose from. All the bearded sizes get some room here, but the tall ones take precedence. The beardless sorts (Siberian, Louisiana, Japanese, and species) are limited to a single page. A hundred daylilies and almost 50 dahlias round out the selection. Prices are reasonable in all sections of the list. In 1988 the catalog will expand to include more extensive descriptions.

North Pine Iris Gardens

308 N. Pine, P.O. Box 595, Norfolk, NE 68701
Telephone: 402-371-3895

Catalog price: $1

More than 400 bearded irises in every size from tall to miniature dwarf, laid out with terse descriptions in a 24-page catalog. Tall varieties dominate the list, but the nursery carries a good selection of standard dwarf types.

Owl Ridge Alpines

Species irises. See under *Alpines and Rock-Garden Perennials*, page 41.

Pleasure Iris Gardens

425 E. Luna, Chaparral, NM 88021
Telephone: 505-824-4299

Catalog price: $1, deductible from first order

Hundreds of unusual iris varieties and species, with a special depth in arilbreds (nearly 200 are available here). A number of rarely offered oncocyclus and regelia species and hybrids comprise another intriguing section of the catalog. The rest of the territory is more familiar: tall and border beardeds, along with strong inventories of Japanese, Louisiana, Siberian, and spuria irises. Offerings tend to be simply described, but more general commentary is plentiful and welcome. Notes on aril iris culture, for example, explain that *aril* is a Greek word meaning "collar." The term refers to the little white collar found around the upper part of the seed.

Powell's Gardens

More than 1,000 bearded irises. See under *Garden Perennials*, page 90.

Rancho de la Flor de Lis

P.O. Box 227, Cerrillos, NM 87010

Catalog price: free

A hefty catalog with an original approach. This collection of more than 1,000 bearded irises is organized chronologically; it starts with the current year's introductions (as most catalogs do) and then spins backward by calendar blocks of five or ten years until it hits the 1930s. Some of the sections are Popularity Parade (1979–1970), Best of the Old (1969–1960), and Fabulous Forerunners (1959–1950). Entries are generously spaced on large white pages. There's plenty to ponder for any iris fancier—but especially one with a taste for floral history.

Redbud Lane Iris Garden

Rt. 1, Box 141, Kansas, IL 61933
Telephone: 217-948-5478

Catalog price: 40¢, deductible from first order

This nursery confesses right up front that it is just a "hobby" garden and doesn't have acres of irises to draw from—but the mom-and-pop owners certainly don't stint on the listings here. Approximately 1,000 iris selections jam the catalog. Tall bearded types get top billing, but smaller beardeds, Siberians, Japanese, and species iris ("*Do not* try to grow these unless you have a knowledge of their culture," warns the text) are all well represented. Almost 200 Louisiana iris cultivars are offered.

Rialto Gardens
1146 W. Rialto, Fresno, CA 93705

Catalog price: free

Scanning this adventurous catalog, which proffers "outstandingly different irises," one easily picks up a sense of mad scientists tinkering in the laboratory. To wit: "Many exciting developments have appeared in the seedling plots since last year. For TB irises we get ever closer to our goals in amoenas, bitones and bicolors based on yellow, orange and brown." Reblooming irises are the specialty here; the 100 or so varieties listed, as laden with exotic color as you might expect, have been starred to show which are the most dependable for spring and fall bloom. A smaller selection of tall beardeds concentrates on intense yellows and oranges.

Riverdale Iris Gardens
7124 Riverdale Road, Minneapolis, MN 55430
Telephone: 612-561-1748

Catalog price: $1, deductible from first order

A catalog organized like a family portrait, with the little ones crouched down front and the grownups standing behind them. The emphasis here is on hardy, diminutive types. Miniature dwarf bearded irises—in a choice of more than 100 varieties—lead off the listings. The standard dwarfs come next, then the intermediate and border bearded and the miniature talls. Five tall types bring up the rear.

Rocknoll Nursery
See under *Alpines and Rock-Garden Perennials*, page 42.

Rockytop Gardens
P.O. Box 41, Eagleville, TN 37060

Catalog price: free

Several hundred painstakingly detailed listings of tall bearded irises. Each flower gets politely dusted with enthusiasm and praise: "A real showoff in California last year . . ." one entry begins. "Beards are bronzy gold. Wide flower. Good bud count. Hooray!"

Schreiner's Gardens
3625 Quinaby Road N.E., Salem, OR 97303

Catalog price: $2, deductible from first order

Iris catalogs don't come any bigger or prettier than this. Page after page of silky photographs make one feel like grabbing a shovel and heading out back for some serious rhizome planting. Hundreds of bearded irises (mostly tall varieties) wheel past, their ruffles drooping into the margins. Descriptive text is vivid; entries are coded to reveal season of bloom, height of stem in inches, and any awards the variety may have earned. Special collections pop up at every turn.

Shepard Iris Garden
3342 W. Orangewood Avenue, Phoenix, AZ 85051
Telephone: 602-841-1231

Catalog price: $1

A collection nicely balanced among different iris types. The roster includes tall and median beardeds, arilbreds, Louisi-anas, and spurias. Descriptions are telegraphic and cultural notes brief.

Anthony J. Skittone
Japanese irises. See under *Bulbs*, page 63.

Skyline Farms
Rt. 3, Box 162, Whitewright, TX 75491
Telephone: 214-364-2840

Catalog price: one first-class stamp

A small slate of bearded and Louisiana irises. The beardeds number about 100 and are tersely described in one, two, or three words. On the beardless side are half a dozen introductions from hybridizer Joseph K. Mertzweiller, who developed the first tetraploid Louisiana iris. (His offerings here include both diploid and tetraploid types.) Minimum order is $20.

Bob Sobek
Box 3125, 37 River Street, Westford, MA 01886

Catalog price: long self-addressed stamped envelope

Standard dwarf, intermediate, and tall bearded irises are the fare on this one-page roster. All the offerings are Mr. Sobek's own introductions.

Sunset Iris Garden
269 Sunset Road S.W., Albuquerque, NM 87105
Telephone: 505-897-2220

Catalog price: $1

More than 400 tall bearded irises, simply laid out in a 21-page booklet. Blooms are carefully described for color, and reblooming varieties are so noted. The nursery specializes in "those varieties that are easy to grow and need no *special* care."

Tow Path Lane Gardens
Ken and Agnes Waite, 6 Tow Path Lane, Westfield, MA 01085

Catalog price: free

A quickie list featuring a few bearded varieties introduced since 1981. The modest prices from this home-style nursery include shipping and handling.

Tranquil Lake Nursery
See under *Daylilies*, page 81.

Valente Gardens
See under *Daylilies*, page 82.

Andre Viette Farm & Nursery
See under *Garden Perennials*, page 92.

The Vine and the Branch
11026 Steele Creek Road, Charlotte, NC 28217
Telephone: 704-588-1788

Catalog price: $1, deductible from first order

A dense 36-page compendium of mingled iris types, set off by a nice plot of daylilies. More than 200 tall bearded irises begin the listings here; each entry contains a line of text and a price, which may range from $2 to $25 or more. Dwarf, intermediate, and arilbred types receive brisk handling. Toward the end the ranks once again swell as Siberian, Louisiana, and Japanese irises trundle past. More than 100 daylilies round out the selection.

Wethersfield Iris Garden
Fred and Mary Gadd, 172 Main Street, Wethersfield, CT 06109
Telephone: 203-529-6036

Catalog price: long self-addressed stamped envelope

This stapled list offers more than 50 tall bearded, arilbred, and aril-median irises. An average of five or six introductions from each of the past ten years are gathered here and de-

scribed in exclusively botanical terms; no general remarks on culture or care embellish the basics.

Wright Iris Nursery
6583 Pacheco Pass Highway, Gilroy, CA 95020
Telephone: 408-848-5991

Catalog price: free

For those gardeners with an aversion to fine print, this catalog may be perfect; all the listings are banged out in capital letters. So you get "GOOD MORNING AMERICA . . . RUFFLED PALE BLUE SELF . . . $4," which may or may not be easier on the eyes. Roughly 150 tall bearded varieties are listed, with reblooming varieties marked as such. A separate list presents about 30 gladioli.

Ivies, Groundcovers, and Climbing Vines

Angelwood Nursery
12839 McKee School Road N.E., Woodburn, OR 97071
Telephone: 503-634-2233

Catalog price: free

More than 100 ivy cultivars listed by name only in a creatively produced brochure (three colored sheets are folded so that they fan out behind a narrow first page). The offerings are listed by categories—variegateds, heart shapes, oddities, fans, bird's-foot, curlies, miniatures, and ivy ivies—and no further descriptions are given. The nursery suggests that those who want to know more about the various cultivars offered write the American Ivy Society (see entry under *Societies and Associations*, page 250).

Bluestone Perennials
Groundcovers. See under *Garden Perennials*, page 86.

Conley's Garden Center
Groundcovers. See under *Wildflowers*, page 174.

Donnelly's Nursery
Ivies. See under *Hostas*, page 104.

Ernst Crownvetch Farms
Rt. 5, Meadville, PA 16335
Telephone: 814-425-7276 or 7897

Catalog price: free

Penngift crown vetch for use as a groundcover. This variety was discovered in 1954 by the Pennsylvania Agricultural Experimentation Station and has been widely tested and used since as an erosion-control plant on steep embankments and on slopes where the natural topsoil has been removed. Today

it is the crown vetch most commonly sold by groundcover nurseries. Ernst offers seed, seedlings in trays, and bare-root field-grown plants. The nursery offers seed for three other soil-conservation plants: Tioga deertongue, Lathco flatpea, and perennial sweetpea.

Evergreen Nursery
1220 Dowdy Road, Athens, GA 30606
Telephone: 404-548-7781 or 800-521-7267

Catalog price: free

Several liriope varieties for groundcover plantings, offered along with English ivy, *Vinca minor*, pachysandra, and such other "groundcovers" as daylily (in five colors, $2 per plant), hosta, mondo grass (*Ophiopogon japonicus*), and *Euonymus fortunei* 'Coloratus'. The various liriopes are described in the nursery's flier; the other plants are simply listed.

D. S. George Nurseries
2491 Penfield Road, Fairport, NY 14450
Telephone: 716-377-0731

Catalog price: free

Clematis vines in every hue from yellow and pink to lavender and purple. Forty named cultivars are written up in the nursery's brochure, and a few are pictured in color.

Gilson Gardens
P.O. Box 277, 3059 US Route 20, Perry, OH 44081

Catalog price: free

Dozens of groundcovers are offered in this neat little booklet, including some that stretch the definition of the term. Hostas and primulas, for example, can be found tucked between the dozens of English ivy and *Vinca minor* cultivars, and garden pinks are listed just after crown vetch. Other interesting selections include dwarf spirea, hardy prickly cactus, and a handful of sedums and sempervivums. All plants can survive zone 5 winters, but the nursery offers no other hardiness information.

Harris Seeds

Clematis plants. See under *General Flowers and Vegetables*, page 20.

Hatten's Nursery, Inc.

Bougainvillea plants. See under *Tropical Plants*, page 169.

Homestead Division of Sunnybrook Farms

Ivies. See under *Hostas*, page 104.

Ivies of the World

P.O. Box 408, Weirsdale, FL 32695
Telephone: 904-821-2201 (days) or 2322 (evenings)

Catalog price: $1.50

A wide-ranging list of ivies that should appeal to both beginners and collectors. Roughly 150 English ivies take up the bulk of the catalog, and shoppers can choose from dozens of gold or silver variegated types or from miniature, bird's-foot, heart-shaped, or curly varieties. The nursery also raises Japanese, Russian, Nepalese, Persian, and Canary Island ivies. Each species is introduced by a paragraph or so of text that explains cold hardiness and special cultural requirements. Each variety is treated to a sentence or two describing foliage and growth.

Miniature Plant World

Ivies. See under *Houseplants*, page 106.

Park Seed Co.

Clematis vines. See under *General Flowers and Vegetables*, page 26.

Peekskill Nurseries

Shrub Oak, NY 10588
Telephone: 914-245-5595

Catalog price: free

A groundcover grower that can supply pachysandra, *Vinca minor*, euonymus, Baltic ivy, and Bar Harbor juniper. All are offered in quantities small enough to cover a corner of the yard or large enough to blanket a roadside.

Perry's

P.O. Box 442, Carpinteria, CA 93013
Telephone: 805-684-5468

Catalog price: $3

More than 200 groundcovers presented in a bright color catalog that makes us wonder why anyone bothers with a lawn at all. From the lovely *Drosanthemum hispidum*, which makes a dense mat of purple blooms in spring, to mondo grass, zoysia grass, sedums, and violets, the list is full of groundcover ideas and solutions. Shoppers will have to order by the flat, and those outside the nursery's delivery area will have to pay an added charge for bare rooting and boxing.

The Plant Kingdom

Tender vines. See under *Houseplants*, page 107.

Prentiss Court Ground Covers

P.O. Box 8662, Greenville, SC 29604
Telephone: 803-277-4037

Catalog price: 25¢

Fifty plus groundcovers presented in a tidy but spare brochure. Several ivies, ajugas, jasmines, and liriopes are offered along with the expected pachysandra, *Vinca minor*, and euonymus. Each plant type is illustrated by a sharp little drawing, but no descriptions are offered, and the planting guide is written in general terms to cover all the listings.

Rice Creek Gardens

Groundcovers. See under *Alpines and Rock-Garden Perennials*, page 41.

Rocknoll Nursery

Groundcovers. See under *Alpines and Rock-Garden Perennials*, page 42.

Sunnybrook Farms Nursery

Ivies. See under *Herbs*, page 103.

Ter-El Nursery

Groundcovers. See under *Garden Perennials*, page 92.

Turnipseed Nursery Farms

P.O. Box 792, Fayettville, GA 30214
Telephone: 404-461-1654

Catalog price: free

A dozen types of groundcover, including English ivy, dwarf mondo grass, three ajuga cultivars, and several liriopes. The firm also sells a small selection of daylilies. A yellow variety—Buried Treasure—was offered at an attractive quantity price in 1987 to encourage its use in mass plantings.

Wayside Gardens

Clematis vines. See under *Garden Perennials*, page 92.

Lilies

B & D Lilies
330 P Street, Port Townsend, WA 98368
Telephone: 206-385-1738

Catalog price: $2

Lilies for the home garden bred both for disease resistance and beauty. Owners Bob and Diana Gibson think many lily buyers are taken in by strains developed for the cut-flower industry, which fall to disease after a couple of seasons in the home garden. Quotes from customers indicate that B & D has gained a satisfied clientele. Along with a big list of hybrids, the firm sells a number of rare species lilies from around the world, grown using modern tissue culture techniques.

Borbeleta Gardens
15974 Canby Avenue, Rt. 5, Faribault, MN 55021
Telephone: 507-334-2807

Catalog price: $3

A big color catalog of lilies, irises, daffodils, and daylilies. Lilies are Borbeleta's forte, and some of the nursery's introductions have gained worldwide acclaim. Almost 200 lily varieties are listed, and more than 50 are illustrated with color photographs. Some older types can be had for $15 a dozen, but prized new introductions can cost as much as $50 a plant. Lily bulbs are shipped in October, irises in July and August, and daylily plants through the summer.

Carroll Gardens
See under *Garden Perennnials*, page 87.

Dunhampton Lily Fields
Mt. Somers, No. 1 R.D., Ashburton, New Zealand

Catalog price: NZ$2

A small but intriguing color catalog for lily enthusiasts who feel the need to examine all corners for novelties and unusual introductions. Many of these plants are available at far less cost from domestic suppliers, but there may be a few surprises worth the extra trouble and expense.

Fairyland Begonia Garden
See under *Begonias*, page 51.

Gardenimport
See under *General Flowers and Vegetables*, page 19.

Russell Graham, Purveyor of Plants
Species lilies. See under *Garden Perennials*, page 88.

Hildenbrandt's Iris Gardens
See under *Irises*, page 110.

Holiday Seeds
Unlabeled seedlings. See under *Hostas*, page 104.

Oregon Bulb Farms
39391 S.E. Lusted Road, Sandy, OR 97055
Telephone: 503-663-3133

Catalog price: $2, deductible from first order

A gorgeous color catalog of hybrid lilies, each pictured in a sharp photograph that makes it seem more beautiful than any we've ever encountered in real life. Many of the crosses are the nursery's own, and some are simply spectacular. The firm has concentrated its efforts on the Asiatic types, which are among the easiest to care for. Smaller selections of aurelian and oriental hybrids are also sold.

Rex Bulb Farms
P.O. Box 774, Port Townsend, WA 98368
Telephone: 206-385-4280

Catalog price: $1

The biggest, the most extensive, and the most heavily illustrated of the lily catalogs, this fat little booklet should be read by anyone thinking of planting some special lilies. Rex offers more than 100 Asiatic hybrids, 50 oriental hybrids, and 25 Chinese and aurelian trumpet types. In addition, the firm offers an excellent selection of species lilies, from the North American *L. canadense* to an array of rarities from China, Japan, Korea, and Tibet.

Riverside Gardens
Rt. 5, Saskatoon, SK, Canada S7K 3J8
Telephone: 306-374-0494

Catalog price: free

Forty hybrid lilies, the bulk of them Asiatic types. Each variety is described in a sentence or two on the typed list. Bulbs are shipped from mid-September to mid-October only.

John Scheepers, Inc.
See under *Bulbs*, page 63.

Anthony J. Skittone
See under *Bulbs*, page 63.

Van Bourgondien Bros.
See under *Bulbs*, page 64.

Mushroom Spawn

Choice Edibles
584 Riverside Park Road, Carlotta, CA 95528
Telephone: 707-768-3135

Catalog price: long self-addressed stamped envelope

Spawn and cultures for growing morel mushrooms. The firm admits that "the procedure for growing any mushroom is unpredictable, at best, and for morels even more so." No guarantees are made, but if you're lucky, maybe you'll be able to produce your own delicacies.

Field & Forest Products
N3296 Kozuzek Road, Peshtigo, WI 54157
Telephone: 715-582-4997

Catalog price: free

An illustrated catalog of mushroom cultivation supplies that brings back memories of science lab. Petri plates, test tubes, potato agar—the firm sells the necessary equipment to get mushrooms started. The folks at Field & Forest are most interested in shiitake mushrooms, and they offer spawn for twelve different strains. Some have intriguing Japanese-sounding names like Three Aromas, Big Light, and West Wind, while the newer strains go by such clinical monikers as 841 and RA-32-E. The catalog offers a nice selection of books for both the mushroom grower and the mushroom hunter.

Fungi Perfecti
P.O. Box 7634, Olympia, WA 98507
Telephone: 206-426-9292

Catalog price: $2.50

Spawn for nearly 30 mushroom species, which, with care, luck, and the right equipment can grow into such exotic edibles as black morel, Baker's paddy straw, enoke-take, wood ear, king stropharia, and various strains of shiitake and oyster mushrooms. Just two pages of the fat catalog are given to spawn. The remaining 50 are stocked with a full laboratory of supplies and a selected library of books. With its inventory of autoclaves, innoculation syringes, sterile shoe shields, flasks, and test tubes, the catalog looks more like a source of hospital supplies than anything aimed at gardeners.

Mushroompeople
P.O. Box 159, Inverness, CA 94937
Telephone: 415-663-8504

Catalog price: $2

Shiitake mushroom spawn in strains for growing outdoors or in the greenhouse. All can be purchased either as plug spawn (¾-inch wooden plugs) or as sawdust spawn. The latter is a little less costly to buy, but will require expensive sterilization equipment to handle and grow. Petri plates, agar, and special shiitake cultivation tools are sold, along with a good collection of books.

Western Biologicals
P.O. Box 46466, Sta. G, Vancouver, BC, Canada V6R 4G7
Telephone: 604-228-0986

Catalog price: $2

Dozens of mushroom species offered either as spawn or as live culture (on malt or nutrient agar medium). Shiitake and oyster mushrooms are sold as log spawn. Supplies, chemicals, equipment, and books are offered to stock the grower's laboratory, and several pages of instructions offer guidance for growing each of the mushroom species sold.

Native Plants of Australia and South Africa

BioQuest International
P.O. Box 5752, Santa Barbara, CA 93150-5752
Telephone: 805-969-4072

Catalog price: $1

Bulbous plants native to South Africa, including a big selection of gladiolus species and many other hard-to-find treasures for the garden, greenhouse, and windowsill. Among the offerings are a dwarf lily-of-the-Nile cultivar, a handful of freesia species, and a choice of fragrant evening-flowering hesperantha.

Peter B. Dow & Company
P.O. Box 696, Gisborne, New Zealand 3800
Telephone: 64-79-83-408

Catalog price: $5

A seed list for the specialist, with almost 4,000 offerings. Seeds are listed by botanical name without description, and most are New Zealand natives or tropical species. Seeds are sold by the packet, by weight, or by count, and the smallest quantity sold for each species ranges in price from about $7 to more than $100. Customers can request the New Zealand native list, the cactus list, the shelter belt and tropical fruit list, the rare palm list, or the rhododendron and azalea list, each of which contains species not in the main catalog.

Feathers Wild Flower Seeds
P.O. Box 13, Constantia, South Africa 7848
Telephone: 27-21-742432

Catalog price: free

A computer printer set for the smallest character size has done some dastardly work here, but, if you give your eyes a rest every few lines, you can work your way through. The reward for the eyestrain is two pages chock-full of seeds for South African native plants, including several dozen protea species and as many leucaspermums, leucodendrons, and ericas (heaths). Seed for several other genera are offered in more limited arrays. Among these are agapanthus, gladiolus, lachenalia, polygala, watsonia, and tritonia.

Harold Grant
90 Wingewarra Street, Dubbo, NSW, Australia 2830
Telephone: 61-68-82-4003

Catalog price: three International Reply Coupons

Seeds of native Australian plants, mostly from western New South Wales, including more than 50 acacia species and al-

most as many eucalyptuses. Trees and shrubs dominate the list, but a dozen "forbs, tufted plants, bulbous plants, and herbaceous perennials" squeeze on near the end, along with about 20 "rockery and ground cover plants." All listings are by botanical name only; flower color is noted in a word or two, and a chart shows the flowering season for each plant.

International Seed Supplies
P.O. Box 538, Nowra, NSW, Australia 2541
Telephone: 61-44-218735

Catalog price: $2

A huge seed list, with hundreds of native Australian plants shuffled in among garden varieties and plants from other continents. Thirty banksia species are offered, along with more than 100 acacias and 200 plus eucalyptus trees and shrubs. Several pages of color highlight the blossoms of some of the more attractive and exotic plants. All listings are followed by a few words describing growth, flower, and cultural needs.

Nindethana Seed Service
RMB 939, Woogenilup, W.A., Australia 6324
Telephone: 61-98-541066

Catalog price: two International Reply Coupons

An extensive list of seeds for plants native to Australia, spanning wildflowers, trees, and shrubs, with many areas of strength in each. Offerings are listed by botanical name only, with no descriptive text.

Nooitgedag Disa Nursery
Disa species native to South Africa. See under *Orchids*, page 128.

D. Orriell, Seed Exporters
45 Frape Avenue, Mt. Yokine, Perth, Australia 6060
Telephone: 61-99-344-2290

Catalog price: $4 in cash

Several descriptive lists of seed for Australian native plants. More than 50 cold-hardy eucalyptus species make up one grouping, a much smaller array of Australian conifers another. Palms, cyads, proteas, acacias, tropical eucalyptus, and flowering perennials and annuals are also offered in profusion. In 1988 the firm will add two lists: one of native plants suitable for bonsai culture and another of pink-flowering small shrubs and plants.

Parsley's Cape Seeds
1 Woodlands Road, P.O. Box 1375, Somerset West,
South Africa 7130
Telephone: 27-24-51-2630

Catalog price: $1 in cash

Seed for hundreds of South African native wildflowers, trees, and shrubs, including a number of gladiolus species. The main list leaves out ericas, pelargoniums, and Proteaceae, which have been assembled on separate lists sent on specific request. The erica list covers more than 100 species, with notes on flower color, shape, plant size, and bloom season. The Proteaceae list includes several genera and dozens of species, and draws in a number of banksia species from Australia. Like the main seed list, the Proteaceae list refers to plants by botanical name only, without description.

Protea Seed & Nursery Suppliers
See under *Proteas*, page 137.

Rust-En-Vrede Nursery
P.O. Box 231, Constantia, South Africa 7848
Telephone: 27-21-74-2574

Catalog price: free

A big list of seeds and bulbs for native South African plants, including many Amaryllidaceae and dozens of agapanthus,

lachenalia, pelargonium, gladiolus, moraea, and watsonia species, all listed by botanical name only. Disa species and hybrids are also offered.

Anthony J. Skittone
Seed for Australian natives. See under *Bulbs*, page 63.

Von Lyncker Nurseries Ltd.
P.O. Box 18200, Wynberg, South Africa 7824
Telephone: 27-21-72-8134

Catalog price: free

A small list of seed for plants indigenous to South Africa, among them several protea and erica species. Offerings from a smattering of other genera include *Watsonia marginata*, *Sparaxis elegans*, *Gloriosa virescens*, and *Podalyria calyptrata*.

West Australian Wildflower Society
Seed Catalog, P.O. Box 64, Nedlands, West Australia 6009

Catalog price: two International Reply Coupons

A lengthy list of seeds for native Australian plants, presented by botanical name only. Among the offerings are more than 80 eucalyptus species and almost as many banksias, melaleucas, and acacias. The list spans some 600 species from scores of different genera.

Orchids

A & P Orchids
Peters Road, Swansea, MA 02777
Telephone: 617-675-1717

Catalog price: free

A straightforward compendium of several hundred orchids, from a nursery that specializes in paphiopedilums. The catalog is sensibly organized by simple and complex hybrid groupings: brachypetalum primary hybrids, complex paphiopedilum hybrids, crosses with red expectancy, green to yellow crosses, and so forth. Cattleya meristems and seedlings are also featured here.

Alberts & Merkel Bros., Inc.
See under *Tropical Plants*, page 168.

Baker & Chantry Orchids
P.O. Box 554, Woodinville, WA 98072
Telephone: 206-483-0345

No catalog or price list

This nursery grows hundreds of masdevallias, paphiopedi-

lums, phragmipediums, and miltonias, but doesn't catalog them on a price list. Interested customers should write and describe what they are looking for, and the nursery will respond with what it has to offer. Some flasks are sold, but most plants are sold as blooming-size specimens.

The Beall Orchid Company
3400 Academy Drive, S.E., Auburn, WA 98002
Telephone: 206-735-1140

Catalog price: free

Several dozen orchid offerings fill these two precisely ordered pages. Mature cattleya seedlings top the list, followed by cattleya community pot specials (hybrids in groups of five or ten plants, sold at a discount), miltoniopsis, oncidium alliance intergenerics, and odontoglossums. Two or three lines of text underline the charms of each plant offered; exclamation points abound. "Very large burgundy flowers, many with black waterfall patterns," a sample entry begins. "These have been some of the most unusual waterfalls we've bloomed to date. One clone had a solid black lip! Excellent vigor in growth with strong spikes."

Bergstrom Orchids
494 Camino Manzanas, Thousand Oaks, CA 91360
Telephone: 805-495-1792

Catalog price: free

A small brochure teeming with several hundred jungle-collected orchids. Encyclias, epidendrums, laelias, and oncidiums are among the largest groupings here. The catalog offers fair warning on the condition of the plants listed. "Most of them are just coming from a tough existence and may be somewhat battered or chewed up," it admits. "Do not be put off by lack of some foliage or discoloration, as this is normal for newly collected plants."

The Big Island Plant Co.
405 W. Washington Street, Suite 89, San Diego, CA 92103
Telephone: 619-232-2600

Catalog price: free

Offers a few popular orchids, including dendrobiums and Atherton vandas, along with a handful of other tropical plants, such as plumerias and white ginger. The catalog was not ready by our press date, but, from our correspondence with the nursery, we expect it to be aimed at the general gardener rather than the specialist.

Boulder Valley Orchids
P.O. Box 45, Niwot, CO 80544-0045
Telephone: 303-444-2117

Catalog price: free

Cattleya and paphiopedilum flasks, listed on a score of pastel pages. Average price per orchid is about $50, but the nursery makes no apologies. "We know these flasks rank with some of the best crosses available in the world today," says the catalog, after disdaining "your usual run-of-the-mill" flowers.

Caribe Orchid Growers
P.O. Box 26, Carolina, PR 00628
Telephone: 809-728-5288

Catalog price: $1, deductible from first order

Here's the scoop from Puerto Rico: "Our greenhouses are located in the foothills of the 'El Yunque Rain Forest' where

tropical sun, constant high humidity and a cooling trade wind provide ideal growing conditions. The abundant sunshine we enjoy year-round helps our orchids to mature much faster, which allows us to sell at very competitive prices." Cattleya seedlings, meristems, mericlones, and miniatures head the list of more than 100 orchid offerings. Phalaenopsis, paphiopedilums, dendrobiums, and vandaceous hybrids and mericlones sway in the breeze toward the back of the catalog. "Beginner's specials" (a mix of three to six orchids selected by the nursery for ease of care) are featured within each general plant category.

Carter & Holmes, Inc.
1 Old Mendenhall Road, P.O. Box 668, Newberry, SC 29108
Telephone: 803-276-0579

Catalog price: $1

Carter & Holmes has been vending exotic blooms since 1943 and now ranks as one of the country's largest orchid suppliers. A small, elegant catalog details its current roster, which stresses the easy-to-grow cattleyas. More than 100 are offered, as mericlones or seedlings, and all are thoroughly described. A dozen delicately tinted photographs, framed in lustrous black at the center of the catalog, show the appeal of these extraordinary plants. Species and unusual hybrids, as well as phalaenopsis seedlings, are also available from the nursery's 16 greenhouses.

Cashen's Orchids
1701 S.E. Cypress Park Lane, Jupiter, FL 33478
Telephone: 305-744-1124

Catalog price: free

More than 100 orchid listings pack the pages of this informal catalog. Species, primary hybrids, mini and standard cattleya crosses, dendrobiums, vandas and ascocendas, and phalaenopsis claim typewritten entries on both sides of six stapled pages. Most are priced moderately, in the $10 to $20 range.

Cedar Hill Orchids
586 Natchez Bend Road, Nashville, TN 37221
Telephone: 615-646-6129

Catalog price: free

A clean, orderly list of nearly 1,000 orchids, including many rare specimens available in limited supply. Printed alphabetically on four sheets of paper, the offerings here show an unusually rich selection of masdevallias, but cattleyas, oncidiums, paphiopedilums, and other orchids balance things out nicely. Botanical names and prices are all you see. Cultural information sheets may be obtained for most major genera; the nursery will help beginners choose plants that are easy to grow.

Charles Island Gardens
P.O. Box 91471, W. Vancouver, BC, Canada V7V 3P2
Telephone: 604-921-7383

Catalog price: free

A modest, sharply focused brochure from a nursery that has taken odontoglossums to its heart. Nineteen hybrids are listed, many in a choice of sizes. In addition, a small batch of miniature cymbidiums, described as "some of the finest meristems from McBeans famous collection," are available in 4-inch pots. Plants sent from Canada to the United States will be shepherded through customs at the Canadian border and mailed—from Blaine or Bellingham, Washington—on a monthly basis.

Clargreen Gardens Ltd.
814 Southdown Road, Mississauga, ON, Canada L5J 2Y4
Telephone: 416-822-0992

Catalog price: $1

A strong array of orchid species (among them 30 paphiopedilums) fill the pages of this compact catalog, along with scores of phalaenopsis, cattleya, and odontoglossum hybrids. Orchid-growing supplies are also sold, including fertilizer, seedling mix, and tree fern boards. Minimum order is $45.

Cloud Forest Orchids
Box 370, Honokaa, HI 96727

Catalog price: free

Fifty orchid crosses of various genera, about evenly split between mericlones and seedlings, make up a list that's a model of simplicity. The Cloud Forest slate occupies a single sheet of paper, leaving just enough room at the bottom of the second side for the nursery owners to sign off with "Aloha and good growing."

Coastal Gardens
137 Tropical Lane, Corpus Christi, TX 78408
Telephone: 512-882-9896

Catalog price: free

A four-page listing of cattleyas, offered both as divisions and as seedlings, along with smaller groupings of phalaenopsis and dendrobiums. Plants are described adequately, in a few words, on the typed list.

Coes' Orchid Acres
4647 Winding Way, Sacramento, CA 95841
Telephone: 916-482-6719

Catalog price: free

Three separate stapled lists provide hundreds of options for the orchid lover: seedlings, rare plants, or blooming-size species and hybrids. Seedlings include cattleya, dendrobium, and oncidium hybrids. The second list covers "rare, awarded, and otherwise very desirable" paphiopedilum and phragmipedium plants; prices are correspondingly elevated. Assorted orchids (including aerangis, brassavola, and phalaenopsis species) round out the selection. Culture notes are free with every order.

Creole Orchids
P.O. Box 24458, New Orleans, LA 70184-4458
Telephone: 504-282-5191

Catalog price: free

Several hundred orchids fill the 15 pages of this catalog. Cattleya alliance claims the biggest single slice, followed by oncidium, vanda, paphiopedilum, dendrobium, cymbidium, and miscellaneous divisions. Both meristems and seedlings are available. All shipments sent priority airmail, out of pot, unless otherwise requested.

Dos Pueblos Orchid Co.
P.O. Box 158, Goleta, CA 93116
Telephone: 805-968-3535

Catalog price: free

A rich listing of more than 70 cymbidium hybrids sold as seedlings. Plants occupy either a 6- or an 8-inch pot and show a minimum of three bulbs. Each entry indicates size, color, and blooming season.

Drago Orchid Corp.
4601 S.W. 127th Avenue, Miami, FL 33175
Telephone: 305-554-1021

Catalog price: free

A six-page listing of cattleya hybrid seedlings, cattleya and laelia species meristems and bulb divisions, and blooming-size vandas—the products of the nursery's extensive breeding program. Seedlings are in 2-, 3-, or 4-inch pots; the vandas occupy 4-inch baskets. Minimum order is $50.

Elmore Orchids
324 Watt Road, Knoxville, TN 37922
Telephone: 615-966-5294

Catalog price: free

Fifty plus orchids presented in a simple descriptive list. Cattleya alliance seedlings and mericlones account for half the inventory; phalaenopsis, dendrobium, and oncidium seedlings balance it out. Pot sizes range from 2 to 5 inches.

Evon Orchids
P.O. Box 17396, San Diego, CA 92117
Telephone: 619-270-1827

Catalog price: free

Founded in 1967 as a grower of cattleya and phalaenopsis for the local cut-flower market, this nursery has since branched out to plant sales and other orchid genera. Ascocendas, cymbidiums, dendrobiums, miltonias, oncidiums, paphiopedilums, doritaenopsis, and vandas—most available in both blooming and seedling size—line the pages of the typed catalog. Listings are plainly set forth with a word or two on flower color. The few drawings give a basic idea of foliage and flower for each genus.

John Ewing Orchids

P.O. Box 1318, Soquel, CA 95073
Telephone: 408-684-1111

Catalog price: free

Phalaenopsis flasks, seedlings, and stem propagations are the fare in this small, neat catalog. The 40 flasks listed contain either 15–20 or 30–35 seedlings ready to be planted. The dozen or so stem propagations, which are true to their name (i.e., not meristems), have been taken from plants of proved quality. The more than 70 seedlings range in size from flats—destined to bloom in two or three years—to 6-inch pots, which should flower in the fall if planted by spring.

Exotics Hawaii, Ltd.

P.O. Box 10416, Honolulu, HI 96816
Telephone: 808-732-2105

Catalog price: long self-addressed stamped envelope

More than 50 mericlones and seedlings, listed in abbreviations that only experts will decipher easily. Cattleyas and dendrobiums account for the majority of the offerings. Most are available in either 2- or 6-inch pots, though a few can be had in community pots.

Farnsworth Orchids

606 N. Lanikai Place, Haiku, Maui, HI 96708
Telephone: 808-572-7528

Catalog price: free

Cattleyas in all shapes and sizes spread their charm through this enticing little booklet, complete with delicate line drawings spaced every few pages. Miniature cattleyas, which seldom grow taller than six inches, win top billing here—more than 40 are carefully described. Compact cattleyas claim 30 or so entries, followed by a modest selection of standard varieties for the traditionalist. A sprinkling of phalaenopsis, vandaceous orchids, and other genera ring the curtain down.

Fennell's Orchid Jungle

26715 S.W. 157th Avenue, Homestead, FL 33031
Telephone: 305-247-4824 or 800-327-2832 (orders only)

Catalog price: $2, $1 deductible from first order

An excellent beginner's booklet, clearly laid out, from a nursery that has been promoting orchid cultivation since its

founding in 1888 in Cynthiana, Kentucky. The catalog guides you through the sometimes baffling world of orchid selection and care; no previous knowledge is assumed. Beginning with "All you need is a sunny window," the text advances simply and deliberately to discuss how much light, water, food, and humidity the plants require. All orchids are listed by type and color, rather than by precise botanical name. Plant selection is left to the nursery, so you can order "your first vanda" or "your first dendrobium," but nothing more exact than that. Not for everyone, this in-loco-parentis approach fits the bill for those easily overwhelmed by orchidiana.

Florália Orquidários Reunidos Ltda.

P.O. Box 501, 24000-Niterói-RJ, Brazil
Telephone: 55-21-719-5800

Catalog price: free

Nursery-grown, flowering-size Brazilian species rub against cattleya alliance mericlones in this two-part catalog—a colorful photo gallery paired with a 25-page price list. Plant descriptions (printed in English) only occasionally trip over the lingual wire strung between the two cultures; mostly they are on the mark and nicely detailed. Laelias and oncidiums account for about half the species listings. Minimum order is $100.

Floratech, Inc.

P.O. Box 28623, Sacramento, CA 95829

A hundred or so orchid seedlings from a new nursery with special strength in phalaenopsis. Listings are color grouped: white, pink, striped, spotted, yellow, and miscellaneous. Several dozen phalaenopsis stem propagations make up a separate category in this somewhat hazy, computer-printed catalog. In addition, a few dendrobium and cattleya seedlings are offered.

Fordyce Orchids

7259 Tina Place, Dublin, CA 94568
Telephone: 415-828-3211 or 447-7171

Catalog price: free

A dense assortment of elite plants and seedlings intended for the hybridizer or connoisseur. "Our adult plant collection is composed primarily of breeding plants, purposely assembled over the years as either proven superior clones with breeding lines I embrace, or carefully selected clones that are as yet unproven as parents but possess great potential; and choice species," explains the unnamed spirit in charge of these several hundred fine-print listings. These orchids are expensive, with some prices shooting as high as $400. Hybridizers will know the ropes, but this is not a suitable garden path for beginners to traipse down.

Fox Orchids, Inc.

6615 West Markham, Little Rock, AR 72205
Telephone: 501-663-4246

Catalog price: free

A folksy 36-page encyclopedia that covers the orchid waterfront—and then some. Cattleyas, vandas, phalaenopsis, paphiopedilums, oncidiums, epidendrums, dendrobiums, intergenerics and miscellaneous plants fill the booklet. In addition, orchid fertilizers and flasking supplies are sold, along with corsages (pins, ribbon, cellophane, shredded wax paper, wire), orchid books, potting material (plant tags, plant sticks, weatherproof pencils), and a collection of reichenbachia orchid plates ("pictures you frame, not plates you eat off of," in the words of the catalog writer). Strictly organized, yet graced with notes of informality here and there, this catalog makes a reassuring pal for novice or intermediate orchidists. Advice is plentiful and to the point.

G & B Orchid Laboratory
2426 Cherimoya Drive, Vista, CA 92084
Telephone: 619-727-2611

Catalog price: free

A nicely balanced but hard-to-read catalog consisting of 15 pages of gray dot-matrix type. Phalaenopsis seedlings listed according to bloom color take up the first few pages, followed by cymbidium meristems, phalaenopsis stem propagations, and various flasks (including cymbidiums, dendrobiums, and phalaenopsis). Flasking and meristem media, chemical supplies, and laboratory glassware are available in profusion.

The Golden Orchid
9100 Fruitville Road, Sarasota, FL 34240-9259
Telephone: 813-377-1058

Catalog price: free

A six-page brochure showcasing nearly 50 orchid hybrids. Cattleyas and cattleya-type mericlones dominate the list; epidendrums, vandas, phalaenopsis, dendrobiums, and a lone catasetum complete the selection. Most plants are agreeably priced in the $5 to $10 range. Various mixed-grouping specials of six plants each offer bargain possibilities; gift certificates are also available.

Great Lakes Orchids
28805 Pennsylvania Road, Romulus, MI 48174
Telephone: 313-941-4696

Catalog price: free

A 26-page booklet dominated by orchid species, including many miniature types and strong selections of masdevallias and paphiopedilums. The several hundred offerings are nicely described, with country of origin, preferred climate, and

bloom season noted in each case. Phalaenopsis, cattleya, and oncidium hybrids are also offered in a range of sizes. Color photographs on the cover effectively whet the appetite.

Green Valley Orchids
Rt. 1, Box 233S, Folsom, LA 70437
Telephone: 504-796-5785

Catalog price: $1, deductible from first order

More than 100 phalaenopsis seedlings dominate the inventory here, listed by the names of the parent plants only and grouped by expected flower color. A few stem propagations and seed-grown phalaenopsis species are also sold, along with about three dozen cattleya alliance meristems and seedlings and a sampling from other genera.

Greenleaf Orchids
158 S. Winterset Avenue, Crystal River, FL 32629
Telephone: 904-795-3785

Catalog price: free

A closely printed typewritten list with chatty overtones. "For those of you who just want some nice, fat, healthy plants we offer the following," reads the text at the top of page one. After a few more words of offhand geniality, the catalog dives into specific deals. Cattleyas are the main order of business: meristems and seedlings in all colors and sizes. Less space is accorded phalaenopsis crosses and species, broughtonia meristems and hybrids, and vanda seedlings. About 200 offerings are splayed across eight pages.

Spencer M. Howard Orchid Imports
11802 Huston Street, N. Hollywood, CA 91607
Telephone: 818-762-8275

Catalog price: free

An exhaustive compendium of more than 500 orchids shoehorned into a 14-page booklet you must squint to decipher. The usual suspects have been rounded up: cattleyas, dendrobiums, epidendrums, laelias, odontoglossums, oncidiums, paphiopedilums, phalaenopsis, vandas, and zygopetalums. Most are offered as blooming-size plants, but a selection of seedlings have staked out some room at the back of the catalog. Plant descriptions include useful information on growing temperature and projected blooming season.

Huronview Nurseries & Garden Centre
1811 Brigden Side Road, Bright's Grove, ON, Canada
N0N 1C0
Telephone: 519-869-4689

Catalog price: free

A balanced, informal offering of more than 200 orchids drawn from the key families of cattleya alliance, oncidium, cymbidium, paphiopedilum, and phalaenopsis. Most plants are in the three- to six-year range. Prices are moderate, from $10 to $20 on the average. The mimeographed booklet also offers orchid supplies such as fertilizer, cork slabs, hanging baskets, wire stakes, sphagnum moss, and a quartet of reference books.

International Growers Exchange
See under *General Flowers and Vegetables*, page 21.

Islander Delights Orchids

14568 Twin Peaks Road, Poway, CA 92064
Telephone: 619-748-0731

Catalog price: free

Three hundred plus orchid hybrids crowd the typewritten pages of this list; oncidium, *Broughtonia sanguinea*, and small cattleya alliance types are featured. The nursery also offers a good collection of species orchids, both seed propagated and jungle collected. Plants are listed by name or parentage only, without description.

J & L Orchids

20 Sherwood Road, Easton, CT 06612
Telephone: 203-261-3772

Catalog price: $1, deductible from first order

Lovers of miniature orchids would be well advised to start their search for happiness in this tidy, voluminous catalog. Several hundred diminutive offerings unfold across 45 neat-as-a-pin pages. Plants that are especially easy to care for are marked as such in the listings; gracefully shaded line drawings on nearly every page add allure to the prose evocations. Masdevallia and dracula species and hybrids—in addition to a wide variety of unusual species gathered from around the world—complement the miniatures.

J & M Tropicals, Inc.

Rt. 1, Box 619-B, Cantonment, FL 32533
Telephone: 904-477-4935

Catalog price: free

A smallish list of plants presented without description. Thirty phalaenopsis seedlings are offered in a range of sizes, along with about 50 species of various genera in flowering size and a handful of vanda crosses. Orchid supplies—fertilizer, vitamins, ring stakes, and teak baskets—are also offered.

J. E. M. Orchids & Ornamentals

6781 165th Street S., Delray Beach, FL 33446
Telephone: 305-498-4308

Catalog price: free

The fruits of orchid crossbreeding fill this 12-page catalog. Oncidium intergenerics; micro, mini, and compact cattleya hybrids and species; dendrobium, phalaenopsis, and vandaceous intergenerics; and catasetum and miscellaneous crossbreeds are listed in abundance. According to the catalog, the crosses are all cold tolerant and enjoy moderate light and well-drained media.

Jemmco, Inc.

P.O. Box 23, St. George, SC 29477
Telephone: 803-563-2427

Catalog price: free

A brief selection of phalaenopsis hybrids sold in community pots for the orchid fancier seeking exotic strains. Proved parents like Capitola and Frank Gottburg are stressed in the breeding program. No descriptions are offered, but listings are categorized by bloom color. A few lines of introductory text explain each category's parentage and general characteristics, so you'll have some idea what you're ordering.

Jimni Orchids, A.C.C.

3738 W. Morten Avenue, Phoenix, AZ 85051
Telephone: 602-841-4767

Catalog price: free

A typed list of a few dozen "windowsill orchids," plants that the nursery claims "require less light, less heat, and flower more often" than the normal greenhouse types. Half the offerings are cattleytonia hybrids; most of the rest are cattleyas and cattleya alliance crosses. All are sold in either blooming size or close to it. Phalaenopsis and oncidium equitants are offered in nursery-selected assortments at low prices.

Jones & Scully, Inc.

18955 S.W. 168th Street, Miami, FL 33187
Telephone: 305-238-7000 or 800-ORCHIDS (orders only)

Catalog price: $5, deductible from first order

The absolute Rolls Royce of orchid catalogs. With its pastel watercolors used as section dividers and its general sheen, the catalog may resemble an annual report from a blue-chip firm coming off a particularly good year, but this elegant 80-page opus is in fact a detailed and comprehensive rundown of everything available for the orchid lover. Nearly 1,000 offerings from a broad range of orchid genera are succinctly evoked by means of informative charts, crisp color photographs, and stylish commentary. Species orchids make up about a third of the listings. Most of the hybrids and seedlings are available in a choice of sizes, and most can be purchased ready to bloom.

Jungle-Gems, Inc.

300 Edgewood Road, Edgewood, MD 21040
Telephone: 301-676-0672

Catalog price: free

This booklet offers potted phalaenopsis (both hybrid and species), cattleya mericlones, oncidiums, cymbidiums, and other orchid types. All receive at least brief descriptions, and a few are singled out for extra praise. Mini-flasks of many of the same plants are also listed; each bottle contains a minimum of five plantlets ready for transplanting into either community or thumb pots.

KamYin SiuBo Orchid
No. 2 Lok Lo Ha, Fo Tan, Shatin, Hong Kong

Catalog price: free

A telegram from the Orient. This list—13 paphiopedilum species listed by botanical name and price alone—doesn't take long to absorb. All plants are flowering size. Minimum order is $100.

Kasem Boonchoo Nursery
109/3, Phaholyotin Soi 15, Sapankwai Bangkok 4, Thailand
Telephone: 66-278-1566 or 5508

Catalog price: free

Cattleya, vanda, ascocenda, and dendrobium crosses, from flasks to blooming-size plants, offered with a good selection of Thai species. Description is limited to a few words on parentage and color. A large accompanying poster features a dozen orchids set like jewels in decorative frames. Minimum order is $100.

Kensington Orchids
3301 Plyers Mill Road, Kensington, MD 20895
Telephone: 301-933-0036

Catalog price: free

Several hundred orchid offerings, densely packed onto both sides of five computer-printed sheets. Room has somehow been made for notes on flower color. Phalaenopsis and doritaenopsis seedlings, both hybrid and species, lead off the list, followed by crowds of cattleyas, cymbidiums, paphiopedilums, and oncidiums. A list of orchid supplies ranges from insecticides to potting materials to reference books.

Khuong Orchids, Ltd.
4444 N. Maxson Road, El Monte, CA 91732
Telephone: 818-448-3754

Catalog price: free

More than 100 orchids, available in community and individual pots or in flasks, on a long descriptive list. Most of the offerings are cattleya and phalaenopsis types (a few species mixed in among the crosses) supplemented by *Brassia verrucosa* and a few vandas and oncidiums. Minimum order is $25.

Kilworth Flowers
County Road 14, Rt. 3, Komoka, ON, Canada N0L 1R0
Telephone: 519-471-9787

Catalog price: free

A rich assortment of orchids, including some rare and hard-to-find specimens. Phalaenopsis seedlings and mericlones

dominate the list, but cattleya and cymbidium cultivars and sophronitis and paphiopedilum species also appear. Blooming-size plants are available in all cases, and brief descriptions note bloom color, mature plant size, and parentage.

Krull-Smith Orchids
2815 Ponkan Road, Apopka, FL 32712
Telephone: 305-886-0915

Catalog price: free

A booklet that's nicely balanced among orchids of various shapes and hues. Several hundred offerings are compactly laid out for your inspection; there's no marginal comment, so you are left alone to browse through the cattleya alliance mericlones (about 50 of these), cattleya seedlings, cattleytonias and miniature cattleyas, phalaenopsis (both stem propagations and seedlings), vandas and ascocendas, paphiopedilums, dendrobiums, and oncidiums. Botanical names are given first, followed by a brief description.

Kultana Orchids
39/6 Soi Wat Nawong, Song Prabha Road, Bangkok 10210, Thailand
Telephone: 66-566-1414, 1720, 1730 or 1732

Catalog price: free

This slick catalog is a feast for the eyes. Lusciously produced, with hundreds of crisp color photographs broken up by soft, billowy watercolors, this 20-page booklet concentrates on orchids as visual spectacle. Apart from the placement of each flower's name beneath its image, descriptive text has been shunned altogether. The selection is broad: vandas, ascocendas, Thai species, dendrobium hybrids, intergenerics, and cattleyas. Minimum order is $100.

Lauray of Salisbury
See under *Houseplants*, page 106.

Laurel Orchids
18205 S.W. 157th Avenue, Miami, FL 33187
Telephone: 305-251-8747

Catalog price: $1, deductible from first order

A nine-page spread of orchids offered in three ways: as inexpensive seedlings, community pot tenants, or blooming-size plants. Cattleyas, ascocendas, and vandas are plentiful in each category, with a few dendrobiums, phalaenopsis, and brassavolas to balance the mix. The text is precise, but tinged with hysteria at times. "Expect the unusual!!!" advises the entry for one vanda cross. "RED!!!" is the color of the next plant cited. Watch for the catalog's ultimate cry: "We like this one—A LOT!!!"

Lenette Greenhouses
4345 Rogers Lake Road, Kannapolis, NC 28081
Telephone: 704-938-2042

Catalog price: free

A chatty, winsome catalog loaded with personal tips and recommendations. Cattleyas, oncidiums, paphiopedilums, phalaenopsis, and vandas are included here. Cattleya and phalaenopsis plants are available in blooming-size, meristem, stud, flask, and seedling forms. (The other orchids are available in one or two forms only.) Throughout, an amiable voice nudges you this way and that and guides your final selections. "Every once in a while a cross comes along that you just really take a liking to," the catalog allows, regarding a certain gold-and-red-flecked cattleya. "This is such a cross."

McBeans Orchids Ltd.
Cooksbridge, Lewes, Sussex, England BN8 4PR
Telephone: 44-273-400-228

Established in 1879, McBeans is one of the world's great orchid nurseries, famed for its extensive breeding program. The export catalog—13 stapled pages inside a glossy jacket—lists approximately 50 recent hybrids, divided among cymbidiums (large-flowered and miniature) and odontoglossums. Entries for each variety toss off a quick line or two of description. A brilliantly colorful pamphlet of cymbidium photographs accompanies the catalog and amplifies its charm.

McClain's Orchid Range
6237 Blanding Boulevard, Jacksonville, FL 32244
Telephone: 904-771-3535

Catalog price: free

This typed list features several dozen cattleya and intergeneric seedlings and mericlones, along with a handful of phalaenopsis and assorted other hybrids. Explanatory material is brief and to the point.

McLane Orchids Inc.
1250 Glen Road, Glen Ridge, W. Palm Beach, FL 33406
Telephone: 305-683-4058

Catalog price: free

The offerings in this modest booklet dart among a few basic branches of the orchid family. Cattleya seedlings and mericlones, oncidiums, dendrobiums, phalaenopsis, and doritaenopsis are offered, along with intergenerics and miscellaneous orchid baskets. A page of helpful hints wraps up the package on a warm note.

Rod McLellan Co.
1450 El Camino Real, S. San Francisco, CA 94080
Telephone: 415-871-5655

Catalog price: $1

Brimming with more than 100 color shots, this is a gorgeous catalog. The company has been in business since 1895 and knows its way around the greenhouse. Each section in the 20-page catalog—phalaenopsis, sophronitis, paphiopedilums, and cattleyas (organzied by hue), large-flowered and miniature cymbidiums, oncidiums, and more—opens with some general discussion, then gets down to specifics. Nearly every listing merits a photograph.

Madcap Orchids
Rt. 29, Box 391UU, Fort Myers, FL 33905
Telephone: 813-694-5900

Catalog price: free

Four hundred orchids crushed together in a businesslike array. The vast majority of the listings are cattleya alliance types, with an emphasis on compact and miniature varieties. Dendrobiums, oncidiums, and vandas are listed almost as an afterthought. Plants are offered in sizes from 2-inch pots to blooming specimens. Minimum order is $25.

Maisie Orchids
183 Temple Street, 5/F Kowloon, Hong Kong

Catalog price: free

A dozen paphiopedilum species offered without comment. The flowering-size orchids may be purchased from either of two columns, labeled "10-Growths" or "100-Growths." Prices in the first column begin at $40 and ascend; prices in the second are nearly ten times higher.

Ann Mann's
9045 Ron-Den Lane, Windermere, FL 32786-9238
Telephone: 305-876-2625

Catalog price: free

A huge assortment of orchids and other tropical plants blackens the 40 pages of this catalog. Nearly 1,000 orchid species and crosses—from cattleyas to oncidiums to vandas—are densely listed by botanical name or parentage with short notes on flower color. Most are sold as mature plants. In addition to the orchids, a rich selection of aroids, bromeliads, ferns, hoyas, and palms droop their verdant foliage here. Fertilizers, insecticides, and fungicides plus baskets, pruning shears, potting media, books, charcoal, cork, cypress slabs, and even a water filtration system are sold to help you give the plants proper care in your home.

Mariposa Orchid Co.
421 Mariposa Drive, Ventura, CA 93001
Telephone: 805-643-1979

Catalog price: free

Phalaenopsis stem propagations supply the heartbeat of this nursery. Many more than 100 varieties and species are arrayed in alphabetical order with a tart line of commentary for each. Quantities of all plants listed are very limited. A handful of phalaenopsis flasks in even shorter supply appear on a supplemental sheet; reservations are required if you want a shot at these.

Mauna Kea Orchids
206 Ainako Avenue, Hilo, HI 96720

Catalog price: free

A brief listing of a dozen cattleya mericlones and seedlings. These are from community pots, ready for planting in individual pots. Each entry specifies the parentage and expected color and characteristics of the offspring.

Paul A. Mulcey
Rt. 2, Box 190, Dallas, PA 18612
Telephone: 717-675-5025

Catalog price: $2 for color catalog, free price list

This nursery functions as a non-exclusive U.S. agent for Vacherot & Lecoufle, the famous French orchid grower. Select varieties of cattleya, phalaenopsis, paphiopedilum, miltonia, and other orchids may be ordered through the Mulcey firm. A series of brief bilingual pamphlets, generally organized by genus, spell out the options; in addition, a sumptuous Vacherot & Lecoufle booklet—containing vivid color photographs—serves to amplify the appeal of these exquisite flowers.

Muses' Tropical Orchids, Inc.
3710 N. Orchid Drive, Haines City, FL 33844

Catalog price: free

Cattleyas and cattleya alliances of all tints are mixed with a modest selection of vandas and species in this descriptive 12-page catalog. Experienced growers will feel more at home here than beginners, as the catalog descriptions assume a high level of expertise.

Nelson's Orchids
Rt. 2, Box 810, Fombell, PA 16123
Telephone: 412-452-6720

Catalog price: free

A mixed bag of orchids, simply listed by name or parentage with only an occasional note about flower color. Cattleya mericlones and crosses make up the largest single category (50 offerings), but vandas, phalaenopsis, dendrobiums, oncidiums, and catasetums also appear. Most plants are offered in 3- or 4-inch pots; a few in blooming size.

Nooitgedag Disa Nursery
7 Sunnybrae Road, Rondebosch, 7700 Cape Town, South Africa
Telephone: 27-21-691919

Catalog price: free

Seed for native South African disa species and for some first- and second-generation crosses. Each of the dozen or so offerings is described in a couple of sentences, and the accuracy of some of the boasts is borne out by pictures on an accompanying color flier.

Oak Hill Gardens
P.O. Box 25, Dundee, IL 60118-0025
Telephone: 312-428-8500

Catalog price: free

Hundreds of orchid species and hybrids pack this informative color-illustrated booklet. The nursery offers an exceptionally large collection of orchid species—more than 300, from dozens of genera. Cattleya, dendrobium, and other hybrids and cymbidium miniatures balance the listings. Bromeliads, flowering houseplants, and indoor foliage plants garner some space as well. A good selection of orchid-growing supplies includes growing media, fertilizers, misters, and books.

Oberon
P.O. Box 99186, Troy, MI 48099-9186
Telephone: 313-531-9572

Catalog price: free

From the test tube to you: a somewhat muddled array of orchids in flask, division, seedling, and mature-plant forms. Cattleyas are sold as bulb divisions and as blooming-size miniatures; paphiopedilums are listed three ways—blooming

size, seedling, and mini-flask. Quantities of most offerings are limited, in many cases restricted to a couple of specimens.

The Orchid Center
P.O. Box 1116, Arcadia, FL 33821
Telephone: 813-494-5896

Catalog price: free

This eight-page brochure resembles a menu in a Chinese restaurant—once you figure out where things are, you'll probably order a nice meal. Cattleya seedlings appear in five color groupings. There are side orders of dendrobium hybrids, phalaenopsis, miniature oncidiums, cattleya mericlones, and dendrobium mericlones. Imported orchids claim more than a page. For dessert, how about some pot stakes, wire baskets, or water-soluble plant food? It's all here, under "Supplies."

Orchid Haven
900 Rossland Road E., Whitby, ON, Canada L1N 5R5
Telephone: 416-668-8534

Catalog price: free

Roughly 100 orchid offerings, neatly organized into eight divisions: blooming-size phalaenopsis, phalaenopsis species (just a couple of entries here), phalaenopsis seedlings and stem propagations, blooming-size cattleyas and meristems, species, and other orchid hybrids. Text for each listing evokes size, shape, and color of the plant. Minimum order is $35.

The Orchid House
1699 Sage Avenue, Los Osos, CA 93402
Telephone: 805-528-1417

Catalog price: free price list, $3 for cultural bulletin

Paphiopedilum fans have found a nesting place in this stylish catalog, from the nursery that is the principal supplier of these cut flowers for the Los Angeles market. The 12 pages are devoted entirely to paphiopedilums and include half a dozen huge color photographs documenting their allure. An extremely detailed cultivation guide consumes a third of the catalog. Prices tend to be high.

Orchid Plant-a-Month Club
P.O. Box 296, Goldens Bridge, NY 10526

Catalog price: free

Members receive an orchid plant each month, the selections chosen to grow well, with proper care, under ordinary household conditions. Full cultural instructions come with each installment.

Orchid Species Specialties
42314 Road 415, Coarsegold, CA 93614
Telephone: 209-683-3239

Catalog price: $1 for main orchid list, $1 for cattleya list, $1 for laelia list

Choice orchid species and varieties (no hybrids), from the simply unusual to the extremely rare. Listings are bunched by genus and note whether an individual plant is awarded or of award quality, endangered, or represents a superior clone. The cattleya list contains nearly 100 species and varieties; the laelia list far fewer. Price and availability of these exotic orchids is generally up in the air—it's recommended that you write or phone for a quotation on plants that interest you.

Orchid World International, Inc.
10885 S.W. 95th Street, Miami, FL 33176
Telephone: 305-271-0268 or 800-367-6720

Catalog price: $10, deductible from first order

At press time this nursery was still hard at work on what it hopes will be the last word in orchid catalogs: a looseleaf binder crammed with color, information, and plants to buy. The nursery sells about 400 phalaenopsis mericlones, as many cattleya hybrids and clones, and a big selection of dendrobiums, oncidiums, and vandas—more than 1,200 offerings in all. About 300 will be illustrated in color, we're told, and all will be thoroughly described. The cultural information will include a complete guide to propagating and potting, a chart showing common insect pests and how to treat them, and the light, temperature, and humidity required by the various orchid types. The looseleaf format will allow for regular (quarterly or biannual) updates.

Orchids & Ferns
7802 Bellaire Boulevard, Houston, TX 77036
Telephone: 713-774-0949

Catalog price: free

A descriptive listing of nearly 200 orchids. Cattleya hybrids garner perhaps two-thirds of the space. Dendrobiums, oncidiums, phalaenopsis, and vandas complete the selection. We're not sure what happened to the ferns.

Orchids Bountiful
826 W. 3800 S., Bountiful, UT 84010
Telephone: 801-295-6064

Catalog price: free

As the name suggests, there's no scarcity of orchids here. Cattleya alliance crosses lead off the typed list, and an assortment of other species and hybrids follows—more than 200 selections in all. Each listing gets a few words of description, with extra attention given to the more unusual species offerings. Books and supplies take up a page at the back.

Orchids by Hausermann, Inc.
2N 134 Addison Road, Villa Park, IL 60181
Telephone: 312-543-6855

Catalog price: $1.25

This 60-page catalog is brisk, colorful, and informative. A hundred plus species orchids start things out, followed by hundreds of hybrids from ascocenda to vanda. Cattleya and phalaenopsis represent a special strength—they run on for 20 pages. With its scores of brilliant color pictures, clear descriptions, and generous growing advice, the catalog is easily handled by beginners. With its wealth of offerings, it is also an important source for experts.

Orchids by M & W
P.O. Box 28, Cullman, AL 35056-0028

Catalog price: free

This catalog is a rather jumbled assortment of unusual orchid species and hybrids listed in no discernible order. Seventy or 80 selections vie for attention, and you'll need to scan the entire roster to be sure of your options. Cattleyas, dendrobiums, phalaenopsis, oncidiums, ascocendas, and laelias are among the offerings.

Orchids by Rowe, Inc.
1251 Orchid Drive Ext., Santa Barbara, CA 93111
Telephone: 805-967-1312

Catalog price: free

A concentrated slate of several dozen cymbidiums. Standard and novelty meristems, species, and seedlings are the main fare, all tenderly evoked; the meristems and seedlings occupy 2½-inch pots, while the species range up to gallon containers. A smattering of paphiopedilum and jewel orchids sneak aboard the roster at the very end. (In addition to cymbidiums, Orchids by Rowe offers a separate listing of several dozen more orchid varieties from Orchids by Burnham, of Devon, England. The latter list includes odontocidiums, miltonias, and oncidiums in flask, seedling, and meristem forms.)

Orchids Limited
4630 North Fernbrook Lane, Plymouth, MN 55442
Telephone: 612-559-6425

Catalog price: free

With small type and a snappy chart, Orchids Limited has managed to present almost 300 orchids, along with cultural information and descriptions, in just a few pages without real crowding. A nice selection of species orchids leads off—more than 100 choices with special strengths among the encyclias and paphiopedilums. The hybrids range from a single aeranthes cross to a handful of vandas, with plenty of cattleya alliances, cymbidiums, dendrobiums, and phalaenopsis in between. Growing instructions, at the front of the catalog, appear to be unusually thorough and clear.

Orchids Orinda
1330 Isabel Avenue, Livermore, CA 94550
Telephone: 415-447-7171

Catalog price: free

A collector's list of phalaenopsis seedlings and meristem clones. The nursery does its own breeding, and each list contains approximately 25 new hybrids, sold as seedlings, and nearly 500 different meristems. The specialty here is intense colors and patterns, though a broad range of flower types are offered. The firm also sells some related species orchids grown from seed. All plants are sold in pots 3 inches or larger, and plants are briefly described on the list.

Orchids Royale
P.O. Box 1289, Carpinteria, CA 93013
Telephone: 805-684-8066

Catalog price: free

Two booklets listing hundreds of orchids, from a nursery with special strength in cymbidiums. The first concentrates (for ten pages) on miltonias, paphiopedilum divisions, and odontoglossums. The second (22 pages) lists cymbidiums. Single-bulb plants are the rule here.

Owens Orchids
P.O. Box 365, Pisgah Forest, NC 28768-0365
Telephone: 704-877-3313

Catalog price: free

The Orchid-A-Month Plan sponsored by this nursery offers you an orchid in the mail each month. Instructions and fertilizer are included in the first shipment. Varieties are unspecified, but will be chosen to suit your location.

Paphanatics, UnLtd.
3319 W. Lincoln Avenue, Suite 103, Anaheim, CA 92801
Telephone: 714-826-8432

Catalog price: free

Flasks of selected blue-ribbon orchids intended for the serious breeder. Several dozen offerings are listed, with a stress on paphiopedilums (including separate headings devoted to vinicolor crosses, novelty, complex whites and pinks, and species). Phalaenopsis and cattleya alliances also merit a nod.

These collections are not cheap—starting at about $50 and shooting through the roof—but each flask is guaranteed to contain at least 25 superior plants.

Penn Valley Orchids
239 Old Gulph Road, Wynnewood, PA 19096
Telephone: 215-642-9822

Catalog price: $1

A comprehensive catalog offering hundreds of rare and exotic orchids. Paphiopedilums dominate the list, which consists mainly of blooming-size plants. Cattleyas and miscellaneous hybrids garner a small fraction of the space. Most plants in the catalog are one of a kind and priced accordingly; cost here ranges from Decent Lunch to Used Car.

Petite Plaisance
P.O. Box 386, Valley Ford, CA 94972
Telephone: 707-876-3496

Catalog price: free

A series of brief brochures make up this nursery's "catalog." The first of these details several dozen blooming-size miltoniopsis crosses and mericlones. A second highlights a selection of 100 cattleya alliance seedlings and mericlones. A third stapled listing concentrates on mixed genera (cattleya, miltoniopsis, and phalaenopsis) flasks, each guaranteed to hold between 40 and 45 plants.

The Plant Shop's Botanical Gardens
18007 Topham Street, Reseda, CA 91335
Telephone: 818-881-4831

A rich blend of orchid flasks and seedlings, conveniently graded on a five-point scale for relative ease of cultivation. Each of the more than 100 flasks offered—with a guaranteed minimum of 25 plants per 500-ml flask—includes cross data and a general note on color and shape. Seedlings are grouped into 2-, 3-, and 4-inch pot sizes. While some of these plants are listed as "ideal for beginners," the list is not, and will require some background in "orchidese" to decipher.

Quality Orchids
P.O. Box 4472, Hialeah, FL 33014

A blunt, no-frills roster of more than 50 mericlones of award-winning orchids of various genera. The plants are shipped in pots of five sizes, from 2 to 6 inches. For those not inclined to wait, a handful of even larger flowering-size plants is also available, at slightly elevated cost.

R. F. Orchids
28100 S.W. 182nd Avenue, Homestead, FL 33030
Telephone: 305-245-4570

A generous array of more vandas than you probably thought existed, from a company that prides itself on maintaining top-quality parentage in its plants. The catalog is elegantly laid out, with 100 plus vandas evoked on trim, photograph-laden pages. A small section devoted to species wheels a sampling of cattleya, dendrobium, epidendrum, laelia, paphiopedilum, phalaenopsis, and other genera into the mix. At the back, cultural requirements of vandas are briefly sketched.

Joseph R. Redlinger Orchids
9236 S.W. 57th Avenue, Miami, FL 33156
Telephone: 305-661-4821

A one-page selection of quart-size orchid flasks—mostly phalaenopsis crosses, but with a sprinkling of other types. Each flask of large plants contains between 60 and 100 specimens ready for potting. Mericlone flasks hold 35 or more plants.

Richella Orchids, Inc.
2881 Booth Road, Honolulu, HI 96813
Telephone: 808-538-6637

Catalog price: free

Community-pot listings galore. Oncidium equitants, dendrobiums, vandaceous orchids, and intergenerics constitute the major headings in this tightly printed 12-page array. The catalog guarantees a minimum of 20 healthy seedlings per pot, ready to be transplanted into separate containers. Individual listings are coded to convey a wealth of data in brisk fashion.

Riverbend Orchids
Rt. 1, Box 590E, Biloxi, MS 39532
Telephone: 601-392-2699

Catalog price: free

A densely printed booklet nearly as tough to decipher as it is rich in contents. Cattleya mericlones, miniatures, and hybrids organized by shade of bloom dominate the listings here. Plants are offered in various sizes—up to and including blooming size. Of more than 200 listings, only a handful fall into the phalaenopsis, dendrobium, oncidium, brassovola, and broughtonia camps.

Royal Ruby Orchids
Route 2, Platt City, MO 64079
Telephone: 816-546-3585

Catalog price: free

Potted orchids, both small specimens and mature plants ready to flower. Cattleyas take up the biggest part of the list, with about 40 hybrids offered. The greenhouse also sells

cymbidiums, phalaenopsis, oncidiums, and a smattering of other types. The list gives brief descriptions, but contains no pictures.

Rust-En-Vrede Nursery
Disa seed. See under *Native Plants of Australia and South Africa*, page 120.

Santa Barbara Orchid Estate
1250 Orchid Drive, Santa Barbara, CA 93111
Telephone: 805-967-1284

It is the stated ambition of this nursery's owners to offer the most extensive listing of famous-name cymbidiums available anywhere in the world. Judging from the catalog, they seem well on their way. More than 1,000 cymbidium offerings—split among division, miniature, and species—are neatly aligned in this specialty booklet. Most plants are established in 6-inch pots. A second booklet from the nursery lists 1,000 other orchids, including cattleyas, dendrobiums, epidendrums, laelias, oncidiums, paphiopedilums, and many more.

Sea Breeze Orchids
P.O. Box 1416, Bayville, NY 11709
Telephone: 516-496-3513 or 628-2764

A compact, tidily arranged list of several hundred orchid species, opening with *Aerangis bilboa* and clicking shut on *Zygopetalum intermedium*. A dozen featured plants are pictured in bright color photographs along the way. Cattleya, dendrobium, laelia, masdevallia, oncidium, and paphiopedilum species are the most bountifully represented genera; many others show up with just a single species. All plants are established and of flowering size.

Sea God Nurseries
P.O. Box 678, Geyserville, CA 95441
Telephone: 707-433-8559

Cattleyas win top billing on this simple roster. About 100 blooming-size plants head the list; pot sizes vary, and the number of mature bulbs per plant is carefully noted. Cattleya seedlings are grouped by color of bloom, with art shades, oranges and yellows, multifloras, and lavenders to pinks garnering an average of about a dozen varieties each. A few laelias supply spice.

Seagulls Landing Orchids
P.O. Box 388, Glen Head, NY 11545
Telephone: 516-367-6336

Catalog price: free

A somewhat scatterbrained catalog offering more than 100 cattleyas, with an emphasis on miniatures. Most plants occupy clay pots; as a result, shipping fees tend to be somewhat higher than the norm.

Alvim Seidel
P.O. Box 1, 89280 Corupá, Santa Catarina, Brazil
Telephone: 55-473-75-1244

This voluminous catalog proffers more than 1,000 orchid species and cultivars, with an emphasis on species. The selection runs both deep and wide: 150 cattleya species are listed, for example (including some rare specimens priced at the $3,000 level), along with plants from dozens of other genera. Although many photographs pepper this catalog—most in muddy black and white, but some sharp, brightly colored shots, too—it's impossible to discern the size and quality of the individual offerings. They are described simply as "nursery grown plants." Catalog pricing is in U.S. dollars; the minimum order is $40, not counting the requisite $6 certification fee. The nursery also carries a large inventory of bromeliads.

George Shorter Orchids
P.O. Box 16952, Mobile, AL 36616
Telephone: 205-653-7469 or 471-6201

An odds-and-ends kind of list marked by informal marginalia—here supplying pot sizes, there alerting the buyer to an irresistible offer and proceeding to sweeten the deal. Cattleyas are the main attraction; miniature cymbidiums plus vanda seedlings and species are offered in lesser numbers. Of the cymbidiums the owner writes, "Let me choose for you & I'll give lg. plts. & one extra as a bonus plt."

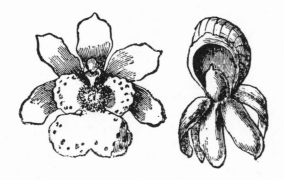

Sidran Orchids
7971 S.W. 122 Street, Miami, FL 33156
Telephone: 305-238-8762

Catalog price: long self-addressed stamped envelope

A basic list of orchid seedlings from a nursery that specializes in ascocenda breeding. Fifty hybrids are introduced with an unusually detailed text, noting in a sentence or two key characteristics of the parent plants and projected traits of the offspring. Most seedlings here are ascocendas, but other orchid types—notably phalaenopsis and vandas—do pop up. Divisions of select awarded plants are also available.

Anthony J. Skittone
Pleiones. See under *Bulbs*, page 63.

Stewart Orchids
P.O. Box 550, Carpinteria, CA 93013
Telephone: 805-684-5448

Catalog price: free

An enticing display of cattleyas, paphiopedilums, miltonias, phalaenopsis, odontoglossums, and unusual species. The 12-page catalog is a model of clarity, with choices ruled and boxed for easy scanning. White, blue, yellow, and purple cattleyas each claim a page.

Dr. Warren Stoutamire
3615 Mogadore Road, Mogadore, OH 44260
Telephone: 216-628-9367

No catalog

Dr. Stoutamire publishes no catalog, but occasionally mails postcards alerting buyers to plants that have just become available. A recent card offered *Disa uniflora* orchids in 4-inch pots, priced at two levels, for either "unexceptional" or "superior" specimens. Write to be put on his mailing list.

Su-An Nursery
P.O. Box 132, Pittsford, NY 14534
Telephone: 716-586-4293

Nearly 100 phalaenopsis seedlings set forth without a lot of fanfare. Varieties are sensibly organized by color groupings, and basic culture information is provided. A few cattleya hybrids are also offered.

Sundance Orchids
817-89th, Rt. 2, Galveston, TX 77551
Telephone: 409-744-4878

Roughly 100 oncidium species, crosses, and mericlones file past in this bare booklet from a nursery that bills itself as the "Equitant Oncidium Place." Shoppers can order specimens in community pots, flasks, or individual pots to flowering size. Descriptions are limited to a few words, and cultural tips to a page, but the nursery suggests a number of articles and books for further reading.

Sunswept Laboratories
P.O. Box 1913, Studio City, CA 91604
Telephone: 818-506-7271

Thirteen stapled pages presenting a rich selection of species and hybrid orchids in flasks. Cattleya, dendrobium, laelia, oncidium, phalaenopsis, and miltonia line up for your inspection. Orchids are shipped in either 250-ml or 500-ml flasks, and generally contain a minimum of 35 seedlings. Entries for a number of the flowers here refer the buyer to color illustrations in *The Orchid Digest*.

Suphachadiwong
18/1 Soi 7, Bangphra Chonburi 20210, Thailand
Telephone: 66-38-311511

Catalog price: $5

An exquisite catalog displaying more than 600 orchids in small, sharp photographs framed in lustrous black. Each image is labeled with its botanical name. A separate 17-page price list, brilliantly detailed and clear, spells out the rest, including exact air-freight charges to various points around the world. Flowering-size plants are listed in the catalog: dendrobiums, paphiopedilums, vanda hybrids, ascocendas, cattleyas, and many more. Minimum order is $100.

T. Orchids
P.O. Box 21-19, Bangkok-21, Thailand
Telephone: 66-573-1747 or 4686

Catalog price: $5 for illustrated catalog, free price list

A thick book that offers just about the last word in orchid variety. The catalog is chatty and rather whimsical, but comes loaded with stellar color photographs on nearly every page. Scores of species orchids from Thailand, Sri Lanka, and the Philippines are richly represented here, in addition to ascocenda, dendrobium, cattleya, phalaenopsis, and intergeneric hybrids. Prices are quoted in U.S. dollars.

TAHAOU
P.O. Box 238, Wilton, CA 95693
Telephone: 916-273-9426

Catalog price: free

The Angraecum House merged with Angraecoid Orchids Unlimited in 1986 to yield this entity, whose tongue-twisting name derives from the first letters of the two components. The 1987 catalog offered more than 40 angraecoid species from Africa and Madagascar, along with about as many hybrids. Entries give descriptions of foliage and flower and an occasional note on culture. A spirit of enthusiasm for these uncommon plants permeates the catalog, and a guide to angraecoid orchid growing is available.

TS Orchids
255 Aipuni Street, Hilo, HI 96720
Telephone: 808-935-4965

Six stapled pages laying out almost 100 seedlings and mericlones, mostly cattleyas. Entries note color and size (from 2-inch pot to blooming size). All plants are shipped bare root.

Taylor Orchids
P.O. Box 267, 21 Blossom Lane, Monroe, MI 48161
Telephone: 313-243-0180

Catalog price: free

Orchid species in profusion, laid out in a straight botanical-names listing. The familiar genera are here: cattleya, masdevallia, paphiopedilum, brassavola, dendrobium, laelia, oncidium, phalaenopsis, along with more unusual genera, such as arundina, lycaste, and xylobium. Altogether, hundreds of listings appear. All plants are well established and close to blooming size.

Tonkin's Orchids, Inc.
119 St. Albans Road, Kensington, CA 94708
Telephone: 415-526-1371

Catalog price: free

An immaculate six-page booklet speckled with nearly 200 award-winning paphiopedilum hybrids. Pricing is a bit unusual. The orchids cost $10 per inch of natural leaf spread, measured at the widest point. Leaf sizes range from five to 28 inches.

Tropical Orchid Farm
P.O. Box 354, Haiku, Maui, HI 96708
Telephone: 808-572-8569

Catalog price: free

Precisely described orchid crosses drawn from phalaenopsis, dendrobium, vanda, and cattleya genera. More than 100 listings fill the eight-page catalog. Each entry includes several lines of informed comment, often splashed with enthusiasm. "How wonderful if this cross comes out," the text for one cattleya exults. "Huge pure whites hoped for. Of course,

people familiar with this type of breeding know that light pinks are likely." A small selection of species orchids also appears. Plant sizes range from 2-inch pots to blooming size.

Tropical World Nursery
7281 S.W. 117th Place, Rt. 1, Boynton Beach, FL 33437
Telephone: 305-732-8813

Catalog price: $1

A ten-foot span of listings printed out on green-and-white-banded computer paper, this catalog offers hundreds of orchid species in about as unwieldy a form as one could imagine. Most of the popular genera (in blooming sizes) are liberally represented, with special strength in laelias and cattleyas. Meristems of named cultivars take up about two feet of the total list.

Tropicals Unlimited
See under *Tropical Plants*, page 171.

Trymwood Orchids
2500 Rockdell Street, La Crescenta, CA 91214
Telephone: 818-248-1835

A dozen or so flasks of cattleya hybrids constitute the heart of the offerings here. Listings predict bloom size and color and leave the guesswork at that. A few meristems are also available in 2-inch pots.

Vacherot & Lecoufle
B.P. No. 8, F-94471, Boissy-Saint-Léger, France
Telephone: 33-1-45-69-10-42

A sumptuous palette of flowers from one of the world's prestige orchid lines, launched more than a century ago. The catalog features sun-drenched photographs scattered through a dozen or so pages, captioned by name and nothing more—among them odontoglossums, cymbidiums, paphiopedilums, cattleyas, phalaenopsis, and miltoniopsis. A thoroughly detailed bilingual (French and English) price list, which includes plants not pictured in the catalog, explains ordering procedures. The minimum order for export is fr250, and an import permit is required (see *Buying Plants from Overseas*, page 9). Paul A. Mulcey (see page 127) can supply many of Vacherot & Lecoufle's plants without the import fuss.

Valley Orchids
Pimpala Road, Morphett Vale, South Australia 5162
Telephone: 618-381-2609

Several hundred cymbidium varieties and crosses presented
in a richly illustrated color catalog. Shoppers can choose
between flasks and single plants with six- or 12-inch leaves.

West Coast Orchids
4905 Cherryvale Avenue, Soquel, CA 95073
Telephone: 408-475-1331

Catalog price: free

Phalaenopsis, odontoglossum, and miltonia crosses—some
described and some simply listed by parentage—on four
typed pages. A handful of phalaenopsis species complements
the hybrids.

Ken West Orchids
P.O. Box 1332, Pahoa, HI 96778
Telephone: 808-965-9895

Catalog price: free

Fifty cattleyas—and the verbiage they elicit—strain the
seams of this modest fine-print brochure. Each listing receives a fat little paragraph of discussion. Plant sizes range
from thumb pot to blooming size. Minimum order is $15;
orders more than $30 earn a bonus plant.

Wilk Orchid Specialties
P.O. Box 1177, Kaneohe, HI 96744
Telephone: 808-247-6733

Catalog price: free

Evenly divided between orchid crosses and mericlones, this
ten-page catalog ranges far and wide. Ascocendas, cattleyas,
and dendrobiums lead the first pack; the mericlones include
a nice selection of oncidium equitants and vanda cultivars.
Fifty or so species complete the list.

Woltmon's Miniature Orchids
P.O. Box 956, 1583 California Avenue, Wahiawa, HI 96786
Telephone: 808-622-1793

Catalog price: free

Approximately 50 miniature cattleya alliance hybrids crowd
both sides of a single sheet of paper. Plants are available
chiefly as seedlings in 2-inch pots, but mericlones and mini-
flasks (containing on average 15–25 plants) also appear. Minimum order is $40.

Guy Wrinkle/Exotic Plants
See under *Tropical Plants*, page 171.

Wyld Court Orchids
Hampstead Norreys, Newbury, Berks., England RG16 0TN
Telephone: 44-635-201283

Catalog price: $1 in cash

Several hundred orchid species set forth in a simple eight-
page booklet organized alphabetically by botanical name.
Angraecum, cattleya, cymbidium, dendrobium, laelia, masdevallia, oncidium, phalaenopsis, and zygopetalum orchids
make up the main categories here. Most plants are of flowering size. Country of origin and temperature preferences—
cool, intermediate, or warm—are duly noted for each offering.

Yamamoto Dendrobiums (Hawaii)
P.O. Box 235, Mountain View, HI 96771
Telephone: 808-968-6955

A lovely color catalog of *Dendrobium nobile* hybrids, offering nearly 100 named varieties. Alternating pages of text and
photographs give the booklet a pleasant, well-ordered density. Listings are detailed and clear, as are the introductory
notes on culture and care.

Zuma Canyon Orchids
5949 Bonsall Drive, Malibu, CA 90265
Telephone: 213-457-9771

Catalog price: $3

Intergeneric phalaenopsis/doritaenopsis hybrids. Pricing for
the plants is by leaf spread, in four-to-seven-inch and eight-
to-12-inch sizes. Community pots are also available. Glossy
color photographs inside the front and back covers supply
enticing detail.

Peonies

Myron D. Bigger

201 North Rice Road, Topeka, KS 66616

Catalog price: free

A typed list of about 60 peony cultivars and a somewhat more limited selection of daylilies. Among the peonies are a few of Mr. Bigger's own introductions, including a white-flowered specimen dubbed 'Myron D. Bigger'. Plants from a number of other sources are also offered. Descriptions are kept to a word or two about bloom color, with no indication of height, bloom season, or the hybridizer's name. The best deal is an assortment of 100 unlabeled daylilies, priced at just $20 in 1987.

Brand Peony Farm

P.O. Box 842, St. Cloud, MN 56302

Catalog price: $1, deductible from first order

A wealth of peonies to choose from, most at very reasonable prices. The catalog is not illustrated, but each plant is described in detail, including flower color, foliage, height, scent, and bloom season. The bulk of the list is made up of double peonies, but a few singles and a dozen Japanese types are offered as well. Old favorites like Karl Rosenfield and Sarah Bernhardt can be had for less than $6 a plant, while such exotics as Fern Leaf, Dakota Princess, and Colleen Marie command much higher rates. A good selection of irises and daylilies is also available.

Busse Gardens

See under *Garden Perennials*, page 86.

Caprice Farm

15425 S.W. Pleasant Hill Road, Sherwood, OR 97140

Telephone: 503-625-7241

Catalog price: $1, deductible from first order

Sixty different peonies presented in a crisp color catalog from a small family-run nursery. The selection ranges from Festiva Maxima, the classic white peony of the last century (introduced in 1851), to newer cultivars like Louise Marx (1981). The emphasis is on older varieties that have proved their worth in the garden. Caprice also sells more than 150 daylily cultivars, including a good selection of miniatures, and a few dozen hostas and Japanese irises. Selected plants of each type are pictured in sharp color photographs, and all are nicely described. This is a catalog to be savored by beginner and expert alike.

Ferncliff Gardens

See under *Dahlias*, page 74.

Gardenimport

See under *General Flowers and Vegetables*, page 19.

Hildenbrandt's Iris Gardens

See under *Irises*, page 110.

Klehm Nursery

Rt. 5, Box 197, S. Barrington, IL 60010

Telephone: 312-551-3715

Catalog price: $2

Peonies are spectacular flowers, and this gorgeous color catalog displays them well. More than 200 varieties are listed, from small rock-garden types to estate, garden, and tree peonies, and most are illustrated in glowing color. Klehm does not deal in the more common types, like Karl Rosenfield and Sarah Bernhardt, but concentrates on newer hybrids. The firm's other specialties are daylilies, hostas, and irises, and big selections of each are included in the catalog, many illustrated in color.

The New Peony Farm

P.O. Box 18105, St. Paul, MN 55118

Telephone: 612-457-8994

Catalog price: free

More than 70 peony cultivars in a simple descriptive booklet. Singles, doubles, semidoubles, and Japanese types are mixed together in strict alphabetical order by name, but a coded system allows readers to scan for the flowers and colors they're interested in. The text provides enough information to guide the shopper, but pictures will have to be sought elsewhere. The nursery ships "three- to five-eye divisions of young quality stock."

Reath's Nursery

P.O. Box 521, 100 Central Boulevard, Vulcan, MI 49892

Catalog price: $1

A nursery that devotes equal attention to herbaceous and tree peonies and that offers many of its own hybrids from both groups. The list of herbaceous peonies includes many from other hybridizers—Glassock, Wild, Murawska, Fay, and

Brand—concentrating more heavily on recent introductions than on old-fashioned strains. Among the tree peonies are a dozen Japanese varieties, a strong selection of Daphnis and Saunders hybrids, and many of Reath's own introductions. The nursery sells a couple of true yellow herbaceous peonies, created by crossing a yellow tree peony with a herbaceous type.

Smirnow's Son
11 Oakwood Drive W., Rt. 1, Huntington, NY 11743
Telephone: 516-421-0836

Catalog price: $2

Smirnow is the premier name in tree peonies, and the nursery's color catalog presents an excellent selection of each of the major types, along with many of its own hybrids. The heart of the catalog lies in the Japanese tree peonies: almost 100 cultivars are offered, about half of them pictured in color. Smaller selections of European and Lutea hybrids also offer many choices. An impressive collection of 100 plus herbaceous peonies, from older cultivars to new hybrids, fills the end of the list.

Tischler Peony Garden
1021 E. Division Street, Faribault, MN 55021
Telephone: 507-334-7242

R. W. Tischler owned and operated the Brand Peony Farm in Faribault for 22 years, until he sold the operation in 1976 to retire. The life of leisure apparently didn't agree with him, as he's now back in the peony patch with his own business. Mr. Tischler apologized to us in a note for the small size of his listing, noting his nursery was "still a one-man job," but in fact he looks like a fair match for the bigger growers. He offers more than 60 varieties, from choice doubles to singles, Japanese types, and newer hybrids—a number of them his own creations.

Andre Viette Farm & Nursery
See under *Garden Perennials*, page 92.

Wayside Gardens
See under *Garden Perennials*, page 92.

Gilbert H. Wild & Son, Inc.
See under *Daylilies*, page 82.

Primroses

Baileys'
P.O. Box 654, Edmonds, WA 98020

Catalog price: free

Exhibition *auricula*, *juliae*, and *vulgaris* hybrid primulas for serious growers. The auriculas make up the meat of this list, with scores of named cultivars organized by flower color. Each offering is briefly described, including name of hybridizer and date of introduction, so that even the uninitiated can take a stab at an order. Experts should use the listing only as a rough guide. The nursery has the resources of many growers available to it, and special requests for unlisted hybrids are encouraged.

Chehalis Rare Plant Nursery
2568 Jackson Highway, Chehalis, WA 98532

Catalog price: long self-addressed stamped envelope

Offers seed for garden and show auriculas in a full palette of colors; double auriculas and *P. florindae* are also available. The list comes on a small slip of paper, with no descriptions and no propagation instructions. Plants are sold at the nursery.

Daystar
See under *Trees and Shrubs*, page 151.

Far North Gardens
16785 Harrison, Livonia, MI 48154
Telephone: 313-422-0747

Catalog price: $2, deductible from first order

An eclectic assortment of seeds and plants, with an emphasis on seeds of primroses, wildflowers, and garden perennials in an intriguing descriptive catalog. The stars of the primrose listings are the Barnhaven Silver Dollar cultivars created in England by Florence Bellis. Seeds for almost 200 other primulas are also sold; these range from show and alpine auriculas to primula species for rock-garden, woodland, bog, and indoor growth. Among the wildflowers sold as plants are bloodroot (both single and double), mayapple, several native orchids, and a dozen trillium species. A number of cultivated perennials and alpines can be found mixed in with the wildflower seed listings. A tiny selection of vegetable seeds runs to the bizarre: tomatillo (or husk tomato), Atlantic Giant pumpkin, baby Asian corn, and dwarf cauliflower.

The real secret of this catalog is found in the last few pages. There, in a long list without descriptions or common names, are seeds for more than 1,000 additional perennials, alpines, and native plants.

Gardenimport
See under *General Flowers and Vegetables*, page 19.

L. S. A. Goodwin & Sons
Goodwins Road, Bagdad, Tasmania, Australia 7030
Telephone: 61-02-68-6233

Not an inch of space is wasted on this densely packed seed list. Seed for more than 1,000 plants—vegetables, flowering annuals, perennials, herbs, trees, and shrubs—are offered in strict alphabetical order in a single-spaced list that extends right to the edge of each page. Some surprises may lurk here, though the annual and perennial flower offerings seem somewhat commonplace. The real specialty of the house is on the back page: seed of hand-pollinated polyanthus primroses, offered in color mixes by strain. Regal Princess scented giant double and single mixed (whew!) make up one packet, Regal Giant ruffled mixed another. Several such offerings give shoppers a gambler's chance of getting some choice flowers in the colors they're after.

Brenda Hyatt
1 Toddington Crescent, Bluebell Hill, Nr. Chatham, Kent, England ME5 9QT
Telephone: 44-634-63251

Catalog price: one International Reply Coupon

An important supplier of show and alpine auriculas. Because of export restrictions, Ms. Hyatt can't send plants to the U.S. or Canada. She does carry a nice selection of hand-pollinated seed, however, sold by flower color or in mixes, and North American customers may find something of interest here. (Unfortunately, named varieties don't come true from seed.) Several other primulas are offered as seed, among them Diana primrose, cowslip, candelabra, and "various unusual primroses." A list of this last category can be had by special request.

Klaus R. Jelitto
Primula seed. See under *Alpines and Rock-Garden Perennials*, page 41.

The Primrose Path
See under *Garden Perennials*, page 91.

Surry Gardens
See under *Garden Perennials*, page 92.

Proteas

The Banana Tree
Protea seed. See under *Tropical Plants*, page 168.

C 'n C Protea
387 Carmen Plaza, Camarillo, CA 93010-6041
Telephone: 805-482-8905

Catalog price: free

A brief specialty seed list intended for the protea devotee. Protea, leucospermum, and leucodendron species make up the one-page list; mixed-seed packets are available within each of the three categories. A small selection of books—concentrating on proteas and wildflowers of South Africa and Australia—completes the list.

International Seed Supplies
Banksia seed. See under *Native Plants of Australia and South Africa*, page 119.

D. Orriell, Seed Exporters
See under *Native Plants of Australia and South Africa*, page 119.

Parsley's Cape Seeds
See under *Native Plants of Australia and South Africa*, page 120.

Protea Gardens of Maui
Rt. 2, Box 389, Kula, HI 96790
Telephone: 808-878-6048 or 6513

Catalog price: free

"Along the chain of Hawaiian Islands about 4,000 feet above the blue Pacific, up in the swirling mists of Haleakala volcano, nestled amidst rock gardens and waterfalls, lie 16 acres of exotic protea plants, with over 150 kinds and species." So Protea Gardens of Maui introduces itself in its small flier that includes pictures as colorful as the prose. The firm tops its price list with bouquets and dried protea wreaths. The live plants are offered with the words "individual requests per species depending on availability." Protea growers will have to follow up with another call or letter to find out just what plants are sold.

Protea Seed & Nursery Suppliers
Mrs. I. M. Bruens, P.O. Box 98229, Sloan Park, South Africa 2152
Telephone: 27-11-7051980

Catalog price: one International Reply Coupon

Seed for dozens of native South African proteas from a range of genera, each species succinctly described. A few banksia species from Australia are listed without notation, and a nice selection of ericas is included with a code to indicate flower color. Seed for several unrelated plants native to South Africa are added at the back of the list, with a note that even more native seeds can be obtained on request.

Anthony J. Skittone
See under *Bulbs*, page 63.

Von Lyncker Nurseries Ltd.
Seed for South African protea species. See under *Native Plants of Australia and South Africa*, page 120.

West Australian Wildflower Society
Banksia seed. See under *Native Plants of Australia and South Africa*, page 120.

Roses

AGM Miniature Roses, Inc.
P.O. Box 6056, Monroe, LA 71211
Telephone: 318-323-1219

A hundred or so miniatures simply offered in booklet form. Rose varieties are classed by color under shades of red, orange, pink, yellow, apricot, white, lavender, bicolors, and blends. A few maxi-minis (slightly larger than miniatures) are also listed. The handful of color photographs here tend to be shadowy and won't be much help to anyone trying to choose one tint of bloom over another.

Antique Rose Emporium
Rt. 5, Box 143, Brenham, TX 77833
Telephone: 409-836-9051

Catalog price: $2

This catalog is a delight. Though the plant selection is geared for the southern gardener, the catalog is filled with historical tidbits and wonderful old illustrations that make it appealing well beyond its targeted region. From such species roses as the true musk and swamp rose to old hybrids like the Archduke Charles and the Marechal Niel, the offerings are steeped in tradition. All plants are own root (grown on their own roots, rather than grafted onto different rootstock), and the nursery asserts that its offerings provide all the beauty of modern hybrids, but with less fuss. Northern gardeners will have to consult an expert or a book before ordering, as no climatic restrictions are noted.

Armstrong Roses
P.O. Box 1020, Somis, CA 93066

Catalog price: free

This luscious catalog, brimming with page after page of life-size color photographs, delights the eye. The company was founded in 1889 by plant breeder John Armstrong and has gone on to develop more than 200 new rose varieties since, including the popular Double Delight. Hybrid teas predominate, but miniatures and roselings (bushier, hardier types cloned from a mother plant) are also represented among the catalog's 60 or so offerings. Each order comes with a booklet of helpful advice on how to water, feed, and prune your plants. The catalog also includes a smattering of garden accessories, such as bronze sundials, faucet handles in the shape of birds, and Swiss-made pruning shears.

David Austin Roses
Bowling Green Lane, Albrighton, Wolverhampton,
England WV7 3HB
Telephone: 44-90-722-3931

Catalog price: $2 in cash

A meaty catalog for those who take their roses seriously. David Austin is both a breeder of new roses and a purveyor of all manner of older species and varieties—almost 700 choices in all. The nursery has concentrated its breeding efforts on crossing old-fashioned roses with modern varieties. Many of the resulting hybrids are described as having the simple, fragrant flowers and bushy, natural growth of the old roses, but with more than one flowering a season. The minimum order is £50, and an import permit is required. Gardeners may want to pool an order. (See *Buying Plants from Overseas*, page 9.)

BDK Nursery
P.O. Box 628, Apopka, FL 32704-0628
Telephone: 305-889-3053

A folksy 20-page catalog of miniatures put out by two self-described "RN's (Rose Nuts)" in Florida. Devoid of photographs, the brochure briefly cites more than 100 miniatures together with a handful of old garden roses. Most entries consist of a spirited line or two of description, and all reflect firsthand experience. "If you want a 'new show off' in your garden . . . pick this one!" exclaims the entry for one miniature. "Heavy bloomer, nice bushy plant, easy to grow, and looks great in a whiskey barrel," reads another.

Peter Beales Roses

London Road, Attleborough, Norfolk, England NR17 1AY
Telephone: 44-953-454707

An encyclopedic catalog of more than 1,000 rose species and cultivars. Peter Beales is the author of *Classic Roses*—one of the better reference books in the field. Rose fanciers will find just about everything they desire in this catalog, from antique species to the latest introductions. All are well described, some are illustrated in color, and the catalog is an education in roses. Minimum order for export is £50, and an import permit must be obtained before ordering. If you choose the most expensive varieties, you could reach the £50 minimum with just ten plants. If you have a small garden, you might consider pooling an order with friends. (See *Buying Plants from Overseas*, page 9.)

W. Atlee Burpee Company

See under *General Flowers and Vegetables*, page 15.

Cants of Colchester

305 Mile End Road, Colchester, Essex, England CO4 5EB
Telephone: 44-206-844008

Cants of Colchester has been in the nursery business since 1765 and has specialized in roses since 1858. More than 200 species and varieties are offered, with a concentration on hybrid tea and floribunda bush roses. Cants carries a nice selection of miniatures. No minimum order is specified, but an import permit must be obtained. Payment must be made in sterling, which can be simplified by charging the order to a credit card. (See *Buying Plants from Overseas*, page 9.)

Carroll Gardens

See under *Garden Perennnials*, page 87.

Donovan's Roses

P.O. Box 37800, Shreveport, LA 71133-7800
Catalog price: long self-addressed stamped envelope

More than 50 varieties are available from Donovan's, with hybrid teas dominating the list. A single page neatly printed on both sides spells out your options: in addition to the

hybrid teas, there are grandifloras, floribundas, shrub, and climbing roses succinctly noted in winsome entries that offer equal measures of caution, ardor, and enthusiasm. Early ordering is recommended; some varieties are in limited supply.

Ferbert Garden Center

806 S. Belt Highway, St. Joseph, MO 64507
Telephone: 816-279-7434

Hybrid teas top the offerings here, with nearly 100 strains arranged alphabetically in a simple three-page typewritten list. Floribundas, grandifloras, and climbers round out the selection. All roses are two-year-old field-grown plants.

Gandy's Roses Ltd.

N. Killworth, Lutterworth, Leicestershire, England LE17 6HZ
Telephone: 44-858-880398

Catalog price: free

A straightforward, no-nonsense catalog from a rose specialist that's been cultivating its blooms since 1876. The catalog's 48 pages list nearly 1,000 varieties and include a couple of color spreads to whet the appetite. Most of the selections are briefly evoked in a line or two of fine-print text; beginners may want some help making choices. Among the offerings are floribunda, grandiflora, hybrid tea, rambler, climbing, and miniature roses. No minimum order is specified, but shipping costs will be exorbitant if just a few plants are imported. (See *Buying Plants from Overseas*, page 9.)

Gloria Dei Nursery

36 East Road, High Falls Park, NY 12440
Telephone: 914-687-9981

Catalog price: free

A modest, family-run operation, Gloria Dei concentrates on one thing—miniature roses—and does it well. More than 100 varieties crowd the pages of this cheery booklet, lightly dusted with evangelical zeal. Each dwarf specimen is summarized in a line or two. There are no pictures, but if you like to think small, you should feel right at home here. Minimum order is three plants.

Greenmantle Nursery

See under *Trees and Shrubs*, page 154.

R. Harkness & Co. Ltd.

The Rose Gardens, Hitchin, Herts., England SG4 0JT
Telephone: 44-462-34027 or 34171

This is a beautiful catalog laid out with a delicacy of touch that can only be described as . . . English. The nursery has been winning rose competitions for more than a century now, and that fecund history shows in the balance and depth of the offerings here, which range from ankle-high miniatures on up. Three hundred varieties—standard, hybrid tea, floribunda, dwarf and patio, shrub, climbers, and ramblers—fill the booklet. Finely boxed photographs exhibit a soft glow on every page. Decriptive text is subtle and precise. Set aside an evening to browse through this catalog; there's plenty to whet, and satisfy, your appetite. An accompanying sheet of instructions on importing roses from Britain—a step-by-step guide for acquiring the necessary import permit—should dispel anxiety on that score. (See also *Buying Plants from Overseas*, page 9.)

Heritage Rose Gardens
16831 Mitchell Creek Drive, Fort Bragg, CA 95437

Catalog price: $1, deductible from first order

A fertile garden patch of dozens of old-fashioned roses—species, gallica (French), damask, centifolia (cabbage), alba (cottage), moss, rambling, bourbon, china, hybrid perpetual, and tea—squeezed into a dense treasure trove of a catalog. Descriptions are vivid and precise. All roses are two-year, field-grown plants on their own roots. A special selection of rare roses for custom rooting—usually available from one to two years after your order is placed—merits a page at the back of the catalog.

High Country Rosarium
1717 Downing Street, Denver, CO 80218
Telephone: 303-832-4026

Catalog price: $1

Since its debut 12 years ago, this nursery has specialized in shrub and old garden roses suited to rugged climates. Tall, thin, and enlivened by tasteful line drawings, the catalog contains 26 roses whose common trait is their hardiness. Among the listings are gallica, damask, moss, hybrid perpetual, Scotch, species, musk, rugosa, and shrub roses. Three collections—including a drought-tolerant mix—are also sold. A cautionary note to the buyer warns, "We sell one-year, own-root roses which are going to be much smaller than the standard grafted rose" on arrival. Have patience: these plants grow rapidly to their full size, then last forever.

Hillier Nurseries (Winchester) Ltd.
See under *Trees and Shrubs*, page 155.

Historical Roses
1657 W. Jackson Street, Painesville, OH 44077
Telephone: 216-357-7270

Catalog price: long self-addressed stamped envelope

A condensed listing of more than 100 antique roses. Old-fashioned shrub roses are the stars, many with the date of first appearance tacked at the end of brief, encoded lines of descriptive text ("B dbl rich pink 1872 FR"). Hybrid perpetuals, floribundas, hybrid teas, and climbers also claim their share of attention in the simple brochure. All roses are two-year-old field-grown plants, budded on multiflora understock.

Hortico, Inc.
723 Robson Road, Rt. 1, Waterdown, ON, Canada L0R 2H0
Telephone: 416-689-6984

Catalog price: free (request rose list)

Hortico is one of of the larger rose suppliers in North America. At first glance the price list looks as if it is for wholesale buyers only, but the fine print shows that the firm accepts smaller orders—even orders for a single plant—and adds a surcharge to the listed price. Small and large orders can be exported to the U.S. Almost 500 cultivars are offered, most of them hybrid teas, floribundas, and modern shrub roses. Some older damasks, gallicas, bourbons, and musks appear on the list, as do a small assortment of miniature and climbing types. Hortico sends out separate lists of perennials (see entry under *Garden Perennials*, page 89) and ornamental shrubs (see entry under *Trees and Shrubs*, page 156.)

Inter-State Nurseries
See under *Trees and Shrubs*, page 156.

Jackson & Perkins Co.
1 Rose Lane, Medford, OR 97501

Catalog price: free

A lovely display of dozens of hybrid teas, grandifloras, floribundas, and more. In business since 1872, Jackson & Perkins claims to be the world's largest rose nursery. The catalog's larger-than-life color photographs of dewy blooms are offset by thorough discussions of each plant's characteristics, including height, color, bud form, bloom size, petal count, stems, foliage, and fragrance. Fruit trees and flowering trees, such as magnolia, plum, and dogwood, are also listed. A separate bulb catalog is mailed in the fall.

Justice Miniature Roses
5947 S.W. Kahle Road, Wilsonville, OR 97070
Telephone: 503-682-2370

Catalog price: free

More than 100 miniature roses grace this 28-page booklet. There are no photos, but a lucid paragraph, complete with advice on best uses for the plant, attends each selection. "Too tall for borders and just right for containers," notes the text on one variety. "The long, wiry stems make for lovely bouquets." A number of collections—generally five or six varieties grouped together—are offered at slightly reduced prices. The nursery guarantees its plants, with one major exception: any miniatures grown indoors. "We have found from sad and costly experience that very few homes are cool and humid enough to sustain rose bushes," the catalog explains with an air of apology.

Keener Classics
205 E. Edgewood, Friendswood, TX 77546

Those on the lookout for hardy, easy-to-care-for, intensely fragrant plants will be interested in this rich collection of more than 100 antique roses. Hybrid perpetual, bourbon, tea, gallica, noisette, and polyantha are the recurring types here; climbing and bush varieties also turn up. Listings note the year of first appearance and approximate size of each rose offered.

W. Kordes' Söhne
2206 Klein Offenseth-Sparrieshoop, West Germany
Telephone: 49-4121-8688

A thick rose catalog practically dripping with color. The blooms have been enlarged to such an extent, and the color punched up so far, that it almost hurts the eyes to look at these pages. Hundreds of cultivars are offered, but the only words of English to help shoppers out come in a brief explanation of export terms. A minimum order of DM100 (about $50) is suggested, to offset the high costs of packing, shipping, and paperwork. (See *Buying Plants from Overseas*, page 9.)

V. Kraus Nurseries, Ltd.
See under *Trees and Shrubs*, page 157.

Krider Nurseries
See under *Trees and Shrubs*, page 157.

E. B. LeGrice Roses Ltd.
Norwich Road, N. Walsham, Norfolk, England NR28 0DR
Telephone: 44-692-402591

In business since 1920, this eminent firm now cultivates more than 400 rose types; they are known for their "offbeat" shades of bloom, including browns, blues, greens, and grays. A zesty catalog spells out your options. Ten chapters—floribundas, miniatures, modern shrubs, and so forth—are individually broken down by color and provide at least a handful of plants under each banner. Marginal notes on cultivation and care are extensive. Minimum order for export is £20.

Liggett's Rose Nursery
1206 Curtiss Avenue, San Jose, CA 95125
Telephone: 408-294-8230

Catalog price: free

A carefully chosen selection of 30 roses, set forth in a smallish catalog printed in dot-matrix type. The nursery prefers varieties that are hardy, bloom profusely, and have proved easy to grow; hybrid teas and floribundas dominate the list. Liggett's offers commercially grown modern roses but, "our main interest still lies with the older roses and the rarer (not commercially grown) modern types," the catalog notes. *Rosa odorata* is the principal understock here; *Rosa manettii* is also used. All plants are either one or two years old.

Lowe's Own-Root Roses
6 Sheffield Road, Nashua, NH 03062
Telephone: 603-888-2214

Catalog price: $2

This catalog is a gold mine for anyone devoted to old garden roses. Highly detailed and authoritative, the no-nonsense booklet presents 2,000 old-fashioned roses, among them albas, bourbons, centifolias, chinas, damasks, damask perpetuals, eglanterias, floribundas, gallicas, hybrid musks, and hybrid perpetuals. Damask perpetuals are the stars of the collection. Very little general discussion informs the catalog—some expertise with roses is assumed—and there are no photographs. Each entry includes the type and name, a note on its color, and the year of introduction. Not much nourishment for the armchair garden plotter, but a feast for the specialist.

MB Farm Miniature Roses, Inc.
Jamison Hill Road, Clinton Corners, NY 12514
Telephone: 914-266-3138

Catalog price: free

As muted and tasteful as the menu in a fine restaurant, this booklet lists its varieties by color in alphabetical order. You may find the color-wheel approach neatly saves you the trouble of picking through the jumbled hues of a conventional catalog: here are the miniature reds (16 choices), here are the yellows (seven in all), here are the whites (six), plus several score more intermediate shades of pink, orange, apricot-coral-peach, and miscellaneous. A scattering of small, dusky photographs lends these uncrowded pages an elegant look. Collections are featured at reduced cost.

McConnell Nurseries, Inc.
See under *Trees and Shrubs*, page 158.

McDaniel's Miniature Roses
7523 Zemco Street, Lemon Grove, CA 92045
Telephone: 619-469-4669

Catalog price: free

A clean and legible arrangement of more than 100 miniature listings shadows one side of a single page. Color of bloom is the organizing principle. Red, white, pink, yellow, orange-apricot-coral, and lavender-mauve each merit their names spelled out in capital letters atop a list; more than half the entries fall under either the red or pink rubrics. Descriptive text is necessarily brief. "Tiny yummy pink flowers," reads the entire listing for one rose.

John Mattock Ltd.

Nuneham Courtenay, Oxford, England OX9 9PY
Telephone: 44-86-738265

Sumptuous color photographs give brilliance to this balanced and comprehensive catalog from a British nursery that's been in the rose business since 1875. Groundcover roses, miniatures, floribundas, climbers, and shrub roses spill across the pages. Roughly every third variety rates a photograph. Descriptive text is clear, precise, and thorough in the English manner; tips on preparing your soil and planting, pruning, and feeding your roses once they are in the ground are generously offered. Because of the difficulties (and the high cost) of exporting roses, the nursery requires a minimum order of £100. This, too, is carefully explained. (See *Buying Plants from Overseas*, page 9.)

Earl May Seed & Nursery Co.

See under *General Flowers and Vegetables*, page 24.

Mike's Roses

Reginald Stocks, 6807 Smithway Drive, Alexandria, VA 22307

Catalog price: free

A rudimentary typewritten list of some 60 roses, filling a page and a half of plain paper. Roses are specified by name, type, color, and year of introduction, with hybrid teas of the past half century holding the edge. Eighteen miniatures make up a minor specialty.

Milaeger's Gardens

See under *Garden Perennials*, page 90.

Miniature Plant Kingdom

4125 Harrison Grade Road, Sebastopol, CA 95472
Telephone: 707-874-2233

Catalog price: $1, deductible from first order

Fifty or so miniature roses listed by name on a single page. With listings from Angela Rippon to Yellow Doll, this catalog is a quick read for the fan of these small beauties.

Miniature Plant World

Miniature roses. See under *Houseplants*, page 106.

Mini-Roses

P.O. Box 4255, Sta. A, Dallas, TX 75208
Telephone: 214-946-3487

Catalog price: free

A slim, monochromatic brochure proffering hundreds of miniature roses—mostly hybrid tea and exhibition types—in a spirit of bonhomie. The majority are best suited for bush growth, but spreading and climbing varieties supplement the mix. The two Texans in charge, who have been tending their sweet-scented plots since 1957, claim that certain benefits accrue to the roses from having had their roots in the Lone Star state. "Our growing season is long—usually February thru November, warm, sometimes HOT, the light, intense, and the days long. This combination gives us sturdy plants grown without winter heat that hold up well in transit. . . ."

Nor'East Miniature Roses, Inc.

58 Hammond Street, Rowley, MA 01969
Telephone: 617-948-7964

Catalog price: free

For shoppers uncertain of exactly where they stand when it comes to miniatures, this catalog makes an excellent primer. Sixty or 70 varieties are spaced throughout 15 pages bursting with color; at an average density of four or five possibilities per page, you never feel overwhelmed by the choices. Most varieties include a postage-stamp-size snapshot placed directly beside the text, so you have some idea of what "currant red" flowers, for example, look like. Ten varieties of miniature tree roses—and a handful of gift items including "mini vases" for tabletop display of your blooms—take up the back page.

Oregon Miniature Roses, Inc.

8285 S.W. 185th Avenue, Beaverton, OR 97007-5742
Telephone: 503-649-4482

A glossy package of approximately 200 miniature roses, about half captured in color photographs with unusually sharp detail. In addition to regular miniatures, the catalog offers a selection of micro-mini roses, climbing miniatures, and patio tree roses.

Carl Pallek & Son Nursery

P.O. Box 137, Virgil, ON, Canada L0S 1T0
Telephone: 416-468-7262

Catalog price: free to Canadian addresses

Canadian customers only. The Palleks sell only roses, about 400 varieties of them, including floribundas, grandifloras, old garden roses, and climbers (no miniatures). Hybrid teas take up the greatest part of the descriptive list. The nursery will ship to any address in Canada, but not to the U.S.

Park Seed Co.

See under *General Flowers and Vegetables*, page 26.

Pickering Nurseries Inc.
670 Kingston Road, Pickering, ON, Canada L1V 1A6
Telephone: 416-839-2111

Catalog price: $1

A rich sampling of varieties drawn from the arc of the rose rainbow makes this lavishly illustrated catalog a delight for the novice or the ace. Hybrid teas, grandifloras, floribundas, polyanthas, hybrid perpetuals, climbers, shrub roses, rugosas, and antiques—each category here contains at least a few specimens. Variety descriptions are careful to note each plant's relative height, merit rating, degree of fragrance, and hue. Planting hints are unusually thorough and well informed. Customers in the U.S. should be aware that rose varieties covered by patent (i.e., those introduced within the past 17 years) will not be exported.

Pixie Treasures Miniature Rose Nursery
4121 Prospect Avenue, Yorba Linda, CA 92686
Telephone: 714-993-6780

Catalog price: free

Large, high-sheen rose portraits steal the show in this otherwise unassuming catalog, which features a teddy bear reaching for a bouquet on the cover. All kinds of miniatures—from micro-mini to striped—are highlighted here. Almost 100 varieties are offered in all. The catalog includes a two-page guide to the proper care of these diminutive plants, with tips on watering, fertilizing, pruning, and extended care.

Rennie Roses
P.O. Box 444, Guelph, ON, Canada N1H 6K5

A crisp one-page selection of miniatures, grouped by color of bloom. Apricot-orange-coral, lavender-mauve, pink-pink blends, red-red blends and orange reds, and yellow and white are the tints to consider. Each listing offers a brief, poetic description. Minimum order is three plants.

Rose Acres
6641 Crystal Boulevard, Diamond Springs, CA 95619
Telephone: 916-626-1722

Catalog price: long self-addressed stamped envelope

A simple typewritten list of nearly 200 roses. Hybrid teas and floribundas are the types best represented, but shrub

roses, miniatures, grandifloras, climbing roses, and polyanthas also appear. Plants are shipped bare root from October through March.

The Rose Garden and Mini Rose Nursery
P.O. Box 203, Cross Hill, SC 29332
Telephone: 803-998-4331

Catalog price: free

This catalog presents approximately 100 miniature roses in an easy-to-read alphabetical format. A third or more of the selections have been honored with the American Rose Society's award of excellence. Helpful comments add bite to the one- or two-line plant descriptions: "A vigorous grower, so give it room," one such listing notes. For those gardeners captivated by things smaller than small, several micro-minis (which attain a maximum height of ten inches) are included.

Rosehill Farm
Gregg Neck Road, Galena, MD 21635
Telephone: 301-648-5538

Catalog price: free

A tidily organized and beautifully illustrated color catalog. Sixty or so miniature roses parade through its dozen slick pages. The selection is well balanced among colors and sizes: white, yellow, lavender and mauve, pink, orange, red, bicolor, and striped, in heights from six inches to two feet. Half a dozen collections complete the roster.

Rosen Tantau
Tornescher Weg 13, 2082 Uetersen bei, Hamburg, West Germany
Telephone: 49-4122-7084

An oversize, color-enriched catalog that is almost overwhelming with its gigantic blowups. Unfortunately, not a word is in English, and shoppers will have to read German even to decode the export terms.

Roses by Fred Edmunds
6235 S.W. Kahle Road, Wilsonville, OR 97070
Telephone: 503-638-4671

More than 100 rose varieties crowd the pages of this handsome, quirky catalog. In contrast to the usual botanical rundown, the listings here bristle with an individual voice and make delightful reading. "Last season this lovely pure-white vanished as quickly as the proverbial snowball in Hades. Since we've had few reports either pro or con, it will be interesting to see what happens this year," one bit of commentary observes. What's available? Hybrid teas, mainly, with a dash of grandifloras, floribundas, and climbers. Perhaps a third of the roses appear in juicy color photographs.

Roses of Yesterday & Today
802 Brown's Valley Road, Watsonville, CA 95076-0398
Telephone: 408-724-3537

Catalog price: $2

Quotations from Ann Landers to Longfellow pepper this utterly charming catalog. Hundreds of old, rare, and unusual rose varieties are featured and evoked in staggering detail for

80 tightly written pages. All descriptions include some general remarks, and many go on to cite the praise of gardeners from around the country. Concerning a variety named "Music Maker," someone writes, "It makes perfect pink flowers for single bud vases and is still flowering after weeks of below freezing Montana nights." Selected modern roses are intermingled with the rest.

Roseway Nurseries, Inc.
P.O. Box 269, Woodland, WA 98674
Telephone: 206-887-4159

Catalog price: $1

A crisp, brightly colored catalog listing more than 120 varieties of roses, from a nursery that has dealt in them for more than 50 years. Hybrid teas and grandifloras dominate the selection here; a handful of floribundas and climbers is also available. The photogenic blooms on display—perhaps a sixth of the total list appear in photographs—exhibit a surreal clarity. Two collections that have been assembled for the strength of their fragrance are a specialty of the house.

Sequoia Nursery/Moore Miniature Roses
2519 E. Noble Avenue, Visalia, CA 93277
Telephone: 209-732-0190

Catalog price: free

A series of colorful pamphlets and brochures jubilantly promoting more than 50 miniature varieties, many of which the nursery owners have bred and introduced to the rose ranks. One such flower, Torch of Liberty, won the Miniature of the Year award in 1987; two others, Sequoia Gold and Ring of Fire, developed in honor of the nursery's recent 50th anniversary, have also been singled out for excellence by the American Rose Society. A tiny vase designed for a single miniature bud, three books on rose cultivation and care, and miniature tree roses are also listed here. The nursery maintains an active breeding program; new varieties pop up all the time.

Springwood Miniature Roses
Rt. 3, Caledon East, ON, Canada L0N 1E0

For Canadian gardeners only (no export), this charming catalog offers more than 100 miniature roses. No photographic displays here, but simple line drawings the size of sealing-wax emblems dot the margins, and each listing is carefully described. Colors range from white through mauve, across shades of yellow, apricot, red, orange, and pink.

Stanek's Garden Center
E. 2929 27th Avenue, Spokane, WA 99223
Telephone: 509-535-2939

Red hybrid tea roses, pink hybrid teas, white, pink, and yellow hybrid teas—you can find what you want instantly in this cleanly organized four-page catalog. More than 100 roses, including grandiflora and floribunda varieties, are grouped by color and type. Climbing, shrub, and tree roses also get an inch or two of space. Listings include parenthetical mention of the American Rose Society's rating for each

rose. Half the catalog is taken up with fruit trees, nut trees, berry plants, and grapevines. All roses sold are two-year specimens, shipped bare root.

Stocking Rose Nursery
785 N. Capitol Avenue, San Jose, CA 95133
Telephone: 408-258-3606

Catalog price: free

More than 200 roses twine through this 24-page catalog, which offers an excellent introduction to rose growing for tenderfeet who don't know a floribunda from a climber. Listings unfold at a leisurely pace, with each rose receiving a paragraph of pointed discussion. Hybrid teas dominate the roster, but grandiflora, polyantha, floribunda, climbing, and tree roses also get a nod. Detailed tips on planting and care proceed step by step through mulching, fertilizing, watering, spraying, pruning, and picking. More than a dozen color photographs serve as reminders of what the slaving in the garden is all about.

Tate Nursery
Rt. 20, Box 436, Tyler, TX 75708
Telephone: 214-593-1020

A glossy brochure detailing more than 70 rose varieties—mostly hybrid teas and grandifloras, with some floribundas, polyanthas, climbers, and shrubs. Each entry consists of a few descriptive words. Rose bushes are guaranteed to bloom the first spring (or be replaced at half the original cost the following spring). The minimum order is three bushes to one address.

Thomasville Nurseries, Inc.
P.O. Box 7, Thomasville, GA 31799
Telephone: 912-226-5568

Catalog price: free

Thomasville specializes in hybrid tea roses, offering 60 named varieties. Floribundas, grandifloras, and a nice selection of climbing roses are also sold. A number of the cultivars can be bought as standard tree roses grafted to an upright three-foot understock. The catalog describes each plant and shows a select few in black-and-white and color photographs.

Two Thomasville sidelines deserve catalogs of their own. More than 200 daylily cultivars are offered, including a good array of miniatures. All but the most recent introductions are priced below $5. The nursery also sells several dozen azaleas, among them a number of Indica and Kurume cultivars and several Gulf Coast natives.

Thousand Flowers Landscaping
405 Edmands Road, Framingham, MA 01701
Telephone: 617-877-3820

Catalog price: long self-addressed stamped envelope

Three dozen old-fashioned roses presented on a simple typed list with basic information about color, height, and date of introduction. The offerings are spread about evenly among gallica, damask, moss, hybrid musk, centifolia, bourbon, and alba types, all but a few dating from before the First World War.

Tillinghast Seed Co.
See under *General Flowers and Vegetables*, page 31.

Tiny Petals Nursery
489 Minot Avenue, Chula Vista, CA 92010
Telephone: 619-422-0385

Catalog price: free

This amiable 14-page catalog from prolific hybridizer Dee Bennett showcases many of her own blooms, including va-rieties dedicated to family and friends. Approximately 100 miniature roses are cited, together with a handful of micro-miniatures, trailers, and climbers. Color photographs document the singular beauty of perhaps a quarter of the varieties offered here; the rest are left to your imagination.

Wayside Gardens
See under *Garden Perennials*, page 92.

Sempervivums and Sedums

Alpenflora Gardens
See under *Alpines and Rock-Garden Perennials*, page 40.

Country Cottage
Rt. 2, Box 130, Sedgwick, KS 67135
Telephone: 316-796-0496

Catalog price: 50¢ or two first-class stamps

Dozens of sempervivum species and cultivars (sold as "chicks"), along with a clutch of sedums. Offerings are adequately described in a sentence or two, and two books are recommended for those who want to see pictures.

Lamb Nurseries
See under *Garden Perennials*, page 89.

Rakestraw's Perennial Gardens & Nursery
See under *Alpines and Rock-Garden Perennials*, page 41.

Red's Rhodies & Alpine Gardens
15920 S.W. Oberst Lane, Sherwood, OR 97140
Telephone: 503-625-6331

Catalog price: two first-class stamps

From the name, we expected rhododendrons and rock-garden plants (and in fact the company does sell both at its nursery), but this mail-order catalog is limited to sedums and sempervivums. Almost 250 species and varieties are listed; all receive a few words of description. A color insert pictures a few of these subtle garden delicacies.

Rocknoll Nursery
See under *Alpines and Rock-Garden Perennials*, page 42.

Jim & Irene Russ
HCR 1, Box 6450, Igo, CA 96047
Telephone: 916-396-2329

Catalog price: 50¢

More than 300 sempervivums and sedums offered in a descriptive booklet with some of the tiniest lettering we've seen. Minimum order is ten plants, but different types may be combined for the total.

Squaw Mountain Gardens
36212 S.E. Squaw Mountain Road, Estacada, OR 97023
Telephone: 503-630-5458

A collector's list of sedums, sempervivums, and related plants for rock-garden use. Roughly 70 sedums are listed and about as many sempervivums, each described in a few words.

Shade Plants

Homestead Division of Sunnybrook Farms
See under *Hostas*, page 104.

Shady Oaks Nursery
700 19th Avenue N.E., Waseca, MN 56093

Catalog price: $1, deductible from first order

"Specialists in plants for shady places." Gardeners with shady lots or shady corners to fill will appreciate the work Shady Oaks Nursery has done to bring together scores of shade-tolerant plants in a single catalog. Hostas are the stars of this show; 70 cultivars can be ordered individually or in special collections. Other attractions include astilbes, campanulas, ferns, trilliums, and a nice selection of trees and shrubs.

Stillpoint Gardens
Box 24, McKnightstown, PA 17343

Catalog price: one first-class stamp

A simple list of shade-tolerant perennials and shrubs, with only the briefest of descriptions. Hostas, daylilies, ferns, azaleas, and rhododendrons are featured, with dozens of species and cultivars offered. About 150 other plants are sold, from junipers and hollies to astilbes and primulas. The perennials are field grown and dug to order. The shrubs are grown in 2- to 4-inch pots. Visitors to the area can see the display gardens on weekends and can stay in the New Salem House Bed and Breakfast, run by the owners.

Sweet Potato Plants

Fred's Plant Farm
Rt. 1, P.O. Box 707, Dresden, TN 38225-0707
Telephone: 901-364-5419

Catalog price: free

Sweet potato plants shipped in the spring, beginning in mid-April. Fred's offered 17 varieties in 1987 and sold them by the dozen, the hundred, or the thousand.

George's Plant Farm
Rt. 1, Box 194, Martin, TN 38237
Telephone: 901-587-9477

Catalog price: free

Fourteen sweet potato varieties sold as plants from mid-April to the end of May. A dozen plants is the minimum order, and advance reservation is required for orders of more than a thousand. In 1987 the nursery added tomato and pepper plants to its inventory.

Margrave Plant Company
Gleason, TN 38229
Telephone: 901-648-5174

Catalog price: free

In business since 1933, this is the oldest of the sweet potato growers we've listed, and we suspect that its flier has served as the model for those of the above two competitors. Margrave sells sweet potato plants in a choice of 15 varieties by the dozen, the hundred, or the thousand. Special offers allow gardeners to save when ordering two different varieties.

Ponzer Nursery
See under *Trees and Shrubs*, page 162.

Steele Plant Company
Gleason, TN 38229
Telephone: 901-648-5476

Catalog price: free

Seven varieties of sweet potato plants are offered in a newspaper-style catalog that introduces us to the entire Steele/

Sanders family. Three generations are now at work at the firm, and a fourth is already toddling through the fields. Steele makes a special pitch to northern growers, claiming that yields in New England can almost match those in the South if gardeners plant quick-maturing varieties. A number of special collections allow gardeners to order small quantities and assorted plants rather than sign up for the normal 25-plant minimum. Steele also sells cabbage, broccoli, cauliflower, brussels sprout, and onion plants.

Trees and Shrubs

Adams County Nursery, Inc.
P.O. Box 108, Aspers, PA 17304
Telephone: 717-677-8105

Catalog price: free

Fruit-tree suppliers for both commercial growers and home gardeners. More than 30 apple varieties are offered, grafted onto a choice of six rootstocks. More than 50 peach and nectarine varieties are listed, along with an array of pear, cherry, plum, and apricot trees. All are sold as year-old specimens.

Alberta Nurseries & Seed Ltd.
General nursery stock for Canadian customers. See under *General Flowers and Vegetables*, page 13.

Alexander's Nurseries
Lilacs. See under *Berry Plants*, page 52.

Alpine Nursery
P.O. Box 5281, 1763 Montana 35, Kalispell, MT
59903-5281
Telephone: 406-752-0732

Catalog price: free

Seedling trees for northern growers, including Colorado blue spruce, Scotch pine, ponderosa pine, European white birch, eastern and western red cedar, and Engleman spruce. You can order some spectacular trees from this catalog if you have the room to grow them. Ponderosa pine and western red cedar can both grow to 200 feet. For the less ambitious, Siberian pea shrub and Tatarian honeysuckle are offered as nice low borders.

Alpine Plants
See under *Garden Perennials*, page 86.

Ames' Orchard and Nursery
6 E. Elm Street, Fayetteville, AR 72701
Telephone: 501-443-0282

Catalog price: $1

For plainspoken honesty, these folks are hard to beat. They talk about the tough climate of the Ozarks, where they're located—scorching summers and bitter cold winters—then admit that those in milder zones west of the Rockies would do better to buy trees from western nurseries that carry less hardy varieties. And while they discuss the finer qualities of their stock, they take pains to point out potential problems. A refreshing change from the glossy, hard-sell approach of some mail-order growers. Ames's specialty is apples, but they also sell peaches, strawberries, blueberries, blackberries, raspberries, and grapes. Their prices are extremely competitive.

Appalachian Gardens
P.O. Box 82, Waynesboro, PA 17268-0082
Telephone: 717-762-4312

Catalog price: free

Ornamental trees and shrubs, offered in a well-written descriptive booklet. The listings include the Franklin tree, several mountain laurels, a small array of azalea and rhododendron hybrids, ten crape myrtle cultivars, and a few viburnum species—almost 200 different plants in all.

Aubin Nurseries, Ltd.
P.O. Box 1089, Carman, MB, Canada R0G 0J0
Telephone: 204-745-6703

Catalog price: free

A nice selection of ornamental shrubs, shade trees, and fruit trees. Some of the shade trees are available as large specimens. The firm shares its expertise by offering a tree-moving service. The nursery also sells roses and garden perennials. Small orders from the U.S. are discouraged, but Aubin will happily ship larger quantities across the border.

Bakers' Tree Nursery
13895 Garfield Road, Salem, OH 44460
Telephone: 216-537-3903

Catalog price: free

Evergreen seedlings for growers with land to fill. The minimum order is 50 trees. If you're planning a Christmas tree farm, planting an unused field, or growing a long windbreak, Bakers' may be the source for you.

The Banana Tree
Banana trees. See under *Tropical Plants*, page 168.

Vernon Barnes & Son Nursery
P.O. Box 250L, McMinnville, TN 37110

Catalog price: free

One- and two-year-old fruit trees, shade and flowering trees, ornamental shrubs, berry plants, and groundcovers. Most of the fruit trees are available on full-size rootstocks only, but a few are sold on dwarfing stock, and six apple varieties are sold as semidwarf trees. Prices are reasonable.

Bass Pecan Company
P.O. Box 42, Lumberton, MS 39455-0042
Telephone: 601-796-2461

Catalog price: free

Pecan trees for home gardeners and commercial growers. Twenty varieties are offered, for planting from zone 9 to the southern part of zone 6. Bass also sells fruit trees, including peach, apple, plum, fig, cherry, apricot, pear, and persimmon.

Bear Creek Nursery
P.O. Box 411, Northport, WA 99157

Catalog price: free

A catalog of fruit and nut trees that is truly rich in information and variety. Bear Creek specializes in antique and unusual apples. More than 70 varieties are kept in stock for normal shipment, and 100 others are available in limited quantities; most are offered on a choice of three different rootstocks. The Bear Creek catalog helps evaluate the choices with descriptions that include taste, texture, keeping quality of the fruit, and the growth habits and cultural requirements of the trees. A three-page section presents a quick education in the selection and care of apple trees.

The nursery's nut-tree department is almost as strong, offering 27 walnut varieties and 16 chestnuts, as well as filberts, hazelnuts, and hickories. A portion of the proceeds from chestnut tree sales goes to support the American Chestnut Foundation, which is working to develop blight-resistant chestnuts. All nut trees are certified for shipment to California.

Bear Creek also sells pear, apricot, and mulberry trees, along with a selection of ornamental and shade trees, flowering shrubs, and other fruiting plants.

Beaver Creek Nursery
P.O. Box 18243, Knoxville, TN 37928
Telephone: 615-922-8561

Catalog price: free

Hard-to-find trees and shrubs for landscaping. Mike Stansberry started the nursery after searching in vain for unusual plants for his own landscaping business, and he has since expanded to offer his discoveries for sale. His list includes brief descriptions (but no illustrations) of such specimens as American smoke tree (*Cotinus obovatus*), Katsura tree (*Cercidiphyllum japonicum*), Kentucky coffee tree (*Gymnocladus dioica*), and Serbian spruce (*Picea omorika*).

Beaverlodge Nursery Ltd.
P.O. Box 127, Beaverlodge, AB, Canada T0H 0C0
Telephone: 403-354-2195

Catalog price: free to Canadian customers

Canadian orders only. Beaverlodge sells a broad array of nursery stock—apple, plum, and cherry trees, saskatoons, gooseberries, and other berry plants, lilacs, hawthorns, honeysuckles, and a selection of hedge shrubs, roses, ornamental and shade trees, evergreens, and garden perennials.

Bergeson Nursery
Fertile, MN 56540
Telephone: 218-945-6988

Catalog price: free

Fruit trees, shade and ornamental trees, hedge shrubs, flowering shrubs, roses, peonies, vines, and berries in a stripped-down price list without descriptions or illustrations. Mail-order shoppers may want to check by letter or telephone for additional offerings, as not all Bergeson's stock is included in the list.

Bernardo Beach Native Plant Farm
Drought-tolerant trees and shrubs. See under *Wildflowers*, page 174.

Boyer Nurseries
405 Boyer Nursery Road, Biglerville, PA 17307
Telephone: 717-677-8558 or 9567

Catalog price: long self-addressed stamped envelope

Fruit trees and flowering trees and shrubs sold from a barebones price list without descriptions or illustrations. The nursery carries a large stock of apple trees, including a big selection of antique varieties, as well as peach, pear, cherry, plum, and apricot trees. The ornamental offerings include Eastern redbud, flowering plum, several flowering crab apples and dogwoods, and 50 azalea and rhododendron cultivars. Strawberry plants are sold at a very good price.

Brooks Tree Farm
9785 Portland Road N.E., Salem, OR 97305
Telephone: 503-393-6300

Catalog price: long self-addressed stamped envelope

Evergreen tree seedlings from around the world, sold in a minimum quantity of 100. Some common species, such as eastern white pine and Colorado spruce, are offered, along with such exotics as giant sequoia, deodar cedar, and Turkish fir. The seed source for each plant is given, and some of these are quite interesting. Noble fir plants are grown from seeds from six different mountain sites, the elevations of which are listed, and the buyer can choose the most appropriate one. Scotch pine is offered from both France and Spain, Bosnian pine from Yugoslavia, nordmann fir from Russia, and alpine fir is grown from seeds collected at an 8,000-foot elevation in Dixie National Forest.

Burgess Seed & Plant Co.
See under *General Flowers and Vegetables*, page 15.

Burnt Ridge Nursery
432 Burnt Ridge Road, Onalaska, WA 98570
Telephone: 206-985-2873

Catalog price: long self-addressed stamped envelope

A smaller nursery with a select list of trees, shrubs, and vines that produce edible fruits or nuts. The firm steers clear of the obvious, offering such exotics as loquat, pineapple guava, golden chinkapin, and monkey puzzle trees, along with several chestnut, hickory, filbert, and fig trees. An indication of hardiness is given for most plants listed.

W. Atlee Burpee Company
See under *General Flowers and Vegetables*, page 15.

C & O Nursery
1700 N. Wenatchee Avenue, P.O. Box 116, Wenatchee, WA 98801-0122
Telephone: 509-662-7164

Catalog price: free

A supplier of fruit trees to commercial growers, C & O will also sell to home gardeners. The emphasis in this glossy catalog is decidedly *not* on the old-fashioned types, but rather on heavy-bearing, long-storing new varieties. Thirty-six different apples are sold on six different rootstocks, along with good selections of peaches, nectarines, apricots, cherries, prunes, plums, and pears. Fruit descriptions and ripening dates are given for all varieties, and information is offered on spacing, planting, pruning, and pollination. Orders of less than $30 are subject to an additional handling charge.

CTP
P.O. Box 10162, Corpus Christi, TX 78410

Catalog price: long self-addressed stamped envelope

CTP stands for Crockett T. Pecos, and he sells seed for about 30 trees and shrubs native to the Southwest. The list spells out only Latin and common names—no descriptions. Among the offerings are Texas ebony (*Pithecellobium flexicaule*), chapatillo (*Amyris texana*), and a few acacia species. Special requests are taken for native cactus species.

California Nursery Company
P.O. Box 2278, Fremont, CA 94536
Telephone: 415-797-3311

Catalog price: free

An unillustrated list of fruit and nut trees with no descriptions. Most of the fruit trees are offered on standard rootstock, but a few of the more popular varieties are also available on dwarfing stock. Both standard and dwarf citrus trees are listed, as well as avocado, artichoke, and kiwi plants, and almost 30 grape varieties. The nut trees include walnuts, pecans, filberts, chestnuts, pistachios, and almonds.

Callahan Seeds
6045 Foley Lane, Central Point, OR 97502
Telephone: 503-855-1164

Catalog price: long self-addressed stamped envelope

An impressive list of tree and shrub seeds from around the world. Callahan started out selling seeds of trees and shrubs from western North America in 1977, but has since expanded to cover the globe. If you have the land, the climate, and the time to grow these trees from seed, Callahan Seeds can offer you the world—more than 500 species in all. Most seeds are sold in 25-gram packets (slightly less than an ounce), and most of the packets sell for less than $5.

Camellia Forest
125 Carolina Forest Road, Chapel Hill, NC 27514
Telephone: 919-967-5529

Catalog price: two first-class stamps

A supplier of ornamental trees and shrubs, primarily for southern growers, with a specialty in camellias. (Northern gardeners can grow these indoors or in a cool greenhouse.) In addition to the camellias, the nursery sells more than 200 tree and shrub species, many of them from China and Japan. Most are hardy only through zones 6 and 7, but a few selections will survive north to zone 3. The list gives the hardiness of each plant and a brief description.

Mark S. Cannon
300 Montezuma Avenue, Dothan, AL 36303
Telephone: 205-792-6970

Hundreds of camellia scions from a man who bills himself as the "originator" of the scion business. He also claims to have "the best of the old and all new varieties." We'll have to take his word for it. The list gives varietal names and prices only; no descriptions. The minimum order is $10.

Carino Nurseries
P.O. Box 538, Indiana, PA 15701
Telephone: 412-463-3350 or 7480

Catalog price: free

Evergreens and a limited number of deciduous trees, sold primarily in lots of 100 or more. Some trees are chosen "specials" and offered in lots of ten, a more manageable quantity for the average homeowner. In 1987 the specials included white dogwood, white birch, blue spruce, Canadian hemlock, Fraser fir, Douglas fir, and American arborvitae.

Cascade Forestry Service
Route 1, Cascade, IA 52033
Telephone: 319-852-3042

Catalog price: free

Seedling and transplant trees in quantities a home gardener can handle. Black walnut, white oak, black cherry, northern pecan, butternut, shellbark hickory, and hazelnut are among the deciduous offerings. White pine, red pine, Scotch pine, Douglas fir, Norway spruce, Colorado blue spruce, white spruce, Black Hill spruce, and Colorado fir make up the evergreen list. Single trees can be ordered, as long as the total reaches a minimum of $20. (Big discounts are given on orders of 100 or 1,000 trees.)

Case Nursery
P.O. Box 155, Ringoes, NJ 08551
Telephone: 201-782-3272

Catalog price: free

A specialized nursery that sells peach and nectarine trees only—28 different peaches and five nectarines. Trees are sold in sizes from two to six feet.

Chestnut Hill Nursery, Inc.
Rt. 1, Box 341, Alachua, FL 32615
Telephone: 904-462-2820

Catalog price: free

Hybrid chestnut trees that the nursery claims are blight resistant. The trees are a cross between a Chinese chestnut and a blight-resistant American chestnut and, according to the nursery's brochure, have the height of the American species with the blight resistance of the Chinese tree. The seedlings are expensive when compared to chestnut trees from other sources, but if the claims made for them are true,

they may be worth the extra cost. The nursery also sells several varieties of grafted oriental persimmons.

Chiltern Seeds
Seed for ornamental trees and shrubs. See under *General Flowers and Vegetables*, page 15.

Clones Unlimited
54 Brook Circle, Glenmoore, PA 19343-9209

Catalog price: free

Hybrid poplar, forsythia, pussy willow, California privet, rose of Sharon, and weeping willow, all sold as unrooted cuttings.

Coènosium Gardens
R. Fincham, 6642 S. Lone Elder Road, Aurora, OR 97002
Telephone: 215-377-1495

Catalog price: $3, refunded on $25 order

A huge catalog of rare and unusual conifers—more than 500 species and cultivars in all—each briefly described and a few illustrated in black-and-white photographs. The majority are dwarf types, which will be of particular interest to rock gardeners. Shoppers will probably want to refer to a good book (or perhaps several) before ordering, to get a better idea of what the plants look like and what conditions they need in order to grow. Mr. Fincham sells a few such texts and urges serious buyers to pay him a visit. Bonsai enthusiasts will find a number of choice junipers and pines ready for bonsai preparation—the junipers rooted, the pines grafted into the root crown.

Cold Stream Farm
2030 Free Soil Road, Free Soil, MI 49411-9752
Telephone: 616-464-5809

Catalog price: free

An assortment of trees and shrubs, including Douglas fir, Hetzi juniper, white cedar, redbud, white and gray dogwood, witch hazel, Osage orange, American and Chinese chestnut, black and red oak, and black walnut. The nursery devotes the better part of its brochure to the promotion of a fast-growing hybrid poplar, billed as "a tree that grandparents can plant and enjoy *with* their grandchildren." Most of the trees are sold as small rooted seedlings, six inches to two feet tall, but some can be ordered as large as five feet. Minimum order is $5.

Colvos Creek Nursery & Landscaping
Rt. 2, Box 176, Vashon, WA 98070

Catalog price: $1, deductible from first order

More than 300 trees and shrubs from a nursery that makes an effort to seek out unusual species and cultivars the owners feel deserve wider use. Many western natives are on the list: weeping Alaska yellow cedar, Pacific wax myrtle, and California honeysuckle (one of those rare plants that prefers dry shade). The nursery has also turned up plently of foreign exotics; it offers dozens of hardy eucalyptus species, as well as plants like Montezuma cypress, cootamundra wattle, and Père David maple.

Cumberland Valley Nurseries, Inc.
P.O. Box 471, McMinnville, TN 37110
Telephone: 615-668-4153

Catalog price: free

A fruit-tree nursery with a specialty in peaches. Cumberland Valley grows a handful of apple, pear, cherry, and pecan varieties and armfuls of peaches. Eighty-four different kinds of peaches are offered on three different rootstocks (Lovell, Nemaguard, and Halford). Thirteen plum types and ten nectarines are offered on the same rootstocks. The price list includes no descriptions, so you'll have to learn what's special about each of the varieties from other sources. Minimum order is $25.

The Cummins Garden
Dwarf conifers. See under *Azaleas and Rhododendrons*, page 44.

Corwin & Letha Davis
20865 Junction Road, Bellevue, MI 49021
Telephone: 616-781-7402

Catalog price: $1 and self-addressed stamped envelope

The dollar will get you a two-by-four-inch slip of paper with prices for pawpaw seeds and seedlings. No indication of the size of the seedlings is given.

Daystar
Rt. 2, Box 250, Litchfield, ME 04350
Telephone: 207-724-3369

Catalog price: $1

Unusual trees and shrubs, dwarf conifers, rhododendrons, heathers, primroses, and rock-garden perennials make up this wide-ranging list. Many of the offerings will be of particular interest to rock gardeners, but you needn't have a rockery to grow the many full-size trees, rhododendrons, heathers, or primulas. Seventy-five heathers were on the 1987 list, with 35 rhododendrons, 25 primulas, and almost 200 trees and shrubs. Plants are listed by botanical name with very brief (two- or three-word) descriptions. Minimum order is $15.

Del's Japanese Maples
4691 River Road, Eugene, OR 97404
Telephone: 503-688-5587 or 2174

Catalog price: free

Two hundred Japanese maples listed by name only (no descriptions). Most are sold as grafts on two-year rootstock in 2¼ by 5-inch pots. Shipments are sent in May only, and supplies of many cultivars are limited. No minimum order.

Bill Dodd's Rare Plants
Trees and shrubs for southern gardeners. See under *Azaleas and Rhododendrons*, page 44.

Earl Douglass
Red Creek, NY 13143
Telephone: 315-754-6621

Catalog price: 25¢

Chestnut seed nuts and seedlings from a man who is working to develop a blight-resistant hybrid from American and Chinese parent trees. The seed nuts are a mix of Manchurian and hybrid nuts (from Manchurian × American hybrids crossed back to the Manchurian trees), and we assume the seedlings are of the same assortment. Mr. Douglass makes no rash claims for the blight-resistance of his trees, instead encouraging customers to try them while he continues to refine his hybrids. His prices are a quarter those of some competitors.

Dutch Mountain Nursery
Trees and shrubs for attracting birds. See under *Wildlife Food Plants*, page 182.

Eastern Plant Specialties
Dwarf conifers. See under *Azaleas and Rhododendrons*, page 44.

Eccles Nurseries, Inc.
Rimersburg, PA 16248-0525
Telephone: 814-473-6265 or 3550

Catalog price: free

Seedling trees, primarily evergreens, sold in quantities of 50 or more. Among the listings are Austrian pine, bristlecone pine, mugho pine, Douglas fir, Fraser fir, Colorado fir, Norway spruce, white spruce, Chinese chestnut, white ash, black walnut, sugar maple, and black locust. Catalog "specials" offer good prices on selected trees in smaller quantities.

Edible Landscaping
Rt. 2, Box 77, Afton, VA 22920

Catalog price: free

An unusual assortment of fruit trees and berry plants in an extremely informative catalog. Offerings include several kiwi cultivars (hardy to zone 3), gooseberries, currants, blackberries, pawpaws, Juneberries, blueberries, Swiss stone pine (which yields pine nuts), persimmons, grapes, figs, mulberries, jujube, and a selection of classic apples (grafted onto dwarfing rootstock). We were impressed by the helpful and honest tone of the catalog and by the extensive instructions given for the care of the lesser-known trees.

Emlong Nurseries Inc.
Stevensville, MI 49127
Telephone: 616-429-3431 or 3612

Catalog price: free

A broad array of nursery stock—fruit, nut, and shade trees, ornamental shrubs, berries, hedge shrubs, grapes, roses, and a small assortment of perennial plants. Though the catalog is wide ranging, the number of varieties offered of each plant is not large. Emlong has much to offer in the area of hedges and flowering trees and shrubs. No minimum order.

Exotica Rare Fruit Nursery
Tropical fruit trees. See under *Tropical Plants*, page 168.

Farmer Seed & Nursery Co.
See under *General Flowers and Vegetables*, page 18.

Fernald's Nursery
Rt. 2, Monmouth, IL 61462
Telephone: 309-734-6994

Catalog price: one first-class stamp

Hardy nut trees for northern growers. Fernald's sells ten varieties of grafted pecans, most of them cut from native Iowa and Illinois parents. Seedlings from the same parent trees are offered at lower prices. In addition to pecans, the nursery sells American and hybrid chestnuts, hazelnuts, black walnuts, butternuts, shellbark and shagbark hickories, and hicans (a pecan and hickory hybrid). No minimum order.

Fiddyment Farms Inc.
5000 Fiddyment Road, Roseville, CA 95678
Telephone: 916-771-0800

Catalog price: free price list

Four species of pistachio trees. Seedlings are shipped between December 15 and January 30. The price list is just that, but explains that a planting guide will be sent with each order.

Henry Field Seed & Nursery Co.
See under *General Flowers and Vegetables*, page 18.

The Fig Tree Nursery
P.O. Box 124, Gulf Hammock, FL 32639
Telephone: 904-486-2930

Catalog price: $1

As the name suggests, fig trees are the specialty here; they're offered in 13 varieties. To complement that strength, the nursery sells a selection of other fruit trees, berries, and ornamentals for southern growers. Among the offerings are Florida 90 strawberries, Orient pears, wisteria, and muscadine grapes.

Flickingers' Nursery
Sagamore, PA 16250
Telephone: 412-783-6528 or 397-4953

Catalog price: free

Evergreen seedlings and transplants sold by the hundred or the thousand (though the nursery will accept an order for 50 trees of one size and kind). The descriptive brochure lists

several species each of fir, pine, and spruce, and both Canadian and Carolina hemlock. Trees are shipped from late March to late April.

Forestfarm
990 Tetherow Road, Williams, OR 97544
Telephone: 503-846-6963

Catalog price: $2

Native plants, perennials, unusual ornamental trees and shrubs, wildlife food plants, and more in a densely packed descriptive list. More than 800 offerings in all. Plants are sold rooted in pots 2 inches square by 6 inches deep, which, the owners feel, allow good-size plants to be shipped economically without the shock of bare-root handling. Each listing is briefly but thoroughly described with the help of a coded system that explains the plant type, its zone hardiness, origin, and special uses (for bonsai, fragrance, or wildlife food, for example). The catalog is sprinkled with quotes, recipes, and drawings, which break up what might otherwise be a formidable mass of offerings.

Dean Foster Nurseries
See under *Berry Plants*, page 53.

Four Winds Growers
P.O. Box 3538, Fremont, CA 94539
Telephone: 415-656-2591

Catalog price: long self-addressed stamped envelope

Dwarf citrus trees, suitable for growth in outdoor containers or for planting in a garden where space is limited. A selection of oranges, tangerines, lemons, grapefruit, limes, tangelos, and kumquats are offered in an informative catalog that provides detailed instructions for care. The nursery cannot ship trees to Florida, Texas, Louisiana, or Arizona.

Fowler Nurseries, Inc.
525 Fowler Road, Newcastle, CA 95659
Telephone: 916-645-8191

Catalog price: free price list, $2 for descriptive catalog

Fruit and nut trees, roses, berries, grapes, and perennial vegetables (artichokes, asparagus, horseradish, and rhubarb). The selection is not huge (only 15 apple varieties and five strawberries), but with plums, persimmons, cherries, peaches, pears (domestic and Asian), apricots, almonds, pecans, walnuts, filberts, and berries to choose from, shoppers will still have plenty to think about. The price list is just that, with no descriptions at all. The catalog could serve as a handbook for starting an orchard or berry farm and will be particularly useful to gardeners in elevated regions of northern California. Trees are shipped between January 15 and March 1. No orders are accepted after January 15. No minimum order.

Foxborough Nursery
3611 Miller Road, Street, MD 21154
Telephone: 301-836-7023

Catalog price: $1

An extensive inventory of dwarf and unusual conifers, broadleaf evergreens, and other trees—about 900 species and cul-

Before Buying a Tree, Try Tasting the Apple

When they shop for unusual apple trees, gardeners are faced with thick catalogs full of attempts to evoke the color, shape, and flavor of hundreds of different fruits in a few words. But, even with the aid of the best descriptions, shoppers end up relying on someone else's perceptions and opinions—someone who may have an entirely different taste for apples. (An apple that tastes divine to one palate may be hopelessly sour to another.) So it makes sound sense for a potential investor in something as personal and long-lasting as an apple tree to try the fruit before placing an order.

Farm stands offer more and more unusual varieties; even our supermarket occasionally stocks Northern Spys and Macouns. But newer varieties and less-common antique strains can be next to impossible to find. Tom and Jill Vorbeck recognized this need when they planned their own orchard and responded by starting Applesource in 1983. It's a mail-order apple business that lets buyers sample a broad range of varieties. With the cooperation of orchards in California, Indiana, Michigan, Kentucky, and Illinois, they offer shoppers more than 60 different varieties, packaged in sampler boxes of six or a dozen

types. Among the listings are such old-fashioned apples as Newtown Pippin (said to be George Washington's favorite), Esopus Spitzenburg, Calville Blanc, and Fameuse (or Snow Apple) as well as a number of new innovations like Blushing Golden, Mutsu, and Holiday.

Not only does the system give buyers a chance to taste apples before they start planting trees, it allows them to try fruit grown in a climate similar to their own. The length of the growing season, the amount of rainfall, and the extremes of summer and winter temperature can all affect fruit flavor. Through Applesource shoppers can order from growers with climatic conditions most like their own.

We should note that Applesource's samplers are also available to people who have no intention of starting an orchard. The samplers make terrific gifts, and the Vorbecks can arrange to ship them for delivery at Thanksgiving or Christmas.

Applesource
Tom Vorbeck, Route 1, Chapin, IL 62628
Catalog price: free

tivars—presented in a catalog geared to the expert gardener. Plants are listed by botanical name without further comment. Buyers must inquire for price, size, and availability.

Fruitwood Nursery
P.O. Box 303, Molena, GA 30258
Telephone: 404-495-5488

Catalog price: long self-addressed stamped envelope

Apple trees for small-scale southern growers. The nursery has tested a number of varieties and chosen six—Granny Smith, Ozark Gold, Crispin, Yates, Mollie Delicious, and Fuji—that are suited to conditions in the South. Minimum order is $12. Orders of 100 or more trees are generally filled on a contract basis, arranged a year in advance of delivery.

Miles W. Fry & Son, Inc.
Frysville, Ephrata, PA 17522
Telephone: 717-354-4501

Catalog price: free

Several different hybrid poplars for quick-growing shade or screen trees. Fry sells specific clones for specific uses (shade or screen) and mixes adapted for northern or southern conditions. All trees are sold as unrooted cuttings, which will require special care for their first year. The nursery also sells plants for groundcover.

Garden World's Exotic Plants
Trees and shrubs for warm climates. See under *Tropical Plants*, page 169.

Louis Gerardi Nursery
1700 E. Highway 50, O'Fallon, IL 62269
Telephone: 618-632-4456

Catalog price: long self-addressed stamped envelope

A specialist in nut trees for northern regions, Gerardi offers more than a dozen varieties of black walnut and almost as many hickories, pecans (from northern sources), and Carpathian walnuts. In the spring of 1987 the nursery had no trees to sell, only scion wood for grafting.

Girard Nurseries
P.O. Box 428, Geneva, OH 44041
Telephone: 216-466-2881

Catalog price: free

A general ornamental nursery source with a specialty in azaleas. Four pages of rhododendrons and azaleas lead off the catalog, many of them Girard's own introductions. A big selection of flowering shrubs complements the azalea collection, and the nursery carries an impressive inventory of ornamental evergreens and shade trees. Bonsai enthusiasts will find more than 30 different dwarfed trees, all root pruned at least once.

Golden Bough Tree Farm
Marlbank, ON, Canada K0K 2L0

Catalog price: $1

A thinking person's catalog of trees, shrubs, and berry plants, sprinkled with quotes and curious facts—even addresses of book suppliers and journals. All plants sold are hardy in Canada, some as far north as zone 1. Specialties include prairie-hardy plums, Amur goldbark cherry (which will survive zone 1b winters), and black willows grown from the seed of the largest specimens in Ontario.

Gossler Farms Nursery
1200 Weaver Road, Springfield, OR 97478-9663
Telephone: 503-746-3922 or 747-0749

Catalog price: $1

Magnolias are the specialty at this nursery, and more than 80 varieties are sold. Flower colors range from pure white to deep purple and wine red. A few of the varieties are on the pricey side, but many nice ones can be had quite reasonably. An accompanying list of "companion plants" ranges from ornamental trees and shrubs like witch hazel (in many colors) and mountain laurel to stewartia. Some specimens, such as camellias and wintersweet, will have to be treated as indoor plants in northern areas.

Harold Grant
Seed for trees and shrubs native to Australia. See under *Native Plants of Australia and South Africa*, page 119.

Greener 'N' Ever Tree Farm and Nursery
P.O. Box 222435, Carmel, CA 93922
Telephone: 408-659-3196

Catalog price: free

Evergreen tree seedlings presented in a straight price list without a hint of description. Most trees are sold as one- or two-year-old seedlings and shipped bare root from January to March, but some are available in "super cell" containers that allow for shipping year-round, and a few are sold in larger containers. The nursery sells many different pines, firs, and spruces, as well as a selection of redwoods, eucalyptus, cypress, and cedar. A separate catalog of tree-farming tools and supplies is also available (see entry under *Tools* on page 239).

Greenmantle Nursery
3010 Ettersburg Road, Garberville, CA 95440
Telephone: 707-986-7504

Catalog price: $3 for catalog, long self-addressed stamped envelope for rose list

Greenmantle Nursery raises fruit and nut trees, berries, and roses, with a special concern for preserving older varieties that grow well in the region of Humboldt County, California. The catalog is almost a textbook on fruit-tree cultivation; its descriptions of the many fruit varieties offered give a lesson in horticultural history as well as present the necessary data on flavor, ripening season, and keeping qualities. Apples and roses seem to be special loves of the nursery owners. More than 50 apples are listed in the catalog, and another 80 can be ordered for custom propagation. Many are the creations of Albert Etter, who lived in nearby Ettersburg and who developed many new apple and strawberry hybrids in the 1920s. The rose list runs to almost 200 varieties, including species roses, gallicas, damasks, albas, chinas, teas, shrubs and bedding roses.

Greer Gardens
Ornamental trees and shrubs. See under *Azaleas and Rhododendrons*, page 45.

Grimo Nut Nursery
Rt. 3, Lakeshore Road, Niagara-on-the-Lake, ON,
Canada L0S 1J0
Telephone: 416-935-9773

Catalog price: $1, deductible from first order

Hardy nut trees for Canadian gardeners, offered in a ten-page descriptive list. Persian walnuts, black walnuts, heartnuts, butternuts, buartnuts (a cross of heartnut and butternut), hazelnuts, chestnuts, hickories, and northern pecans are sold as seedlings or grafted trees, most in a choice of several named varieties. A long introduction provides cultural instructions, and a chart compares the hardiness, flavor, nut size, and bearing quality of all the varieties sold.

Gurney Seed & Nursery Co.
See under *General Flowers and Vegetables*, page 19.

Hanchar's Superior Trees
P.O. Box 407, Carrolltown, PA 15722
Telephone: 814-472-4382

Hanchar's offers seedlings of 30 different tree species, most of them North American natives. The nursery built a new greenhouse in 1987, and has begun to offer some container-grown seedlings, which the proprietors feel are superior to field-grown trees shipped bare root. Hanchar's stock includes eastern redbud, thornless honey locust, and Japanese zelkova, along with a selection of pines, oaks, spruces, and maples.

Hancock's
Rt. 4, Box 4788, Manchester, TN 37355

Catalog price: free

A one-page list of nursery stock: raspberry bushes, clematis and jasmine vines, amaryllis and calla lily bulbs, and a few evergreen shrubs.

Harmony Farm Supply
P.O. Box 451, Graton, CA 95444
Telephone: 707-823-9125

Catalog price: $2

This nursery promotes "edible tree crops" and steers clear of ornamentals. Here you'll find fruit and nut trees, berries, and grapes, the varieties chosen for culture in northern California. While some parts of the list aren't huge (only 25 apple varieties are sold), California gardeners will find plenty of selections suited to their special conditions: citrus, figs, feijoas, and fruit trees that will produce without long, cold winters. To help customers succeed with their new orchards, Harmony sells tools, supplies, and books; to help them enjoy their success, the firm sells a selection of strainers, stoners, slicers, and dehydrators. The catalog gives plenty of advice and explanation.

Hastings
See under *General Flowers and Vegetables*, page 20.

Heard Gardens, Ltd.
5355 Merle Hay Road, Johnston, IA 50131
Telephone: 515-276-4533

Catalog price: free

We've never been there, but Heard Gardens must be a fragrant place to visit in late April and early May, when the lilacs are in flower. A simple catalog lists almost 40 lilac varieties, with blooms ranging from white to magenta to deep purple to—of course—lilac. A handful of "rare and unusual" trees are also offered for shipping, including Greencolumn maple, a cultivar of black sugar maple available only from Heard.

Hidden Springs Nursery
Rt. 14, Box 159, Cookeville, TN 38501
Telephone: 615-268-9889

Catalog price: 45¢ (specify edible landscaping list)

A descriptive list of "edible landscaping" plants—mostly fruit trees and berries. Only a few cultivars of each type are sold, the selections made for hardiness and disease resistance. The only apples sold, for example, are Old Faithful (an exceptionally large tree), Ben Davis, and King David. Among the more unusual offerings are several kiwi and mayhaw cultivars. Most of the plants are tube or container grown and sent with roots intact. A separate herb and fuchsia list costs 40¢. (See entry under *Fuchsias*, page 85.)

Hillier Nurseries (Winchester) Ltd.
Ampfield House, Ampfield, Romsey, Hants., England
SO51 9PA
Telephone: 44-794-68733

The Hillier catalog seems almost inviting on the outside, with its small format and color cover, but inside it is crammed with tiny listings for more than 4,000 trees and shrubs (including 300 plus roses and almost as many azaleas and rhododendrons). If your eyes are sharp, you know your Latin names, and you master the coded descriptive system, browsing through these pages may prove to be a horticultural feast. But most of us will need a magnifying glass and a copy of *Hortus Third* to make sense of it all. As cold hardiness is not the problem in England that it is in North America, winter tolerances are not mentioned. Before ordering, it might be wise to consult a reference book or an expert to see if your selections are likely to survive. Hillier imposes no minimum order on exports, but does charge a minimum of £15 for export shipping. (See *Buying Plants from Overseas*, page 9.)

Hilltop Trees, The Nursery Corporation
P.O. Box 578, Hartford, MI 49057
Telephone: 616-621-3135

This slick color catalog is aimed more at the commercial fruit grower than the home gardener, but the firm does fill retail orders of $75 (five trees) or more. Many of the selections are patented varieties, and the descriptions praise qualities like "early coloring," "russet resistant," and "full coloring," which promise to bring extra profit in the market. Home growers can extract more pertinent information from the lengthy descriptions, however, and Hilltop offers a big selection: 80 apple varieties on a choice of eight rootstocks, and dozens of pears, peaches, plums, cherries, nectarines, and apricots.

Holly Hills, Inc.
Dwarf conifers. See under *Azaleas and Rhododendrons*, page 46.

HollyDale Nursery
P.O. Box 26, Pelham, TN 37366
Telephone: 615-467-3121 or 800-222-3026

Peaches, plums, nectarines, and pecans, presented in a bare-bones price list. The nursery will sell trees by the thousand, and they'll ship a single tree for a backyard orchard. Almost 90 peach varieties are offered on a choice of two rootstocks.

Jerry Horne
Palms. See under *Tropical Plants*, page 169.

Hortica Gardens
See under *Bonsai*, page 56.

Hortico, Inc.
723 Robson Road, Rt. 1, Waterdown, ON, Canada L0R 2H0
Telephone: 416-689-6984

Catalog price: free (request shrub list)

A massive list of trees and shrubs, with the emphasis on the shrubs. We count more than 1,000 listings, offered as seedlings and transplants in various stages of growth. Plants are listed by botanical names only, without descriptions, so buyers may need to consult a reference book to figure out what's what. Prices are quoted per 100, but a note at the top of each page indicates how to adjust the fee for a smaller order. Even single-plant orders will be accepted. Both small and large orders can be exported to the U.S. Hortico sends out separate lists of perennials (see entry under *Garden Perennials*, page 89) and roses (see entry under *Roses*, page 140).

Hughes Nursery
1305 Wynooche W., Montesano, WA 98563

Catalog price: $1.50

More than 100 Japanese and other maples in a price list with brief descriptions. The Japanese names have been translated, and they have a pleasantly different ring to them: Lonely Person, Floating Clouds, Guards at a Boundary, and Heat Waves. Some of the trees will grow as tall as 30 feet, while others can be used for bonsai.

International Seed Supplies
Seed for native Australian trees and shrubs. See under *Native Plants of Australia and South Africa*, page 119.

Inter-State Nurseries
P.O. Box 208, Hamburg, IA 51640-0208
Telephone: 314-754-4525 or 800-843-5091 (orders only)

Catalog price: free

A glossy color catalog of nursery stock for the general home gardener. The spring catalog, sent out in late winter, offers ornamental trees and shrubs, garden perennials, berry plants, fruit trees, and a big selection of roses (hybrid teas, floribundas, and climbing types). A summer catalog presents daylilies, peonies, a limited selection of fall bulbs, and several pages of bearded irises.

Ison's Nursery & Vineyards
Brooks, GA 30205
Telephone: 404-599-6870

Ison's sells fruiting nursery stock, with a concentration on muscadine grapes (hardy north to zone 6). Twenty-two muscadine varieties are listed with extensive instructions for their care. Other offerings include apple, pear, plum, cherry, apricot, peach, fig, walnut, and pecan trees and an assortment of berry plants.

Izard Ozark Natives
Seed for trees and shrubs native to the Ozarks. See under *Wildflowers*, page 175.

Jackson & Perkins Co.
See under *Roses*, page 140.

Jersey Chestnut Farm
58 Van Duyne Avenue, Wayne, NJ 07470

Three varieties of budded Chinese chestnut trees described on a single-page flier. Two of the cultivars, Jersey Gem and Henry VIII, are the nursery's own creations. All three are hardy to southern zone 4 and are not affected by blight. The nursery also sells persimmon trees.

Johnson Nursery
Route 5, Ellijay, GA 30540
Telephone: 404-273-3187

Catalog price: free

A glossy color catalog of fruit trees, grapes, and berries. Peaches dominate the list, running from the antique Georgia Belle and White English to modern introductions like Sunbrite and Johnson's own JD. The rest of the catalog holds apples, plums, pears, Asian pears, almonds, walnuts, cherries, and apricots. Minimum order is $15.

J. W. Jung Seed Co.
See under *General Flowers and Vegetables*, page 21.

Kelly Nurseries
Dansville, NY 14437
Telephone: 716-335-2211 or 800-828-6977 (orders only)

Catalog price: free

A big color catalog full of all manner of nursery stock—trees, shrubs, berry plants, and garden perennials. Most of the offerings are illustrated by attractive color photographs. (The pictures of fruit and berries are so luscious they drove us to the kitchen for a snack.) Among the ornamentals are roses, azaleas, native mountain laurels, evergreens, and such flowering trees as golden chain tree, redbud, and tree wisteria. The nursery is geared to serving the home gardener and is happy to accept small orders.

V. Kraus Nurseries, Ltd.
Carlisle, ON, Canada L0R 1H0
Telephone: 416-689-4022

Catalog price: free

A simple typed list without descriptions sets forth more than 400 trees and shrubs. Shade trees and ornamental shrubs dominate the list, though a smattering of fruit trees and berry plants are tucked into the final pages. Buried in the center of the list is an impressive collection of roses—nearly 200 different hybrid teas, grandifloras, floribundas, shrub, and miniature roses. The nursery will ship retail orders to the U.S., but cannot send any of the larger trees across the border.

Krider Nurseries
P.O. Box 29, Middlebury, IN 46540
Telephone: 219-825-5714

Catalog price: free

Roses lead the way in this general nursery catalog. More than 100 modern cultivars are offered, mostly hybrid teas, but including a small assortment of floribunda, climbing, and miniature roses. A few of the stars are treated to big color pictures. The rest of the catalog presents shade, flowering, and fruit trees, berry plants, and an assortment of ornamental shrubs.

Michael & Janet Kristick
155 Mockingbird Road, Wellsville, PA 17365
Telephone: 717-292-2962

Catalog price: free

On the first page of their tree list, the Kristicks suggest four reference books on Japanese maples and ornamental conifers. Without the books, their list will make little sense. Indeed, this list is more of a starting point for further correspondence than a genuine catalog. Prices are not given, some of the offerings may not actually be available, and the Kristicks grow many other plants that are not on the list. Trees are listed by botanical names only; no common names and no descriptions are given. For gardeners who know their conifers and Japanese maples, the Kristicks have much to offer—more than 150 Japanese maple cultivars and hundreds of rare evergreens.

Lakeshore Tree Farms Ltd.
Rt. 3, Saskatoon, SK, Canada S7K 3J6
Telephone: 306-382-2077

Catalog price: $1 in Canadian funds

A color catalog of trees, shrubs, and garden perennials for Canadian customers. Lakeshore carries a well-rounded selection of nursery stock—fruit and shade trees, evergreens, vines, flowering shrubs, hedges, berry plants, and about 50 different perennials.

Lawson's Nursery
Rt. 1, Box 294, Ball Ground, GA 30107
Telephone: 404-893-2141

Catalog price: free

James Lawson's fruit-tree nursery looks to be a labor of love. He grows more than 80 antique apple types and grafts or buds each of the trees himself onto seven different rootstocks. His efforts seem to be directed almost exclusively toward the home gardener and the smaller orchardist. Many of the trees are available only in limited quantities, and most are grafted onto dwarfing rootstocks. The descriptive catalog details the qualities of the fruit and offers some historical background. In addition to the apples, Mr. Lawson sells some pear, plum, and cherry trees and a few blueberry varieties.

Lennilea Farm Nursery
Rt. 1, Box 683, Alburtis, PA 18011
Telephone: 215-845-2077

Catalog price: free

A single photocopied sheet lists Lennilea's stock of grafted nut trees. The nursery sells shagbark and shellbark hickory, northern pecan, heartnut, Chinese chestnut, chinkapin, and filbert trees, with pawpaws and saskatoons for those who want fruit. Many more plants are sold only at the nursery, which is located "near the church in the beautiful little country village of Huff's Church, PA." Sounds nice. Those who make the trip will find ornamental trees and shrubs, perennials, gardening supplies, and, in the spring, annual flower and vegetable plants.

W. O. Lessard Nursery
Banana trees. See under *Tropical Plants*, page 170.

Henry Leuthardt Nurseries, Inc.
P.O. Box 666, E. Moriches, NY 11940
Telephone: 516-878-1387

Catalog price: free

A nursery with a European flair, Leuthardt sells both old and new fruit-tree varieties, many of them of French and Swiss origin. Atlantic Queen, for example, is an old French pear, and Berne Rose is a Swiss apple similar to Baldwin. Such standard apples as McIntosh, Cortland, and Macoun are listed alongside hard-to-find older types like Black Gilliflower, Spitzenberg (Thomas Jefferon's favorite), and Ribston Pippin. In addition to apple and pear trees, the nursery sells plums, cherries, peaches, nectarines, grapes, and berry bushes. Perhaps the most unique Leuthardt offerings are the espaliered fruit trees. Unfortunately, by the time our 1987 catalog arrived in February these had been sold out for the year. Interested buyers may have to order these far in advance.

Living Tree Center
P.O. Box 797, Bolinas, CA 94924
Telephone: 415-868-2224

Catalog price: long self-addressed stamped envelope for price list, $6 for descriptive catalog and journal, deductible from first order

The Living Tree Center puts out one of the most unusual nursery catalogs we have come across. The first half of the booklet is taken up by descriptions of the 66 apple varieties offered and by notes on chilling requirements, rootstocks, and planting methods. The second half of the book, the journal, presents articles with titles like "Orgone Energy Used to Enhance Plant Growth" and "Earth Energies, Megaliths, Sacred Sites, and Human Consciousness." Most of the apple varieties offered are older types, and the catalog gives some interesting historical insights.

Louck's Nursery
P.O. Box 102, Cloverdale, OR 97112

Catalog price: one first-class stamp

Louck's sells rare and unusual Japanese maples, but unfortunately could not get us a copy of its catalog before our press deadline.

Louisiana Nursery
Rt. 7, Box 43, Opelousas, LA 70570
Telephone: 318-948-3696 or 942-6404

Catalog price: $3.50 (specify magnolia and general plant list)

Magnolias are the star attraction here, in an encyclopedia of species and cultivars—more than 400 in all—and in a wide palette of colors. The 60 pages of the catalog that follow are put under the wry heading "Companion Plants." Here the reader will find hundreds of other flowering trees and shrubs and scores of garden perennials, each briefly described. Zonal hardiness is not noted, and some plants, like giant papyrus, will not survive a cold winter. Other specialties include camellias, azaleas, hollies, jasmines, bamboos, and hibiscus. A separate catalog of daylilies and irises is available for $2 (see entry under *Daylilies*, page 79). A list of scion wood and bud wood can also be had for $2.

McConnell Nurseries
Port Burwell, ON, Canada N0J 1T0

Catalog price: free (to Canadian customers only)

Sears's entry into the mail-order nursery business, McConnell will sell to Canadian customers only. The luscious color catalog serves up a menu of fruit and nut trees, berry plants, ornamental trees and shrubs, and garden perennials, the selections aimed at the general home gardener rather than the specialist. Roses get a little extra attention; 40 hybrid teas and climbing roses spread their petals over ten sparkling pages. The perennial selections take up almost half the catalog, ranging from daylilies and lupines to chrysanthemums and giant phlox. Customers can call in their orders to any local Sears store.

McFayden Seeds
Trees and shrubs for Canadian customers. See under *General Flowers and Vegetables*, page 24.

McGregor Nursery Sales
See Lakeland Nursery Sales under *General Flowers and Vegetables*, page 22.

Maplewood Seed Co.
6219 S.W. Dawn Street, Lake Oswego, OR 97035

Catalog price: long self-addressed stamped envelope

Just as the name suggests, this firm sells seed for maple trees. A bare-bones list lays out the choices: more than 100 species and cultivars, most of them Japanese maple (*Acer palmatum* and *A. japonicum*) cultivars.

Rider Nursery

Rt. 2, Box 90A, Farmington, IA 52626

Telephone: 319-878-3313

Catalog price: free

Two dozen strawberry varieties lead off this nursery's pamphlet-style price list. Other edibles on the list include fruit trees on dwarf and standard rootstocks, grapevines, blueberries, raspberries, and blackberries. The firm also sells shade trees, ornamental trees and shrubs, and roses. Prices are very competitive.

Saginaw Valley Nut Nursery

8285 Dixie Highway #3, Birch Run, MI 48415

Catalog price: long self-addressed stamped envelope

Hardy nut trees for northern growers. Most of the offerings are named cultivars with the origin and cold hardiness of the parents identified. More than a dozen strains of black walnut appear on the list. Other offerings include Persian walnuts, heartnuts, butternuts, Chinese chestnuts, hazelberts (hazel-filbert crosses), shagbark hickories, and northern pecans. Buyers have a choice of seeds, seedlings, or grafted specimens. The list gives very short descriptions of the various strains.

St. Lawrence Nurseries

Rt. 2, Potsdam, NY 13676

Telephone: 315-265-6739

Catalog price: free

This nursery is situated in northern New York, well into zone 4, and the trees offered are hardy to at least -30° F. The cold winters have eliminated some popular items from the list—Bartlett pears aren't sold, and none of the fruit trees are grafted onto dwarfing rootstock—but the owners have sought out a wealth of cold-hardy alternatives. They sell 125 apple varieties and 15 pears, several of them the nursery's own introductions. And they carry a bountiful array of grapes, cherries, grafted plums, blueberries, and other fruiting shrubs from around the world. The search for hardy nut trees has led them to a half dozen named black walnuts and a handful of other northern natives. The nursery sells American chestnut seedlings from apparently blight-resistant parents. No minimum order. Canadian orders welcomed. Catalogs are mailed during January and February only.

Salter Tree Farm

Rt. 2, Box 1332, Madison, FL 32340

Telephone: 904-973-6312 or 4640

Catalog price: long self-addressed stamped envelope

Native southeastern trees and shrubs for the home landscape. Some of these plants will thrive as far north as Illinois and New England, and some won't survive in northern Georgia. The list gives the common and botanical names of the plants, plus the price and inventory of the various sizes available. Gardeners will have to call or write with questions about the cultural needs of particular species. Among the offerings: live oak, pignut hickory, fever tree, Ashe magnolia, blue beech, and a half dozen native rhododendron species. A smattering of lilies, groundcovers, and wildflowers are sold as companion plants.

Santa Barbara Seeds

P.O. Box 6520, Santa Barbara, CA 93160-6520

Catalog price: long self-addressed stamped envelope

Seed for exotic and unusual fruit-bearing trees and shrubs. Care to grow your own coffee crop? How about guavas, cherimoyas, or loquats? If you have the patience to grow from seed, this firm can get you started. No cultural instructions are given in the price list. Instead the owners "encourage resource research, if prior knowledge is not on hand."

Savage Farms Nurseries

P.O. Box 125, McMinnville, TN 37110

Catalog price: free

A general line of trees and shrubs, with all the plants pictured in color. Fruit trees are a specialty of sorts—13 apples and nine peaches are offered—but the selection tends to ramble on with a little of this and a little of that. You'll find most of the popular flowering trees and shrubs, shade trees, hedge shrubs, nut trees, berry plants, and evergreens, along with a few perennials and wildflowers. The firm sends the same catalog out under the name Lee's Nursery.

F. W. Schumacher Co.

36 Spring Hill Road, Sandwich, MA 02563-1023

Telephone: 617-888-0659

Catalog price: free

Tree and shrub seeds in a list headlined "For Nurserymen and Foresters." The average home gardener won't want the trouble of raising trees from seed, and many of the packets here cost more than a seedling tree from a nursery. But for specialists the list may hold some rare finds and some real values. Schumacher sells seeds for more than 50 azalea and rhododendron species and for over 75 named cultivars. More than 80 pines are offered, along with 20 cotoneasters and a dozen dogwood species.

Shady Oaks Nursery

See under *Shade Plants*, page 146.

Simpson Nurseries

P.O. Box 160, Monticello, FL 32344

Telephone: 904-997-2516 or 800-874-3571

Catalog price: free

Pecan trees, fruit trees, and ornamentals sold in quantity. The minimum order is ten of a given variety, so this nursery will be of interest only to those starting or expanding an orchard or planning a major landscaping project. Plants are listed by varietal name without description.

Sonoma Antique Apple Nursery

4395 Westside Road, Healdsburg, CA 95448

Telephone: 707-433-6420

Catalog price: free

More than 60 varieties of antique apples and pears, available on a choice of rootstocks from dwarf to standard. Each strain is described in a short paragraph, including some historical background. Mingling with the antique apples are a few stray modern varieties, like Fuji, Spigold, and Liberty. Among the real antiques are Calville Blanc (1598), Lady (1600), and Seek-No-Further (1748). The nursery offers a number of English cider apples and will custom graft trees from a supplemental list of 30 antique eating appples, some of them quite rare. Other fruiting offerings include apricots, cherries, peaches, plums, figs, persimmons, and grapes. Each year the firm sells a limited number of espaliered fruit trees, but they disappear quickly. To get an advance listing of next summer's varieties and forms, send your name and address to the nursery, "attention: espalier."

Southmeadow Fruit Gardens

Box SM, Lakeside, MI 49116

Telephone: 616-469-2865

Catalog price: free price list, $8 for illustrated catalog

An incredibly extensive list of old-fashioned fruit trees—nearly 250 apple varieties and more than 40 pears, all of them available on a choice of rootstocks. The breadth of this list puts most other nurseries to shame, and some of the varieties are available nowhere else. The selection ranges from the very old to the merely antique to the relatively modern. The 16th-century Calville Blanc and 17th-century Lady apples were among the five choices on the nursery's

first list back in 1951, and they still get encouraging plugs from year to year. Several commercial orchard varieties have now been added to the inventory, but are sold only on dwarfing rootstocks. In addition to apples and pears, Southmeadow sells peaches, plums, cherries, medlars, currants, gooseberries, and grapes.

The price list describes only a few featured varieties; the rest are simply listed. The full catalog ($8) gives descriptions of each variety offered, includes some historical background, and contains black-and-white illustrations of most.

Southwestern Native Seeds

See under *Wildflowers*, page 180.

Joel W. Spingarn

39 Beeholm Road, W. Redding, CT 06896

Catalog price: $1, deductible from first order

Two hundred dwarf and pygmy conifers, many of them rarities. Mr. Spingarn's list gives no descriptions, not even common names, but he does recommend some books for further reading.

Spring Hill Nurseries

6523 N. Galena Road, Peoria, IL 61632

Catalog price: free

Spring Hill Nurseries and Breck's (see entry under *Bulbs*, page 59) are run from the same Peoria, Illinois, address. Breck's handles the bulbs and Spring Hill the general nursery stock. The Spring Hill catalog is a glossy color affair, with crisp, enticing pictures of every offering. The inventory ranges from roses and fruit trees to wildflowers and garden perennials, with a plenty of stops in between. While the firm doesn't offer great depth in any department—three peony cultivars are offered, two types of strawberries, and six flowering trees—it spreads itself so broadly that there is much to choose from anyway.

Stallings Nursery

910 Encinitas Boulevard, Encinitas, CA 92024

Telephone: 619-753-3079

Catalog price: $2, deductible from first order

A big list of subtropical flowering shrubs and perennials that can be grown as outdoor plants in areas with only occasional light frosts. Gardeners elsewhere may want to consider this as a source for potted plants to be moved indoors for the winter. More than 1,000 species and varieties are offered, including dozens of hibiscus cultivars and a score of jasmines. The catalog includes no pictures and describes only some of the listings.

Stanek's Garden Center

Fruit and nut trees. See under *Roses*, page 144.

Stark Bro's Nurseries & Orchards Co.

Louisiana, MO 63353-0010

Telephone: 314-754-5511 or 800-325-4180 (orders only)

Catalog price: free

Fruit trees, berry plants, and landscaping trees and shrubs in a luscious color catalog that pictures many of the fruits life size. If the mouth-watering photographs don't tempt you to place an order, they may well drive you to the refrigerator for a snack. Stark sells about 30 apple varieties and almost 20 peaches, along with a range of other fruits and berries. Many are modern cultivars, and even some of the old varieties are promoted as "improved" through modern breeding. The nursery has made a special effort to stock fruit varieties that will bear well in the southern states. A page in the catalog is devoted to plants for zones 8 and 9. Among the nonfruiting offerings are roses, lilacs, and a selection of shade trees.

Stern's Nurseries, Inc.
607 W. Washington Street, Geneva, NY 14456
Telephone: 315-789-7371

Catalog price: long self-addressed stamped envelope

Stern's is the firm that makes Miracle-Gro plant food, and the nursery operation has been dubbed Miracle-Gardens. No catalog is issued, just a bare-bones price list that presents a limited selection of roses, flowering shrubs, berry plants, daylilies, and peonies.

Stillpoint Gardens
See under *Shade Plants*, page 146.

Stonehurst Rare Plants
1 Stonehurst Court, Pomona, NY 10970
Telephone: 914-354-4049

Catalog price: $1

"The arboretum of dwarf and unusual conifers," Stonehurst sells more than 1,000 different dwarf conifers from a list that includes no descriptions, sizes, or prices. This is a source for serious collectors, and buyers will have to inquire as to price and availability of each plant desired. The firm makes no suggestions as to reference books that might show pictures of the offerings, urging instead that interested customers find a way to visit the nursery. A separate list of more than 100 choice Japanese maples is available for a long self-addressed stamped envelope. The firm is building up an inventory of rare dwarf rhododendrons, but does not yet have enough to offer by mail.

T & T Seeds Ltd.
Nursery stock for Canadian customers. See under *General Flowers and Vegetables*, page 30.

Thompson and Morgan
Tree and shrub seeds. See under *General Flowers and Vegetables*, page 31.

Tillinghast Seed Co.
See under *General Flowers and Vegetables*, page 31.

Trans-Pacific Nursery
Rt. 1, Box 299, Sheridan, OR 97378
Telephone: 503-843-3588

Catalog price: free

This nursery sells "rare & exotic" plants, most of which can survive outdoors only where winters are mild. Gardeners whose plots dip much below freezing may be interested in the plants for indoor or greenhouse culture. We can't claim familiarity with these plants, but we can give you some examples: Australian blackwood (*Acacia melanoxylon*), monkey puzzle tree (*Araucaria araucana*) from Tierra del Fuego, scarlet ginger lily (*Hedychium longicornutum*) from Malaysia, and several eucalyptus species.

James Trehane & Sons Ltd.
Stapehill Road, Hampreston, Wimborne, Dorset, England BH21 7NE
Telephone: 44-202-873490

Catalog price: $2

A nursery deeply involved with camellias. James Trehane sells about 250 *japonica*, *reticulata*, and hybrid camellias, and that number represents years of winnowing the list down to those specimens the firm feels are the very best. Referring to the scores of varieties that have been dropped from the inventory over the years, the catalog coldly notes "frankly, many . . . deserved oblivion." The firm will export to the U.S. and Canada with the required documentation (see *Buying Plants from Overseas*, page 9).

Tripple Brook Farm
See under *Garden Perennials*, page 92.

Turtle Springs Farm
P.O. Box 7454, Tifton, GA 31793-7454
Telephone: 912-382-1134

Catalog price: $1

The nursery changed its name from Turtle Creek Farms in 1987, but still sells what it terms "rare and worthy plants for the Southeast." Among those worthy of mentioning here: Chinese tallow tree (*Sapium sebiferum*), maiden's blush (*Pinckneya bracteata*, a rare flowering shrub from coastal Georgia), and a number of new crape myrtle cultivars. The firm puts in a special plug for swamp cypress (*Taxodium distichum*), which, though a swamp plant in the wild, will grow in almost any southern landscape and in fact is drought tolerant. The descriptive list is mailed in January, a supplemental plant list in September.

Valley Nursery
P.O. Box 4845, Helena, MT 59601

Catalog price: 25¢

More than 200 cold-hardy trees and shrubs presented on a names-only list. Interested customers are asked to write or call for prices and sizes. The inventory includes a number of honeysuckles, roses, lilacs, viburnums, mountain ashes, and flowering crab apples, as well as a selection of evergreens and fruit trees.

Vans Pines
W. Olive, MI 49460
Telephone: 616-399-1620

Pine, spruce, and fir seedlings sold by the hundred and the thousand. A few deciduous trees, such as black walnut, English oak, and white birch, are also sold in quantity. This is not a source for the average home planter.

Vermont Fruit Tree Co.
Rt. 1, River Road, New Haven, VT 05472
Telephone: 802-388-3912

Twenty apple varieties for northern orchardists, grafted onto semidwarfing rootstock. Old and new varieties are represented, from Spitzenberg and King of Tomkins County to Jonagold and Freedom. Some orchard-planning tips are given in the catalog, and more detailed instructions are sent with each order.

Vineland Nurseries
P.O. Box 98, Vineland Station, ON, Canada L0R 2E0
Telephone: 416-562-4836

Catalog price: $1

Vineland Nurseries sells what it calls "special plants for small spaces": dwarf and unusual evergreens, heathers, rhododendrons, Japanese maples, and hardy bamboos. More than 300 species and varieties are listed by botanical name in a simple typed booklet with telegraphic descriptions that rarely extend beyond a couple of words. Shoppers in the area can choose from an even larger selection. Many of the rhododendrons grown aren't offered to mail-order customers, and a number of the larger specimens in the catalog are too big for shipping.

Washington Evergreen Nursery
P.O. Box 388, Leicester, NC 28748
Telephone: 704-683-4518 or 803-747-1641 (winter)

Catalog price: $2, deductible from first order

Two hundred dwarf conifers, each described in some detail in a text that covers size, shape, color, and texture. The catalog has no pictures, but the nursery has a slide library and will lend slides to interested customers. False cypress (*Chamaecyparis*) cultivars are well represented on the list, with more than 60 offerings. A number of companion plants are sold, including a good selection of mountain laurel cultivars, hollies, boxwoods, evergreen azaleas, and rhododendrons.

Waynesboro Nurseries
P.O. Box 987, Waynesboro, VA 22980
Telephone: 703-942-4141

Catalog price: free

Fruit and nut trees, berry plants, and ornamentals in a catalog filled with lovely hand-tinted color illustrations. Apples, peaches, cherries, grapes, and berries are pictured larger than life in vivid color, and descriptions point out qualities of interest to home growers. The ornamental offerings include a number of azaleas, spireas, lilacs, weigelas, yews, junipers, and flowering crab apples. Plants are sold singly or in quantity. Minimum order is $20.

Wayside Gardens
See under *Garden Perennials*, page 92.

West Australian Wildflower Society
Seed for Australian trees and shrubs. See under *Native Plants of Australia and South Africa*, page 120.

Western Maine Nurseries, Inc.
1 Evergreen Drive, Fryeburg, ME 04037
Telephone: 207-935-2161

Catalog price: free

Evergreen seedlings—firs, pines, spruces, and larches—sold in lots of 100 or more. Most are field-grown plants, shipped bare root, but some of the trees can be ordered as smaller seedlings in trays. The $75 minimum order limits the appeal of this nursery to planters with plenty of land.

Westside Exotics
P.O. Box 156, Westley, CA 95387
Telephone: 209-894-3492 or 575-2168

Catalog price: long self-addressed stamped envelope

A one-page specialty list of hardy palms intended for the Central Valley of California—and any other areas with comparable climates. Approximately 40 species are offered as cuttings and a dozen as seeds. Text is nonexistent, so you'd better know your palms by their botanical names.

Wiley's Nut Grove Nursery
2002 Lexington Avenue, Mansfield, OH 44907
Telephone: 419-756-0697

Catalog price: long self-addressed stamped envelope

Hardy northern nut trees, including Chinese chestnuts, butternuts, black walnuts, Persian walnuts, hickories, and pecans. Trees are sold as seedlings or as grafted stock. Some larger specimens, too big for shipping, are sold at the nursery, which is located at 1116 Hickory Lane in Mansfield.

Windy Ridge Nursery
P.O. Box 301, Hythe, AB, Canada T0H 2C0
Telephone: 403-356-2167

Catalog price: $2, deductible from first order

Fruiting stock and a few ornamentals for the far north from a grower in the Peace River region. Raspberries, currants, strawberries, gooseberries, saskatoons, cherries, plums, apples, and hazelnuts are the fruiting offerings. The ornamentals include lilacs, potentillas, and Russian olive. All stock has been wintered in the ground, so it should survive conditions at least as harsh as those found in Hythe. Only saskatoons are shipped to the U.S., and the minimum export order is $100 (which will buy 20 one-foot plants).

Winterthur Museum & Gardens
Direct Mail Dept., Winterthur, DE 19735
Telephone: 703-387-2457 or 800-556-4567

Catalog price: $1

Prized plants from the Winterthur Gardens offered in a combination nursery and gift catalog. Henry F. du Pont spent decades collecting rare specimens for his garden and creating new hybrids, and some of the most popular of his plantings are propagated for sale to the public. Among them are a handful of Mr. du Pont's own azalea hybrids, a pale yellow forsythia, the dawn redwood (*Metasequoia glyptostroboides*), and the princess tree (*Paulownia tomentosa*), a large, showy flowering tree from China and Japan that is now much sought after for its lumber. A few unusual garden perennials are also offered, including candelabra primrose (*Primula japonica*) and Ozark phlox (*Phlox pilosa ozarkana*). (For a description of Winterthur's gift offerings, see entry under *Gifts for Gardeners*, page 214.)

Womack's Nursery Co.
Rt. 1, Box 80, De Leon, TX 76444-9660
Telephone: 817-893-6497

Pecan trees, fruit trees, berry plants, and grapevines for Texans and other southern growers. Pecans get top billing here; 15 cultivars are offered as budded trees in sizes from two to nine feet. (Trees over five feet must be picked up at the nursery or sent by truck.) Fruit offerings include 25 peaches and somewhat smaller selections of apples, apricots, figs, persimmons, pears, and plums. The firm sells nearly 30 different grape varieties, among them a few T. V. Munson cultivars developed in the early 1900's specifically for Texas growing conditions. The catalog describes each offering carefully, and offers a couple of pages of planting and growing advice. The minimum order is $15.

Woodland Nurseries
2151 Camilla Road, Mississauga, ON, Canada L5A 2K1
Telephone: 416-277-2961

Catalog price: $1, deductible from first order

More than 200 ornamental trees and shrubs listed by botanical name only in an uninviting list. Shoppers who need more guidance can order the nursery's booklet, *Choice Ornamentals for All Seasons*, for $3.50. It describes all the plants on the list and includes a special section on the care of rhododendrons and azaleas (of which the nursery sells about 40 varieties). The minimum order for shipment is $50, and the nursery will ship to U.S. customers.

Woodlanders, Inc.
1128 Colleton Avenue, Aiken, SC 29801
Telephone: 803-648-7522

Catalog price: two first-class stamps for price list, $1.50 for descriptive catalog

The Woodlanders price list is a somewhat daunting ten-page register of more than 600 trees, shrubs, perennial wildflowers, and ferns, organized by botanical name with curt, abbreviated descriptions. The descriptive catalog lifts the lid on many of the mysteries, but serious shoppers will want to consult an illustrated reference book as they browse. Recognizing this, the firm has added a code to both the price list and the catalog, noting books in which illustrations and more detailed descriptions can be found. A terrific idea! The Woodlanders inventory is weighted toward species native to the southeastern U.S., but also includes a number of foreigners that will grow well in that region.

M. Worley Nursery
98 Braggtown Road, York Springs, PA 17372
Telephone: 717-528-4519 or 4434

Fruit trees, berry plants, and a smaller selection of shade trees and ornamentals in a compact descriptive catalog. Worley sells a wide array of apple and peach cultivars. In addition to the popular modern apples, the nursery grows about 50 old-fashioned types, budded on semidwarfing rootstock. The other fruiting offerings run from cherries, nectarines, plums, and pears to strawberries, blueberries, and grapevines. The landscaping trees include sweet gum, a few native maples and oaks, and a handful of flowering crab apples. There is no minimum order, but a $6 minimum shipping charge applies to orders of fewer than ten trees.

Yerba Buena Nursery
Trees and shrubs native to California. See under *Wildflowers*, page 181.

Zilke Brothers Nursery
Baroda, MI 49101
Telephone: 616-422-2666

Zilke Brothers sells trees and shrubs for home gardeners. The inventory is more limited than some, but it ranges from fruit and nut stock to ornamentals and shade trees and seems to touch most of the bases along the way. A dozen apple varieties are offered on semidwarfing rootstock, along with peaches, cherries, plums, pears, grapevines, and berry plants. Thirty roses (mostly hybrid teas) lead off the ornamental list, followed by such flowering trees and shrubs as redbud, cotoneaster, coralberry, and more than a dozen flowering crab apples. The shade trees include mountain ash, sunburst locust, and a number of maple species. The nursery requires no minimum order.

Tropical Plants

Alberts & Merkel Bros., Inc.
2210 S. Federal Highway, Boynton Beach, FL 33435
Telephone: 305-732-2071

Catalog price: three catalogs, $1 each

In business since 1890, this nursery offers an immense selection of things tropical. Three stapled lists direct you to the main botanical camps: orchids, bromeliads, and foliage plants. The first list includes cattleya, phalaenopsis, vanda, dendrobium, oncidium, and species orchids, available as seedlings and mericlones. Text is spare but ample. The second list lays out about 200 bromeliad species and cultivars and pictures a few in color. The third provides hundreds of further options, including anthuriums, dieffenbachias, dracaenas, philodendrons, and ferns.

Charles Alford Plants
P.O. Box 1048, Plymouth, FL 32768

Catalog price: free

A tiny selection of staghorn ferns and orchids. The three ferns, grown on cypress plaques from spores and well established, are the house specialty. The orchids include a cattleya hybrid, *Laelia tenebrosa*, and *Catasetum expansum*. Mr. Alford plans to add more staghorns to his inventory over the next few years.

Anything Grows Greenhouse
1609 McKean Road, Ambler, PA 19002
Telephone: 215-542-9343

Catalog price: $2, deductible from first order

This nursery offers a series of specialty lists. The largest of these is devoted to approximately 300 sansevieria cultivars, described in detail. A second presents 50 or so *Euphorbia milii* hybrids. The $2 fee buys the entire set of lists.

The Banana Tree
715 Northampton Street, Easton, PA 18042
Telephone: 215-253-9589

Catalog price: 75¢

For those gardeners able to provide the requisite well-drained soil, abundant light, high humidity, and consistent heat in the 75° F range, this booklet is bulging with bananas and related tropical plants. More than a score of banana trees (offered as corms) are listed. In addition, hundreds of rare seeds spill across these 20 pages: euphorbias, proteas, and

yuccas, to name just a few. Descriptions are thorough and precise.

Beahm Epiphyllum Gardens
Epiphyllums, rhipsalis, and hoyas. See under *Epiphyllums and Hoyas*, page 82.

John Brudy Exotics
3411 Westfield Drive, Brandon, FL 33511
Telephone: 813-684-4302

Catalog price: $1, deductible from first order

An idiosyncratic seed catalog full of tropical flowering vines, woody shrubs, hanging-basket specimens, tub plants, and trees. The author of this 16-page catalog takes you by the hand and steers you through a jungle of rare items—everything from the African baobab tree ("often hollow, the trunk was sometimes used as a jail") to giant snake lily ("for daring gardeners . . . something for your largest pot!!"). Cultural instructions for each offering are thoughtfully supplied.

Peter B. Dow & Company
Seeds. See under *Native Plants of Australia and South Africa*, page 119.

Endangered Species
P.O. Box 1830, Tustin, CA 92681
Telephone: 714-544-9505

Catalog price: $5

A quirky roster of rare varieties of bamboos, palms, cycads, phormiums, sansevierias, succulents, and exotic foliage plants including grasses, shrubs, and trees. Hundreds of listings pepper the catalog—many illustrated with line drawings. The introductory text is zesty, offbeat, and fun to read. "If you want common, ordinary, no-risk plants with instant delivery and an iron-clad guarantee, you have come to the wrong source," the owners note at one point. "Growing and shipping rare plants involve some risk, otherwise the plants would not be rare!" Prices are on the high side.

Exotica Rare Fruit Nursery
P.O. Box 160, Vista, CA 92083
Telephone: 619-724-9093

Catalog price: long self-addressed stamped envelope

Plants and fruit trees from around the world comprise a fragrant slate. Banana, papaya, guava, mango, and jelly palm are just a few of the fruit offerings. A few low-chill apple varieties are the closest the nursery comes to "ordinary" plants. On the nutty side, almonds, cashews, and macadamias add to the mix of more than 50 exotic specimens, listed simply by name. Flowering shrubs and vines also appear. Plants are available in one-, five-, and 15-gallon sizes.

Garden World's Exotic Plants
2503 Garfield Street, Laredo, TX 78043
Telephone: 512-724-3951

Catalog price: $1

Thirty kinds of bananas begin this catalog, which offers a potpourri of warm-weather plants. Citrus trees, bamboos, hibiscus, bougainvilleas, and cacti are all offered in an array of choices. Tropical and subtropical pepper seeds—ranked from mild to extremely hot—make up a category of their own.

Glasshouse Works
Church Street, Box 97, Stewart, OH 45778-0097
Telephone: 614-662-2142

Catalog price: $1.50

A voluminous list of 1,000 plus plants, both "traditional and unusual." Among the "traditional" offerings are about 70 begonias and as many peperomias. More "unusual" are the scores of rare ferns, terrarium gesneriads, euphorbias, and sansevierias. Plants are alphabetized by botanical name and nicely described. To aid readers in locating their special wants, the nursery has broken out three categories: foliage and flowering plants (the largest), succulents, and hardy plants and shrubs. In addition to these general offerings, specialty lists—on variegated plants, crown of thorns, or unusual sansevierias, for example—are mailed throughout the year.

Green: Plant Research
P.O. Box 735, Kaaawa, HI 96730
Telephone: 808-237-8672

Catalog price: free

More than 100 asclepiads fill this specialty list, clearly set

forth in an eight-page booklet. Plants—which are offered as unrooted cuttings—have been gathered from many sources throughout the southern Pacific. Calotropis, dischidias, and hoya are the chief genera here, with hoyas the most prevalent by far.

Robert B. Hamm
See under *Begonias*, page 51.

Hatten's Nursery, Inc.
6401 Overlook Road, Mobile, AL 36608
Telephone: 205-342-0505

Catalog price: long self-addressed stamped envelope

Bougainvillea fans should know about this small, concentrated slate of the heat-loving vines from Brazil. More than a score of varieties appear, including single-flowered, variegated-foliage, and double-flowered types. Descriptive text, while brief, lets you know the color and character of blooms to expect.

Jerry Horne
10195 S.W. 70th Street, Miami, FL 33173
Telephone: 305-270-1235

Catalog price: long self-addressed stamped envelope

An orderly listing of bromeliads, ferns, palms and cycads, and miscellaneous varieties adding up to roughly 200 rare specimens. The nursery prides itself on the size and toughness of its plants—which have been grown exposed to the weather in "shadehouses" covered by screen. Varieties are listed simply, with a single line of abbreviated text, but the accompanying notes on caring for your purchases are quite detailed.

J. L. Hudson, Seedsman
See under *General Flowers and Vegetables*, page 20.

Hurov's Tropical Seeds
P.O. Box 1596, Chula Vista, CA 92012
Telephone: 619-426-0091

Seeds for hundreds of tropical indoor and outdoor plants gathered by H. R. Hurov and friends on "expeditions throughout the tropical and subtropical world." Plants are listed by botanical name, followed by a sentence or two of text describing place of origin, qualities, and popular uses. Some examples from the list: *Polygonum cuspidatum* from Taiwan, used to help heal broken bones, and *Velozia candida* from Brazil, "an outstanding houseplant."

KEO Entities, Exotic Tropical Seeds
348 Chelsea Circle, Land O' Lakes, FL 33539

A smattering of seeds drawn from the exotic end of the scale and simply presented on a couple of pages. The contents are a mixed bag, ranging from a Chinese fly-catching vine to the popular Indian rubber tree. Cigar plant, Japanese pine, dwarf ornamental pomegranate, Philippine monkey banana, passion flower, sacred bamboo—the list goes on. Why not plant them all in the backyard and drive your neighbors nuts with envy?

W. O. Lessard Nursery

19201 S.W. 248th Street, Homestead, FL 33031

Catalog price: $1, deductible from first order

Thirty-one varieties of banana, from Apple Banana to Nino. Each entry merits a paragraph of discussion that tells you just about everything you'd care to know: height at maturity, size and quality of fruit, leaf tint and shape—even the plant's wind tolerance.

Ann Mann's

See under *Orchids*, page 127.

Mellinger's Inc.

See under *Trees and Shrubs*, page 159.

D. Orriell, Seed Exporters

Seed for Australian native plants. See under *Native Plants of Australia and South Africa*, page 119.

T. A. Patton

P.O. Box 721242, Houston, TX 77272

Catalog price: free

Several dozen exotic tropical seeds, offered with a promise to liven up your windowsill or garden plot. The seeds are nicely described on two stapled pages. What can you get? Strawberry guava ("edible purplish red to yellow one-inch fruit"), passion flower ("an exquisite blue flowering vine"), and New Zealand cork ("large heart-shaped soft leaves"), for starters. Seeds are guaranteed fresh and come with growing directions.

The Plumeria People

P.O. Box 820014, Houston, TX 77282-0014
Telephone: 713-496-2352

Catalog price: $1

Gardeners able to provide well-drained soil, regular feeding, and plenty of sun may wish to consider adding plumeria (or frangipani) blossoms to their patio gardens. Dozens of rooted and unrooted cuttings, organized by color of bloom, dominate the first third of this richly scented catalog. Hibiscus,

bougainvilleas, gingers, daylilies, and assorted bulbs and rhizomes complete the listings. The catalog is shot through with poetry and casual remarks that lend it a dose of charm. Gardening supplies—including books, rooting hormone, and pruners—fill a few pages at the end.

Reasoners

P.O. Box 1881, Oneco, FL 34264
Telephone: 813-756-1881

Catalog price: $1

More than 100 hybrid grafted hibiscus varieties offered by a family of pioneering Florida horticulturists who have been tending to the needs of hibiscus lovers for roughly a century now. The list gives the botanical name, then indicates the color and type of bloom (single, double, spotted, splashed . . .) for each plant. Those new to the game may want to order a copy of the booklet *What Every Hibiscus Grower Should Know*, also available here.

Santa Barbara Seeds

See under *Trees and Shrubs*, page 163.

Spaulding Bulb Farm

1811 Howey Road, Sebring, FL 33872
Telephone: 813-385-0318

If you're hungry for caladium bulbs, pull up a chair. More than 50 varieties are presented here, neatly classed by color of bloom: red, pink, and white. Fancy-leaf types predominate, but strap- and lance-leaf strains also appear. A helpful index of do's and dont's for potted caladiums, together with detailed remarks on caladium planting and care, points you in the right direction.

Stallings Nursery

See under *Trees and Shrubs*, page 164.

Sunshine Caladium Farms

P.O. Box 905, Sebring, FL 33870
Telephone: 813-385-0663

Catalog price: free

Caladium bulbs sold in quantities of 25 or more. Thirty cultivars are offered, each pictured in color in the firm's brochure.

Trans-Pacific Nursery

See under *Trees and Shrubs*, page 165.

James Trehane & Sons Ltd.

Camellias. See under *Trees and Shrubs*, page 165.

Tropical Seeds

2525 Date Street #803, Honolulu, HI 96826
Telephone: 808-949-6934

Catalog price: $1

A diverse selection of exotic tropical seeds makes this five-page catalog interesting to leaf through. From bird of paradise ("stemless plant with strange, birdlike flowers"), through royal poinciana ("a spectacular picture when in bloom"), to guava ("flesh of the fruit is solid pink and can be used for juice, jelly or jam"), the abundant text casts the score of freshly collected seeds in an appealing light. Why not order Kona coffee and Maui onion, and concoct a nice little meal?

Tropicals Unlimited
595 Uluhaku Street, Kailua, HI 96734

Catalog price: $1

This slim catalog presents a mix of tropical plants, seeds, and reference books. Seeds are the most plentiful, with about two dozen species listed and described. Plants range from anthurium to macadamia nut—and include cattleya, dendrobium, and vandaceous orchids.

Westside Exotics
Palms. See under *Trees and Shrubs*, page 166.

Guy Wrinkle/Exotic Plants
11610 Addison Street, N. Hollywood, CA 91601
Telephone: 818-766-4820 or 3643

Catalog price: $1, deductible from first order

Several hundred succulents, orchids, bromeliads, and cycads crowd the pages of this rudimentary dot-matrix catalog. Most listings are for plants, but miscellaneous bulbs are also available. The approach is minimalist—in most cases botanical names and sizes only.

Water Lilies

Kurt Bluemel, Inc.
See under *Grasses*, page 97.

Eco-Gardens
See under *Garden Perennials*, page 87.

Lilies of the Valley Water Gardens
P.O. Box 22363, Carmel, CA 93923
Telephone: 408-624-5279

Catalog price: $1.50, deductible from first order

Hardy water lilies, ornamental grasses, water irises, bog and marsh plants, and water aquatics with such appealing names as water snowflake, floating heart, and azure water hyacinth. The water lilies form the core of the list, and they're offered in a choice of 23 varieties from the showy white Gonnere to the creamy orange Comanche and the crimson-flowered Gloriosa. Many other tropical species can be obtained on request. The typed catalog gives clear descriptions of each plant and goes into some detail on planting and pond maintenance. A few selected blooms are pictured on the color cover. Fertilizers, fish foods, pumps, strainers, and books are offered, as well as an intriguing product called Fido-Shock, which keeps "the playful pup and predatory pussy" out of the pool and deters that "*mortal enemy* of the water gardener, the RACCOON!"

Lilypons Water Gardens
P.O. Box 10, Lilypons, MD 21717-0010
Telephone: 301-874-5133

Catalog price: $4

The many stunning color photographs of water-lily blossoms in this catalog are almost enough to make us dam up the driveway and flood the whole yard. Lavender, scarlet, fuchsia, and clear white blooms are displayed in life-size views that

are better than we're ever likely to get from our own muddy embankments. Almost 40 hardy lilies are offered, along with as many tropicals (both day- and night-blooming types) and a rainbow of lotuses. Bog plants, irises, and submerged water plants fill in the edges and center of the pond. Lilypons can also supply you with pools, fountains, statuary, fish (one large pair of koi can set you back $200), pumps, filters, and numerous (and probably necessary) odds and ends.

Moore Water Gardens
Port Stanley, ON, Canada N0L 2A0
Telephone: 519-782-4052

Catalog price: free

Hardy and tropical water lilies, lotuses, underwater plants, and shallow-water or bog plants offered in a descriptive catalog. A few of the prettier blooms appear in color on the front and back covers. None of the plants can be shipped to the U.S. Non-Canadian customers will have to content themselves with the selection of pools, pumps, fountains, planting tubs, underwater lights, and books.

Paradise Water Gardens
14 May Street, Whitman, MA 02382
Telephone: 617-447-4711 or 3803

Catalog price: $2

"Everything for the water garden," reads the headline on this big color catalog, and it looks like an earnest boast. Scores of fiberglass and plastic pools and waterfalls lay the foundation, followed by pumps, filters, fountains, statuary, and, of course, plants. The company offers a good selection of hardy and tropical water lilies, many of them pictured in color, along with lotuses, underwater plants, and marsh and bog plants like Imperial taro, Japanese iris, and cattail.

S. Scherer & Sons
104 Waterside Avenue, Northport, NY 11768
Telephone: 516-261-7432

Catalog price: free

This catalog doesn't cost anything, but it doesn't offer any pictures either. Seventeen hardy lilies are offered and about as many tropicals, each listed with a few words of bloom description. The nursery sells statuary, fiberglass pools, pumps, fountains, outdoor lighting, and a good selection of plants for the muddy region at the edge of the pool. Those who live nearby can pick up cut lily flowers "ready to be placed in your pool. . . . a great idea for wedding parties and special occasions when you need an immediate effect."

Slocum Water Gardens
1101 Cypress Gardens Boulevard, Winter Haven, FL 33880
Telephone: 813-293-7151

Catalog price: $2

Visitors to Florida's Cypress Gardens may want to stop and see the nearby display pools at Slocum Water Gardens. Those who can't make the trip can shop by mail in this beautiful color catalog. Seventeen lotus varieties are offered, most of them pictured in stunning color photographs. Thirty-five hardy lilies are described and more than 50 tropicals, again lavishly illustrated in big color photographs. For those who want to really impress the neighbors, the nursery offers the Victoria lily, a massive tropical species that grows leaves big enough to stand on. (At London's Kew Gardens these show lilies rate their own greenhouse.) The catalog is equally comprehensive in its offerings of marsh and bog plants, underwater plants, goldfish and koi, fiberglass pools, plastic liners, fountains, waterfalls, pumps, filters, and planting tubs.

Stapely Water Gardens
Stapeley, Nantwich, Cheshire, England CW5 7LH
Telephone: 44-270-628111

A large color catalog of water lilies, marsh plants, oxygenating aquatic plants, and pool supplies. Nearly 50 water lilies are described and pictured in a section that makes no distinction between tropical and hardy types. U.S. and Canadian customers will have to ignore the fish offerings and the many molded pools, as these can't be exported.

William Tricker, Inc.
P.O. Box 31267, Independence, OH 44131
Telephone: 216-524-3491 or 3492

William Tricker moved to the United States from England in 1885, and, while working as a gardener on Staten Island, began experiments in hybridizing tropical water lilies. He started his own nursery ten years later, and the business that carries his name claims to be the country's oldest water-garden specialist. (In past years, though not in 1987, it has also claimed title as the world's largest.) Tropical lilies are Tricker's forte. Fifty varieties are offered, with enchanting names like Eldorado, Persian Lilac, and Leopardess; the color pictures show blooms to match the magic of the titles. (The modern trend, we should note, is toward duller names that don't ring with the old romantic resonance. Mrs. Martin Randig, for example, doesn't have the spark of Indigo Zan-

zibar, Amethyst, and Lilac Queen.) The hardy-lily inventory is made up of almost 30 varieties, and the catalog goes on to peddle the massive Victoria lily, a number of lotus cultivars, and dozens of marsh and shallow-water plants. Pools, supplies, fish, and books round out the list.

Van Ness Water Gardens
2460 N. Euclid Avenue, Upland, CA 91786-1199
Telephone: 714-982-2425 or 981-5045

Catalog price: $2

A color-filled water-gardening catalog that can also serve as a textbook on the subject. The plant and supply offerings are interspersed with pages of cultural advice, pool-construction tips, and guidance on maintaining proper water quality for fish and plants. Sixty tropical lilies are offered and almost 40 hardy types, many of them shown in lavish color photographs that occasionally cover an entire page. In crimson reds, creamy whites, and soft purples, the flowers are pictured with such crisp realism that we can almost smell them (and without having to wade up to our waists in mud to get so close). The nursery sells a somewhat smaller line of marsh and bog plants and a veritable supermaket of supplies, equipment, books, and pool accessories.

Water Lily World
2331 Goodloe, Houston, TX 77093
Telephone: 713-692-8734

Catalog price: $3

A dozen tropical water lilies and as many hardy varieties presented in a typed descriptive list with no illustrations. The marsh- and aquatic-plant listings include a few identifying dawings, but nothing like the rich color of competing catalogs. Water Lily World carries a big line of pumps, pools, and supplies, and these "extras" take up most of the room in the assemblage of stapled sheets that serves as the firm's catalog.

Waterford Gardens
74 E. Allendale Road, Saddle River, NJ 07458
Telephone: 201-327-0721

Catalog price: $3.50

In our book this catalog takes top honors for stunning color photography and elegant page layout. The gorgeous sapphire bloom of Blue Beauty spread its dew-dropped petals across the entire opening page of the 1987 catalog, and dozens of other show-stopping pictures followed close behind. The firm offers 35 tropical lilies and 20 hardy varieties in a way that makes the flowers look like the last word in botanical perfection. Lotuses, marsh plants, and floating aquatics are sold to round out the planting. A full inventory of pools, liners, books, and supplies also appears. Plenty of advice is offered to the gardener planning a water garden, including step-by-step instructions for installing a plastic-lined pool and planting tips for each lily type.

The WaterWorks
111 E. Fairmount Street, Coopersburg, PA 18036
Telephone: 215-282-4784

Catalog price: $1

A demure and understated catalog that limits its illustrations to some simple line drawings. Fifteen hardy water lilies are offered and as many tropicals, each with a sentence of de-scription. Several lotus species and varieties, a handful of bog plants, and a selection of perennials for around the pool fill out the plant list. The bulk of the catalog is given over to pools, planting containers, pumps, and other supplies, including many Tetra products.

Wicklein's Aquatic Farm and Nursery, Inc.
1820 Cromwell Bridge Road, Baltimore, MD 21234
Telephone: 301-823-1335

Catalog price: $1

Two dozen hardy water lilies, almost as many tropicals, and a handful of lotus varieties lead off this descriptive catalog, which confines its illustrations to a few drawings. Tropical bog plants such as giant papyrus and violet-stemmed taro are offered, along with hardy wetland plants like Japanese sweet-flag and arrowhead and a number of plants meant for higher ground. The firm sells pumps, filters, pools, and supplies and offers plenty of instruction and advice.

Wildflowers

W. R. Aimers, Ltd.
Rt. 1, King, ON, Canada L0G 1K0
Telephone: 416-833-5282

Catalog price: free

Wildflower seed sold in mixes or by individual species. The mixtures have been selected for various regions of Canada (but can also be planted in corresponding climatic areas of the northern U.S.) and for different garden uses, such as flowers for cutting and for drying. Most of Aimers's seeds are for flowers that do best when planted in sunny borders or open fields.

Alpine Plants
Sierra natives. See under *Garden Perennials*, page 86.

Appalachian Wildflower Nursery
Rt. 1, Box 275A, Reedsville, PA 17084
Telephone: 717-667-6998

Catalog price: long self-addressed stamped envelope for plant list, $1 for descriptive catalog

This nursery sells unusual wildflowers from around the world, mixed in with a smattering of trees and shrubs. A few cultivated varieties are sold along with their wild cousins. The catalog lists phlox species from the Rockies and the Appalachians, primulas from the Alps and southern China,
and irises from the Altay mountains of Tadzhik, in the U.S.S.R. All stock is raised at the nursery in Pennsylvania.

Applewood Seed Co.
P.O. Box 10761, Edgemont Sta., Golden, CO 80401
Telephone: 303-431-6283

Catalog price: free

An expansive selection of wildflower seeds in a nicely illus-trated catalog. The seeds are available sorted by species or in an array of mixes designed for different regions and grow-ing conditions. Seven different regional mixes are sold, along with assortments chosen for low growth, high growth, and suitability for dry, wet, sunny, or shady conditions. Some of the seeds and mixes are sold in packets, but most come only in larger quantities for area plantings.

Baldwin Seed Co.
P.O. Box 3127, Kenai, AK 99611

Catalog price: $1.50

A fascinating and beautiful catalog of native Alaskan wild-flowers. Each plant is nicely described, and many are illus-trated with simple but lovely multicolor engravings. Our catalog came with a sample packet of dwarf pink poppy seed (*Papaver alborosium*), a rare miniature poppy that grows to a height of about six inches. (Because this species is listed as threatened, the seeds Baldwin sends come from nursery-grown plants.) Almost 60 different species are offered, including Alaska gentian (*Gentiana platypetala*), arctic daisy (*Chrysanthemum arcticum*), and mountain harebell (*Campanula lasiocarpa*), some of which will be of particular interest to rock gardeners.

Beersheba Wildflower Gardens

P.O. Box 551, Stone Door, Beersheba Springs, TN 37305
Telephone: 615-692-3575

Catalog price: free

Native wildflower plants, including some relatively rare species. Beersheba sells pink ladyslipper, trout lily, Turk's-cap lily, jack-in-the-pulpit, and five species of trillium. More than 50 plants are listed by common and botanical names, and some are illustrated in color. Prices are reasonable.

Bernardo Beach Native Plant Farm

Star Route 7, Box 145, Veguita, NM 87062
Telephone: 505-345-6248

Catalog price: four first-class stamps

Drought-tolerant plants, including wildflowers, trees, and shrubs. Most of the offerings are natives of the southwestern U.S., and all are selected for growth in that region. Among the natives are cliffrose (*Cowania mexicana*), Apache plume (*Fallugia paradoxa*), dwarf coyotebush (*Baccharis pilularis*), and several sages. The imports include jujube, blue spurge (*Euphorbia myrsinites*), and dwarf plumbago (*Ceratostigma plumbaginoides*). Minimum order for shipping is $20.

Boehlke's Woodland Gardens

W. 140 N. 10829 Country Aire Road, Germantown, WI 53022

Catalog price: 50¢

An attractive catalog of native wildflowers, ferns, and a few cultivated perennial varieties. Among the wildflowers are white trout lily (*Erythronium albidum*), great merrybells (*Uvularia grandiflora*), shooting star (*Dodecatheon meadia*), and skunk cabbage (*Symplocarpus foetidus*). Each plant is well described with growing requirements clearly spelled out, and the list is separated into sun-loving and shade-tolerant species and plants for wet, marshy spots. The catalog is illustrated by black-and-white pencil drawings of selected offerings.

The Botanic Garden Seed Co. ✓

9 Wyckoff Street, Brooklyn, NY 11201
Telephone: 718-624-8839

Catalog price: free

Wildflower seeds distinguished by the most beautiful packages we have seen. The primary selection includes poppy, foxglove, dame's rocket, evening primrose, sweet pea, and several others (showing that the term "wildflower" is not defined clinically here). The Art Nouveau–style packets are so attractive you may be hesitant to tear them open, but the company also sells the artwork as postcards and posters, so you needn't hold back. An even bigger variety of wildflower seed is sold in "postcard packets," which can be mailed as inexpensive gifts. For a more extravagant gift, some of the

seeds are sold as collections packed with "goatskin" (actually sheepskin) gloves and wooden-handled cultivators in wicker garden hampers.

Joseph Brown

Star Rt., Box 226, Gloucester Point, VA 23062
Telephone: 804-642-4602

Seeds for more than 200 native trees, shrubs, and wildflowers, including more than 20 native orchids. Plants are listed by botanical name only; no common names, no descriptions, and no pictures appear. Gardeners in the area can buy plants at the nursery (phone ahead for an appointment), but only seeds are shipped.

John Chambers

15 Westleigh Road, Barton Seagrave, Kettering, Northants., England NN15 5AJ
Telephone: 44-933-681-632

Catalog price: free

A densely packed, unillustrated catalog of British wildflower seeds. No descriptions are given, beyond a code to indicate annuals, biennials, and perennials, so the reader will have to do some research to identify the nearly 500 selections. Most seeds are listed by common name only, which will make the shopper's job just that much harder. U.S. and Canadian customers must send payment in British sterling or charge their order to a Visa or Access card.

Colorado Alpines, Inc.

See under *Alpines and Rock-Garden Perennials*, page 40.

Conley's Garden Center

Boothbay Harbor, ME 04538
Telephone: 207-633-5020

Catalog price: $1.50, deductible from first order

A substantial list of native wildflowers, groundcovers, and ferns. A few of the offerings, such as the lilies, trilliums, and ladyslippers, are sold as bulbs, but most are shipped in flats of three or ten plants. Sixty-seven different wildflower species are offered, 28 ferns, and 16 species of groundcovers and vines. Among the listings are yellow and showy ladyslipper, painted trillium, and bird's foot violet. The miminum order is $25.

The Crownsville Nursery
See under *Garden Perennials*, page 87.

E & H Products
71-301 Highway 111, Suite 1, Rancho Mirage, CA 92270

Catalog price: free

Wildflower seed sold in regional mixes and by species. Separate mixes are available for the southwestern desert, the California coast, the Pacific Northwest, the western mountains, California interior valleys, the San Francisco Bay area, the northeastern states, the southeastern states, and the midwestern states (including Texas). Seeds for more than forty individual species are also sold. All seeds and mixes can be had in quarter-ounce packets or in larger quantities.

Eco-Gardens
See under *Garden Perennials*, page 87.

Far North Gardens
Seeds for more than 1,000 wildflowers and garden perennials. See under *Primroses*, page 136.

Forestfarm
See under *Trees and Shrubs*, page 152.

Gardens of the Blue Ridge
P.O. Box 10, Pineola, NC 28662
Telephone: 704-733-2417

Catalog price: $2

A descriptive list of native wildflowers, ferns, trees, and shrubs, illustrated with a few color photographs. The roughly 250 offerings are grouped by plant type—such as ferns, orchids, and rhododendrons—and by cultural requirements—such as bog plants and plants suitable for rock gardens. The nursery gardens are open to the public year-round, but are at their best from May through October.

Draig Goch Seed Co.
Box 113, Newfield, NY 14867

Catalog price: 50¢

The name suggests Welsh imports, but Draig Goch offers seed for wildflowers native to the northeastern U.S. In a simple typed brochure illustrated with small drawings, the nursery presents its roughly 40 offerings, which range from moth mullein (*Verbascum blattaria*), a tall sun-loving plant, to herb-robert (*Geranium robertianum*), a diminutive pink geranium that thrives in woodland conditions. Draig Goch can supply small quantities of seed for many other species not listed in the catalog and can collect seed to order.

Russell Graham, Purveyor of Plants
See under *Garden Perennials*, page 88.

Green Horizons
218 Quinlan #571, Kerrville, TX 78028
Telephone: 512-257-5141

Catalog price: one first-class stamp

Texas wildflower seed sold by the packet, the ounce, or the pound. The brochure lists about two dozen species—such as

Mexican hats (*Ratibida columnaris*), firewheel (*Gaillardia pulchella*), and golden wave (*Coreopsis tinctoria*)—but notes that others are available in bulk. The back side of the brochure lists books and wildflower note cards.

Griffey's Nursery
1670 Highway 25/70, Marshall, NC 28753
Telephone: 704-656-2334

Catalog price: free

A simple pamphlet, its descriptions limited to three or four words, but one that holds some treasures. Here the range of wildflowers is extended to encompass native flowering shrubs and trees, such as flame azalea, tulip tree, and flowering raspberry. The true wildflower offerings include many native orchids, violets, and trilliums. Some of the listings are not widely sold: white turtlehead (*Chelone glabra*), wood betony (*Pedicularis canadensis*), and *Streptopus roseus*, to list three. Native ferns are also available. The nursery sometimes goes by the name The Three Laurels.

High Altitude Gardens
Seed for western natives. See under *General Flowers and Vegetables*, page 20.

International Growers Exchange
See under *General Flowers and Vegetables*, page 21.

Izard Ozark Natives
P.O. Box 454, Mountain View, AR 72560
Telephone: 501-368-7439

Seeds for wildflowers, shrubs, and trees native to the Arkansas and Missouri Ozarks. Almost 100 species are offered, including wild senna (*Cassia marilandica*), compass plant (*Silphium laciniatum*), Arkansas yucca, fringe tree (*Chionanthus virginicus*), and smoke tree (*Cotinus obovatus*). The firm sells a number of books on growing and identifying native plants and on harvesting wild herbs and food plants.

Lafayette Home Nursery, Inc.
Lafayette, IL 61449
Telephone: 309-995-3311

This nursery, one of the Midwest's biggest dealers in seed for prairie restoration, celebrated its 100th birthday in 1987. Seeds for scores of wildflower species are offered, some for

woodland planting and some for open prairie growth. (Among the names that caught our eye: rattlesnake master, prairie thimbleweed, and compass plant). Perhaps more important to the prairie gardener are the many native grass seeds offered, for such plants as prairie switchgrass, little bluestem, and Indian grass. For those who live in the area, the nursery offers an installation service. The firm will even send out a burn-control adviser for plantings that require periodic burning.

Larner Seeds

P.O. Box 407, 235 Fern Road, Bolinas, CA 94924
Telephone: 415-868-9407

Catalog price: 75¢

The motto here is "seeds for the western landscape." Most of the seeds offered are California natives, and many, like arroyo lupine, desert bluebell, and California poppy, will thrive under dry conditions. In 1987 the firm moved to the coastal town of Bolinas, and as a result a number of coastal and wet-area plants have started creeping onto the list. Some tree seeds are offered, including seeds of several California oaks. The owners' interest in drought-tolerant wildflowers has also led them to a number of native American vegetables that can be grown with a minimum of irrigation, including Hopi blue corn, Hopi melon, chia, and tepary beans.

Two pamphlets, *Notes on Growing California Wildflowers* and *Notes on Natural Design*, will be sent with the catalog for an additional $1.25 (for a total of $2).

Las Pilitas Nursery

Star Rt., Box 23X, Santa Margarita, CA 93453
Telephone: 805-438-5992

Catalog price: free price list, $4 for descriptive catalog

Three hundred California natives, arranged alphabetically by botanical name, make up this list. Wildflowers, trees, and shrubs are shuffled together on the price list, and most readers will need either the descriptive catalog or a reference work to know just what all the plants are. The descriptive catalog gives cultural instructions and descriptions of all plants offered.

Most of the offerings are sold as nursery stock in 3½-inch pots. Larger plants can be had at the nursery, in containers up to 15 gallons, but these are not available for shipping. Seeds are offered for 30 of the wildflower species.

Little Valley Farm

Rt. 1, Box 287, Richland Ctr., WI 53581
Telephone: 608-538-3180

Catalog price: 25¢

A small, attractive catalog of native wildflowers and shrubs. Some of the wildflower offerings are sold as plants, and some can be ordered as seeds. Each listing is illustrated with a small line drawing, and the text gives a description and cultural instruction. Most of the wildflowers are prairie natives, with a few wetland and woodland dwellers thrown in for balance. The farm sells a number of books on the care and identification of native plants.

Lofts Seed, Inc.

P.O. Box 146, Bound Brook, NJ 08805
Telephone: 201-356-8700 or 800-526-3890

Catalog price: free

Lofts blends several wildflower seed mixes for different regions of North America. The regions are somewhat broader than those of some competitors. Canada, for example, is covered by a single mix, as is the northern U.S. The plants in each mix are selected to do well in open, sunny areas, and some grass seed is included to help prevent erosion while the plants are getting started.

McLaughlin's Seeds

P.O. Box 550, Mead, WA 99021-0550

Catalog price: $1 (specify wildflower list)

Seeds for more than 100 wildflowers of the Pacific Northwest and northern Rocky Mountains. The catalog is a newspaper-size descriptive list with a few black-and-white photographs. The seeds are available in packets or in larger quantities, and a few mixes are sold—one for shade, one for coastal gardens, and one comprised of plants found along the Lewis & Clark trail. A separate herb catalog is sent out for $1 (see entry under *Herbs*, page 101).

Maver Nursery

See under *Garden Perennials*, page 89.

Midwest Wildflowers

P.O. Box 64, Rockton, IL 61072

Catalog price: 50¢

Seeds for more than 150 North American wildflower species, listed by botanical and common name. A booklet accompanying the list provides pictures and descriptions of a dozen of the most popular plants. No descriptions are given of the other offerings. Seeds are sold in packets by species and are not offered in mixes or in bulk quantities.

Moon Mountain Wildflowers

P.O. Box 34, Morro Bay, CA 93442
Telephone: 805-772-2473

Catalog price: $1

This descriptive catalog presents about 50 wildflowers, many of them illustrated by attractive pencil drawings. Instructions are given for starting the seeds and for growing all plants. Among the listings are a number of plants native to

Europe, such as rocket larkspur and scarlet flax, that have either naturalized here or that grow well in wild plantings. The listings are divided into annuals and perennials, and the native range of each plant is noted. Several regional mixes are sold, about half of them for the varied climates of California. Seeds are sold in packets or in larger quantities by weight.

Mountain Ornamental Nursery
P.O. Box 83, Altamont, TN 37301
Telephone: 615-692-3424

A wholesale supplier of ornamental trees and shrubs, wildflowers, and ferns. For the gardener with a large landscaping project, the nursery may be able to fill some holes at a reasonable price. More than 50 wildflowers are offered, the minimum order being 25 of a single variety. All plants are listed by common name only, and in a few cases a note or call to the nursery might be in order to be sure the plants offered are really the species wanted. Seedling trees and shrubs are sold in quantities of 250 or more, which will put them out of reach for most home gardeners. For the record, the offerings include bladdernut, native azaleas, witch hazel, redbud, hornbeam, and about 40 other nut and shade trees and ornamental trees and shrubs.

Mountain West Seeds
Box 1471, Cheyenne, WY 82003
Telephone: 307-634-6328

Catalog price: 25¢

Seed for Rocky Mountain and prairie wildflowers, many of which are suitable for rock gardens. The 1987 list spanned 24 species, including cliffbush (*Jamesia americana*) and mountain phacelia (*Phacelia sericea*). The list changes from year to year depending on the supply. Seeds are sold in packets and are not available in bulk quantities.

Native Gardens
Rt. 1, Box 494, Greenback, TN 37742
Telephone: 615-856-3350

Catalog price: $1, deductible from first order

In 1987 the Native Gardens list came in the form of a poster-size chart of about 75 wildflowers, coded to provide descriptions and cultural information in condensed form. In 1988 the nursery plans to issue a more complete descriptive catalog. Most of the offerings can be had as either seeds or plants, and many of the plants are available in a choice of sizes, either potted or field grown. Among the offerings are woodbine, Tennessee coneflower, fire pink, and blue lobelia.

Native Plants, Inc.
1697 W. 2100 N., P.O. Box 177, Lehi, UT 84043
Telephone: 801-768-4422 or 531-1456

Catalog price: free

Native wildflower and grass seed for landscaping use and erosion control. The minimum order is $50, so gardeners planning a small wildflower patch needn't inquire. The firm is set up to provide seed for land reclamation projects, road-side seeding, and any other large-scale plantings. For shoppers planning a major wildflower project, the color catalog lists seeds for more than 100 wildflower species and as many native grasses. The firm provides custom mixes (for a price), soil tests, and reclamation consulting services.

Native Seeds, Inc.
14590 Triadelphia Mill Road, Dayton, MD 21036
Telephone: 301-596-9818

Catalog price: free

Seed for 27 sun-loving wildflowers available by individual species or in regional mixes. Scarlet larkspur is on the list, as is prairie aster, butterfly weed, California poppy, and Texas bluebonnet. If you are ordering by species, seeds can be had in small packets. The mixes, available for regions and for individual states, must be ordered in quantities of half a pound or more. A descriptive brochure with a few color photographs accompanies the price list.

Natural Gardens
113 Jasper Lane, Oak Ridge, TN 37830

Catalog price: $1, deductible from first order

About 70 native species are described in detail in an unillustrated catalog. The plants are about evenly divided between woodland and field types. Among those that attracted our attention are swamp haw (*Viburnum nudum*), heal all (*Prunella vulgaris*), and beautyberry (*Callicarpa americana*). Most of the offerings are sold as plants in 2-inch pots. Some can also be bought as seed.

New England Wild Flower Society, Inc.
Seed List, Hemenway Road, Framingham, MA 01701
Telephone: 617-877-7630 or 237-4924

Catalog price: long self-addressed stamped envelope with two first-class stamps

As part of its effort to encourage gardeners to use more wildflowers in their home landscapes, each spring the New England Wild Flower Society sells seeds for more than 150 wildflowers native to North America. Requests for the seed list should be sent in January. Late requests and requests sent without the stamped envelope will not be honored. The wide-ranging offerings include seven native rhododendron species (and two albino variants), scarlet monkey flower (*Mimulus cardinalis*), albino prairie blazing star (*Liatris pycnostachya* 'Alba'), dog-hobble (*Leucothoe fontanesiana*), and wild hydrangea (*Hydrangea arborescens*). Be sure to look at the coded propagation instructions when ordering: a few plants need at least two years to germinate. (See entry under *Societies and Associations*, page 261, for information on membership.)

Niche Gardens
Rt. 1, Box 290, Chapel Hill, NC 27514
Telephone: 919-967-0078 (weekday evenings)

Catalog price: $1, deductible from first order

A tidy, nicely written descriptive catalog of about 100 southeastern natives. The plants are propagated at the nursery and shipped in 4-inch, quart, or gallon pots. Among the more unusual offerings: white great lobelia (*Lobelia siphilitica* 'Alba'), downy lobelia (*L. puberula*), pale purple coneflower (*Echinacea pallida*), and fairy lily (*Zephyranthes atamasco*). Each year the nursery includes a few trees and shrubs that it feels deserve more attention from gardeners.

North Eastern Ferns and Wild Flowers
Mark Hayden, P.O. Box 292, Newfields, NH 03856
Telephone: 603-772-1136

A hundred northeastern wildflowers and 30 native ferns listed without descriptions or illustrations. Some of the ferns are rare or unusual species, such as mountain wood fern (*Dryopteris spinulosa* var. *dilatata*), giant wood fern (*Dryopteris goldiana*), and Braun's holly fern (*Polystichum braunii*). Among the wildflowers are cubeseed iris (*Iris prismatica*), mayapple (*Podophyllum peltatum*), more than a dozen native groundcovers, five trilliums, and five native orchids.

Northplan Seed Producers
P.O. Box 9107, Moscow, ID 83843
Telephone: 208-882-8040

Catalog price: long self-addressed stamped envelope

Northplan introduces itself as a supplier of seed for "disturbed land restoration," for planting on mined land, overgrazed ranges, and test-drilling sites. But many of the seeds are also suited to home gardens, and some are available only in packets for small-scale projects. Cascade iris, pearly everlasting, and mountain thermopsis are among the flowers sold in small quantities only. The firm offers several wildflower mixes—with names like Blue Mountain, Palouse Prairie, Great Plains, and Boise Basin—designed for planting in western prairie and mountain areas. The seed list stretches well beyond the bounds of the normal wildflower supplier. Seeds for more than 100 native trees and shrubs are offered, along with about 50 different range and reclamation grasses. The firm also publishes a vegetable seed catalog under the name Mountain Seed and Nursery.

Oakridge Nurseries
P.O. Box 182, E. Kingston, NH 03827
Telephone: 603-642-8227

Catalog price: $1

A compact color brochure (with some of the tiniest type we've come across) lists 35 northeastern wildflowers and 19 native ferns. The nursery sells trailing arbutus (*Epigea repens*), wood lily (*Lilium philadelphicum*), white turtlehead (*Chelone glabra*), and a number of unusual woodland ferns. All plants are described; a few are illustrated with color photographs.

Orchid Gardens
6700 Splithand Road, Grand Rapids, MN 55744
Telephone: 218-326-6975

Catalog price: 50¢

Though the name is Orchid Gardens, this nursery sells only three native orchid species and makes an effort to discourage shoppers from ordering them. To buy any of the orchids, gardeners must order other wildflowers and ferns of equal value, and even then the nursery restricts the orchid orders to two plants of each species per year. Ladyslipper fanciers should really have no trouble with those restrictions. The nursery sells more than 100 other wildflowers and 14 native ferns, some of which are bound to entice even the hard-core orchid fan. Violets are a particular specialty here. Ten native species are offered, including the rare Selkirk's violet. Plants are succinctly described, and a coded system is used to give growing instructions.

Painted Meadows Seed Company
P.O. Box 1865, Kingston, PA 18704
Telephone: 717-283-2911

Catalog price: free

A single wildflower seed mix designed for use in the eastern U.S., "north of Florida and east of the Mississippi River." The mix combines a dozen wildflowers with clover and fescue grass.

Panfield Nurseries, Inc.

322 Southdown Road, Huntington, NY 11743
Telephone: 516-427-0112

Catalog price: long self-addressed stamped envelope

A wholesale source of wildflowers and ferns, primarily woodland species. Plants are shipped bare root during the dormant season (October 1 through December 15 and February 15 through March 30). Write only if you plan a large planting. The firm sells a full line of nursery stock and gardening supplies at its store.

Passiflora Wildflower Company

Rt. 1, Box 190-A, Germanton, NC 27019
Telephone: 919-591-5816

Catalog price: $1

Thirty wildflower species are laid out in an attractive color brochure that makes each plant look like a prize. Most are sun lovers that can be used for naturalizing an open field or for giving a native look to a well-lit flower bed. Gardeners can order either seeds or nursery-grown plants. Three seed mixtures and a handful of helpful books are also sold.

The Theodore Payne Foundation

10459 Tuxford Street, Sun Valley, CA 91352
Telephone: 818-768-1802

Catalog price: long self-addressed stamped envelope

Seed for more than 100 wildflowers listed by botanical name without description. As a concession to the novice gardener, common names are included in the list, and a few plants are broken out as the "most popular and showy species of easy culture." (Among these, blazing star, baby blue eyes, and gold variant of California poppy.) Strong areas here include 12 species of lupine, six penstemons, and some unusual wild poppies. The foundation sells a few mixes, including four that have been selected for color (blue and lavender, blue and gold, gold, and rainbow). Seeds, including the mixes, are sold in packets, by the ounce, or by the pound.

Plants of the Southwest

See under *General Flowers and Vegetables*, page 27.

Prairie Moon Nursery

Rt. 3, Box 163, Winona, MN 55987
Telephone: 507-452-5231 or 4990

Catalog price: two first-class stamps

Prairie wildflowers sold as either plants or seeds. The catalog gives the moisture requirements of each plant, but offers no descriptions and doesn't point out which plants need sun and which prefer shade. With some expertise—or a reference book—this should be an important plant source. Almost 150 wildflower species are listed, as are 17 grasses and sedges.

Prairie Nursery

P.O. Box 365, Westfield, WI 53964
Telephone: 608-296-3679

Catalog price: $1, deductible from first order

More than 60 prairie wildflowers in an illustrated descriptive catalog. A dozen of the plants are pictured in dramatic color photographs. Many others are identified with clear line drawings. The descriptions sometimes wax poetic (on the sky-blue aster: "brilliant blue flowers mirror the late summer sky, covering the prairie with an azure blanket") but always give solid information about plant height, flower color, moisture, and soil requirements. Offerings are sold as both plants and seeds. Seeds can be bought by the packet, the ounce, or the pound; plants are sold in quantities of three or more. The minimum order is $15.

The Primrose Path

See under *Garden Perennials*, page 91.

Putney Nursery, Inc.

Putney, VT 05346
Telephone: 802-387-5577

Catalog price: $1, deductible from first order

Wildflowers, perennials, ferns, and herbs presented in a small color catalog. Most of the offerings are sold as small field-grown plants. Seeds are sold for some of the wildflowers and all the annual herbs, and a wildflower mix is available for covering larger areas. The plant list shuffles wildflowers and cultivated garden perennials, jumping from cottage pink to wild geranium to baby's breath. More than 100 species and varieties are sold as nursery stock, and the $6 minimum order allows gardeners to fill even the smallest bare patch in a border.

Clyde Robin Seed Co.

P.O. Box 2366, Castro Valley, CA 94546
Telephone: 415-581-3468

Catalog price: $2

The producers of the Meadow-in-a-Can wildflower mix, sold in many gift catalogs, Clyde Robin also sells wildflower seeds by species in its own color catalog. More than 90 different plants are listed, many of them pictured in clear color photographs, and all are sold in garden-size packets. Wildflower purists may object to finding cultivated varieties of oriental poppy and lupine on the list, but plenty of genuine natives are there as well, and gardeners are free to pick and choose. Several regional mixes are offered, along with one for shady areas and one made up exclusively of short species.

Rocknoll Nursery
See under *Alpines and Rock-Garden Perennials*, page 42.

Rocky Mountain Seed Service
P.O. Box 215, Golden, BC, Canada V0A 1H0

Catalog price: $1

Seeds for almost 150 plants native to British Columbia. Most are wildflowers, but some trees and shrubs have found their way onto the list. The owners admit that some of the plants are extremely difficult to propagate from seed, particularly the native orchids and wintergreen. Fern spores are also offered, and these require special care as well. A number of compatible non-natives are sold, many of them small relatives of native species, which may be of interest to rock gardeners. The catalog gives brief descriptions of all offerings as well as basic cultivation instructions.

John Scheepers, Inc.
See under *Bulbs*, page 63.

Shady Oaks Nursery
See under *Shade Plants*, page 146.

Siskiyou Rare Plant Nursery
See under *Alpines and Rock-Garden Perennials*, page 42.

Southwestern Native Seeds
Box 50503, Tucson, AZ 85703

Catalog price: $1

Seeds for more than 300 wildflowers, succulents, trees, and shrubs native to the Southwest, presented in a coded list that gives an amazing amount of information in a few short pages. Plants are divided into desert, mountain, and tropical species, and the code supplies data on the county of origin, elevation and hardiness, size, special characteristics, and recommended uses. Rock gardeners will find some rare mountain species here, cactus fanciers some unusual natives, and dry-area homeowners some fascinating alternatives to common nursery stock.

Stock Seed Farms
Rt. 1, Box 112, Murdock, NE 68407
Telephone: 402-867-3771

Catalog price: free

Seeds for native prairie wildflowers and grasses presented in a descriptive brochure. Ten different grasses are offered, including buffalo grass, Indian grass, and big bluestem. The wildflower offerings include a dozen prairie perennials and a few self-seeding annuals. Grass seed is sold by the pound, wildflower seed by the packet or the ounce. The firm sells a number of brochures and books on prairie grasses and wildflowers and two "Bit O' Prairie" gift sacks—seed mixes packed in attractive calico print bags.

Strand Nursery Co.
Rt. 3, Box 187, Osceola, WI 54020
Telephone: 715-294-3779

Catalog price: one first-class stamp

Native ferns and wildflowers sold in quantities of 20 plants or more. Strand sells a dozen different ferns and 20 wildflower species on a list with short descriptions.

Sunlight Gardens
Rt. 3, Box 286-B, Loudon, TN 37774
Telephone: 615-986-6071

Catalog price: free price list, $2 for descriptive catalog

More than 80 native wildflowers and 20 companion garden perennials. The full catalog gives a thorough description of each plant, including cultural information, and points out which plants are easy to grow. For many of the offerings the catalog descriptions suggest companion plants. Blackberry lily, for example, is recommended for planting with butterfly weed, coneflower, gaillardia, sundrop, and fire pink. Sunlight Gardens does not hold to a purist wildflowers-only philosophy. The owners think many of the native plants look best in a perennial border and that many perennials shine when planted with wildflowers. The nursery does hold to one restriction: no plants sold are gathered in the wild; all are nursery grown.

Sunshine Seed Company
Rt. 2, Box 176, Wyoming, IL 61491
Telephone: 309-286-7356

Catalog price: $1

Native wildflower and grass seed sold in bulk for area plantings. The stripped-down list of 60 prairie species and 20 woodland plants consists of botanical and common names only, no pictures and no descriptions.

Tripple Brook Farm
See under *Garden Perennials*, page 92.

Twin Peaks Seeds
1814 Dean Street, Eureka, CA 95501

Catalog price: free

A small list of western wildflower seeds sold by the packet. Arroyo lupine, scarlet bugler, grand lianthus, and showy penstemon are among the offerings. Each plant is described in a couple of sentences, including a few words on culture.

Valley Creek

P.O. Box 475, Circle Drive, McArthur, OH 45651
Telephone: 800-992-7396 (7397 in Ohio)

Catalog price: free

Wildflower seeds sold in regional mixes and by individual species. No packets are offered; the smallest quantity listed is one-sixth of a pound. All the flowers are briefly described, and a few are illustrated in color. In 1988 the firm will expand its offerings to include lawn and gardening supplies, herbs and spices, and gift items.

The Vermont Wildflower Farm

P.O. Box 5, Route 7, Charlotte, VT 05445-0005
Telephone: 802-425-3931

Catalog price: free

Several wildflower seed mixtures, for sunny, shady, wet, or dry areas and for different regions of the country. A new mix in 1987 was a combination for cut flowers. The mixtures are sold by the ounce or the pound. Seed for 24 individual wildflower species can be bought in packets. The farm maintains a six-acre display garden, open to the public seven days a week from mid-May to mid-October.

Vick's Wildgardens

P.O. Box 115, Gladwyne, PA 19035
Telephone: 215-525-6773

Catalog price: $1

Many of the illustrations in this book are reproduced from the catalogs of James Vick, a Rochester, New York, seedsman whose firm was one of the country's largest seed suppliers during the second half of the 19th century. Vick's Wildgardens is a sort of family offshoot, started in 1930 by a Vick relative who had worked in the original seed firm as a child. The older firm is gone now, but Vick's Wildgardens keeps the family name alive in the gardening business. The descriptive catalog lists almost 100 native wildflowers and ferns, each pictured with a small drawing and a few featured with color photographs. Vick's deals primarily in woodland plants, offering a handful of trilliums, ladyslippers, and native lilies. Spring shipments go out in March and April, fall shipments in September and October.

Wayside Gardens

See under *Garden Perennials*, page 92.

We-Du Nurseries

See under *Garden Perennials*, page 93.

The Wildflower Source

P.O. Box 312, Fox Lake, IL 60020

Catalog price: $1, deductible from first order

Woodland and shade-loving wildflowers, each described in some detail on a typewritten price list. Eight trillium species, a handful of hardy native orchids, and such plants as mottled wild ginger (*Asarum shuttleworthii*), white turtlehead (*Chelone glabra*), and crested iris (*Iris cristata*) are among the features. Prices are quite reasonable.

Wildginger Woodlands

P.O. Box 1091, Webster, NY 14580

Catalog price: $1, deductible from first order

More than 150 wildflowers, mostly woodland species, sold as seeds and as nursery stock. The offerings include a dozen native violets (and some cultivated varieties), eight trilliums, and a selection of asters, wild geraniums, mulleins, and ladyslippers. Thirty ferns are sold, either as plants or as spores. All seed and spore orders must be placed in the early spring, by March 15, as they are collected and packed to order.

Wildwood, Inc.

Rt. 3, Box 165, Pittsboro, NC 27312

Catalog price: long self-addressed stamped envelope

Thurman Maness has toyed with mother nature at his wildflower nursery, crossing cardinal flower (*Lobelia cardinalis*) with blue lobelia (*L. siphilitica*) to create hybrids with unique fuchsia-colored blooms. He claims that the hybrids are easier to grow than their wild parents; they have a tolerance for drier soil and a greater resistance to disease. Mr. Maness sells the natural forms of both plants and white variants of each. His list also includes hardy ferns and a small selection of other wildflowers. Minimum order is $10. No export and no credit cards.

Windrift Prairie Shop

Rt. 2, Daysville Road, Oregon, IL 61061
Telephone: 815-732-6890

Catalog price: two first-class stamps

A hundred native wildflowers sold as seeds or plants for prairie restoration. The list gives both botanical and common names and notes whether plants will grow in wet, medium, or dry prairie habitats. No other description or cultural information is offered; instead the firm sells some inexpensive books and pamphlets that tell the full story. The minimum plant order is three of the same species; seeds are sold in packets or by weight.

Woodlanders, Inc.

See under *Trees and Shrubs*, page 167.

Wyrttun Ward

See under *Herbs*, page 103.

Yerba Buena Nursery

19500 Skyline Boulevard, Woodside, CA 94062
Telephone: 415-851-1668

Catalog price: free

Yerba Buena offers more than 250 trees, shrubs, and perennials native to California, along with a big selection of native and exotic ferns. The business is run primarily as a retail nursery, but plants will be shipped by UPS or airmail to customers who live too far away to visit. Interested long-distance shoppers will have to inquire about shipping charges when they place their orders. The price list does not include descriptions, illustrations, or cultural instructions.

Wildlife Food Plants

Dutch Mountain Nursery

7984 N. 48th Street, Rt. 1, Augusta, MI 49012
Telephone: 616-731-5232

Catalog price: long self-addressed stamped envelope

A bare-bones list of 100 trees and shrubs that produce berries or nuts that birds like to eat. Many also provide cover and nesting sites. Among the offerings are red and white snowberry, Franklin tree, Kentucky coffee tree, Carolina allspice, and an assortment of dogwoods, cherries, serviceberries, and viburnums. The list gives common and botanical names, mature height, zone hardiness, and the size of the plants sold.

Forestfarm

See under *Trees and Shrubs*, page 152.

Glendale Enterprises

Rt. 3, Box 77P, DeFuniak Springs, FL 32433
Telephone: 904-859-2141 or 2341

Catalog price: $1

Seed for chufa and velvet beans, promoted as excellent food plants for wild turkeys and other wildlife. The literature that accompanies the price list gives a little information about providing for the needs of wild turkeys and explains what chufa and velvet beans are. The brochure also talks up the partridge pea (*Cassia fasciculata*) as a crop for game birds, but doesn't quote prices.

Kester's Wild Game Food Nurseries, Inc.

P.O. Box V, Omro, WI 54963
Telephone: 414-685-2929

Catalog price: $2

An educational catalog of dozens of plants that animals, birds, and fish like to eat or use as cover. The nursery's specialty is marsh and water plants. Its wetland offerings include Sago pondweed (*Potamogeton pectinatus*), wild celery (*Vallisneria spiralis*), and arrowhead (*Sagittaria latifolia*), all relished by ducks, geese, and swans. Perennial and annual grains are offered to attract deer, quail, and turkeys. Cultural instructions are given for all the plants, and many are pictured. A lengthy text at the back of the catalog explains how to create a complete habitat for wildlife, including the strategic planting of trees, shrubs, and other shelter plants.

Wildlife Nurseries

P.O. Box 2724, Oshkosh, WI 54903-2724
Telephone: 414-231-3780

Catalog price: free

Marsh and water plants for attracting ducks. The catalog starts out with a few pages of pictures of the owners on various hunting trips. If their plants attracted all the ducks they bagged in the snapshots, they must have figured out what the birds like. Among the offerings are wild celery, Wapato duck potato ("best muskrat food available"), and giant wild rice.

PART II:

Gardening Supplies

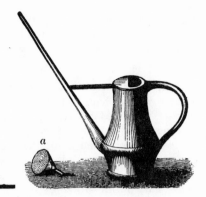

General Gardening Supplies

Allen, Sterling & Lothrop
See under *General Flowers and Vegetables*, page 13.

Archia's Seed Store
See under *General Flowers and Vegetables*, page 14.

Bountiful Gardens
See under *General Flowers and Vegetables*, page 14.

Bunton Seed Co.
See under *General Flowers and Vegetables*, page 14.

W. Atlee Burpee Company
See under *General Flowers and Vegetables*, page 15.

Charley's Greenhouse Supply
1569 Memorial Highway, Mt. Vernon, WA 98273
Telephone: 206-428-2626

Catalog price: $2

A big catalog of greenhouse and general gardening supplies offered in retail quantities for the home gardener. Charley's sells fans, heaters, lighting equipment, shading material, and meters for greenhouse owners, as well as books, tools, plastic pots, and propagating trays that can be used by gardeners who haven't yet built their solariums.

J. Collard
P.O. Box 40098, Long Beach, CA 90804-6098
Telephone: 213-433-0495

Catalog price: free

J. Collard put out its first mail-order catalog in the fall of 1987, a fold-out brochure offering tools, supplies, and other garden accessories. Among the selections were three ornamental wrought-iron hose guides, a selection of stainless-steel tools from Burgon & Ball in England, a small painted garden bench and companion planter, and a sectional picket fence to guard the Christmas tree from pets and toddlers.

Composting Fast-Easy
709 W. Stonecrest Circle, St. Joseph, MO 64506
Telephone: 816-233-0332

Catalog price: self-addressed stamped envelope

A composter made from a standard 50-gallon barrel. Buy the complete composter, or buy the base and supply your own barrel. The base raises the barrel and allows it to be rotated to mix the compost inside.

Crary Co.
P.O. Box 1779, Fargo, ND 58107
Telephone: 701-282-5520 or 800-362-3145 ext. 151

Catalog price: free

A raised barrel-type composter called the Compostumbler. The barrel holds 60 gallons and is perched on a stand so that a wheelbarrow can be rolled directly under the door for unloading.

Dalen Products, Inc.
11110 Gilbert Drive, Knoxville, TN 37932
Telephone: 615-966-3256

Catalog price: free (ask for retail price list)

Dalen manufactures the inflatable owls and snakes that have become so popular over the past few years. The firm also makes mulch materials, a tomato collar that funnels water down to the plant's roots, and nylon netting to use for trellises, fencing, and pest control. Dalen sells primarily on a wholesale basis, but will sell directly to customers who write.

Dan's Garden Shop
See under *General Flowers and Vegetables*, page 16.

Day-Dex Co.
4725 N.W. 36th Avenue, Miami, FL 33142
Telephone: 305-635-5241 or 5259

Catalog price: free

Tiered plant benches for growing and displaying potted plants. Legs and frames are made of galvanized steel, shelving of galvanized wire mesh.

Dominion Seed House
Supplies for Canadian customers. See under *General Flowers and Vegetables*, page 16.

Early's Farm and Garden Centre
See under *General Flowers and Vegetables*, page 18.

Evergreen Garden Plant Labels
Bloom-stalk supports. See under *Plant Labels and Markers* page 233.

Farmer Seed & Nursery Co.
See under *General Flowers and Vegetables*, page 18.

F & R Farrell Co.

P.O. Box 133, Harrisburg, OH 43126-0133

Telephone: 614-877-3678

Catalog price: free

Farrell sells a rosebush winterizer, and its brochure leaves some mystery about exactly what it is. We're told how to prepare the roses to go in it (we're to tie their branches together in a bundle), and we're told that we should fill the space between the bush and the winterizer with peat moss, but nowhere are we told what the winterizer is made of or what it looks like. The firm illustrates its other product, a heavy-duty plastic growing flat.

Henry Field Seed & Nursery Co.

See under *General Flowers and Vegetables*, page 18.

Florist Products Inc.

2242 N. Palmer Drive, Schaumburg, IL 60173

Telephone: 312-885-2242

Catalog price: free

A full line of growing supplies offered in retail quantities at reasonable prices. We have ordered tools and potting soil from Florist Products and can vouch for the firm's claim that orders are filled promptly, within 48 hours. We have also compared a lot of prices and can state that better deals are hard to find. The firm offers Felco pruners, for example, at prices close to those of the larger wholesale suppliers. The catalog listings range from plastic pots and seedling flats to redwood planters, fertilizers, insecticides, light stands, sprayers, bird seed, and such greenhouse equipment as heaters and exhaust fans. The firm often advertises under the initials FPI.

Full Circle

P.O. Box 6, Redway, CA 95560

Telephone: 707-923-3988

Catalog price: $2

Horticultural supplies, mostly for indoor growers. The firm sells lights, hydroponic systems, fertilizers, trays, pruners, and both natural and chemical insect controls. Many of the offerings are of special interest to marijuana growers.

Gardener's Supply Co.

See under *Tools*, page 239.

Gro-Tek

Tufts Road, Box 518A, S. Berwick, ME 03908

Telephone: 207-676-2209

Catalog price: $1

A limited but very nice selection of greenhouse and garden supplies, including many innovative solar heat-storage products. Gro-Tek sells plans, hardware, and glazing panels for self-built greenhouses and sun rooms, along with accessories for heating and cooling. The firm sells plastic pots and flats, organic fertilizers and pest controls, books on plant propagation and greenhouse gardening, watering heads, trickle-irrigation kits, and an indoor watering hose. A small collection of hand tools includes the Cape Cod weeder, an L-shaped cutting tool.

Growing Naturally

P.O. Box 54, Pineville, PA 18946

Telephone: 215-598-7025

Catalog price: free

Supplies for the gardener who prefers organic soil improvements and pest controls. Growing Naturally sells a good selection of organic pesticides and insect traps, beneficial insects, natural soil conditioners, and fertilizers, along with a more limited array of general gardening supplies. Among the special features here are an inexpensive cold frame, a composter, an electric heat mat, a cider press, plastic and metal plant markers, and ornamental faucet handles in animal shapes.

Gurney Seed & Nursery Co.

See under *General Flowers and Vegetables*, page 19.

Harris Seeds

See under *General Flowers and Vegetables*, page 20.

Hubbard Folding Box Co.

15980 Rush Creek Road, Osseo, MN 55369

Catalog price: free

A metal-reinforced folding wooden box that could be used for moving plants, storing tools, or gathering fruit. Between uses the box folds flat.

Johnny's Selected Seeds

See under *General Flowers and Vegetables*, page 21.

J. W. Jung Seed Co.

See under *General Flowers and Vegetables*, page 21.

Orol Ledden & Sons

See under *General Flowers and Vegetables*, page 23.

A. M. Leonard, Inc.

See under *Tools*, page 240.

Living Wall Gardening Co.

2044 Chili Avenue, Rochester, NY 14624

Telephone: 716-247-0070

Catalog price: free

Living Wall has taken the concept of the side-pocket barrel strawberry planter into another realm. The firm makes stacking barrel planters in a variety of shapes that can be set up practically anywhere and can be combined into some amazing and wonderful creations. The color catalog shows flower- and vegetable-covered towers, walls, and arches that remind us of the Tournament of Roses parade. They've even got pictures of tomato plants floating on platforms in swimming pools. No soil or fertilizer is needed. According to the catalog, each unit "comes filled with a special inorganic growing medium unlike any other . . . which should last perhaps forever . . . and can be manufactured almost any place on the face of the earth." Small single units can be planted on rooftops or used as hanging planters where space is tight.

McDermott Garden Products
Box 129, 1300 S. Grand Avenue, Charles City, IA 50616
Telephone: 515-228-5086

Catalog price: free

Enameled steel planters for raised-bed gardening and a rotating drum composter. The planters come in either 14- or 28-inch heights and are intended more for production gardening than for patio display. The composter is covered with wire mesh, both for improved air circulation and to allow gardeners to check up on the decomposition process.

McFayden Seeds
Supplies for Canadian customers. See under *General Flowers and Vegetables*, page 24.

Marion Designs
594 Front Street, N. Marion, MA 02738
Telephone: 617-748-2540

Catalog price: $1, deductible from first order

Redwood potting benches, plant stands, and shelved display tables, described and pictured in a color flier.

Earl May Seed & Nursery Co.
See under *General Flowers and Vegetables*, page 24.

The Meyer Seed Company
See under *General Flowers and Vegetables*, page 25.

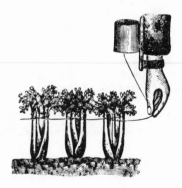

Mill Hill Gardens
Rt. 1, Northfield, VT 05663

Catalog price: free

Sells Wallo' Water plant protectors—water-filled clear plastic cylinders that act as miniature solar greenhouses for individual plants in the garden. Set them up over seedlings in the early spring and the plants are heated by day and protected from frost by night. When the danger of frost is past, the protectors can be emptied and flattened for storage.

Modern Homesteader
1825 Big Horn Avenue, Cody, WY 82414
Telephone: 800-443-4934 or 307-587-5946

Catalog price: free

Handy products for the garden, yard, and ranch. Picnic tables, outdoor benches, two-wheeled garden carts, and a gazebo are sold as affordable build-them-yourself kits. Those who put up garden produce will find a steam canner, two juice-extracting pots, and a vacuum sealer that seals plastic bags for the freezer. Two western-style outdoor bells can be set up to call wayward weeders in for dinner. A horseshoe boot scraper will knock the dirt from their shoes before they come in the house.

The Natural Gardening Company
27 Rutherford Avenue, San Anselmo, CA 94960
Telephone: 415-456-5060

Catalog price: $1

A slim but choice catalog of tools, seeds, pest controls, fertilizers, books, and birdhouses for the gardener who prefers the natural approach. Just two types of fertilizer are offered: bat guano and a soluble seaweed powder. The pest-control page displays three of Safer's organic products, the tools are from Spear & Jackson of England, and the seed offerings are European vegetable, herb, and salad-green collections from Le Marché Seeds International. To help growers start their seeds on the right foot, the firm offers a soil-block maker. Bird lovers can choose from a glass hummingbird feeder, West German birdhouses made of cement and sawdust, and a hanging ceramic birdbath.

Northern Hydraulics, Inc.
P.O. Box 1219, Burnsville, MN 55337
Telephone: 612-894-9510 or 800-533-5545

Catalog price: free

Hydraulic log splitters, portable tent-style greenhouses, sprinkler timers, sprayers, garden carts, and outdoor clothing in a big catalog that's also filled with automotive equipment, go-carts, generators, and other decidedly ungarden-like gadgets.

Ontario Seed Company, Ltd.
See under *General Flowers and Vegetables*, page 26.

Park Seed Co.
See under *General Flowers and Vegetables*, page 26.

Patio Pacific, Inc.
24433 Hawthorne Boulevard, Torrance, CA 90505-6506
Telephone: 213-378-9286 or 800-334-3667

Catalog price: free

Pet doors in a score of styles, from a dozen different manufacturers. Patio Pacific is so sure that they have the best prices around that they'll beat by ten percent any deal you can find locally. The easiest models to install fit in the gap of a slightly opened sliding glass door. More permanent models must be built into a wooden door.

Peaceful Valley Farm Supply

11173 Peaceful Valley Road, Nevada City, CA 95959
Telephone: 916-265-FARM

Catalog price: $2, deductible from first order

A bulky catalog of natural pest controls, fertilizers and soil amendments, and such supplies as sprayers, cold frames, pruning tools (dozens of them), composters, Japanese gardening tools, and power shredders. The firm puts most of its energy into the pest controls, offering scores of beneficial organisms, biological and botanical insecticides, mineral-based fungicides, and plenty of clever traps and repellents. Peaceful Valley also sells seeds and nursery stock (see entry under *Trees and Shrubs*, page 161).

Plant Collectibles

103 Kenview Avenue, Buffalo, NY 14217

Catalog price: $1

A somewhat limited collection of growing supplies that includes seed-starting flats and cell packs, Jiffy-Pots, plastic pots, plant food from Stern's and Peters, Safer's insecticidal soap, chemical pesticides, and leaf polish.

Porter & Son

See under *General Flowers and Vegetables*, page 27.

Pot Lock

1032 21st Street, Rock Island, IL 61201

Catalog price: long self-addressed stamped envelope

A locking device for securing potted plants to their shelves. The lock prevents pots from blowing over in the wind and discourages theft of valuable plants and containers. In 1987 six locks sold for $9, postpaid.

Science Associates

P.O. Box 230, Princeton, NJ 08542
Telephone: 609-924-4470 or 247-7234

Catalog price: $1

Accurate instruments for measuring weather conditions. The catalog pictures dozens of thermometers, including maximum-minimum meters for monitoring air and soil temperatures, remote temperature indicators, and thermographs that chart conditions over a long period. Hygrometers, psychrometers, barometers, wind indicators, and precipitation gauges complete the weather station.

R. H. Shumway's

See under *General Flowers and Vegetables*, page 29.

Southeastern Wood Products Co.

P.O. Box 113, Griffin, GA 30224
Telephone: 404-227-7486 or 800-722-7486

Catalog price: free

Roll-on wood fencing made of six-foot wooden slats woven together with galvanized wire—a quick and inexpensive way to buy privacy for your yard.

T & T Seeds Ltd.

Supplies for Canadian customers. See under *General Flowers and Vegetables*, page 30.

Tillinghast Seed Co.

See under *General Flowers and Vegetables*, page 31.

Trade-Wind Instruments

Ron Tyler, 1076 Loraine Street, Enumclaw, WA 98022
Telephone: 206-825-2294

Catalog price: free

Marine and meteorological instruments for the gardener who wants to keep careful track of garden conditions. Several anemometers are offered (for measuring wind speed), along with a rain gauge. A tide clock will probably be of little use to inland tillers.

Tregunno Seeds Limited

See under *General Flowers and Vegetables*, page 31.

Vermont Bean Seed Co.

See under *General Flowers and Vegetables*, page 33.

The Vermont Country Store, Mail Order Office

P.O. Box 3000, Manchester Ctr., VT 05255-3000
Telephone: 802-362-4647

Catalog price: free

This chunky little catalog is crammed with useful items that have stood the test of time: rubber doorstops, cotton night-shirts (and nightcaps), enameled steel breadboxes, and reconditioned Electrolux vacuum cleaners. A few of the offerings may be useful to gardeners; there's Bag Balm salve for dry, chapped hands (and for cows' udders), a maximum-minimum thermometer, and an old-fashioned apple corer.

Beekeeping Supplies

Brushy Mountain Bee Farm, Inc.
Rt. 1, Box 135, Moravian Falls, NC 28654
Telephone: 919-921-3640 or 800-BEESWAX

Catalog price: free

A complete line of beekeeping supplies at reasonable prices (about 25 percent lower than those of the leading suppliers). In addition to hive components, gloves, helmets, extractors, and the usual line of supplies, the firm sells books, slide shows, and videotapes. Even gardeners who do their best to steer clear of bees may be interested in some sideline items: the classic Carolina porch rocker (the kind John F. Kennedy used), an oak porch swing, and a selection of wooden birdhouses and feeders.

The A. I. Root Co.
P.O. Box 706, Medina, OH 44258-0706
Telephone: 216-725-6677 or 6678

Catalog price: free

The main name in beekeeping supplies, A. I. Root sells just about everything an apiarist could want—hives, smokers, coveralls, veils, tools, and books—in a catalog liberally sprinkled with advice.

Sunnybrook Farms Nursery
Old-fashioned coiled-straw beehive. See under *Herbs*, page 103.

Sunstream Bee Supply
P.O. Box 225, Eighty Four, PA 15330
Telephone: 412-222-3330

Catalog price: 50¢, deductible from first order

A full line of beekeeping supplies, from jars and labels to hives and extractors. Sunstream sells complete wooden hives as well as all components at comparatively low prices. Coveralls, veils, books, sting treatments, and plastic honey bears are also offered.

Birdhouses and Feeders

Atlas Gift Manufacturing
2731 E. Latimer Street, Tulsa, OK 74110
Telephone: 918-836-8018

Catalog price: free

Hand-painted polymer birdhouses made to look like miniature buildings. Selections include a log cabin, a general store, a barn, a gingerbread house, and a thatched cottage. Atlas even offers a feeder that looks like a tiny carousel, with colorful birds circling around it.

Autumn Innovations
P.O. Box 18426, Greensboro, NC 27419
Telephone: 919-852-0753

Catalog price: free

English birdhouses, feeders, and dovecotes with real thatched roofs and rustic log-and-branch construction. Autumn Innovations also imports a garden trug (made of birch ply) and a spherical sundial.

Bird 'n Hand
40 Pearl Street, Framingham, MA 01701
Telephone: 617-879-1552

Catalog price: free

A nice selection of birdseed and feeders, along with such auxiliary devices as a birdbath water heater and a birch and pewter birdcall. The firm sometimes advertises under the name Farmers' Exchange.

Brushy Mountain Bee Farm, Inc.
See under *Beekeeping Supplies*, above.

Country Ecology

P.O. Box 59, Center Sandwich, NH 03227
Telephone: 603-284-7142

Catalog price: free

Three styles of birdhouses made of weathered pine and bark slabs. One is designed for bluebirds, another for tree swallows, and a third for such small birds as chickadees, nuthatches, titmice, and western house finches. All houses are priced at $21 postpaid in 1988.

Duncraft

Penacook, NH 03303
Telephone: 603-224-0200

Catalog price: free

Dozens of birdhouses and feeders, offered in a color catalog along with seed and suet. The feeders come in a range of styles for attracting birds from hummingbirds to finches to woodpeckers. Most of the feeders are made of clear plastic. The birdhouses include a pine chickadee dwelling shaped like an acorn, a redwood house for wrens, and some deluxe resorts for purple martins.

Europa Enterprises

99 Frenchtown Road, E. Greenwich, RI 02818
Telephone: 401-884-4442

Catalog price: free

The popular line of bird feeders from K-Feeders. These are clear plastic tube-style feeders, with holes and perches spaced down the sides. We own the three-tube model with a squirrel-baffle top, which has kept the birds happy and has managed to foil the squirrels.

Hyde Bird Feeder Company

56 Felton Street, P.O. Box 168, Waltham, MA 02254
Telephone: 617-893-6780

Catalog price: free

Bird feeders in many styles, from clear plastic silo types to a wooden design made to look like a New England covered bridge. Several hummingbird feeders are offered, along with one birdhouse, made from a cored bark-on log. Hyde also offers some books on bird-watching and a selection of seed.

Mr. Birdhouse

2307 Highway 2 W., Grand Rapids, MN 55744
Telephone: 218-326-3044

Catalog price: free

Easy-care aluminum martin houses, with lots of features the birds are said to prefer. According to the brochure, the vented aluminum construction is cooler than many wooden houses, and the non-porous surface discourages parasites. Plenty of tiny railings give the birds places to perch.

The Natural Gardening Company

See under *General Gardening Supplies*, page 187.

Plow & Hearth

See under *Tools*, page 241.

Harley Warrick

42440 Green Street, Belmont, OH 43718
Telephone: 614-484-4826

No catalog

To residents of Ohio, West Virginia, and western Pennsylvania, the Mail Pouch tobacco barn sign is a familiar sight. Its exhortation, "Chew Mail Pouch tobacco. Treat yourself to the best." was once brushed by dozens of painters from coast to coast. Today, the tobacco company has trimmed its painting staff to one man, Harley Warrick, who continues the tradition of lettering the huge signs on barns just as they've been painted for decades. In his spare time (on rainy days and over the winter) Mr. Warrick builds and letters miniature Mail Pouch barns in the form of birdhouses, feeders, and mailboxes. We bought a birdhouse a few years back and can report that it is perfect in every detail, and a charming piece of Americana. Send orders only, as Mr. Warrick has no brochure. Each little barn sells for $27, postpaid.

Wild Bird Supplies

4815 Oak Street, Crystal Lake, IL 60012
Telephone: 815-455-4020

Catalog price: free

An abundance of bird feeders, seed, birdhouses, and books in a compact black-and-white catalog. Choose from wood feeders, plastic tube feeders, wire barrier feeders (that keep squirrels and larger birds from the food), suet feeders, and six different hummingbird feeders. A heated birdbath provides water all winter. A half dozen aluminum martin houses are offered, from 12-room economy units to a 24-room castle. Other houses and nesting shelters are specially designed for robins, bluebirds, wrens, flickers, and chickadees.

Bonsai Supplies

The Bonsai Associates, Inc.
Mill Centre, Suite 106, 3000 Chestnut Avenue
Baltimore, MD 21211
Telephone: 301-235-5336

Catalog price: $2, deductible from first order

An excellent selection of tools, supplies, and books for bonsai practitioners. More than a dozen Japanese pruners and shears, specially designed for trimming branches, knobs, and roots, are offered, among them the classic loop-handled shears now popular even with gardeners who have never snipped a bonsai branch. The firm also sells a small collection of plants for bonsai culture.

Bonsai by Sylvia
P.O. Box 3326, Deland, FL 32720
Telephone: 904-734-2618

Catalog price: $1

Dozens of bonsai pots, each pictured and described, and organized by the Japanese cities of origin. Sylvia balances her list with a good selection of bonsai tools, soil components and fertilizers, and a few books.

Bonsai Creations
2700 N. 29th Avenue, #204, Hollywood, FL 33020-1513
Telephone: 305-962-6960

Catalog price: $2.50

A big catalog of bonsai supplies and plants that stretches its borders to include many Japanese tools for coarser garden applications—pruning saws, flower scissors, and heavy-duty pruning shears. A good variety of specialty bonsai tools is offered, along with an array of stands, pots, and miniature ceramics. The book list includes titles on bonsai, Japanese gardens, and ikebana. In the nursery department shoppers can choose from several dozen plants offered in pre-bonsai condition or as cultured bonsai specimens.

The Bonsai Farm
See under *Bonsai*, page 56.

Heritage Arts
16651 S.E. 235th Street, Kent, WA 98042
Telephone: 206-631-1318

Catalog price: $2

An extensive collection of ceramic containers, cutting tools, and other bonsai supplies. Almost 50 different shears and specialized cutters are offered, from the elegant loop-handled Japanese scissors to wire- and root-cutting tools that look like instruments of torture. The most important tools are

also offered in sets. The container selection takes up several pages, each design pictured in a photograph. The inventory is about evenly split between unglazed vessels and those with a solid-color finish.

International Bonsai Containers
412 Pinnacle Road, Rochester, NY 14623
Telephone: 716-334-2595

Catalog price: free

A color catalog of Japanese ceramic bonsai containers and trays. Plastic water basins, cutting tools, training wire, and books are also offered.

John Palmer Bonsai Company
P.O. Box 29, Sudbury, MA 01776
Telephone: 617-443-5084

Catalog price: free

Bonsai books, tools, containers, supplies, and accessories in an exceptionally helpful catalog. All offerings are illustrated in black-and-white photographs and are well described in the text. We were particularly impressed by the book selection, which in 1987 ranged from Bloomer's *Timeless Trees: The U.S. National Bonsai Collection* to Gelderen and Smith's *Conifers*, and to books on Japanese gardens, parks, and wood-block prints.

Shanti Bithi Nursery
See under *Bonsai*, page 57.

Spring Hollow
10109 Deal Road, Williamsburg, MI 49690
Telephone: 616-267-5161 or 946-2578

Catalog price: $1

Plastic containers for training bonsai trees. The shapes mimic those of classic Japanese ceramic containers, but at a fraction of the price.

Books

agAccess
P.O. Box 2008, Davis, CA 95617
Telephone: 916-756-7177

Catalog price: free

A broad array of new books on such subjects as pest control, nursery and greenhouse management, floriculture, fruit and vegetable production, beekeeping, forestry, and weed science. The catalog contains just a sampling of the titles sold; the firm represents more than 600 publishers worldwide. From gift books like the *Royal Horticultural Society Diary* to texts on biotechnology and farm machinery, agAccess seems to have something to offer most gardeners. Professionals will have the longest shelves to scan.

Agriculture Canada, Communications Branch
Ottawa, ON, Canada K1A 0C7
Telephone: 613-995-5222 or 8963

Catalog price: free

Agriculture Canada publishes about a dozen instructional booklets for home gardeners and more than 200 titles on commercial agriculture, which are distributed free of charge (with a cap of five booklets per request). Write or call for the catalog of publications. Some more extensive bound volumes are sold for a nominal charge. Canadian gardeners should also be aware that a number of helpful publications dealing with the specific requirements of growers in different regions can be had from the provincial governments.

The American Botanist
P.O. Box 143, Brookfield, IL 60513
Telephone: 312-485-7805

Catalog price: $1 for a year of price lists

Used and out-of-print books on gardening and agriculture, with special strengths in garden history, herbals, horticulture, and landscape design. New lists are mailed every few months, each holding several hundred titles. Some recent titles sell for just a few dollars; a few early 19th-century botanicals carry tags of $1,000 and more.

Anchor & Dolphin Books
P.O. Box 823, 30 Franklin Street, Newport, RI 02840
Telephone: 401-846-6890

Catalog price: $1

A slim, stylish booklet that presents more than 100 nicely described antiquarian volumes on landscape architecture and garden history. Many books date from the late 19th and early 20th centuries, but more contemporary treatises do slip in. Charles Eliot's Boston park system proposal (circa 1893) was listed in a recent catalog opposite Harold Bruce's *The Gardens of Winterthur in All Seasons*, published in 1968. The list never includes all titles in stock, and customers are urged to visit the shop or send a want list.

Carol Barnett-Books
3128 S.E. Alder Court, Portland, OR 97214
Telephone: 503-239-5745

Catalog price: free

Used books on all things green and botanical—trees, flowers, shrubs, ferns, and more. Descriptions are economical. "Planting trees in masses" is the terse summary of a typical book. Most books listed are 20th-century releases; a few dip back to the 1800's.

Bell's Book Store
536 Emerson Street, Palo Alto, CA 94301
Telephone: 415-323-7822

Catalog price: $2.04 for rose book list

This 40-page catalog brims over with detailed and informed synopses of almost 150 new and antiquarian books on old garden roses. Each listing is taken in hand, weighed for its gist and style, and returned to the shelf. The catalog thus offers the best sort of personal commentary and guidance; its enthusiasm for the books is infectious. "This woman grew roses for many years," says the text about a certain Mrs. Foote who produced a rose book several decades ago. "In the process she used her eyes and developed firm opinions on how to obtain the best results." The voice behind the catalog takes pains to recommend some books for beginners and others for those farther along the garden path.

Beth L. Bibby - Books
1225 Sardine Creek Road, Gold Hill, OR 97525
Telephone: 503-855-1621

Catalog price: $2, refunded on orders of $20 or more

A rich selection of nearly 500 new and used books ("in good or better condition, or as indicated") devoted to gardening, horticulture, and natural history. Listings are brief—generally a single phrase encapsulating the book's contents—and spread across ten pages tightly printed on both sides. Prices tend to be modest; most books listed date from the past 50 years.

Bountiful Gardens
New books on organic gardening. See under *General Flowers and Vegetables*, page 14.

Warren F. Broderick - Books
695 4th Avenue, P.O. Box 124, Lansingburgh, NY 12182
Telephone: 518-235-4041

Catalog price: six first-class stamps

A specialty list devoted to vintage works on garden design and history, including garden art, architecture, and plant exploration as well as garden classics. More than 200 titles appear in three cumulative catalogs (from each of the past three years); the relative values of the works are judged with a note of authority. These classic volumes do not come cheap—prices per book run to $100 and more.

Brooklyn Botanic Garden
1000 Washington Avenue, Brooklyn, NY 11225-1099
Telephone: 718-622-4433

Catalog price: free

Past issues of the Brooklyn Botanic Garden's journal, *Plants & Gardens*, make an excellent library of compact reference books. Send a postcard for a complete list. (See entry under *Magazines*, page 273, for a more complete description.) The organization also offers a video/booklet set for children, *Get Ready, Get Set, Grow: A Kid's Guide to Good Gardening*. The set includes a 15-minute videocassette and two booklets, one for the child gardener and one for the supervising adult.

Builders Booksource
1801 Fourth Street, Berkeley, CA 94710
Telephone: 415-845-6874

Catalog price: $1, deductible from first order

New books on carpentry and construction, including several titles on decks and patios.

Capability's Books
Box 114, Highway 46, Deer Park, WI 54007
Telephone: 715-269-5346

Catalog price: free

Over 700 current garden books sorted into more than 70 categories for easy reference. Sections on individual plant types (African violets, dahlias, fuchsias, geraniums, and Japanese maples, etc.) as well as on such topics as plant hunters, greenhouses, pruning and propagation, and watering systems pack this chunky, encyclopedic catalog. Some headings contain one or two well-described books; others have dozens to offer. Several garden videos are also available, and this part of the list is expanding.

Russell L. Ciochon
P.O. Box 1966, Iowa City, IA 52244-1966
Telephone: 602-577-0232

Catalog price: free

A dozen rare botanical books sandwiched in among several hundred natural history volumes on ornithology, herpetology, mammalogy, ichthyology, and entomology. *The Land of the Blue Poppy: Travels of a Naturalist in Eastern Tibet*, first published in 1913 and here described as a "plant-hunting classic," is typical of the fare.

The Garden Book Club
250 W. 57th Street, New York, NY 10107
Telephone: 212-582-6912

Catalog price: free

A book club that operates along the lines of the Book-of-the-Month Club. Each month a bulletin detailing main and alternate selections will be mailed to you; your only obligation is to purchase four books during the first year of membership. Coffee-table volumes on garden history and design, reference books, specialty works, and how-to books (how to grow herbs, for instance, or cultivate wildflowers) shade the editorial mix. In 1987 the club offered *Hortus Third* at an incredibly low price as an inducement to membership. Write for current information.

V. L. T. Gardner
30026 Avenida Celestial, Rancho Palos Verde, CA 90274
Telephone: 213-541-1372

No catalog or list

New and used books on gardening. Gardner puts out no lists, but will search for your wants.

The Growing Company
P.O. Box 1276, Los Angeles, CA 90069
Telephone: 213-659-GROW

Catalog price: free

"The Garden Organizer," a green-and-white three-ring binder designed to sort out the many details of the active gardener's life, may help those who find themselves buried by their own good intentions at times. The binder has grids for mapping garden plots and for keeping track of what's been planted. It also provides space for charting scheduled chores and envelopes for filing odds and ends (clippings, warranties, seed packets, etc.) that gardeners accrue.

Harper Horticultural Slide Library
219 Robanna Shores, Seaford, VA 23696
Telephone: 804-898-6453

Catalog price: $1.50

Horticultural slides for sale or rent. Pamela Harper is the co-author of the book *Perennials: How to Select, Grow & Enjoy*, and the 250 photographs from that book make up one of the offered sets. Smaller sets are available in such categories as "herbs," "groundcover plants," "plants for flower arrangers," and "wildflowers of the eastern U.S.A." The slide sets can be rented by the week or purchased outright. Individual slides of thousands of plants are also offered for sale.

Hatchards
187 Piccadilly, London, England W1V 9DA
Telephone: 44-1-439-9921

Hatchards operates a chain of bookstores in Great Britain; the firm's books are available to North Americans through its mail-order catalog. A lean patch of garden books—slightly more than a dozen—pops up at the heart of this stylish booklet; all of them are recent releases from British publishers. The focus is on traditional English gardens, with several volumes on noted estate and botanical gardens. Wildflowers and old roses are also likely to earn spots on the list, along with titles by noted British garden scribes.

Honingklip Nurseries & Book Sales
13 Lady Anne Avenue, Newlands 7700 South Africa
Telephone: 27-21-644410

Catalog price: free

Books on South African plants, mostly new, but a few old and out-of-print titles. Offerings range from inexpensive pamphlets on growing proteas to a limited-edition leather-bound volume on mimetes. Prices on the export list are quoted in U.S. dollars.

Hurley Books
Rt. 1, Box 160, Westmoreland, NH 03467
Telephone: 603-399-4342

Catalog price: $1

Several hundred used and antiquarian books on agriculture, horticulture, animal husbandry, and rural living. Titles range from 20th-century books on fruit growing and sheep farming to 19th-century volumes on window gardening and fertilizers (Samuel L. Dana, *A Muck Manual for Farmers*, 1851). A few rare botanical titles from the 18th and early 19th century command higher prices.

International Specialized Book Services, Inc.
5602 N.E. Hassalo Street, Suite T, Portland, OR 97213
Telephone: 503-287-3093 or 800-547-7734

Catalog price: free

An eclectic mix of new books on gardening imported from around the world, with a special emphasis on publishers from Australia and New Zealand. Five or six titles per page provide ample space for detailed descriptions (and, in many cases, excerpts from reviews). The selection ranges far and wide, from *How to Propagate Plants* to *Fuchsias in Australia*. A nice catalog for browsers.

Ivelet Books Limited
18 Fairlawn Drive, Redhill, Surrey, England RH1 6JP
Telephone: 44-737-64520

Catalog price: free

This firm specializes in out-of-print, rare, and antiquarian books on gardening and mails three or four catalogs a year. Landscape gardening is a central preoccupation here; garden design and history take a minor role. Hundreds of volumes—a few dating back to the 1600's, but most published in this century—are nicely described. Payment by credit card simplifies the problem of currency exchange.

Ian Jackson
P.O. Box 9075, Berkeley, CA 94709
Telephone: 415-548-1431

Catalog price: free

A whimsical, far-ranging catalog of roughly 150 used and antiquarian books on botany and gardening. (The cover of the spring 1987 catalog featured a wonderful turn-of-the-century snapshot captioned "Nora de Generes, age 11, and her six-pound beet.") The description of a book titled *The Two Oldest Trees* (1914) gives play to Mr. Jackson's distinctive style of commentary: "A choice specimen of sequoia-inspired vanity publishing, and perhaps the most inane of the half-dozen such books produced by California enthusiasts in the first quarter of this century, when the possession of a Model T Ford, a Kodak camera, a picnic basket, obedient female relatives to give scale to the trees, and—for research purposes—access to a Funk and Wagnalls encyclopedia, was all that an aspiring man of the trees required." Many books of greater botanical merit are also offered.

Johnny's Selected Seeds
New books on vegetable gardening. See under *General Flowers and Vegetables*, page 21.

K & L Cactus Nursery
New books on cacti and succulents. See under *Cacti and Succulents*, page 68.

Myron Kimnach
1600 Orlando Road, San Marino, CA 91108

Three specialty catalogs—on ferns, succulents, and bromeliads—offer both new and used books. The first scans more than 100 volumes concerned with ferns; the second a comparable number of works on cacti and other succulents; the third offers roughly 40 books on bromeliads. In addition to books, back issues of society and scientific journals are offered, many of them hard-to-find publications from foreign sources. Mr. Kimnach graciously provides addresses so that customers can subscribe and receive future issues.

Kohan-Matlick Productions
1016 N. Sycamore Avenue, Hollywood, CA 90038
Telephone: 818-843-3648 or 213-876-4055

Catalog price: free

Sells a videocassette on the care of cymbidium orchids.

Norman Levine's Editions
Boiceville, NY 12412
Telephone: 914-657-7000

Catalog price: $1

This immense catalog contains a small green plot—fewer than 100 used books devoted to gardening and horticulture, out of many thousands listed. Title, author, and year is about all the assistance you get; those seeking specific works may get lucky, but others will feel lost. Most books are of recent vintage.

Kenneth M. Lewis
32255 N. Highway 99W, Newberg, OH 97132
Telephone: 503-538-2051

Catalog price: free

"Old, rare, common, and new" books on lilies, mushrooms, cacti, and botany. Mr. Lewis will send a list of what he has, or he'll search for specific books if you send your wants.

Lion's Head Books

Academy Street, Salisbury, CT 06068
Telephone: 203-435-9328

No catalog or list

New and used books on gardening. Send your want list.

Daniel Lloyd

Heather Lea, 4 Hillcrest Avenue, Chertsey, Surrey
England KT16 9RD
Telephone: 44-1-940-2512

Catalog price: $1, deductible from first order

A nice, fat catalog bursting with gardening and botanical books—old and new. Listings here are well organized under a slew of sub-heads; descriptive material is scarce. Roughly 2,000 titles in all await your perusal. "Enquiries" are welcomed. Travelers to London who make the trip to Kew Gardens can visit the Lloyd shop at 9 Morlake Terrace in Kew.

McQuerry Orchid Books

5700 W. Salerno Road, Jacksonville, FL 32244
Telephone: 904-387-5044

Catalog price: free

This catalog offers several hundred old and new orchid books, with a stress on classic and antique color-plate volumes. Clearly laid out, the 16-page booklet contains titles both for hobbyists and advanced growers. Books on individual genera, as well as those devoted to particular geographic regions ("Africa & Madagascar," for example) are given distinct headings. Descriptions tend to be cursory. The firm publishes and distributes the *You Can Grow Orchids* series by Mary Noble—and sells the books by mail. McQuerry also sells antique orchid prints; inquire if interested.

Matrix

P.O. Box 1176, Southport, CT 06490

Catalog price: free

A series of instructional videocassettes on gardening.

Timothy Mawson

Main Street, New Preston, CT 06777
Telephone: 203-868-0732

Catalog price: $1

Three hundred new, used, and antiquarian garden and flower books. The emphasis is on garden history and on historic titles; costly early 19th-century volumes are sold as well as more affordable facsimiles and modern histories. James Maddock's 1810 handbook on flower culture, *The Florist's Directory*, is sold alongside a new edition of Georgina Masson's *Italian Gardens*. A few new and old books on particular plant types—such as rhododendrons, primroses, and roses—offer practical fare as well as history.

Necessary Trading Co.

New books on organic gardening. See under *Pest Controls*, page 231.

Orchid Sundries

Books on orchids. See under *Indoor Gardening Supplies*, page 224.

The Original Home Gardener's Video Catalog

P.O. Box 410777, San Francisco, CA 94141
Telephone: 415-558-8688 or 800-331-6304

Catalog price: free

A large selection of instructive videos for the home gardener. Nearly 40 tapes, from 15 to 60 minutes in length, cover general gardening, houseplants, fruits and vegetables, flowers (including flower arranging), and landscaping themes. Experts narrate the videos, and British gardener John Bryan appears in this capacity in many of them. Available in either VHS or Beta formats.

Pomona Book Exchange

Highway 52, Rockton, ON, Canada L0R 1X0
Telephone: 519-621-8897

Catalog price: $1

Nearly 1,000 used and antiquarian books on gardening, botany, natural history, and biology proceed alphabetically by author in this densely packed catalog. Commentary, when it does appear, is terse. Arizona cacti fight for air on the same page with *Flora of the Assyrian Monuments* (1894). Offerings range in age and cost from rare 18th- and early 19th-century volumes priced at $500 and up to relatively recent books offered for less than $10. The firm is happy to deal with U.S. customers.

Putterin Press

Dept. 3X5, P.O. Box 72, Burlingame, CA 94011
Telephone: 415-343-8426

Catalog price: free

Sells a five-year garden diary. Each calendar page is broken into five horizontal bands, so that notes can be compared with the events of previous years.

Rainbow Gardens Nursery & Bookshop

New books on cacti and succulents. See under *Epiphyllums and Hoyas*, page 83.

Richters

New books on herbs. See under *Herbs*, page 102.

Savoy Books

P.O. Box 271, Bailey Road, Lanesborough, MA 01237

Catalog price: free

Antiquarian books on horticulture and agriculture, many of them rare and quite expensive. The firm concentrates on books published from the 16th through the 19th centuries.

Second Life Books

P.O. Box 242, Quarry Road, Lanesborough, MA 01237
Telephone: 413-447-8010

Catalog price: $1

An antiquarian bookseller who deals both in horticultural titles and works on history, politics, travel, and revolution.

Each catalog lists almost 200 horticultural works, many of them rarities, such as an 1833 letter from James Fenimore Cooper to a friend in France asking for help in setting up a New York winery with French grapes. Offerings are fully described, and their contents (and conditions) appraised in an authoritative voice. Many volumes date from the mid and late 19th century; some are even older.

Robert Shuhi - Books

Box 268, Morris, CT 06763
Telephone: 203-567-5231 or 9384

Catalog price: $1

A confusing list of 1,200 plus used books of which roughly 50 are on gardening. Twelve extra-long stapled pages covered on both sides and—replete with hand-written notations—advance from "Archeology" to "Travel." Gardening books here include both obscure and classic volumes; most are 20th-century releases.

Timber Press

9999 S.W. Wilshire, Portland, OR 97225
Telephone: 503-292-0745

Catalog price: free

An exceptional assortment of new books on a broad range of botanical subjects, all published or imported by Timber Press. From conifers and azaleas to proteas and water lilies, Timber Press has growing manuals and definitive reference works.

Twin Oaks Books

4343 Causeway Drive, Lowell, MI 49331
Telephone: 616-897-7479

Catalog price: free

A hefty catalog of reference works—either new or difficult to obtain—for the serious orchidist. Hundreds of books are described in staggering detail; the majority are new releases. Titles are assessed in a cozy gardener-to-gardener style. "Calm yourself . . . this is a new book on Paphs . . . but it is not the book," the catalog remarks offhandedly at one point, and that tone is typical.

United States Government Printing Office

Superintendent of Documents, Washington, DC 20402
Telephone: 202-783-3238

Catalog price: free (specify SB-301)

Some of the best deals on basic gardening information are to be had from the U.S. government. List SB-301 includes a score of books and pamphlets with such titles as Growing Vegetables in the Home Garden, Selecting and Growing House Plants, Mulches for Your Garden, Building Hobby Greenhouses, and Control of Insects on Deciduous Fruits and Tree Nuts in the Home Orchard, Without Insecticides.

Separate handbooks are offered on the care of camellias, boxwoods, azaleas and rhododendrons, bunch grapes, and summer flowering bulbs. Another larger list of publications on farms and farming, SB-161, can also be had for the asking. Gardeners who want an official copy of the USDA hardiness-zone map should send 25¢ and ask for Miscellaneous Publication #814.

Gary Wayner, Bookseller

Rt. 3, Box 18, Ft. Payne, AL 35967-9501
Telephone: 205-845-5866

Catalog price: $1

A fine-print catalog of more than 400 new and used natural-history volumes, with some mosses and flowers tucked in among the gnats and reptiles. Listings include title, author, year, and price.

Wilkerson Books

31 Old Winter Street, Lincoln, MA 01773
Telephone: 617-259-1110

Catalog price: $1, deductible from first order

Several hundred gardening and landscape volumes clearly presented in a small booklet. Selections range from early 20th-century guides like Making a Rock Garden (1912) to more recent works on the order of Eleanor Perenyi's Green Thoughts (1981).

Elisabeth Woodburn

Booknoll Farm, Box 398, Hopewell, NJ 08525
Telephone: 609-466-0522

Catalog price: request catalog order form

Elisabeth Woodburn rules the roost when it comes to old and rare books on horticulture (she even has an excellent collection of new titles, including hard-to-find imports). In her converted barn/library in Hopewell she shelves some 13,000 volumes. She makes the inventory available to mail-order customers through a small library of specialized descriptive price lists. Send for the current list of lists, or use the following price guide to request the ones you want directly. The general 19th-century book list costs $2. The wildflower, vegetable, and fruit lists cost $2 each; the catalogs of orchid, rock-garden, and fragrance books cost $1 each.

Gary W. Woolson, Bookseller

Rt. 1, Box 1576, Hampden, ME 04444
Telephone: 207-234-4931

Catalog price: free

An eccentric medley of more than 200 used books in the general field of horticulture. Some volumes listed are a decade old, some were published in the 19th century. Descriptions are thorough.

Cider and Wine Presses

Growing Naturally
See under *General Gardening Supplies*, page 186.

Happy Valley Ranch
Rt. 2, Box 83, Paola, KS 66071
Telephone: 913-849-3103

Catalog price: $1

Cider and wine presses in a range of sizes and styles. The featured model is a double-tub combination presser and grinder that turns whole apples to pulp on one side while on the other side the pulp is pressed into cider.

Jaffrey Manufacturing, Inc.
P.O. Box 226, Mt. Vernon, NH 03057
Telephone: 603-532-8448

Catalog price: free

Jaffrey makes a single cider and wine press with a combined grinder and presser top. The frame and tub are made of rock maple; the tub is big enough to hold a bushel of pulp. The firm also sells a wooden wheelbarrow, maple syrup, and wooden buckets. The buckets are made with pine staves and oak bands and look like they'd make attractive planters or useful picking containers. The wheelbarrow has old-fashioned styling but modern hardware: the rubber tire spins on ball bearings and greased fittings.

Computer Aids

CompuGarden, Inc.
1006 Highland Drive, Silver Spring, MD 20910

Catalog price: free

Garden-planning software for use on an IBM PC or compatible home computer. The software prepares a vegetable garden plan based on the information the user provides and includes maps, schedules, cultural notes for each of the plants chosen, and fertilizer guides. Space on the program allows the gardener to keep a journal; a comprehensive vegetable encyclopedia, prepared by the New York Botanical Garden, offers plenty of backup information. Gardeners without access to computers can fill out a questionnaire and let CompuGarden run the program. The firm will send a 100-page personalized garden plan in a three-ring notebook.

Computer/Management Services
1426 Medinah Court, Arnold, MD 21012

Catalog price: free

Computer software for orchid hobbyists that allows them to keep organized records of their plants. The program, called Orchidata, lets growers keep notes on all aspects of their plants and organizes the listings by a quality rating or by parentage. The program can be used on an IBM PC or compatible home computers with at least 156K of memory. Another program, called Collectr, can be used to keep track of collections of any type of plant (or stamps, coins, dolls, etc.), allowing space for collectors to enter information on date purchased, price paid, source, and a description of each item.

Ortho Information Services
575 Market Street, Rm. 3188, San Francisco, CA 94105

Catalog price: free

A computerized gardening aid that brings software into the backyard. The program, which includes a full-color 192-page book for reference, guides you through the stages of planning a garden by absorbing criteria of flower color and shade, and then sifting 700 plant varieties for those suited to your area. Complete instructions are included in the accompanying book. The single-disk program may be used on an IBM, Commodore, or Apple (IIe, IIc, or Mac) computer.

Fertilizers

Actagro
4111 N. Motel Drive, Suite 101, Fresno, CA 93722
Telephone: 209-275-3600

Catalog price: free

Sells Hortopaper roll-on mulch, a biodegradable material made from peat moss and cellulose fiber. When covered with a thin layer of soil and kept moist, the material eventually breaks down to humus. Hortopaper comes in rolls 15 to 400 feet long, in three-foot squares, or in nitrogen-enriched plant rings that fertilize with each watering.

Avant Horticulture Products
P.O. Box 15233, West Palm Beach, FL 33416-5233
Telephone: 305-686-7054 or 800-334-7979

Catalog price: free

Reacted liquid fertilizers, which, according to the firm's literature, contain dipotassium amino phosphonate, a molecular combination of nitrogen, phosphate, and potassium. Other fertilizers supply these nutrients in combination with salts and minerals that can build up to harmful levels in the soil. Avant claims its plant foods are free of such toxic elements as chlorine, nickel, lead, and cadmium. It further claims that the nutrients in its reacted fertilizers are used more efficiently by plants.

Cape Cod Worm Farm
Worm castings. See under *Worms*, page 244.

Clarel Laboratories, Inc.
513 Grove Street, Deerfield, IL 60015
Telephone: 312-945-4013

Catalog price: free

Liquid-concentrate plant foods specifically formulated for houseplants. Granny's Bloomers is a low-nitrogen fertilizer that promotes blooming in mature African violets. (High-nitrogen fertilizers result in lush foliage growth but few blooms.) Cactus Juice does a similar job on cacti, Sitting Pretty helps ferns along, and Jungle Juice gives a little more nitrogen to foliage plants.

Crosby Associates
44 Broadview Terrace, Chatham, NJ 07928
Telephone: 201-635-8139

No catalog or price list

Publishes a weatherproof laminated chart showing the fertilizer requirements of various plants throughout the year. Titled the "Master Fertilizer and Soil Improvement Guide," it sells for $2.50 postpaid.

Earthborne Farm
Rt. 1, Box 289, Greenup, IL 62428
Telephone: 217-923-3035

Catalog price: free

Soil improvement shouldn't be limited to the application of compost and fertilizer. Earthborne Farm sells seed for hairy vetch and winter oats for use as a green manure crop over the fall and winter. The seed is sown after the summer harvest and is plowed under in the spring.

Farm Products Associates
P.O. Box 128, Boston, MA 02117
Telephone: 617-946-0085

Catalog price: free

"Products to and from the dairying industry." Gardeners will be most interested in a single product *from* the dairying industry—a blend of cow manure and peat moss for use as a soil improver. Called PMM 50/50, it is sold in 22-liter bags. Write for the UPS-shipped price or for the name of a local supplier.

The Fertrell Co.
P.O. Box 265, Bainbridge, PA 17502
Telephone: 717-367-1566

Catalog price: free

Blue Label plant food sold by the 50-pound bag or by the ton. The firm also makes a couple of liquid fertilizers from fish meal and seaweed; these are sold in quart bottles and in larger containers. The price list spells out only the basic nitrogen-phosphorus-potassium analysis.

Green Earth Organics
9422 144th Street E., Puyallup, WA 98373-6686
Telephone: 206-845-2321

Catalog price: $1

Organic fertilizers and minerals, offered in an educational catalog with recipes for mixing the various raw materials into balanced treatments for particular garden needs. The firm also offers a good selection of natural pest controls and a couple pages of tools.

Growing Naturally
Organic soil conditioners. See under *General Gardening Supplies*, page 186.

I. F. M.
See under *Pest Controls*, page 231.

Lexigrow
Box 1491, Indianapolis, IN 46206-1491
Telephone: 317-844-5691

Catalog price: $2, deductible from first order, for sample

Sells Lexigrow time-release fertilizers—pellets that dissolve over periods of four months to two years—and Leximulch, a nonwoven polypropylene fabric. The $2 sample measures about two by three inches.

Living Acres
New Sharon, ME 04955
Telephone: 207-778-2390

Sells a liquid seaweed extract for use as a seed and rooting treatment and as a foliar spray. A compost made of dairy and poultry manures decomposed with other organic materials is also sold. The firm expects to have an organic potting mix on the market by early 1988.

Miracon Co.
P.O. Box 3360, Westport, CT 06880

Catalog price: free

Sells a soluble plant fertilizer called Nature's Miracle and a liquid foliar spray called Planteen, both for use on houseplants. No indication is given in the literature of what the plant foods are made of or of what their nitrogen, phosphorus, and potassium contents are. We're told only that Nature's Miracle is a "natural, organic soil conditioner. . . rich in protein."

Mother Nature's
Box 1055, Avon, CT 06001

Catalog price: free

Worm castings, recommended by Mother Nature's as a propagating medium, houseplant food, or garden fertilizer. The castings are sold in eight- and 32-pound bags and in larger quantities wholesale.

The Natural Gardening Company
Bat guano. See under *General Gardening Supplies*, page 187.

Necessary Trading Co.
See under *Pest Controls*, page 231.

North American Kelp
Cross Street, Waldoboro, ME 04572
Telephone: 207-832-7506

Catalog price: free

Fertilizers and soil conditioners made from seaweed and fish meal. A seaweed meal is made to be mixed into the soil, a liquid seaweed extract can be used as a soil fertilizer or a foliar spray, and a fish-and-seaweed mix provides the hormones of seaweed and the nutrients of fish waste. All the products can be used on houseplants or in the garden.

North Country Organics
P.O. Box 107, Newbury, VT 05051
Telephone: 802-866-5562

Catalog price: free

A broad range of organic fertilizers and soil amendments made for specific garden uses—one is formulated for starting vegetable seeds, another as a winter food for grass hays, another for flowering houseplants. The most popular blend, Harvest King, is a high-nutrient (5-3-4) general-purpose food for the vegetable garden or orchard. A few natural pest controls round out the list.

Ohio Earth Food, Inc.
13737 Duquette Avenue N.E., Hartville, OH 44632
Telephone: 216-877-9356

Catalog price: free

Organic fertilizers and soil additives and a selection of natural pest controls. Soil conditioners are sold either in components, such as dried blood, seaweed powder, and fish emulsion, or in mixes for specific purposes. The pest controls range from diatomaceous earth and tree tanglefoot to rotenone and thuricide. All offerings are briefly described.

Peaceful Valley Farm Supply
See under *General Gardening Supplies*, page 188.

Plantjoy
3562 E. 80th Street, Cleveland, OH 44105
Telephone: 216-641-1200

No catalog

Peruvian bird and bat guano in 23-ounce containers. The 1987 price was $8.10 per container, postpaid.

Ringer Research
9959 Valley View Road, Eden Prairie, MN 55344-3585
Telephone: 612-892-5430 or 800-654-1047

Catalog price: free

Natural fertilizers and soil additives specifically formulated for lawns, trees, vegetable gardens, flower beds, berry patches, roses, African violets, and foliage houseplants. The 24-page color catalog graphically displays the hazards of chemical fertilizers (brown, thatched lawns) and the benefits of Ringer's formulas (gorgeous roses, juicy strawberries). The firm sells composting supplies and formulas to aid decomposition, along with a selection of natural pest controls and a few tools.

Shady's Greenhouse
44 Pine Street, Franklin, MA 02038

Catalog price: $1 and self-addressed stamped envelope for fertilizer formula

This catalog *is* the product. On four pages we're given formulas for a cut-flower preservative, fertilizers for azaleas and potted plants, a first-aid paint for tree and shrub damage, a rabbit repellent, and several other useful garden mixtures. Supplies for all can be purchased at drugstores, hardware stores, supermarkets, or feed and grain suppliers.

Spray-N-Grow, Inc.
P.O. Box 722038, Houston, TX 77272
Telephone: 713-771-5760

Offers a liquid foliar spray that promotes fruiting and flowering, and a fungicidal spray. No clue is given as to what's in either formula, and the literature is somewhat unclear on how its main product, Spray-N-Grow foliar spray, actually works. According to the brochure, it's "a biological catalyst which either causes the phytochrome pigment embedded in the chloroplast to enlarge or causes new stomata to form, increasing the plant's ability to make sucrose."

Flower-Arranging Supplies

Dorothy Biddle Service
Greeley, PA 18425-9799
Telephone: 717-226-3739

Catalog price: 25¢

Flower-arranging supplies from the family of the late Dorothy Biddle, in her time a well-known author and lecturer on the subject. Lots of turtles (or needlepoints) are listed, along with scissors, snips, and wire cutters (for artificial stems). Many of the offerings will be of interest even to those who leave their flowers on the plant: knee pads, gloves, and an indoor watering hose.

Country House Floral Supply
P.O. Box 86, Bvl. Station, Andover, MA 01810
Telephone: 617-475-8463

Catalog price: $1

A good selection of unusual vases, containers, and bases for use in flower arranging, along with an array of shears and pruners, weighted flower holders, and such supplies as tape, wire, and stakes. The firm offers a selection of books on flower arranging, many of them on ikebana.

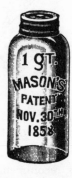

Food-Preservation Supplies

Allen, Sterling & Lothrop
See under *General Flowers and Vegetables*, page 13.

Ball Corporation
Box 2005, Dept. PK 6A, Muncie, IN 47302

No catalog

Ball is the biggest name in home canning, as most vegetable gardeners are aware. The firm's jars and lids are sold at most stores, but its comprehensive guide to canning, the *Ball Blue Book*, is sold only by mail. The book provides a clear and thorough introduction to canning, including charts and recipes that can be referred to year after year. In 1987 Ball charged $2.50 for the book, postpaid.

Farmer Seed & Nursery Co.
See under *General Flowers and Vegetables*, page 18.

Gardener's Kitchen
Box 412-7, Farmington, CT 06034

Catalog price: free

Canning lids and rings, including the regular #70 size, the wide-mouth #86, and the smaller #63. As far as we can tell, Gardener's Kitchen is the only commercial source for the #63 lids and rings. Now if only they'd make rings for our old glass-topped Mason jars.

Gurney Seed & Nursery Co.
See under *General Flowers and Vegetables*, page 19.

Harmony Farm Supply
See under *Trees and Shrubs*, page 155.

McFayden Seeds
Kitchen supplies for Canadian customers. See under *General Flowers and Vegetables*, page 24.

Earl May Seed & Nursery
See under *General Flowers and Vegetables*, page 24.

Mellinger's Inc.
See under *Trees and Shrubs*, page 159.

Modern Homesteader
See under *General Gardening Supplies*, page 187.

Tillinghast Seed Co.
See under *General Flowers and Vegetables*, page 31.

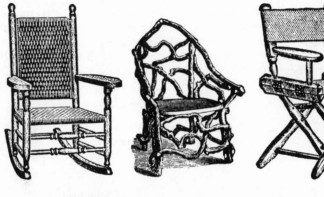

Furniture

Adirondack Store & Gallery
Drawer 991, Lake Placid, NY 12946
Telephone: 518-523-2646

Catalog price: free

Adirondack-style furniture made of oak or rock maple. The firm sells both the classic Adirondack chair and a folding version (made by Willsboro Wood Products), along with a companion line that includes settee, chaise, side table, picnic table set, and porch swing. The gallery also deals in one-of-a-kind rustic twig furniture, both new and antique. Interested customers should call or write to find out more details about the twig products; they are never available in enough quantity to include in the catalog.

The Alsto Company
Steel shell-back lawn chairs. See under *Tools*, page 236.

Bench Craft
36 Newport Drive, Wayne, PA 19087
Telephone: 215-640-1213

Catalog price: free

Bench Craft makes the elegant Lutyens garden bench and chair of mahogany and offers them with either a natural finish or painted white. The firm sells hardwood planters of a compatible design.

Brushy Mountain Bee Farm
Porch swing and Carolina rocker. See under *Beekeeping Supplies*, page 189.

Capability
Box 228, 238 Davenport Road, Toronto, ON, Canada M5R 1J6
Telephone: 416-962-1859

Catalog price: free

Some of the most beautiful teak and mahogany garden furniture we have seen, offered with a wide range of quality cast-stone ornaments, lead-look planters made of fiberglass, and other products for adding last decorative touches to a garden. The wooden furniture includes English garden benches and chairs, and some elegant variants on the basic designs (the Lutyens bench is among those sold, along with some we think even more lovely). Some smaller folding pieces for balconies and terraces should be available in the spring of 1988. The cast-stone ornaments are made by Minsterstone of England (sold in the U.S. by Ascot Designs—see entry under *Garden Ornaments*, page 207). Pedestals, pots, vases, benches, sundials, sculpture, birdbaths, and fountains are offered, mostly in the neoclassical style. Capability will sell only some of its furniture by mail but will steer customers interested in the rest of the line to local architects or landscape designers.

Charleston Battery Bench, Inc.
191 King Street, Charleston, SC 29401
Telephone: 803-722-3842

Catalog price: free

"Authentic reproductions" of the cast-iron and cypress benches made in Charleston since the 1880's. The firm bought the molds for the ornamental cast-iron ends when the original maker went out of business 30 years ago. It now casts the ends by the original method and finishes the benches with slats made of South Carolina cypress. The entire bench is immersion-painted in "the traditional Charleston dark green color."

Clapper's
Teak garden furniture. See under *Tools*, page 237.

Colonial Williamsburg
Reproduction of an 18th-century garden bench. See under *Garden Ornaments*, page 208.

Columbia Cascade Timber Co.
1975 S.W. Fifth Avenue, Portland, OR 97201
Telephone: 503-223-1157 or 800-547-1940

Catalog price: free (request TimberForm catalog)

TimberForm outdoor furniture, planters, and play structures, intended primarily for use in municipal parks. Benches are offered in dozens of styles, many of them variations on the wooden-slatted bench with cast-iron ends. Picnic tables and checkerboard table and chair sets are offered, the supports designed to be embedded in the earth or in concrete.

Country Casual
17317 Germantown Road, Germantown, MD 20874
Telephone: 301-540-0040 or 800-872-8325

Catalog price: $2

Teak garden furniture imported from England and a cherry Mayan-style outdoor chair made in the U.S. The teak furniture is available in a range of styles, including a choice of classic English park benches and the more ornamental Lutyens bench. Country Casual sells chairs, tables, swings, and planters to round out its list. All the furniture is pictured in the 24-page color catalog.

Cypress Street Center
350 Cypress Street, Fort Bragg, CA 95437
Telephone: 707-964-4940

Catalog price: free

Adirondack chairs and loveseats made of redwood. Some assembly is required, and the catalog demonstrates the extent of this work in a series of photographs. We ordered a pair of chairs, and can report that the assembly work involved screwing in about thirty Phillips-head screws. Shoppers can look at the catalog and judge for themselves whether they'll need to summon a handy friend. The chairs are nicely finished and the prices are reasonable. The firm also sells planters, benches, and a serving (or work) cart.

Erkins Studios, Inc.
Teak garden furniture and stone benches. See under *Garden Ornaments*, page 208.

Florentine Craftsmen
Cast aluminum furniture. See under *Garden Ornaments*, page 208.

The Frontier Furnishings Co., Inc.
554 E. Broadway, Alton, IL 62002
Telephone: 618-465-8868

Catalog price: free

Adirondack-style furniture made of white oak and another simpler line of chairs and benches made of cedar. The Adirondack line includes chair, rocker, chaise, loveseat, settee, glider, and porch swing, all sold unfinished at very reasonable prices. Finishing is offered at extra cost.

The Garden Concepts Collection
Painted mahogany furniture. See under *Garden Ornaments*, page 209.

Gardener's Eden
See under *Gifts for Gardeners*, page 212.

Gardener's Supply Co.
Steel shell-back lawn chairs. See under *Tools*, page 239.

Green Hand Tools
Teak benches for Canadian customers. See under *Tools*, page 239.

Hangouts
2888 Bluff Street #312, Boulder, CO 80301
Telephone: 800-426-4688 or 303-449-8896

Catalog price: free

Colorful Yucatan hammocks woven from cotton with nylon end strings. These hammocks have a fine weave, which is quite comfortable for long-term lazing about. They do not have the wooden spreader found on rope hammocks. This makes them a little more difficult to get in and out of, but also more portable. Choose from five sizes—from child-scale to a large double model.

Heartwood Furniture
P.O. Box 117, Worcester, NY 12197-0117
Telephone: 607-397-8758

Catalog price: free

Heartwood Furniture presents its SCooP folding lawn chair as an original design. A few other canvas-back and sling beach chairs are also offered, as well as some small folding

The Adirondack Chair: A Garden Classic

After more than 50 years of popularity, the Adirondack chair has earned a sort of heirloom status. Many of us remember sitting in one on our grandparents' porches, and more and more of us are now buying them for our own decks and yards. Judging by the number of mail-order companies that sell them, Adirondacks must be among the most popular pieces of quality yard furniture on the market.

The origins of the design are difficult to pinpoint with any certainty, but we have been able to document a couple of milestones in its evolution. In 1905 Harry C. Bunnell was granted a patent for "a chair of the bungalow type adapted for use on porches, lawns, at camps, and also adapted to be converted into an invalid's chair." His patent sketch shows a chair with the general outlines of the seat we know today, but with much refinement still to come. Bunnell made the chairs in Westport, in upper New York state, during the first two decades of the century, and many were purchased for resorts and camps in the nearby Adirondacks. Called "Bunnell chairs" at first, they gradually became known as "Adirondack chairs."

In 1932 Sears, Roebuck & Co. introduced the chair to its customers as "The Very Latest Wood Lawn Furniture." The model pictured in the catalog is virtually identical to the designs still being sold, except that the catalog version was painted in alternating stripes of orange and green. The company launched the chair and a companion settee with a color illustration (only a few items in the catalog were singled out for color treatment) and with lavish doses of praise. "New — Modern — Colorful! Ideal for private homes, clubs, tennis or country clubs. Artistically designed, generously proportioned, extremely comfortable."

Through the 1930's the chair spread across the country, both through the Sears catalog and through firms that offered kits for home assembly. By the 1940's it had become a lawn fixture, and today it is no longer "New" and "Modern," but has taken on the timeless look of a classic.

Sears made its version from "selected hardwood" and charged just $3.98. Many mail-order firms now carry the chair in redwood, teak, oak, mahogany, or maple, at prices that range up to $200.

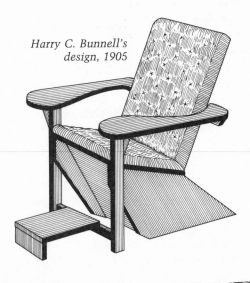

Harry C. Bunnell's design, 1905

The Sears, Roebuck & Co. version, 1932

drawings by Mary Reilly

tables. The SCooP chair is made of either mahogany or redwood, the other furniture of cherry, oak, or unspecified hardwood.

David Kay, Inc.
See under *Gifts for Gardeners*, page 213.

The Live Oak Railroad Co.
111 E. Howard Street, Live Oak, FL 32060
Telephone: 904-362-4419

Catalog price: free

Victorian wood-slatted outdoor benches with cast-iron ends.

One model is a reproduction of a bench found at railroad depots; another copies the street bench of Charleston, South Carolina. The third and most ornate design is of unnamed origin. The company also sells a cast-iron mailbox and a hitching post.

Kenneth Lynch & Sons, Inc.

Stone, iron, and teak benches. See under *Garden Ornaments*, page 209.

Modern Homesteader

Outdoor furniture in kit form. See under *General Gardening Supplies*, page 187.

Nampara Gardens

Japanese-style redwood bench. See under *Garden Ornaments*, page 210.

Newport Woodworks

767 East Main Road, Middletown, RI 02840
Telephone: 401-849-6850

Catalog price: free

Some unusual and beautiful garden benches, made of teak or mahogany, offered with a gazebo, an arched bridge (up to 40 feet long), a porch swing, and a teak table and chair set. Two of the benches are inspired by medieval wheelbarrow seats—they have small wooden wheels under the legs on one end and handles projecting out from the other. Newport's versions are handsome, well-proportioned benches that the firm suggests "can be moved to catch the sun, down a garden row as you work, or left to grace some private corner of your garden." Another, more elegant, bench combines a long, arched back with rounded ends in a design that looks as though it would settle comfortably into a Gertrude Jekyll garden.

Plow & Hearth

See under *Tools*, page 241.

Reed Bros.

Turner Station, Sebastopol, CA 95472
Telephone: 707-795-6261

Catalog price: $7

Hand-carved redwood furniture that is truly unusual. A garden bench, for example, has a back worked from a solid slab of wood into a curved, scrolly shape decorated with leaves and squirrels in high relief. The arms, legs, and seat have been similarly shaped, though, for the sake of comfort, the seat has been spared relief carving. Other designs feature carvings of seashells, birds, and flowers. A few simpler models feature curving legs and arms and leave the carving at a few rudimentary ornamental gouges. Prices reflect the tremendous amount of handwork involved. Some smaller items—planters, garden stakes, and baskets—are more readily affordable.

Smith & Hawken

Teak and Adirondack-style furniture. See under *Tools*, page 241.

Southern Statuary & Stone

See under *Garden Ornaments*, page 210.

Telescope Casual Furniture, Inc.

Granville, NY 12832
Telephone: 518-642-1100

Catalog price: free

This firm started out in Telescope, Pennsylvania, in 1903 as a manufacturer of cots. It has since moved from Pennsylvania and has moved on from cots to director's chairs and aluminum outdoor furniture, but it remembers the early days in its name. The firm is now one of the major manufacturers of director's chairs and aluminum-frame outdoor chairs and tables. The big color catalog shows dozens of chair styles, all lightweight and portable, and all of contemporary design.

Twin Oaks Hammocks

Rt. 4, Box 169, Louisa, VA 23093
Telephone: 703-894-5125

Catalog price: free

Traditional Pawley Island rope hammocks made by members of two Virginia "kibbutz-like" communities. Twin Oaks makes most of the rope hammocks sold by other catalogs. The basic models are woven of polypropylene fiber that won't rot or mildew outdoors, spread by oak bars at each end. The smallest size fits one six-footer, the largest holds two or more. A more portable model, without the wooden spreader bars, offers an alternative for backpackers. Twin Oaks also makes a "hammock chair" with an oak frame and woven-rope seat that looks both original and comfortable.

Vermont Castings, Inc.

7009 Prince Street, Randolph, VT 05060
Telephone: 802-728-3181

Catalog price: free

Vermont Castings is famous for its cast-iron wood stoves, which don't have much use in the vegetable patch. But the firm also makes a beautiful iron and teak garden bench. While other benches of this type have iron ends and wooden slats, Vermont Castings' version mixes those materials for a more integrated look. The cast-iron ends are topped by wooden armrests, and the back holds iron uprights between top and bottom teak slats. The result is a handsome and distinctive seat that will look at home in either old-fashioned or modern settings.

Walpole Woodworkers
767 East Street, Walpole, MA 02081
Telephone: 617-668-2800 or 800-343-6948

Catalog price: $1 for furniture catalog, $3 for building catalog, $5 for fencing catalog

This firm has everything needed to fence and furnish your yard and offers a range of storage sheds and picnic shelters to fill that unused corner. The firm's fencing offerings range from white picket to split rail, and include high solid screens, low ornamental walls, and a wide selection of gates and arbors. The furniture line concentrates on log-construction chairs, rockers, and picnic-table sets made of cedar. We've rocked in the firm's two-seat covered swing and can attest to its comfort. Chaises, stools, porch swings, and children's swing sets round out the list.

Westwind Manufacturing Inc.
P.O. Box 948, Kemp, TX 75143
Telephone: 214-498-6753

Catalog price: free

Redwood furniture sold from a price list without descriptions or illustrations. We called to get more information and were promised a set of photographs, but after two months we're still waiting. The firm also sells plant stands, window shelves, and gazebos.

White Flower Farm
Teak garden furniture. See under *Garden Perennials*, page 93.

Wikco Industries, Inc.
Rt. 2, Box 154, Broken Bow, NE 68822
Telephone: 308-872-5327

Catalog price: free

Makes a wrought-iron garden bench, "an exact copy of the wrought iron benches found in parks and gardens at the turn of the century." This seat is not to be confused with the cast-iron benches made elsewhere. Wikco makes its bench by heating and curving bands of iron, not by casting molten metal. The seat and back are composed of horizontal iron slats, the entire bench finished with white, green, or brown paint. The firm also makes a "slide hammer" log splitter,

which may be the answer for those whose aim with axes and mauls is less than perfect.

Willsboro Wood Products
P.O. Box 336, Willsboro, NY 12996
Telephone: 518-963-8623 or 800-342-3373

Catalog price: free

Rustic log-construction furniture made of cedar and folding maple Adirondack chairs and settees. All are finished with a smooth sanding that makes them look fine indoors as well as out and are sent "in their natural state." A coating of oil or clear polyurethane will make them look a little more civilized and will better protect the wood, whether from rain outdoors or spilled drinks inside. The color catalog is a beauty, showing each of the pieces to its best advantage.

Wood Classics, Inc.
Rt. 1, Box 455E, High Falls, NY 12440
Telephone: 914-687-7288

Catalog price: free

Several different outdoor furniture styles, all made of teak and mahogany—woods the firm claims have no equal for outdoor use. The classic English garden bench leads off the color catalog (with chair and porch swing to match), followed by the Adirondack chair (with settee, footrest, and table). Other offerings include a bench and chair set modeled on 18th-century Chippendale furniture, a picnic table and benches inspired by Shaker designs, and a more contemporary line dubbed "Versailles." All the furniture can be purchased fully assembled or in kit form at considerable savings.

Woodventure, Inc.
15 Island Drive, Savannah, GA 31406
Telephone: 912-354-8857

Catalog price: free

Outdoor furniture made of either teak or pine. The Adirondack chair is one member of the line, and the other designs have a similar rugged yet comfortable look. Settees are made with double-welled curved backs and with contoured seats. A service cart looks perfect with the Adirondack chair and might complete a set if you already own the chairs. Prices are on the high side.

Garden Carts

Bishop-Klein Industries, Inc.
Collapsible garden cart. See under *Tools*, page 237.

Carts Warehouse
200 Center Street, P.O. Box 3, Point Arena, CA 95468
Telephone: 707-882-2422

Catalog price: free

Carts Warehouse started out selling kits and plans for sturdy two-wheeled garden carts. The firm still sells the kits, in four cart sizes, and now also offers finished carts from other manufacturers—Garden Way, Stanley Forge, and Sotz. If you're looking for a garden cart, the Carts Warehouse brochure lets you compare the features of these leading makers and offers their carts at prices almost as low as the manufacturers' own—sometimes lower. For handy types, the kits can be a real savings.

Country Manufacturing, Inc.
P.O. Box 104, Fredericktown, OH 43019
Telephone: 614-694-9926

Catalog price: free

Carts, wagons, sprayers, and spreaders, most of them designed to be towed behind a small garden tractor. The smallest cart holds six cubic feet and dumps easily with a foot-released door panel. The largest wagon is seven feet long and 38 inches wide and dumps with the help of a hydraulic jack.

FXG Corporation
3 Sullivan Street, Woburn, MA 01801
Telephone: 617-933-8428

Catalog price: free

FXG offers just one product, the Log 'n' Lawn garden cart. It looks very similar to such two-wheeled, box-top designs as the Garden Way cart. But unlike other devices, the Log 'n' Lawn cart's plywood box snaps off for conversion to a log carrier.

Garden Way Manufacturing Co.
See under *Tools*, page 238.

Gardener's Supply Co.
See under *Tools*, page 239.

Homestead Carts
6098 Topaz Street N.E., Salem, OR 97305
Telephone: 503-390-5586 or 393-4779

Catalog price: free

Two-wheeled garden carts with plywood box tops and pneumatic tires. A few extra touches distinguish these carts from the competition: covered handles, a steel reinforcing bar that keeps the sides from splaying out, and an added steel support beam under the center of the main bed. Even more options are offered at additional cost: a steel bed liner and an extra rear panel to keep bulky loads from spilling.

Jaffrey Manufacturing, Inc.
Wooden wheelbarrows. See under *Cider and Wine Presses*, page 197.

Mardon Industries, Inc.
Route 122, Lyndonville, VT 05851
Telephone: 802-626-9311

Catalog price: free

Two-wheeled garden carts with plywood box tops. The design looks very similar to the cart offered by Garden Way, and the price is a little lower. But shipping charges are scaled so that western customers end up paying out most of the savings in increased freight.

Modern Homesteader
Kits for two-wheeled carts. See under *General Gardening Supplies*, page 187.

The Stanley Forge Co., Inc.
P.O. Box 23156, Stanley, KS 66223
Telephone: 913-681-2073 or 800-255-5013

Catalog price: free

Two-wheel, box-top garden carts that look as tough as most, but cost a little less.

Wisconsin Wagon Co.
507 Laurel Avenue, Janesville, WI 53545
Telephone: 608-754-0026

Catalog price: free

Offers two scale models of a turn-of-the-century wooden wheelbarrow, one built for children aged five to seven, and a slightly smaller version for four-year-olds. Both are made with oak boxes, maple handles, and steel ball-bearing wheels. A full-scale replica of the Janesville ball-bearing coaster wagon—the four-wheeled pull wagon of choice from 1900 through the 1930's—will bring back memories for experienced gardeners. It would make a nice gift for a grandchild or a novel garden cart. The firm also sells scooters and cradles beautifully crafted from wood.

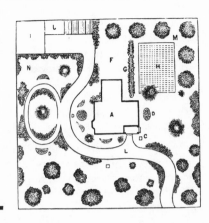

Garden Design and Plant-Finding Services

Historical Landscapes
Rt. 2, Box 242A, Bernville, PA 19506
Telephone: 215-488-6613

Catalog price: free

Historically authentic landscape design for people who want to create a period environment around their houses. The service is aimed primarily at owners of older buildings, but designs can be drawn up to complement even the most modern structure. Interested customers are asked to fill out a detailed questionnaire and to provide photographs and diagrams of the house and grounds. The final design takes the form of a carefully drawn plan, accompanied by descriptions and historical background on each of the plants.

North Star Seed and Plant Search
Sandy Olson, Rt. 1, Box 2310, Troy, ME 04987
Telephone: 207-948-2401

Catalog price: long self-addressed stamped envelope

A plant-searching service for gardeners who want to track down hard-to-find plants, from childhood favorites to new varieties spotted at flower shows or in display gardens. The firm has a computer bank with sources for more than 50,000

plants and seeds, including herbs, vegetables, native plants, garden perennials, annual flowers, bulbs, roses, grasses, ferns, ornamental trees and shrubs, fruits, nuts, and berries.

ProCreations
8129 Earhart Boulevard, New Orleans, LA 70118
Telephone: 800-245-8779 or 504-486-7787

Catalog price: free

Makers of the Plan-A-Flex Landscape Designer, an exact-scale design kit with reusable peel-and-stick symbols. The kit won't be much help in choosing plants for the border, but it will aid in organizing the yard. Stick-on symbols are provided for "several types of trees, shrubs, and plants," as well as for outdoor furniture, lighting, surfacing, fencing, and pool, patio, and decking materials. The 1987 price was $33.95, postpaid. Call or write for the current rate. Similar kits are offered for designing kitchens, baths, and entire houses.

Seeds Blüm
Plant-finding service. See under *General Flowers and Vegetables*, page 29.

Garden Ornaments

American Sundials, Inc.
P.O. Box 677, Point Arena, CA 95468
Telephone: 707-884-3082

Catalog price: long self-addressed stamped envelope

Sand-cast bronze sundials in a variety of styles, all of them flat circles with an old-fashioned look. All but one carry sayings like "Amidst the flowers I tell the hours" and "I count only the sunny hours."

Ascot Designs
286 Congress Street, Boston, MA 02210
Telephone: 617-451-9173

Catalog price: free

Cast-stone garden ornaments imported from Minsterstone in England. Containers, birdbaths, benches, fountains, sundials, and balustrading are offered, mostly in the neoclassical style. A few Japanese- and Chinese-style sculptures and bowls are also included in the catalog. Ascot Designs will do custom work and will search for genuine antique ornaments. Canadian customers can order Minsterstone products from Capability in Toronto (see entry under *Furniture,* page 201).

Autumn Forge
1104 N. Buena Vista Avenue, Orlando, FL 32818
Telephone: 305-293-3302

Catalog price: $1, deductible from first order

Hand-forged iron plant hangers and dinner bells in traditional and contemporary designs. A number of other items are made for indoor use, among them fireplace tool sets, hooks, and candle holders.

Autumn Innovations
Sundials. See under *Birdhouses and Feeders,* page 189.

Capability
See under *Furniture,* page 201.

Carillon
Rt. 2, Box 122, Banks, OR 97106
Telephone: 503-647-2731

Catalog price: free

Wind chimes made of aged copper. Carillon sells two basic designs in a range of sizes. One dangles plain chiming tubes from an ornamental top that has the look of a Chinese pagoda roof or the peak of a turreted Victorian house. The second clangs its clapper against flat triangular chimes, hand painted with folksy decorations.

Peter Catchpole, Blacksmith
Riverview Road, Gaylordsville, CT 06755
Telephone: 203-354-5425

No catalog

Makes a swivel plant bracket with an old-fashioned look. Many other items can be commissioned, from plant hooks to estate entrance gates.

Colonial Williamsburg
P.O. Box CH, Williamsburg, VA 23187
Telephone: 804-220-7467

Catalog price: free

Reproductions of 18th-century antiques, mostly from the collections of Colonial Williamsburg. Decorative household items take up the most space in the color catalog; among them are a few vases and jars that may be of interest to gardeners. A few pieces more directly related to the garden are also included in each catalog: an 18th-century garden bench, a ceramic birdhouse, a sundial, an assortment of botanical prints, and books on historic gardens.

Robert Compton, Ltd.
Star Rt., Box 6, Bristol, VT 05443
Telephone: 802-453-3778

Catalog price: $2, deductible from first order

Ceramic fountains inspired by natural forms, designed for both indoor and outdoor use. One suggests a stack of mushrooms, another a tower of calla lily blooms. Three designs are offered in a choice of sizes, from just over two feet to almost seven feet in height. The color brochure presents clear pictures of each design.

Dressler & Co.
P.O. Box 67, Silver City, NV 89428
Telephone: 702-847-0519

Catalog price: free

A cast-iron boot scraper in a Victorian design. The 1987 price was $21.95, postpaid. Write for the current charge.

Erkins Studios, Inc.
604 Thames Street, Newport, RI 02840
Telephone: 401-849-2660

Catalog price: $4

A veritable supermarket of garden ornaments, fountains, and teak garden furniture. If the budget will allow, shoppers can pick out a cherub-strewn garden pool, hand carved of Italian marble. Somewhat less expensive (though still earnestly priced) are the many smaller carved-stone sculptures, the cast-stone ornaments, urns, and fountains, and the lead statues and cisterns. Most of the offerings are reproductions or imitations of classic European designs. A separate brochure pictures an unusual and attractive inventory of terracotta pots, planters, urns, jars, and pedestals. Furniture seekers will find benches of Carrara marble and of cast stone and a complete line of teak garden furniture imported from England.

Florentine Craftsmen
46-24 28th Street, Long Island City, NY 11101
Telephone: 718-937-7632 or 212-532-3926

Catalog price: $3

Florentine Craftsmen has blended neoclassical reproductions with more recent pieces in an interesting catalog of garden ornaments, fountains, and outdoor furniture. The newer sculptures have the same sort of "cute" appeal as Hummell figurines, and if your taste can't handle Hummells you probably won't like many of these. (One fountain pumps water over an umbrella held by a pair of children in farmer-type boots and rain garb.) All the pieces, whether old or new in design, are made to last, of either cast stone, lead, or carved stone. The furniture includes some Victorian chairs and tables reproduced in cast aluminum and some newer cast-aluminum and wrought-iron pieces that are attempts to modernize such old styles as rustic twig furniture and ornate rattan.

Why Not?
108 Tamalpias Avenue, Berkeley, CA 94706
Telephone: 415-841-5027

Catalog price: free

Handmade, brightly painted wooden whirligigs in a flock of styles. An Indian paddles his canoe, a roadrunner spins its legs, a washerwoman works vigorously over her tub, and eagles, dragons, penguins, witches, pheasants, and whales twist in the wind. We were taken by the flutter-winged flamingo, a kinetic version of this garden standby. We've resisted the call of the flamingo for years now, but the question is a good one: why not?

Garden Structures

Ashland Barns
990 Butler Creek Road, Ashland, OR 97520
Telephone: 503-488-1541

Catalog price: $4, deductible from first order

Plans for barns, garden sheds, workshops, and garages. The catalog shows a sketch of each design and a basic floor plan with the overall dimensions. The buildings range from cute little barn-style sheds to eight-stall, two-story horse barns and even complete houses.

Bow House, Inc.
Randall Road, Bolton, MA 01740
Telephone: 617-779-2271 or 6464

Catalog price: $2

Gazebos, belvederes, arbors, garden bridges, and other fanciful garden structures offered in kit form. The belvedere, a screened- or glassed-in gazebo, is one of the firm's most popular creations, and we can see why. With its curved, steeply pointed roofline it really is a beauty. If you are after a true "folly," as these strange garden structures were once called, you might choose a miniature domed and columned Greek temple.

Child Life Play Specialties, Inc.
P.O. Box 527, Holliston, MA 01746
Telephone: 617-429-4639 or 800-462-4445

Catalog price: free

Children's play structures presented in an oversize color catalog. Swing sets, slides, playhouses, sandboxes, and seesaws are offered, constructed of pressure-treated fir and cedar with a coating of green enamel.

Creative Playgrounds, Ltd.
P.O. Box 431, Sun Prairie, WI 53590
Telephone: 608-837-7363

Catalog price: free

Timbergym wooden play structures. The smallest takes up a six-by-eight-foot area of yard space, the largest a twelve-by-twenty-foot plot. Along with ladder and swing structures, the firm sells a sandbox and a teeter-totter.

Dalton Pavilions, Inc.
7260-68 Oakley Street, Philadelphia, PA 19111
Telephone: 215-342-9804

Catalog price: free

Three styles of gazebos and a pagoda, all made of western red cedar. The structures are offered in kit form, but local dealers can often arrange for installation. The firm sends inquirers a color brochure showing each of the designs in attractive settings and provides the name of a local dealer who can quote prices and shipping charges.

The Garden Concepts Collection
See under *Garden Ornaments*, page 209.

Newport Woodworks
See under *Furniture*, page 204.

Sun Designs
P.O. Box 206, Delafield, WI 53018-0206
Telephone: 414-567-4255

Catalog price: long self-addressed stamped envelope

Sun Designs sells idea books and plans for outdoor structures, from gazebos and bridges to doghouses and privies.

The brochure describes the four idea books, which show color sketches of the constructions and rough floor plans. Detailed plans are sold for any you decide to build. *Gazebos* ($9.45 postpaid) pictures dozens of gazebos and a selection of strombrellas (covered garden seats and swings), arbors, and unusual birdhouses and feeders. *Backyard Structures* ($10.45 postpaid) covers storage sheds, cabanas, trash-can enclosures, doghouses, barns, and a small chapel. *Bridges & Cupolas* and *Privy* each sell for $9.45 postpaid. Check prices if ordering after 1988.

Vintage Woodworks
513 S. Adams, Fredericksburg, TX 78624
Telephone: 512-997-9513

Catalog price: $2

If you're a fan of Victorian gingerbread, you'll love the Vintage Woodworks catalog. Page after page of elaborate spandrels, brackets, shingles, arches, balusters, rails, and posts are offered. Incorporate them into your own design for a romantic garden structure, or buy a complete gazebo package. Vintage Woodworks' prefabricated gazebo is the frilliest and airiest design we have seen, its sides ornamented in high Victorian style with wide-open balusters and spandrels, its roof made of spaced slats that let the breeze flow through.

Vixen Hill Manufacturing Company
Main Street, Elverson, PA 19520
Telephone: 215-286-0909

Catalog price: $2

Gazebos in several sizes and styles, shipped in prefabricated sections for relatively simple assembly (no nailing is required; the parts are bolted together through pre-drilled holes). The smallest model will seat three or four comfortably, the largest could fit a good-size brass band. One elaborate design includes a two-tiered roof; a narrow row of spandrels below the upper eave releases summer heat. A small glassed-in model can be used as a greenhouse or a three-season study.

Walpole Woodworkers
Fencing, storage sheds, and picnic shelters. See under *Furniture*, page 205.

Westwind Manufacturing Co.
Redwood gazebos. See under *Furniture*, page 205.

Yards of Fun
P.O. Box 119, N. Manchester, IN 46962
Telephone: 219-982-6067

Catalog price: free

Children's swing sets, climbing gyms, playhouses, and sandboxes, made of unpainted pressure-treated lumber. Write for information, and you'll get a color catalog with the name of the nearest distributor.

Gifts for Gardeners

Bittersweet Farm
6294 Seville Road, Seville, OH 44273
Telephone: 216-887-5293

Catalog price: $1

A hand-lettered, homespun-feeling catalog, featuring the handcrafted products of a family farm. Flowers and herbs adorn a selection of hats, wreaths, ornamental hearts, and baskets. Simple line drawings give you an idea of what the items look like; a brief paragraph of commentary fills in the rest. "Our wreath for spring is done on a silver king base, with all pastel colored flowers, everything that reminds us of nice summer days ahead," reads one entry—and this is typical of the catalog's pleasantly relaxed tone.

The Botanic Garden Seed Co.
Wildflower seed gift baskets. See under *Wildflowers*, page 174.

Brookfield Nursery & Tree Plantation
P.O. Box 2490, Christiansburg, VA 24068-2490
Telephone: 703-382-9099 or 800-443-TREE

Catalog price: free

Freshly cut Christmas trees. Choose from white pine, Fraser fir, or blue spruce in either "home size" or "apartment size." White pine wreaths are sold with or without bows.

Gardener's Eden
P.O. Box 7307, San Francisco, CA 94120-7307
Telephone: 415-421-4242

Catalog price: free

Williams-Sonoma's entry into the gardening supply field. The firm has made a name for itself with its carriage-trade kitchen-supply catalog, and with Gardener's Eden it has followed the same path into the garden. Catalog shoppers will find nothing so mundane as plastic pots here. Gardener's Eden offers Portuguese terracotta pots decorated in high relief, wooden barrel planters from England, and the same metal flower buckets that commercial florists use in Paris. Teak garden benches are presented in the color catalog, along with an unusual set of rustic bent-chestnut furniture from Spain, a two-seated garden swing, an Adirondack chair made of teak, and a replica of the deck chair used on the *Queen Elizabeth II*. Those looking for something useful will find knee pads, Japanese flower shears, Felco pruners in left- and right-handed models, waterproof garden shoes and boots, and a canvas fruit-picking bag. The Christmas catalog includes a beautiful cast-iron tree stand and a number of living wreaths.

W. M. Green & Company

P.O. Box 278, Robersonville, NC 27871
Telephone: 800-482-5050 or 800-682-5050

Catalog price: free

A general gift catalog that regularly features items of interest to gardeners—planters, sundials, wind chimes, and ornamental hose guides.

Gumps

250 Post Street, San Francisco, CA 94108-9915
Telephone: 800-334-8677 or 415-467-3818

Catalog price: $3

A high-ticket catalog of jewelry and fine home furnishings that always includes a few items of interest to well-heeled gardeners. Among the 1987 offerings were two bronze Japanese garden lanterns, some beautiful hand-painted porcelain planters, and a handful of glass and ceramic vases. We should warn shoppers that the prices at Gumps are on the high side; the vases range from $20 to more than $500.

David Kay, Inc.

Suite 114, 921 Eastwind Drive, Westerville, OH 43081
Telephone: 614-891-2030 or 800-872-5588

Catalog price: free

Gifts for Home & Garden is the title of David Kay's color catalog, and its pages are filled with useful and attractive accessories for use outdoors and in. The list changes with some regularity, but past seasons have brought teak benches and oak Adirondack chairs, a ceramic birdhouse in the form of a miniature pagoda, a flower-arranging kit in a natural wicker basket, sundials, wind chimes, garden bridges, planters, wildflower wreaths, and a set of child-size garden tools. Write and see what's for sale this season.

Mrs. McGregor's Garden Shop

4801 First Street N., Arlington, VA 22203
Telephone: 703-528-8773

Catalog price: free

Gifts for Gardeners, Mrs. McGregor's catalog is called, but there's nothing stopping us from ordering for ourselves. Teak planters and garden boxes are pretty enough to bring into the living room and tough enough to leave outdoors. Choose from several different styles and sizes. Other offerings include a lead garden hare, aprons, metal plant markers, a long-handled bulb planter, wind chimes, and a cast-aluminum wall fountain.

Natural Art Forms, Inc.

1716 Old Metairie Street, Metairie, LA 70001
Telephone: 504-578-0214 or 800-843-2839

Catalog price: $2

Gold and silver earrings, pins, and pendants in the shapes of orchid blooms. These botanically correct representations look like just the thing to wear to American Orchid Society conventions.

The Nature Company

P.O. Box 2310, Berkeley, CA 94702
Telephone: 800-227-1114

Catalog price: free

The Nature Company catalog changes from season to season, but it always holds something special for gardeners. The summer 1987 booklet offered Soleri wind chimes, posters of flowers, birds, butterflies, and fruit, a plant press, a choice of unusual sundials, and the Brooklyn Botanic Garden's video, *Get Ready, Get Set, Grow!*, an introduction to gardening for kids.

Navand

36 Fairview Avenue, Hawthorne, NJ 07506
Telephone: 201-423-5950 or 800-527-2925

Catalog price: $1

Navand doesn't have a catalog, but for $1 it will send a collection of photographs of its gift offerings, all of which have an orchid motif. Orchid wind socks, jewelry boxes, neckties, scarves, atomizers, aprons, and greeting cards are sold. If you don't find the orchid you want among those attractions, Navand will hand paint almost any orchid on a quilted pillow.

Pleasant Hill Farm

20454 S. Springwater Road, Estacada, OR 97023
Telephone: 503-631-2918

Catalog price: $1

Holly and evergreen wreaths and unassembled greens for holiday decorating. Boxes of loose holly are offered, along with fresh cedar greens, pinecones, juniper branches, and mistletoe.

Plow & Hearth

See under *Tools*, page 241.

Seeds Blüm

Seed, herb, and potato gift packs. See under *General Flowers and Vegetables*, page 29.

Serenity Herbs

Box 42, Monterey Stage, Gt. Barrington, MA 01230
Telephone: 413-528-4595

Catalog price: $1

Products made from herbs and dried flowers—wreaths, garlands, sachets, and nosegays, along with a selection of teas, culinary herbs, herb vinegars, and natural dyes. A small library of books completes the selection.

Signals

333 Sibley Street, Suite 626, St. Paul, MN 55101
Telephone: 800-424-9424

Catalog price: free

Books, videos, clothing, and gift items derived from public television programming. For gardeners the 1987 catalog offered *Victory Garden* T-shirts and sweatshirts, a *Victory Garden* wind sock, *Victory Garden* mugs, and a *Victory Garden* video. Other items of interest included a flower-pressing kit and wind chimes.

There's Always the Garden

32 W. Anapamu Street #267, Santa Barbara, CA 93101
Telephone: 805-687-6478

Catalog price: free

T-shirts, sweatshirts, and canvas tote bags silkscreened with various ornamental designs around the firm's name and motto: "There's always the garden."

Norm Thompson

P.O. Box 3999, Portland, OR 97208
Telephone: 800-547-1160

Catalog price: free

Norm Thompson's catalog is mostly filled with clothing that would be ruined by a few minutes of weeding, but the firm always tosses in a few items for yard and garden use. The spring 1987 booklet included a mahogany and canvas folding chair, a four-wheeled garden scooter (which looks much more comfortable than the knee-pad approach), a hummingbird feeder, wind chimes, and several wildflower-seed mixtures.

Tom Thumb Workshops

P.O. Box 332, Chincoteague, VA 23336
Telephone: 804-824-3507

Catalog price: $1

Potpourris, potpourri containers, dried flowers, essential oils, and gift items made from pressed flowers.

Winterthur Museum & Gardens

Direct Mail Dept., Winterthur, DE 19735
Telephone: 703-387-2457 or 800-556-4567

Catalog price: $1

Winterthur's color gift catalog offers planters, vases, horticultural prints, garden ornaments, and a pewter-topped glass potpourri jar, all based loosely on the collection at the Winterthur Museum. The catalog also includes many of the plants grown in the Winterthur Gardens (see entry under *Trees and Shrubs*, page 166).

Gloves and Gardening Clothing

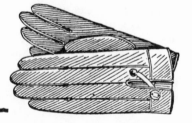

Clothcrafters, Inc.

P.O. Box 176, Elkhart Lake, WI 53020
Telephone: 414-876-2112

Catalog price: free

A grab bag of cloth products for both indoor and outdoor use. For gardeners, the firm sells denim knee pads fastened behind the legs with Velcro straps, insect netting (by the yard or made up into roomy head bags), and a handy tool belt. PlyBan breathable polyethylene is sold in 50-foot strips for use as row covers. The material is said to act as a mini-greenhouse

to protect plants from frost in the spring. After their work is done, gardeners may be interested in Clothcrafters' aprons and chefs' hats.

Green Mountain Glove Company, Inc.

P.O. Box 25, Randolph, VT 05060
Telephone: 802-728-9160

Catalog price: free

One of the very few suppliers of heavy-duty goatskin gloves, which are noted for their durability, warmth, and pliability.

Many other catalogs offer "lanolin-enriched goatskin" gloves, which are actually made of sheepskin and are far less rugged. Green Mountain's gloves are made of full-grain goatskin and will hold up under the strain of heavy gardening chores. Wool and cotton liners are offered for added warmth.

Emi Meade, Importer
16000 Fern Way, Guerneville, CA 95446

Catalog price: free

European-style gardening clogs in bright colors of molded polyurethane. A cork insole provides some cushioning and helps keep the shoes on your feet. Emi Meade also offers an abrasive block called Atomcoll, which is used like a pumice stone to smooth rough skin and calluses.

Putnam's
Main Street, Wilton, NH 03086
Telephone: 603-654-6564

Catalog price: free

Putnam's is a small country clothing store that sells a few of its more unique offerings by mail—bug hats, Carter's overalls and dungarees, cotton work shirts, engineer's caps, and "goatskin" gloves (they're actually sheepskin).

Greenhouse Supplies

Acme-Hardesty Co.
910 Benjamin Fox Pavilion, Jenkintown, PA 19046
Telephone: 800-223-7054

Catalog price: free

Industrial charcoal for use in potting mediums. This source will be of most interest to larger-scale greenhouse growers, orchid enthusiasts, and hydroponic gardeners. Write for a brochure or call for the name of a local distributor.

Aquamonitor
Mist irrigation system. See under *Irrigation Equipment*, page 226.

Arctic Glass & Millwork, Inc.
I-94 at County Road T, Hammond, WI 54015
Telephone: 715-796-2292

Catalog price: $2, deductible from first order

Insulated double-pane windows and doors for sun rooms and greenhouses. The $2 fee buys a price list and a couple of articles with design ideas and installation instructions.

Bio-Energy Systems Co.
P.O. Box 191, Ellenville, NY 12428-0191
Telephone: 914-647-6700

Catalog price: free

Manufacturer of the Gro-Mat root-zone heating system for greenhouse growers. The firm sends a questionnaire with its literature and asks prospective customers to fill it out so that prices can be quoted on a customized system. Home gardeners without sun rooms or greenhouses need not apply. The first question shows four basic greenhouse types and asks customers to circle the one that looks most like their own.

Biotherm Engineering
P.O. Box 6007, Petaluma, CA 94953
Telephone: 707-763-4444 or 800-GET-HEAT

Catalog price: free

Two types of root-zone or under-bench heating systems. The firm's original Biotherm system is custom designed to a gardener's greenhouse, based on the answers to a four-page questionnaire. In 1987 a simpler Gardentherm system was added to the line; it's a prepackaged kit covering 65 square feet. The smaller system runs on standard 115-volt electrical current and is more appropriate for smaller greenhouses and sun rooms. Gardentherm comes in a choice of two-, three-, or four-foot widths.

Bramen Co., Inc.
Thermostatically controlled ventilator. See under *Tools*, page 237.

Brighton By-Products Co., Inc.
P.O. Box 23, New Brighton, PA 15066
Telephone: 412-846-1220 or 800-245-3502

Catalog price: $5

A thick and comprehensive catalog of growing supplies, mostly in wholesale quantities. Seed-starting trays, for example, are sold in 100-sheet packs. Tools are sold singly, however, as are such greenhouse supplies as heaters and ventilating fans, and the firm sells Agritape root-zone heaters in reasonable lengths.

Charley's Greenhouse Supply
See under *General Gardening Supplies*, page 185.

Grow-n-Energy

P.O. Box 1114, Matthews, NC 28106

Catalog price: one first-class stamp

Plastic pots, flats, seed-starting supplies, and other tools and equipment for both greenhouse and outdoor gardeners. Chemical pesticides and fertilizers are offered, along with stakes, plant markers, soil meters, and misting nozzles.

Don Mattern

267 Filbert Street, San Francisco, CA 94133
Telephone: 415-781-6066

Catalog price: free

Sells the Herrmidifier greenhouse humidifier. Only one model is available, a seven-pound plastic and brass unit capable of wetting between 5,000 and 7,000 cubic feet of greenhouse space. A humidistat control can be set to keep humidity at fixed settings between 20 and 80 percent.

Memory Metals, Inc.

84 W. Park Place, Stamford, CT 06901
Telephone: 203-357-9777

Catalog price: free

Self-powered thermostatic vent opener that uses a modern metal technology called "shape memory." The metal coil that opens and closes the vent has been "trained" to "return to predetermined shapes at selected temperatures." Those who want to know more can read the *Scientific American* article (November 1979) the firm sends out in its information packet.

Premium Seed and Horticultural Supply Co.

915 E. Jefferson Street, Louisville, KY 40206
Telephone: 502-582-3897

Catalog price: $1.50

A general line of growing supplies, catering both to home gardeners and commercial growers. The firm offers hobby greenhouses from the Texas Greenhouse Company (as well as the tent-type Solar Dome) and full-size structures from Nexus in widths from 15 to 40 feet. Supplies range from pesticides (chemical and organic), fertilizers, plastic pots and flats, tools, and sprinklers to greenhouse heaters, fans, and coolers, root-zone heaters, conveyor belts, and industrial-size shredders. The firm also sells vegetable seeds (see entry under *General Flowers and Vegetables*, page 27).

Pro-Grow Supply Co.

12675 W. Auer Avenue, Brookfield, WI 53005
Telephone: 414-781-1150

Catalog price: free

Electric soil sterilizers, root-zone heating mats, and soil mixers. You'd have to mix a lot of soil to justify the cost of the massive mixers, but the heaters come as small as 22 by 22 inches, and, even with the thermostat controls, they aren't ruinously expensive.

Rodco Products Co., Inc.

P.O. Box 944, Columbus, NE 68601
Telephone: 402-563-3596

Catalog price: free

Manufacturers of a temperature monitor that measures conditions at two locations and displays the readouts on a alarm-clock-like device that can be set up anywhere in the house—up to 1,000 feet from the sensors. The device can be programmed to set off an alarm when either of the sensors detects conditions either too warm or too cold. It can be used to watch for frost in the garden or to detect overheating in the greenhouse (or to check attic, pool, or hot-tub heat). It will also give a readout of the day's high and low temperatures.

Skagit Gardens

1695 Johnson Road, Mt. Vernon, WA 98273

Catalog price: $2, deductible from first order

"Professional horticultural tools and supplies for the recreational grower." At last, a wholesale supply house that home gardeners can write to without disguising their stationery. Skagit Gardens sells molded fiber containers in sizes up to 14 gallons, cedar hanging baskets, Rootcubes and Horticubes growing media, several root-zone heating systems, budding and grafting knives, plastic and wooden plant labels, Felco pruners, Japanese bonsai and garden tools, and a flatbed greenhouse cart.

Standard Humidifier

100 Ashton Street, Pawtucket, RI 02860
Telephone: 401-722-0238

Catalog price: free

Humidifiers and humidistats for large and small greenhouses. The smallest humidifier puts out two quarts per hour, the largest three gallons.

Stuppy, Inc., Greenhouse Supply Div.

P.O. Box 12456, N. Kansas City, MO 64116
Telephone: 800-821-2132 (800-892-5044 in Missouri)

Catalog price: $2.50

A phonebook-thick catalog crammed with greenhouse supplies. The book starts off with a display of steel-framed quonset greenhouses, the smallest of which is 17 feet wide. Big selections of coverings, hardware, and equipment are offered to complete the job. Commercial growing supplies fill the rest of the book: propagating mats, plastic pots, handcarts, sprayers, and irrigation systems. The firm offers few tools beyond those needed to apply greenhouse coverings. Orders under $25 pay an added handling charge.

Superior Autovents
17422 La Mesa Lane, Huntington Beach, CA 92647

Catalog price: free

A solar-powered vent opener that will lift a 32-pound vent up to 13 inches.

Village Green Enterprises
P.O. Box 424, Davis, CA 95617
Telephone: 916-758-5402

Catalog price: $3

Shade cloth for sun rooms and greenhouses. The fabric is made of vinyl-coated polyester in a range of colors and can be ordered in either 73 or 95 percent shade density. The cloth is cut to fit the sun room and comes with roller bar, pulleys, control lines, and all hardware necessary for installation.

Yonah Manufacturing Co.
P.O. Box 280, Cornelia, GA 30531
Telephone: 404-778-8654

Catalog price: free

Polypropylene shade cloth in a range of weaves that provide shade from 30 to 92 percent density. The cloth is cut and sewn to fit the customer's greenhouse or awning measurements and is finished with binding and grommets.

Greenhouses

Clover Greenhouses
200 Weakley Lane, P.O. Box 789, Smyrna, TN 37167
Telephone: 615-459-3863 or 800-251-1206

Inexpensive freestanding plastic-covered greenhouses. The smallest model is 12 feet square, the largest 30 by 148 feet. Clover offers all materials needed to build the structures and such ancillary equipment as fans, heaters, humidifiers, irrigation systems, and a hydroponic lettuce-growing system.

E. R. & Son Farm
Small tent-style greenhouses. See under *Tools*, page 238.

Everlite Greenhouses
9305 Gerwig Lane, Guilford Industrial Center
Columbia, MD 21046
Telephone: 301-381-3880

Catalog price: $5

Aluminum-frame greenhouses in dozens of styles and sizes. If you don't find what you want in the catalog, Everlite is willing to create custom designs. The firm makes attached sun rooms and conservatories and freestanding greenhouses in styles from the plainest frame structures to frilly octagonal Victorians. The extensive catalog gives the impression that Everlite is knowledgeable about horticultural matters. Two contrasting greenhouses are pictured, one for cacti and another for tropical orchids, and the text explains that Everlite advised on the appropriate choice of covering material and climate-control equipment for each. The firm also makes plenty of greenhouses for people, not for plants. The catalog cover shows a Burger King restaurant with a wraparound solarium.

Four Seasons Solar Products
5005 Veterans Memorial Highway, Holbrook, NY 11741
Telephone: 800-368-7732

Catalog price: free

Wood- and aluminum-frame attached greenhouses or sun rooms. The color catalog shows many custom installations, all of them being used for living rather than horticultural purposes. The firm puts interested customers in touch with local franchised design and remodeling centers. Canadian customers should contact Mr. Cole at 506 McNicoll Avenue, Willowdale, ON M3H 2E1 (416-493-7773).

Gardener's Supply Co.
See under *Tools*, page 239.

Gothic Arch Greenhouses
P.O. Box 1564, Mobile, AL 36633-1564
Telephone: 205-432-7529

Catalog price: free

Freestanding and attached greenhouses with a distinctive arched framework and Gothic peak. The frame is made of either redwood or red cedar, the covering of fiberglass-reinforced acrylic plastic. With their translucent coverings, these are more appropriate for growing plants than for use as living spaces. The firm also offers shade cloth and benches as well as heating, cooling, and ventilating systems.

Greenhouse Specialties Co.
16195 S.W. 184th Street, Miami, FL 33187-4906

Catalog price: free

Plans and supplies for simple and inexpensive wood-frame greenhouses. The customer follows the plans to build the structure from locally purchased lumber and buys the finishing hardware and supplies from Greenhouse Specialties. The covering offered is a clear acrylic fiberglass called Lacolite. The firm sells heaters, exhaust fans, thermostats, and timers to complete the job.

Gro-Haus Industries, Ltd.
P.O. Box 244, Central Bridge, NY 12035
Telephone: 518-868-2061

Catalog price: free

Small freestanding and lean-to greenhouses for home gardeners, designed for easy assembly. The frame is aluminum, the covering Lexon Thermoclear sheeting, a clear plastic material in a reinforced double-wall formation. The smallest lean-to unit measures four by nine feet, the largest freestanding greenhouse 12 by 12 feet. Modular four-foot additions can extend the length of any unit. The firm offers such accessories as bench frames, basket-hanger poles, heaters, and ventilation fans.

Gro-Tek
See under *General Gardening Supplies*, page 186.

Hydro-Gardens, Inc.
See under *Hydroponic Growing Supplies*, page 222.

Inland Harbors Inc.
P.O. Box 35068, Minneapolis, MN 55435
Telephone: 612-941-8280 or 800-544-2525

Catalog price: free

Boating equipment and trailer accessories take up most of the space in this catalog, but Inland Harbors also sells a portable tent-type greenhouse and a selection of work gloves and boots that may be of interest to gardeners.

Janco Greenhouses, J. A. Nearing Co., Inc.
9390 Davis Avenue, Laurel, MD 20707-1993
Telephone: 301-498-5700

Catalog price: $2

Freestanding and attached aluminum-frame greenhouses in dozens of styles, some made for living and some for growing plants. The horticultural greenhouses are made with ventilation sashes at the roofline and can be equipped with fans, heaters, and thermostatic controls. The color catalog shows each design in clear pictures and diagrams and explains the features and recommended uses.

Lindal Cedar Sunrooms
P.O. Box 24426, Seattle, WA 98124
Telephone: 206-725-0900

Catalog price: free

Cedar-frame sun rooms. Thick wooden beams and frame supports give these sun rooms an inviting, comfortable feeling. Those looking for a solarium that combines living space with sunny plant windows may want to give this brochure a look.

Lord & Burnham
CSB 3181, Melville, NY 11747
Telephone: 914-591-8800

Catalog price: $2

Greenhouses and solariums from one of the premier names in the business. Lord & Burnham has been building and installing greenhouses since 1856 and has many fine 19th-century structures in its portfolio (including Jay Gould's grand Gothic-style conservatory at the Lyndhurst estate, near Tarrytown, New York—the first steel-framed greenhouse in the United States). Today the firm makes a full line of aluminum-frame solariums and hobby greenhouses, while still offering custom-designed structures on a larger scale. The structures and additions are built with ventilation and shading appropriate to their ultimate uses, and Lord & Burnham is eminently experienced in building environments healthy for plants as well as for people. Canadian customers should write the company at 325 Welland Avenue, St. Catharines, ON L2R 6V9, or call 416-685-6573.

Machin Designs
557 Danbury Road, Wilton, CT 06897
Telephone: 203-834-9566

Catalog price: $5

We admit to a passion for 19th-century greenhouses, with their airy, curved lines and fussy embellishments, and Machin Designs has hit a soft spot with its Victorian-style constructions. These greenhouses are gorgeous. (And, we suspect, expensive. No prices are given in the catalog.) The typical Machin Designs conservatory is built with a white aluminum framework, the roof of which arches up over straight walls in an S-curve to a sharp peak. Many variations are available, from straight-sloped roofs to simple arches to larger and more elaborate structures in which the roof elements are repeated in an ornate step-like design.

Northern Greenhouse Sales

P.O. Box 42SP, Neche, ND 58265
Telephone: 204-327-5540

Catalog price: three first-class stamps for brochure and fabric sample

Mag Smith and Bob Davis sell a strong, rip-stop, woven polyethylene greenhouse covering, and to encourage customers to buy it they send out a packet of suggestions on designing and building inexpensive greenhouses. They made the frame of their own 50 by 12-foot greenhouse out of rebar—the cheap iron rods used to strengthen concrete—at a cost of only $100. Smith and Davis are delighted to receive pictures of the creative structures their customers come up with. Canadian customers should write to the firm at Box 1450, Altona, MB R0G 0B0.

Pacific Coast Greenhouse Mfg. Co.

8360 Industrial Avenue, Cotati, CA 94928
Telephone: 707-795-2164

Catalog price: $1

Freestanding and attached redwood-frame greenhouses from a builder with three generations of experience in glasshouse manufacture. The greenhouses arrive in pieces, with glazing installed in the frames, and the buyer takes responsibility for installation. Pacific Coast's designs involve no fancy curved glass, and the firm claims the structures are a simple matter to put up. ("Because the glazing is already in place," reads the catalog, "installation goes about five times faster than an unglazed system. Our easy to follow instructions amount to two pages. Compare that with the book-length instructions you receive with aluminum greenhouse kits.") The firm also supplies the equipment necessary to make the structures plantworthy: heaters, coolers, humidifiers, vent openers, and fans.

Premium Seed and Horticultural Supply Co., Inc.

See under *Greenhouse Supplies*, page 216.

Santa Barbara Greenhouses

1115J Avenida Acaso, Camarillo, CA 93010
Telephone: 805-482-3765

Catalog price: free

Straight-sided redwood-frame greenhouses. The simplest and least expensive hobby models are covered with acrylic fiberglass panels. Fancier versions have tempered plate-glass walls. Both lean-to and freestanding models are available, the smallest just seven by four feet. Buyers are responsible for putting the structures up, but, with the exception of the foundation, construction looks very basic. The firm sells benches, heaters, fans, misters, thermostats, and shade cloth.

Stuppy, Inc., Greenhouse Supply Div.

See under *Greenhouse Supplies*, page 216.

Sturdi-Built Manufacturing Company

11304 S.W. Boones Ferry Road, Portland, OR 97219
Telephone: 503-244-4100

Catalog price: $2, deductible from first order

Small and medium-size redwood-frame greenhouses designed for horticultural use. Several models are offered, from simple squared structures to barn-shaped buildings and a round model (which looks something like a yurt, for those with memories of the 1960's). All but the round design can be purchased as freestanding greenhouses or as attached lean-tos. Sturdi-Built ships in unglazed prefabricated sections—roof, side, and end-wall sections, with pre-hung door. Glass must be installed in the finished frame.

Sun System Greenhouses

75 Austin Boulevard, Commack, NY 11725
Telephone: 516-543-7600

Catalog price: free

Aluminum-frame greenhouses covered with double-pane glass. The color brochure shows only attached lean-to models (from three by seven feet to 13 feet square), and it shows more pools and sofas than plants. These greenhouses can obviously be used for horticulture, but that isn't the priority of Sun System's sales department. Greenhouse accessories like heaters and ventilation fans will have to be purchased elsewhere.

Suncraft, Inc.

414 South Street, Elmhurst, IL 60126
Telephone: 312-852-5554

Catalog price: $1

Curved-eave aluminum-and-glass greenhouses. The basic low-cost package leaves frame cutting and drilling to the buyer, but much of that work can be done at Suncraft for an additional fee. Buyers can choose from attached greenhouses, six or eight feet wide and seven to 20 feet long, or from freestanding greenhouses at twice the width. The firm offers Modine gas-fired heaters as well.

Sunglo Solar Greenhouses
4441 26th Avenue W., Seattle, WA 98199
Telephone: 206-284-8900 or 800-647-0606

Catalog price: free

Aluminum-frame greenhouses made with a double-wall acrylic covering that's both sturdy ("strong enough to support a Volkswagen") and energy efficient. Double-pane glass is also available at extra cost for those who want transparent windows. Lean-to models are available in widths of five to ten feet and freestanding greenhouses in widths from eight to 15 feet. Fans, heaters, benches, shelves, and shading materials are also sold.

Texas Greenhouse Co.
2717 St. Louis Avenue, Ft. Worth, TX 76110
Telephone: 817-926-5447

Catalog price: $1

Small redwood-frame greenhouses for hobby gardeners and larger aluminum-frame structures for big-volume growers. The two hobby models are unusually handsome designs and appear to be efficiently laid out. One is made with a Gothic arch roofline, covered with corrugated fiberglass, enclosing a base ten by 12 feet. The other has slightly sloping straight walls, glass panes attached with aluminum glazing strips, roof vents, and a floor area of eight by 11 feet. The aluminum-frame greenhouses are offered with curved or angled eaves, as freestanding structures or lean-tos in practically any size. Other redwood-frame greenhouses are offered, but a catalog was not available to us by press time. The firm supplies a wide range of accessories to make its buildings plant habitable.

Turner Greenhouses
P.O. Box 1260, Goldsboro, NC 27530-1260
Telephone: 919-734-8345

Catalog price: free

Inexpensive aluminum-frame greenhouses designed to be covered with either flat acrylic-fortified fiberglass or polyethylene. Freestanding models are available in eight- or 14-foot widths, and a seven-foot lean-to design offers a cheaper alternative. Turner claims the buildings are easy to put up (though the brochure hints that a few friends will make the job more pleasant). The lightweight construction simplifies the work of building a foundation—a simple wood-beam or concrete-block base will do. The firm sells benches, heaters, coolers, exhaust fans, humidifiers, and other equipment to make the plants comfortable.

Vegetable Factory, Inc.
71 Vanderbilt Avenue, New York, NY 10169
Telephone: 212-867-0113 or 800-221-2550

Catalog price: $2

Aluminum-frame, double-glazed sun rooms and greenhouses. Those building lean-to structures for human use can cover the sun rooms with clear Plexi-DR. For horticultural use, a less expensive flat fiberglass can be used. The greenhouses can be made in just about any size and shape, from tiny units that extend out from a raised window to freestanding structures 24 feet wide.

Horticultural Tours

Leona Bee Tours & Travel
Glendale Federal Bank Building
18305 Biscayne Boulevard, Suite 211, Miami, FL 33160
Telephone: 305-935-3101

Catalog price: free

Tours for orchid enthusiasts. In 1987 Ms. Bee organized trips to Mexico to coincide with the Mexico Orchid Show in Cuernavaca, and to Vanuatu in the South Pacific. One highlight of all of her "Orchid Adventure" tours is the opportunity to collect native orchids in remote locales.

Boxwood Tours
P.O. Box 1129, Paoli, PA 19301
Telephone: 215-296-9742

Catalog price: free

Boxwood Tours will arrange and plan customized garden tours of the United States and Great Britain. The firm promises that "groups will visit sites that are off the beaten path, enjoy gracious accommodations, and dine at first-class restaurants."

California Kiku Tours
Scott Hitchman, P.O. Box 661694, Sacramento, CA 95866
Telephone: 916-485-8478

Catalog price: free

Mr. Hitchman organized a chrysanthemum tour of Japan in the fall of 1987. Call or write to find out about future trips.

Country Inn Tours
2930 Camino Diablo, Walnut Creek, CA 94596
Telephone: 415-932-1391 or 800-227-2432

Catalog price: free

Garden tours of England. The July 1987 tour stopped at many famous gardens in London and the south of England, among them such commercial nurseries as the Harkness Rose Nursery and David Austin's Roses, where tour members were able to do some plant shopping. Alan Bloom and Beth Chatto gave personal tours of their gardens. Write for information on future tours.

Cox & Kings Travel
21 Dorset Square, London, England NW1 6QG
Telephone: 44-1-724-6624

Catalog price: free

Dozens of tours each year that cater to travelers interested in botany and wildflowers. In 1987 Cox & King led separate tours to Rhodes, Crete, Majorca, Corfu, Corsica, the Swiss Alps, the Italian Dolomites, the Seychelles Islands, and the Spanish Pyrenees. All the trips begin and end in London. Write for information about future tours.

Paul Gripp
1350 More Ranch Road, Santa Barbara, CA 93111
Telephone: 805-967-9798 or 1284

Catalog price: free

Mr. Gripp runs the Santa Barbara Orchid Estate (see entry under *Orchids*, page 131), and, in addition to offering plants from his nursery, he occasionally offers orchid tours and courses. In the spring of 1987, for example, he led a California native orchid hunt, with stops at San Simeon, Big Sur, Point Lobos, the Russian River, and Yosemite.

Limewalk Tours
120 Lake Street, Burlington, VT 05401
Telephone: 802-863-5790

Catalog price: free

European tours that take in plenty of gardens without overdoing it. An August 1987 trip to Scotland included a balance of visits to historic sites and exceptional gardens.

Raoul Moxley Travel
76 Elmbourne Road, London, England SW17 8JJ
Telephone: 44-1-672-2437

Catalog price: free

Botanical tours and expeditions that fly from and return to London. Trips range in length from six days to a full month, depending upon the area visited. Write for the brochure, which is mailed in September.

Serendipity Garden Tours
3 Channing Circle, Cambridge, MA 02138
Telephone: 617-354-1879

Catalog price: free

Offers several garden and wildflower tours each year. 1987 began with a spring trip to view gardens in the San Francisco Bay area, continued with summer ventures to England, the Austrian Alps, the Colorado Rockies, Switzerland, Ireland, and Scotland, and wrapped up with a month-long excursion to Australia and New Zealand.

Thranhardt Travel Service
P.O. Box 5425, Athens, GA 30604
Telephone: 404-549-7081

Catalog price: free

European tours with stops at both historic and horticultural sites. A September 1987 trip roamed through England, Wales, and Scotland, taking in castles and gardens. According to the brochure, "Lectures on propagation, the origins of plant names, plant explorers, and cheese-making often find their way into the itinerary. . . . A wrap-up often includes libation at the local pub."

Hydroponic Growing Supplies

Applied Hydroponics
3135 Kerner Boulevard, San Rafael, CA 94901
Telephone: 415-459-7898 or 800-634-9999

Catalog price: free

Containers, pumps, nutrients, ceramic pellets, and lighting equipment for hydroponic growers. The catalog devotes the most space to lighting equipment, which ranges from halide and sodium bulbs and reflectors to Vita-Lite fluorescent tubes. Track mounts, meters, and timers are also sold.

Applied Hydroponics of Canada
2215 Walkley, Montreal, PQ, Canada H4B 2J9
Telephone: 514-489-3803

Catalog price: $2, deductible from first order

An extensive inventory of hydroponic supplies, many of them appropriate for the hobbyist and home gardener. The catalog includes books, growing mediums, nutrients, containers, pumps, and lighting equipment. The firm sells Floralite light stands, Wonderlite mercury bulbs, and Duro-Lite's Plant-Lite bulbs and Vita-Lite tubes. Orders are welcomed from Canadian and U.S. customers.

CropKing Inc.
P.O. Box 310, Medina, OH 44258
Telephone: 216-725-5656

Catalog price: free

Plastic-covered greenhouses and hydroponic growing-system supplies, primarily for commercial growers. The smallest greenhouse measures 14 by 18 feet, small enough for many backyards. CropKing sells a complete line of greenhouse equipment and supplies, including hydroponic growing sys-

tems. The firm also offers training workshops in hydroponic growing and includes a subscription to a hydroponic growers' newsletter with each package sale.

Green Thumb Hydro-Gardens
P.O. Box 1314, Sheboygan, WI 53081
Telephone: 414-459-8405

Catalog price: free

A modular hydroponic growing system for home gardeners. The firm recommends the system for use "on a balcony, patio, a flat roof, in the yard, around a house trailer, or in a home greenhouse." The firm offers kits in several sizes and configurations, and components for expansion.

Harvest Glow Systems, Inc.
32 E. Fillmore Avenue, St. Paul, MN 55107
Telephone: 612-291-7383 or 800-328-8322 ext. 420

Small-scale hydroponic systems for home growers. The featured window unit is a complete system in a three-foot tray, including a submerged pump. The company also sells self-watering plastic planters, a portable tent-type greenhouse, sodium and metal halide lights, and a small selection of vegetable seeds chosen for hydroponic growing.

Hydro-Gardens, Inc.
P.O. Box 9707, Colorado Springs, CO 80932
Telephone: 303-495-2266 or 2267

Catalog price: free

Hydro-Gardens sells everything for hydroponic gardeners, from a two-foot covered window unit to a 20-foot polyethylene- or fiberglass-covered greenhouse and the systems to fill it. The big catalog is filled with kits, components, hardware, nutrients, and greenhouse equipment.

Windowsill Gardens
Grafton, NH 03240
Telephone: 603-523-7762

Catalog price: free

Small, windowsill-size "Nutriponic" pots and planters, utilizing a system the firm calls "a combination of conventional soil gardening and hydroponics." The planters are essentially two containers stacked together; the upper part holds soil, and the bottom holds a liquid nutrient. A kit comes with planter, instruction book, planting medium, and a bottle of nutrient.

Indoor Gardening Supplies

Aquamonitor

Mist irrigation system for orchid propagation. See under *Irrigation Equipment*, page 226.

Bowman African Violets

P.O. Box 6712, Malibu, CA 90264

Telephone: 213-456-8370

Catalog price: free

Specially designed pots for African violet culture. They hold a reservoir of water and ration it to the plants as needed. To fill the pots, Bowman offers its own African violet soil mix and a leaf-support ring. The firm also sells a small selection of African violet plants.

Dr. James Brasch

Box 354, McMaster Univ., Hamilton, ON, Canada L8S 1C0

Catalog price: $1

Hormones, fungicides, and fertilizers for use in orchid culture. The featured hormone product, Keikigrow, "when applied to a dormant bud on the flower spike of phalaenopsis orchids, will induce the formation of a meristematic duplicate right on the plant."

Clargreen Gardens Ltd.

Orchid-growing supplies. See under *Orchids*, page 122.

DoDe's Gardens, Inc.

1490 Saturn Street, Merritt Island, FL 32953

Telephone: 305-452-5670

Catalog price: two first-class stamps

General growing supplies for houseplants and African violets: potting soil, plant food, insecticides, plant trays and seed-starting inserts, light stands, and books. All products are illustrated and described in a 16-page catalog.

Fischer Greenhouses

See under *African Violets and Other Gesneriads*, page 35.

G & B Orchid Laboratory

Orchid-propagation supplies. See under *Orchids*, page 124.

Glass Roots

J. Kevin Donahue, Ridge Road, Deerfield, NH 03037

Telephone: 603-463-7973

Catalog price: free

Handcrafted plant rooters, all far more attractive than the odd assortment of juice glasses we've been using. The hand-

blown glass vessels are mounted in wrought-iron hangers, which in the brochure are shown twisted with rooting ivy.

The Green House

1432 W. Kerrick Street, Lancaster, CA 93534

Telephone: 805-948-1959

Catalog price: free

Sells the Gro-Cart light stand for raising plants indoors where window light is not sufficiently strong. The stand has three four-foot-wide shelves, each 20 inches deep. The price list includes a quote for UPS shipping to the customer's address.

Holz-Ems Nursery Supplies

P.O. Box 6695, Dept. 304, Orange, CA 92667

Telephone: 714-771-5379

Catalog price: free

Galvanized wire pot hangers and orchid stakes. Send $6 for a sample pack and catalog or write for the price list. The minimum order is $35, which buys a lot of stakes, so only serious growers should inquire.

House of Violets

936-940 Garland Street S.W., Camden, AR 71701

Telephone: 501-836-3016

Catalog price: free

Sells the Swift Moist-Rite planter, a square self-watering flower pot designed for the moisture needs of African violets. The pot should take good care of plants with similar water requirements.

Huronview Nurseries & Garden Centre
Orchid-growing supplies. See under *Orchids*, page 124.

Indoor Gardening Supplies
P.O. Box 40567, Detroit, MI 48240
Telephone: 313-427-6160

Catalog price: free

Light stands, fluorescent fixtures, plastic pots and trays, and an array of timers, soil-testing meters, thermometers, and humidity indicators. The light-stand selection is the best we've seen. Many different styles are offered, in sizes from multishelf units to single self-supported fluorescent fixtures. Some tall, narrow units look like a practical solution for apartments where space is tight.

J & M Tropicals, Inc.
Orchid-growing supplies. See under *Orchids*, page 125.

J. F. Industries
Rt. 4, Box 309-1, Pryor, OK 74361
Telephone: 918-434-6768

Catalog price: self-addressed stamped envelope

African violet leaf supports, designed to fasten to the outside of the pot with an arrangement of rubber bands. The green plastic supports are made in five sizes.

Jerromes Sales/Leasing
P.O. Box 900862, Dallas, TX 75390-0862
Telephone: 214-821-1406 or 229-9375

Catalog price: free

Disposable leaf wipes for houseplants. They clean dust from the leaves with a mild cleanser and oil solution.

Ken-Bar, Inc.
24 Gould Street, Reading, MA 01867
Telephone: 617-944-0003

Catalog price: free

Maker of the Agritape root-zone heating system, an electrically powered heater embedded in a thin plastic film. The system is most economical for smaller growers and looks like an interesting option for windowsill gardeners. The strips come in widths of three or 11 inches and can be cut to any length. The complete system includes a base of Styrofoam insulation, a cover of aluminum mesh screen, and a thermostat-controlled transformer. Ken-Bar also sells row covers and plastic mulches, but in quantities that will put them out of reach for most home gardeners.

Kensington Orchids
Orchid-growing supplies. See under *Orchids*, page 126.

Maine Bentwood Products
Blinn Hill Road, Box 391, E. Pittston, ME 04345
Telephone: 207-582-2592

Catalog price: free

Hanging teardrop plant shelves made of cedar. The outside frame of the unit is bent into a teardrop shape, with straight shelves set inside.

Ann Mann's
Orchid-growing supplies. See under *Orchids*, page 127.

Morel Chemicals
P.O. Box 1167, Englewood, FL 33533

Catalog price: $1

Culture media specially formulated for germinating and replating orchids. Seven different formulas are offered, which, used in various strengths and in combination with differing amounts of dextrose and mashed bananas, provide for the needs of most of the important orchid genera. Morel believes that this genera-specific approach is superior to the all-purpose media generally offered.

OFE International, Inc.
P.O. Box 164402, Miami, FL 33116
Telephone: 305-253-7080

Catalog price: free

A color catalog rich with orchid-growing supplies. Dozens of growing media are offered for different orchids and for different size plants, from basic mixes of tree-fern fiber, redwood chips, and fir bark for mature plants to finer and more complex mixes for seedlings and for phalaenopsis culture. All the mix ingredients are also offered separately for growers who think they have better ideas. The pot department includes tree-fern pots, slatted cedar baskets (for vandaceous orchids), clay pots with slits up the sides, cork slabs, wire baskets with coconut-fiber liners, and some common plastic pots and flats. The catalog also delves deeply into fertilizers, insecticides, fungicides, and hormone preparations.

Oak Hill Gardens
Orchid-growing supplies. See under *Orchids*, page 128.

The Orchid Center
Orchid-growing supplies. See under *Orchids*, page 128.

Orchid Sundries
250a Nine Mile Ride, Wokingham, Berks., England
RG11 3PA
Telephone: 44-734-733883

Catalog price: free

A wide selection of supplies for orchid cultivation presented in a descriptive brochure. Fertilizers, insecticides, fungicides, growing media, and pots are offered, along with such greenhouse equipment as thermostats, fans, and misters. North American customers will have to inquire about export restrictions and duties. The second half of the catalog is taken up by books on orchids, and these we know can be imported without duty or trouble.

Plants 'N' Things
See under *African Violets and Other Gesneriads*, page 37.

Public Service Lamp Corp.
410 W. 16th Street, New York, NY 10011
Telephone: 212-989-5557 or 800-221-4392

Catalog price: free

Wonderlite mercury-vapor flood lamps that fit in standard screw-base sockets and emit full-spectrum lighting for plant growth.

Roberts Flower Supply
12390 Root Road, Columbia Station, OH 44028
Telephone: 216-236-5571

Catalog price: free

A new business that sells more than 130 orchid-related items in a simple descriptive price list. Among the offerings are growing media in both raw form and in mixes, fertilizers, wire hangers and supports, plastic pots, teak and cedar vanda baskets, and watering aids.

Scientific Glass Company
P.O. Box 25125, Albuquerque, NM 87125
Telephone: 505-345-7321

Orchid growers take note: here is a distiller/filtration system for purifying tap water. The firm claims the system will remove 99.7 percent of the impurities from water once it's up and running.

Spiral Filtration
747 N. Twin Oaks Valley Road #13, San Marcos, CA 92069
Telephone: 619-744-3012

Catalog price: free

Water purifiers for orchid growers. Several systems are offered, geared to cope with municipal water supplies or with well water. All work by reverse osmosis.

Tropical Plant Products
P.O. Box 7754, Orlando, FL 32804
Telephone: 305-293-2451 or 2453

Catalog price: free

Orchid-growing supplies, including growing media, fertilizers, fungicides, pots, wire baskets, and an exceptional collection of tree-fern products—from slabs, balls, and pots to planters carved into monkey shapes by Mayan Indians.

Verilux Inc.
P.O. Box 1512, Greenwich, CT 06836
Telephone: 203-869-3750

Catalog price: free

Manufacturer of the Verilux TruBloom fluorescent lamp, a full-spectrum plant light with a balanced white color

(6000K). The firm claims that the lamps promote compact growth and that they induce plants to hold their blooms longer than they would under competing lights. Verilux's bulbs have received good reviews from indoor growers (attested to by the packet of articles sent with the brochure). They are available only by mail and must be ordered in case quantities (six of one size per case).

The Violet House
P.O. Box 1274, Gainesville, FL 32601
Telephone: 904-377-8465

Catalog price: free

Supplies for African violet growers, including potting materials, fertilizers, rooting compounds, pest controls, reservoir planters, soil and weather meters, leaf supports, and African violet seed. The firm will ship just about anywhere in the world.

The Violet Showcase
3147 S. Broadway, Englewood, CO 80110
Telephone: 303-761-1770

Catalog price: $1

A big selection of growing supplies and books for African violet devotees. The container inventory includes plastic pots and tubs, wicking trays, reservoir planters, and ornamental ceramic pots shaped like baskets and seashells. A number of plant stands are offered as well as a good choice of fertilizers and remedies. If you still can't get your violets up to snuff, the firm sells artificial violets made of silk. For a description of the nursery's plant listings, see entry under *African Violets and Other Gesneriads*, page 39.

Volkman Bros. Greenhouses
See under *African Violets and Other Gesneriads*, page 39.

Irrigation Equipment

Aquamonitor
P.O. Box 327, Huntington, NY 11743
Telephone: 516-427-5664

Catalog price: free

A mist irrigation system with a built-in sensor that controls water flow. The mister keeps humidity high and controls daytime temperature, factors important to orchid growers and rose propagators. The system is most often used in greenhouses, though Aquamonitor claims it can also be useful for outdoor plant propagation.

Aquatic Systems, Inc.
619e E. Gutierrez Street, Santa Barbara, CA 93103
Telephone: 805-965-5125 or 800-445-8457

Catalog price: free

A drip irrigation system in kits designed for both home gardeners and larger-scale growers. The firm sells a complete line of backup components, including timers, adapters, filters, solvents, and fertilizer injectors.

C & C Products
Rt. 3, Hereford, TX 79045
Telephone: 806-276-5338

Catalog price: free

The Big Drop watering system. We're tempted to call this a sprinkler, but C & C makes a point of distinguishing it from those devices. Its slogan: "We don't sprinkle . . . we water." The Big Drop waterer spews larger drops than a standard sprinkler. It can be raised to cover a 60-foot circle, lowered to water a 40-foot span, or tilted to water a narrow strip.

The Dramm Company
Long-handled watering nozzles. See under *Tools*, page 237.

Drip Irrigation Garden
16216 Raymer Street, Van Nuys, CA 91406
Telephone: 818-989-5999

Catalog price: 25¢

Drip-irrigation kits and components. Three starter kits provide 50 feet of tubing and the necessary connectors, plugs, filters, and drippers. Gardeners can put together larger or smaller systems from the list of components. Micro-sprinklers for irrigating lawns and groundcovers are also offered.

Ever-Tite Coupling Co.
254 W. 54th Street, New York, NY 10019
Telephone: 212-265-1420

Catalog price: free

Snap-shut hose couplings for those who have to connect and disconnect hoses and irrigation equipment frequently. The cam-locking couplings seal tight without twisting and threading.

Fogg-It Nozzle Co.
P.O. Box 16053, San Francisco, CA 94116
Telephone: 415-665-1212

Catalog price: free

A misting nozzle designed to fit on an ordinary garden hose, offered either by itself or with extension handles and shut-off valves. The nozzles are available in many garden-supply stores, but the firm will also sell directly to customers by mail.

Green Grow, Inc.
Box 53596, Lubbock, TX 79453
Telephone: 800-527-2716 or 806-745-3344

Catalog price: free

Drip-irrigation kits and components. The catalog describes the benefits of drip irrigation in some detail and gives instructions for choosing and installing your own system.

Harmony Farm Supply
P.O. Box 451, Graton, CA 95444
Telephone: 707-823-9125

Catalog price: $2

Offers a full line of drip- and micro-sprinkler irrigation equipment, with an introductory text that explains how to design a system to answer particular irrigation needs and how to choose among the hundreds of components offered. The firm also carries a good selection of beneficial insects and other biological pest controls.

International Irrigation Systems
LPO 160, 1555 Third Avenue, Niagara Falls, NY 14304
Telephone: 416-688-4090

Catalog price: free

Sells Irrigro drip-irrigation systems in kits and components. The main feature of the system is the porous Irrigro tubing, which "weeps water along its full length." Because the systems require no additional drip outlets, they are relatively inexpensive. The basic garden kit contains 100 feet of tubing, eight feet of header hose, and the necessary plugs and connectors. Canadian customers should contact the firm at P.O. Box 1133, St. Catharines, ON L2R 7A3.

International Trading Corp.
362 Commonwealth Avenue, Boston, MA 02115
Telephone: 617-424-7033

Catalog price: $2

Sirotex hose and sprinkler systems, which look like a match for the more commonly available Gardena systems. Hoses come with coil reels or portable roll-up boxes (which look like oversize measuring tapes made of red and gray plastic). Sprinklers come in a range of designs, from hand-held spray nozzles to oscillating and spinning types to a stationary mister. Other attachments convert the hose into a garden shower or a carwash. One of the selling points is Sirotex's Quick-Fit coupling system, which snaps hoses to sprinklers without twisting and which automatically shuts off the water when uncoupled.

Lone Fir Farms
Star Rt., Box 461, Gales Creek, OR 97117-9800
Telephone: 503-357-7688

Catalog price: self-addressed stamped envelope

Low-volume, low-pressure sprinklers sold at reasonable prices.

MOR
P.O. Box 504, Kiryat-Gat, 82-I04, Israel

Catalog price: $1, deductible from first order

Modular sprinkler and mister systems designed for low-volume operation. The featured sprinkler head is produced to operate at specific flow rates, from ten to 40 gallons an hour. Gardeners choose the rate when they order. A half dozen other sprinklers and sprayers are offered that spew a range of drop sizes to different distances under different water pressures.

Miser Irrigation Systems
P.O. Box 94616, Lincoln, NE 68509-4616
Telephone: 402-467-1369

Catalog price: free

Miser drip-irrigation systems designed for vegetable and flower gardens. Several beginning kits are offered, along with a big line of components. The Miser system drips water from

emitter attachments rather than from holes in the hose itself, so water can be directed to trickle out only where needed. The system can be set up to water potted plants. Wind chimes and an ornamental windmill are offered as sidelines.

Misti Maid, Inc.
5500 Boscell Common, Fremont, CA 94538
Telephone: 415-656-5777

Low-volume irrigation systems that can be designed to combine drip emitters, soaker hoses (porous tubing), micro-sprinklers, and misters. Starter kits let gardeners try the different methods of watering either alone or in combination. Those more confident of their needs can shop from the big list of components.

Moss Products Inc.
P.O. Box 72, Palmetto, FL 33561
Telephone: 813-729-5433

Catalog price: free

Drip-, mist-, and micro-spray irrigation systems. Kits offer gardeners a taste of each method, but come with only 24 feet of tubing. Bigger systems can be assembled from the component list. Most of the offerings in the general brochure are designed for the home garden, but overhead misters and sprinklers are also sold for greenhouse use.

Plastic Plumbing Products, Inc.
17005 Manchester Road, P.O. Box 186, Grover, MO 63040
Telephone: 314-458-2226

Catalog price: $1, deductible from first order

Sells the Rain Run drip-irrigation system, which can be purchased as a kit with 100 feet of tubing or in components. The firm has a larger catalog of irrigation equipment that it was not able to send us by our deadline.

Quality Sprinkler
P.O. Box 7064, Kennewick, WA 99336
Telephone: 509-547-0051 or 800-345-9038

Catalog price: free

Four rotary sprinklers with a choice of bases. The primary model for lawn and garden spray comes in either metal or high-impact plastic and can be affixed to a spike, a three-foot tripod stand, or a ground-level sled base. A "pop-up" sprinkler is designed to be embedded in the lawn, and a low-angle waterer is made to spray under trees.

Raindrip, Inc.
P.O. Box 2173, Chatsworth, CA 91313-2173
Telephone: 818-718-8004 or 800-544-3747

Catalog price: free

Drip- and micro-sprinkler irrigation systems. Raindrip claims its systems are less prone to clogging because of its "turbulent flow" drippers and points out that its pressure regulator maintains an even flow of moisture under a range of temperature conditions. Several kits are available for vegetable gardens, trees and shrubs, and container plants. A full line of components is sold for gardeners who want to custom design their systems or who want to add on to existing equipment.

Rose Tender
1049 Mockingbird Lane, Van Wert, OH 45891

Low-angle sprinklers that water roses at their bases and leave no water spots on the upper leaves. The basic model shoots water in a full circle; one attachment confines the flow to two sides for watering narrow beds; another sprays water higher for watering lawns.

Sides Irrigation
Box 510, 832 Oak Street, Coffeeville, MS 38922
Telephone: 601-675-8218

Catalog price: free

Trickle- and micro-spray irrigation supplies, from 50- and 100-foot starter kits from Submatic to components like fertilizer applicators, pressure gauges, and back-flow preventers. Systems can be tailored to water vegetable gardens, orchards, lawns, and hanging plants.

Spot Systems
5812 Machine Drive, Huntington Beach, CA 92649-1101
Telephone: 714-891-1115 or 800-854-7649

Catalog price: free

Drip- and micro-sprinkler irrigation systems for small and large growers. Several kits are offered, or tubing can be bought in 100-foot coils (or 2,500-foot reels) with the necessary emitters, misters, and low-volume sprinklers. A pressure regulator keeps the system running evenly.

Submatic Irrigation Systems
P.O. Box 246, Lubbock, TX 79408
Telephone: 806-747-9000 or 800-858-4016

Catalog price: free

Drip- and sprinkler-irrigation systems that should satisfy the needs of large-scale growers as well as backyard gardeners with a few thirsty vegetables. A beginner's kit with 50 feet of tubing and 25 drip emitters offers the most basic watering solution. Far more extensive and elaborate systems can be built from the components, which include ten different drip emitters, a handful of micro-sprinklers, larger-area impact sprinklers (some in pop-up housings for lawn use), as well as a full line of couplings, plugs, elbows, adapters, valves, and filters. Prices range from $15 for the smallest kit to more than $15,000 for the largest filter.

Trickle Soak Systems
P.O. Box 38, Santee, CA 92071-0038
Telephone: 619-449-6408

Catalog price: $2.50, deductible from first order

This firm produces the fattest of the irrigation catalogs (and the most expensive, if you don't place an order). Page after page of hoses, couplings, emitters, and more extravagant valves and filters are offered, in a range of choices that will leave novices bewildered. A dozen types of plastic hose are offered, for example, in a pyramid of sizes, with no explanation of why one is preferable to another. Fifteen different drip emitters and an array of sprinklers and foggers are similarly displayed with a minimum of description. Gardeners who know these ropes may find exactly what they need.

The Urban Farmer Store
2121 Taraval Street, San Francisco, CA 94116
Telephone: 415-661-2204

Catalog price: $1

The folks at the Urban Farmer Store want us to understand drip irrigation before we buy, and the introduction they send out with their brochure offers a clear and concise analysis of the subject. The differences between various emitters and other components are discussed, as well as strategies for planning a system that best solves the problems individual gardeners face. The firm sells no kits, but the text helps gardeners sort through the many emitters, micro-sprinklers, filters, pressure regulators, and fertilizer injectors that are offered.

Outdoor Lighting

Genie House

P.O. Box 2478, Red Lion Road, Vincentown, NJ 08088
Telephone: 609-859-0600

Catalog price: free

Handcrafted outdoor lighting fixtures made of glass panes framed by antiqued copper, brass, and tin. The designs are inspired by colonial lanterns and candle holders and are available in wall- or post-mounted models.

Hanover Lantern

Hoffman Products, Inc., 470 High Street, Hanover, PA 17331

Outdoor post- and wall-mounted lighting fixtures in a variety of styles. One model suggests a Japanese lantern, another a ship's beacon, and one a colonial street lamp. Several are more contemporary looking. All are offered with, or can be converted to, a low-voltage (12-volt) electrical system, which is safer where there is a chance that the wiring might be pierced by digging pets and children or by adults working in the yard.

Philip Hawk & Company

159 E. College Avenue, Pleasant Gap, PA 16823
Telephone: 814-355-7177

Catalog price: $3

Hand-carved stone lanterns inspired by traditional Japanese designs, but interpreted with more modern lines. Mr. Hawk presents his work in an attractive black-and-white portfolio, each piece pictured on a separate sheet. 1987 prices ranged from $1,100 to $3,600, excluding shipping.

Heritage Lanterns

70A Main Street, Yarmouth, ME 04096
Telephone: 207-846-3911

Catalog price: $2, deductible from first order

As its name suggests, Heritage Lanterns sells lighting fixtures in old-fashioned styles. Some are reproductions of actual colonial lamps; some are derivations from old designs. Most of the lanterns in this color catalog are made for outdoor use, and most can be mounted either atop a post or on a wall. The firm is best known for its onion-globe lamp, an unusual lantern with a blown-glass light ball sandwiched between an antiqued metal base and the top socket.

Nightscaping

1705 E. Colton Avenue, Redlands, CA 92373
Telephone: 714-794-2121

Catalog price: $2

Specialty outdoor, indoor, and underwater lighting in a slick color catalog that offers bits of design guidance along with the merchandise. Most of Nightscaping's fixtures are modern designs, and many are meant to be concealed by plantings, their light drawing attention to features of the garden rather than the lighting hardware itself. Exceptions are the "El Camino," a reproduction of the bell-shaped lamp found on California's El Camino Real, and the "Tikiliter," a combination kerosene torch and electric floodlight. All the lights are designed for use with 12-volt wiring, a safer outdoor option than standard household current. Several transformers and timers are offered to help you complete your installation.

Strassacker Bronze, Inc.

See under *Garden Ornaments*, page 210.

Wendelighting

2445 N. Naomi Street, Burbank, CA 91504
Telephone: 818-995-8066

Catalog price: free

This operation makes some deluxe projection lighting devices for indoor use (for spotlighting artwork and architectural features) as well as an outdoor walk reflector that beams light up from an inconspicuous ground-level fixture.

WoodForm, Inc.

9705 N.E. Colfax Street, Portland, OR 97220
Telephone: 503-253-9626 or 800-624-5091

Catalog price: free

Garden lighting mounted in subdued and unobtrusive wooden posts (the fixtures shine from carved-out holes). As you thumb through the catalog, the posts grow thicker, and at about the midway point they begin to be referred to as bollards. We looked the word up and learned that bollards are the wharf posts to which ships tie their lines. The thickest bollards from WoodForm are about 11 inches across; the tallest stand seven feet high. The firm makes benches and trash receptacles that complement the look of the lights.

Pest Controls

All Pest Control
6030 Grenville Lane, Lansing, MI 48910
Telephone: 517-646-0038

Catalog price: free

Biological pest controls in quantities suitable both for home gardeners and large commercial growers. *Nosema locustae*, for example, a biological insecticide that affects grasshoppers and crickets, can be bought to treat a single acre or 10,000 acres. The price list is amazingly informative, explaining how all the treatments work and how to put them to the best use. In addition to biological insecticides, the firm sells traps, netting, diatomaceous earth, botanical and mineral pesticides, organic fertilizers, and composting aids.

Alternative
Biological pest controls. See under *Tools*, page 236.

Beneficial Insectary
245 Oak Run Road, Oak Run, CA 96069
Telephone: 916-472-3715

Ladybugs, trichogramma wasps, lacewings, and praying mantises offered as natural pest controls. The one-page flier explains how each of the bugs helps out in the garden and how they should be cared for.

Bio-Control Co.
P.O. Box 337, Berry Creek, CA 95916
Telephone: 916-589-5227

Catalog price: free

This firm's letterhead pictures an enlarged ladybug crawling along a stem toward a tiny aphid. That lopsided gladiatorial spirit sets the tone for this educational brochure. Ladybugs, lacewings, trichogramma wasps, and praying mantises are sold, with brief chapters describing the behavior and care of each. The firm also sells a solution it calls Bio-Control Honeydew, which it claims attracts and nourishes beneficial insects and "stimulates some to produce or lay eggs."

Bio-Resources
1210 Birch Street, Santa Paula, CA 93060
Telephone: 805-525-0526

Catalog price: free

Beneficial insects, offered in a descriptive brochure that explains which pest bugs each of them eats and what care they need to get established in your garden. The firm sells lacewing larvae, trichogramma wasps, predatory mites, whitefly parasites (*Encarsia formosa*), fly parasites, ladybugs, and mealybug predators (*Cryptolaemus montrouzieri*).

Bonide Chemical Co.
2 Wurz Avenue, Yorkville, NY 13495
Telephone: 315-736-8231

Catalog price: free

Chemical pesticides, fungicides, and herbicides, along with a few biological and organic control measures. The color catalog shows dozens of products from tree-wound paint and organic compost aids to malathion, flying-insect sprays (chemical insecticides), and rotenone (an organic insecticide).

Down to Earth
850 W. 2nd Street, Eugene, OR 97402
Telephone: 503-485-5932

Catalog price: free (request insect control brochure)

Organic insect controls. Down to Earth sells the full line of Safer's insecticidal soaps, including the standard garden formula, a formula for fruits and vegetables, a cryptocidal soap to eliminate mosses and lichens from walks and woodwork, and a pet soap to control fleas, lice, and ticks. The firm sells ladybugs for the control of aphids and spider mites and *Bacillus thuringiensis* for whiteflies, caterpillars, and worms.

The Dramm Company
Sprayers. See under *Tools*, page 237.

E. R. & Son Farm
Sprayers. See under *Tools*, page 238.

Great Lakes IPM
10220 Church Road N.E., Vestaburg, MI 48891
Telephone: 517-268-5693

Catalog price: free

Traps and lure for monitoring insect populations. A few of the listings, such as the Japanese beetle trap, can be used to help reduce insect infestations, but most are intended as measuring devices to check the effectiveness and aid in the scheduling of other insect-control measures.

Green Earth Organics
Natural pest controls. See under *Fertilizers*, page 198.

The Greener Thumb
Organic pest controls. See under *Tools*, page 239.

Growing Naturally
Organic pest controls. See under *General Gardening Supplies*, page 186.

Harmony Farm Supply
Organic pest controls. See under *Irrigation Equipment*, page 226.

I. F. M.
333-B Ohme Garden Road, Wenatchee, WA 98801
Telephone: 509-662-3179 or 1922

Catalog price: free

A richly informative catalog of natural pest controls and organic soil additives and fertilizers. To start gardeners off on the right foot, the firm offers a range of soil and plant-tissue tests, including checks for toxic residues. The fertilizer offerings range from bone meal and bat guano to green manure seed and foliar-spray fertilizers. Beneficial predators and parasites, botanical pesticides, and traps make up the pest-control section of the list. The extensive text gives directions for using each method. A comprehensive guide to natural pest management for orchardists takes up several pages of the booklet.

Insects Limited, Inc.
10505 N. College Avenue, Indianapolis, IN 46280-1438
Telephone: 317-846-3399

Catalog price: free

Insect traps and pheromone lures. The minimum order is $50, which will buy more traps than most yards can hold.

InterNet, Inc.
2730 Nevada Avenue N., Minneapolis, MN 55427
Telephone: 612-541-9690 or 800-328-8456

Catalog price: free

Plastic netting for keeping birds away from crop plants.

The Natural Gardening Company
Organic pest controls. See under *General Gardening Supplies*, page 187.

Natural Gardening Research Center
Hwy. 48, P.O. Box 149, Sunman, IN 47041

Catalog price: free

Dozens of clinical color pictures in this catalog show the ravages of garden pests and diseases. After a couple of pages, the views of rotting fruit and shriveled leaves have us crying for mercy—which the firm offers in abundance in the form of organic pest controls and cures. This is a terrific introduction to organic controls for beginners, and veterans will find this firm's offerings as comprehensive as any. Organic fertilizers complement the pest-control end of the list, and seed and nutrients are offered for a chemical-free lawn.

Nature's Control
P.O. Box 35, Medford, OR 97501
Telephone: 503-899-8318

Catalog price: free

Beneficial insects for the control of garden pests. Four different species of predatory mites, each thriving under different climatic conditions, make meals of spider mites. Ladybugs and green lacewing larvae munch on aphids, scales, and other soft-bodied insects. Other predatory offerings eat whitefly scales and mealybugs. Whitefly traps and insecticidal soap help out when the predators are between snacks.

Necessary Trading Co.
New Castle, VA 24127
Telephone: 703-864-5103

Catalog price: $2

An extensive inventory of biological pest controls, organic fertilizers, composting equipment, and books. Pest controls include (among many others) diatomaceous earth (for slugs), grasshopper spore disease, milky spore disease (for Japanese beetles), nematodes (for grubs), natural poisons like rotenone, pyrethrin, and sabadilla, beneficial insects, as well as fly-swatters, traps, and netting. The "soil-building" department is just as well stocked, and the book collection looks like an important resource for anyone who gardens without chemicals.

Ohio Earth Food, Inc.
Natural pest controls. See under *Fertilizers*, page 199.

Peaceful Valley Farm Supply
Organic pest controls. See under *General Gardening Supplies*, page 188.

Rincon-Vitova Insectaries, Inc.
P.O. Box 95, Oak View, CA 93022
Telephone: 805-643-5407 or 800-248-BUGS

Catalog price: free

Beneficial insects from a firm that's been supplying them to commercial growers since 1948. A descriptive brochure for home gardeners counts among its offerings green lacewings, trichogramma wasps, mealybug predators, whitefly parasites,

ladybugs, predatory mites, and fly parasites, each of which eats quantities of various garden pests. The brochure describes the appetite of each bug.

Rocky Mountain Insectary
P.O. Box 152, Palisade, CO 81526

Catalog price: free

Sells pedio wasps (*Pedioblus foveolatus*), which in their larval stage feed on the Mexican bean beetle.

Safe-N-Sound
P.O. Box 153, 116 Main Street, Garrison, IA 52229
Telephone: 319-477-5041 or 800-255-2255 ext. CAGE

Catalog price: free

Wire-mesh traps for capturing but not injuring bothersome animals. Once trapped, they can be relocated to a place where they'll no longer be yard and garden pests. One model is big enough for a coyote or a lynx, another small enough for field mice. A solid-covered sheet-metal trap is recommended when a skunk is the quarry.

Seabright Enterprises
4026 Harlan Street, Emeryville, CA 94608
Telephone: 415-655-3126

Catalog price: free

Sells a sticky paste called Stikem Special, which can be used to trap flying insects, to keep birds from roosting in unwanted spots (they don't like the feel of the substance on their feet), and to keep crawling and climbing creatures out of trees (you paint a barrier ring around the base of the trunk). The material is odorless and can be used with scented lures.

Spalding Laboratories
760 Printz Road, Arroyo Grande, CA 93420
Telephone: 805-489-5946

Catalog price: free

Sells predatory insects that feed on the pupa of pest flies (primarily manure- and filth-breeding flies). Several different predatory species are lumped together by the firm and sold in a mixture it calls Fly Predators. A cone-shaped mesh fly trap is also sold. These pest flies are more of a problem for animal farmers than home gardeners, but, if your gardening involves manure or if you are bothered by flies around your composter, perhaps these predators will be a help.

Techfence
P.O. Box A, Marlboro, NJ 07746-0139
Telephone: 201-462-6101

Catalog price: free

High-tensile electric fencing that can be used to keep pets and farm animals in or problem animals out. Gardeners will probably be most interested in the fences as pest-control barriers; the mild shock will keep deer, racoons, and other marauders out of the garden.

Unique Insect Control
5504 Sperry Drive, Citrus Heights, CA 95621
Telephone: 916-961-7945 or 967-7082

Catalog price: free

An array of beneficial insects in a brochure with extensive explanatory text. Ladybugs, praying mantises, fly parasites, green lacewings, and trichogramma wasps are offered, and customers are given full instructions on how to establish them in the garden. Red earthworms are also sold, along with a few odd tools and books.

W-W Grinder, Inc.
Power sprayers. See under *Tools*, page 242.

West Coast Ladybug Sales
P.O. Box 903, Gridley, CA 95948
Telephone: 916-534-0840

Catalog price: self-addressed stamped envelope

Ladybugs, praying mantises, lacewings, trichogramma wasps, and fly parasites for use as organic pest controls. The price list is sent with copies of several articles on beneficial insects (some from competitors' catalogs) and instructions on how to care for the bugs when they arrive.

Plant Labels and Markers

AE Products
45 Burr Farms Road, Westport, CT 06880

No catalog or price list

Stiff plastic plant markers, 9/16 inch wide, sold in 30-inch strips that gardeners can cut to suit their purposes. In 1987 100 strips cost $15 postpaid. Write for current prices.

Economy Label Sales Co.
P.O. Box 350, Daytona Beach, FL 32015
Telephone: 904-253-4741 or 800-874-4465

Catalog price: $2

Plastic plant labels and garden markers in dozens of styles. Gardeners can choose from flexible wraparound labels in many widths and lengths or stiff pot labels to stick in the soil. All labels are sold by the thousand. The firm will print on any label for an extra charge.

EON Industries
P.O. Box 853, Holland, OH 43528

Catalog price: free

Metal garden markers in two styles and several sizes. All have galvanized standards and zinc nameplates. The nameplates can be written on with grease pencil or with a fine-pointed permanent marker such as Sanford's Sharpie pen. EON sells its markers in boxes of 25 or by the hundred and thousand.

Evergreen Garden Plant Labels
P.O. Box 922, Cloverdale, CA 95425

Catalog price: free

Permanent garden markers with enameled-aluminum nameplates made to order. Evergreen will make nameplates for any registered iris, rose, daylily, daffodil, or peony cultivar (and for any species on that list of plants). The plates include the varietal name and beneath it the hybridizer's name and the year of introduction. If you want plates made for other plants or for unregistered cultivars, inquire about custom prices. Evergreen also sells an inexpensive galvanized metal bloom-stalk support, which looks like a savior for delphiniums, gladioli, and other fragile plants. The supports are 30 inches tall, with an open hook at the top.

Harlane Company
See under *Tools*, page 239.

International Nursery Labels
7000 Soquel Drive #333, Aptos, CA 95003
Telephone: 408-684-1007

Catalog price: self-addressed stamped envelope

Plastic wraparound plant labels and stiff plastic markers sold either plain or printed. The minimum order for plain labels is 500 of a single style. Printed labels must be ordered by the thousand. White and yellow are the standard colors, but the firm can make them from red, green, orange, or pink plastic for a small extra charge.

A. M. Leonard, Inc.
See under *Tools*, page 240.

Paw Paw Everlast Label Co.
P.O. Box 93-C, Paw Paw, MI 49079-0093

Catalog price: free

Zinc plant labels in an array of sizes and shapes. The simplest tags are made to tie on or wrap around the plant. Several others come on wire standards for inserting in the dirt; the tallest of these is almost two feet from point to nameplate. The firm claims that the zinc nameplates properly marked with pencil or crayon will remain legible for years.

F. R. Unruh
37 Oaknoll Road, Wilmington, DE 19808
Telephone: 302-994-2328

Catalog price: self-addressed stamped envelope

Metal plant markers sold by the hundred. The nameplates are either white- or green-enameled aluminum and can be ordered in two sizes (two by three inches or two by six inches). The wire stakes come in heights of 4½ or 11½ inches.

Planters

Allen, Sterling & Lothrop
Wooden barrels and tubs. See under *General Flowers and Vegetables*, page 13.

Bench Craft
Hardwood planters. See under *Furniture*, page 201.

The Bradbury Barrel Co.
P.O. Box A, Bridgewater, ME 04735
Telephone: 207-429-8141

Catalog price: free

Wooden barrels and tubs in a range of sizes, offered in raw form or with plastic liners. The containers are intended as merchandise displays for stores and supermarkets, but they also make excellent planters. Be prepared to buy a few, however. The minimum order is $100.

Erkins Studios, Inc.
Stone and terracotta planters. See under *Garden Ornaments*, page 208.

Jaffrey Manufacturing, Inc.
Wooden buckets. See under *Cider and Wine Presses*, page 197.

David Kay, Inc.
See under *Gifts for Gardeners*, page 213.

Living Wall Gardening Co.
See under *General Gardening Supplies*, page 186.

Kenneth Lynch & Sons, Inc.
Cast-stone planters. See under *Garden Ornaments*, page 209.

Mrs. McGregor's Garden Shop
Teak planters. See under *Gifts for Gardeners*, page 213.

Miller Nurseries
Wooden barrels. See under *Trees and Shrubs*, page 159.

Reed Bros.
Hand-carved redwood planters. See under *Furniture*, page 204.

Joe Reed, Woodsmith
Georgetown, ME 04548

Catalog price: $1, deductible from first order

"Chateau" planter boxes with a European flair. Most have ball finials on the corners; one is decorated with Portuguese tiles. The boxes are finished with polyurethane deck enamel, white on the outside and green on the inside, and fitted with plastic inserts.

San Luis Plastics Products
P.O. Box 12559, San Luis Obispo, CA 93406
Telephone: 805-549-0700

Catalog price: free

Stacking plastic barrel planters with side pockets, which allow gardeners to plant in "high-rise" format where garden space is limited. These look like good vessels for growing strawberries, smaller vegetables, or flowers on patios, balconies, or porches.

Smith & Hawken
Italian terracotta planters. See under *Tools*, page 241.

Southern Statuary & Stone
See under *Garden Ornaments*, page 210.

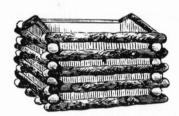

Sweetbriar Logs
507 Mt. Holyoke Avenue, Pacific Palisades, CA 90272
Telephone: 213-459-LOGS

Catalog price: free

Planters made to look like tree stumps and fallen logs. The owners got the idea for these unusual containers on a camping trip. After years of experimentation, they've managed to make convincing reproductions of actual logs, complete with rough bark, wormholes, knots, scars—even growth rings and saw marks on the ends. We haven't seen the planters in person, but from the photographs these look like museum-quality copies of trailside specimens. Shoppers who want to add a sylvan touch to a flower bed, wildflower garden, or porch can choose from vertical stumps (from seven inches to three feet tall), hollowed-out fallen logs (from three to eight feet long), or from hanging stumps and wall pockets. All are made of high-density polyurethane foam. If the logs are to be used indoors, brass caps are put over the drainage holes.

Prints, Posters, and Cards

Arts & Flowers of Cider Hill Farm

Rt. 1, Box 1066, Windsor, VT 05089-9728
Telephone: 802-674-5293

Catalog price: $1

Prints and cards of botanical watercolors by Gary and Sarah Milek. Gary is the artist in the partnership, Sarah the herbalist. Together they've produced a series of attractive paintings, among them a garden of culinary herbs, an arrangement of wedding herbs, and a profusion of wildflowers. The $1 fee buys a set of sample cards and a price list of the larger prints.

Colonial Williamsburg

Reproductions of 18th-century botanical prints. See under *Garden Ornaments*, page 208.

Graven Images

R. & L. Johnson, 4211 Seneca, Chattanooga, TN 37409
Telephone: 615-821-7473

Catalog price: $1

Rubber stamps of plants, flowers, trees, bugs, and birds. The stamped prints make an artistic production out of the simplest letter or postcard. Once you've mastered the basic technique, you can try inking the stamps in multiple colors with the use of watercolor pens. Or try combining the prints by adding leaves to flowers and planting your creations in stamped flowerpots.

Island Designs

25 Cleftstone Road, Bar Harbor, ME 04609
Telephone: 207-288-4250

Catalog price: $1

Embossed greeting cards printed in soft colors and picturing dozens of different flowers and animals. Poppies, lupines, morning glories, and ladyslippers are among the subjects, each design subtly textured and raised from the surface in the embossing process. All the cards are illustrated in the color flier.

Larkspur Graphics

P.O. Box 10-4680, Anchorage, AK 99510
Telephone: 907-274-0404

Catalog price: free

Andie Thrams creates an exceptionally beautiful single-sheet calendar featuring flowers that grow wild in Alaska. Wild iris, arctic lupine, and wild calypso orchid have been featured in past years. The 1988 calendar pictures the chocolate lily. Ms. Thrams has only strayed from the course twice, when she illustrated the California poppy and alstroemeria, neither of which ranges naturally in her state. Each calendar is hand printed in soft silkscreened colors, in compositions that make the most of the flowers' natural forms. Past years' designs can be had as note cards.

Richters

Culinary herb posters. See under *Herbs*, page 102.

Susan Riecken

P.O. Box 102, Cambridge, MA 02140

Catalog price: $1

An artist whose chosen medium is the hand-carved rubber stamp and whose inspirations come from the garden and the kitchen. Every year she publishes a desk calendar laced with quotes on gardening and charming color prints of flowers, vegetables, fruits, tools, and kitchen implements. The quotes are culled from 18th- and 19th-century garden texts and from such writers as Thomas Jefferson, Gilbert White, Flora Thompson, and Isabella Beeton. The pictures combine a sharpness of detail and a subtle blending of color with a wonderful homespun appeal. Riecken also prints a poster called "Thinking of a Garden," as well as correspondence cards and gift cards, all printed in color. The information packet comes with color samples of her work.

Rubber Stamps of America

P.O. Box 567, Saxtons River, VT 05154
Telephone: 802-869-2622

Catalog price: free

This firm sells exquisite little rubber stamps of wildflowers and wild beasts. About a dozen wildflower designs by artist Vivian Day are offered, along with stamp pads in an array of exotic colors.

Soil- and Disease-Testing Services

Critter Creek Laboratory
400 Critter Creek Road, Lincoln, CA 95648
Telephone: 916-645-8520

Catalog price: free

Disease testing for orchids. The firm will test for cymbidium mosaic virus and for tobacco mosaic virus and will develop tests for any other orchid virus disease. In addition to its testing services, the firm sells test kits.

Freedom Soil Lab
P.O. Box 1144, Freedom, CA 95019-1144
Telephone: 408-724-4427

Catalog price: free

A soil-testing service that measures nitrogen, phosphorus, potassium, calcium, magnesium, sulphur, toxic salts, pH, and humus. The results are sent out with recommendations for correcting any problems that may be detected.

Micro Essential Laboratory, Inc.
4224 Avenue H, Brooklyn, NY 11210
Telephone: 718-338-3618

Catalog price: free

An extensive line of test kits for indicating levels of acidity, humidity, iodine, chlorine, and other chemical and climatic conditions. The Hydrion pH soil tester is the one that will be of interest to most gardeners. It comes with a reference chart showing the pH preferences of several hundred house and garden plants. When you write to the firm, be sure to ask for the retail price list.

Tools

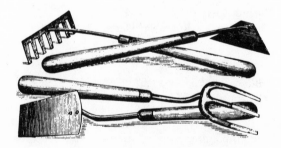

The Alsto Company
P.O. Box 1267, Galesburg, IL 61401
Telephone: 309-343-6181 or 800-447-8192 (orders only)

Catalog price: free

Adjustable-width rakes, programmable sprinklers, long-handled weeders—the Alsto's catalog is full of garden-tool innovations. Their long-handled bulb planter is the cheapest we've seen, and the Bionic Ear, a telescopic listening device, would make some bird-watcher/gardener a most surprising birthday present. Alsto's sells sheepskin gloves, cast-iron boot scrapers, and classic steel shell-back lawn chairs at reasonable prices.

Alternative
3439 E. 86th Street, Suite 259D, Indianapolis, IN 46240
Telephone: 800-423-0876

Catalog price: free

Hand tools, measuring devices, sprayers, and biological pest controls laid out in a small color brochure. The firm sells a good selection of pruning equipment—Felco pruners, pruning saws, long-handled clippers, and lopping shears—along with an array of weather meters, including thermometers, rain gauges, and humidity indicators. Among the pest controls offered are beneficial insects, insecticidal soap, sticky traps, and animal repellents.

Garden Way cart is the one that looks like a big wooden box mounted on two bicycle wheels. With the wheels on the sides, these carts are less strain to use than the traditional wheelbarrow, as the weight of the load rests efficiently on the wheels rather than on the user's arms and back. We've never tried the Troy-Bilt tillers, but we know they are widely used, and Garden Way's literature is full of letters from happy customers. The largest tillers, the six-, seven-, and eight-horsepower models, can be converted into log splitters, generators, and even two-wheeled tractors for dragging heavy carts. The Tomahawk chipper isn't quite that versatile, though it is capable both of shredding leaves for compost and of chipping heavy branches. If you write for any of these products, be prepared for a steady stream of mail. Garden Way has a vigorous sales staff.

Gardener's Eden

Left-handed Felco pruners. See under *Gifts for Gardeners,* page 212.

Gardener's Supply Co.

128 Intervale Road, Burlington, VT 05401-9984
Telephone: 802-863-1700

Catalog price: free

A practical-minded color catalog of tools and supplies for gardeners more interested in results than style. The firm sells a metal soil-block maker, a paper pot system for starting seeds, Gardena sprinklers, and a choice of row covers, composters, and sprayers. Gardener's Supply sells its own two-wheeled garden cart, which looks both well built and well priced. The tool selection includes a push mower from Denmark, an array of innovative weeders and hoes, and an interesting two-handled, foot-driven soil loosener. The furniture collection seems to change with each season, but in 1987 the company carried the classic shell-back steel lawn chairs. Gardener's Supply distributes the Northern Light greenhouse, a small structure that can be installed by two people in a day. Interested shoppers should write for the greenhouse information packet.

Gardening Naturally

Route 102 Industrial Park, Stockbridge, MA 01262
Telephone: 413-298-4272 or 800-325-0055

Catalog price: free

Sells the Gardener gas- and electric-powered rototiller, billed as "the only two-axle, counter-rotating tine tiller you can get." The firm claims its tiller is more maneuverable than other front- and rear-tine tillers, and therefore better suited to small gardens. Three models are offered, each capable of tilling to a ten-inch depth.

Green Hand Tools

2301 Avenue C North, Saskatoon, SK, Canada S7L 5Z5
Telephone: 306-665-6707

Catalog price: $2, deductible from first order (sent to Canadian customers only)

An elegant catalog of tools and teak garden benches. The firm offers shovels, spades, and garden forks made by Bulldog Tools of England, German shears and loppers, and a fascinating collection of hand tools from Japan. It carries the Gardena watering system and an array of Gardena's modular tools. Proper tool care is emphasized throughout the catalog. Drawings demonstrate the proper use of unusual tools, and the text explains how to care for wooden handles and metal parts. To aid in proper care and storage, Green Hand sells hooks for hanging tools out of the weather and a wooden scraper for cleaning dirt from metal blades.

The Greener Thumb

109 E. 20th Street, Littlefield, TX 79339

Catalog price: free

Fine-quality tools and organic pest controls, offered by a venture launched in 1987. Greener Thumb sells Spear & Jackson's line of carbon-steel digging tools, True Friends' pruning shears, loppers, hedge shears, and pruning saws, and some innovative hoes and weeders from other makers. The firm sells Attack and Bonide pest controls, among them beetle traps, sticky bars for flying insects, and milky spore disease, which kills Japanese beetle grubs.

Greener'N Ever Tree Farm and Nursery

P.O. Box 222435, Carmel, CA 93922
Telephone: 408-624-2149

Catalog price: free

Greener'N Ever publishes two catalogs, one of trees (described here under *Trees and Shrubs,* page 154) and one of tools for tree growers. The tool catalog offers pruning saws, shears, and knives, loppers, shovels, planting bars, long-handled dibbles, hoedads, and sprayers.

Greenleaf Technologies

P.O. Box 12726, Memphis, TN 38182-0726
Telephone: 901-521-1758

Catalog price: free

Portable battery-operated sprayers mounted on two-wheeled dollies. The sprayers are available in two and a half-, five-, and 15-gallon sizes.

Harlane Company

266 Orangeburgh Road, Old Tappan, NJ 07675

Catalog price: free

Felco pruners at exceptionally low prices, a battery-powered pH meter for testing soil and water, and a staked plant label with a removable nameplate. Harlane will print registered rose names on the label plates at about ten cents a label. Permanent marking pens are offered for labeling other plants.

Kemp Company
160 Koser Road, Lititz, PA 17543
Telephone: 717-627-7979 or 800-441-5367

Catalog price: free

Kemp makes three models of gas-powered shredder/chippers that it actively sells to home gardeners as tools for making compost and mulch from yard debris. The color brochure not only explains the benefits of Kemp's machines, it offers an education in composting and mulching.

Kinco Manufacturing
170 N. Pascal, St. Paul, MN 55104
Telephone: 612-644-4666

Catalog price: free

Sells the Kinco sickle-bar mower, a lethal-looking machine designed for cutting tall grass, weeds, and even small saplings.

The Kinsman Company, Inc.
River Road, Point Pleasant, PA 18950
Telephone: 215-297-5613

Catalog price: free

Tools and other useful garden equipment. Kinsman offers a full line of Sheffield Pride gardening tools—spades, forks, shovels, hoes, trowels, and clipping shears in stainless and carbon steel—along with English watering cans, German birdhouses made from sawdust and concrete, garden arches and arbors, composters, cold frames, and electric chipper/shredders. Shoppers in the area may want to visit the warehouse shop in Doylestown. Call 215-348-0840 for business hours and directions.

Karl Kuemmerling, Inc.
129 Edgewater Avenue N.W., Massillon, OH 44646
Telephone: 216-477-3457 or 800-338-2266

Catalog price: free

Tools and supplies for people who work with trees. Kuemmerling sells dozens of saws, loppers, and pruners, along with mauls, wedges, peaveys, and some mean-looking weed- and brush-clearing tools. The selection of sprayers and buckskin

gloves will probably be of more interest to gardeners than the climbing spurs and safety straps.

A. M. Leonard, Inc.
6665 Spiker Road, Piqua, OH 45356
Telephone: 513-773-2694 or 800-543-8955

Catalog price: free

A comprehensive catalog of tools and supplies aimed primarily at people in the plant business. Home gardeners can skip over many of the pages, but there's plenty here that will do as good a job at home as in a commercial orchard or greenhouse. Scores of pruners, hoes, trowels, and horticultural knives are offered, along with propagating mats, carts, magnifiers, plant supports, and labels. Quantity discounts can cut prices way down.

Mantis Manufacturing Co.
1458 County Line Road, Huntington Valley, PA 19006
Telephone: 215-355-9700 or 800-344-4030

Catalog price: free

Makes a lightweight tiller/cultivator with a number of attachments that allow the machine to perform other tasks. As a tiller, the Mantis will dig down six to eight inches. With an edging blade it cuts a clean edge between lawn and garden. With the trimmer attachment it converts to a hedge trimmer. Other attachments transform the tool into a lawn aerator or dethatcher and a furrower.

Meridian Equipment Corp.
4-40 Banta Place, Fair Lawn, NJ 07410
Telephone: 201-794-8362

Catalog price: free

Fine-quality garden tools imported from Sheffield Pride of England. Gardeners can choose from top-of-the-line stainless-steel blades and forks or from merely deluxe tools forged from carbon steel. All are equipped with high-strength metal-cored polypropylene handles. Spades, forks, hoes, rakes, and shears are presented in a color catalog that makes everything look sharp and shiny. In a tucked-in flier, Meridian also offers Pawley's Island rope hammocks, wall-mounted hose reels, wind socks, and an inventive ball-bearing hose guide that slides hoses around tender plants without excessive friction.

The Natural Gardening Company
See under *General Gardening Supplies*, page 187.

Walter F. Nicke
P.O. Box 433, McLeod Lane, Topsfield, MA 01983

Catalog price: 50¢

Walt Nicke's Garden Talk, as this catalog is titled, somehow manages to mix classic old-fashioned tools with modern plastic gadgets and top-of-the-line quality implements with far cheaper models in a way that seems sensible and right. The firm sells stainless-steel tools from Sheffield Pride of England, along with a plastic version of the Sussex garden trug. It offers six different weeding tools that have been clawing the earth for at least a century along with an oak-look plastic planter. We don't mind the constant shift of gears because everything here has been chosen to be useful.

Almost every page holds something that looks as if it could solve a nagging garden problem. Other features that caught our eye include plant supports made by the Scottish War Blind, strap-on knee pads, thatched birdhouses from England, and a book on gardening for the handicapped.

Nicol & Associates
65 Newtown Avenue, Stratford, CT 06497
Telephone: 203-375-1067

Catalog price: free

Makers of the Tiny Tim seed dispenser, a device for portioning small seeds into pots and trays. It looks something like a cake decorator and is used in much the same way, with the thumb controlling the plunger. An adjustable nozzle can be set to match the size of the seed being handled. Send for the flier, or send $3.50 (postpaid) for the dispenser (check price after 1988).

North Star Evergreens
P.O. Box 253, Park Rapids, MN 56470
Telephone: 218-732-5818 or 800-336-3361

Catalog price: free

This big catalog of tools and supplies for tree farmers also includes many useful items for the garden. Tucked behind tree balers and industrial-size sprayers the diligent shopper will find Felco pruners (at very low prices), Wilkinson Sword trowels and hand forks, a long-handled bulb planter, weed and brush hooks, and such useful forestry tools as loppers, pruning saws, and planting bars. Pike poles, cant hooks, and peaveys are sold for those who dream of the big woods.

Ozark Handle & Hardware
P.O. Box 426, Eureka Springs, AR 72632
Telephone: 501-423-6888

Catalog price: $2, deductible from first order

All manner of wooden tool handles, from hammers and axes to shovels, hoes, and wheelbarrows. Twenty different shovel handles were listed in 1987, almost all of them available in an assortment of lengths and thicknesses. Accurate drawings of each handle help mail-order buyers pick out replacements for broken or damaged tools. (We're sure the proprietors would ask, "Why wait for them to break?" A bold line of the cover reads, "Remember the handle shortage of '77.")

Plow & Hearth
560 Main Street, Madison, VA 22727
Telephone: 703-948-7010 or 6821

Catalog price: free

The Plow & Hearth catalog tends to a gardener's needs year-round. Fireplace accessories, teakettles, and Barbour oiled jackets (called "greasy coats" by our friends in Scotland) get us through the cold months. When the weather warms up, the firm moves outdoors with an excellent selection of garden tools, supplies, outdoor furniture, and birdhouses. Plow & Hearth took over Green River Tools in 1986 and now offers a pared-down version of that wonderful inventory—scythes, soil-block makers, stirrup and Dutch hoes, thistle pullers, children's tools, and the Double-Digger two-handled soil loosener. Other utilitarian offerings include a garden cart, a porous soaker hose, cold frames, and composters. Of more recreational appeal are kerosene patio torches, planters, wind chimes, bocce balls, and an excellent line of garden furniture, including a folding Adirondack chair, oak gliders and porch swings, rustic cedar table and chair sets, teak and iroko benches, and Victorian-style slatted benches made with cast-aluminum ends. For the birds, Plow & Hearth offers martin houses, hummingbird feeders, German birdhouses made of sawdust and cement, and a hanging ceramic birdbath.

R & H Products, Inc.
P.O. Box 722, Richboro, PA 18954
Telephone: 215-355-4325 or 887-2196

Catalog price: free

Sells a small hand tool called the Wonder Weeder, promoted as a "multipurpose garden tool" for weeding, cultivating, edging, furrowing, and planting. We think other tools must do some of those jobs better, but it does look like a useful weeder.

Rachet-Cut
P.O. Box 303, Milldale, CT 06467

Catalog price: free

Florian pole pruners, loppers, and a hand pruner, all made with a ratchet action that increases their cutting power. The same brochure is sent out by American Standard Company in neighboring Plantsville, Connecticut.

Scotchmen
Rt. 1, Pottstown, PA 19464
Telephone: 215-495-6282

Catalog price: free

Sells a gas-powered chipper/shredder and a wheel-mounted sprayer. Scotchmen takes pains to distinguish its chipper/shredder from smaller electric models, which it calls "outdoor kitchen shredders." Boasts the brochure, "Throw a rock into an electric and see what happens. Throw a rock into a Scotchmen, and it's instantly pulverized!"

Smith & Hawken
25 Corte Madera, Mill Valley, CA 94941
Telephone: 415-383-4050

Catalog price: free

Smith & Hawken always manages to put together an exceptional assortment of tools, supplies, and outdoor furniture for its regular seasonal catalogs, and it always manages to make everything look and sound better than anything we've seen elsewhere. The firm sells the Lutyens garden bench, for example, and prints a picture of it that makes it look bigger and more perfectly designed than the very same bench as offered by other catalogs. And Smith & Hawken comes up with many things the competition doesn't have: a child-size Adirondack chair, a lovely teak garden bench with a back of overlapping circular arches, Italian terracotta planters with built-in reservoirs to keep plants from drying out, a genuine Sussex trug made of willow and chestnut (not plywood), and a long-handled bulb planter specially designed and built for the firm by Bulldog Tools of England. Other Smith & Hawken specialties include Japanese pruning tools and shears, the Crocodile machete, galvanized metal flower buckets of the type used by Parisian florists, Yucatan hammocks, copper watering cans, and Gardena sprinklers. The firm is the only one we've come across that sells sheepskin gloves by their proper name (other catalogs sell them as "lanolin-rich" goatskin).

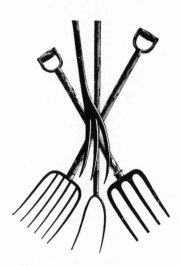

Sporty's Tool Shop
Clermont Airport, Batavia, OH 45103-9747
Telephone: 513-732-2411 or 800-543-8633 (orders only)

Catalog price: free

Sporty's Tool Shop started out as a supplier to pilots, and the catalog still has plenty of aeronautical offerings: leather flight jackets, weather instruments, and a pilot's flight bag. (If you write to Sporty's Pilot Shop you'll get a complete catalog of the stuff.) But the general list has expanded to include an abundance of items for groundlubbers. In 1987 Sporty's sold water timers, hose reels, rope hammocks and swings, kerosene patio torches, and a water broom that turns the garden hose into a hydraulic sweeper. A particular Sporty's favorite is a heavy-duty mailbox. Pictures show the box holding up nicely as two M-80s go off inside it and as a 15-ton bulldozer drives over it.

Sunbird Products
P.O. Box 144, Millersburg, OH 44654
Telephone: 216-674-2966 or 800-445-5668

Catalog price: free

Makes a small gas-powered tiller/cultivator for home gardens that digs down "six inches or more." Attachments can convert the machine into a snow thrower, a hedge trimmer, a water pump, a lawn aerator/dethatcher, a blower/broom, a power sprayer, or a string trimmer.

W-W Grinder, Inc.
P.O. Box 4029, Wichita, KS 67204
Telephone: 316-838-4229 or 800-835-2127

Catalog price: free

Several models of chipper/shredders with escalating capacities and prices. All have big hoppers that allow loose material to be piled in easily without much spillage. The largest models can reduce three-inch branches to chips at a rate of 96 bites per second. The firm also makes power sprayers. A 12-gallon model can be pulled by hand; the 55-gallon machine can be towed by a riding tractor or set in the back of a pickup truck.

Warnico/USA
59 Rutter Street, Rochester, NY 14606
Telephone: 716-458-2840

No catalog

Sells a weeding tool called the Easy Weeder. The firm has no catalog or brochure, but will quote prices if you write.

White Flower Farm
See under *Garden Perennials*, page 93.

Winona Attrition Mill Co.
1009 W. 5th Street, Winona, MN 55987
Telephone: 507-452-2716

Catalog price: free

Shredders for converting yard waste to compost. The machines can be purchased with gas engines on mobile cart mounts, like other shredders, or they can be ordered without the mounts (for stationary installation over the compost pile) and without engines (for hookup to the power drive of a garden tractor).

Woodstock Soapstone Co., Inc.
Airpark Road, Box 37H, W. Lebanon, NH 03784
Telephone: 603-298-5955

Catalog price: free

Manufactures the Yellowbird, a rear-tined rotary tiller that digs a 15-inch swath down to a depth of eight inches. The machine converts to a cultivator by replacing the tiller blades with a three-pronged attachment that "moves back and forth just under the surface of the soil."

Topiary Frames

Exotic Blossoms
P.O. Box 2436, Philadelphia, PA 19147-0436
Telephone: 215-271-2440

Catalog price: free

Vine-covered wire topiary frames in the shape of airplanes, toadstools, sailboats, and a regular Noah's ark of animals. Buy the frames alone and plant them yourself, or order them already growing. (No indication is given of what plants the firm uses when it supplies planted topiary.)

The Ivy League
P.O. Box E, Wakefield, MA 01880
Telephone: 617-246-3635 or 800-356-2468

Catalog price: free

Wire topiary frames planted with small-leaved vines. Shapes includes cats, turtles, dolphins, hearts, and many others, some freestanding, others mounted on wood bases or strung for hanging. Pins and empty frames are also sold.

Topiary, Inc.
41 Bering Street, Tampa, FL 33606

Catalog price: free

Wire forms in various animal shapes for making simple vine-covered topiary. The forms are filled with sphagnum moss and potting soil and planted with creeping fig ("a similar small-leaf vine will do"). Buy the forms empty or planted.

Vine Arts
P.O. Box 03014, Portland, OR 97203
Telephone: 503-289-7505

Catalog price: $1.25

Wire frames for creating topiary in animal shapes from small-leaved vines. The brochure consists of a single piece of paper with sketches of some of the shapes and an attached price list.

Worms

Cape Cod Worm Farm
30 Center Avenue, Buzzards Bay, MA 02532
Telephone: 617-759-5664

Catalog price: self-addressed stamped envelope

Earthworms and worm castings. The worms are sold as "bait-size" breeders or as all-size bed runs, and gardeners can save a little money by going for the smaller wrigglers. The worm castings make a rich soil additive for potted plants or for the garden and lawn.

Carter Worm Farm
Plains, GA 31780
Telephone: 912-824-7707

Catalog price: free

Hugh A. Carter runs this operation, and yes, he is related to the former president—he's a cousin. Perhaps it's the ambition in the family blood, but Mr. Carter does not content himself with selling a few worms here and there to fishermen and gardeners; his brochure tries to convince us to buy enough to start our own worm farms. ("Big Money in Fishworms," reads the headline, over a text enlivened by loads of capital letters.) Of course Mr. Carter does sell the worms in garden (and fishing) quantities of 1,000 or more.

Fain's Bait Farm
Rt. 2, Box 182, Edison, GA 31746-9410
Telephone: 912-835-2542

Catalog price: free

Fain's Bait Farm is pushing its new gray nightcrawler, a "large type fishworm, that does not have to be pampered." The brochure notes that the worm "has more moves than a hula dancer. Especially good for catfish, young bass, trout." While Fain's sales pitch is aimed at fishermen, we have it on good authority that the worm will also dance in the garden.

PART III:

Societies and Magazines

Societies and Associations

African Violet Society of America, Inc.
P.O. Box 3609, Beaumont, TX 77704
Telephone: 409-839-4725

Annual dues: $13.50, $18 Canada and overseas

Membership includes a subscription to the bimonthly *African Violet Magazine*, which contains color-illustrated articles on African violet culture, reviews of new cultivars, and news of exhibitions and upcoming events. At the annual meeting members may attend workshops and go on nursery tours. Local chapters and affiliates hold regular meetings and shows year-round.

The Alabama Wildflower Society
Rt. 2, Box 115, Northport, AL 35476

Annual dues: $5

The society provides a forum for those interested in Alabama's native flora to meet and exchange information and to work for the protection of wild habitats. Members receive two newsletters a year with articles on growing wildflowers and observations on rare plants in their natural locations. Local chapter meetings and field trips are held throughout the state.

Alaska Native Plant Society
Verna Pratt, P.O. Box 141613, Anchorage, AK 99504
Telephone: 907-333-8212

Annual dues: $10

The society's monthly newsletter, *Borealis*, is published October through May. It presents articles on native trees and wildflowers and notes on society business. One recent issue contained detailed instructions for growing Alaska wild iris from seed. Monthly meetings are held in Anchorage from October to May. The summer months are taken up by field trips, and the newsletter in those months is given over to field-trip schedules. Seed sales to members.

Aloe, Cactus & Succulent Society of Zimbabwe
P.O. Box 8514, Causeway, Harare, Zimbabwe

Annual dues: $10, Can$11 Canada

Publishes an annual journal, *Excelsa*. The 1987 issue ran to 108 pages, many of them color illustrated, with articles such as "Lithops and Migrating Cranes" (by Desmond Cole),

"Cacti and Succulents on Stamps," and "The Evolution of Cycads." Members also receive a biannual newsletter and are invited to lectures, slide shows, garden meetings, tours, and expeditions (all in Zimbabwe).

Alpine Garden Club of British Columbia
Denys C. Lloyd, 3281 W. 35th Avenue, Vancouver, BC, Canada V6N 2M9

Annual dues: Can$13

Local members may participate in meetings and field trips. All members receive the club's bulletin, mailed five times a year, and a chance to join in the annual seed exchange.

Alpine Garden Society
E. M. Upward, Lye End Link, St. John's, Woking, Surrey, England GU21 1SW
Telephone: 44-4862-69327

Annual dues: £12 U.S. and Canada, £10 U.K.

The *Quarterly Bulletin of the Alpine Garden Society* is filled with articles on mountain expeditions, the culture of specific plants, reviews of books and symposia, and other subjects of interest to rock gardeners, laced throughout with full-page color photographs. Though the title sounds imposing, the articles make easy and fascinating reading, even for the nonexpert. Members may also participate in a seed distribution each winter (which offers nearly 4,000 species) and are invited to shows, local meetings, and tours to mountain areas all over the world. The society publishes a number of books and guides.

American Bamboo Society
1101 San Leon Court, Solana Beach, CA 92075
Telephone: 619-481-9869

Annual dues: $15

A bimonthly newsletter contains articles on bamboo culture as well as notices of meetings, new publications, and conferences. The Pacific Northwest chapter publishes its own newsletter (available for $5 from Larry Rueter, 8829 Gothic Way, Everett, WA 98204-2223). An annual or biannual journal contains more substantial writings on bamboo. Members may buy seeds, plants, and books, may take advantage of the society's library, and may visit its bamboo greenhouse at

Quail Botanical Gardens in Encinitas, California. An annual source list directs members to bamboo nurseries, and four local chapters (in Florida, California, and Washington) hold meetings and organize local activities.

American Begonia Society
8922 Conway Drive, Riverside, CA 92503
Telephone: 714-687-3728

Annual dues: $15, $20 Canada and Mexico, $35 overseas

The bimonthly journal, *The Begonian*, publishes articles on collection expeditions, new cultivars, and begonia culture, all illustrated with black-and-white photographs. The eastern and southwestern regional affiliates also publish separate newsletters with information on local events and articles of interest to begonia fans. The society sponsors seed sales to members, maintains a slide library, and runs a begonia bookstore in Riverside, California. Plants are sold at national and regional conventions. Several local branches maintain display gardens, the most spectacular of which is the Begonia Museum on the campus of Southampton University in Southampton, New York.

American Bonsai Society, Inc.
P.O. Box 358, Keene, NH 03431
Telephone: 603-352-9034

Annual dues: $18, $22 Canada and overseas

The society's quarterly journal, *Bonsai*, is laid out with the elegance of its subject and is filled with illustrated articles on styling, soils, pots, wiring, and collecting. Interviews with bonsai masters are a regular feature. *ABStracts*, a quarterly newsletter, contains notes on meetings and events. The society maintains a slide and video library, sponsors a book service, and holds an annual convention where members may shop for plants, pots, and tools and attend workshops and demonstrations.

American Boxwood Society
P.O. Box 85, Boyce, VA 22620
Telephone: 703-837-1758

Annual dues: $15

The Boxwood Bulletin, the society's quarterly magazine, contains articles on boxwood culture and garden plantings as well as notes on events and meetings. (The *Bulletin* is available without membership for $8.) An annual meeting is held each year in May, generally at the Blandy Experimental Farm in Boyce, Virginia, where the society maintains a library and display garden (with more than 80 boxwood cultivars). A buyer's guide is sold for $3 postpaid.

American Bryological and Lichenogical Society
Dept. of Biology, Texas A&M Univ., College Station, TX 77843-3258

Annual dues: $30, $35 Canada and overseas

An organization devoted to the scientific study of mosses, liverworts, and lichens. Field trips and readings are held in conjunction with the annual summer meeting. The quarterly journal, *The Bryologist*, is somewhat scholarly in tone. A more informal bulletin, *Evansia*, is directed toward amateurs and is available for an additional $5 per year.

American Camellia Society
P.O. Box 1217, Fort Valley, GA 31030-1217
Telephone: 912-967-2358

Annual dues: $15 U.S. and Canada, $16.50 overseas

Members receive *The Camellia Journal*, published quarterly, and the 250-page *Yearbook*. The *Journal* carries articles on new camellia cultivars, treatments for pests and diseases, reviews of meetings and publications, and notices of upcoming events. At the society's headquarters in Fort Valley, members may use the library of rare horticultural books and view the camellia display garden. Local chapters hold meetings and shows in most of the southern states and in California.

American Community Gardening Association
c/o Chicago Botanic Garden, P.O. Box 400, Glencoe, IL 60022
Telephone: 312-835-0250

Annual dues: $15

An association of garden organizers and neighborhood leaders that will be of interest to anyone actively involved in community gardening. Members receive the quarterly *Journal of Community Gardening*, a recent issue of which contained articles on teaching gardening skills to Southeast Asian immigrants, heirloom vegetables grown by native Americans, and interviews with community gardeners in Providence, Rhode Island. Regional conferences are held throughout the year, along with an annual conference.

American Daffodil Society, Inc.
Rt. 3, 2302 Byhalia Road, Hernando, MS 38632
Telephone: 601-368-6337

Annual dues: $10 U.S. and Canada, $7.50 overseas

Members receive *The Daffodil Journal*, a color-illustrated quarterly. A recent issue contained an article on grower Grant Mitsch, another on wild daffodils of Spain and Portugal, and reviews of dozens of new cultivars. The society also rents slides, sells old and new books, maintains a lending library, and offers advice on daffodil culture for the garden and for show. Members may attend the annual convention and may keep in touch with other enthusiasts through round-robin letter circuits.

American Dahlia Society
M. Martinolich, 159 Pine Street, New Hyde Park, NY 11040
Telephone: 516-742-3890

Annual dues: $8 U.S. and Canada, $9 overseas

Publishes the quarterly *Bulletin of the American Dahlia Society*, which is largely given over to society business and notes of upcoming shows and meetings. Every issue includes at least one article on dahlia care; these range from insect problems to growing habits to raising dahlias from seed. The society holds an annual banquet and meeting each spring and a national show in the late summer. The 75 local affiliates also hold regular meetings and shows and have access to the society's slide library. New members receive a copy of the booklet *Classification and Handbook of Dahlias*, which explains the standard classification system and describes 1,500 cultivars.

American Fern Society

Dr. David Barrington, Dept. of Botany, Univ. of Vermont, Burlington, VT 05405

Annual dues: $6, $8 Canada and overseas

All members receive *Fiddlehead Forum*, a bimonthly bulletin with articles of interest to fern growers and notes on society business. Those interested in delving into a more scientific study of ferns may send an additional $4 ($6 for foreign addresses) for a subscription to the quarterly *American Fern Journal*, which contains scholarly articles on the subject. The society makes packets of fresh spore available to members at nominal cost or by exchange, sponsors field trips, and encourages local study groups.

American Fuchsia Society

County Fair Building, 9th Avenue & Lincoln Way, San Francisco, CA 94122

Annual dues: $12.50 ($25 for overseas airmail)

The monthly *American Fuchsia Society Bulletin* contains articles on fuchsia care, sources for buying plants, and notices of local branch activities. Twenty-six branches are spread across California, and an affiliated group in Eugene makes the society accessible to Oregonians. All branches hold regular meetings; many sponsor shows, workshops, and plant sales. The society sells books on fuchsias and maintains a lending library of books and slides.

American Ginger Society

P.O. Box 100, Archer, FL 32618

Telephone: 904-495-9168

Annual dues: $15 U.S. and Canada, $20 overseas

Members may participate in plant exchanges and tours of ginger collections and will receive the biannual magazine, *Ziginber*. The magazine is still in the planning stages as we write, but will be issued in 1988. It will publish illustrated articles on growing and eating ginger.

American Gloxinia & Gesneriad Society, Inc.

Lois N. Russell, 5320 Labadie, St. Louis, MO 63120

Annual dues: $12, $15 Canada

Membership includes a subscription to *The Gloxinian*, a color-illustrated bimonthly journal with articles on the culture of unusual gesneriads, notes from members culled from round-robin letters, and schedules of upcoming events. New members receive a copy of the handbook *To Know and Grow Gesneriads*. Slides are available for loan to members, and plants and seeds are sold at chapter conventions (held throughout the U.S. and Canada).

American Gourd Society

P.O. Box 274, Mt. Gilead, OH 43338-0274

Telephone: 419-946-3302

Annual dues: $3

The Gourd, the society's magazine, comes out three times a year. A recent issue included articles on gourd birdhouses, Balinese painted gourds, and a thumb piano made from a gourd. The society sells inexpensive bulletins on gourd care and on such subjects as making gourd planters and preserving color in ornamental gourds. Two fall shows are sponsored, in Mt. Gilead, Ohio, and Cary, North Carolina, and a spring meeting is held in Mansfield, Ohio. Seeds and gourds are offered for sale in a sheet mailed with *The Gourd*.

American Hemerocallis Society

Elly Launius, 1454 Rebel Drive, Jackson, MS 39211

Annual dues: $12.50

New members receive an information-filled booklet, *Welcome to the World of Daylilies*, which lists sources by region of the country, explains the many daylily awards, offers a beginning course on daylily culture, and rates the top 100 cultivars by member popularity. *The Daylily*, the Society's quarterly journal, is a 120-page color-illustrated booklet crammed with growing tips, interviews, articles, and reviews of new cultivars. The society sells books on daylilies and rents slides. Members are automatically put in touch with one of the fifteen regional affiliates, which hold regular meetings, publish local newsletters, and maintain display gardens. A national convention, held annually, includes garden tours, lectures, and clinics.

American Hibiscus Society

P.O. Box 12073, St. Petersburg, FL 33733-2073

Annual dues: $10

Publishes a quarterly journal, *The Seed Pod*, which contains news of member activities and articles on hibiscus culture. The society maintains a seed bank for members and sponsors an annual convention and show. Local chapters hold regular meetings at which plants and books may be purchased.

American Horticultural Society

P.O. Box 0105, Mt. Vernon, VA 22121

Telephone: 703-768-5700

Annual dues: $20, $35 Canada and overseas

Members receive *American Horticulturist*, a glossy bimonthly magazine full of articles of interest to home gardeners. Recent issues have included stories on careers in horticulture, vireya rhododendrons, raising giant pumpkins, and plant-derived pesticides. Every other month the society fills in with a newsletter of the same title, which is shorter, offers how-to advice, and prints a schedule of upcoming events. The society sponsors a free seed program in January, offers discounted horticultural books, and maintains a library and display garden at its headquarters at River Farm in Alexandria, Virginia.

American Hosta Society
Jack Freedman, 3103 Heatherhill Drive S.E., Huntsville, AL 35802
Telephone: 205-324-7149

Annual dues: $12.50, $15 Canada and overseas

Publishes *The Hosta Journal*, a thick biannual magazine with articles on hosta hybridizers, culture, and pest problems as well as reviews of new introductions. The society runs an annual popularity poll that allows members to rate the top 100 cultivars. Lectures, garden tours, and plant sales are all features of the annual convention.

American Iris Society
Carol Ramsey, 6518 Beachy Avenue, Wichita, KS 67206

Annual dues: $9.50

Members receive the quarterly *AIS Bulletin*, a 100-page illustrated journal with features on iris culture, new varieties, hibridizing techniques, and exhibition advice. New members are automatically enrolled in one of the 24 regional affiliates, which hold regular meetings, conduct garden tours, support round-robin letters, and sponsor lectures, workshops, and slide shows. The national society publishes a number of books and cultural brochures and makes experts available to answer individual gardening questions.

The American Ivy Society
P.O. Box 520, W. Carrollton, OH 45449-0520
Telephone: 513-434-7069

Annual dues: $15, $19 Canada, $23 overseas

The *Ivy Journal*, published three times a year, includes articles on ivy culture and history, descriptions and hardiness tests of unusual varieties, and notes on member activities. The society answers members' questions about any ivy subject, identifies cultivars from cuttings, publishes pamphlets on many aspects of ivy culture (including a source list), and sponsors an annual convention.

American Orchid Society
6000 S. Olive Avenue, West Palm Beach, FL 33405
Telephone: 305-585-8666

Annual dues: $28, $34 Canada and overseas

Members receive the monthly *American Orchid Society Bulletin*, a richly illustrated color magazine full of articles of interest to both novice and expert growers. New members are sent the society's *Handbook on Orchid Culture*, an extremely useful booklet that tells how to care for the most popular orchid genera. Those who want more scientific reading may subscribe to *Lindleyana* (see entry under *Magazines*, page 000). The society publishes a number of booklets on a range of orchid topics, offers books to members at a discount, and oversees a network of almost 500 local affiliates worldwide. With 23,000 members in 66 countries, the society is one of the largest horticultural organizations in the world.

American Penstemon Society
Orville Steward, P.O. Box 33, Plymouth, VT 05056

Annual dues: $7.50, $8 Canada and overseas

Publishes the biannual *Bulletin of the American Penstemon Society*, a unillustrated 60-page booklet with articles on penstemon culture and notes on society business. The society runs a seed exchange, maintains a book and slide library, sponsors field trips, and invites all members to its annual meeting. New members are sent a copy of the pamphlet *Manual for Beginners with Penstemons*.

American Peony Society
250 Interlachen Road, Hopkins, MN 55343

Annual dues: $7.50

In its effort to promote interest in peony culture, the society gives seeds to members (for a nominal handling charge), donates plants to arboretums, and publishes the quarterly *American Peony Society Bulletin*, which contains articles of interest to peony growers at all levels of expertise. The annual convention includes a national peony show. Local conventions and exhibitions are held throughout "the peony growing belt." Among the society's publications are a handbook of peony culture and a historical checklist of more than 5,000 cultivars.

American Plant Life Society
P.O. Box 985, National City, CA 92050

Annual dues: $20

Serves gardeners interested in "the Amaryllidacaea and related monocot plant families" (bulbous plants like amaryllis, cyrtanthi, gladioli, alstroemerias, irises, lilies, and daffodils). Members receive a quarterly newsletter with short articles, book and supplier reviews, and notes on upcoming events as well as the more extensive yearbook *Herbertia*, a thick color-illustrated booklet that contains extensive articles on wild species and garden culture. The society sponsors a seed distribution each winter and holds an annual convention. Local chapters also hold meetings and conventions.

American Pomological Society
103 Tyson Building, University Park, PA 16802
Telephone: 814-863-2198

Annual dues: $12

Members receive the quarterly *Fruit Varieties Journal*, a magazine with extensive and detailed articles on the culture of fruit trees and berry plants. Some of these will make dense reading for novices, but each issue contains a couple of articles that can be appreciated by the home grower. Members may also get discounted subscriptions to other fruit-growers' magazines through the society and will have access to scion lists and reprints of articles from other journals.

American Primrose Society
Brian Skidmore, 6730 W. Mercer Way, Mercer Island, WA 98040

Annual dues: $10, or £7.50 U.K.

Primroses, the society's quarterly journal, contains articles on primrose culture, history, collection expeditions, and important growers, as well as information on meetings and society business. Black-and-white illustrations appear throughout. Members may participate in the annual seed exchange and may attend chapter meetings, local exhibitions, and the society's annual convention. New members receive a cultural chart detailing the growing requirements of many primula species.

American Rhododendron Society
Paula L. Cash, 14885 S.W. Sunrise Lane, Tigard, OR 97224
Telephone: 503-620-4038

Annual dues: $20

Publishes a color-illustrated quarterly journal, which usually contains at least a dozen short articles of general interest, along with schedules of meetings and shows and notes on other society affairs. The society organizes an annual convention, which alternates between East and West Coast cities and is occasionally held in Canada. Members may attend local chapter meetings and regional conferences and may participate in the annual seed exchange or draw on the society's pollen bank. Slide programs on various subjects are available for rental. Local chapters sponsor plant and cutting sales, maintain libraries and display gardens, organize tours, and compile lists of suppliers.

American Rock Garden Society
Buffy Parker, 15 Fairmead Road, Darien, CT 06820

Annual dues: $20

The annual seed exchange of the American Rock Garden Society is one of the greatest amateur endeavors in the field of horticulture. Seed for more than 5,000 species and varieties are submitted by members from all over the world and distributed by a hard-working group of volunteers. In addition to a chance to participate in the seed exchange, members receive the quarterly *Bulletin of the American Rock Garden Society*, an illustrated journal with articles on the natural habitats of alpine plants, on garden culture, and on many other subjects of interest to rock gardeners. At the annual spring meeting members may attend lectures and field trips, buy plants, and meet fellow enthusiasts. The society maintains a slide library, and, by arrangement with the Pennsylvania Horticultural Society, lends books by mail. Books may also be purchased through the society's mail-order bookstore. Twenty regional chapters hold their own meetings, lectures, plant sales, shows, and garden visits.

American Rose Society
P.O. Box 30,000, Shreveport, LA 71130-0030
Telephone: 318-938-5402

Annual dues: $25 U.S. and Canada, $40 overseas

Membership includes a subscription to *The American Rose*, a monthly magazine full of color photographs and articles on rose culture, as well as a copy of the annual *Handbook for Selecting Roses*, an encoded directory of hundreds of cultivars, and the *American Rose Annual*, an information-packed book with the results of regional garden trials of new introductions. The society maintains a 118-acre display garden in Shreveport and sponsors two national meetings and shows each year. Several district branches and scores of local societies hold additional conventions and shows.

American Society for Horticultural Science
701 N. St. Asaph Street, Alexandria, VA 22314-1998
Telephone: 703-836-4606

Annual dues: $20

Publishes two bimonthly journals, *HortScience* and the *Journal of the American Society for Horticultural Science*. Each contains dozens of scholarly articles on scientific studies relating to commercial horticulture.

Aril Society International
Donna Downey, 5500 Constitution N.E., Albuquerque, NM 87110
Telephone: 505-255-8207

Annual dues: $6

Affiliated with the American Iris Society. Members receive the *Yearbook*, an illustrated booklet with articles, a membership roster, and notes on society business, along with three issues of the society's newsletter. The society organizes an annual rhizome sale.

Arkansas Native Plant Society
Sue Clark, P.O. Box 10506, Conway, AR 72032

Annual dues: $5

Members receive a biannual newsletter, *Claytonia*, which runs notices of upcoming meetings, field trips, and workshops. Meetings, at which members may buy plants, are held in April and October.

Australian Fuchsia Society
The Secretary, P.O. Box 97, Norwood, S.A., Australia 5067

Annual dues: Aus$4

Publishes a quarterly *Journal* with articles on fuchsia care. A booklet, *Succeeding with Fuchsias in South Australia*, may be ordered for an additional Aus$1.50. Local members may participate in meetings, workshops, and shows.

Australian Geranium Society
27 Chichester Street, Maroubra, NSW, Australia 2035

Annual dues: Aus$8

Sends members a quarterly *Journal*, with roughly 20 pages of articles and records of society business. A recent issue contained articles on methods of propagation from leaf cuttings and a feature on compact trailing ivy-leaved geraniums. Local members may attend monthly meetings and the society's two shows, and may join tours and nursery visits.

Australian Rhododendron Society
P.O. Box 21, Olinda, Victoria, Australia 3788
Telephone: 61-751-1980

Annual dues: Aus$15

The Rhododendron, the society's quarterly journal, is a color-illustrated affair with articles on Australian rhododendron gardens and growers. Foreign members may participate in an annual seed sale, but will probably find it inconvenient to visit the society's display garden in Olinda or buy plants at local meetings.

Azalea Society of America, Inc.

P.O. Box 6244, Silver Spring, MD 20906
Telephone: 301-593-2415

Annual dues: $15

Publishes *The Azalean*, a quarterly journal with extensive articles on azalea culture, notes on recent introductions, and news of chapter activities. The national society maintains a slide library. Local chapters host plant and cutting sales, lectures, garden tours, and the annual society meeting.

Bio-Dynamic Farming & Gardening Association

Roderick Shouldice, P.O. Box 550, Kimerton, PA 19442
Telephone: 215-327-2420

Annual dues: $20, $25 Canada, $26 overseas

Members receive the quarterly journal *Biodynamics*, which publishes articles on biodynamic gardening methods (a philosophy of gardening that stresses improving soil with crop rotations and special composts). The association publishes books on the subject and sells compost preparations and a compost starter.

The Bio-Integral Resource Center

P.O. Box 7414, Berkeley, CA 94707
Telephone: 415-524-2567

Annual dues: $30, $35 Canada, $40 overseas

An organization that "publishes information on all aspects of environmentally sound pest control." Home gardeners and other non-professional members are sent *Common Sense Pest Control Quarterly*, an illustrated 32-page journal with thorough articles on combating garden pests using organic techniques. Professional members receive *The IPM Practitioner*, published ten times a year, with articles that focus on the protection of crop plants. Back issues, books, and pamphlets are also sold.

Bonsai Clubs International

Virginia Ellerman, 2636 W. Mission Road #277, Tallahassee, FL 32304

Annual dues: $15, $18 Canada and overseas

A coordinating body for the many local bonsai clubs across the U.S. and Canada. Members receive *Bonsai Magazine*, a glossy black-and-white bimonthly with articles on bonsai styles and techniques and news of local club activities. New members are steered to an area club wherever possible. Bonsai Clubs International sponsors an annual meeting with workshops, lectures, and seminars, maintains a lending library of slides and books, publishes a source guide, and offers advice to members who want to start a local club.

Botanical Club of Wisconsin

Theodore S. Cochrane, Treasurer, 449 Jean Street, Madison, WI 53703

Annual dues: $5

A club open to anyone with an interest in botany or Wisconsin wildflowers. Members receive the quarterly *Bulletin* and may participate in meetings and field trips.

The Botanical Society of South Africa

Kirstenboch, Claremont, Cape, South Africa 7735
Telephone: 27-21-771725

Annual dues: R21

U.S. and Canadian members receive the quarterly journal *Veld & Flora*, a color-illustrated magazine with articles on plants native to South Africa. While North American members can't easily make the meetings and plant sales, they may buy books from the society and participate in the annual seed distribution. All members receive 15 packets of seeds each year. The seed list and the seeds can be sent by airmail for an additional R6.20.

Boxwood Society of the Midwest

Missouri Botanical Garden, P.O. Box 299, St. Louis, MO 63166

Annual dues: $10

Members receive a boxwood identification guide, the biannual *Bulletin*, with articles on boxwood care, and a chance to join the fall field trip and attend the annual spring meeting. Most member activity centers on work with the boxwood collection at the Missouri Botanical Garden.

British & European Geranium Society

Ray Plowright, 1 Roslyn Road, Hathersage, Sheffield, England S30 1BY

Annual dues: $5, £3 Canada and overseas

Membership includes the *Year Book* and three issues of *The Geranium Gazette*, an unillustrated journal with articles on new cultivars, geranium culture, society news, and letters from members. New members receive the booklet *Geraniums*, which provides a sound introduction to the care and identification of the various geranium types. The society offers books and seeds to members.

The British Cactus & Succulent Society

Miss W.E. Dunn, 43 Dewar Drive, Sheffield, England S7 2GR

Annual dues: $15 or £6

Publishes the *British Cactus & Succulent Journal*, an illustrated quarterly magazine filled with articles aimed at both experts and novices. A recent issue contained writings on cold-hardy cacti, succulent collections in German public gardens, the cultivation of conophytums, bringing coryphantus to flower, and the hallucinogenic properties of peyote. North American members may not be able to take advantage of the many branch activities, but they may be on the receiving end of the annual seed distribution, and they may shop from the society's mail-order book list.

British Fuchsia Society

Ron Ewart, 29 Princess Crescent, Dollar, Scotland FK14 7BW

Annual dues: £5

Members receive a copy of the society's *Annual*, two issues of the *Bulletin*, free passes to society shows, free advice on fuchsia culture, and a chance to shop from the society's mail-order book list. Fuchsia photographers may enter slide competitions.

British Pelargonium & Geranium Society
Jan Taylor, 23 Beech Crescent, Kidlington, Oxford, England OX5 1DW

Annual dues: $10

Members receive the society's quarterly journal and are sent free seed upon joining and upon renewal. The Society holds regular meetings and shows and organizes outings.

The Bromeliad Society, Inc.
Linda Harbert, 2488 E. 49th Street, Tulsa, OK 74015

Annual dues: $15, $20 Canada and overseas

The bimonthly *Journal of The Bromeliad Society* is a thick color-illustrated affair with articles of interest to hobbyists as well as scientists. In addition, the society offers members seeds and a number of informational booklets. Members are encouraged to participate in the activities of local affiliated societies.

Bromeliad Study Group of Northern California
Daniel Arcos, 1334 S. Van Ness Avenue, San Francisco, CA 94110

Annual dues: $10 U.S. and Canada, $20 overseas

The study group meets monthly and sponsors field trips. In conjunction with three other similar California groups it publishes *The Bromeliad Hobbyist*, a monthly journal with articles on bromeliad culture that is illustrated with tipped-in color photographs. Bromeliad enthusiasts who live in the area of San Diego, Long Beach, or San Gabriel should write for information about the study groups in those cities.

Brooklyn Botanic Garden
See *Plants & Gardens* under *Magazines*, page 273.

Cactus & Succulent Society of America
Virginia Martin, 2631 Fairgreen Avenue, Arcadia, CA 91006

Annual dues: $26 U.S. and Canada, $28 overseas

Members receive the bimonthly *Cactus and Succulent Journal* (see entry under *Magazines*, page 268), a newsletter, and invitations to biannual conventions and the annual plant show. The society maintains a non-circulating library at Whittier College, in Whittier, California. In 1987 the society started a seed exchange, though it may not be available to all members for a couple of years. Those who are already subscribers to the *Journal* may become active members of the society for only $6 ($7 overseas).

California Horticultural Society
Elsie Mueller, 1847 34th Avenue, San Francisco, CA 94122
Telephone: 415-566-5222

Annual dues: $25, $30 Canada and overseas

Membership includes a subscription to *Pacific Horticulture* (see entry under *Magazines*, page 273), a monthly bulletin, and the opportunity to participate in the annual seed exchange, join field trips, and attend monthly lecture meetings at which plants are displayed and sold. A circulating library is available at each monthly meeting.

California Rare Fruit Growers, Inc.
The Fullerton Arboretum, California State Univ. Fullerton, Fullerton, CA 92634

Annual dues: $10, $15 overseas

An organization for gardeners interested in unusual deciduous fruits, subtropical fruits, and tropical fruits for greenhouse culture. Members receive a quarterly journal, *The Fruit Gardener*, and an annual, both with articles on choosing and growing unusual fruit trees. Recent issues have included features on mangoes, dates, figs, and coffee berries, along with pest-control notes, recipes, book reviews, and source lists. The society holds an annual winter meeting, sponsors a summer field trip and plant sale, and maintains a seed bank for members. A dozen local chapters also hold regular meetings.

Canadian Gladiolus Society
P.O. Drysdale, 3770 Hardy Road, R.R. 1, Agassiz, BC, Canada

Annual dues: Can$8

Publishes an *Annual* in January and a *Fall Bulletin* in September. The *Annual* contains notes from members on local shows across Canada as well as articles on caring for and exhibiting gladioli.

Canadian Iris Society
Mrs. D. Fenner, Hillsdale Farm, R.R. 1, Mt. Forest, ON, Canada N0G 2L0

Annual dues: Can$3 (Canadian members only)

The society maintains an iris display garden at the Royal Botanical Gardens in Hamilton, Ontario, and its activities are centered there and in the Toronto area. Shows are held in both cities in June, at the height of flowering season for tall bearded irises. Members may also attend meetings and plant auctions, and all receive the society's quarterly newsletter.

Canadian Orchid Society
128 Adelaide Street, Winnipeg, MB, Canada R3A 0W5

Annual dues: US$25 U.S., Can$25 Canada, US$28 overseas

Publishes the quarterly *Canadian Orchid Journal*, with brief articles on the care of different orchid types and notes on the activities of local orchid societies.

Canadian Prairie Lily Society
A. E. Delahey, R.R. 5, Saskatoon, SK, Canada S7K 3J8

Annual dues: Can$4

The society organizes an annual lily show and periodic field trips, sponsors fall bulb sales to members, and publishes a quarterly newsletter, a six-page typed affair with short articles and society news.

Canadian Rose Society
Dianne Lask, 686 Pharmacy Avenue, Scarborough, ON, Canada M1L 3H8

Annual dues: Can$15

Members receive three issues of *Rosarian* magazine and a copy of the *Rose Annual*. The society maintains several demonstration gardens and a library. At meetings members may buy plants and books.

The Canadian Wildflower Society
James A. French, 35 Bauer Crescent, Unionville, ON, Canada L3R 4H3
Telephone: 416-477-3992

Annual dues: US$15 U.S., Can$15 Canada, Can$25 overseas

Devoted to the study, cultivation, and conservation of native plants. The quarterly magazine, *Wildflower*, is filled with pictures and articles on various wildflower subjects. A two-part series in 1987 supplied descriptions of all known trillium species, along with information on habitat and culture. The spring issue contained a list of U.S. and Canadian seed sources. The society sells books to members, organizes workshops and field trips, and runs a plant sale at its annual May meeting.

Center for Plant Conservation
125 The Arborway, Jamaica Plain, MA 02130
Telephone: 617-524-6988

Annual dues: contribution of $30 or more suggested

A non-profit organization working to save endangered plant species, run as a consortium of 19 botanical gardens. Contributors receive a quarterly newsletter with articles on rare and endangered plants and on the conservation efforts of the cooperating aboretums.

Colorado Native Plant Society
P.O. Box 200, Fort Collins, CO 80522

Annual dues: $8

Devoted to the appreciation and preservation of Colorado's native flora. Members may participate in field trips, seminars, workshops, and classes and are encouraged to become involved in activities related to plant conservation. The quarterly newsletter, *Aquilegia*, contains articles on various wildflowers and schedules of upcoming field trips and workshops. The society holds an annual meeting; local chapters meet more frequently.

Connecticut Horticultural Society
150 Main Street, Wethersfield, CT 06109
Telephone: 203-529-8713

Annual dues: $12

An organization for anyone with an interest in gardening and horticulture. The society holds monthly lecture meetings, spring and fall plant sales, periodic workshops, and weekend garden visits. Members may join several tours each year, from a December poinsettia-viewing excursion to Longwood Gardens to lengthier horticultural trips abroad. The monthly

newsletter keeps members posted on the many society activities and includes book reviews, seasonal growing tips, and a regular herb column. The society's library is open to members and the public on weekday afternoons.

The Cottage Garden Society
Mrs. Philippa Carr, 15 Faenol Avenue, Abergele, Clwyd., Britain LL22 7HT

Annual dues: $10 U.S., £4 Canada, £3 U.K.

Formed in 1982 "for the benefit of owners of small gardens who want to keep alive the tradition of gardening in the cottage style." The quarterly *Newsletter* serves as a forum for the exchange of information on old-fashioned flower varieties and for the exchange of seeds. Members in Great Britain may attend local chapter meetings.

The Cryptanthus Society
2355 Rusk, Beaumont, TX 77702

Annual dues: $10, $15 Canada and overseas

An international organization that puts cryptanthus enthusiasts in touch with fellow growers around the world. The quarterly *Journal* carries articles on newly discovered species, new hybrids, cryptanthus culture, and notes on the activities of local societies. A lending slide library is available to members.

The Cycad Society
1161 Phyllis Court, Mountain View, CA 94040

Annual dues: $10

The Cycad Society Newsletter is published quarterly and contains information on society activities and articles on various cycad subjects. A library is maintained at the Selby Botanical Garden in Sarasota, Florida, and members may draw on the resources of the society's seed and pollen banks.

Cyclamen Society
Dr. D. Bent, 9 Tudor Drive, Otford, Kent, England TN14 5QP
Telephone: 44-9592-2322

Annual dues: £5.50

Members receive a biannual journal, which contains articles on cyclamen species and cultivars, some illustrated in color. The society sponsors a seed sale and exchange every September and offers members a few books. As many cyclamen species are in danger of extinction in the wild, the society works actively to ensure their survival by lobbying to close loopholes in international export laws and by maintaining a directory of rare plants in cultivation. Members are invited to meetings, shows, and an annual conference weekend.

The Cymbidium Society of America, Inc.
6881 Wheeler Avenue, Westminster, CA 92683

Annual dues: $15

Publishes a bimonthly color journal, *The Orchid Advocate*, which contains articles on the culture and exhibition of cymbidiums, paphiopedilums, and "other selected genera" (a dendrobium was the only "other" orchid that made it into the issue we saw). In 1987 the journal ran a series of articles on commercial growers and a two-part guide to the ethics of collecting wild species. Many branches maintain libraries and offer plants for sale at meetings. Overseas members who want the journal sent by air mail should add $15 to the dues.

The Delphinium Society
Mrs. Shirley Bassett, "Takakkaw," Ice House Wood, Oxted, Surrey, England RH8 9DW

Annual dues: US$6 U.S. and Canada

Members receive a packet of hand-pollinated delphinium seed and *The Delphinium Society Yearbook*, a thick color-illustrated booklet with articles on delphinium care, notes on new cultivars, reviews of shows and competitions, and notes on society business. Members are also given the opportunity to buy additional delphinium seed. North American members may have the yearbook and seed list sent by air mail for an additional $6.

Dwarf Iris Society
Lynda Miller, 3167 E. US 224, Ossian, IN 46777
Telephone: 219-597-7403

Annual dues: $3

A section of the American Iris Society. Members receive two newsletters, a chance to be on round-robin letter circuits, and an invitation to the annual meeting, held during the American Iris Society convention. The society maintains several display gardens.

Epiphyllum Society of America
Betty Berg, P.O. Box 1395, Monrovia, CA 91016
Telephone: 805-259-4637

Annual dues: $6 U.S. and Canada, $12 overseas

Publishes a bimonthly bulletin and maintains a library for members. Plants are sold at meetings.

Friends of the Devonian Botanic Garden
Univ. of Alberta, Edmonton, AB, Canada T6G 2E1

Annual dues: Can$15

Membership includes a subscription to the quarterly journal *Kinnikinnick*, an opportunity to shop from the garden's seed and perennial plant lists in February and May, and a chance to join in a round-robin letter circle. The dues also help to support the Devonian Botanic Garden. The issue of *Kinnikinnick* that we received included a lengthy article on the new saskatoon cultivar, Smoky, a story on early native-American horticulture on the Plains, and a report on research into biological weed control.

Friends of the Farm
Hopewell Farms, Rt. 1, Box 32, Dalton City, IL 61925
Telephone: 217-864-2679

Annual dues: $15

An organization that works to promote organic practices in commercial farming. A four-page monthly newsletter, *Tuning In*, contains articles on natural pest controls, open-pollinated vegetables, and natural soil improvement methods.

The approach, however, is more political than instructional, and the articles are fairly light on practical advice. More than 40 demonstration farms throughout the U.S. are affiliated with the organization.

Friends of the Fig Society
5715 W. Paul Bryant Drive, Crystal River, FL 32629
Telephone: 904-795-0489 or 404-253-6362

Annual dues: $5

An organization of more than 100 fig enthusiasts throughout the U.S. "and a couple of foreign countries." Members receive *The Fig Leaf*, a twelve-page quarterly newsletter full of letters from members and articles on fig culture. The spring 1987 issue devoted six pages to thorough descriptions of several unusual fig varieties. The society encourages plant exchanges between members and keeps a library of books on figs.

Friends of the Trees Society
P.O. Box 1466, Chelan, WA 98816

Annual dues: $5 (plus $5 for airmail overseas)

The *Friends of the Trees Yearbook* is a veritable *Whole Earth Catalog* of forestry and self-sufficient gardening. Articles on various gardening subjects share space with extensive directories of organizations, suppliers, magazines, and books. An article on planting trees with a hoedad, for example, is followed by a dozen sources of manual tree-planting equipment and reviews of as many books on reforestation. The society also publishes the *Actinidia Enthusiasts Newsletter* for growers and fans of kiwi fruit ($3 per issue, annual), a seed catalog ($1.50), and a few other books and pamphlets.

Garden History Society
Mrs. Anne Richards, 5 The Knoll, Hereford, England HR1 1RU

Annual dues: £13.50 or US$30, £12 U.K.

The society organizes tours for members, sponsors lectures and conferences, and publishes the biannual *Garden History*, a journal rich with scholarly articles on historical gardens and related matters. To keep up with the many society activities, members receive three newsletters a year.

Gardenia Society of America
Box 879, Atwater, CA 95301

Annual dues: $5

Publishes a biannual newsletter, *Gardenia News*, which offers information on new varieties and sources. Experts are available to answer members' questions.

Georgia Botanical Society
Mrs. Eleanor F. Lehner, 1645 Kellogg Springs Drive, Dunwoody, GA 30338

Annual dues: $15

Members may participate in regular field trips and such special events as an October fungi walk, a winter tree-identification program, and a spring wildflower weekend. The society publishes a quarterly newsletter and a biannual magazine, *Tipularia*.

Gesneriad Hybridizers Association
4115 Pillar Drive, Rt. 1, Whitmore Lake, MI 48189

Annual dues: $5

An affiliate of the American Gloxinia and Gesneriad Society. Members receive *Crosswords*, a triannual journal with articles on new hybrids and features on important hybridizers. The association's annual meeting takes place during the A.G.G.S. convention.

Gesneriad Society International
P.O. Box 102, Greenwood, IN 46142

Annual dues: $12.50, $15.75 Canada and overseas

Membership includes a subscription to *Gesneriad Sainpaulia News*, a 64-page bimonthly magazine filled with articles on gesneriad culture, some illustrated in color. The society sponsors seed sales and exchanges and offers books and plants for sale to members. Round-robin letter circuits allow members to keep in touch with each other, and experts are available to answer specific cultural questions.

The Hardy Plant Society
Garden Cottage, 214 Ruxley Lane, West Ewell, Surrey, England KT17 9EU

Annual dues: £6

Members receive two issues of *The Hardy Plant*, a fat little magazine with informative articles on perennials, gardens, and other subjects of interest. Three newsletters containing information on society activities and meetings are also mailed to members. Members may take part in the annual seed exchange and may attend meetings, slide lectures, and garden tours when in Great Britain.

Hardy Plant Society of Oregon
Connie Hanni, 33530 S.E. Bluff Road, Boring, OR 97009

Annual dues: $12

Though based in Oregon, the society welcomes members wherever they live. Membership includes two issues of the society's newsletter, which contains articles, news, and source lists, and a chance to join field trips and attend meetings, workshops, and lectures.

Hawaiian Botanical Society
Dept. of Botany, Univ. of Hawaii at Manoa, 3190 Maile Way, Honolulu, HI 96822

Annual dues: $7.50

The society provides a forum and meeting place for gardeners interested in plants of Hawaii and other Pacific islands. Three or four newsletters are sent out each year, with articles on newly discovered or endangered species, botanical studies of plant habitats, and notes on society business. Nine meetings are held each year; there are also occasional society-sponsored forays to gardens and wild spots.

The Heather Society
Mrs. A. Small, Denbeigh, All Saints Road, Creeting St. Mary, Ipswich, Suffolk, England IP6 8PJ

Annual dues: US$10, Can$14, or £6

Members receive a *Bulletin* three times a year, with notes on society business and member activities, as well as the annual *Yearbook*, a thick booklet with articles on nurseries and growers, tips on heather culture, notes on new cultivars, book reviews, and an index to articles on heather in other magazines and journals. The society maintains a trial garden at Harlow Car Gardens in Harrogate and is working on a display garden at the R.H.S. Garden at Wisley. A number of booklets on heather culture and garden design are available to members at reasonable prices.

Heliconia Society International
c/o Flamingo Gardens, 3750 Flamingo Road, Ft. Lauderdale, FL 33330

Annual dues: $20

Publishes a color-illustrated *Bulletin* with articles on heliconia and related plants (Musaceae, Strelitziaceae, Lowiaceae, Zingiberaceae, Costaceae, Cannaceae, and Marantaceae). The spring 1987 issue contained an account of a heliconia-viewing trip to Costa Rica, an article on the culture of *Canna* × *ehemannii*, and a report on some experiments in growing *Heliconia stricta* from seed. Members may attend an annual June conference, at which plants are sold.

Herb Research Foundation
P.O. Box 2602, Longmont, CO 80501
Telephone: 303-449-2265

Annual dues: $25, $30 Canada and overseas

Members receive the quarterly journal *HerbalGram*, which contains articles on the botany, chemistry, and pharmacology of herbs. The journal seems to be aimed at commercial growers and producers of herbal products, particularly herbal remedies, though the articles are written at a level that can be appreciated by even casual readers.

The Herb Society of America, Inc.
2 Independence Court, Concord, MA 01742

Annual dues: $28

An organization for gardeners interested in the cultivation, history, and use of herbs. The society tries to steer clear of any advice on the medicinal use of herbs. *The Herbarist*, the society's annual, contains articles on such subjects as herbal moth repellents and historic gardens. Thirty pages of the 1987 issue were devoted to an article on the Botanic Garden in Cambridge, Massachusetts, which was maintained from 1805 to 1834. Members also receive a quarterly newsletter and may participate in the activities of local units (by invitation only).

Heritage Roses Group
See addresses below

Annual dues: $5, $5.25 Canada, $5.75 overseas

"A fellowship for those who care about old roses." Rather than bind the fellowship into a single organization, the group has split it up so that prospective members must track down the appropriate address from a list of seven regional coordinators. Here they are: Northeast—Lily Shohan, Rt. 1, Box 228, Clinton Corners, NY 12514. North Central—Henry Najat, 6365 Wald Road, Monroe, WI 53566. Northwest—Mary Rae Mattix, 120 N. Barner Drive, Centralia, WA 98531. Southwest—Margaret Blodgett, 1452 Curtis Street, Berkeley, CA 94702 or Miriam Wilkins, 925 Galvin Drive, El Cerrito, CA 94530. South Central—Mitzi VanSant, 4806 Evans Avenue, Austin, TX 78751. Southeast—Charles A. Walker, Jr., 1512 Gorman Street, Raleigh, NC 27606. Members receive an unillustrated quarterly journal, *The Rose Letter*. The different regional coordinators put out supplier lists and answer questions about old roses.

Hobby Greenhouse Association
609 Palomino Circle, Paso Robles, CA 93446

Annual dues: $10, $12 Canada, $14 overseas

Publishes *Hobby Greenhouse*, a quarterly newsletter that usually runs to 24 pages. The summer 1987 issue contained articles on window greenhouses, the praying mantis, bromeliads, dendrobiums, rhipsalis, and African violet culture. Members are invited to participate in round-robin letters and may send specific gardening questions to the association's board of experts.

The Holly Society of America, Inc.
304 N. Wind Road, Baltimore, MD 21204

Annual dues: $15

Members receive the *Holly Society Journal*, a 40-page illustrated quarterly split between notes on society business and articles on such subjects as holly arboreta, new cultivars, and collecting expeditions. At the annual meeting members may join in a holly auction and cutting exchange. During the rest of the year they may attend chapter meetings and garden tours. The society offers a number of books and pamphlets on holly culture and identification.

Home Orchard Society
P.O. Box 776, Clackamas, OR 97015

Annual dues: $10

Organized "to promote the science, culture and pleasure of fruit-bearing trees, shrubs, vines, and plants in the home landscape." Membership includes a subscription to *Pome News*, a quarterly journal, and an invitation to the March meeting, which includes a scion exchange and rootstock sale. In the fall classes are given in backyard orchard techniques.

Horticultural Society of New York
128 W. 58th Street, New York, NY 10019
Telephone: 212-757-0915

Annual dues: $25 for basic membership, $50 for full membership

Basic membership includes a subscription to the society's bimonthly *Newsletter*, a discount on all classes, books, and plants offered by the society; use of the library, and invitations to tours, shows, and the annual meeting. Full membership also includes a subscription to *Garden* magazine (see

entry under *Magazines*, page 270), two first-day tickets to the New York Flower Show, and borrowing privileges at the society library.

The Hoya Society International
Chistine M. Burton, P.O. Box 54271, Atlanta, GA 30308

Annual dues: inquire

The society publishes a quarterly newsletter, offers books for sale, and maintains a library. Members may participate in round-robin letters.

Hydroponic Society of America
P.O. Box 6067, Concord, CA 94524

Annual dues: $25 U.S. and Canada, $35 overseas

Members receive a bimonthly newsletter as well as a volume with the transcripts of talks given at the annual conference. Occasional greenhouse tours and speaker meetings are organized, and we're told that regional chapters are being formed. The newsletters contain several pages of advertisements from suppliers of hydroponic equipment.

Hydroponic Society of Victoria
Dr. B. C. Hanger, P.O. Box 174, Ferntree Gully, Victoria, Australia 3156

Annual dues: Aus$20

Publishes a monthly newsletter, much of which is taken up with articles from other sources. A recent issue featured stories on growing *Aloe vera* hydroponically, the merits of various growing media, and greenhouse culture of roses. Books and plants are sold at meetings.

Ikebana International
C.P.O. Box 1262, Tokyo 100-91, Japan
Telephone: 81-3-293-8188

Annual dues: 7,000 yen

A worldwide organization devoted to the promotion of ikebana, the Japanese art of flower arranging. Members receive three issues of *Ikebana International*, a colorful magazine with articles by experts in various schools of flower arranging. Each issue includes a big picture gallery of exceptional arrangements. The Tokyo office will put interested members in touch with local chapters so that they may take part in workshops and meetings. Chapter members may also pay dues more conveniently through their local organizations.

Illinois Native Plant Society
Dept. of Botany, Southern Illinois Univ., Carbondale, IL 62901-6509

Annual dues: $10 U.S. and Canada

Publishes a quarterly newsletter, *The Harbinger*, which contains reports on meetings, short articles on native plants, and a schedule of upcoming field trips, programs, and chapter meetings. Members also receive two issues of *Eringenia*, a journal with more comprehensive articles. The society offers discounts to members on a wide range of natural history books.

Indigenous Bulb Growers' Association of South Africa
P.O. Box 141, Woodstock, Cape Town, South Africa 7915
Annual dues: R5

Members receive the annual *IBSA Bulletin* with articles that sometimes range beyond the confines of indigenous South African plants. Local benefits include a chance to attend meetings, collecting trips, and plant and seed sales.

Indoor Citrus & Rare Fruit Society
W. Doty, 176 Coronado Avenue, Los Altos, CA 94022
Annual dues: $15 U.S. and Canada, $18 overseas

Publishes a 24-page quarterly newsletter, each issue of which includes articles on citrus culture, upcoming society activities, and seed and book offers for members. The society will also track down sources of seeds and plants at the request of individual members and will direct them to books and articles with information on specific species and varieties.

The Indoor Gardening Society of America, Inc.
R. Morrison, 5305 S.W. Hamilton Street, Portland, OR 97221
Annual dues: $10 U.S. and Canada, $12 overseas

The Indoor Garden, the society's bimonthly journal, contains articles on various indoor plants, with information on choosing plants and caring for them on a windowsill or under lights. Featured in two recent issues were bromeliads, caladiums, trailing African violets, crossandra, and loquat trees. Shorter notes and letters from readers touched on an even wider range of plants, including episcias, cacti, and orchids. The society offers a good selection of books and cultural guides to members, organizes an annual seed exchange, and encourages round-robin letters.

International Aroid Society
Box 43-1853. S. Miami, FL 33143
Annual dues: $15, $18 Canada and overseas

Membership includes a subscription to *Aroideana*, an illustrated quarterly journal with scholarly articles on aroids. U.S. members also receive a monthly newsletter, and those in the Miami area may attend monthly meetings at Fairchild Tropical Garden and may use the society's library.

International Camellia Society
Thomas H. Perkins III, P.O. Box 750, Brookhaven, MS 39601
Telephone: 601-833-7351
Annual dues: $11 U.S. and Canada

Members receive the annual *International Camellia Journal*, a thick color-illustrated book with articles on camellia culture and gardens around the world. The society is truly an international organization, with membership coordinators in England, Italy, France, Spain, Portugal, West Germany, Australia, New Zealand, Japan, and South Africa. An international conference is held every other year, each time in a different country (in Italy in 1988).

International Carnivorous Plant Society
Fullerton Arboretum, Fullerton, CA 92634
Telephone: 714-738-5006
Annual dues: $10 U.S. and Canada, $15 overseas

Publishes the *Carnivorous Plant Newsletter*, a quarterly journal with color and black-and-white photographs and articles that range from cultural advice for beginners to more advanced articles on taxonomy. The society maintains a seed bank and sells seeds to members.

International Dwarf Fruit Tree Association
A-338-A Dept. of Horticulture, Michigan State Univ., E. Lansing, MI 48824
Annual dues: $45

An organization devoted to promoting the popularity and understanding of dwarf fruit trees; the membership is made up primarily of commercial growers and research scientists. A conference is held each year, and the proceedings are issued as an annual publication. Members also receive bimonthly newsletters.

International Geranium Society
4610 Druid Street, Los Angeles, CA 90032
Telephone: 213-222-6809
Annual dues: $12.50

Geraniums Around the World, the society's color-illustrated quarterly journal, contains articles on all aspects of geranium culture. Seven branches in California hold monthly meetings; the society hosts an annual meeting and banquet. Members may order seeds for unusual species and varieties from the society's seed bank.

International Lilac Society
P.O. Box 315, Rumford, ME 04276
Telephone: 207-562-7453
Annual dues: $10

Members receive the monthly *Lilac Newsletter* and a copy of the *Annual Meeting Proceedings*. For an additional $5 they may order the society's *Register of Cultivar Names*, which lists all known lilac cultivars, with synonyms, parentage, breeders, and dates of introduction. The society holds an annual meeting, organizes a plant sale, and offers lilac seed to members. Canadian members may send dues in Canadian funds to Charles Holetich, Box 399 Royal Botanical Gardens, Hamilton, ON, L8N 3H8.

International Ornamental Crabapple Society
Thomas L. Green, Morton Arboretum, Lisle, IL 60532
Telephone: 312-968-0074
Annual dues: $15

Publishes a quarterly journal, *Malus*, with articles on unusual species and varieties, cultural notes, and reports on society business. The winter issue contains the proceedings of the annual meeting, held each August.

The International Palm Society
P.O. Box 368, Lawrence, KS 66044

Annual dues: $15

Membership includes a subscription to *Principes*, a 50-page quarterly journal with articles on the natural habitats of palms, conservation of rare species, commercial uses of palms in cultivation, and other subjects of interest to palm enthusiasts. Most articles are illustrated with black-and-white photographs. The society maintains a seed bank for members and offers a selection of books for sale by mail.

International Society for Horticultural Science
De Dreijen 6, 6703 BC Wageningen, Netherlands
Telephone: 31-8370-21747

Annual dues: US$25 or 50 Dutch guilders

Publishes the quarterly journal *Chronica Horticulturae*, with scientific articles on various botanical subjects. A recent issue contained papers on soil compaction, fire blight, carbon dioxide levels in the greenhouse, and diseases of apricot trees.

Kansas Wildflower Society
Mulvane Art Center, Washburn Univ., Topeka, KS 66621

Annual dues: $10

An organization devoted to promoting awareness and conservation of Kansas's wildflowers. Members may join dozens of field trips and may attend lectures and workshops on various wildflower subjects. A quarterly newsletter compiles articles on plants and natural habitats.

Los Angeles International Fern Society
P.O. Box 90943, Pasadena, CA 91109-0943

Annual dues: $15 U.S. and Canada, $19 overseas

Publishes a bimonthly journal and offers spore and books to members by mail. Plants are sold at monthly meetings and exhibited at an annual show.

Louisiana Iris Society of America
Betty Jamieson, 26 Cambre Circle, Hot Springs Village, AR 71909

Annual dues: $3

A section of the American Iris Society; gardeners must be members of the larger organization to join this one. For their $3, members receive two newsletters, a chance to participate in round-robin letters, and an invitation to the annual meeting, held to coincide with the American Iris Society's convention. Several display gardens are in the works.

The Maine Organic Farmers and Gardeners Association
P.O. Box 2176, Augusta, ME 04330

Annual dues: $20

Membership includes a subscription to *The Maine Organic Farmer & Gardener* (see entry under *Magazines*, page 272) as well as a bimonthly newsletter and access to expert advice and technical assistance. The association actively promotes the use of safe and sustainable organic growing methods. A research library is open to members.

Marigold Society of America, Inc.
P.O. Box 112, New Britain, PA 18901

Annual dues: $10

The society sends gift seeds to members every spring, answers marigold questions, maintains a display garden at River Farm in Mt. Vernon, Virginia, and publishes the quarterly *Amerigold Newsletter*, with articles on shows, marigold cultivars, and important growers and a calendar of society events. The annual meeting is held each July "at a place of particular horticultural interest." Lompoc, California, was the chosen spot in 1987 because of its importance as a center of the marigold seed business. (There's a family connection here: William Morris, the society's president, is my uncle.)

The Massachusetts Horticultural Society
Horticultural Hall, 300 Massachusetts Avenue, Boston, MA 02115
Telephone: 617-536-9280

Annual dues: $35

Membership includes a subscription to *Horticulture* magazine (see entry under *Magazines*, page 271), a bimonthly newsletter, borrowing privileges at the world's oldest and largest horticultural library, access to the society's plant hotline (a free cultural advice service), free admission to the spring flower show and to many botanical gardens across North America, and invitations to garden tours, classes, and workshops. After spending many hours in the library at Horticultural Hall during the research for this book, we can recommend it as one of the finest places on earth for the curious gardener.

Michigan Botanical Club
Mathaei Botanical Gardens, 1800 Dixboro Road, Ann Arbor, MI 48105

Annual dues: $12

Members receive *The Michigan Botanist*, a quarterly journal, may attend monthly slide lectures from September to April, and may join regular field trips.

Minnesota Native Plant Society
220 Biological Sciences Center, 1445 Gortner Avenue, Univ. of Minnesota, St. Paul, MN 55108

Annual dues: $8 (U.S. members only)

The society sponsors field trips and plant-identification workshops, holds monthly meetings from October to May, and publishes the triannual newsletter *Minnesota Plant Press*, which offers a calendar of upcoming events, articles on native plants, and book reviews. Members may participate in an annual seed exchange and seedling sale.

Minnesota State Horticultural Society
161 Alderman Hall, 1970 Folwell Avenue, St. Paul, MN 55108
Telephone: 612-373-1031

Annual dues: $15 U.S. and Canada, $20 overseas

Publishes *The Minnesota Horticulturist*, a color magazine with articles on a range of subjects of interest to general home gardeners. A recent issue included stories on edible wild plants, the Eloise Butler Wildflower Garden, a plan for a compact composter, and seasonal garden reminders. Nine issues are mailed each year. Members may borrow books from the society's library by mail, may attend shows, workshops, and tours, and may call or write the society for advice on gardening problems.

Mississippi Native Plant Society
Travis Salley, 202 N. Andrews Avenue, Cleveland, MS 38732
Telephone: 601-843-2330
Annual dues: $5

Sponsors periodic field trips, holds occasional meetings, and publishes a quarterly newsletter with notes on society business and some articles on wildflowers.

National Chrysanthemum Society
H.B. Locke, 2 Lucas House, Craven Road, Rugby, Warwickshire, England CV21 3JQ
Annual dues: £9

Members receive spring and fall *Bulletins*, with cultural articles, reports on society activities, and reviews of new cultivars, along with a summer *Year Book*, which holds more extensive articles and a few color pictures. Members may attend the meetings of regional groups, are given free passes to national shows, and may write for advice on cultural problems.

National Chrysanthemum Society, Inc. USA
Galen L. Goss, 5012 Kingston Drive, Annandale, VA 22003
Annual dues: $8.50

Publishes *The Chrysanthemum*, a quarterly journal filled with articles on chrysanthemum culture, notes on new varieties, and advice for exhibitors. Each new member is sent a copy of the *Beginner's Handbook*, a color-illustrated guide to choosing and growing chrysanthemums. The society sells a number of other books and pamphlets, including a register and classification guide that describes 2,000 cultivars. Members are invited to attend the annual show, which features tours and speakers in addition to the exhibition. Slides may be rented.

National Gardening Association
180 Flynn Avenue, Burlington, VT 05401
Telephone: 802-863-1308
Annual dues: $18, $24 Canada and overseas

Publishes *National Gardening*, a glossy monthly magazine loaded with articles on growing fruits and vegetables and illustrated with color photographs throughout. A recent issue included a comparison of different raspberry varieties, an article on corn earworms, advice on growing perennial flowers from seed, and the regular monthly "Seed Swap" and "Seed Search" columns with lists of plants that members are looking for or have for trade. The association publishes a number of books, all available for sale to members, and operates a call- or write-in garden problem-solving service.

National Junior Horticultural Association
441 E. Pine Street, Fremont, MI 49412
Annual dues: none

Membership is open to young people, ages 6 to 22, who want to learn more about plants and horticulture. While the association encourages an interest in gardening as a hobby, its ultimate goal is to help members discover career opportunities in horticulture. Members receive the irregular (two or three issues a year) newsletter *Going & Growing*.

National Oleander Society
P.O. Box 3431, Galveston, TX 77552-0431
Annual dues: $5

Members receive the quarterly newsletter *The Nerium News*, with articles on oleander culture, and may send for free seeds with a self-addressed stamped envelope. Cuttings will also be supplied for a nominal fee. The society has compiled a slide show of Galveston's oleanders, which it will lend to members for the cost of postage. Monthly meetings are held in Galveston; the society sponsors occasional field trips.

The National Sweet Pea Society
L. H. O. Williams, Acacia Cottage, Down Ampney, Cirencester, Glos., England, GL7 5QW
Telephone: 44-793-750385
Annual dues: £10 U.S. and Canada, £9 U.K.

The society hosts at least two exhibitions each year, to which members are admitted free of charge, and organizes regular meetings and lectures. Members receive a copy of the booklet *How To Grow Sweet Peas*, two issues of the society's *Bulletin*, and the thick, color-illustrated *Annual*.

National Wildflower Research Center
2600 FM 973 North, Austin, TX 78725
Telephone: 512-929-3600
Annual dues: $25

Lady Bird Johnson donated the land and the initial funding for the National Wildflower Research Center in 1982, and the organization has since grown with donations from across the country. Members receive the quarterly newsletter *Wildflower*, and, beginning in the fall of 1987, the biannual *Wildflower Journal*. Members may ask for seed source lists, compiled for each state, and may order books, T-shirts, note cards, and wildflower sculptures. The research center will either sell or lend slides and will answer questions about wildflower care. Members are invited to special events, tours, and seminars, and have a standing invitation to visit the display gardens and research plots in Austin.

Native Plant Society of New Mexico
P.O. Box 5917, Santa Fe, NM 87502
Annual dues: $8

An organization "dedicated to promoting a greater appreciation of native plants in their environment and to the preservation of endangered species." Members receive a bimonthly newsletter that starts out with an action-packed calendar of upcoming events. Field trips, plant sales, slide shows, local meetings, and an annual statewide meeting keep New Mexico wildflower fans in the thick of things virtually every week of the year. A couple of articles in each issue may help while away the hours in between activities. The society sells a few books to members at a discount; the sales list is published periodically in the newsletter.

Native Plant Society of Oregon

Dan Luoma, 2912 N.W. Arthur, Corvallis, OR 97330
Telephone: 503-758-8063

Annual dues: $10

Works to encourage the enjoyment and protection of Oregon's native plants. Members receive a quarterly newsletter with a schedule of field trips, workshops, flower shows, and chapter meetings as well as informative articles on nomenclature, plant explorers, and the natural habitats of wildflowers. The society holds an annual statewide meeting for all members and offers a number of gift items for sale, including note cards, posters, and T-shirts.

Native Plant Society of Texas

1204 S. Trinity Street, Decatur, TX 76234

Annual dues: $15

The society and its regional chapters organize field trips to parks, preserves, botanical gardens, and research centers; sponsor work sessions that include plant surveys, habitat restoration, and plant rescues in areas about to be developed; and host lectures and symposia. The bimonthly *Texas Native Plant Society News* keeps members posted on all activities and provides a forum for seed sales and exchanges. Articles focus on important parks and native plant preserves and on proposed developments that threaten important habitats.

New England Botanical Club, Inc.

22 Divinity Avenue, Cambridge, MA 02138

Annual dues: $25

Membership includes a subscription to *Rhodora*, a quarterly journal with scholarly articles focusing on New England plant life. The spring 1987 issue, for example, contained an 80-page article on the rare flora of Massachusetts, studies of *Dahlia congestifolia* and of the invasion of eastern North America by *Carex praegracilis*, a story on Maria L. Owen, a 19th-century Nantucket botanist, and book reviews and notes on upcoming meetings and conferences. The club maintains a large herbarium of New England plants and a library.

New England Wild Flower Society, Inc.

Garden in the Woods, Hemenway Road, Framingham, MA 01701
Telephone: 617-877-7630 or 237-4924

Annual dues: $25

The Garden in the Woods, the society's 45-acre wildflower preserve, contains more than 1,500 native species and varieties, many of them rare and endangered. Anyone may visit and wander the trails; members are entitled to free admission. Membership also includes a subscription to the bian-

nual journal *Wild Flower Notes*, with articles on many aspects of gardening with wildflowers. A quarterly newsletter keeps members informed of lectures, educational programs, and tours. Members may borrow books and slides from the society's library and are offered a discount on plants, books, and gifts. (Plants are not sold by mail.) Among the society's publications are some excellent guides to propagating and cultivating native plants. Every winter the society organizes a wildflower seed sale open to the general public (see entry under *Wildflowers*, page 177.)

New Jersey Native Plant Society

P.O. Box 1295R, Morristown, NJ 07960

Annual dues: $10

Publishes a quarterly newsletter and organizes field trips, workshops, plant exchanges, and symposia. Founded in 1983, the society is currently planning a wildflower garden, but has not yet settled on the location. A recent issue of the newsletter included articles on wild columbines, the germination of milkweed, and several natural areas threatened by development.

North American Fruit Explorers

Rt. 1, Box 94, Chapin, IL 62628

Annual dues: $8, $10 Canada and overseas

An organization of fruit-growing enthusiasts interested in finding, testing, and preserving superior fruit and nut varieties "regardless of their commercial importance." The society's quarterly journal, *Pomona*, contains reports from members and experts on their trials of various cultivars as well as informative articles on fruit culture, propagation techniques, and breeding procedures. New members are sent a copy of *The Handbook for Fruit Explorers*, a 146-page reference guide to amateur pomology. Annual meetings are held at important fruit-development centers, such as the New York State Fruit Testing Station and Oregon State University. Local chapters hold more frequent meetings, and some sponsor orchard visits. Members may borrow books by mail from the society's library, and exchange scion and bud wood through ads in *Pomona*.

North American Gladiolus Council

R. A. Vogt, 9338 Manzanita Drive, Sun City, AZ 85373

Annual dues: $7.50 U.S. and Canada, $10 overseas

Publishes the *North American Gladiolus Council Bulletin*, a 100-page quarterly journal with articles that range from cultural advice for beginners to hybridizing procedures and results of scientific research. Many local affiliates hold meetings and exhibitions.

North American Heather Society

Alice E. Knight, 62 Elma-Monte Road, Elma, WA 98541

Annual dues: $10

Members receive the quarterly newsletter *Heather News*, which contains botanical articles, notes on heather culture, features on species and cultivars, and information about society activities. Several local chapters hold regular meetings (a strong eastern chapter is based in Northampton, Massachusetts), and the national organization holds an annual meeting. Several regional display gardens are in the works.

North American Lily Society
Mrs. Dorothy Schaefer, P.O. Box 476, Waukee, IA 50263
Telephone: 515-987-1371

Annual dues: $12.50

New members are put in touch with regional societies, which hold meetings in almost every state and province in North America and which publish their own newsletters. The society sends members its quarterly *Bulletin*, a 50-page booklet with articles on different lily species and cultivars, cultural advice and notes on diseases and pests, and stories about public lily gardens. The society maintains a library and slide collection, sponsors a seed exchange, and encourages round-robin letters. The annual meeting includes speakers, garden tours, and a flower show.

North Carolina Wild Flower Preservation Society
Mrs. S. M. Cozart, 900 W. Nash Street, Wilson, NC 27893

Annual dues: $5

Publishes a biannual journal with articles on native plant habitats and wildflower culture and notes on society business. Spring and fall meetings are held; these include speakers, slide shows, and field trips. Other field trips are organized by local groups throughout the year. Seed and plant exchanges among members are encouraged. The society sells its *North Carolina Native Plant Propagation Handbook* for $3.

Northern Nevada Native Plant Society
P.O. Box 8965, Reno, NV 89507
Telephone: 702-358-7759

Annual dues: $7.50

Members are invited to participate in meetings, workshops, and a wide range of field trips, from picnics to mountain bike trips and overnight hikes. They also receive a monthly newsletter with short articles and a schedule of events as well as the irregularly published journal *Mentzelia* and occasional reprints of out-of-print papers. Plant sales are held occasionally during the year, and each fall the society sponsors a free seed distribution to members.

Northern Nut Growers Association
Kenneth Bauman, 9870 S. Palmer Road, New Carlisle, OH 45344

Annual dues: $15 U.S. and Canada, $17 overseas

An organization for both home and professional nut growers. The association publishes a quarterly newsletter, *The Nutshell*, with brief articles on such subjects as northern pecans, nutcracker collections, and blight-resistant chestnuts as well as news of association business. The *Annual Report* contains more substantial articles and usually runs to almost 200 pages. The association also publishes a book, *Nut Tree Culture in North America*, available for $17.50 postpaid ($18.50 to overseas addresses). Members are invited to the annual meeting in August, where they may attend lectures and demonstrations, visit important plantings, and view exhibits of new cultivars and equipment.

Ohio Native Plant Society
Ann Malmquist, 6 Louise Drive, Chagrin Falls, OH 44022

Annual dues: $7.50

The society sponsors lectures, field trips, and an annual dinner, maintains a display garden at the Garden Center of Greater Cleveland, and publishes a bimonthly journal. Seeds, plants, and books are sold to members.

Pennsylvania Horticultural Society
325 Walnut Street, Philadelphia, PA 19106
Telephone: 215-625-8250

Annual dues: $30

An organization devoted to the needs and interests of general home gardeners. Members receive the bimonthly color magazine *The Green Scene*, a recent issue of which included stories on potato culture, pressing flowers, ferns in the garden, cotton farming in New Jersey, and the restoration of a 17th-century garden. A monthly newsletter keeps members informed about upcoming lectures, workshops, field trips, garden visits, and tours (including some that venture abroad). The society maintains a library and gift shop and runs a horticultural hotline to answer questions about plant care. Members receive a free ticket to the Philadelphia Flower Show in March and to the P.H.S. Harvest Show in September.

Peperomia Society International
5240 W. 20th Street, Vero Beach, FL 32960

Annual dues: $5 U.S. and Canada, $8 overseas

Publishes a quarterly journal, *The Gazette*, with pictures and descriptions of peperomias, articles on propagation and cultivation, round-robin summaries, and information on plant sources. Members may exchange cuttings through notices in *The Gazette* and may join in round-robin letters.

Permaculture Institute of North America
4649 Sunnyside Avenue N., Seattle, WA 98103
Telephone: 206-547-6838

Annual dues: $25

An organization devoted to promoting sustainable agriculture in North America. Members receive four issues of *The Permaculture Activist*, a newsletter with articles on permaculture techniques and farms that have successfully applied them, reports on member activities, and notices of upcoming events and workshops. The institute operates a mail-order book service which offers about two dozen titles ranging from general gardening texts to specialized works on water management, forestry, and, of course, permaculture.

Puget Sound Dahlia Association
Roger L. Walker, 544 129th Avenue S.E., Bellevue, WA 98005

Annual dues: $10

Members receive a monthly bulletin and the annual journal *Dahlias of Today*. Plants and books are sold at meetings, and the association maintains a display garden at Volunteer Park in Seattle. Membership is limited to residents of the Northwest.

Rare Fruit Council International, Inc.
13609 Old Cutler Road, Miami, FL 33158
Telephone: 305-238-1360

Annual dues: $20

An organization devoted to furthering interest in tropical fruits. Membership includes a monthly newsletter with detailed articles on fruit culture and news of society activities. A recent issue contained a dozen pages on the mango, including an analysis of different cultivars, an illustrated guide to grafting, and a recipe for fresh mango ice cream. Members are invited to meetings, seminars, workshops, field trips, and an annual plant sale. In addition to the group centered in Miami, chapters have been formed in Palm Beach and Tampa Bay, Florida, and in Australia. The association has a display garden as well as a library at its headquarters.

Reblooming Iris Society
John Weiler, 1146 W. Rialto, Fresno, CA 93705

Annual dues: $3

A specialist group affiliated with the American Iris Society. The Reblooming Iris Society holds an annual symposium on remontant irises, publishes the biannual *Reblooming Iris Recorder*, holds a plant auction, and publishes a checklist of remontant iris cultivars.

Rhododendron Society of Canada
H. G. Hedges, R.R. 2, St. George, ON, Canada N0E 1N0

Annual dues: US$15 U.S., Can$15 Canada

The society sponsors an annual spring meeting; three regional affiliates gather more frequently. Members may participate in a seed exchange and may use the society's library. Two issues of the *Bulletin* are published each year, containing articles on rhododendron and azalea care and breeding.

Rhododendron Species Foundation
P.O. Box 3798, Federal Way, WA 98063-3798
Telephone: 206-927-6960 or 838-4646

Annual dues: $25

More than 1,700 forms of 475 rhododendron species grow in the foundation's 24-acre garden at Federal Way, the largest such collection in North America. Membership dues aid the foundation in its work of discovering, collecting, preserving, and distributing rare species. Members get free admission to the garden, a chance to participate in plant, seed, and pollen distributions, and invitations to attend classes and lectures. The foundation sends a quarterly newsletter to members and publishes a number of books and prints that it offers for sale.

The Royal National Rose Society
Chiswell Green, St. Albans, Herts., England AL2 3NR
Telephone: 44-727-50461

Annual dues: £8.50

Publishes *The Rose*, a color-illustrated quarterly journal with articles on rose care and breeding and reviews of new and old cultivars. New members receive copies of two introductory booklets, *How To Grow Roses* and *The Rose Directory*. The society maintains a display garden at St. Albans, where members may see more than 1,700 varieties in a garden setting. Members also receive free passes to the British National Rose Festival and to other society shows held throughout Great Britain and may use the society's extensive research library.

Saintpaulia International
P.O. Box 549, Knoxville, TN 37901

Annual dues: $12.50, $15.75 Canada and overseas

Members receive the bimonthly magazine *Gesneriad Saintpaulia News*, which is also a benefit of membership in the Gesneriad Society International. Local chapters hold meetings, workshops, tours, and plant sales. The national society holds an annual meeting, which includes speakers on various topics and an African violet exhibition.

Saskatchewan Orchid Society
M. Swartz, 221 Delayen Place, Saskatoon, SK, Canada S7N 2T9

Annual dues: Can$10

Publishes a bimonthly newsletter with growing tips, information on orchid culture, news of society events, and notes from other Canadian orchid societies. The society maintains a library, sells plants and books, and offers orchid growing supplies to members at good discounts.

Scottish Rock Garden Club
Miss K. M. Gibb, 21 Merchiston Park, Edinburgh, Scotland EH10 4PW

Annual dues: £5 or US$12

Members receive two issues of the club's color-illustrated journal and have access to the club's experts for answers to rock-gardening questions. Those in the area may participate in garden outings, plant sales, monthly meetings, and slide lectures. North American members may take part in the annual seed sale.

Seed Savers Exchange
Kent Whealy, Rt. 3, Box 239, Decorah, IA 52101

Annual dues: $12, US$16 Canada and Mexico, $24 overseas

A non-profit organization working to save heirloom and endangered vegetable varieties from extinction. Members receive two publications, the 256-page *Winter Yearbook* and the *Fall Harvest Edition*, which present articles on seed saving, interviews with collectors and growers, and "plant finder" ads from gardeners looking for and offering plants that have disappeared from commercial seed catalogs. Both volumes serve to connect the exchange's 600 members and to facilitate the exchange of the roughly 4,000 rare vegetable varieties they are growing and saving. The exchange's comprehensive directory to heirloom vegetable sources, *The Garden Seed Inventory*, is available for $15 postpaid. The exchange plants about a third of its inventory of rare seeds on its two-acre plot in Decorah each year, and visitors are welcome to visit during the summer and see the more than 1,000 varieties grown there.

Sempervivum Fanciers Association
Dr. C. William Nixon, 37 Oxbow Lane, Randolph, MA 02368

Annual dues: $12 U.S. and Canada, $14 overseas

Members receive a quarterly newsletter with articles on sempervivum cultivars, companion plants, and other subjects of interest as well as an annual membership list. Free hybrid seed is usually sent to members in the fall. The association does not yet hold regular meetings.

The Sempervivum Society
11 Wingle Tye Road, Burgess Hill, W. Sussex, England RH15 9HR
Telephone: 44-46-6848

Annual dues: £7.50

Publishes a biannual journal, *Houseleeks*, which contains articles on the botany of sempervivums as well as writing of more general interest. Many of the articles are illustrated in color. A quarterly newsletter offers schedules of upcoming events of interest to sempervivum fanciers around the world and includes less formal articles than are found in *Houseleeks*. The society publishes several books and helps to maintain a living reference collection of more than 1,000 species and cultivars. Plants and offsets from the collection are periodically offered to members for sale.

The Society for Japanese Irises
Mrs. Andrew C. Warner, 16815 Falls Road, Upperco, MD 21155
Telephone: 301-374-4788

Annual dues: $3.50

A section of the American Iris Society. Each year members receive two copies of *The Review*, a 20-page publication, one page of which is given over to reports of society business and the balance to articles on Japanese iris cultivars and advice on their care. The society rents slides and organizes round-robin letters. The annual meeting is held at the American Iris Society convention.

Society for Louisiana Irises
P.O. Box 40175, Univ. of Southern Louisiana, Lafayette, LA 70504

Annual dues: $7.50

Membership includes a subscription to the society's *Bulletin*, a color-illustrated journal issued irregularly. A quarterly newsletter is mailed at more reliable intervals. The society's annual meeting is held in April on the campus of the University of Southwestern Louisiana. The society publishes a checklist of Louisiana iris cultivars and in 1988 will complete a comprehensive book on Louisiana irises, which will contain many color plates.

Society for Pacific Coast Native Iris
4333 Oak Hill Road, Oakland, CA 94605

Annual dues: $4

A section of the American Iris Society devoted to furthering information about Pacific Coast irises. Membership is lim-

ited to members of the American Iris Society. The Society for Pacific Coast Native Iris publishes a biannual *Almanac*, with articles on native iris species and hybrids developed from them. Iris seed is offered for sale to members in the fall.

Society for Siberian Irises
Gunther Stark, 631 G24 Highway, Norwalk, IA 50211

Annual dues: $2.50

A section of the American Iris Society. Members receive two issues of *The Siberian Iris*, a journal with articles on various aspects of Siberian iris culture, illustrated with black-and-white photographs. A lending slide library is available to members, and round-robin letters allow growers with similar interests to share their observations.

South African Fuchsia Society
Box 193, Hilton, South Africa 3245

Annual dues: US$18

Members are sent three issues *Fuchsia Fanfare*, a 20-page journal with articles on fuchsia care and handy tips in letters from members. South African members may attend meetings and may use the society's library and borrow from its collections of slides and videos.

Southern California Botanists
Alan Romspert, Dept. of Biology, California State Univ. Fullerton, Fullerton, CA 92634
Telephone: 714-773-3614 or 2428

Annual dues: $8

A group devoted to the study of native California plants. *Crossosoma*, its bimonthly journal, usually runs to 12 pages, with articles and notices of upcoming events. The group funds research projects and often publishes the resulting studies in the journal. Members may take part in numerous field trips and may attend occasional slide presentations and the annual symposium.

Southern California Camellia Society
Mel Belcher, 7475 Brydon Road, La Verne, CA 91750
Telephone: 714-593-4894

Annual dues: $15

Members are sent four issues of the *Camellia Review*, a 20- to 30-page journal with articles on camellia culture and notes on exceptional varieties. The society also publishes the official camellia nomenclature book. Chapters hold monthly meetings from November through April and shows each weekend during the bloom months of January, February, and March.

Southern California Horticultural Institute
P.O. Box 49798, Barrington Sta., Los Angeles, CA 90049

Annual dues: $18

Membership includes a subscription to *Pacific Horticulture* (see entry under *Magazines*, page 273) and to a monthly bulletin with news of upcoming events. Meetings are held on the second Thursday of each month in Friendship Hall, near the southeast entrance to Griffith Park. The agenda may include a talk by a plant authority, plant sales and exhibits, book sales, and a plant raffle. Members are invited to attend occasional horticultural seminars and garden tours.

Southern Garden History Society
Old Salem, Inc., Drawer F, Salem Sta., Winston-Salem, NC 27101
Telephone: 919-724-3125
Annual dues: $15

Founded in 1982, the society seeks to "stimulate interest in Southern garden and landscape history and in the preservation and restoration of historic gardens and landscapes." Its quarterly newsletter, *Magnolia*, reports on the activities of member groups throughout the South. The editors plan to expand it soon to include longer articles, research pieces, and essays. At the annual meeting in April, members may hear reports on research and restoration projects and may visit nearby gardens of historic interest.

Species Iris Group of North America
Florence Stout, 150 N. Main Street, Lombard, IL 60148
Annual dues: $3.50

A section of the American Iris Society. The group issues a 40-page *Bulletin* each spring and fall and organizes an annual seed exchange. The seed list is mailed free to members, and the seeds may be ordered for a nominal charge. The group holds its annual meeting at the American Iris Society convention.

Spuria Iris Society
Floyd Wickenkamp, 10521 Bellarose Drive, Sun City, AZ 85351
Annual dues: $3

A section of the American Iris Society. Members receive two newsletters a year and may participate in a round-robin letter circuit. The society publishes several books and pamphlets, including a comprehensive checklist of spuria iris cultivars. The annual meeting is held at the American Iris Society convention.

Tennessee Native Plant Society
Dept. of Botany, Univ. of Tennessee, Knoxville, TN 37996
Telephone: 615-974-2256
Annual dues: $8

Founded to "promote interest in plant identification, folklore, growing native plants from seeds and cuttings, landscaping with natural plants, preserving native areas, and protecting rare plants." Members may join in a number of field trips during the year and may attend meetings (three or four, usually held in Nashville). The society publishes a bimonthly newsletter with articles on such subjects as wild berries, botanical photography, drying and pressing wildflowers, and planning a wildflower garden. Books are offered at a discount to members, and wildflower nurseries advertise in the newsletter.

Texas Horticultural Society
P.O. Box 10025, College Station, TX 77840
Telephone: 409-779-1051
Annual dues: $10

A society that straddles the fence between serving home gardeners and commercial growers. A recent issue of its monthly journal, *The Texas Horticulturist*, contained articles on employer sanctions in the Immigration Control and Reform Act, a program to control oak wilt disease, purple coneflowers for the perennial border, and the effect of an April freeze on the state's fruit and nut crops. The advertisements reflect the society's diverse membership: the offerings range from garden bulbs to a massive tractor-mounted sprayer. The society sells vegetable seed in the winter and early spring.

The Toronto Cactus & Succulent Club
P.O. Box 334, Brampton, ON, Canada L6V 2L3
Telephone: 416-767-6433
Annual dues: Can$10

The Club holds eight meetings a year in downtown Toronto and publishes eight newsletters, each with cultural articles, book reviews, and news of club activities. Seeds and books are sold at the meetings, and members sell and exchange plants among themselves. The club has a library for members. Its annual June show is open to the public; an annual picnic is for members only.

Victoria Orchid Society
P.O. Box 337, Victoria, BC, Canada V8W 2N2
Annual dues: Can$8.50

Members meet each month to buy and sell plants, have problems diagnosed, and listen to a talk or slide presentation. A monthly *Bulletin* reviews the meetings, announces upcoming events, and offers some information on orchid culture and unusual orchid species. Other benefits of membership include beginners' classes and a chance to pool orders and buy exotic plants from wholesale suppliers.

Vinifera Wine Growers Association
P.O. Box P, The Plains, VA 22171
Telephone: 703-754-8564
Annual dues: $17 U.S. and Canada, $20 overseas

An organization for home gardeners and others interested in small-scale vineyards and wine making. The association's quarterly *Journal* is a thick booklet filled with articles on wine-making history and practical advice, much of it aimed at the home grower—a tremendous value at $15. In addition, many basic instructional booklets are available to members at no charge. The Highburg Vineyard, a model home vineyard, is open to visitors by appointment. The association holds an annual seminar with experts in grape growing and wine making, and sponsors an annual wine festival in the Middleburg, Virginia, area.

Virginia Wildflower Preservation Society
P.O. Box 844, Annadale, VA 22033

Annual dues: $10

"An organization of amateurs and professionals who share an interest in Virginia's wild plants and habitats and a concern for their protection." Members may participate in field trips, workshops, classes, plant rescues, and the society's annual meeting. A quarterly *Bulletin* contains articles on efforts to save wildflower habitats, on wildflower culture, and on other subjects of interest. A recent issue held a reflection on the preparation of the *Atlas of Virginia Flora*, a discussion of the real value of plant rescues, a report on acid rain, and a hard-nosed appraisal of the wildflower meadows promoted by many wildflower seed firms.

Washington Native Plant Society
Dept. of Botany KB-15, Univ. of Washington, Seattle, WA 98195
Telephone: 206-543-1942

Annual dues: $10

Publishes the quarterly newsletter *Douglasia*, which contains schedules of upcoming field trips and chapter meetings as well as articles on plant conservation, botanical gardens with strong native plant collections, and such related topics as recycling. The society also publishes a series of *Occasional Papers* that hold more lengthy studies of Washington's native plants. The first was published in 1983, the second in late 1986, so these really are occasional.

Water Lily Society
Charles B. Thomas, P.O. Box 104, Buckeyestown, MD 21717

Annual dues: $15 U.S. and Canada, £15 U.K. and Europe

Publishes the quarterly *Water Garden Journal*, with articles on water plants, fish, and other water-gardening subjects, along with book reviews and reports on society business.

Members exchange seed through announcements in the *Journal*, and commercial members offer plants for sale. Members may attend lectures and slide presentations at the annual symposium, held at a noted botanical garden (in 1988 at Harlow Car Gardens in Harrogate, England).

Western Horticultural Society
P.O. Box 60507, Palo Alto, CA 94306
Telephone: 415-941-1332

Annual dues: $20

Membership includes a subscription to *Pacific Horticulture* (see entry under *Magazines*, page 273). The society holds monthly meetings at which plants are raffled and organizes field trips and garden visits. Members are kept informed of society activities through a monthly newsletter.

Wildflower Garden Club
S. Karabelnikoff, 7435 Old Harbor Road, Anchorage, AK 99504

Annual dues: $7.50

Holds monthly meetings during the winter, garden tours and field trips during the summer. Sponsors plant sales and maintains a display garden at the Municipal Greenhouse on Debarr Road in Anchorage.

Wyoming Native Plant Society
P.O. Box 1471, Cheyenne, WY 82003

Annual dues: $7

An organization of people concerned with protecting the native plants and ecosystems of Wyoming. This is an outdoor-oriented society; its summer meeting is a weekend camping and hiking get-together (held in 1986 in the Flaming Gorge National Recreation Area). Members receive three newsletters a year with articles on such topics as nomenclature, the flora of particular parks and wild areas, and descriptions of rare and endangered species.

Magazines

Actinidia Enthusiasts Newsletter
See Friends of the Trees Society, page 255.

Agricultural Research
Superintendent of Documents, U.S. Government Printing Office, Washington, DC 20402
Telephone: 301-344-3280

Annual subscription: $11, $13 Canada, $13.75 overseas

A monthly journal of articles on scientific research relating to agriculture, presented in language understandable to general gardeners. A recent issue carried reports on leafy spurge, efforts to create new blueberry varieties, and a new method of measuring vitamin K. The journal is illustrated with black-and-white photographs throughout.

African Violet Magazine
See African Violet Society of America, Inc., page 247.

Amaranth Today
Rodale Press, Inc., 33 E. Minor Street, Emmaus, PA 18098
Telephone: 215-967-5171

Annual subscription: $15, $21 Canada and overseas

A quarterly newsletter with articles of interest to commercial growers of amaranth: markets, nutritional analyses, and cultural advice.

The American Bee Journal
Hamilton, IL 62341
Telephone: 217-847-3324

Annual subscription: $11.75, $17.40 Canada and overseas

"The Beekeeper's Companion Since 1861." A monthly 60-page journal filled with how-to articles on beekeeping. A recent issue contained stories on selling honey, queen rearing in northern California, and the Mackenson instrumental insemination device. Columns on new gadgets, advice for beginners, and reports on the world honey market are regular features.

American Horticulturist
See American Horticultural Society, page 249.

The American Rose
See American Rose Society, page 251.

Amerigold Newsletter
See Marigold Society of America, Inc., page 259.

Arnoldia
The Arnold Arboretum, Jamaica Plain, MA 02130-2795

Annual subscription: $12, $15 Canada and overseas

A quarterly color-illustrated magazine published by the Arnold Arboretum of Harvard University. Articles range from popularly written stories on trees and shrubs to scholarly papers. A recent issue contained a lengthy piece on hollies and a research report titled "Clonal and Age Differences in the Rootings of *Metasequoia glyptostroboides* Cuttings." An excellent publication for anyone seriously interested in trees.

Aroideana
See International Aroid Society, page 258.

Australian Orchid Review
Graphic World Pty Ltd, 14 McGill Street, Lewisham, NSW, Australia 2049

Annual subscription: US$22 ($33 airmail)

A color-illustrated quarterly with articles on orchid care and reports on unusual species and new hybrids. The magazine is also crowded with advertisements from orchid suppliers from around the world.

Avant Gardener
Box 489, New York, NY 10028

Annual subscription: $15

A monthly newsletter filled with new ideas culled from other general and scientific publications, with an emphasis on cultural advice and the "discovery" of underused plants for the garden. The June 1987 issue presented 50 unusual trees and garden perennials, with cultural advice and sources for each, selected by Dr. J. C. Raulston, director of the North Carolina State University Arboretum. A more typical issue contained articles on the culture of shiitake mushrooms, an analysis of commercial potting mixes, new magnolia cultivars, sinningias, and trees for city streets.

The Azalean
See Azalea Society of America, Inc., page 252.

Baer's Garden Newsletter
John Baer's Sons, Box 328, Lancaster, PA 17603

Annual subscription: $3.50

A four-page newsletter, published quarterly, with garden tips, book reviews, and other items of interest to home gardeners.

The firm also publishes the annual *Agricultural Almanac*, which has been providing garden advice since 1825.

The Begonian
See American Begonia Society, page 248.

Biodynamics
See Biodynamic Farming & Gardening Association, page 252.

Bonsai
See American Bonsai Society, Inc., page 248.

Bonsai Magazine
See Bonsai Clubs International, page 252.

Borealis
See Alaska Native Plant Society, page 247.

The Boxwood Bulletin
See American Boxwood Society, Inc., page 248.

British Cactus & Succulent Journal
See the British Cactus & Succulent Society, page 252.

The Bromeliad Hobbyist
See Bromeliad Study Group of Northern California, page 253.

John E. Bryan Gardening Newsletter
John E. Bryan Inc., 1505 Bridgeway, Suite 107, Sausalito, CA 94965-1967

Annual subscription: $30 U.S. and Canada, $45 overseas

A monthly eight-page newsletter consisting of an editorial, a monthly garden guide, and book reviews. The garden guide is the real substance of the newsletter; it offers practical seasonal advice for taking care of a broad range of garden and indoor plants.

The Bryologist
See American Bryological and Lichenological Society, page 248.

Bulletin of American Garden History
P.O. Box 397A, Planetarium Station, New York, NY 10024

Annual subscription: $7

A quarterly journal with articles on exhibits, gardens, plant sources, and resouces for research as well book reviews and other news of interest to garden historians. Several articles in 1986 and 1987 were devoted to California garden history.

The Bu$iness of Herbs
P.O. Box 559, Madison, VA 22727
Telephone: 703-948-7169

Annual subscription: $18 U.S. and Canada, $26 overseas

A 24-page bimonthly newsletter full of articles and reports that should be of interest to both the commercial grower and the serious home herb gardener. Recent issues have included a story on the effect of the nuclear accident at Chernobyl on international herb markets, a plan for an herb-drying room, and an article on growing French tarragon. A calendar lists symposia, herb festivals, and pertinent garden society meetings across the U.S.

Cactus and Succulent Journal
Abbey Garden Press, Box 3010, Santa Barbara, CA 93130-3010
Telephone: 805-963-3228

Annual subscription: $20 U.S., Canada, and Mexico, $21 overseas

A bimonthly magazine rich with material for cactus and succulent lovers. Each issue runs to about 50 pages and is filled with articles on unusual species and varieties, all well illustrated with photographs, some in color. The editors blend articles on plant care for beginners with more scholarly botanical reports for those who have delved deeper in the field. Abbey Garden Press also carries an excellent selection of books on cacti and succulents.

The Camellia Journal
See American Camellia Society, page 248.

Camellia Review
See Southern California Camellia Society, page 264.

Carnivorous Plant Newsletter
See International Carnivorous Plant Society, page 258.

Chronica Horticulturae
See International Society for Horticultural Science, page 259.

The Chrysanthemum
See National Chrysanthemum Society, Inc. USA, page 260.

Common Sense Pest Control Quarterly
See Bio-Integral Resource Center, page 252.

Country Home
Magazine Group of Meredith Corp., 1716 Locust Street, Des Moines, IA 50336

Annual subscription: $15, $21 Canada and overseas

A lavish, color-filled magazine that comes out every other month with articles on home decorating, antiques, and travel, along with one or two picture stories on gardening and landscaping.

Country Journal
Historical Times, Inc., P.O. Box 392, Mt. Morris, IL 61054

Annual subscription: $17, $22 Canada and overseas

What was once a magazine of New England country life is now a diffuse journal with stories on such subjects as saguaro cactus, thunderstorms, home food drying, and ice cream recipes. The same colorful production standard has been maintained through the change, and the magazine still makes light but informative reading. Several articles of direct interest to gardeners appear in each issue. Two regular columns, "Hardy Trees and Shrubs" and "The Vegetable Garden," offer seasonal suggestions. The magazine comes out monthly.

Crossosoma
See Southern California Botanists, page 264.

Crosswords
See Gesneriad Hybridizers Association, page 256.

The Cultivar
The Agroecology Program, Univ. of California, Santa Cruz, CA 95064
Telephone: 408-429-4140
Annual subscription: free

The Agroecology Program at the University of California, Santa Cruz, is "a research and education group working towards the development of ecologically, socially, and economically sustainable agricultural systems." *The Cultivar*, its biannual newsletter, contains news of pertinent legislative activity, research reports, and articles on such subjects as the biological control of the codling moth and the link between herbicide exposure and cancer. Each issue profiles several organizations around the world with similar goals.

The Daffodil Journal
See American Daffodil Society, Inc., page 248.

Dahlias of Today
See Puget Sound Dahlia Association, page 262.

The Daylily
See American Hemerocallis Society, page 249.

Desert Plants
Boyce Thompson Southwestern Arboretum, P.O. Box AB, Superior, AZ 85273
Telephone: 602-689-2811
Annual subscription: $15, $20 Canada, Mexico, and overseas

A thick journal with extensive articles on desert plants and the traditional food crops of the Southwest. The writing is scholarly yet always readable, and the topics are routinely fascinating, even to a New Englander with no expertise in the botany of succulents. Past volumes have delved into such subjects as the saguaro and the harvest of its fruit by the Papago Indians, the history of corn in cultivation and a study of its wild relatives, and a year-round study of pollen harvested by honey bees near Tucson. All articles are well illustrated, often in color, and the issues generally extend to 64 pages. A subscription includes four issues, which may not exactly correspond to a calendar year.

Bev Dobson's Rose Letter
Beverly R. Dobson, 215 Harriman Road, Irvington, NY 10533
Telephone: 914-591-6736
Annual subscription: $9 U.S. and Canada, $13.50 overseas

A bimonthly newsletter with reviews of shows, suppliers, and books, discussions of judging practices, and articles on personalities in the rose world, commercial growers, and other subjects of interest to rose fanciers. Bev Dobson also publishes an annual *Combined Rose List*, which lists more than 5,000 rose varieties and the nurseries that sell them.

Douglasia
See Washington Native Plant Society, page 266.

Economic Botany
The New York Botanical Garden, Bronx, NY 10458-5126
Annual subscription: $45, $50 Canada and overseas

A quarterly journal "devoted to past, present, and future uses of plants by people." Each issue runs to more than 200 pages, with extensive articles on such topics as the marama bean seed crop in Texas, the argan tree as a desert source of edible oil, and archaelogical evidence of coca use in Peru. The writing is scholarly, and many of the subjects covered will be of only slight interest to the average home gardener.

Evansia
See American Bryological and Lichenological Society, page 248.

Excelsa
See Aloe, Cactus & Succulent Society of Zimbabwe, page 247.

Fairchild Tropical Garden Bulletin
10901 Old Cutler Road, Miami, FL 33156
Telephone: 305-667-1651
Annual subscription: $6

A slim quarterly journal, each issue of which holds two or three articles on various subjects loosely related to the garden's collection. The titles in a recent issue were "Carnivorous Plants: An Introduction," "Florida's Native Cycad, *Zamia pumila*," and "Trinidad and Tobago: Sister Islands in the Caribbean." Residents of the area may want to become members for an additional fee, which will entitle them to free admission and access to shows, tours, and workshops.

Farm & Ranch Living
P.O. Box 572, Milwaukee, WI 53201
Telephone: 414-423-0100
Annual subscription: $10

A new bimonthly magazine aimed at farmers and would-be farmers. The color-filled articles emphasize the charms of farm life, with regular features like "The Most Interesting Rancher I've Ever Met" and "The Prettiest Place in the Country." This is not a "how-to" publication; it focuses instead on people and lifestyles.

Fiddlehead Forum
See American Fern Society, page 249.

The Fig Leaf
See Friends of the Fig Society, page 255.

Flower and Garden
4251 Pennsylvania Avenue, Kansas City, MO 64111
Annual subscription: $6, $9 Canada and overseas

A general-interest bimonthly gardening magazine with color-illustrated articles on such subjects as planning a vegetable garden, mulching, lawn care, growing houseplants, and how to plant and care for flowers like roses, daylilies, chrysanthemums, and irises. A recent issue had stories on planting for wildlife, saving wildflowers, and visiting public gardens.

The Four Seasons
Regional Parks Botanic Garden, Tilden Regional Park,
Berkeley, CA 94708-1199

Annual subscription: $10

"An occasional journal devoted to natural history, biology, ecology, conservation, botany, and horticulture, with emphasis on California's native plants." In the past, issues have been published approximately annually, and have included thoroughly researched articles on such subjects as the Port Orford cedar, the interdependence of hound's tongue and the long-nosed flies, and several articles on manzanitas. Subscription orders should be made payable to East Bay Regional Park District.

Fruit Varieties Journal
See American Pomological Society, page 250.

Fuchsia Fanfare
See South African Fuchsia Society, page 264.

Garden
Subscription Dept., Botanical Garden, Bronx, NY 10458

Annual subscription: $12, $14.50 Canada and overseas

A bimonthly magazine that presents fascinating articles on public gardens, botanical research, garden flowers, and the preservation of rare species, all illustrated with color and black-and-white photographs. Examples of past articles include stories on a new near-blue rose; on the search for silphion, a spice plant used by the ancient Greeks but now apparently extinct; on Charleston's Magnolia Plantation; and on wintering fig trees in the north by burying them on their sides in trenches.

The Garden
Home & Law Publishing Ltd., Greater London House, Hampstead Road, London, England NW1 7QQ

Annual subscription: £17.50

The monthly journal of the Royal Horticultural Society, a benefit of membership in the society but also available by subscription. Each issue holds more than 50 pages of color-illustrated writing on such topics as rock gardening, tulip care, Chinese gardening tools and techniques, and flowering plums and cherries. Book reviews are a regular feature.

Garden Design
P.O. Box 836, Peterborough, NH 03458-9990

Annual subscription: $20 U.S. and Canada, $25 overseas

A lavish color magazine published quarterly by the American Society of Landscape Architects. Several exquisite gardens are featured in photographic portfolios in each issue, ranging from an English-style perennial garden in New Jersey, to the hillside landscaping around a geometric contemporary house in Michigan, to the sculpture garden at Peggy Guggenheim's palazzo in Venice. Book reviews, sample garden plans, and articles on specific plant types round out the glossy 100-page package.

Garden History
See Garden History Society, page 255.

Gardening Newsletter by Bob Flagg
P.O. Box 2306, Houston, TX 77005

Annual subscription: $12.95

A monthly newsletter that focuses on plants and gardening in the Gulf Coast region—zones 8, 9, and 10. Several articles appear in each issue on such subjects as choosing pecan varieties, the care of crape myrtles, and planting summer bulbs. Recipes and monthly garden reminders are regular features.

The Geranium Gazette
See British & European Geranium Society, page 252.

Geraniums Around the World
See International Geranium Society, page 258.

Gesneriad Saintpaulia News
See Gesneriad Society International, page 256, and Saintpaulia International, page 263.

The Gloxinian
See American Gloxinia & Gesneriad Society, Inc., page 249.

The Green Scene
See Pennsylvania Horticultural Society, page 262.

Greener Gardening, Easier
E. Dexter Davis, Horticulturist, 26 Norfolk Street, Holliston, MA 01746

Annual subscription: $12, Can$15 Canada

A monthly newsletter for gardeners in the northeastern states and the eastern provinces. Each issue holds a calendar of upcoming events in the region, reminders of things to do in the garden, book and catalog reviews, news of research findings, and discussions of plants, gardening techniques, tools, and sources.

Gurney's Gardening News
2nd & Capitol, Yankton, SD 57079

Annual subscription: $5.95 (U.S. subscriptions only)

Published six time a year by the Gurney Seed & Nursery Co. In a tabloid format, the *News* presents 32 pages of gardening advice with an emphasis on vegetables and food crops. Recipes, descriptions of unusual vegetables, and stories on successful gardeners are regular features. The publication contains such a wealth of information for such a low price that we're willing to excuse the frequent plugs for Gurney as a source for most plants mentioned.

The Hardy Plant
See the Hardy Plant Society, page 256.

Harrowsmith
7 Queen Victoria Road, Camden East, ON, Canada K0K 1J0 or The Creamery, Charlotte, VT 05445
Telephone: 613-378-6661 or 802-425-3961

Annual subscription: see below

Harrowsmith began as a Canadian magazine, but now puts out a separate U.S. edition slightly different in content. Both editions are published six times a year. Canadian subscriptions are $16 a year (in Canadian funds, sent to the Camden East address). U.S. subscriptions are $18 a year (in U.S. funds, sent to the Charlotte address). Overseas subscriptions are $24 a year (in Canadian funds, sent to the Camden East address). The magazine presents articles on country living and gardening with an emphasis on natural and organic methods. Gardening articles have ranged from heirloom houseplants and northern watermelons to no-mow lawns and scarecrows. All stories are illustrated in color.

Heather News
See North American Heather Society, page 261.

The Herb Quarterly
P.O. Box 275, Newfane, VT 05345

Annual subscription: $24, $26.50 Canada and overseas

A magazine for gardeners with an interest in growing and using herbs. Each issue presents 48 pages of articles on subjects like growing plants from seed, herbal bath preparations and cough syrups, Japanese parsley, dandelion, medicinal mints, and recipes.

The Herb, Spice, and Medicinal Plant Digest
L. E. Craker, Dept. of Plant and Soil Sciences, Stockbridge Hall, Univ. of Massachusetts, Amherst, MA 01003
Telephone: 413-545-2347

Annual subscription: $6

A quarterly journal aimed at commercial herb growers. The summer 1987 issue had articles on legal issues in labeling herbs for sale, on fertilizing perennial herbs with organic mulches, and on the potential for sales of herb plants through garden centers. Subscription orders should be made payable to the University of Massachusetts.

HerbalGram
See Herb Research Foundation, page 256.

The Herbarist
See the Herb Society of America, Inc., page 256.

Herbertia
See American Plant Life Society, page 250.

Horticulture
Subscription Dept., P.O. Box 2595, Boulder, CO 80323
Telephone: 800-525-0643

Annual subscription: $18, $24 Canada and overseas

An excellent general gardening magazine that covers a wide range of subjects of interest to home gardeners. Articles deal with the care and maintenance of trees, shrubs, vegetables, and flowers; features show exceptional public and private gardens; regular columns review tools and books. Each winter the magazine reviews new flower and vegetable introductions from commercial suppliers. Recent issues have included stories on Scotland's Logan Botanic Garden, windowsill herb gardens, winterizing roses, Japanese stone walkways, forcing bulbs indoors, and treatments for tomato pests and diseases. *Horticulture* comes out monthly and is filled with color and black-and-white photographs.

HortIdeas
G. & P. Williams, Rt. 1, Box 302, Gravel Switch, KY 40328

Annual subscription: $10, $12 Canada and Mexico, $15 overseas

A monthly newsletter that culls news from hundreds of sources. Each issue offers 12 pages crowded with information on pest control measures, new and unusual plants and where to buy them, slide shows and videos for sale or rent, hardiness ratings of various tree and shrub cultivars, research results from scientific journals, novel suggestions for improving lawns and gardens, book reviews, and much more. We think it's a terrific value. Send $1 for a sample issue if you'd like to see it before subscribing.

HortScience
See American Society for Horticultural Science, page 251.

Hortus
P.O. Box 90, Farnham, Surrey, England GU9 8SX

Annual subscription: £28 U.S. and Canada

A quarterly journal of essays on gardening that takes the form of a small book. Each issue runs to about 128 pages and contains about 20 pieces on such subjects as garden history, design, and nomenclature. Among the writers are such luminaries as Dame Sylvia Crowe, Beth Chatto, Anthony Huxley, Will Ingwersen, Jane Brown, and Stephen Lacey. Few practical articles are included, but some recommend unusual species and cultivars, and all make wonderful reading with plenty of food for thought. We find it the perfect bedside book.

The Hosta Journal
See American Hosta Society, page 250.

House & Garden
Box 5202, Boulder, CO 80322

Annual subscription: $24, $38 Canada, $41 overseas

A slick, upscale monthly magazine that puts more emphasis on the *House* side of its title than the *Garden*. Each issue contains at least one picture story on a garden.

Houseleeks
See the Sempervivum Society, page 264.

The IPM Practitioner
See Bio-Integral Resource Center, page 252.

The Indoor Gardener
See the Indoor Gardening Society of America, Inc., page 258.

International Bonsai
Wm. N. Valavanis, 412 Pinnacle Road, Rochester, NY 14623
Telephone: 716-334-2595

Annual subscription: $20, $25 Canada and overseas

A glossy color magazine published four times a year, with articles on different bonsai styles and on techniques for use with particular plants. Drawings illustrate the technical articles, and some extraordinary mature specimens are pictured in crisp photographs. Each issue is devoted largely to a particular plant or style. In the past these have included satsuki azaleas, Japanese black pines, hawthorns, the formal upright style, and the slanting style. All back issues are available.

Ivy Journal
See the American Ivy Society, page 250.

Journal of Garden History
Taylor & Francis, Inc., 242 Cherry Street, Philadelphia, PA 19106-1906

Subscription: $112 (for two years)

A scholarly quarterly with extensive articles on garden history that range from studies of plantings in ancient Rome to papers on 19th-century horticulturists. Restoration projects are often featured, with detailed accounts of the research that went into them. Many of the articles are illustrated.

The Kew Magazine
Timber Press, 9999 S.W. Wilshire, Portland, OR 97225
Telephone: 503-292-0745

Annual subscription: $50 U.S. and Canada

Founded as the *Botanical Magazine* in 1787, *The Kew Magazine* is the world's oldest botanical periodical in continuous publication. Since its inception the magazine has been a showcase for fine botanical illustration, and today each issue includes a half dozen full-page color reproductions of plant portraits by leading artists. Articles range from historical subjects to stories on endangered species and new plant discoveries. The magazine appears quarterly. British and other foreign subscription inquiries should be sent to The Kew Magazine, Basil Blackwell Ltd., 108 Cowley Road, Oxford, England OX4 1JF.

Kinnikinnick
See Friends of the Devonian Botanic Garden, page 255.

Lilac Newsletter
See International Lilac Society, page 258.

Lindleyana
The American Orchid Society Inc., 6000 S. Olive Avenue, West Palm Beach, FL 33405
Telephone: 305-585-8666

Annual subscription: $20, $22 Canada and overseas

A new scientific quarterly, launched at the end of 1986. The American Orchid Society intends *Lindleyana* to "embrace all aspects of orchid research: systematics, physiology, phytochemistry, cytology, anatomy and morphology, pollination biology, and evolution." It will include papers, book reviews, monographs, and proceedings of symposia.

Living off the Land, A Subtropic Newsletter
P.O. Box 2131, Melbourne, FL 32902-2131

Annual subscription: $12.60 U.S. and Canada, $15.75 overseas

Each issue deals with a different subtropical fruit, including instructions for planting and care and recipes for using the harvest. The issue we received treated the calamondin, a sour-tasting citrus that can be used in relishes, pies, marmalades, and breads. Past issues have covered papaya, banana, lychee, pineapple, chayote, and many other exotics. All back issues (more than 70 so far) are for sale. The last page of each issue is given over to a seed exchange. The newsletter comes out every other month.

Magnolia
See Southern Garden History Society, page 265.

The Maine Organic Farmer & Gardener
P.O. Box 2176, Augusta, ME 04330

Annual subscription: $8, $14 Canada and overseas

A publication of The Maine Organic Farmers and Gardeners Association and a benefit of membership in that society. Ostensibly a journal for professional growers in Maine, the thick bimonthly tabloid is packed with articles that will be of interest to any gardeners who have chosen a natural approach to plant care. Articles delve into such subjects as organic lawn care, wildflower gardening, attracting bluebirds, gypsy moth control, and rotation grazing.

Malus
See International Ornamental Crabapple Society, page 258.

Mentzelia
See Northern Nevada Native Plant Society, page 262.

The Minnesota Horticulturist
See Minnesota State Horticultural Society, page 259.

Mother Earth News
P.O. Box 3122, Harlan, IA 51593

Annual subscription: $18, $21 Canada and overseas

The self-proclaimed "Original Country Magazine," *Mother Earth News* runs articles on wild animals, draft horses, and owner-built homes as well as many stories of more direct interest to gardeners. Recent issues have included a plan for a wooden yard cart, a critique of different hoes, a guide to growing potatoes, and a number of recipes for pickles. In the winter of 1987 the magazine presented a two-part review of the spring seed catalogs, comparing the companies in one issue and rating their new varieties in the next. *Mother Earth News* is published bimonthly and is printed in color throughout.

National Gardening
See National Gardening Association, page 260.

The Nerium News
See National Oleander Society, page 260.

New England Gardener
P.O. Box 2699, Nantucket, MA 02584

Annual subscription: $14.95, $17.95 Canada and overseas

A beautiful and informative little newsletter, published monthly for gardeners throughout the Northeast. Special attention is paid to coastal conditions; a recent issue contained a lengthy article on shrubs suitable for planting near the shore. Other subjects covered range from the care of oriental poppies and dahlias to growing vegetables in containers and planning a flower border to peak for a June wedding.

The New Farm
Rodale Press, Inc., 33 E. Minor Street, Emmaus, PA 18098

Annual subscription: $15, $19 Canada, $23 overseas

Published seven times a year, *The New Farm* is aimed at organic growers, with articles on such subjects as free organic fertilizers, sludge, biological pesticides, soil-saving weed control, and soybean and wheat crops for livestock feed. Each issue is about 48 pages long, illustrated with black-and-white photographs.

The Nutshell
See Northern Nut Growers Association, page 262.

The Orchid Advocate
See the Cymbidium Society of America, Inc., page 254.

Orchid Digest
Mrs. Norman H. Atkinson, P.O. Box 916, Carmichael, CA 95609-0916

Telephone: 916-485-8317

Annual subscription: $18

A lavish quarterly magazine with articles on orchid propagation and care, newly described species, and seasonal notes, illustrated with scores of beautiful color plates. The writing ranges from stories for beginners, like "Cattleyas, Tropical America's Gift to the Orchid World," to more advanced pieces such as "A Peculiar Means of Vegetative Reproduction by *Phalaenopsis stuartiana.*"

The Orchid Review
Mr. Christopher Bailes, Katukelle House, Victoria Village, Trinity, Jersey, Channel Islands, Great Britain

Annual subscription: US$32.50 or £19

A monthly journal that keeps up with the activities of British orchid societies and presents illustrated articles on orchid culture and breeding. A representative issue in the spring of 1987 included lengthy features on the creation of the pleione cultivar Shantung and on the collection of Eric Young as well as reports on awards from the Royal Horticultural Society and on the Orchid Society of Great Britain's fall show.

Orquideologia
Jardin Botanico "Joaquin Antonio Uribe," Carrera 52 No. 73-182, Apartado Aereo 4725, Medellin, Colombia

Annual subscription: $25 (plus $7 for airmail to U.S., Canada, and Mexico, and $10 for airmail to Europe)

Subscribers receive three color-illustrated issues a year, the articles printed in both Spanish and English. It would be wise to write for current subscription rates, as the fees above were valid only through 1987. The issue we saw included three articles: "New Species of *Lepanthes* from Panama," "New Species in the *Pleurothallidinae* from Colombia," and "New Species of *Pleurothallis* from Colombia."

Pacific Horticulture
P.O. Box 22609, San Francisco, CA 94122

Annual subscription: $12, $14 Canada and Mexico, $16 overseas

An excellent quarterly magazine, each issue of which is reliably filled with in-depth articles on a fascinating range of topics, all nicely illustrated with color and black-and-white photographs. The summer 1987 issue held stories on garden ornament, the cobra lily, the rhododendron collection at Hendricks Park, the Monterey cypress, and Maria Merian, a 17th-century naturalist.

Plants & Gardens
Brooklyn Botanic Garden, 1000 Washington Avenue, Brooklyn, NY 11225

Annual subscription: $20 for subscribing membership

Members receive the quarterly journal *Plants & Gardens*, each issue of which treats a different gardening subject in great detail. Several articles by experts in the field are combined with photographs and clear diagrams in an 80- to 100-page booklet that can serve as a basic reference work. Past volumes have covered rock gardening, ferns, African violets, outdoor container gardening, mulches, pruning, dwarf conifers, and more than 100 other topics. All the booklets are available as back issues, and a collection of several makes a sound gardening library. Members are also mailed *Plants & Gardens News*, a quarterly newsletter with information about classes, meetings, and the occasional plant and seed "dividends" that are also benefits of membership.

The Plantsman
Home & Law Publishing Ltd., Greater London House, Hampstead Road, London, England NW1 7QQ

Annual subscription: £13.50 U.S. and Canada

A quarterly journal with a scholarly tone, published in association with the Royal Horticultural Society. Examples of past articles include "Notes on the Genus *Cryptanthus,*" "Orchids Hardy in the British Isles," and "An Australian *Restio.*" Each article runs to a dozen or so pages, each issue to more than 50 pages.

Pome News
See Home Orchard Society, page 257.

Pomona
See North American Fruit Explorers, page 261.

Practical Gardening
Competition House, Farndon Road, Market Harborough, Leics., England LE1 9NR

Telephone: 44-858-34567

Annual subscription: £17.50 U.S. and Canada

A monthly magazine with a popular orientation. The design looks something like *Seventeen* magazine, but the contents are pure gardening. All the articles take a practical approach: a feature on greenhouses surveys new models and advises readers in their choice; a story on alstroemeria tells how to grow the lilies; a piece on tools tells which are the most essential. Each issue spans some 90 pages, but packs in so many stories that it seems like much more.

Primroses

See American Primrose Society, page 250.

Principes

See the International Palm Society, page 259.

The Rhododendron

See Australian Rhododendron Society, page 251.

Rhodora

See New England Botanical Club, Inc., page 261.

Rodale's Organic Gardening

Rodale Press, Inc., 33 E. Minor Street, Emmaus, PA 18049

Annual subscription: $13, $16 Canada, $21 overseas

A monthly magazine with a how-to approach. Presents organic gardening techniques in simple, easy-to-read articles that rarely take more than a few minutes to finish. Rodale's style is not to preach, but to explain and to do it in the manner of the popular "mainstream" magazines, so that readers are hardly aware they're being offered natural and alternative solutions to gardening problems. From pest-control measures and composting tips to recipes and historical stories, the magazine covers the territory of a general gardening publication.

Rosarian

See Canadian Rose Society, page 254.

The Rose Letter

See Heritage Roses Group, page 256.

The Seed Pod

See American Hibiscus Society, page 249.

The Siberian Iris

See Society for Siberian Irises, page 264.

Solanaceae

3370 Princeton Court, Santa Clara, CA 95051

Annual subscription: $5 U.S. and Canada, $10 overseas

A quarterly journal that provides a forum for the exchange of experience and expertise among fans of Solanaceae, a large family of fruits and vegetables that includes potatoes, tomatoes, eggplants, and peppers as well as such exotics as the tamarillo, the pepino dulce, and some 2,000 other species. The writing in the journal we received wanders from an article on McDonald's french fries to a list of Solanaceae species traditionally grown or gathered by southwestern Indians. Subscribers may buy from the organization's bank of rare and unusual seeds and may participate in exchanges with other readers.

Southern Living

P.O. Box 523, Birmingham, AL 35201
Telephone: 800-633-8628 (800-292-8667 in Alabama)

Annual subscription: $19.95 in 19 southern states, $24 in rest of U.S., Canada, and overseas

A home and garden magazine "For People Who Love the South." Subscriptions to addresses north of the Mason-Dixon line and west of Texas are gently discouraged with a higher rate. A typical issue gives a dozen pages over to gardening topics, out of a total of more than 200. A recent issue contained stories on roses, carrots, and fall-flowering perennials along with a schedule of southern garden events.

Sunset Magazine

80 Willow Road, Menlo Park, CA 94025

Annual subscription: $14 in 13 western states, $18 in other states, $25.75 foreign

A home, garden, and travel magazine for residents of the West. Four editions are produced for different regions, and the gardening articles are targeted to the growing conditions of the areas covered. Each monthly issue contains more than 60 articles, about a dozen of which relate directly to the garden. Recipes, plans for outdoor constructions, and stories about public parks expand the roster. The stories are generally short and practical, and most are illustrated in color.

Veld & Flora

See the Botanical Society of South Africa, page 252.

The Washington Park Arboretum Bulletin

The Arboretum Foundation, Univ. of Washington XD-10, Seattle, WA 98195
Telephone: 206-325-4510

Annual subscription: write for current rates

An informative quarterly magazine sent to supporters of the Washington Park Arboretum. Articles on such subjects as plants of the Mediterranean suitable for growing in American gardens and on the effects of nuclear testing on vegetation in the Marshall Islands make the journal of interest even to gardeners who live far from Seattle. Book reviews and notes on developments at the arboretum fill out each 32-page issue.

Wild Flower Notes

See New England Wild Flower Society, Inc., page 261.

Wildflower

See the Canadian Wildflower Society, page 254.

Wildflower Journal

See National Wildflower Research Center, page 260.

World Pumpkin Confederation Newsletter

See "Growing the Big Ones," page 32.

Zingiber

See American Ginger Society, page 249.

Index